Saxon Math
Intermediate 3

Teacher's Manual
Volume 2

Stephen Hake

A Harcourt Achieve Imprint

www.SaxonPublishers.com
1-800-284-7019

Acknowledgements

This book was made possible by the significant contributions of many individuals and the dedicated efforts of talented teams at Harcourt Achieve.

Special thanks to Chris Braun for conscientious work on Power Up exercises, Problem Solving scripts, and student assessments. The long hours and technical assistance of John and James Hake were invaluable in meeting publishing deadlines. As always, the patience and support of Mary is most appreciated.

– *Stephen Hake*

Staff Credits

Editorial: Joel Riemer, Hirva Raj, Paula Zamarra, Smith Richardson, Robin Adams, Brooke Butner, James Daniels, Dave Baceski, Cecilia Colome, Pamela Cox, Gayle Lowery, Leslie Bateman, Michael Ota, Stephanie Rieper, Ann Sissac, Chad Barrett, Heather Jernt

Design: Alison Klassen, Joan Cunningham, Alan Klemp, Julie Hubbard, Lorelei Supapo, Andy Hendrix, Rhonda Holcomb

Production: Mychael Ferris-Pacheco, Jennifer Cohorn, Greg Gaspard, Donna Brawley, John-Paxton Gremillion

Manufacturing: Cathy Voltaggio, Kathleen Stewart

Marketing: Marilyn Trow, Kimberly Sadler

E-Learning: Layne Hedrick

ISBN 13: 978-1-6003-2725-4 (Teacher's Manual Set)
ISBN 10: 1-6003-2725-7 (Teacher's Manual Set)

ISBN 13: 978-1-6003-2601-1 (Teacher's Manual, Vol. 2)
ISBN 10: 1-6003-2601-3 (Teacher's Manual, Vol. 2)

© 2008 Harcourt Achieve Inc. and Stephen Hake

All rights reserved. No part of the material protected by this copyright may be reproduced or utilized in any form or by any means, in whole or in part, without permission in writing from the copyright owner. Requests for permission should be mailed to: Paralegal Department, 6277 Sea Harbor Drive, Orlando, FL 32887.

Saxon is a trademark of Harcourt Achieve Inc.

3 4 5 6 7 8 9 059 12 11 10 09 08

SAXON MATH™
Intermediate 3

CONTENT OVERVIEW

Teacher's Manual, Volume 1

The New Look of Results	T4
Proven Results	T6
Unique Program Structure	T8
• Lesson Structure	
• Daily Problem Solving	
• Ongoing Assessment	
Support for All Students	T18
• Differentiated Instruction	
• Adaptations for Saxon Math	
Components	T22
Professional Development	T24
Table of Contents	T25
Content by Strand	T37
Problem Solving Overview	1A
Section 1: Lessons 1–10, Investigation 1	7A
Section 2: Lessons 11–20, Investigation 2	59A
Section 3: Lessons 21–30, Investigation 3	114A
Section 4: Lessons 31–40, Investigation 4	169A
Section 5: Lessons 41–50, Investigation 5	223A
Section 6: Lessons 51–60, Investigation 6	277A
English/Spanish Math Glossary	T588
Index	T596

Teacher's Manual, Volume 2

Table of Contents	T5
Content by Strand	T17
Section 7: Lessons 61–70, Investigation 7	328A
Section 8: Lessons 71–80, Investigation 8	385A
Section 9: Lessons 81–90, Investigation 9	440A
Section 10: Lessons 91–100, Investigation 10	494A
Section 11: Lessons 101–110, Investigation 11	540A
English/Spanish Math Glossary	T588
Index	T596

ABOUT THE AUTHOR

Stephen Hake has authored six books in the **Saxon Math** series. He writes from 17 years of classroom experience as an elementary and secondary teacher and as a math specialist in El Monte, California. As a math coach, his students won honors and recognition in local, regional, and statewide competitions.

Stephen has been writing math curriculum since 1975 and for Saxon since 1985. He has also authored several math contests including Los Angeles County's first Math Field Day contest. Stephen contributed to the 1999 National Academy of Science publication on the Nature and Teaching of Algebra in the Middle Grades.

Stephen is a member of the National Council of Teachers of Mathematics and the California Mathematics Council. He earned his BA from United States International University and his MA from Chapman College.

Table of Contents
Integrated and Distributed Units of Instruction

Section 1 — Lessons 1–10, Investigation 1

		Page	TEKS Strands Focus
	Lesson Preparation • Problem Solving Overview	1A 1	N, A, UP
Overview	Lessons 1–10, Investigation 1	7A	
Lesson 1	Lesson Preparation • Months and Years • Calendar Activity Make a Calendar	7G 7	A, UP
Lesson 2	Lesson Preparation • Counting Patterns Activity Skip Counting	13A 13	A, UP
Lesson 3	Lesson Preparation • Reading a Clock to the Nearest Five Minutes Activity Setting a Clock	17A 17	M
Lesson 4	Lesson Preparation • Number Line • Thermometer Activity Reading and Recording Temperature	21A 21	A, G, M, UP
Lesson 5	Lesson Preparation • Fractions of an Hour Activity Fractions of an Hour	28A 28	N, M
Lesson 6	Lesson Preparation • Addition	33A 33	N, UP
Lesson 7	Lesson Preparation • Subtraction	38A 38	N, UP
Lesson 8	Lesson Preparation • Addition and Subtraction Fact Families	44A 44	N
Lesson 9	Lesson Preparation • Unknown Addends	48A 48	N, UP
Lesson 10	Lesson Preparation • Adding Three Numbers	52A 52	N, UP
Investigation 1	Lesson Preparation • Pictographs and Bar Graphs Activity Pictograph and Bar Graph	56B 56	PST
Cumulative Assessment	Power-Up Test 1, Cumulative Test 1, Performance Task 1		Standards Benchmark Check Point

TEKS Strands Key:
N = Number, Operation, and Quantitative Reasoning
A = Patterns, Relationships, and Algebraic Thinking
G = Geometry and Spatial Reasoning
M = Measurement
PST = Probability and Statistics
UP = Underlying Processes and Mathematical Tools

Section 2 — Lessons 11–20, Investigation 2

TEKS
Page | **Strands Focus**

		Page	Strands Focus
Overview	Lessons 11–20, Investigation 2	59A	
Lesson 11	Lesson Preparation • Place Value Activity Place Value	59G 59	N, UP
Lesson 12	Lesson Preparation • Reading and Writing Numbers Through 999	65A 65	N
Lesson 13	Lesson Preparation • Adding Two-Digit Numbers Activity Regrouping	69A 69	N, UP
Lesson 14	Lesson Preparation • Subtracting Two-Digit Numbers Activity Regrouping for Subtraction	75A 75	N, UP
Lesson 15	Lesson Preparation • Rounding to the Nearest Ten and Hundred	79A 79	N
Cumulative Assessment	Power-Up Test 2, Cumulative Test 2, Test-Day Activity 1		
Lesson 16	Lesson Preparation • Adding Three-Digit Numbers	85A 85	N, UP
Lesson 17	Lesson Preparation • Comparing and Ordering, Part 1	92A 92	N, UP
Lesson 18	Lesson Preparation • Some and Some More Stories, Part 1	97A 97	N, UP
Lesson 19	Lesson Preparation • Subtracting Three-Digit Numbers, Part 1	102A 102	N, UP
Lesson 20	Lesson Preparation • Some Went Away Stories, Part 1	108A 108	N, UP
Investigation 2	Lesson Preparation • Working with Money Activity Money Exchanges	112B 112	N, UP
Cumulative Assessment	Power-Up Test 3, Cumulative Test 3, Performance Task 2		*Standards Benchmark Check Point*

TEKS Strands Key:
N = Number, Operation, and Quantitative Reasoning
A = Patterns, Relationships, and Algebraic Thinking
G = Geometry and Spatial Reasoning
M = Measurement
PST = Probability and Statistics
UP = Underlying Processes and Mathematical Tools

Section 3 — Lessons 21–30, Investigation 3

		Page	TEKS Strands Focus
Overview	Lessons 21–30, Investigation 3	114A	
Lesson 21	Lesson Preparation • Naming Dollars and Cents • Exchanging Dollars, Dimes, and Pennies *Activity* Exchange Pennies for Dimes	114G **114**	N, PST
Lesson 22	Lesson Preparation • Adding Dollars and Cents	119A **119**	N, UP
Lesson 23	Lesson Preparation • Subtracting Three-Digit Numbers, Part 2	124A **124**	N, UP
Lesson 24	Lesson Preparation • Column Addition	130A **130**	N, UP
Lesson 25	Lesson Preparation • Counting Dollars and Cents *Activity* Counting Money	134A **134**	N, A
Cumulative Assessment	Power-Up Test 4, Cumulative Test 4, Test-Day Activity 2		
Lesson 26	Lesson Preparation • Subtracting Dollars and Cents	140A **140**	N, UP
Lesson 27	Lesson Preparation • Comparing and Ordering, Part 2	146A **146**	N, UP
Lesson 28	Lesson Preparation • Subtracting Across Zeros *Activity* Subtracting Across Zeros	152A **152**	N, UP
Lesson 29	Lesson Preparation • Fractions of a Dollar	156A **156**	N
Lesson 30	Lesson Preparation • Estimating Sums and Differences	161A **161**	N
Investigation 3	Lesson Preparation • More About Pictographs *Activity* Class Pictograph	166B **166**	PST
Cumulative Assessment	Power-Up Test 5, Cumulative Test 5, Performance Task 3	*Standards Benchmark Check Point*	

TEKS Strands Key:
N = Number, Operation, and Quantitative Reasoning
A = Patterns, Relationships, and Algebraic Thinking
G = Geometry and Spatial Reasoning
M = Measurement
PST = Probability and Statistics
UP = Underlying Processes and Mathematical Tools

Section 4 — Lessons 31–40, Investigation 4

		Page	TEKS Strands Focus
Overview	Lessons 31–40, Investigation 4	169A	
Lesson 31	Lesson Preparation • **Writing Directions** Activity Giving Directions	169G **169**	UP
Lesson 32	Lesson Preparation • **Reading and Writing Numbers Through 999,999** Activity Reading and Writing Big Numbers	174A **174**	N, UP
Lesson 33	Lesson Preparation • **More About Number Lines** Activity Making A Timeline	180A **180**	G, UP
Lesson 34	Lesson Preparation • **Length: Inches, Feet, and Yards** Activity Inches, Feet, Yards	185A **185**	A, M
Lesson 35	Lesson Preparation • **Measuring to the Nearest Quarter Inch** Activity Inch Ruler	191A **191**	M, UP
Cumulative Assessment	Power-Up Test 6, Cumulative Test 6, Test-Day Activity 3		
Lesson 36	Lesson Preparation • **Some and Some More Stories, Part 2**	197A **197**	N, UP
Lesson 37	Lesson Preparation • **Estimating Lengths and Distances** Activity Estimating and Measuring Lengths	201A **201**	M, UP
Lesson 38	Lesson Preparation • **Reading a Clock to the Nearest Minute**	206A **206**	M, UP
Lesson 39	Lesson Preparation • **Stories About Comparing**	211A **211**	N, G, UP
Lesson 40	Lesson Preparation • **Missing Numbers in Subtraction** • **Some Went Away Stories, Part 2**	216A **216**	N, UP
Investigation 4	Lesson Preparation • **Scale Maps** Activity Scale Map	221B **221**	M, UP
Cumulative Assessment	Power-Up Test 7, Cumulative Test 7, Performance Task 4		**STANDARDS BENCHMARK CHECK POINT**

TEKS Strands Key:
N = Number, Operation, and Quantitative Reasoning
A = Patterns, Relationships, and Algebraic Thinking
G = Geometry and Spatial Reasoning
M = Measurement
PST = Probability and Statistics
UP = Underlying Processes and Mathematical Tools

Section 5 — Lessons 41–50, Investigation 5

		Page	TEKS Strands Focus
Overview	Lessons 41–50, Investigation 5	223A	
Lesson 41	Lesson Preparation • Modeling Fractions Activity Fraction Manipulatives	223G **223**	N
Lesson 42	Lesson Preparation • Drawing Fractions	228A **228**	N
Lesson 43	Lesson Preparation • Comparing Fractions, Part 1 Activity Comparing Fractions	233A **233**	N
Lesson 44	Lesson Preparation • Fractions of a Group	239A **239**	N
Lesson 45	Lesson Preparation • Probability, Part 1 Activity Probability Demonstration	244A **244**	PST, UP
Cumulative Assessment	Power-Up Test 8, Cumulative Test 8, Test-Day Activity 4		
Lesson 46	Lesson Preparation • Fractions Equal to 1 • Mixed Numbers	249A **249**	N
Lesson 47	Lesson Preparation • Equivalent Fractions Activity Equivalent Fractions	254A **254**	N
Lesson 48	Lesson Preparation • Finding Fractions and Mixed Numbers on a Number Line Activity Fractions on the Number Line	260A **260**	N, G
Lesson 49	Lesson Preparation • Comparing Fractions, Part 2	265A **265**	N, UP
Lesson 50	Lesson Preparation • Probability, Part 2	270A **270**	PST
Investigation 5	Lesson Preparation • Probability Games	275B **275**	PST, UP
Cumulative Assessment	Power-Up Test 9, Cumulative Test 9, Performance Task 5		*Standards Benchmark Check Point*

TEKS Strands Key:
N = Number, Operation, and Quantitative Reasoning
A = Patterns, Relationships, and Algebraic Thinking
G = Geometry and Spatial Reasoning
M = Measurement
PST = Probability and Statistics
UP = Underlying Processes and Mathematical Tools

Section 6 — Lessons 51–60, Investigation 6

			Page	TEKS Strands Focus
Overview		Lessons 51–60, Investigation 6	277A	
	51	Lesson Preparation • **Rectangles** Activity Rectangle List	277G **277**	G, UP
	52	Lesson Preparation • **Length and Width** Activity Measuring Length and Width	282A **282**	G, M
	53	Lesson Preparation • **Rectangular Grid Patterns** Activity Rectangular Patterns	287A **287**	A, M
	54	Lesson Preparation • **Multiplication as Repeated Addition**	292A **292**	N, A, M
	55	Lesson Preparation • **Multiplication Table** Activity Using a Multiplication Table	297A **297**	N, A
Cumulative Assessment		Power-Up Test 10, Cumulative Test 10, Test-Day Activity 5		
	56	Lesson Preparation • **Multiplication Facts: 0s, 1s, and 10s** Activity Zeros, Ones, and Tens	302A **302**	N, A
	57	Lesson Preparation • **Arrays** Activity Arrays	306A **306**	N, A
	58	Lesson Preparation • **Perimeter**	311A **311**	M, UP
	59	Lesson Preparation • **Multiplication Facts: 2s and 5s**	316A **316**	N, A
	60	Lesson Preparation • **Equal Groups Stories, Part 1**	321A **321**	N, UP
Investigation 6		Lesson Preparation • **More About Bar Graphs**	326B **326**	PST
Cumulative Assessment		Power-Up Test 11, Cumulative Test 11, Performance Task 6		Standards Benchmark Check Point

TEKS Strands Key:
N = Number, Operation, and Quantitative Reasoning
A = Patterns, Relationships, and Algebraic Thinking
G = Geometry and Spatial Reasoning
M = Measurement
PST = Probability and Statistics
UP = Underlying Processes and Mathematical Tools

Section 7 — Lessons 61–70, Investigation 7

		Page	TEKS Strands Focus
Overview	Lessons 61–70, Investigation 7	328A	
Lesson 61	Lesson Preparation • Squares • Multiplication Facts: Square Numbers *Activity* Squares on a Grid	328G **328**	N, A, M
Lesson 62	Lesson Preparation • Area, Part 1 *Activity* Area	334A **334**	N, A, M
Lesson 63	Lesson Preparation • Area, Part 2 *Activity* Estimating Area in Square Feet	340A **340**	N, M
Lesson 64	Lesson Preparation • Multiplication Facts: 9s	345A **345**	N, A, UP
Lesson 65	Lesson Preparation • Angles *Activity* Angles	350A **350**	G, UP
Cumulative Assessment	Power-Up Test 12, Cumulative Test 12, Test-Day Activity 6		
Lesson 66	Lesson Preparation • Parallelograms	355A **355**	G, M, UP
Lesson 67	Lesson Preparation • Polygons	361A **361**	G, M, UP
Lesson 68	Lesson Preparation • Congruent Shapes *Activity* Congruent Shapes	368A **368**	G, UP
Lesson 69	Lesson Preparation • Triangles *Activity* Make Equilateral and Right Triangles	373A **373**	G, UP
Lesson 70	Lesson Preparation • Multiplication Facts: Memory Group *Activity* Flash Cards	378A **378**	N, A, UP
Investigation 7	Lesson Preparation • Symmetry, Part 1 *Activity* Symmetry, Part 1	383B **383**	G, UP
Cumulative Assessment	Power-Up Test 13, Cumulative Test 13, Performance Task 7		

Standards Benchmark Check Point

TEKS Strands Key:
- N = Number, Operation, and Quantitative Reasoning
- A = Patterns, Relationships, and Algebraic Thinking
- G = Geometry and Spatial Reasoning
- M = Measurement
- PST = Probability and Statistics
- UP = Underlying Processes and Mathematical Tools

Section 8	Lessons 71–80, Investigation 8	Page	TEKS Strands Focus
Overview	Lessons 71–80, Investigation 8	385A	
Lesson 71	Lesson Preparation • **Rectangular Prisms**	385G **385**	G, UP
Lesson 72	Lesson Preparation • **Counting Cubes** Activity Counting Cubes	390A **390**	M, UP
Lesson 73	Lesson Preparation • **Volume** Activity Volume	394A **394**	M, UP
Lesson 74	Lesson Preparation • **Weight: Ounces, Pounds, and Tons** Activity Weighing Objects	399A **399**	M, UP
Lesson 75	Lesson Preparation • **Geometric Solids** Activity Solids	404A **404**	G, UP
Cumulative Assessment	Power-Up Test 14, Cumulative Test 14, Test-Day Activity 7		
Lesson 76	Lesson Preparation • **Multplication Facts: 11s and 12s** Activity Modeling 11s and 12s	410A **410**	N, A, UP
Lesson 77	Lesson Preparation • **Multiplying Three Numbers** Activity Multiplying to Find Volume	416A **416**	M, UP
Lesson 78	Lesson Preparation • **Multiplying Multiples of Ten**	421A **421**	N, UP
Lesson 79	Lesson Preparation • **Length: Centimeters, Meters and Kilometers** Activity Metric Units of Length	425A **425**	M, UP
Lesson 80	Lesson Preparation • **Mass: Grams and Kilograms** Activity Metric Units of Mass	431A **431**	M, UP
Investigation 8	Lesson Preparation • **More About Geometric Solids** Activity Classifying Solids	436B **436**	G, UP
Cumulative Assessment	Power-Up Test 15, Cumulative Test 15, Performance Task 8		STANDARDS BENCHMARK CHECK POINT

TEKS Strands Key:
N = Number, Operation, and Quantitative Reasoning
A = Patterns, Relationships, and Algebraic Thinking
G = Geometry and Spatial Reasoning
M = Measurement
PST = Probability and Statistics
UP = Underlying Processes and Mathematical Tools

Section 9 — Lessons 81–90, Investigation 9

		Page	TEKS Strands Focus
Overview	Lessons 81–90, Investigation 9	440A	
Lesson 81	Lesson Preparation • Multiplying Two-Digit Numbers, Part 1 Activity Doubling Money	440G **440**	N, UP
Lesson 82	Lesson Preparation • Fair Share Activity Fair Share	445A **445**	N, UP
Lesson 83	Lesson Preparation • Finding Half of a Number	450A **450**	N, A, UP
Lesson 84	Lesson Preparation • Multiplying Two-Digit Numbers, Part 2	455A **455**	N, UP
Lesson 85	Lesson Preparation • Using Manipulatives to Divide by a One-Digit Number Activity Equal Groups	460A **460**	N, UP
Cumulative Assessment	Power-Up Test 16, Cumulative Test 16, Test-Day Activity 8		
Lesson 86	Lesson Preparation • Division Facts • Multiplication and Division Fact Families	465A **465**	N, A
Lesson 87	Lesson Preparation • Capacity Activity Measuring Capacity	471A **471**	N, M, UP
Lesson 88	Lesson Preparation • Even and Odd Numbers Activity Even and Odd Numbers	476A **476**	N, UP
Lesson 89	Lesson Preparation • Using a Multiplication Table to Divide by a One-Digit Number	481A **481**	N, UP
Lesson 90	Lesson Preparation • Equal Groups Stories, Part 2	486A **486**	N, UP
Investigation 9	Lesson Preparation • Symmetry, Part 2 Activity 1 Creating Symmetrical Figures Activity 2 Lines of Symmetry	491B **491**	G, UP
Cumulative Assessment	Power-Up Test 17, Cumulative Test 17, Performance Task 9		*Standards Benchmark Check Point*

TEKS Strands Key:
N = Number, Operation, and Quantitative Reasoning
A = Patterns, Relationships, and Algebraic Thinking
G = Geometry and Spatial Reasoning
M = Measurement
PST = Probability and Statistics
UP = Underlying Processes and Mathematical Tools

Section 10 — Lessons 91–100, Investigation 10

		Page	TEKS Strands Focus
Overview	Lessons 91–100, Investigation 10	494A	
Lesson 91	Lesson Preparation	494G	
	• Multiplying Three-Digit Numbers, Part 1	494	N, UP
	Activity Estimation by Volume		
Lesson 92	Lesson Preparation	499A	
	• Parentheses	499	N
	• Using Compatible Numbers, Part 1		
Lesson 93	Lesson Preparation	504A	
	• Estimating Products	504	N, UP
Lesson 94	Lesson Preparation	508A	
	• Using Compatible Numbers, Part 2	508	N
Lesson 95	Lesson Preparation	512A	
	• Using Estimation to Verify Answers	512	N, UP
Cumulative Assessment	Power-Up Test 18, Cumulative Test 18, Test-Day Activity 9		
Lesson 96	Lesson Preparation	516A	
	• Rounding to the Nearest Dollar	516	N, UP
Lesson 97	Lesson Preparation	520A	
	• Multiplying Three-Digit Numbers, Part 2	520	UP
Lesson 98	Lesson Preparation	525A	
	• Estimating by Weight or Mass	525	N, A, M
	Activity Estimating by Mass		
Lesson 99	Lesson Preparation	530A	
	• Effects of Estimation	530	N
Lesson 100	Lesson Preparation	534A	
	• Multiplying Dollars and Cents	534	UP
Investigation 10	Lesson Preparation	538B	
	• Evaluating Estimates	538	N, UP
	Activity Evaluating Estimates		
Cumulative Assessment	Power-Up Test 19, Cumulative Test 19, Performance Task 10		*Standards Benchmark Check Point*

TEKS Strands Key:
N = Number, Operation, and Quantitative Reasoning
A = Patterns, Relationships, and Algebraic Thinking
G = Geometry and Spatial Reasoning
M = Measurement
PST = Probability and Statistics
UP = Underlying Processes and Mathematical Tools

Section 11 — Lessons 101–110, Investigation 11

		Page	TEKS Strands Focus
Overview	Lessons 101–110, Investigation 11	540A	
Lesson 101	Lesson Preparation • Dividing Two-Digit Numbers	540G 540	N, A, UP
Lesson 102	Lesson Preparation • Sorting	545A 545	UP
Lesson 103	Lesson Preparation • Ordering Numbers Through 9,999	549A 549	N, UP
Lesson 104	Lesson Preparation • Sorting Geometric Shapes	553A 553	G, UP
Lesson 105	Lesson Preparation • Diagrams for Sorting	559A 559	G, UP
Cumulative Assessment	Power-Up Test 20, Cumulative Test 20, Test-Day Activity 10		
Lesson 106	Lesson Preparation • Estimating Area, Part 1	564A 564	M
Lesson 107	Lesson Preparation • Drawing Enlargements Activity Drawing Enlargements	569A 569	UP
Lesson 108	Lesson Preparation • Estimating Area, Part 2 Activity Estimating Area with a Grid	573A 573	M
Lesson 109	Lesson Preparation • Points on a Grid	577A 577	A
Lesson 110	Lesson Preparation • Dot-to-Dot Design Activity Dot-to-Dot Design	582A 582	A, UP
Investigation 11	Lesson Preparation • Planning a Design	586B 586	UP
Cumulative Assessment	Power-Up Test 21, Cumulative Test 21, Performance Task 11	Standards Benchmark Check Point	

TEKS Strands Key:
N = Number, Operation, and Quantitative Reasoning
A = Patterns, Relationships, and Algebraic Thinking
G = Geometry and Spatial Reasoning
M = Measurement
PST = Probability and Statistics
UP = Underlying Processes and Mathematical Tools

QUICK REFERENCE

Place Value

Thousands			,	Ones		
Hundred Thousands	Ten Thousands	Thousands	,	Hundreds	Tens	Ones
___	___	___	,	___	___	___

Comparison Symbols

>	greater than
<	less than
=	equal to

Time

Length

Metric
1 kilometer = 1000 meters
1 meter = 100 centimeters

Customary
1 yard = 3 feet
1 foot = 12 inches

Mass and Weight

Metric
1 kilogram = 1000 grams

Customary
1 ton = 2000 pounds
1 pound = 16 ounces

Capacity

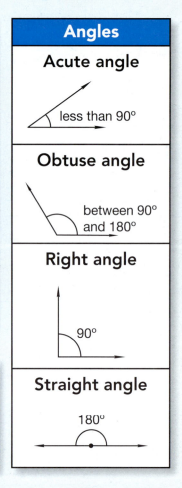

Arithmetic with Two Numbers

Addition	addend + addend = sum	addend + addend ――― sum
Subtraction	greater − lesser = difference	greater − lesser ――― difference
Multiplication	factor × factor = product	factor × factor ――― product
Division	dividend ÷ divisor = quotient	divisor) dividend with quotient on top

Angles

Acute angle — less than 90°

Obtuse angle — between 90° and 180°

Right angle — 90°

Straight angle — 180°

Lines and Segments

line	segment	parallel Lines	perpendicular
A B	D E		

Content by Strand

This chart gives you an overview of the instruction of math concepts by strand in **Saxon Math** *Intermediate 3*. The chart shows where in the textbook each topic is taught and references the New Concepts section of a lesson or the instructional part of an Investigation.

Numbers and Operations	LESSON NUMBER
Numeration	
digits	11, 32
read and write whole numbers, decimals, fractions, and mixed numbers	5, 12, 29, 32, 41
place value to hundred thousands	11, 12, 32, Investigation 4
find the value of a collection of coins and bills	21, 22, 25, 81, Investigation 2
number line (whole numbers, fractions, mixed numbers)	4, 15, 17, 27, 33, 48
expanded form	11, 13, 14
model a fractional part of a whole, group, or set	5, 29, 41, 42, 43, 44, 46, 47, 48, 49
name a fractional part of a whole, group, or set	5, 29, 41, 44, 46, 47, 48, 49
equivalent fractions	43, 46, 47
comparison symbols (=, <, >)	17, 27, 43, 49, 99
compare and order whole numbers, decimals, and fractions	17, 27, 39, 43, 49, 99, 103, Investigation 10
Basic operations	
model addition and subtraction	6, 7, 9, 13, 14, 16, 19
add and subtract whole numbers	6, 7, 8, 9, 10, 13, 14, 16, 18, 19, 20, 23, 24, 25, 26, 28, 36, 40, 92, 94, 95
add and subtract decimal numbers	21, 22, 26, 29, 92
mental math strategies	1–120
regroup in addition, subtraction, and multiplication	14, 16, 19, 21, 28, 60, 84, 91, 97, 101
model multiplication	54, 55, 57, 60, 61, 62, 63, 76, 77, 78, 86
multiply whole numbers	54, 55, 56, 57, 59, 60, 61, 62, 63, 64, 70, 76, 77, 78, 81, 84, 86, 91, 93, 94, 95, 97, 101
multiplication as repeated addition	54, 59
model division	82, 85, 86, 101
division notations: division box, division sign, and division bar	82, 83, 85, 86, 89, 90, 101

Content By Strand   T17

Numbers and Operations, Continued	LESSON NUMBER
Properties of numbers and operations	
even and odd numbers	88, 102, 105
square numbers	61
parentheses	92
inverse operations (fact families)	8, 9, 40, 83, 86, 89
Estimation	
round whole numbers	15, 30, 93, 94, 95, 99
round to the nearest dollar	96
estimate sums, differences, products	30, 92, 93, 94, 95, 99
compatible numbers	92, 94

Algebra	
Patterns and relations	
use/describe/extend a whole number or geometric pattern	2, 3, 4, 33, 34, 38, 53, 59, 61
patterns in multiplication	54, 55, 59, 61, 64, 76, 78, 91
extend a table	25, 34, 63, 76, 98
Number sentences and unknowns	
solve addition number sentences using concrete and pictorial models	6, 9, 13, 16, 36 58
solve subtraction number sentences using concrete and pictorial models	7, 14, 19, 28, 39
solve multiplication number sentences using concrete and pictorial models	55, 57, 60, 61, 62
solve division number sentences using concrete and pictorial models	82, 85
write/solve number sentences given a problem situation	6, 7, 8, 9, 18, 20, 30, 36, 39, 40, 60, 63, 64, 73, 78, 79, 81, 84, 85, 89, 90
solve number sentences with unknowns	9, 36, 40, 86, 90

Geometry	LESSON NUMBER
Describe properties and relationships of lines	
parallel, perpendicular	66, 71, 105, Investigation 4
Identify/describe angles	
acute, obtuse, right, or straight	65, 66, 69, 105
2-Dimensional figures	
identify/describe polygons by their attributes	40, 51, 53, 66, 67, 68, 69, 104
congruence	68, 71
classify triangles	69, 104
classify quadrilaterals	51, 66, 104
3-Dimensional figures	
identify/describe geometric solids by their attributes	71, 75, 104, Investigation 8
Points and coordinate geometry	
name and graph points on a line	4, 15, 17, 27, 33, 48
name and graph ordered pairs	109, 110, Investigation 11
identify symmetry	Investigation 7, Investigation 9
Measurement	
Measuring physical attributes	
use customary units of length, area, volume, weight, capacity	34, 35, 37, 52, 58, 62, 63, 73, 74, 87, 98, 106, 108, Investigation 4
use metric units of length, area, volume, mass, capacity	79, 80, 87, 98, 106, 108
use temperature scales: Fahrenheit, Celsius	4, *
measure time	3, 5, 38, *
choose appropriate unit of measurement	34, 74, 79, 80, 87

* These concepts are presented in Power Ups in lessons throughout the book.

Content By Strand   T19

Measurement, Continued	LESSON NUMBER
Solving measurement problems	
perimeter of polygons	58, 66, 67, 79
area of rectangles	52, 53, 62, 63
estimate area	62, 63
volume of rectangular prisms	72, 73, 77
Use appropriate measurement instruments	
ruler (U.S. customary and metric)	34, 35, 37, 52, 58, 66, 73, 79, Investigation 4
thermometer	4, *
Data Analysis and Probability	
Data interpretation, collection and representation	
collect data	Investigation 3, Investigation 6
display data	105, Investigation 1, Investigation 3, Investigation 6
pictographs	Investigation 1, Investigation 3
bar graphs	Investigation 1, Investigation 6
Probability	
describe events as more likely, less likely, or equally likely to occur	45, 50, Investigation 5
Problem Solving	
four-step problem-solving process	1–110
problem-solving strategies	1–110

* These concepts are presented in Power Ups in lessons throughout the book.

Saxon Math Intermediate 3

NOTES

SECTION 7 OVERVIEW

Lesson Planner

Lesson	New Concepts	Materials	Resources
61	• Squares • Multiplication Facts: Square Numbers	• Manipulative kit: color tiles	• Power Up 61
62	• Area, Part 1		• Power Up 62 • Lesson Activity 23
63	• Area, Part 2	• 1-foot construction paper squares (2 per group) • Grid paper	• Power Up 63
64	• Multiplication Facts: 9s		• Power Up 64
65	• Angles	• Manipulative kit: ruler • Straws (1 per student)	• Power Up 65
Cumulative Assessment			• Cumulative Test 12 • Power-Up Test 12 • Test-Day Activity 6
66	• Parallelograms	• Manipulative kit: ruler	• Power Up 66
67	• Polygons	• Manipulative kit: ruler	• Power Up 67
68	• Congruent Shapes		• Power Up 68
69	• Triangles		• Power Up 69 • Lesson Activity 24
70	• Multiplication facts: Memory Group	• Student fraction circles	• Power Up 70 • Lesson Activity 25
Cumulative Assessment			• Cumulative Test 13 • Power-Up Test 13 • Performance Task 7
Inv. 7	• Symmetry, Part 1	• Manipulative kit: color tiles or pattern blocks	• Lesson Activity 26

 All resources are also available on the Resources and Planner CD.

Additional Resources

- Instructional Masters
- Reteaching Masters
- Resources and Planner CD
- Calculator Activities
- Assessment Guide
- Performance Tasks
- Instructional Transparencies
- Answer Key CD
- Power Up Workbook
- Written Practice Workbook

LESSONS 61–70, INVESTIGATION 7

Math Highlights

Enduring Understandings — The "Big Picture"

After completing Section 7, students will understand that:

- square numbers can be represented by arrays of square units that form square figures.
- certain attributes of geometric figures are measurable using standard units.
- geometric figures can be described using formal vocabulary.
- two-dimensional geometric figures are classified according to attributes including size of angles and number of sides.

Essential Questions

- How is a square number related to a pattern of square arrays?
- How can we use standard measurement tools such as a ruler to compare the attributes of geometric figures?
- Why is it important to use formal vocabulary when describing geometric figures?
- What are some attributes used to classify polygons?

Math Content Highlights	Math Processes Highlights

Number Sense
• Multiplication *Lessons 61, 64, 70*
• Estimation *Lesson 63*
 	
Algebraic Thinking
• Identifying Patterns on a Table *Lesson 63*
 	
Geometry and Measurement
• Finding Area *Lessons 62, 63*
• Types of Angles *Lesson 65*
• Describing and Classifying Two-Dimensional Geometric Figures *Lessons 66–69*
• Finding and Creating Lines of Symmetry *Inv. 7*
	Problem Solving
	• Strategies
	  – Draw a Picture or Diagram *Lessons 62, 63*
	  – Find or Extend a Pattern *Lessons 65, 70*
	  – Make or Use a Table, Chart, or Graph *Lessons 64–66*
	  – Make an Organized List *Lesson 63*
	  – Make It Simpler *Lessons 67–69*
	  – Work Backwards *Lesson 66*
	  – Work a Simpler Problem *Lesson 67*
	  – Write a Number Sentence *Lessons 61, 62, 64*
	• Real-World Applications *Lessons 61–70, Inv. 7*
	
	Communication
	• Analyze *Lessons 63, 70*
	• Discuss *Lessons 67, 68, Inv. 7*
	• Explain *Lesson 65*
	• Generalize *Lessons 62, 64*
	• Verify *Lesson 64*
	
	Connections
	• Math and Other Subjects
	  – Math and History *Lesson 61*
	  – Math and Geography *Lessons 63–65, 69*
	  – Math and Science *Lessons 64, 65, 69, Inv. 7*
	
	Representation
	• Represent *Lessons 61, 62, 64, 65, 68, 69*
	• Manipulative Use *Lessons 61, 63, 65, 68*

SECTION 7

Differentiated Instruction

Support for differentiated instruction is included with each lesson. Specific resources and features are listed on each lesson planning page. Features in the Teacher's Manual to customize instruction include the following:

Teacher's Manual Support

Alternative Approach	Provides a different path to concept development. *Lessons 61–63, 65, 66, 68*
Manipulative Use	Provides alternate concept development through the use of manipulatives. *Lessons 61–63, 65–70*
Flexible Grouping	Provides suggestions for various grouping strategies tied to specific lesson examples. *TM page 387A*
Inclusion	Provides ideas for including all students by accommodating special needs. *Lessons 62, 65, 67–69*
Math Language	Provides a list of new and maintained vocabulary words along with words that might be difficult for English learners. *Lessons 61–70, Inv. 7*
English Learners	Provides strategies for teaching specific vocabulary that may be difficult for English learners. *Lessons 61–70, Inv. 7*
Errors and Misconceptions	Provides information about common misconceptions students encounter with concepts. *Lessons 63, 66–68, Inv. 7*
Extend the Example	Provides additional concept development for advanced learners. *Lessons 61–64, 66–68*
Extend the Problem	Provides an opportunity for advanced learners to broaden concept development by expanding on a particular problem approach or context. *Lessons 61, 63–70*
Early Finishers	Provides additional math concept extensions for advanced learners at the end of the Written Practice. *Lessons 61, 62, 66, 67, 69, 70*
Investigate Further	Provides further depth to concept development by providing additional activities for an investigation. *Inv. 7*

Additional Resources

The following resources are also available to support differentiated instruction:
- Adaptations for Saxon Math
- English Learner Handbook
- Online Activities
- Reteaching Masters

Technology

Student Resources
- Student Edition eBook
- Calculator Activities
- Online Resources at www.SaxonMath.com/Int3Activities
  — Real World Investigations
  — Online Activities *Lessons 61–70, Inv. 7*
  — Online Calculator Activity

Teacher Resources
- Resources and Planner CD
- Test and Practice Generator CD
- Monitoring Student Progress: eGradebook CD
- Teacher Manual eBook CD
- Answer Key CD
- Adaptations for Saxon Math CD
- Online Resources at www.SaxonMath.com

LESSONS 61–70, INVESTIGATION 7

Cumulative Assessment

The assessments in Saxon Math are frequent and consistently placed to offer a regular method of ongoing testing.

Power-Up Test: Allow no more than ten minutes for this test of basic facts and problem solving skills.

Cumulative Test: Next administer this test, which checks mastery of concepts in previous lessons.

Test-Day Activity and Performance Task: The remaining class time can be spent on these activities. Students can finish the Test-Day Activity for homework or complete the extended Performance Task in another class period.

After Lesson 65

Power-Up Test 12

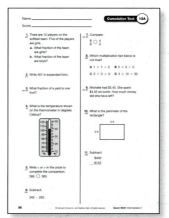
Cumulative Test 12

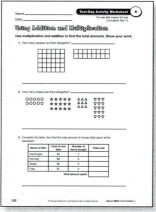
Test-Day Activity 6

After Lesson 70

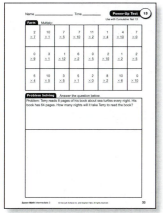
Power-Up Test 13

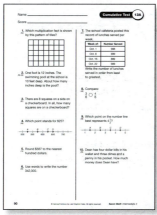
Cumulative Test 13

Performance Task 7

Evidence of Learning — What Students Should Know

By the conclusion of Section 7, students should be able to demonstrate the following competencies:

- Learn multiplication facts using concrete models. **TEKS (3.4)(A)**
- Identify patterns in multiplication facts using models. **TEKS (3.6)(B)**
- Identify and extend whole-number and geometric patterns to make predictions and solve problems. **TEKS (3.6)(A)**
- Use pictorial or concrete models of square units to determine the area of two-dimensional surfaces. **TEKS (3.11)(C)**
- Use standard units to find the perimeter of a shape. **TEKS (3.11)(B)**
- Identify, classify, and describe two-dimensional geometric figures by their attributes. **TEKS (3.8)**

Reteaching

Students who score below 80% on assessments may be in need of reteaching. Refer to the Reteaching Masters for reteaching opportunities for every lesson.

Section Overview 7   328D

SECTION 7

Benchmarking and Tracking Standards

Benchmark Tests

Benchmark Tests correlated to lesson concepts allow you to assess student progress after every 20 lessons. An End-of-Course Test is a final benchmark test of the complete textbook. The Benchmark Tests are available in the Assessment Guide.

Monitoring Student Progress: eGradebook CD

To track TEKS mastery, enter students' scores on Cumulative Tests and Benchmark Tests into the Monitoring Student Progress: eGradebook CD. Use the report titled *Benchmark Standards Report* to determine which TEKS were assessed and the level of mastery for each student. Generate a variety of other reports for class tracking and more.

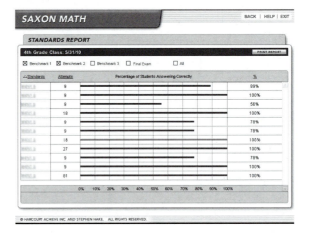

Test and Practice Generator CD

Test items also available in Spanish.

The Test and Practice Generator is an easy-to-manage benchmarking and assessment tool that creates unlimited practice and tests in multiple formats and allows you to customize questions or create new ones. A variety of reports are available to track student progress toward mastery of the TEKS throughout the year.

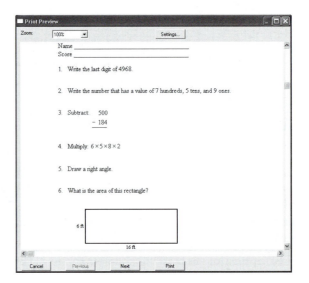

Northstar Math offers you real time benchmarking, tracking, and student progress monitoring.

Visit **www.northstarmath.com** for more information.

328E   Saxon Math Intermediate 3

LESSONS 61–70, INVESTIGATION 7

Content Trace

Lesson	New Concepts	Practiced	Assessed	Looking Forward
61	• Squares • Multiplication Facts: Square Numbers	Lesson 62 Lessons 61, 62, 63, 64, 65, 68, 69, 72, 73, 76, 80, 94	Test and Practice Generator	Lessons 62, 63, 66, 81, 84, 91, 97, 106, 108, 109
62	• Area, Part 1	Lessons 62, 64, 65, 67, 68, 72, 73, 77, 78, 79, 80, 81, 82, 83, 85, 87, 88	Tests 14, 15, 17	Lessons 63, 68, 72, 73, 106, 108
63	• Area, Part 2	Lessons 63, 64, 65, 69, 70, 72, 91, 92, 94, 97, 98, 99, 104, 105, 106, 107	Tests 20, 21	Lessons 64, 66, 68, 72, 73, 75, 106, 108
64	• Multiplication Facts: 9s	Lessons 64, 65, 66, 67, 69, 71, 72, 73, 75, 76, 78, 79	Test 14	Lessons 70, 73, 76, 78, 81, 84, 91, 97
65	• Angles	Lessons 65, 66, 72, 74, 77, 80, 90, 107	Tests 14, 15, 16, 19, 21	Lessons 66, 67, 68, 69, 73, 104, Inv. 7
66	• Parallelograms	Lessons 66, 68, 69, 70, 72, 80, 81	Test 15	Lessons 67, 68, 69, 104, Inv. 7, 9
67	• Polygons	Lessons 67, 68, 69, 70, 74, 80, 82, 84, 90, 103	Test 14, 16, 20	Lessons 68, 69, 75, 104, Inv. 7, 9
68	• Congruent Shapes	Lessons 69, 70, 71, 77, 86	Test 28	Lessons 69, 75, 104, Inv. 7, 9
69	• Triangles	Lessons 69, 70, 71, 77, 79, 86, 107	Test and Practice Generator	Lessons 75, 104, 106, 108, 109, Inv. 7, 9
70	• Multiplication Facts: Memory Group	Lessons 70, 71, 72, 73, 74, 75, 76, 77, 78, 79, 80, 81, 82	Tests 14, 15	Lessons 73, 76, 77, 78, 81, 84, 89, 91, 97
Inv. 7	• Symmetry	Lessons 71, 72, 73, 75, 80, 85, 90, 101	Test and Practice Generator	Lessons 75, 104, Inv. 8, 9

LESSON 61

Planning & Preparation

- **Squares**
- **Multiplication Facts: Square Numbers**

Objectives
- Use square numbers of objects to make square patterns.
- Learn multiplication facts for square numbers through 12×12.
- Identify the pattern of square numbers on a multiplication table.
- Write a multiplication fact represented by a given array.

Prerequisite Skills
- Recognize a square as a special type of rectangle.
- Use a multiplication table to find products.

Materials

Instructional Masters
- Power Up 61

Manipulative Kit
- Color tiles
- Rulers

Teacher-provided materials
- Grid paper*

  *optional

Texas Essential Knowledge and Skills

(3.4)(A) learn and apply multiplication facts through 12 by 12 using concrete models and objects

(3.6)(A) identify and extend geometric patterns to make predictions and solve problems

(3.6)(B) identify patterns in multiplication facts using concrete objects, pictorial models

(3.11)(C) use pictorial models of square units to determine the area of two-dimensional surfaces

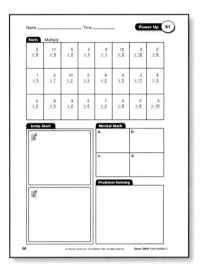

Power Up 61

Reaching All Special Needs Students

Special Education Students	At-Risk Students	English Learners	Advanced Learners
• Adaptations for Saxon Math	• Alternative Approach (TM) • Reteaching Masters	• English Learners (TM) • English Learner Handbook	• Early Finishers (SE) • Extend the Activity (TM) • Extend the Example (TM) • Extend the Problem (TM) • Online Activities

TM = Teacher's Manual
SE = Student Edition

Math Language

New	Maintained	English Learners
square number	factor product square	special

328G Saxon Math Intermediate 3

Problem Solving Discussion

Problem

Jill listened to her favorite radio station from 4:00 p.m. to 5:00 p.m. During that hour, the radio station played 3 commercials. Each commercial lasted 4 minutes. Altogether, how many minutes of commercials did the radio station play between 4:00 and 5:00?

Focus Strategy  **Write a Number Sentence**

Understand Understand the problem.

"What information are we given?"

1. Jill listened to the radio from 4:00 p.m. to 5:00 p.m.
2. The station played 3 commercials.
3. Each commercial lasted 4 minutes.

"What are we asked to do?"

We are asked to find how many minutes of commercials the station played between 4:00 and 5:00.

Plan Make a plan.

"How can we use the information we know to solve the problem?"

We can *write a number sentence* to find the total number of minutes.

Solve Carry out the plan.

"How long was each commercial?"

4 minutes

"How many commercials were played during the hour Jill listened to the radio?"

3 commercials

"What kind of number sentence can we write to find the total?"

We can write an addition number sentence.

"What addition number sentence can we write to solve this problem?"

4 minutes + 4 minutes + 4 minutes = 12 minutes

Check Look back.

"Did we complete the task?"

Yes, we found the total number of commercial minutes played by the radio station between 4:00 and 5:00 (12 minutes).

"Is our answer reasonable?"

Yes, we know that our answer is reasonable because 3 commercials playing for 4 minutes each have a total length of 4 + 4 + 4 = 12 minutes.

"What problem solving strategy did we use, and how did it help us?"

We *wrote a number sentence* to find the total length of the commercials.

"Can we use multiplication instead of addition to solve this problem?"

Yes, this is also an equal-groups problem. We can write this number sentence:

3×4 minutes = 12 minutes.

LESSON 61

Power Up

Facts
Distribute **Power Up 61** to students. See answers below.

Jump Start
Before students begin the Mental Math exercise, do these exercises as a class.

Mental Math
Encourage students to share different ways to mentally compute these exercises. Strategies for exercises are listed below.

a. Think 6 + 4 = 10
   10 + 6 + 4 = 10 + 10 = 20

c. Think $1.00 − $0.50 + $0.05
   $1.00 − $0.45 = $1.00 − $0.50 + $0.05
   = $0.50 + $0.05 = $0.55

   Count Up
   $0.45 + $0.05 = $0.50 + $0.50 = $1.00
   $0.05 + $0.50 = $0.55

Problem Solving
Refer to **Problem-Solving Strategy Discussion**, p. 328H.

- Squares
- Multiplication Facts: Square Numbers

Texas Essential Knowledge and Skills
(3.4)(A) learn and apply multiplication facts through 12 by 12 using concrete models and objects
(3.6)(A) identify and extend geometric patterns to make predictions and solve problems
(3.6)(B) identify patterns in multiplication facts using concrete objects, pictorial models
(3.11)(C) use pictorial models of square units to determine the area of two-dimensional surfaces

Power Up

facts Power Up 61

jump start
 Count up by 7s from 0 to 70.
Count up by 10s from 5 to 95.

Write two multiplication facts using the numbers 2, 12, and 24. $2 \times 12 = 24$; $12 \times 2 = 24$

Draw a rectangle that is 1 inch long and 1 inch wide.
See student work.

mental math

a. **Number Sense:** 10 + 6 + 4   20

b. **Time:** It is 2:45 p.m. How many minutes is it until 3:00 p.m.?   15 min

c. **Money:** One yo-yo costs $0.45. Shantessa bought one yo-yo with $1.00. How much change did she receive? $0.55

d. **Money:** Find the value of these bills and coins: $13.05

328 *Saxon Math* Intermediate 3

Facts Multiply:

2 × 8 = **16**	11 × 5 = **55**	5 × 0 = **0**	2 × 4 = **8**	2 × 1 = **2**	12 × 2 = **24**	5 × 12 = **60**	2 × 6 = **12**
1 × 5 = **5**	5 × 7 = **35**	10 × 2 = **20**	5 × 3 = **15**	9 × 2 = **18**	4 × 5 = **20**	2 × 11 = **22**	6 × 5 = **30**
5 × 2 = **0**	8 × 5 = **40**	3 × 2 = **6**	5 × 5 = **25**	7 × 2 = **14**	5 × 9 = **45**	0 × 8 = **0**	5 × 10 = **50**

problem solving

Jill listened to her favorite radio station from 4:00 p.m. to 5:00 p.m. During that hour, the radio station played 3 commercials. Each commercial lasted 4 minutes. Altogether, how many minutes of commercials did the radio station play between 4:00 and 5:00? 12 minutes

New Concepts

Squares

Tiles are often used to cover floors, shower walls, and counter tops. Many tiles are shaped like **squares.** Remember that a square is a special kind of rectangle with four sides of equal length. We can arrange square tiles to make larger squares.

Example 1

We can make square patterns using 1 tile, 4 tiles, or 9 tiles.

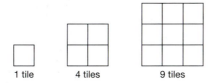

1 tile   4 tiles   9 tiles

How many tiles are needed to make the next square pattern in this sequence?

We add one more row and column of tiles. We count **16 tiles.**

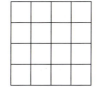

Generalize Can you name another number of tiles that can make a square pattern? sample: 25, 36

Multiplication Facts: Square Numbers

Numbers like 1, 4, and 9 are sometimes called **square numbers.** A **square number** is the product of two identical factors. We can write these numbers as multiplication facts.

$1 \times 1 = 1$ $2 \times 2 = 4$ $3 \times 3 = 9$

Lesson 61   329

New Concepts

Real-World Connection

"You have seen tile floors before. Where else have you seen squares arranged in a pattern to make a larger square?"

Write students' responses on the board. sample: stamps on a sheet of stamps, panes of glass in a window, a quilt

Explanation

Inform students that when a larger square is made out of smaller squares, the large square must have an equal number of rows and columns.

"If we had 5 rows and 3 columns, would we have a square?" no

"What would we call this shape?" a rectangle

Example 1
Connection

Guide students to identify the number of rows and columns in each square pattern pictured.

"What do you notice about the square patterns?" The number of rows and columns increases by 1 each time; The number of rows and columns is equal in each figure.

Extend the Example

"Look at the number of tiles that make these square patterns."

Write the numbers of the first six squares on the board or overhead: 1, 4, 9, 16, 25, 36.

"What pattern do you see for these numbers?" samples: 1×1, 2×2, 3×3, 4×4, 5×5, 6×6; The numbers alternate between even and odd.

(continued)

Math Background

Numerous interesting arithmetic facts relating to squares exist. For example, square numbers arise when we add odd numbers in the following way:

$1 + 3 = 4$
$1 + 3 + 5 = 9$
$1 + 3 + 5 + 7 = 16$
$1 + 3 + 5 + 7 + 9 = 25$

Notice that the square number on the right-hand side of each of these equations is exactly the number of addends on the left-hand side of each equation multiplied by itself. (For example, $25 = 5 \times 5$ and $1 + 3 + 5 + 7 + 9$ contains exactly five addends, which are the first five odd counting numbers.)

English Learners

Special means to be different or unusual. Say:

"Why do you think we call a square a special kind of rectangle?" sample: A square is a rectangle, but all 4 sides of a square are the same length.

Ask:

"What might be some reasons for your family to take a special trip far away?" samples: wedding, vacation

Ask students to discuss a special meal or tradition in their family.

Lesson 61   329

New Concept (Continued)

Activity
Extend the Activity

Draw a square array representing 3 × 3 = 9 on the board. Have students do the same at their desks. Tell students to make a bigger square by adding one row and one column as you do the same on the board.

"How many little squares did we add to the big square?" 7

Now repeat the process to get a larger square.

"How many little squares did we add to the big square this time?" 9

Repeat the process once more.

"How many little squares did we add to the big square this time?" 11

Help students recognize the sequence of odd numbers you have just uncovered. Explain that the number is odd because the additional row and column that are added each time to get a larger square share one small square.

Example 2

Remind students that we multiply *factors* to get the *product*. Have students check the answer using repeated addition.
4 + 4 + 4 + 4 = 16
5 + 5 + 5 + 5 + 5 = 25

(continued)

Activity
Squares on a Grid

Materials: color tiles

Use tiles to build squares that show all the square numbers from 1 to 25. You can start with the square numbers 1, 4, and 9. Write a multiplication fact for each square.

On a multiplication table, the square numbers appear diagonally across the table. Each square number is the product of two identical factors.

	0	1	2	3	4	5	6	7	8	9	10	11	12
0	0	0	0	0	0	0	0	0	0	0	0	0	0
1	0	1	2	3	4	5	6	7	8	9	10	11	12
2	0	2	4	6	8	10	12	14	16	18	20	22	24
3	0	3	6	9	12	15	18	21	24	27	30	33	36
4	0	4	8	12	16	20	24	28	32	36	40	44	48
5	0	5	10	15	20	25	30	35	40	45	50	55	60
6	0	6	12	18	24	30	36	42	48	54	60	66	72
7	0	7	14	21	28	35	42	49	56	63	70	77	84
8	0	8	16	24	32	40	48	56	64	72	80	88	96
9	0	9	18	27	36	45	54	63	72	81	90	99	108
10	0	10	20	30	40	50	60	70	80	90	100	110	120
11	0	11	22	33	44	55	66	77	88	99	110	121	132
12	0	12	24	36	48	60	72	84	96	108	120	132	144

Example 2

Find each product.

a. 4 × 4   b. 5 × 5

We can make square patterns or use a multiplication table to find the products.

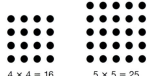

4 × 4 = 16   5 × 5 = 25

Alternative Approach: Using Manipulatives

In addition to tiles, students can use grid paper to represent square numbers. Give each student a piece of grid paper. Have them square the numbers 1–12 and outline the number of boxes on the graph paper to show the square represented by the multiplication fact. Suggest that students label each small square within one of the larger squares.

Example 3

The square number 121 is the product of which two identical factors?

We see on the multiplication table that 121 is the product of 11 × 11.

Lesson Practice

1; 4; 9; 16; 25; 36; 49; 64; 81; 100; 121; 144

a. Copy and complete each multiplication fact below.

1 × 1	2 × 2	3 × 3	4 × 4
5 × 5	6 × 6	7 × 7	8 × 8
9 × 9	10 × 10	11 × 11	12 × 12

▶ b. This square is made with 10 rows of 10 tiles. How many tiles are in this square? 100 tiles

▶ c. Here is a sequence of square numbers. What are the next three numbers in the sequence?

1, 4, 9, 16, __25__, __36__, __49__, ...

Written Practice — Distributed and Integrated

1. Square tiles covered the front porch. How many tiles were used? 24
(53)

2. Write a multiplication fact for the array of tiles in problem 1. 6 × 4 = 24
(57)

Formulate Write number sentences for problems 3 and 4. Then write a complete sentence to answer each question.

▶ 3. Fresh pies were on sale for $7.99. If the regular price was $9.87, how much is saved by buying them on sale? $9.87 − s = $7.99; sample: Buying a pie on sale saves $1.88.
(20, 26)

▶ 4. Ruben took six big steps to cross the room. About how many feet is it across the room? (Each big step is about a yard, which is three feet.) 6 × 3 ft = f; sample: It is about 18 ft across the room.
(34, 60)

Lesson 61   331

New Concept (Continued)

Lesson Practice

Guided Practice

Use these problems as guided practice to check the students' understanding of today's concept.

Problem b

Students can skip count by 10s ten times to solve this problem.

Problem c

Suggest that students find these numbers on a multiplication table and see if there is a pattern that can be followed to find the next three numbers.

Extend the Problem

"What is the 8th term in this sequence?" 64

"What is the 10th term?" 100

Closure The questions below help assess the concepts taught in this lesson.

"If we see 3 rows of tiles and 6 columns of tiles, are we looking at a picture of a square number?" no

"How do we know?" The number of tiles in the columns and rows are equal in a square number.

Discuss real-world situations where finding a square number might be helpful. Examples are given below.

- We need to find the number of tiles to buy for a square floor.
- We need to find out how many boxes with a square bottom will fit in a square storage area.

Written Practice

Math Conversations
Independent Practice and Discussions to Increase Understanding

Problems 3 and 4 Formulate

3. Students may need help recognizing this as a "some went away" story.

   "The price started at $9.87 and then some went away."

4. Students should recognize this as an "equal groups" story. There are 6 groups, or big steps, with 3 feet in each group:
   6 steps × 3 feet in each step = total feet.

(continued)

Lesson 61   331

Written Practice (Continued)

Math Conversations
Independent Practice and Discussions to Increase Understanding

Problem 6 Multiple Choice
Test Taking Strategy
Point out the word "not" in the question. That means that every answer choice except one will be equal to 16. Point out to students that 8 is multiplied by one number in choice **B** and a different number in choice **C**. These two products will be different, so only one will be 16. Either **B** or **C** must be the answer.

"If someone thinks 8 times 8 is 16, what mistake did they make?" They confused multiplication with addition.

Problem 12 Represent
Hold up a sheet of paper as an example of a rectangle and trace its perimeter with your finger.

Problem 13
Encourage students to perform the multiplications by memory and then check their answers with a multiplication table or tiles to complete the problems.

Extend the Problem
"Which one of these problems represents a square number?" problem **c**.

(continued)

---

5. The odometer of John's car showed this display:
(32)

a. Write the number of miles shown using digits. 50,674 miles

b. Use words to state the number of miles the car has been driven. fifty thousand, six hundred seventy-four miles

6. Multiple Choice Which of these multiplications does *not* equal 16? c
(56, 59, 61)

  A 16 × 1   **B** 8 × 2   **C** 8 × 8   **D** 4 × 4

7. Order these events from first to last. Then make a timeline from 1950 to 2000 to display the events. 1964, 1969, 1974, 1997; See student work.
(33)

  1976: Mars *Viking* probe launched   1997: Mars *Sojourner* probe launched

  1969: Moon landing   1964: First space walk

8. What number is shown by the base ten blocks? 213
(11)

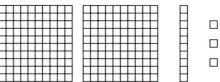

9. What fraction of the marbles in the bag are blue? $\frac{3}{7}$
(44)

10. If Chad picks one of the marbles in problem **9** without looking, which color is he more likely to pick: white or blue? white
(50)

11. Compare these two fractions: $\frac{3}{7}$ ⊙ $\frac{4}{7}$ <
(49)

12. **Represent** Draw a rectangle 3 inches long and 2 inches wide. What is the perimeter of the rectangle? See student work; 10 in.
(52, 58)

13. Find each product:
(59, 61)

  a. 9 × 6   54   **b.** 9 × 5   45   **c.** 7 × 7   49

Add or subtract, as shown:

14. (21, 22) 38¢ + 75¢ + $1 $2.13

15. (23) $450 − $375 $75

16. (16) $463 + $98 $561

17. (55, 61) 11 × 11   121

▶ **18.** (2, 32) **Conclude** Find the next four numbers in this sequence:

200, 400, 600, __800__, __1,000__, __1,200__, __1,400__, …

19. (32) Write 73,492 in expanded form.   70,000 + 3,000 + 400 + 90 + 2

20. (40) A flock of 95 birds hopped around the park. Some flew away to find more food. Then there were 67 birds in the park. How many birds flew away? Write and solve a subtraction number sentence to find the answer.   95 − d = 67; 28 birds

Real-World Connection

Roberto's team scored 59 points in a basketball game. Ian's team scored fewer points than Roberto's team. Could the total number of points scored by both teams be 123? Explain.   no; sample: The total number of points cannot be 123 because 59 + 64 = 123 and 64 > 59.

Lesson 61   333

Understanding square numbers and the construction of squares prepares students for

- **Lessons 62 and 63,** area.
- **Lesson 66,** parallelograms.
- **Lessons 81 and 84,** multiplying two-digit numbers.
- **Lessons 91 and 97,** multiplying three-digit numbers.
- **Lessons 106 and 108,** estimating area.
- **Lesson 109,** points on a grid.

Written Practice (Continued)

Math Conversations
Independent Practice and Discussions to Increase Understanding

▶ **Problem 18** **Conclude**
"In this problem, we are skip counting by what number?" 200

Help students see that skip counting by 200s is the same as skip counting by 2s except that there are two zeros attached:

2, 4, 6, 8 ⟶ 200, 400, 600, 800

Errors and Misconceptions

▶ **Problem 3**
Some students may struggle with the terms "regular price" and "sale price." Let them know that to find how much is saved, the sale price is subtracted from the regular price.

▶ **Problem 12**
Students often forget to record the units for perimeter. Remind them that perimeter is named with both a number and a unit of length such as inches or feet.

Suggest to students that they start by finding the number that can be added to 59 to get a sum of 123. Then have them answer the question and explain their answers.

Lesson 61   333

LESSON 62

Planning & Preparation

• Area, Part 1

Texas Essential Knowledge and Skills

(3.4)(A) apply multiplication facts through 12 by 12 using objects

(3.6)(B) identify patterns in multiplication facts using concrete objects and pictorial models

(3.11)(B) use standard units to find the perimeter of a shape

(3.11)(C) use concrete and pictorial models of square units to determine the area of two-dimensional surfaces

Objectives
- Explain the differences between a shape's perimeter and its area.
- Use square units to measure area.
- Draw rectangles on a grid and determine their areas.
- Multiply the length and width of a rectangle to find its area in square units.

Prerequisite Skills
- Find the perimeters of rectangles.
- Use multiplication to find the numbers of small squares inside a rectangular grid pattern.
- Write a multiplication fact represented by a given array.
- Use manipulatives such as counters or color tiles to model arrays.

Materials
Instructional Masters
- Power Up 62
- Lesson Activity 23

Manipulative Kit
- Rulers
- Color tiles*

  optional

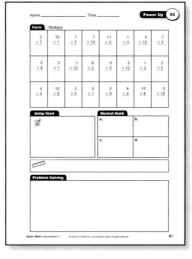

Power Up 62

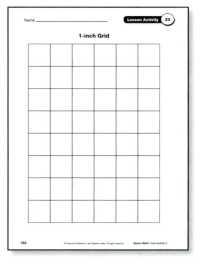

Lesson Activity 23

Differentiated Instruction

Reaching All Special Needs Students

Special Education Students	At-Risk Students	English Learners	Advanced Learners
• Inclusion (TM) • Adaptations for Saxon Math	• Alternative Approach (TM) • Reteaching Masters	• English Learners (TM) • English Learner Handbook	• Extend the Example (TM) • Early Finishers (SE) • Online Activities

TM=Teacher's Manual
SE=Student Edition

Math Language

New	Maintained	English Learners
area	length	recall
dozen	perimeter	
square inch	width	
square unit		

334A *Saxon Math* Intermediate 3

Problem Solving Discussion

Problem

A **dozen** is twelve. Ms. Kalinski arranged two dozen muffins in a 4 × 6 array. Then the children ate some of the muffins. This diagram shows the muffins that are remaining. How many muffins did the children eat? How many muffins are left? Use a "some went away" pattern to solve the problem.

Focus Strategies

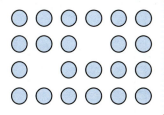 Draw a Picture or Diagram

 Write a Number Sentence

Understand Understand the problem.

"What information are we given?"

1. A dozen is twelve.
2. There are two dozen muffins in a 4 × 6 array.
3. Some muffins have been eaten.

"What are we asked to do?"

We are asked to find how many muffins were eaten. We are also asked to use a "some went away" pattern to find how many muffins remain.

Plan Make a plan.

"How can we use the information we know to solve the problem?"

To find the number of muffins that were eaten, we will *use the diagram*. To find the number of muffins that remain, we can *write a number sentence*. We need to subtract the number of muffins that were eaten from the beginning number.

Solve Carry out the plan.

"How many muffins were eaten?"

We look at the diagram and find that 2 muffins were eaten.

"How many muffins is two dozen?"

A dozen is 12, so two dozen is 12 + 12, or 24 muffins.

"What number sentence can we write?"

24 muffins − 2 muffins = 22 muffins

Check Look back.

"Did we complete the task?"

Yes, we found that 2 muffins were eaten and that 22 muffins remained.

"What problem solving strategies did we use, and how did they help us?"

We *used a diagram* to find how many muffins were eaten. Then, instead of counting the muffins that remained, we *wrote a number sentence* to calculate the answer.

Alternate Strategy

Act It Out or Make a Model

Have students use counters or color tiles to model the problem. Each counter or tile can stand for one muffin. Students can create a 4 × 6 array and then remove two counters/tiles to model the problem.

LESSON 62

Power Up

Facts
Distribute **Power Up 62** to students. See answers below.

Jump Start
Before students begin the Mental Math exercise, do these exercises as a class.

Mental Math
Encourage students to share different ways to mentally compute these exercises. Strategies for exercises are listed below.

a. Compare Numerators and Denominators
Compare the denominators.

$5 = 5$

Denominators are the same so compare the numerators.

$2 < 4 \rightarrow \frac{2}{5} < \frac{4}{5}$

c. Think $22 + 10 + 1$

$22 + 11 = 22 + 10 + 1 = 32 + 1 = 33$

Problem Solving
Refer to **Problem-Solving Strategy Discussion**, p. 334B.

LESSON 62 • Area, Part 1

> **Texas Essential Knowledge and Skills**
> (3.4)(A) apply multiplication facts through 12 by 12 using objects
> (3.6)(B) identify patterns in multiplication facts using concrete objects and pictorial models
> (3.11)(B) use standard units to find the perimeter of a shape
> (3.11)(C) use concrete of square units to determine the area of two-dimensional surfaces

Power Up

facts Power Up 62

jump start
Count down by 3s from 30 to 0.
Count down by 4s from 40 to 0.

Write the year "two thousand eleven" as digits. 2011

Draw a $3\frac{1}{2}$-inch segment on your worksheet. Record the length next to the segment. See student work; $3\frac{1}{2}$ in.

mental math

a. **Fractions:** Compare these fractions using the symbol <, >, or =.

$\frac{2}{5} \;\boxed{<}\; \frac{4}{5}$

b. **Money:** $\$1.50 + \$1.00$ $\$2.50$

c. **Number Sense:** $22 + 11$ 33

d. **Time:** It is afternoon. Kim began reading a book at the time shown on the clock. She stopped reading 2 hours later. What time did she stop reading the book? 6:10 p.m.

problem solving

A **dozen** is twelve. Ms. Kalinski arranged two dozen muffins in a 4×6 array. Then the children ate some of the muffins. This diagram shows the muffins that are remaining.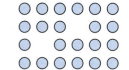

How many muffins did the children eat? How many muffins are left? Use a "some went away" pattern to solve the problem. 2 muffins; 22 muffins are left

---

334 Saxon Math Intermediate 3

Facts Multiply:

2 × 7 **14**	10 × 1 **10**	7 × 5 **35**	7 × 10 **70**	11 × 2 **22**	1 × 4 **4**	4 × 10 **40**	7 × 0 **0**
0 × 9 **0**	3 × 1 **3**	1 × 12 **12**	6 × 2 **12**	0 × 5 **0**	2 × 10 **20**	1 × 2 **2**	2 × 5 **10**
5 × 4 **20**	10 × 5 **50**	3 × 5 **15**	5 × 1 **5**	2 × 0 **0**	8 × 2 **16**	10 × 6 **60**	0 × 10 **0**

New Concept

In Lesson 58 we measured the perimeter of a rectangle. Recall that the perimeter of a rectangle is the distance around it. To measure perimeter, we add the lengths of the four sides of the rectangle.

In this lesson we will measure the **area** of a rectangle. The area of a rectangle is the amount of surface inside it. To measure area, we count the number of squares of standard size that fit inside the rectangle.

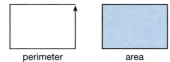

perimeter   area

Here we show the perimeter and area of a 3-inch by 2-inch rectangle.

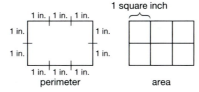

The perimeter of the rectangle is 10 inches, but the area is 6 square inches.

Notice that we use the words **square inches** to describe the area. Below we show an area equal to one square inch.

To measure small areas, we can use square inches. To measure larger areas, we can use square feet or square yards.

Lesson 62   335

Math Background

Is there a difference between a 4-inch square and 4 square inches?

Yes, the term 4-inch square describes a square with sides 4 inches long. Four square inches describes an area, but the area does not need to be the shape of a square; the terms are not synonyms. A 4-inch square has an area of 16 square inches, not 4 square inches.

4 square inches

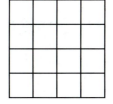
4-inch square

English Learners

To **recall** means to think back and remember something. Ask:

"Who can recall a multiplication fact with 4 as a factor?"

Ask volunteers to recite one of the facts for 1×4 through 12×4.

Ask:

"Who can recall the number of inches in one foot?" 12 inches

Ask students to recall a favorite story they have read.

New Concept

Observation

Explain to students that we call the measurements of the outside edge of a shape the perimeter and the surface inside the shape the area. Use the example of a fence around a yard. The fence is the perimeter of the yard and the yard inside of the fence would be the area.

Ask students to use one finger to trace the perimeter of their desktops. Then ask students to use their open hand to wipe the whole area of their desktop.

Active Learning

Have students stand and model the concepts of perimeter and area by forming rectangles. First, have the students hold hands and form two pairs of equal lines: one equal pair in the front and back and the other equal pair on the right and left. If students are left out, send them to the board to make a sketch of the others. Have each line join together to form the rectangle. Draw a rectangle on the board and label the sides with the number of students in each line.

"For our rectangle, what do we call the number we get by adding up the number of students in each line?" perimeter

Next have the students stand in a rectangular array. If their desks are arranged in rows and columns, just have them stand by their desks. Again send students to the board who are left out of the pattern to draw the rectangle.

"Now you have formed a different rectangle. What do the number of students represent for this rectangle?" area

End the activity by discussing how the two rectangles differed in size and why.

(continued)

New Concept (Continued)

Activity
Distribute one copy of Lesson Activity 23 to each student.

Discussion
"Would the area or perimeter be different if we switched the length and width to get a 3-inch by 6-inch rectangle?" Neither would be different.

"Why not?" sample: It does not matter in which order we add to find the perimeter or multiply to find the area.

Math Connection
Point out to students that the rectangles they are making on grid paper can represent arrays. Have them identify the number of rows and columns and name a multiplication fact to fit each rectangle.

For the *Generalize* question, remind students about the connection between arrays and area.

Example
"Why do units of inches make sense for this problem?" sample: Photographs are measured in inches.

Extend the Example
"What is the perimeter of this rectangle?" 24 inches

Lesson Practice

Guided Practice
Use these problems as guided practice to check the students' understanding of today's concept.

Problem a — Multiple Choice
Test-Taking Strategy

Ask students to eliminate incorrect answers and explain their reasoning. **A** can be eliminated because area is the space inside, not the lines around the outside. **C** can be eliminated because we could not measure the space inside in circles. **D** can be eliminated because we measure in square units and all rectangles are not squares.

Problem b
"Instead of counting each square, how can we find the number of stickers Stan used?" We can multiply 5×6.

(continued)

336 Saxon Math Intermediate 3

Activity

Area

On **Lesson Activity 23**, trace over grid lines to make the rectangles described below. Next to each rectangle, write its perimeter and area. Be sure to name the area in square inches.

1. Near the top of the grid, trace a 5-inch by 2-inch rectangle. What is its perimeter and area? 14 inches; 10 square inches
2. Trace a 6-inch by 3-inch rectangle. What is its perimeter and area? 18 inches; 18 square inches

Generalize Write a number sentence using the numbers 5, 2, and 10. Write another number sentence using the numbers 3, 6 and 18. What kind of sentences did you write? What do you think is another way to find the area of a rectangle besides counting squares? $5 \times 2 = 10$; $6 \times 3 = 18$; multiplication; area of rectangle = length × width

Example

A 5-inch by 7-inch photograph has an area of how many square inches?

One way to find the area is to make 7 rows of 5 squares and count the number of squares. Another way to find the area of a rectangle is to multiply the length and width of the rectangle.

7 in. × 5 in. = **35 square inches**

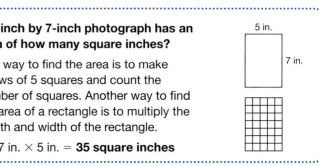

Lesson Practice

a. **Multiple Choice** To measure area, we count **B**
   A segments.   B squares.   C circles.   D rectangles.

b. Stan covered the front cover of a journal with 1-inch square stickers. What was the area of the front cover? 30 sq. in.

336 Saxon Math Intermediate 3

Alternative Approach: Using Manipulatives

Divide students into groups and give each group 36 color tiles.

"Make a rectangle that has a perimeter of 26 tiles and an area of 36 square tiles." Students should make a rectangle of 9 rows by 4 columns or 4 rows by 9 columns.

"Now, make a rectangle that has a perimeter of 24 tiles but still has an area of 36 square tiles." Students should make a square of 6 rows by 6 columns.

Explain that two rectangles can have the same area but different perimeters.

"Do you think two rectangles could have the same perimeter but different areas?" yes

"Use your tiles to form two rectangles with equal perimeters of 12 units but with different areas." Students should build rectangles that are 5×1, 4×2, or 3×3.

▶ c. Silvia placed a stamp that was 1 square inch in the corner of a 3-inch by 5-inch envelope. Altogether, how many stamps would be needed to cover the front of the envelope? **15 stamps**

d. What is the perimeter and area of a 6-inch by 4-inch rectangle? **20 inches; 24 square inches**

Written Practice
Distributed and Integrated

▶ 1. (**Formulate**) Miguel bought 8 boxes of tiles for $10 per box. What was the cost of all ten boxes? Write a number sentence. Then write a complete sentence to answer the question. $10 × 8 = □; The boxes cost $80.
(56, 60)

2. a. What fraction of the tiles are blue? $\frac{5}{9}$
(44)
   b. What fraction of the tiles are white? $\frac{4}{9}$

3. Compare the two fractions in problem 2. $\frac{5}{9} > \frac{4}{9}$ or $\frac{4}{9} < \frac{5}{9}$
(49)

4. Barry made this rectangle out of one-inch square tiles.
(52, 62)
   a. How long is the rectangle? **5 inches**
   b. How wide is the rectangle? **4 inches**
   c. How many tiles did he use? **20 tiles**
   d. What is the area of the rectangle? **20 sq. in.**

5. What is the perimeter of the rectangle in problem 4? **18 inches**
(58)

▶ 6. **Multiple Choice** Which of these multiplication facts equals 10? **c**
(59, 61)
   A 5 × 5   **B** 9 × 1   **C** 2 × 5   **D** 8 × 2

Lesson 62   337

Inclusion

Build It and Count It

Some students may need additional real-world experiences to internalize the meaning of area.

Materials: 35 color tiles per student

- Use tiles to build rectangles with 7 rows of 5, 3 rows of 5, and 6 rows of 4.
- Find the area of each rectangle by skip counting the rows or columns.
- Some students may need to actually move each group of tiles as they count.
- Write the area on a card or small paper and place it on top of the tiles.

New Concept (Continued)

Lesson Practice

Problem c
Encourage students to use multiplication and the measurements of the envelope to determine the answer. Tell them that connecting the problem to arrays may help.

Closure — The questions below help assess the concepts taught in this lesson.

"What is the difference between area and perimeter?" The perimeter is the measurement around a shape. The area measures the surface inside the shape.

"How do we find the area of a rectangle?" We can build the rectangle and count the number of tiles, or we can multiply the length and the width.

"If we have a rectangle that is 4 inches by 5 inches, what is the area?"
20 square inches

Discuss real-world situations where finding area might be helpful. Examples are given below.

- A real estate agent needs to know how much space is inside a house, so she must find the area.
- We want to plant a garden and need to know how much fertilizer to buy.

Written Practice

Math Conversations
Independent Practice and Discussions to Increase Understanding

Problem 1 (Formulate)
Help students recognize this as an "equal groups" story.

"We have 8 boxes, or groups, and ten dollars for each box. So, we have 8 groups of 10."

Problem 6 Multiple Choice
Test-Taking Strategy

In this question students will have to calculate each answer choice and then choose the correct answer.

(continued)

Lesson 62   337

Written Practice (Continued)

Math Conversations
Independent Practice and Discussions to Increase Understanding

Problem 8
Remind students that they only need to add a zero after the other factor when multiplying by 10.

Problem 12 (Represent)
Have students write the multiplication fact shown by each square to help them see the sequence of squared numbers. Students can also think of the pattern as "growing squares" one row and column at a time.

Problem 13 (Conclude)
Alternate Method

"What are the multiplication number sentences we would write for the squares in problem 12?" $1 \times 1 = 1$, $2 \times 2 = 4$, $3 \times 3 = 9$

"What multiplication number sentences will help us find the next two numbers in the sequence?" $4 \times 4 = 16$, $5 \times 5 = 25$

(continued)

---

7. What number is shown by this model? 203

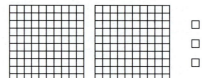

8. Multiply:
   a. 10×6 60
   b. 10×12 120

9. What is the place value of the 6 in 825,630? hundreds

10. Point A represents what mixed number on this number line? $9\frac{3}{4}$

11. For a school fundraiser Roderick sold 132 key rings and 95 T-shirts. How many more key chains did Roderick sell than T-shirts? Write and solve a greater-lesser-difference number sentence to find the answer. $132 - 95 = d$; 37 key rings

▶ 12. (Represent) Draw the next square in this sequence:

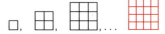

▶ 13. (Conclude) The square numbers in problem 12 are 1, 4, 9, ... What are the next two numbers in this sequence? 16, 25

14. What multiplication fact is shown by this array? $6 \times 3 = 18$ or $3 \times 6 = 18$

   x x x x x x
   x x x x x x
   x x x x x x

15. 36¢ + 95¢ + $2 $3.31

16. $300 − $104 $196

17. Write the mixed number $4\frac{1}{2}$ using words.   four and one half

18. Find the missing addend.
    a. $10 + m = 25$ 15
    b. $24 + n = 34$ 10

19. Write 25,760 in expanded form. $20,000 + 5,000 + 700 + 60$

338 Saxon Math Intermediate 3

20. Multiple Choice Which number sentence could you use to find
(40) the amount of money Kurt spent on pencils? B

Kurt had $10.75. He bought six pencils. Then he had $4.80.

A $10.75 + $4.80 = ☐   B $10.75 − ☐ = $4.80

C ☐ − $4.80 = $10.75   D $4.80 + $10.75 = ☐

Real-World Connection

Bryan's teacher asked him to sharpen 55 pencils. When he was finished, he handed out 32 pencils to his classmates and gave the rest to the teacher. The next day, Bryan sharpened another 55 pencils. This time he gave all of the pencils to his teacher. How many sharpened pencils did Bryan give his teacher altogether? 78 pencils

Understanding area and how to multiply length and width prepares students for

- **Lesson 63,** finding area in square feet and square yards
- **Lesson 68,** congruent shapes
- **Lesson 72,** finding volume by counting cubes
- **Lesson 73,** finding volume
- **Lessons 106 and 108,** estimating area

Written Practice (Continued)

Errors and Misconceptions

Problem 4d
Students often forget to report the units for area. Remind them that area is named using both a number and a unit such as square inches.

Point out to students that this is a two-step problem. Have them use numbers, pictures, or words to show how they found the number of pencils Bryan gave his teacher.

LESSON 63

Planning & Preparation

• Area, Part 2

Texas Essential Knowledge and Skills

(3.4)(A) apply multiplication facts through 12 by 12 using concrete models and objects

(3.11)(C) use concrete and pictorial models of square units to determine the area of two-dimensional surfaces

Objectives
- Use multiplication to find areas measured in square feet and square yards.
- Create a scale drawing of a rectangular surface on grid paper to find its area in square feet or square yards.
- Find the number of square feet in one square yard.

Prerequisite Skills
- Explain the differences between a shape's perimeter and its area.
- Use square units to measure area.
- Draw rectangles on a grid and determine their areas.
- Multiply the length and width of a rectangle to find its area in square units.

Materials
Instructional Masters
- Power Up 63

Manipulative Kit
- Color tiles

Teacher-provided materials
- 1-foot construction paper squares
- Grid paper

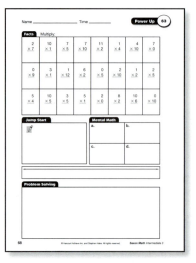

Power Up 63

Reaching All Special Needs Students

Special Education Students	At-Risk Students	English Learners	Advanced Learners
• Adaptations for Saxon Math	• Alternative Approach (TM) • Error Alert (TM) • Reteaching Masters	• English Learners (TM) • English Learner Handbook	• Extend the Example (TM) • Extend the Problem (TM) • Online Activities

TM = Teacher's Manual

Math Language

Maintained	English Learners
perpendicular	carpet

340A *Saxon Math* Intermediate 3

Problem Solving Discussion

Problem

If a coin is flipped, it can land showing either "heads" or "tails." Emilio will flip a quarter two times. One possibility is that the first flip will be heads and the second flip will also be heads.

Another possibility is that the first flip will be heads and the second flip will be tails.

What are the other possibilities Emilio can get by flipping a quarter two times? Copy and complete the tree diagram at right to help you find the combinations.

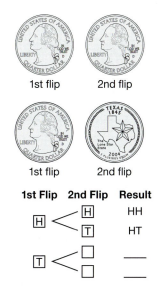

1st flip   2nd flip

1st flip   2nd flip

1st Flip	2nd Flip	Result
H	H	HH
	T	HT
T	☐	___
	☐	___

Focus Strategies

Draw a Picture or Diagram

Make an Organized List

Understand — Understand the problem.

"What information are we given?"

A coin flip can be either heads or tails. Emilio will flip a quarter two times. We are given a tree diagram and two possible outcomes: "heads, heads" and "heads, tails."

"What are we asked to do?"

We are asked to complete the tree diagram to find the other possible outcomes.

Plan — Make a plan.

"What problem solving strategies will we use?"

We will *draw a tree diagram* and *make an organized list* of the coin-flip combinations.

Solve — Carry out the plan.

"How do we complete the tree diagram?"

For each possible first coin-flip result, the second flip can be either heads or tails. The results of a second flip for a first flip of heads are already recorded on the tree diagram. We record the results of a second flip for a first flip of tails by writing H and T in the empty spaces on the diagram. Then we list the possible combinations of two coin flips by reading along the branches of the tree diagram. The four possible results of flipping a coin two times are HH, HT, TH, and TT. The two combinations we were looking for are TH and TT.

1st Flip	2nd Flip	Result
H	H	HH
	T	HT
T	H	TH
	T	TT

Check — Look back.

"Are our answers reasonable?"

Yes, it makes sense that there are four possible outcomes for two flips of a coin. For each of the two possible first flips, there are two possibilities for the second flip. This is a total of $2 \times 2 = 4$ possible outcomes.

Lesson 63

LESSON 63

Power Up

Facts
Distribute **Power Up 63** to students. See answers below.

Jump Start
Before students begin the Mental Math exercise, do these exercises as a class.

Mental Math
Encourage students to share different ways to mentally compute these exercises. Strategies for exercises are listed below.

  c. **Think of dimes**
   12 dimes − 4 dimes = 8 dimes
   $1.20 − 40¢ = $0.80 or 80¢

  d. **Count and Write the Fraction**
   total number of parts = 5
   number of shaded parts = 4
   $\frac{4 \text{ parts shaded}}{5 \text{ total parts}} = \frac{4}{5}$

Problem Solving
Refer to **Problem-Solving Strategy Discussion**, p. 340B.

LESSON 63 • Area, Part 2

Texas Essential Knowledge and Skills
(3.4)(A) apply multiplication facts through 12 by 12 using concrete models and objects
(3.11)(C) use concrete and pictorial models of square units to determine the area of two-dimensional surfaces

Power Up

facts   Power Up 63

jump start
Count up by square numbers from 1 to 144.
Count up by 100s from 0 to 2000.
Draw an array to show the multiplication fact 2 × 3. *See student work.*
Label the number line by 5s from 0 to 50. *0, 5, 10, 15, 20, 25, 30, 35, 40, 45, 50*

mental math
a. **Estimation:** Round 289 to the nearest hundred. *300*
b. **Calendar:** How many days are in 5 weeks? *35 days*
c. **Money:** $1.20 − 40¢ *80¢*
d. **Fractions:** What fraction of the rectangle is shaded? $\frac{4}{5}$

problem solving
If a coin is flipped, it can land showing either "heads" or "tails." Emilio will flip a quarter two times. One possibility is that the first flip will be heads and the second flip will also be heads.

1st flip   2nd flip

Another possibility is that the first flip will be heads and the second flip will be tails.

1st flip   2nd flip

340   *Saxon Math* Intermediate 3

Facts   Multiply:

2 × 7 = 14	10 × 1 = 10	7 × 5 = 35	7 × 10 = 70	11 × 2 = 22	1 × 4 = 4	4 × 10 = 40	7 × 0 = 0
0 × 9 = 0	3 × 1 = 3	1 × 12 = 12	6 × 2 = 12	0 × 5 = 0	2 × 10 = 20	1 × 2 = 2	2 × 5 = 10
5 × 4 = 20	10 × 5 = 50	3 × 5 = 15	5 × 1 = 5	2 × 0 = 0	8 × 2 = 16	10 × 6 = 60	0 × 10 = 0

What are the other possibilities Emilio can get by flipping a quarter two times? Copy and complete the tree diagram at right to help you find the combinations.

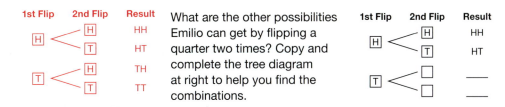

New Concept

In Lesson 62 we used square inches to measure the areas of small rectangles. To measure larger areas, like the area of a floor, we often use **square feet** or **square yards**.

If a floor is covered with one-foot square tiles, we can find the area of the floor in square feet by counting tiles.

Example 1

The floor of a small room is covered with one-foot square tiles. Bill counted 10 tiles along one wall and 8 tiles along a perpendicular wall. How many tiles covered the whole floor? What was the area of the room?

There are 8 tiles in each of the 10 rows. There are 10 × 8 = 80 tiles. The tiles are one-foot squares, so the area of the floor is **80 square feet**.

Activity

Estimating Area in Square Feet

Use two one-foot squares to help you estimate the areas of some rectangular surfaces in the classroom, such as a desktop, tabletop, the inside surface of a door or window, or a bulletin board.

1. Name the object you measured on a piece of grid paper.
2. Draw a picture of its rectangular surface, with each square on the grid paper representing one square foot on the actual object.

Math Background

Various units have been introduced to measure area, including square inches, square feet, and square yards. Students should be aware that other units are frequently used to measure area, including square miles and acres for measuring larger quantities (such as tracts of land).

New Concept

Instruction

On the board, draw three squares: a square with sides 1 inch long, a square with sides 1 foot long, and a square with sides 1 yard long. Label the squares 1 square inch, 1 square foot, and 1 square yard, respectively.

Point out the differences in size and relate the squares to units of measurement the students are familiar with: inches, feet, and yards. Remind students that a square that is 1 inch high and 1 inch wide is 1 square inch. Point to the square foot and ask,

"What is the width and height of this square?" It is 1 foot wide and 1 foot high.

Point to the square yard and ask,

"What is the width and height of this square?" It is 1 yard wide and 1 yard high.

• **Example 1**

"We gave the answer in square feet because we found out how many 1-foot squares covered the area."

• **Activity**

Pre-cut one-foot squares from construction paper. Supply each pair or small group of students with two squares. Demonstrate how to play "leap frog" with the squares in order to find the length along two sides of a rectangular surface.

Also demonstrate how to record the measurement on grid paper, using each square on the paper to represent a one-foot square on the actual object.

(continued)

New Concept (Continued)

Discussion

For the *Analyze* question, have students sketch a square and then divide it into 3 equal columns with 3 equal rows. The intersecting lines form smaller squares that model the square feet in one square yard.

"**Is a square yard bigger than three square feet?**" Yes, a square yard measures 3 feet on each side, so it has an area of 9 square feet.

"**How many square inches are in a square foot?**" 144 square inches; a square foot is 12 inches by 12 inches; 12 × 12 = 144.

Real-World Connection

Read the following list of items aloud and have students respond with the unit of measure they think should be used to describe each item.

- The bed of a truck square feet
- A football field square yards
- A hamster cage square inches
- A mural square feet
- A rug square inches or feet
- A movie screen square feet or yards
- A wash cloth square inches

Example 2

Use color tiles to find the answer.

Error Alert

Students may be tempted to multiply the number of square feet by 3 to get the number of square yards. Remind students that there are 9 square feet in a square yard, not 3.

Alternate Method

Use grid paper to solve the problem with one square on the graph paper equal to one square foot.

Lesson Practice

Guided Practice

Use these problems as guided practice to check the students' understanding of today's concept.

Problem a Error Alert

When counting tiles to determine area, students often forget to report the units. Be sure that students give the answer in square feet. Remind them that area is named using both a number and a unit.

Problem b

Extend the Example

For advanced learners, have them find how many square feet are in 20 square yards. 180 square feet (Think 9 × 2 = 18 and 18 × 10 = 180, or find the number of square feet in 10 square yards and double the number.)

(continued)

342   Saxon Math Intermediate 3

---

3. Write its estimated area.
4. Describe how you found the area.

9 square feet; sample: We can arrange 9 one-foot squares to make a square with sides 1 yard long.

Carpeting is often sold by the square yard. A square that has sides 1 yard long has an area of one square yard.

Analyze There are 3 feet in one yard. How many square feet are in a square yard? How do you know?

Example 2

The picture shows a piece of carpet that is 3 yards long and two yards wide.

2 yd
3 yd

a. The carpet covers an area of how many square yards?

b. The carpet covers an area of how many square feet?

a. A 3-yard by 2-yard rectangle has an area of **6 square yards**.

2 yd
3 yd

b. Each square yard equals 9 square feet. So 6 square yards is 6 × 9 square feet, which is **54 square feet**.

6 ft
9 ft

Lesson Practice

a. The floor of a small room is covered with one-foot square tiles. Bill counted 6 tiles along one wall and 8 tiles along a perpendicular wall. How many tiles cover the whole floor? What is the area of the room? 48 square feet

b. How many square yards of carpet are needed to cover the floor of a room that is 4 yards wide and 5 yards long? You can use color tiles to help you answer this question. 20 square yards

c. One square yard is 9 square feet. Copy and complete the table below.

Square yards	1	2	3	4	5	6
Square feet	9	18	27	36	45	54

342   Saxon Math Intermediate 3

Alternative Approach: Using Manipulatives

Students can use color tiles to construct a visual model of area. Tell them to think of the tiles as square units. Remind students to write their answers in whatever square unit of measurement the problem calls for.

English Learners

Carpet is a soft floor covering. Ask:

"**If a piece of carpet is 4 × 5 feet, how many square feet is it in total?**" 4 × 5 = 20 square feet

Ask:

"**Where have you seen carpet on the floor?**" samples: homes, schools, libraries, offices

Ask students to tell what color carpet they would like to have in their room.

Written Practice *Distributed and Integrated*

1. **(37, 60)** Monica walked from her garage to the street to estimate the length of her driveway. She took ten big steps. Each big step was about 3 feet. About how many feet long is her driveway? *about 30 ft*

2. **(36)** (Formulate) Jimmy's great-grandfather is 84 years old. He retired when he was 65 years old. How many years has he been retired? Write a number sentence. Then write a complete sentence to answer the question. *65 + r = 84; Jimmy's grandfather has been retired 19 years.*

One-foot square tiles covered the sidewalk. See the picture at right to answer problems **3–5**.

3. **(53)** a. How long is the sidewalk? *10 ft*

   b. How wide is the sidewalk? *3 ft*

4. **(63)** What is the area of the sidewalk? *30 sq. ft*

5. **(56, 57)** What multiplication fact is shown by this array of squares? *3 × 10 = 30*

6. **(55) Multiple Choice** Which of these multiplication facts equals 20? **A**

   A 2 × 10   **B** 19 × 1   **C** 5 × 5   **D** 10 × 10

7. **(11) Multiple Choice** Which shows five ones and six hundreds? **D**

   A 56   **B** 560   **C** 650   **D** 605

8. **(40)** Find the missing number: ☐ − 398 = 245. *643*

9. **(56)** Multiply:
   a. 6 × 10   *60*
   b. 16 × 10   *160*

10. **(32)** What is the place value of the 4 in 412,576?   *hundred thousands*

Lesson 63   343

New Concept (Continued)

Closure The questions below help assess the concepts taught in this lesson.

"If we want to find the number of square yards in a rectangle and the length and width are given in yards, what do we do?"
We multiply the length times the width.

"Which is larger, a square yard or a square foot?" a square yard

"Why do you think carpet is sold by the square yard instead of the square inch?" sample: The numbers would be too great if carpet were sold by the square inch. There are 144 × 9 square inches in a square yard (1296 square inches).

Discuss real-world situations where we need to use square feet and square yards. Examples are given below.

- The floor spaces of buildings are usually measured in square feet.
- Carpet and other flooring materials are often sold by the square yard.

Written Practice

Math Conversations
Independent Practice and Discussions to Increase Understanding

Problem 2 (Formulate)

Students may think of a timeline to solve this problem: later − earlier = difference.

Or they can write it as a "some and some more" problem:

years up to retirement + some more years after retirement = his age now

Problem 6 Multiple Choice
Test-Taking Strategy

Be sure that students read the problem carefully and note that the question asks them which multiplication is equal to 20. So students must check each answer in turn and eliminate the ones not equal to 20.

Suggest that students picture the multiplications as arrays made of tiles.

"Which arrays equal 20?"

(continued)

Lesson 63   343

Written Practice (Continued)

Math Conversations
Independent Practice and Discussions to Increase Understanding

Problem 11 (Analyze)

Students should represent one square yard as an array of 3 columns and 3 rows. Then by counting the elements of the array or by multiplying 3 × 3, students can determine the answer.

Extend the Problem

"If the square measured 2 yards on each side, what would the area be in square yards?" 4 square yards

"What would the area be in square feet?" 36 square feet

Problem 12 (Analyze)
Extend the Problem

"If the square measured 2 yards on each side, what would the perimeter be in yards?" 8 yards

"What would the perimeter be in feet?" 24 feet

Problem 15
Alternate Method

Students can skip count to find the answers.

"Skip count by 4s to find the 8th term in the sequence." 32

"Skip count by 3s to find the 9th term in the sequence." 27

"Skip count by 6s to find the 7th term in the sequence." 42

Errors and Misconceptions

Problem 7

The problem asks for five ones and six hundreds. Since the ones are mentioned first, students may look for an answer that gives 5 as the first digit. Instruct students first to look for an answer that has five ones.

Problem 11

Remind students who continue to answer "3" that square feet measure area, not length. Have the students use their colored tiles to model this problem.

---

344   Saxon Math Intermediate 3

(Analyze) Look at the square to answer problems **11** and **12**.

▶ **11.** One yard is 3 feet. The picture shows one square yard. How many square feet is one square yard?   9 sq. ft.

1 yd

▶ **12. a.** What is the perimeter of the square in yards?   4 yards

  b. What is the perimeter of the square in feet?   12 feet

13. Draw a picture to represent the mixed number $2\frac{1}{3}$.   See student work.

14. Write the two fractions shown by the shaded circles. Then compare the fractions. $\frac{1}{2}; \frac{4}{8}; \frac{1}{2} = \frac{4}{8}$

▶ **15.** Find each product on a multiplication table:
  a. 4 × 8   32   **b.** 3 × 9   27   **c.** 7 × 7   49

Add or subtract, as shown:

16. $498 + $679 $1,177

17. $0.87 + $0.75 + $0.93 $2.55

18. $5.00 − $3.46 $1.54

19. $323 − $100 $223

20. When Ismael came into class after lunch, he noticed the clock. Write the time in digital form.   12:53 p.m.

---

344   Saxon Math Intermediate 3

Looking Forward

Working with square yards and square feet prepares students for

- **Lesson 64,** multiplying by 9.
- **Lesson 66,** working with parallelograms.
- **Lesson 68,** identifying congruent shapes.
- **Lesson 72,** counting cubes to find volume.
- **Lesson 73,** finding volume.
- **Lesson 75,** identifying geometric solids.
- **Lessons 106 and 108,** estimating area.

LESSON 64

Planning & Preparation

Texas Essential Knowledge and Skills
- (3.4)(A) learn/apply multiplication facts through 12 by 12 using objects
- (3.6)(B) identify patterns in multiplication facts using pictorial models
- (3.14)(A) identify the mathematics in everyday situations

• Multiplication Facts: 9s

Objectives
- Identify patterns in the 9s facts on the multiplication table.
- Learn different methods to practice the 9s facts.
- Apply 9s multiplication facts to convert square yards to square feet.

Prerequisite Skills
- Understand the relationship between repeated addition and multiplication.
- Use "product" and "factor" to describe numbers in multiplication number sentences and on the multiplication table.
- Use a multiplication table to find products of given multiplication problems.

Materials
Instructional Masters
- Power Up 64

Manipulative Kit
- Rulers

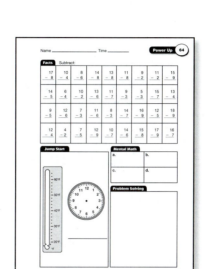

Power Up 64

Differentiated Instruction

Reaching All Special Needs Students

Special Education Students	At-Risk Students	English Learners	Advanced Learners
• Adaptations for Saxon Math	• Reteaching Masters	• English Learners (TM) • English Learner Handbook	• Extend the Example (TM) • Extend the Problem (TM) • Online Activities

TM=Teacher's Manual

Math Language

Maintained	English Learners
dozen	fold

Lesson 64   345A

LESSON 64

Problem Solving Discussion

Problem

Juan rides his bike around the block along the path shown. Two times around the block is 1 mile. How many times around the block must Juan ride to travel 3 miles?

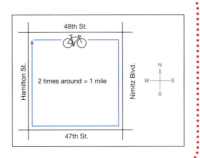

Focus Strategies

 Write a Number Sentence

 Make or Use a Table, Chart, or Graph

Understand *Understand the problem.*

"What information are we given?"

We are shown a map of the block where Juan rides his bike. Two times around the block is 1 mile.

"What are we asked to do?"

We are asked to find how many times around the block equals 3 miles.

Plan *Make a plan.*

"How can we use the information we know to solve the problem?"

We know that 2 times around the block is 1 mile. We can *write a number sentence* to find the number of times around the block to travel 3 miles.

Solve *Carry out the plan.*

"If 2 times around the block is 1 mile, how many times around the block equals 3 miles?"

Three miles is 2 + 2 + 2 times around, which is 6 times around.

"How can we make a table that shows the number of times around the block for each mile that Juan rides?"

We can make a table with a row for miles and a row for times around the block. We continue the pattern of counting up by 2s as shown in this table:

Miles	1	2	3	4	5	6	7	8
Times around	2	4	6	8	10	12	14	16

Check *Look back.*

"Did we complete the task?"

Yes, we found how many times Juan must ride his bike around the block to travel 3 miles.

"Is our answer reasonable?"

Yes, we know that our answer is reasonable because each mile is 2 times around. So 3 miles is 2 + 2 + 2 = 6 times around.

"What problem solving strategies did we use?"

We *wrote a number sentence* to find the answer. We *made a table* to show the pattern.

Alternate Strategy

Find/Extend a Pattern

Students may also find the number of times Juan must ride around the block by counting up by 2s.

Saxon Math Intermediate 3

LESSON 64

- Multiplication Facts: 9s

Texas Essential Knowledge and Skills
(3.4)(A) learn/apply multiplication facts through 12 by 12 using objects
(3.6)(B) identify patterns in multiplication facts using pictorial models
(3.14)(A) identify the mathematics in everyday situations

Power Up

facts Power Up 64

jump start
Count down by 3s from 45 to 0.
Count down by 9s from 90 to 0.

It's night. Draw hands on your clock to show 10:48. Write the time in digital form.   10:48 p.m.

The daily high on Monday was 36°F. On Tuesday it was 6 degrees warmer. Mark your thermometer to show the high temperature on Tuesday.   42°F

mental math

a. **Number Sense:** 43 + 9   52

b. **Money:** 90¢ + 90¢ $1.80 or 180¢

c. **Money:** $10.00 − $2.00 $8.00

d. **Patterns:** What is the next number in the pattern below?   14

| 12 | 14 | 13 | 15 | ___ |

problem solving
Juan rides his bike around the block along the path shown. Two times around the block is 1 mile. How many times around the block must Juan ride to travel 3 miles?   6 times

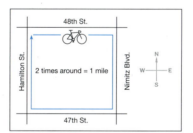

Lesson 64   345

LESSON 64

Power Up

Facts
Distribute **Power Up 64** to students. See answers below.

Jump Start
Before students begin the Mental Math exercise, do these exercises as a class.

Mental Math
Encourage students to share different ways to mentally compute these exercises. Strategies for exercises are listed below.

a. Think 43 + 10 − 1
   43 + 9 = 43 + 10 − 1 = 53 − 1 = 52

b. Add the 9s and put a zero in the ones place.
   9 + 9 = 18, so 90¢ + 90¢ = 180¢

d. Look for a Pattern.
   The pattern is add 2, subtract 1, add 2, subtract 1. To find the next number, we subtract 1 from 15; 15 − 1 = 14. The next number is **14**.

Problem Solving
Refer to **Problem-Solving Strategy Discussion**, p. 345B.

Facts Subtract:

17 − 8 9	10 − 4 6	8 − 6 2	14 − 8 6	13 − 8 5	11 − 8 3	9 − 2 7	11 − 2 9	15 − 9 6
14 − 5 9	6 − 4 2	10 − 2 8	13 − 6 7	11 − 7 4	9 − 3 6	5 − 3 2	15 − 7 8	13 − 4 9
9 − 5 4	12 − 6 6	7 − 3 4	11 − 6 5	8 − 3 5	14 − 7 7	16 − 9 7	12 − 5 7	18 − 9 9
12 − 4 8	4 − 2 2	7 − 5 2	12 − 9 3	10 − 7 3	14 − 6 8	15 − 8 7	17 − 9 8	16 − 7 9

Lesson 64   345

New Concept

Instruction

Begin this lesson by reviewing addition of numbers that add up to nine.

Emphasize that

$$1 + 8 = 9$$
$$2 + 7 = 9$$
$$3 + 6 = 9$$
$$4 + 5 = 9$$

First see if students can list the numbers on their own before providing assistance. Remind students that the order of the addends does not affect the sum, so listing four facts is enough. This can be emphasized by showing students the following:

$$1 + 8 = 9 = 8 + 1$$

Explanation

There is another trick for finding the product when we multiply by 9s up to 9×10. The first digit of each product is 1 less than the number that is multiplied by 9. Write $9 \times 6 = \square$ on the board or overhead.

"Five is one less than 6, so we know the first digit is five. The sum of the two digits will be nine, so we also know that the second digit is four."

Write the answer, 54, on the board. Using this method, have students determine the answer for 9×7 and 9×9.

Discussion

Have students write the multiplication facts for 9 in two columns. The first column should start at the top with $9 \times 2 = 18$ and end at the bottom with $9 \times 5 = 45$. The second column should start at the bottom with $9 \times 6 = 54$ and end at the top with $9 \times 9 = 81$. Ask students:

"How could we write $9 \times 1 = 9$ so that we could include it in our table with $9 \times 10 = 90$?" $9 \times 1 = 09$

(continued)

New Concept

Look down the 9s column of a multiplication table for patterns. Starting with the product of 9×2, notice how the digits in the tens place count up and the digits in the ones place count down. Also notice how the two digits of each product have a sum of 9. These two patterns continue through 9×10.

	0	1	2	3	4	5	6	7	8	9	10	11	12
0	0	0	0	0	0	0	0	0	0	0	0	0	0
1	0	1	2	3	4	5	6	7	8	9	10	11	12
2	0	2	4	6	8	10	12	14	16	18	20	22	24
3	0	3	6	9	12	15	18	21	24	27	30	33	36
4	0	4	8	12	16	20	24	28	32	36	40	44	48
5	0	5	10	15	20	25	30	35	40	45	50	55	60
6	0	6	12	18	24	30	36	42	48	54	60	66	72
7	0	7	14	21	28	35	42	49	56	63	70	77	84
8	0	8	16	24	32	40	48	56	64	72	80	88	96
9	0	9	18	27	36	45	54	63	72	81	90	99	108
10	0	10	20	30	40	50	60	70	80	90	100	110	120
11	0	11	22	33	44	55	66	77	88	99	110	121	132
12	0	12	24	36	48	60	72	84	96	108	120	132	144

$9 \times 2 = 18$
$9 \times 3 = 27$
$9 \times 4 = 36$
$9 \times 5 = 45$
$9 \times 6 = 54$
$9 \times 7 = 63$
$9 \times 8 = 72$
$9 \times 9 = 81$

Generalize Look at the products from 9×2 through 9×9. Can you find another pattern?

sample: The order of the digits in the products of 9×2 through 9×5 are the reverse of the order of the digits in the products of 9×6 through 9×9.

Here is a fun way to find the nines multiplication facts from 9×2 to 9×9 using your fingers. Hold your hands out in front of you and imagine that your fingers are numbered 1 through 10 from left to right.

To find 3 × 9, fold down the number 3 finger. The fingers to the left of the folded finger count as tens. There are two of them. Two tens is 20. The fingers to the right of the folded finger count as ones. There are seven. Twenty and seven is 27.

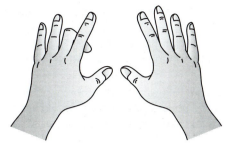

Example 1

Find each product:

a. 7 × 9   b. 8 × 9

Until we have learned the nines facts, we can use a multiplication table or patterns to find the products.

a. 7 × 9 = **63**   b. 8 × 9 = **72**

Example 2

One square yard is 9 square feet. A rug that is 8 square yards covers how many square feet?

2 yd

4 yd

Each square yard is 9 square feet, so we multiply 9 square feet by 8.

8 × 9 square feet = **72 square feet**

Lesson Practice   Find each product.

a. 9 × 3   27   b. 9 × 4   36   c. 9 × 6   54

d. 9 × 10   90 ▶   e. 9 × 11   99 ▶   f. 9 × 12   108

Lesson 64   347

 **English Learners**

To **fold** means to bend something over upon itself. Ask:

"Take a piece of paper and fold it in half. Fold that piece in half. Fold it one more time. Open it up. How many rectangles do you have?" 8 rectangles

Ask:

"What other things do we fold?"
samples: sheets, clothes, tortillas

Show students how to fold a letter in thirds to fit in an envelope and let them practice.

New Concept (Continued)

Using your fingers to find the nines facts works for 9 × 1 through 9 × 10. Students should both understand and memorize the multiplication facts for 9s. This method is a fun way to start the process.

Example 1
Remind students that a multiplication problem can be written with either number first. Some students may find it easier to think of the problems as 9 × 7 or 9 × 8 and use the 9s row in the multiplication table instead of the 9s column.

Example 2
"When we convert from yards to feet, we always multiply by 9 because 1 square yard covers the same area as 9 square feet."

Students may want to use their tiles to remind them of this fact.

Extend the Example
"A rug has an area of 8 square yards. Find possible values for its perimeter. Draw a picture or use tiles to help you solve the problem." Students may make a rug which is 8 × 1 (perimeter 18 yards) or 2 × 4 (perimeter 12 yards).

Lesson Practice

Guided Practice
Use these problems as guided practice to check the students' understanding of today's concept.

Problems e and f
Have students use a multiplication table to find the answers.

Alternate Method
Students can think of 9 × 11 as 9 × 10 plus 9 × 1 and 9 × 12 as 9 × 10 plus 9 × 2.

(continued)

Lesson 64   347

New Concept (Continued)

Closure The questions below help assess the concepts taught in this lesson.

"What did we learn about the nines multiplication facts through 9 × 10 that makes them easy to remember?" The sum of the digits in the products is 9; The first digit of the product is one less than the multiplier; We learned a trick to find the facts using our fingers.

"What are some reasons we might need to multiply by 9?" sample: to convert from square yards to square feet

Discuss real-world situations where knowledge of multiplying by 9 is useful. Examples are given below.

- To convert from square yards to square feet, multiply by 9.
- There are 9 calories in one gram of fat. To find the number of calories from fat in a food item, take the grams of fat and multiply by 9.

Written Practice

Math Conversations
Independent Practice and Discussions to Increase Understanding

Problem 1 Formulate
Students should recognize this as an "equal groups" story.

"We have four tickets, or groups, with a $9 cost for each ticket."

Problem 7 Represent
Inform students that the comparison will be easiest if they draw the two rectangles one above the other. Demonstrate how to draw congruent rectangles and divide them into halves and thirds. Shade one section of each rectangle.

(continued)

Written Practice — Distributed and Integrated

1. (Formulate) Tickets for the movie were $9 each. Mr. Chen bought 4 tickets. How much did the tickets cost? Write a number sentence. Then write your answer in a complete sentence.
(60, 64) $9 × 4 = p$; sample: The tickets cost $36.

2. Mr. Chen paid for the movie tickets in problem **1** with two $20 bills. How much money should he get back? $4
(14, 20)

3. Using square tiles with sides 1 foot long, Miguel covered one square yard with 9 tiles. How many tiles does Miguel need to cover 3 square yards? 27
(63, 64)

4. (Represent) Draw a square with sides 3 inches long.
(35)

5. What is the perimeter of the square you drew in problem **4**? 12 in.
(58)

6. What is the area of the square you drew in problem **4**?
(62) 9 square inches

7. (Represent) Draw two rectangles that are the same size and shape. Shade $\frac{1}{2}$ of one rectangle. Shade $\frac{1}{3}$ of the other rectangle. Then compare these fractions: See student work.
(42, 43)

$$\frac{1}{2} > \frac{1}{3}$$

8. A dozen eggs in a carton is an array. This array illustrates what multiplication fact? $6 × 2 = 12$ or $2 × 6 = 12$
(57)

9. If one egg is removed from the carton in problem **8**, then what fraction of a dozen eggs is left? $\frac{11}{12}$
(44)

10. (Conclude) Copy and continue this table to find the number of eggs in 4 dozen:
(2)

Number of Dozen	1	2	3	4
Number of Eggs	12	24	36	48

11. Find each product:
(64)
   a. 9×10 90
   b. 7×9 63
   c. 9×4 36

12. Find each product:
(61)
   a. 9×9 81
   b. 8×8 64
   c. 7×7 49

13. Find 77 on a multiplication table. Which two numbers have a
(55) product of 77?   7 and 11

14. Use your ruler to find the length of segment AB. $2\frac{1}{4}$ inches
(35)

A ●—————————————● B

15. $999 + $999 $1,998
(16)

16. $100 − $91 $9
(28)

▶ **17.** $9 + 9 + 9 + 9 + 9 + 9$ 54
(10, 54)

18. How many nickels equal a quarter? A nickel is what fraction of a
(44) quarter?   5, $\frac{1}{5}$

Look at the spinner to answer problems **19** and **20**.

▶ **19.** The spinner is least likely to stop on which number?   3
(50)

▶ **20.** (Verify) Todd thinks the sections with 1 are $\frac{3}{6}$ of the
(47) spinner. James thinks the sections with 1 are $\frac{1}{2}$ of the
spinner. Who is right? Why?   Both Todd and Jim are right
because $\frac{3}{6} = \frac{1}{2}$.

Lesson 64   349

Multiplying by 9s using various methods prepares students for

- **Lesson 70,** learning the memory group of multiplication facts.
- **Lesson 73,** finding volume.
- **Lesson 76,** multiplying by 11s and 12s.
- **Lesson 78,** multiplying multiples of ten.
- **Lessons 81 and 84,** multiplying two-digit numbers.
- **Lessons 91 and 97,** multiplying three-digit numbers.

Written Practice (Continued)

Math Conversations
Independent Practice and Discussions to Increase Understanding

Problem 10 Conclude
Students can complete the table by skip counting by 12s. Skip counting by 12s is like skip counting by 10 and adding 2.
$24 + 10 = 34; 34 + 2 = 36$

Problem 17
Encourage students to use multiplication to solve.

Extend the Problem
"If we were to add three more 9s, what would the answer be?"   81

Problem 19
Extend the Problem
"Which number is the spinner most likely to stop on?"   1

Problem 20 Verify
Have students draw two circles that are the same size, one divided into sixths and another divided into halves. By shading three of the six parts of one circle and one half of the other circle, students should be able to compare the fractions and see that $\frac{1}{2}$ equals $\frac{3}{6}$.

Errors and Misconceptions

Problems 5 and 6
Students often forget to add units when reporting perimeter and area. Remind them that perimeter and area are named using both a number and a unit. Perimeter should be reported in units and area in square units.

Problem 7
Students must be sure to draw congruent rectangles and divide them correctly. Remind students that the small side of the comparison symbol points to the smaller number.

LESSON 65

Texas Essential Knowledge and Skills
(3.8) describe two-dimensional geometric figures by their attributes
(3.15)(A) explain observations using objects

Planning & Preparation

• Angles

Objectives
- Identify right angles, acute angles, and obtuse angles.
- Use proper vocabulary such as "vertex" and "side" to describe attributes of the angles.
- Model acute, right, and obtuse angles using concrete objects.

Prerequisite Skills
- Identify line segments as parallel or perpendicular.

Materials
Instructional Masters
- Power Up 65

Manipulative Kit
- Ruler
- Student clocks*

Teacher-provided materials
- Straws
- Index cards*

   *optional

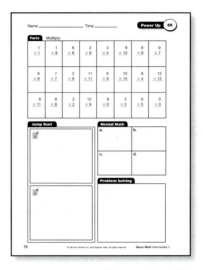

Power Up 65

Reaching All Special Needs Students

Special Education Students	At-Risk Students	English Learners	Advanced Learners
• Inclusion (TM) • Adaptations for Saxon Math	• Alternative Approach (TM) • Reteaching Masters	• English Learners (TM) • English Learner Handbook	• Extend the Problem (TM) • Online Activities

TM = Teacher's Manual

Math Language

New	Maintained	English Learners
acute angle	side	right angle	bend
angle	straight angle		
obtuse angle	vertex		

350A *Saxon Math Intermediate 3*

Problem Solving Discussion

Problem

Chris is hiking along a trail in the mountains. As he hikes, he counts the blue signs that mark the trail. The table at right shows the number of signs he sees along the way.

Copy the table on your paper. Continue the pattern to predict how many signs Chris will see if he hikes 7 miles.

Distance	Total Number of Signs
1 mile	8
2 miles	16
3 miles	24
4 miles	32

Focus Strategies

 Make or Use a Table, Chart, or Graph

 Find/Extend a Pattern

Understand *Understand the problem.*

"What information are we given?"

1. Chris sees blue signs as he hikes along a trail.
2. We are shown a table that tells the total number of signs he has seen for each number of miles.

"What are we asked to do?"

We are asked to continue the pattern in the table to predict the total number of signs Chris will count if he hikes 7 miles.

Plan *Make a plan.*

"What problem solving strategy can we use?"

We will *use the table* to *find* and *extend the pattern*.

Solve *Carry out the plan.*

"What pattern do you see in the table?"

The total number of signs is a pattern that counts up by 8s.

"What does the table look like if we continue the pattern?"

We add 3 rows to count up to a distance of 7 miles. Then we continue the pattern of counting by 8s in the right-hand column.

"How many signs do we predict Chris will see if he hikes 7 miles?"

56 signs

Distance	Total Number of Signs
1 mile	8
2 miles	16
3 miles	24
4 miles	32
5 miles	40
6 miles	48
7 miles	56

Check *Look back.*

"Did we complete the task?"

Yes, we copied the table and continued the pattern to predict that Chris would see a total of 56 signs if he hiked 7 miles.

"Is our answer reasonable?"

Yes, we know that our answer is reasonable because Chris sees 8 signs each mile, so for 7 miles, he would see 7 × 8 signs = 56 signs.

Alternate Strategy
Write a Number Sentence

Encourage students to use multiplication to solve the problem. Each mile of the hiking trail contains 8 signs. So for 7 miles, there are 7 groups of 8 signs. Thus, Chris sees 7 × 8 signs = 56 signs.

Lesson 65 350B

LESSON 65

Power Up

Facts
Distribute **Power Up 65** to students. See answers below.

Jump Start
Before students begin the Mental Math exercise, do these exercises as a class.

Mental Math
Encourage students to share different ways to mentally compute these exercises. Strategies for exercises are listed below.

a. Compare the Digits from Left to Right
  thousands: 1 = 1
  hundreds: 0 < 4
  1,045 < 1,405

b. Think 3 + 6 and 6 + 3 equal 9 and Solve.
  3 + 6 + 6 + 3
  = 9 + 9 = 18

Problem Solving
Refer to **Problem-Solving Strategy Discussion**, p. 350B.

Distance	Number of Signs
1st mile	8
2nd mile	16
3rd mile	24
4th mile	32
5th mile	40
6th mile	48
7th mile	56

LESSON 65 • Angles

Texas Essential Knowledge and Skills
(3.8) describe two-dimensional geometric figures by their attributes
(3.15)(A) explain observations using objects

Power Up

facts   Power Up 65

jump start
- Count up by 6s from 0 to 60.
- Count up by 12s from 0 to 120.
- Write two multiplication facts using the numbers 4, 9, and 36. $4 \times 9 = 36$; $9 \times 4 = 36$
- Write $714.20 as words.   seven hundred fourteen dollars and twenty cents

mental math

a. **Number Sense:** Compare these numbers using the symbol <, >, or =.
  1,045 < 1,405

b. **Number Sense:** 3 + 6 + 6 + 3   18

c. **Money:** $1.20 + $1.00 $2.20

d. **Number Line:** Which point shows the number 210?   X

problem solving

Chris is hiking along a trail in the mountains. As he hikes, he counts the blue signs that mark the trail. The table at right shows the number of signs he sees along the way.

Copy the table on your paper. Continue the pattern to predict how many signs Chris will see if he hikes 7 miles.   56 signs

Distance	Total Number of Signs
1 mile	8
2 miles	16
3 miles	24
4 miles	32

Facts   Multiply:

1 × 1 = 1	1 × 9 = 9	6 × 6 = 36	2 × 9 = 18	4 × 4 = 16	9 × 10 = 90	8 × 9 = 72	9 × 7 = 63
9 × 9 = 81	7 × 7 = 49	3 × 9 = 27	11 × 11 = 121	6 × 9 = 54	10 × 10 = 100	9 × 4 = 36	12 × 12 = 144
9 × 11 = 99	8 × 8 = 64	2 × 2 = 4	12 × 9 = 108	9 × 0 = 0	3 × 3 = 9	9 × 5 = 45	0 × 0 = 0

New Concept

An **angle** is an open figure with two **sides** that meet at a **vertex**.

Angles

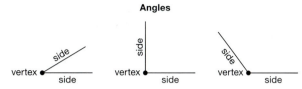

Remember that square corners are called right angles. To show that an angle is a right angle, we can draw a small square in its corner.

Generalize How many right angles does a rectangle have?
4

An angle that is smaller than a right angle is an **acute angle**.

Acute Angles

An angle that is larger than a right angle is an **obtuse angle**.

Obtuse Angles

An angle that looks like a straight line is a **straight angle**.

New Concept

Instruction
Remind students that rectangles have right angles. Tell them that angles are not always part of a shape or a closed figure. Two sides, lines, line segments, or rays that meet at a point also form angles.

Draw the following examples on the board for reference:

Emphasize that a vertex does not have to be the corner of a shape by pointing to the vertex of each example.

Memory Cues
Acute angle: A mnemonic for remembering the term and its meaning is "a cute little angle."

Right angle:

> "When we walk and turn right, we turn a corner. Right angles make square corners."

Obtuse angle: Explain to students that *obtuse* also means "blunt" or "dull" and that it describes objects that are not very sharp. Obtuse angles have measures greater than a right angle, so they are less sharp than a right angle or an acute angle.

After discussing the *Generalize* question, challenge students to draw a closed figure with four right angles that is *not* a rectangle. They should conclude that it is impossible.

(continued)

Math Background

In this lesson, students generalize and extend what they learned about angles in their study of rectangles. This knowledge will later be applied to triangles and other polygons. Continued progress through more advanced geometry will depend on the ability to recognize the properties of geometric figures and classify shapes according to these properties. Knowledge and understanding of formal vocabulary enables students to articulate geometric relationships.

New Concept (Continued)

Activity
Direct students to hold straws so that you can see the angle you describe. Have students make each type of angle a few times.

Leave a straw unbent so it forms a 180° angle (a straight angle). Show it to students and ask,

"Is this an angle?" yes

Example
Hold up a straw in the same orientation and angle as in part **c**. Reorient the angle so that the vertex is on the opposite side.

"Is this angle acute, obtuse, or right?" obtuse

"Does it matter if the vertex is on the right or the left? Explain." no; sample: We only need to look at how far apart the sides are to decide if an angle is acute, obtuse, or right.

Lesson Practice

Guided Practice
Use these problems as guided practice to check the students' understanding of today's concept.

Problem b
Extend the Problem
"What kind of angle is each angle of a square?" a right angle

"Does a circle have angles? Explain." no; sample: A circle does not have two straight lines meeting at a vertex.

Closure The questions below help assess the concepts taught in this lesson.

"What is an angle?" An angle is an open figure with two sides that meet at a vertex.

"We learned four terms to describe angles. Which term describes an angle that makes a square corner?" a right angle

"Which term describes an angle smaller than a right angle? ... larger than a right angle?" an acute angle; an obtuse angle

"Which term describes an angle that looks like a straight line?" a straight angle

Discuss real-world situations where different types of angles are used. Examples are given below.

- We need to have right angles for a baseball diamond or the squares in a game of hopscotch or four-square.
- Acute angles are used to measure the steepness of a hill or a ramp.

Angles

Materials: one straw for each student

By bending straws we can make models of angles. The point where the straw bends is the vertex.

As a class, bend straws to form acute angles, right angles, and obtuse angles as you teacher directs.

Example
Label each angle as acute, right, or obtuse.

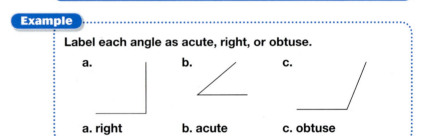

a. right   b. acute   c. obtuse

Lesson Practice

a. What is the name of the point where the sides of an angle meet? vertex

▶ b. What kind of angle is each angle of a rectangle? right angle

Name each type of angle shown below.

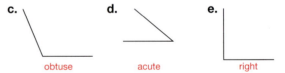

obtuse   acute   right

 Alternative Approach: Using Manipulatives

Use the student clock to practice making angles.

"Show 8:52 on your clock. What type of angle do the hands make?" an acute angle

"Show 6:10 on your clock. What type of angle do the hands make?" an obtuse angle

"Show 3:00 on your clock. What angle do the hands make?" a right angle

"Show 11:27 on your clock. What angle do the hands make?" an obtuse angle

Continue the activity by having students name times while the class determines if the clock hands make acute, obtuse, or right angles.

English Learners

To **bend** means to force a straight form into a curved or angled form. Say:

"Bend your fingers. Bend your arm. Bend your knees."

Students should follow the directions. Ask:

"What materials are hard to bend? What materials are easy to bend?" samples: steel, wood, rock; plastic, cloth, aluminum foil

Have students practice bending their fingers to make shadow animals.

Written Practice — Distributed and Integrated

1. Cynthia wants to put tiles on a floor that is 12 feet long and 9 feet wide. Each tile has sides one foot long. What numbers can Cynthia multiply to find how many tiles she needs to cover the entire floor?   9 and 12
(62, 63)

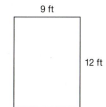

2. What is the area of the rectangle in problem **1**?   108 square feet
(55, 64)

A wading pool at the park has the shape of figure *ABCD*. Look at this picture to answer problems **3–5**.

3. Angle *B* is a right angle.
(65)
    a. Which angle is acute?   Angle *C*

    b. Which angles are obtuse?   Angles *A* and *D*

▶ **4.** (Explain) Is the pool the shape of a rectangle? Explain your answer.   no; sample: The angles are not all right angles.
(51, 65)

▶ **5.** Sides *AB* and *BC* are each 12 feet long. Side *CD* is 13 feet long. Side *AD* is 7 feet long. What is the perimeter of the pool?   44 ft
(58)

▶ **6.** There is a row of tiles along the edge of the pool. There are 3 tiles in one foot. How many tiles are there in 10 feet?   30 tiles
(56, 60)

7. Deanna saw some coins in the pool. What was the total value of the coins?   52¢
(25)

8. Three of the 7 children in the pool were girls.
(44)
    a. What fraction were girls? $\frac{3}{7}$

    b. What fraction were boys? $\frac{4}{7}$

Lesson 65   353

Written Practice

Math Conversations
Independent Practice and Discussions to Increase Understanding

▶ **Problem 4** (Explain)
Have students list the properties of a rectangle. Students may list others, but only the first two are necessary.

1. four right angles
2. four sides
3. opposite sides are of equal length

If any one of these does not apply to the shape of the pool, then students know that it is not a rectangle.

▶ **Problem 5**
Encourage students to draw the pool from problem **5** and label the corners A, B, C, and D to assist in solving the problem. Have them label each side with the correct measurement.

▶ **Problem 6**
Students can multiply or skip count to solve this problem.

(continued)

Inclusion

Name the Angle
Some students may have difficulty with the vocabulary in this lesson. Help them develop a visual reminder.

Materials: index cards

- Students draw a small box in the bottom left corner of the card to indicate a right angle. Label this "right angle."
- In the middle of the card, students draw an acute angle and label it.
- On the right side of the card, students draw an obtuse angle and label it.
- Students can use this card whenever they need to name an angle. They place the "right angle" corner of the card on the angle. They can easily see that if the card fits the angle, it is a right angle. If the angle shows outside the card, it is an obtuse angle. If they can only see one side of the angle, it is an acute angle.

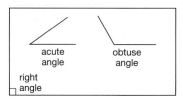

Lesson 65   353

Written Practice (Continued)

Math Conversations
Independent Practice and Discussions to Increase Understanding

▶ **Problem 12** (Analyze)
Help students see that the shaded part ends between two tick marks and that the answer will be between the numbers used for skip counting.

Extend the Problem
"The next morning, Gina looked at the thermometer. The temperature had dropped by 9°F. What was the new temperature of the pool?" 85°F − 9°F = 76°F

▶ **Problem 13** (Represent)
Suggest that students begin by drawing one line segment $\frac{1}{2}$ inch long. Next draw $\frac{3}{4}$-inch segments from both ends of the first segment to form right angles. Draw a line segment connecting the remaining ends of the $\frac{3}{4}$-inch segments to complete the rectangle.

▶ **Problem 19** Multiple Choice
Test-Taking Strategy
Ask students which choice is different from the others and why. **C**; sample: $\frac{10}{11}$ is different because all other answers have the same number on the top and bottom of the fraction.

Errors and Misconceptions

▶ **Problem 2**
Students often forget to add units when reporting area. Remind them that area is named using both a number and a unit such as square inches or square feet.

---

9. Compare the two fractions in problem 8. $\frac{3}{7} < \frac{4}{7}$ or $\frac{4}{7} > \frac{3}{7}$
(43)

10. Sam looked at the clock. The pool closes at 5:00 o'clock. In how many minutes does the pool close? **20 min**
(3)

11. Name the fraction or mixed number shown on each number line.
(48)

a. 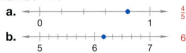 $\frac{4}{5}$

b. 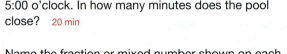 $6\frac{1}{6}$

▶ 12. (Analyze) Gina looked at the thermometer in the pool to find the temperature of the water. How warm was the water? **85°F**
(4)

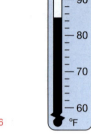

▶ 13. (Represent) Draw a rectangle $\frac{3}{4}$ inches long and $\frac{1}{2}$ inch wide. **See student work.**
(35, 52)

14. Find each product.
(61)
a. 3 × 3 **9**   b. 4 × 4 **16**   c. 6 × 6 **36**

15. Find each product.
(64)
a. 3 × 9 **27**   b. 9 × 4 **36**   c. 9 × 8 **72**

16. 81 − ☐ = 50   **31**
(40)

17. 81 + ☐ = 150   **69**
(9)

18. 9 + 9 + 9 + 9 + 9 + 9 + 9   **63**
(10)

▶ 19. **Multiple Choice** Which fraction does *not* equal 1?   **c**
(46)

A $\frac{2}{2}$ B $\frac{3}{3}$ C $\frac{10}{11}$ D $\frac{12}{12}$

20. Point *B* represents what number on this number line?   **535**
(33)

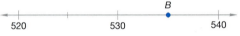

354   Saxon Math Intermediate 3

Looking Forward

Identifying right, acute, and obtuse angles, drawing different angles, and recognizing angles in various flat shapes prepares students for

- **Lesson 66,** working with parallelograms.
- **Lesson 67,** identifying polygons.
- **Lesson 68,** finding congruent shapes.
- **Lesson 69,** identifying types of triangles.
- **Investigation 7,** finding lines of symmetry.
- **Lesson 73,** finding volume.
- **Lesson 104,** sorting geometric shapes.

Cumulative Assessments and Test-Day Activity

Assessments
Distribute **Power-Up Test 12** and **Cumulative Test 12** to each student. Have students complete the **Power-Up Test** first. Allow 10 minutes. Then have students work on the **Cumulative Test.**

Test-Day Activity
The remaining class time can be spent on **Test-Day Activity 6.** Students can begin the activity in class and complete it as homework.

LESSON 66

Planning & Preparation

Texas Essential Knowledge and Skills
(3.8) identify, classify, and describe two-dimensional geometric figures by their attributes and compare two-dimensional figures by their attributes using formal geometry vocabulary
(3.11)(B) use standard units to find the perimeter of a shape
(3.14)(A) identify the mathematics in everyday situations

• Parallelograms

Objectives
- Identify and classify parallelograms.
- Compare and contrast parallelograms and other quadrilaterals.
- Find pairs of parallel sides on parallelograms.
- Identify acute and obtuse angles in parallelograms.
- Name polygons using letters at their vertices.

Prerequisite Skills
- Describe line segments as parallel or perpendicular.
- Identify right angles, acute angles, and obtuse angles.
- Find parallel and perpendicular sides of rectangles.

Materials

Instructional Masters
- Power Up 66

Manipulative Kit
- Ruler
- Color tiles or counters*

Teacher-provided materials
- Straws*
- Pipe cleaners*
- Strips of cardboard joined with brads*
- Index cards*

  *optional

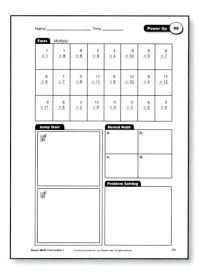

Power Up 66

Differentiated Instruction

Reaching All Special Needs Students

Special Education Students	At-Risk Students	English Learners	Advanced Learners
• Adaptations for Saxon Math	• Alternative Approach (TM) • Error Alert (TM) • Reteaching Masters	• English Learners (TM) • English Learner Handbook	• Extend the Example (TM) • Extend the Problem (TM) • Early Finishers (SE) • Online Activities

TM=Teacher's Manual
SE=Student Edition

Math Language

New	Maintained	English Learners
parallelogram	parallel right angle	pair

Lesson 66   355A

LESSON 66

Problem Solving Discussion

Problem

Matt likes to solve crossword puzzles. He has a book of puzzles. He started at the beginning of the book and solves one puzzle each day. Matt solved Puzzle #4 on Monday. On what day did Matt solve Puzzle #1?

Focus Strategies

 Work Backwards

 Make or Use a Table, Chart, or Graph

Understand *Understand the problem.*

"What information are we given?"

1. Matt solves one crossword puzzle each day.
2. He started at the beginning of the book (Puzzle #1).
3. Matt solved Puzzle #4 on Monday.

"What are we asked to do?"

We are asked to find the day on which Matt solved Puzzle #1.

Plan *Make a plan.*

"What problem solving strategy can we use?"

We can *work backwards* and *make a table* to keep track of our work.

Solve *Carry out the plan.*

"If Matt solved Puzzle #4 on Monday, on what day did he solve Puzzle #3?"

We first count back one day to Sunday. We make a table to keep track of our count:

"On what day did Matt solve Puzzle #2?"

We count back one more day to Saturday.

"On what day did Matt solve Puzzle #1?"

We count back one more day and find that he solved Puzzle #1 on Friday.

Puzzle	#1	#2	#3	#4
Day	Friday	Saturday	Sunday	Monday

Check *Look back.*

"Did we complete the task?"

Yes, we found the day on which Matt solved Puzzle #1 (Friday).

"Is our answer reasonable?"

Yes, Matt solves one puzzle each day. He solved Puzzles #1, #2, #3, and #4 on Friday, Saturday, Sunday, and Monday, respectively.

"What problem solving strategies did we use, and how did they help us?"

We *worked backwards* to find the starting point when we knew the ending point. We *made a table* to help us keep track of each step of our solution.

Saxon Math Intermediate 3

LESSON 66

• Parallelograms

Texas Essential Knowledge and Skills
- (3.8) identify, classify, and describe two-dimensional geometric figures by their attributes and compare two-dimensional figures by their attributes using formal geometry vocabulary
- (3.11)(B) use standard units to find the perimeter of a shape
- (3.14)(A) identify the mathematics in everyday situations

Power Up

facts   Power Up 66

jump start
- Count up by halves from 5 to 10.
  Count up by fourths from 2 to 4.
- Draw an array to show the multiplication fact 1×4.
  See student work.
  Write these numbers in order from least to greatest.
  595, 625, 655, 695
       625   695   655   595

mental math

a. **Fractions:** Compare these fractions using the symbol <, >, or =.
$$\frac{1}{2} \;\;\bigcirc\;\; \frac{2}{4}$$
(=)

b. **Number Sense:** $32 - 9$ 23

c. **Number Sense:** $36 - 8$ 28

d. **Probability:** CeeCee spins the spinner one time. What color is the spinner most likely to land on? green

problem solving

Matt likes to solve crossword puzzles. He has a book of puzzles. He started at the beginning of the book and solves one puzzle each day. Matt solved Puzzle #4 on Monday. On what day did Matt solve Puzzle #1? Friday

Lesson 66   355

LESSON 66

Power Up

Facts
Distribute **Power Up 66** to students. See answers below.

Jump Start
Before students begin the Mental Math exercise, do these exercises as a class.

Mental Math
Encourage students to share different ways to mentally compute these exercises. Strategies for exercises are listed below.

b. Think $32 - 10 + 1$
$32 - 9 = 32 - 10 + 1 = 22 + 1 = 23$

c. Think $36 - 10 + 2$
$36 - 8 = 36 - 10 + 2 = 26 + 2 = 28$

Problem Solving
Refer to **Problem-Solving Strategy Discussion,** p. 355B.

Facts   Multiply:

1 × 1 **1**	1 × 9 **9**	6 × 6 **36**	2 × 9 **18**	4 × 4 **16**	9 × 10 **90**	8 × 9 **72**	9 × 7 **63**	
9 × 9 **81**	7 × 7 **49**	3 × 9 **27**	11 × 11 **121**	6 × 9 **54**	10 × 10 **100**	9 × 4 **36**	12 × 12 **144**	
9 × 11 **99**	8 × 8 **64**	2 × 2 **4**	12 × 9 **108**	9 × 0 **0**	3 × 3 **9**	9 × 5 **45**	0 × 0 **0**	

Lesson 66   355

New Concept

Connection

Draw the following figures on the board or overhead:

"Are all of these shapes rectangles? Why or why not?" no; sample: A rectangle must have four sides and four right angles. Not all of these shapes have four sides and four right angles.

"Which of these shapes have at least two sets of parallel lines?" Students should indicate the square, rectangle, parallelogram, and octagon.

"Are the shapes you indicated all parallelograms? Explain." no; sample: A parallelogram has four sides and the octagon has more than four sides.

For the second *Classify* question, remind students that squares are rectangles because they have four sides and four right angles. Any flat shape that meets this definition will be a rectangle.

"Just as a square is a type of rectangle, a rectangle is a type of parallelogram. Is a square a type of parallelogram?" Yes; a square has two sets of parallel sides.

Error Alert

When classifying shapes, students often make the mistake of applying a definition in reverse: "If all rectangles are parallelograms, then all parallelograms are rectangles." Squares are rectangles because they have four sides and four right angles. Squares and rectangles are both parallelograms because they have four sides and two sets of parallel sides. The reverse is not always true because a parallelogram is not required to have any right angles, so some parallelograms will not be squares or rectangles.

(continued)

New Concept

Waylon has some tiles shaped like this:

The tile has 4 sides.

Classify Is the shape a rectangle? How do you know? No, the shape does not have right angles.
Recall that a rectangle has four right angles. This shape does not have four right angles, so it is not a rectangle. We call this four-sided shape a parallelogram. A **parallelogram** is a four-sided flat shape that has two pairs of parallel sides.

One pair of parallel sides   The other pair of parallel sides

Classify Look at the figures below. Is a rectangle a parallelogram? Rectangles are also parallelograms because rectangles have two pairs of parallel sides.

Example 1

Which of these figures is *not* a parallelogram?

A   B   C   D

A parallelogram has two pairs of parallel sides. We see two pairs of parallel sides in shapes **A**, **B**, and **C**.

A   B

C

356 Saxon Math Intermediate 3

Math Background

Students have learned that the area of a rectangle is found by multiplying its length by its width. The area of a parallelogram is exactly the same as the area of a rectangle with a length equal to the base and a width equal to the height. This connection between the area of a parallelogram and the area of a rectangle can be seen by drawing a parallelogram on the board, removing" a right triangle from one side of the parallelogram, and then "transplanting" that same right triangle to the other side of the parallelogram. The new figure will be a rectangle with a length equal to the base of the parallelogram and a width equal to the height of the parallelogram, so the areas of the two figures must be the same.

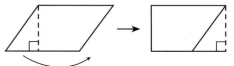

However, shape **D** has only one pair of parallel sides.

Shape D is not a parallelogram.

Example 2

What is the perimeter of this parallelogram?

The parallel sides of a parallelogram are equal in length.

2 in. + 4 in. + 2 in. + 4 in. = 12 in.

The perimeter of the parallelogram is **12 in.**

We can name an angle of a parallelogram by the letter at its vertex. We can name a side by the letters at the ends of the line segment.

Example 3

a. Which angles of this parallelogram are acute and which are obtuse?

b. Which side is parallel to side **AB**?

a. Acute angles are less than right angles, so the acute angles are **angle A** and **angle C**. Obtuse angles are greater than right angles, so the obtuse angles are **angle B** and **angle D**.

b. The side parallel to side **AB** is side **DC**.

Lesson 66   357

New Concept (Continued)

Example 1
"Do all parallelograms have four right angles? Explain." no; Some parallelograms have four right angles. A parallelogram only needs to have two sets of parallel sides.

Extend the Example

Have students identify each of the shapes in the example. Some of the shapes can be classified as more than one type of figure.
- **A:** rectangle, parallelogram
- **B:** parallelogram
- **C:** square, rectangle, parallelogram
- **D:** Students with advanced knowledge may correctly classify this as a quadrilateral or trapezoid.

Alternate Method

When identifying shapes as parallelograms, students can trace the shape and use a ruler or straightedge to continue the edges outside the figure. If a shape is a parallelogram, the lines will never intersect or appear to get closer. If the shape is not a parallelogram, the extended lines will cross outside the figure, move closer together, or move farther apart. Have students perform this method on the shapes in example 1. The extended lines for the first three shapes should never intersect. The last shape will have a pair of intersecting lines above the shape and diverging lines beneath.

Example 2
Example 2 identifies another way to determine if a 4-sided shape is a parallelogram. If students measure the length of opposite sides and find that they are equal in length, then the shape is a parallelogram.

Example 3
Extend the Example

Point out that the angles opposite each other in a parallelogram are equal, the obtuse angle is opposite the other obtuse angle, and the acute angle is opposite the other acute angle.

"What would happen if the acute angle were opposite the obtuse angle?"

Have students draw such a figure.

"Do you still have a parallelogram? Explain." no; sample: When the acute angle is opposite the obtuse angle, the figure cannot have two sets of parallel sides.

(continued)

 English Learners

A **pair** is two corresponding things that match or are made to be used together. Say:

"If you had ten pairs of socks, how many socks would you have in all?"
10 × 2 = 20 socks

Ask:

"What are some things we use in pairs?" samples: earrings, gloves, shoes, socks

Have students name a pair of numbers whose sum is ten.

 Alternative Approach: Using Manipulatives

Here are two ways to construct a model parallelogram:

1. Use 4 straws and 4 pipe cleaners to construct the rectangle.

2. Use 4 strips of cardboard jointed with brads to form a rectangle.

Shift the sides of the rectangle to show that opposite sides remain parallel even though the angles are not right angles.

New Concept (Continued)

Lesson Practice

Guided Practice

Use these problems as guided practice to check the students' understanding of today's concept.

Problem a
Invite students to draw their parallelograms on the board. Students may also use straws or pipe cleaners to construct their parallelograms.

Problem b
Remind students that opposite parallel sides in a parallelogram are equal in length.

Problem f
Extend the Problem
Have students classify each angle in this parallelogram.
Angle *Q* and angle *S* are acute.
Angle *R* and angle *T* are obtuse.

Closure — The questions below help assess the concepts taught in this lesson.

"What are parallel lines?" Parallel lines are straight lines that stay the same distance apart.

"What is a parallelogram?" A parallelogram has two sets of sides parallel to each other.

"Does every parallelogram have four right angles?" no

"What are parallelograms with four right angles called?" rectangles

Discuss real-world situations where parallelograms are used. An example is given below.

- Some parking lots have "angled parking" spaces that are each in the shape of a parallelogram.

Written Practice

Math Conversations
Independent Practice and Discussions to Increase Understanding

Problem 1
Help students recognize this as an "equal groups" story.

"Gwen has three groups, or boxes, with 40 tiles in each group."

(continued)

358   Saxon Math Intermediate 3

Lesson Practice

a. Draw a parallelogram that does *not* have right angles.
See student work.

b. What is the perimeter of the parallelogram on the right? **14 in.**

c. **Multiple Choice** Which shape below is *not* a parallelogram? **B**

A   B   C   D

d. Which shapes in problem c are rectangles? **A, C**

e. Which angles in this parallelogram are obtuse? angles *R* and *T*

f. Which side of this parallelogram is parallel to side *QT*? side *RS*

Written Practice — Distributed and Integrated

1. **Formulate** Gwen has 3 boxes of tiles with 40 tiles in each box. Write a number sentence to show how many tiles are in all 3 boxes. $3 \times 40 = 120$ tiles
(60, 24)

2. **Multiple Choice** Gwen sees this tile pattern around the edge of a shower. What are the next two tiles in the pattern? **A**
(2)

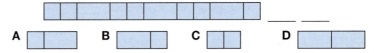

A   B   C   D

3. Write two addition facts and two subtraction facts using 7, 8, and 15. $7 + 8 = 15$; $8 + 7 = 15$; $15 - 8 = 7$; $15 - 7 = 8$
(8)

4. **Multiple Choice** Which shape is *not* a parallelogram? **B**
(66)

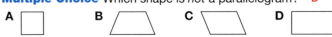
A   B   C   D

5. One square yard equals 9 square feet. How many square feet is 9 square yards? **81 square feet**
(60, 64)

358   Saxon Math Intermediate 3

Inclusion

What Is a Parallelogram?

Some students may have difficulty with the vocabulary in this lesson. Help them develop a visual reminder.

Materials: index cards, crayons

- Write "Parallelogram" on the board and have students copy it at the top of their card.

- Students draw a rectangle. They trace each pair of opposite sides with a crayon, using a different color for each pair. For example, they might trace the top and bottom sides with a red crayon, and the right and left sides with a blue crayon.

- Students draw a square and trace each pair of opposite sides with a crayon, using a different color for each pair.

- Students draw a parallelogram with two obtuse and two acute angles, tracing opposite sides as above.

- Students can refer to this card whenever they need to identify a parallelogram.

For exercise, Sasha walks around the park every day. Look at the picture of the park for problems **6–9**.

6. What is the shape of the park?   parallelogram
(66)

7. a. Which angles are acute?   angle A and angle C
(65)

    b. Which angles are obtuse?   angle B and angle D

8. What is the perimeter of the park?   700 yards
(58)

9. Which side of the park is parallel to side AB?
(40, 66) side DC or side CD

▶ **10.** It takes Sasha 14 minutes to walk around the park twice. She started walking at 3:20 p.m. The clock shows the time she finished. Write the time in digital form.   3:34 p.m.
(38)

▶ **11.** Blaine opened a box of 40 tiles and used 28 of the tiles. How many tiles are left?   12 tiles
(20)

12. Use your inch ruler to measure the segments below to the nearest quarter inch.
(35)

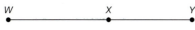

    a. How long is segment WX? $1\frac{1}{2}$ inches

    b. How long is segment XY? $1\frac{1}{4}$ inches

    c. How long is segment WY? $2\frac{3}{4}$ inches

13. There are three colors of marbles in a bag. Kyle picks one marble without looking. Which color is he least likely to pick?   red
(50)

Marbles in Bag

Color	Number
red	2
blue	3
green	5

Written Practice (Continued)

Math Conversations

Independent Practice and Discussions to Increase Understanding

▶ **Problem 10**

Extend the Problem

Ask advanced learners,

"If Sasha walked for 49 minutes, how many times would she have walked around the park?"   7 times

"What time would it be if she started walking at 3:20 p.m.?"   4:09 p.m.

▶ **Problem 11**

Extend the Problem

"Draw a rectangle that Blaine could have made with 28 tiles."

Students may also use tiles to solve this problem. They should draw or build a rectangle that is 7 × 4 or 2 × 14.

(continued)

Written Practice (Continued)

Math Conversations
Independent Practice and Discussions to Increase Understanding

▶ **Problem 19 Multiple Choice**
Test-Taking Strategy

For a fraction to be equal to $\frac{1}{2}$, the denominator must be even so it can be equally divided into two groups. Since the problem asks which fraction is *not* equal to $\frac{1}{2}$, we look first for fractions with odd denominators.

Errors and Misconceptions

▶ **Problem 5**
It is a common mistake to multiply by three when converting from square feet to square yards. Remind students that to correctly convert from square feet to square yards, they must multiply by nine.

▶ **Problem 20**
Students often make the mistake of counting tick marks instead of segments along the number line. Because point A is on the second of four tick marks, this would result in the incorrect answer of $\frac{2}{4}$, or $\frac{1}{2}$. Caution students to avoid counting tick marks and to count segments instead.

Students can use tiles or counters to represent the pencils. Suggest that they count by quarters to find how much she spent. Then have them use the manipulatives to show how many pencils Tammy had left.

---

14. Look at the table in problem **13** to answer **a** and **b**.
(44)
    a. How many marbles are in the bag?   10

    b. What fraction of the marbles are blue? $\frac{3}{10}$

15. $3.75 + $4.29 $8.04   **16.** $200 − $81 $119
(22)   (28)

17. $9 + 9 + 9 + 9 + 9 + 9 + 9 + 9$ 72
(10, 54)

18. Write a fraction equal to 1 that has a denominator of 10. $\frac{10}{10}$
(46)

▶ **19. Multiple Choice** Which fraction is *not* equal to $\frac{1}{2}$?   C
(47)
    A $\frac{2}{4}$ **B** $\frac{3}{6}$ **C** $\frac{4}{7}$ **D** $\frac{5}{10}$

20. Point A represents what fraction? $\frac{2}{5}$
(48)

Early Finishers
Real-World Connection

Tammy bought 7 pencils for 25 cents each. Then she bought 4 more pencils and gave 3 to her brother. How many pencils does Tammy have left? How much did she spend on the pencils altogether? You may use your manipulatives to help find the answer.   8 pencils; $2.75

Looking Forward

Drawing and constructing parallelograms, recognizing angles within parallelograms, and identifying different shapes prepares students for

- **Lesson 67,** identifying polygons.
- **Lesson 68,** finding congruent shapes.
- **Lesson 69,** identifying types of triangles.
- **Investigations 7 and 9,** identifying lines of symmetry.
- **Lesson 104,** sorting geometric shapes.

LESSON 67

> **Texas Essential Knowledge and Skills**
>
> (3.8) identify, classify, and describe two-dimensional geometric figures by their attributes and compare two-dimensional figures by their attributes using formal geometry vocabulary
>
> (3.11)(B) use standard units to find the perimeter of a shape
>
> (3.14)(C) select/develop an appropriate problem-solving plan/strategy, including working a simpler problem

Planning & Preparation

• Polygons

Objectives
- Classify figures as examples or nonexamples of polygons.
- Identify and describe polygons by their attributes.
- Use proper vocabulary to name polygons.
- Find the perimeters of polygons.

Prerequisite Skills
- Find the perimeters of rectangles.
- Identify right angles, acute angles, and obtuse angles.
- Identify, classify, and describe rectangles, squares, and parallelograms by their attributes.
- Find parallel or perpendicular sides of quadrilaterals.

Materials

Instructional Masters
- Power Up 67

Manipulative Kit
- Ruler
- Pattern blocks*

Teacher-provided materials
- Index cards*

  *optional

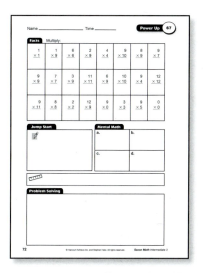

Power Up 67

Differentiated Instruction

Reaching All Special Needs Students

Special Education Students	At-Risk Students	English Learners	Advanced Learners
• Inclusion (TM) • Adaptations for Saxon Math	• Error Alert (TM) • Reteaching Masters	• English Learners (TM) • English Learner Handbook	• Extend the Example (TM) • Extend the Problem (TM) • Early Finishers (SE) • Online Activities

TM = Teacher's Manual
SE = Student Edition

Math Language

	New	Maintained	English Learners
circle hexagon octagon	pentagon polygon quadrilateral	parallelogram	intersection

Lesson 67 361A

LESSON 67

Problem Solving Discussion

Problem

Liz asked her father to download her 3 favorite songs from the Internet. Each song costs 99¢. How much will all 3 songs cost?

Focus Strategy  Work a Simpler Problem

Understand *Understand the problem.*

"What information are we given?"

1. Liz wants to download 3 songs.
2. Each song costs 99¢.

"What are we asked to do?"

We are asked to find the cost of all 3 songs.

Plan *Make a plan.*

"How can we use the information we know to solve the problem?"

We can use number sense to *make the problem simpler.*

Solve *Carry out the plan.*

"What price is close to 99¢?"

The price 99¢ is close to $1.

"If each song cost $1, how much would 3 songs cost?"

Three songs would cost $3.

"Each song is 1¢ less than a dollar, so how many cents less than $3 would 3 songs be?"

Each song is 1¢ less than a dollar, so 3 songs would be 3¢ less than $3.

"How much is 3¢ less than $3?"

We count backwards: $2.99, $2.98, $2.97.

Check *Look back.*

"Did we complete the task?"

Yes, we found that the total price of 3 downloaded songs that cost 99¢ each is $2.97.

"Why did we use the price $1 to help us solve the problem?"

We made our calculation with the amount $1 because it is a simpler number to work with than 99¢.

"Does our answer make sense?"

Yes, our answer makes sense, because $3 \times \$1 = \$3$, and $2.97 is a little less than $3.

Alternate Strategy
Act It Out

Students can work in pairs to *act out* this problem using their money manipulatives. They can make three groups of 99¢, combine the groups, and find the total.

361B *Saxon Math* Intermediate 3

LESSON 67

• Polygons

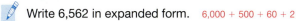

Texas Essential Knowledge and Skills
(3.8) identify, classify, and describe two-dimensional geometric figures by their attributes and compare two-dimensional figures by their attributes using formal geometry vocabulary
(3.11)(B) use standard units to find the perimeter of a shape
(3.14)(C) select/develop an appropriate problem-solving plan/strategy, including working a simpler problem

Power Up

facts   Power Up 67

jump start
- Count down by 7s from 70 to 0.
- Count up by square numbers from 1 to 144.
- Write 6,562 in expanded form.   6,000 + 500 + 60 + 2
- Draw a $2\frac{1}{4}$-inch segment on your worksheet. Record the length next to the segment.   See student work; $2\frac{1}{4}$ in.

mental math
a. **Number Sense:** 10 + 4 + 7   21
b. **Number Sense:** 45 + 6   51
c. **Money:** $10.00 − $4.50 $5.50
d. **Measurement:** What is the perimeter of the square?   12 in.   3 in.

problem solving

Focus Strategy: Work a Simpler Problem

Liz asked her father to download her 3 favorite songs from the Internet. Each song costs 99¢. How much will all 3 songs cost?

(**Understand**) We are asked to find the cost of 3 songs that are 99¢ each.

(**Plan**) We can *work a simpler problem.*

(**Solve**) The price 99¢ is close to $1. We can pretend that each song costs $1. This means 3 songs would cost $3. Each song is 1¢ less than a dollar, so 3 songs is 3¢ less than $3. We count backwards: $2.99, $2.98, **$2.97.**

Lesson 67   361

LESSON 67

Power Up

Facts
Distribute **Power Up 67** to students. See answers below.

Jump Start
Before students begin the Mental Math exercise, do these exercises as a class.

Mental Math
Encourage students to share different ways to mentally compute these exercises. Strategies for exercises are listed below.

a. **Look for Numbers that Add to 10.**
Think 4 + 7 = 1 + 3 + 7 = 1 + 10
Use substitution to solve the problem.
10 + 4 + 7 = 10 + 1 + 10 = 11 + 10 = 21

b. Think 45 + 5 + 1.
45 + 6 = 45 + 5 + 1 = 50 + 1 = 51

Problem Solving
Refer to **Problem-Solving Strategy Discussion**, p. 361B.

Facts   Multiply:

1 × 1 = 1	1 × 9 = 9	6 × 6 = 36	2 × 9 = 18	4 × 4 = 16	9 × 10 = 90	8 × 9 = 72	9 × 7 = 63
9 × 9 = 81	7 × 7 = 49	3 × 9 = 27	11 × 11 = 121	6 × 9 = 54	10 × 10 = 100	9 × 4 = 36	12 × 12 = 144
9 × 11 = 99	8 × 8 = 64	2 × 2 = 4	12 × 9 = 108	9 × 0 = 0	3 × 3 = 9	9 × 5 = 45	0 × 0 = 0

New Concept

Explanation
Tell students that the term *polygon* comes from ancient Greek and means "many angled." Polygons are closed figures that can contain any number of angles. Write the following word prefixes on the board.

"tri-" means 3
"quad-" means 4
"penta-" means 5
"hexa-" means 6
"octa-" means 8

Ask for volunteers to look up these prefixes in the dictionary and read their definitions aloud. Write the definitions next to the prefixes and use them to ask the students,

"How many arms would an octopus have?" 8

"What would I mean if I said that my wallet is a trifold?" sample: It folds up into three layers.

Discussion
"Can a circle be a polygon?" no

"Why not?" It has no straight sides.

"Can a polygon have a right angle?" yes

"Can you think of an example?" sample: A rectangle is a polygon with four right angles.

Example 1
Error Alert

Students most often mistakenly call shapes with curved lines polygons. Draw a triangle on the board and label each side with one of the characteristics of a polygon (closed, flat, straight sides). Leave this triangle on the board so students can reference it for the practice problems.

Real-World Connection

"There is a building in Washington, D.C., called The Pentagon. How many sides do you think this building has?" 5 sides

"The pyramids of Egypt have four visible faces, and each face has three sides. What polygon makes up each of these faces?" a triangle

"A snowflake is a flat crystal with six sides. What would you call this polygon?" a hexagon

(continued)

362   Saxon Math Intermediate 3

Check We made our calculation with the amount $1 because it is a simpler number to work with than 99¢. Our answer makes sense, because 3 × $1 = $3, and $2.97 is a little less than $3.

New Concept

A **polygon** is a closed, flat shape with straight sides.

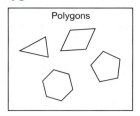
Polygons

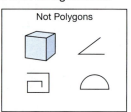
Not Polygons

Discuss Is a polygon always a parallelogram? Why or why not?

no; sample: A polygon can be a parallelogram if it has 4 sides and 2 pairs of parallel sides, but a polygon does not always have 4 sides and might have sides that are not parallel.

Example 1

Explain why these shapes are *not* polygons.

a.   b.   c.

a. The shape is not closed.
b. The shape is not flat.
c. The shape is curved.

In example 1, the figure in part **c** is a special curved figure we may know called a **circle.** A circle is a flat, closed shape, but it does not have straight sides. It is not a polygon.

362   Saxon Math Intermediate 3

Math Background

Students learned about hexagons and octagons in this lesson. They may not know the names of other polygons with more than four sides. For example, a heptagon is a seven-sided polygon, a decagon has ten sides, and a dodecagon has twelve sides. Although it does not have a special name, it is interesting to note that Archimedes incorporated the use of a 96-sided polygon in his studies related to pi.

Polygons are named by their number of sides.

Polygons

Name	Example	Number of sides
Triangle	△	3
Quadrilateral	▭	4
Pentagon	⬠	5
Hexagon	⬡	6
Octagon	⯄	8

Example 2

Kathleen arranged pattern blocks to make the design. What is the shape of each pattern block in the design?

Each pattern block in the design has 6 sides. A 6-sided polygon is a **hexagon**.

Example 3

a. Mrs. Lopez saw this sign and stopped at the intersection. What is the shape of the sign?

b. If each side of the stop sign is 12 inches long, what is the perimeter of the stop sign?

a. The sign has 8 sides. An 8-sided polygon is an **octagon**.

b. We add eight 12-inch sides or we multiply 12 inches by 8.

$$8 \times 12 \text{ in.} = 96 \text{ in.}$$

The perimeter of the stop sign is **96 inches**.

Lesson 67 363

English Learners

An **intersection** is where two streets or lines cross. Draw a diagram of intersecting streets on the board. Say:

"Why might you find a stop sign at an intersection?" A stop sign is there in case cars are coming from more than one direction.

Draw several pairs of intersecting lines on the board. Ask volunteers to point to the intersection of each pair.

New Concept (Continued)

Example 2
Extend the Example

Call students' attention to the six hexagons surrounding the center hexagon.

"How many pattern blocks would we need to make another ring of hexagons around the design?" 12 more blocks

Students can use pattern blocks or make a sketch to assist in solving this extension problem.

"Can you guess how many more pattern blocks we would need to go around the design once more?" 24

"What pattern do you see?" sample: We double the number of tiles found in the previous ring each time we add a ring.

Example 3
Real-World Connection

Ask students if they have encountered any other signs that are in the shape of a polygon. Have students describe the sign and name the polygon. List their responses on the board. Some examples would be a yield sign in the shape of a triangle or a speed limit sign in the shape of a rectangle. Students can sketch signs from memory at their desks.

(continued)

Lesson 67 363

New Concept (Continued)

Example 4
"The word quad means "four." When we see the word quadrilateral we should think of the number four."

Example 5
Extend the Example

"How many sides does this polygon have?" six sides

"Is this polygon a hexagon? Explain." yes; sample: A hexagon is a polygon with six sides. The shape of the playground is a polygon and it has six sides.

Explain that the polygons students saw earlier in this lesson were *regular polygons*. They are called regular because all their angles are equal and the lengths of all their sides are equal.

"What is another name for a regular quadrilateral?" a square

Lesson Practice

Guided Practice
Use these problems as guided practice to check the students' understanding of today's concept.

Problem b
Explanation

"A prefix is a beginning sound which can be attached to the beginning of another word. The prefix tri- means "three," so a triangle has three angles."

Problem c Multiple Choice
Test-Taking Strategy

Since all of these figures are different, students must apply the definition of a polygon to each shape to eliminate all invalid choices.
A: meets the definition
B: not a polygon because it is not a flat shape
C: not a polygon because it does not have straight sides
D: not a polygon because the figure is not closed

(continued)

Example 4

These four shapes are all what type of polygon?

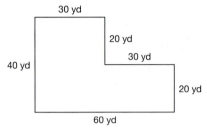

Each polygon has 4 sides. Any polygon with 4 sides is a **quadrilateral**.

Example 5

Simon ran the perimeter of the playground once. How far did he run?

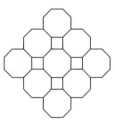

We add the length of each side to find the total distance around the playground.

60 yd + 20 yd + 30 yd + 20 yd + 30 yd + 40 yd = 200 yd

Simon ran **200 yards**.

Lesson Practice

a. Miguel arranged two kinds of polygons to make this pattern. Name the two types of polygons. octagon and square or quadrilateral

b. Draw a 3-sided polygon. What is the name for a polygon with 3 sides? See student work; triangle

c. **Multiple Choice** Which of these figures is a polygon? A

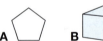
A B C D

Naming Polygons

Some students may have difficulty remembering the names of common polygons. Students can work in pairs to practice.

Materials: index cards

- Each student should create a set of flashcards with the name of the polygon on one side and a picture of the corresponding shape on the other.

- Place students in pairs and have them take turns identifying the names of each of the polygons on the flashcards. Encourage students to help each other find ways to remember the names of each shape.

d. Each side of the hexagon is 12 in. What is its perimeter? 72 in.

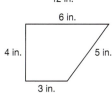

▶ e. What is the perimeter of the quadrilateral? 18 in.

Written Practice   *Distributed and Integrated*

1. Paul finished two tile jobs. For the first job, he was paid $400. For the second job, he was paid $535. How much was he paid for both jobs? $935
(18)

2. How much more was Paul paid for the second job in problem **1** than for the first job? $135
(39)

▶ 3. **Estimate** Madison pays $590 each month for rent and $285 for her car. Estimate the total Madison pays for rent and for her car each month. $900
(30)

4. Jenny was born in 1998. How old will she be on her birthday in 2008? 10 years old
(28, 39)

5. Gabe bought a postcard and gave the clerk a dollar. He got back two quarters, two dimes, and three pennies.
(25, 40)
   a. How much money did Gabe get back? 73¢
   b. How much did the postcard cost? 27¢

6. Arrange these numbers in order from least to greatest. 236, 263, 326, 362
(27)
   263   326   362   236

Lesson 67   365

New Concept (Continued)

Problem e
Extend the Problem
"Which sides of the quadrilateral are parallel?" The 3-inch side and the 6-inch side

"Which angles are right angles?" The angle between the 6-inch side and the 4-inch side and the angle between the 3-inch side and the 4-inch side

Closure The questions below help assess the concepts taught in this lesson.

"What are three characteristics of a polygon?" closed, flat, straight sides

"What is a polygon with 6 sides called?" a hexagon

"Is a parallelogram always a polygon?" yes

"How would you find the perimeter of an octagon?" sample: add the lengths of all 8 sides

"What can any polygon with 4 sides be called?" a quadrilateral

Discuss real-world situations where understanding polygons would be helpful. Examples are given below.
- We want to build a fence around a yard.
- We make a holiday card in an unusual shape.
- We want to explain the difference between home plate and the other bases in baseball.

Written Practice

Math Conversations
Independent Practice and Discussions to Increase Understanding

Problem 3 **Estimate**
Students should first round each number to the nearest hundred and then add. 590 rounds to 600, and 285 rounds to 300.

Extend the Problem
"About how much would Madison pay for two months of rent and car payments?" $1,800

(continued)

Lesson 67   365

Written Practice (Continued)

Math Conversations
Independent Practice and Discussions to Increase Understanding

Problem 7 Multiple Choice
Test-Taking Strategy

Since all of these figures are different, students must apply the definition of a polygon to each shape to eliminate all invalid choices.
A: not a polygon because the figure is not closed
B: not a polygon because it does not have straight sides
C: not a polygon because it is not a flat shape
D: meets the definition

Problem 11 Multiple Choice
Test-Taking Strategy

Students should look at the smallest and largest numbers being added. Mark out any choice that does not have a 3 in the thousands place and any choice that does not have a 5 in the ones place. This eliminates choices **A** and **D**. Students then need to look for a 4 in the hundreds place to determine that **B** is correct.

Problem 12 (Conclude)

Students should recognize this pattern as skip counting by 9s or multiples of 9.

"What multiplication facts could we write to find the next three numbers in this sequence?" $9 \times 6 = 54$; $9 \times 7 = 63$; $9 \times 8 = 72$

Problem 16 Multiple Choice
Test-Taking Strategy

Students should count the number of sides for each polygon to determine the pattern. The first shape has three sides. The second has four sides. The third has five sides.

"How many sides does the next shape have?" six

Extend the Problem

"What is the name of each of these polygons?" triangle, square (or rectangle/parallelogram/quadrilateral), pentagon, hexagon

(continued)

---

7. Multiple Choice Which of these figures is a polygon? **D**
(67)

8. a. What fraction of an hour is 15 minutes? $\frac{1}{4}$
(5)
b. How many minutes is $\frac{3}{4}$ of an hour? 45 min

9. a. What is the numerator of $\frac{3}{4}$? 3
(41)
b. What is the denominator of $\frac{3}{4}$? 4

10. The picture below shows three equal groups of tiles. Write a multiplication fact that shows the total number of tiles. $3 \times 6 = 18$
(54, 60)

11. Multiple Choice Which number equals $3{,}000 + 400 + 5$? **B**
(32)
A 3,450   **B** 3,405   **C** 3,045   **D** 30,405

12. (Conclude) What are the next three numbers in this sequence? 54, 63, 72
(2, 64)

$$9, 18, 27, 36, 45, \_\_\_, \_\_\_, \_\_\_, \ldots$$

13. Which multiplication fact is shown by this array? $7 \times 4 = 28$
(57)

14. 32¢ + 58¢ + 25¢ $1.15
(22, 24)

15. $360 − $296 $64
(23)

16. Multiple Choice Which polygon is next in this sequence? **A**
(2, 67)

366   Saxon Math Intermediate 3

17. Show how to write this addition as multiplication, and then find
(54, 55) the total. $7 \times 8 = 56$

$$8 + 8 + 8 + 8 + 8 + 8 + 8$$

18. Which point best represents 16 on the number line? **B**
(33)

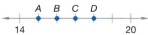

19. Use your inch ruler to find the length of this paper clip to the
(35) nearest quarter inch. $1\frac{1}{4}$ inch

▶ **20.** A square tile has sides 6 inches long.
(58, 62)
  a. What is the perimeter of the tile? 24 in.
  b. What is the area of the tile? 36 sq. in.

6 in.

6 in.

Early Finishers
Real-World Connection

Four friends ran a race. Tony ran faster than Bill. Bill ran faster than CJ. Ryan ran faster than Tony. Who won the race? Who came in last? Draw a picture to show how you got your answer.
Ryan; CJ; See student work.

Lesson 67 367

Working with polygons and learning about different types of polygons prepares students for

- **Lesson 68,** identifying congruent shapes.
- **Lesson 69,** identifying types of triangles.
- **Investigations 7 and 9,** identifying lines of symmetry.
- **Lesson 75,** identifying geometric solids.
- **Lesson 104,** sorting geometric shapes.

Written Practice (Continued)

Math Conversations
Independent Practice and Discussions to Increase Understanding

▶ **Problem 20**
Extend the Problem

"If we placed four 6-inch tiles in a row, what would the perimeter of the shape be in inches?" Each long edge would be $6 \times 4 = 24$ inches. Each short edge would be 6 inches. $24 + 24 + 6 + 6 = 60$ inches

"What would the perimeter of this shape be in feet?" 5 feet

"What would the area of this shape be in square inches?" $36 \times 4 = 144$ square inches

Students may need to draw a picture or use tiles to solve these problems.

Errors and Misconceptions

▶ **Problem 8b**
Students often get confused when figuring amounts of time smaller than one hour. Refer students to the classroom clock and ask them to picture shading $\frac{3}{4}$ of it. The location at which the shading ends marks the time equal to $\frac{3}{4}$ of an hour.

▶ **Problem 11**
Students may get confused by the missing value in the tens place. Remind students that if there is not a digit in a place value when the number is written in expanded form, there is a zero in that digit of the number.

Have students show the picture they drew. Ask them to use the picture to explain who won the race and who came in last.

Lesson 67 367

LESSON 68

Planning & Preparation

Texas Essential Knowledge and Skills
(3.8) compare two-dimensional figures by their attributes using formal geometry vocabulary
(3.9)(A) identify congruent two-dimensional figures
(3.14)(A) identify the mathematics in everyday situations
(3.16)(B) explain the solution process

• Congruent Shapes

Objectives
- Identify pictorial models of congruent figures.
- Find congruent shapes or objects in the classroom.

Prerequisite Skills
- Use proper vocabulary to name polygons.
- Identify, classify, and describe polygons by their attributes.
- Identify right angles, acute angles, and obtuse angles.
- Find parallel or perpendicular sides of quadrilaterals.

Materials

Instructional Masters
- Power Up 68

Manipulative Kit
- Geoboards (student and overhead)*
- Rulers

Teacher-provided materials
- White paper
- Construction paper
- Scissors

optional

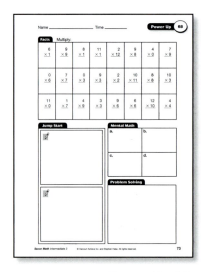

Power Up 68

Reaching All Special Needs Students

Special Education Students	At-Risk Students	English Learners	Advanced Learners
• Inclusion (TM) • Adaptations for Saxon Math	• Alternative Approach (TM) • Error Alert (TM) • Reteaching Masters	• English Learners (TM) • English Learner Handbook	• Extend the Example (TM) • Extend the Problem (TM) • Online Activities

TM=Teacher's Manual

Math Language

New	Maintained	English Learners
congruent	side	flip

368A *Saxon Math* Intermediate 3

Problem Solving Discussion

Problem
The DVDs were priced at $9.99 each. At this price, how much would 2 DVDs cost? Explain how you found your answer.

Focus Strategy Make It Simpler

Understand *Understand the problem.*

"What information are we given?"

DVDs are priced at $9.99 each.

"What are we asked to do?"

We are asked to find the cost of 2 DVDs and to explain how we found our answer.

Plan *Make a plan.*

"What problem solving strategy can we use?"

We can use number sense to *make the problem simpler*.

Solve *Carry out the plan.*

"What whole-dollar price is close to $9.99?"

The price of 1 DVD is close to $10.00.

"If each DVD were priced at $10.00, how much would 2 DVDs cost?"

$20.00

"How many cents less than $20.00 is the cost of 2 DVDs?"

One DVD costs 1¢ less than $10.00, so 2 DVDs cost 2¢ less than $20.00.

"Counting 2¢ backward from $20.00, what do we find is the total cost of 2 DVDs?"

We count backward two cents to $19.98.

Check *Look back.*

"Is our answer reasonable?"

Yes, we know that our answer is reasonable because $19.98 is close to $20.00. If we round the price of each DVD to $10.00, it is easy to see that 2 DVDs cost about $20.00.

"What problem solving strategy did we use, and how did it help us?"

We *made the problem simpler* by rounding the price. This helped us to solve the problem mentally.

Alternate Strategy
Write a Number Sentence

Students can also write a number sentence to add the prices:
$9.99 + $9.99 = $19.98.

LESSON 68

Power Up

Facts
Distribute **Power Up 68** to students. See answers below.

Jump Start
Before students begin the Mental Math exercise, do these exercises as a class.

Mental Math
Encourage students to share different ways to mentally compute these exercises. Strategies for exercises are listed below.

c. Add and Attach Two Zeros
7 + 7 = 14
700 + 700 = 1,400

d. Count and Write the Fraction
total parts: 3
parts shaded: 2
The fraction is $\frac{2}{3}$.

Problem Solving
Refer to **Problem-Solving Strategy Discussion**, p. 368B.

LESSON 68 • Congruent Shapes

Texas Essential Knowledge and Skills
(3.8) compare two-dimensional figures by their attributes using formal geometry vocabulary
(3.9)(A) identify congruent two-dimensional figures
(3.14)(A) identify the mathematics in everyday situations
(3.16)(B) explain the solution process

Power Up

facts   Power Up 68

jump start
- Count up by 4s from 0 to 40.
- Count up by 8s from 0 to 80.
- Write two multiplication facts using the numbers 8, 5, and 40. $8 \times 5 = 40; 5 \times 8 = 40$
- Write the greatest 3-digit number that uses each of the digits 7, 5, and 8. What is the value of the digit in the ones place?   875; 5

mental math
a. **Money:** $2.37 + $1.00 $3.37
b. **Calendar:** How many days are in 10 weeks?   70 days
c. **Number Sense:** 700 + 700   1,400
d. **Fractions:** What fraction of the circle is shaded? $\frac{2}{3}$

problem solving
The DVDs were priced at $9.99 each. At this price, how much would 2 DVDs cost? Explain how you found your answer. $19.98; sample: We can find the answer by rounding $9.99 to $10.00 and then finding the cost of 2 DVDs for $10.00 each. The cost would be $20.00. Then we count back one cent for each DVD to $19.98.

368   Saxon Math Intermediate 3

Facts   Multiply:

6 × 1 = **6**	9 × 9 = **81**	8 × 1 = **8**	11 × 1 = **11**	2 × 12 = **24**	9 × 8 = **72**	4 × 0 = **0**	7 × 9 = **63**
0 × 6 = **0**	7 × 7 = **49**	0 × 3 = **0**	9 × 3 = **27**	2 × 2 = **4**	10 × 11 = **110**	8 × 8 = **64**	10 × 3 = **30**
11 × 0 = **0**	1 × 7 = **7**	4 × 9 = **36**	3 × 3 = **9**	9 × 6 = **54**	6 × 6 = **36**	12 × 10 = **120**	4 × 4 = **16**

New Concept

If figures are the same size and shape, we say they are **congruent**.

Congruent Triangles   Not Congruent Triangles

yes; sample: Since they are both squares, they are the same shape. Since they have the same perimeter, the sides are the same length, so the squares are the same size.

Discuss Two squares have the same perimeter. Will the two squares be congruent? Why or why not?

Example 1

Which pair of figures is not congruent?

A   B

C   D

The figures in **A, B,** and **C** are congruent. The figures in **D** are not congruent because they are not the same size.

If congruent figures are turned or flipped, they are still congruent. These three triangles are congruent.

Example 2

Which parallelogram below is not congruent to this parallelogram?

A   B   C   D

Lesson 68   369

New Concept

Instruction
Explain to students that congruent shapes are exactly alike in terms of size and shape. Other characteristics such as color, shading, or orientation (flips, rotations) do not affect their congruence.

Example 1
Extend the Example

"Are the triangles in A congruent to the triangles in C?" No; even though they are both triangles, they are not the same shape or size.

Active Learning

Divide students into pairs. Give each student white paper, construction paper, pencils, and scissors. Tell students that each pair will make shapes that are congruent.

Each student should draw a closed figure on the construction paper and cut it out. They should exchange figures with their partner, and their partner should trace the figure once on the white paper. Then flip, move, or rotate the figure, and trace it a second time nearby. Have students tape their congruent shapes to the wall or board as a visual cue for future reference.

Example 2
Math Language

The way a shape is flipped or turned is called its orientation. Orientation means the direction something is facing, usually with respect to the cardinal directions. Make sure students understand that since a shape's "orientation" does not affect its shape or size, changing the orientation does not change congruence.

(continued)

Math Background

The different ways that a figure may be changed while maintaining congruence are known as *congruence transformations* or *isometries*. Isometries for flat figures are usually described as rotations (turning), translations (moving), and reflections (flipping). If a figure is moved *and* flipped, the isometry is called a *glide reflection*. Each of these changes may be described mathematically relative to a grid. Another isometry is an *identity map*. This is simply the exact same figure in the exact same orientation and location. A figure is congruent to itself.

English Learners

To **flip** means to turn something over to the other side, sometimes with a tossing or flicking action. Say:

"Who can flip on the lights? At your desk, flip over your math book."

Observe students or student volunteers performing these actions.

Ask:

"What are some foods that you must flip over to cook?" sample: pancakes, tortillas, omelets

Have students flip coins with a partner.

Lesson 68   369

New Concept (Continued)

Lesson Practice

Guided Practice

Use these problems as guided practice to check the students' understanding of today's concept.

Problem a
Extend the Problem

"If two things are different colors, can they still be congruent? Explain." yes; sample: Shape and size are not changed by the color.

Problem c Multiple Choice
Test-Taking Strategy

Students should imagine tracing the given triangle, cutting it out, and then trying to place it over the triangle in each answer choice. Any choices that do not match should be marked out. Only congruent triangles will be left.

Problem d Error Alert

Students often overlook congruent shapes that are not oriented the same. Remind students that congruent figures are the same size and shape and may be turned or flipped.

Closure — The questions below help assess the concepts taught in this lesson.

"What does congruent mean?" Congruent means that figures or objects are the same size and shape.

"If two figures are the same size and shape but are facing different directions, are they congruent?" Yes, congruent figures can be flipped or turned.

Discuss real-world situations where congruence is important. Examples are given below.

- A mold is made of an artist's sculpture so that the same shape can be reproduced again and again.
- The same puzzle-piece shapes are used for a jigsaw puzzle with different designs pasted on the pieces.

Recall that a parallelogram is a four-sided, flat shape that has two pairs of parallel sides. The parallelograms in A, B, and D are congruent to the figure in example 2 because they are all the same size and the same shape. Choice **C** is not congruent because it is a different size.

Congruent Shapes

Look around the room for two shapes or objects that are congruent. Name the shapes or objects on your paper. Sketch both of them.

Lesson Practice

a. What two words complete the definition? size, shape
   Congruent figures are the same ___ and ___.

b. Draw a triangle that is congruent to this triangle. See student work.

c. **Multiple Choice** Which triangle below is congruent to the triangle in problem **b**? A

   A   B   C   D

d. **Multiple Choice** Which pair of figures is *not* congruent? B

   A   B
   C   D

Written Practice Distributed and Integrated

1. Mary wanted to buy a new rose bush. The red one cost $8.49. The yellow one cost $7.89. The red one cost how much more than the yellow one? $0.60
   (39)

2. Mary decided to buy the yellow rose bush for $7.89. Tax was 55¢. What was the total price including tax? $8.44
   (18, 22)

370 Saxon Math Intermediate 3

Alternative Approach: Using Manipulatives

Geoboards can also be used to model congruent shapes. Make a shape on your geoboard and have students make the same shape on theirs. An overhead geoboard may also be used. Point out to students that when the geoboard is rotated, the shape is still congruent. Practice by creating various shapes for students to mimic.

Inclusion

Congruent Pairs

Students who have difficulty identifying congruent shapes will benefit from this hands-on activity.

Materials: construction paper, scissors

- Place students in groups and give them construction paper. Have each student cut out pairs of identical shapes. These will represent congruent figures after they have been mixed up.

- Have each group mix together their pairs of shapes and spread them out. Then have students take turns finding congruent pairs from the pile.

3. Mary gave the clerk $9.00 to pay for the rose bush in problem **2**.
   (28, 25) What coins did she probably get back in change?   2 quarters, 1 nickel, 1 penny

Mary planted roses in her square rose garden. Look at the picture to help you answer problems **4–6**.

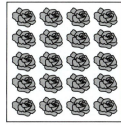

▸ 4. What is the perimeter of the garden?   28 yd
   (58)

5. What is the area of the garden?   49 sq. yd
   (62)

▸ 6. The array of rose bushes in the garden represents what multiplication fact?   4 × 5 = 20
   (57)

7 yd

7. The table below shows the numbers and colors of roses in Mary's garden.
   (44)

Red	Pink	Yellow	White	Peach
6	5	3	2	4

What fraction of the roses in the garden are yellow? $\frac{3}{20}$

8. Compare the fraction of roses that are red to the fraction that are pink. $\frac{6}{20} > \frac{5}{20}$
   (49)

9. Mary waters the roses for 20 minutes in the morning. The clock shows when she stopped watering. Write the time in digital form.   7:37 a.m.
   (38)

▸ 10. **Multiple Choice** Which shape below is *not* a polygon?   C
   (67)

A   B   C   D

Lesson 68   371

Written Practice (Continued)

Math Conversations
Independent Practice and Discussions to Increase Understanding

Problem 4
"What number sentence might you use to find the perimeter of the garden?" 7 + 7 + 7 + 7 = 28 or 4 × 7 = 28

Problem 5
"What number sentence could you use to find the area of the garden?" 7 × 7 = 49

Problem 6
Make sure students understand that this question pertains to the array of the bushes, not to the dimensions of the garden.

Problem 10   Multiple Choice
Test-Taking Strategy
Students should look for the one shape that is different from the others. Students should notice that choice **C** is different because the figure is not closed.

(continued)

Written Practice (Continued)

Math Conversations
Independent Practice and Discussions to Increase Understanding

Problem 11 Multiple Choice
Test-Taking Strategy
Students can eliminate any choices that do not match the color pattern. The figure indicates that the next shape is blue, so students can mark out answer choices **A** and **B**. Students can then mark out choices based on the orientation of the triangle, which alternates from pointing up to pointing down.

Problem 12
Extend the Problem
"What do we call a polygon with five sides?" a pentagon
"With six sides?" a hexagon
"With eight sides?" an octagon

Problem 13 Conclude
Students may also answer that the shape is a polygon or quadrilateral. Let students know that we want to choose the most precise name for the shape. Just as they would want to be called by their own names instead of "boy/girl" or "human," students should call shapes by their most precise names.

Problem 20 Represent
Help students see that there are three $\frac{1}{2}$ inches in $1\frac{1}{2}$ inches. Have them examine their rulers to check. Students should then divide their rectangle into three sections, each $\frac{1}{2}$ inch wide.

Extend the Problem
"What fraction of the rectangle is unshaded?" $\frac{1}{3}$

Errors and Misconceptions

Problems 4 and 5
Because the square contains rows of four rosebushes and columns of five rosebushes, students may ignore the "7 yd" notation or the fact that the garden is a square and incorrectly list the perimeter as 18 yards and the area as 20 square yards.

---

11. Multiple Choice Tran used tiles shaped like triangles and parallelograms to make this border. What are the next two tiles in the pattern? c
(2, 67)

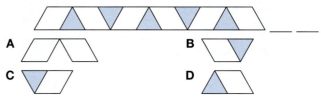

A B C D

12. What is another name for this three-sided polygon?
(67) triangle

13. (Conclude) These two triangles fit together to make what four-sided shape? parallelogram
(66)

14. Use digits and symbols to write a fraction equal to 1 with a denominator of 8. Then write the fraction using words. $\frac{8}{8}$; eight eighths
(46)

15. Find each product.
(56, 59)
a. 5×0 0   b. 5×7 35   c. 7×10 70

16. Write the addition below as multiplication, and then find the total. $7 \times 7 = 49$
(54, 61)

$7 + 7 + 7 + 7 + 7 + 7 + 7$

17. $78 + 78 + 78$ 234
(24)

18. $500 - 234$ 266
(28)

19. (Represent) Draw a rectangle that is $1\frac{1}{2}$ inches long and $\frac{3}{4}$ inches wide. See student work.
(35, 52)

20. (Represent) Divide the rectangle you drew in problem **19** into three equal parts and shade $\frac{2}{3}$ of the rectangle. See student work.
(42)

Looking Forward

Identifying congruent shapes, drawing congruent shapes, and recognizing congruent shapes in differing orientations prepares students for

- **Lesson 69,** identifying types of triangles.
- **Investigations 7 and 9,** identifying lines of symmetry.
- **Lesson 75,** identifying geometric solids.
- **Lesson 104,** sorting geometric shapes.

LESSON 69

Planning & Preparation

Texas Essential Knowledge and Skills

(3.8) identify, classify, and describe two-dimensional geometric figures by their attributes and compare two-dimensional figures by their attributes using formal geometry vocabulary

(3.9)(A) identify congruent two-dimensional figures

(3.14)(A) identify the mathematics in everyday situations

(3.16)(B) explain the solution process

• Triangles

Objectives
- Identify, classify, and describe triangles as equilateral, isosceles, or scalene.
- Identify triangles with a right angle as right triangles.
- Make concrete models of different types of triangles.

Prerequisite Skills
- Use proper vocabulary to name polygons.
- Identify, classify, and describe polygons by their attributes.
- Identify right angles, acute angles, and obtuse angles.

Materials
Instructional Masters
- Power Up 69
- Lesson Activity 24

Manipulative Kit
- Rulers

Teacher-provided materials
- Square pieces of paper
- Index cards*

  *optional

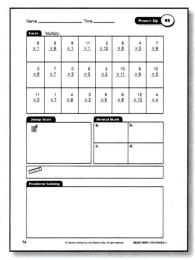
Power Up 69

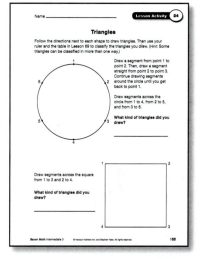
Lesson Activity 24

Differentiated Instruction

Reaching All Special Needs Students

Special Education Students	At-Risk Students	English Learners	Advanced Learners
• Inclusion (TM) • Adaptations for Saxon Math	• Reteaching Masters	• English Learners (TM) • English Learner Handbook	• Extend the Problem (TM) • Early Finishers (SE) • Online Activities

TM = Teacher's Manual
SE = Student Edition

Math Language

New		Maintained	English Learners
decade	right triangle	congruent	refer
equilateral triangle	scalene triangle	polygon	
isosceles triangle	triangle		

Lesson 69   373A

LESSON 69

Problem Solving Discussion

Problem

Francesca and Sophie are going to the theater to see a movie. The movie is 1 hour 59 minutes long. The previews before the movie last 15 minutes. What is the total length of the previews and the movie? Explain how you found your answer.

Focus Strategy  **Make It Simpler**

Understand Understand the problem.

"What information are we given?"

1. The movie is 1 hour 59 minutes long.
2. The previews before the movie last 15 minutes.

"What are we asked to do?"

We are asked to find the total length of the previews and the movie. We are also asked to explain how we found our answer.

Plan Make a plan.

"What problem solving strategy can we use?"

We can *make the problem simpler* by rounding the length of the movie to the nearest hour.

Solve Carry out the plan.

"What whole number of hours is close to 1 hour 59 minutes?"

2 hours

"If the movie were 2 hours long, what would be the total length of the movie and previews?"

The total length would be 2 hours 15 minutes.

"What is the exact length of the previews plus the movie?"

We rounded up the length of the movie by 1 minute, so we need to count back 1 minute to 2 hours 14 minutes.

Check Look back.

"Explain how we found our answer. Is our answer reasonable?"

Yes, our answer is reasonable because the length of the movie (1 hour 59 minutes) is 1 minute less than 2 hours. We rounded 1 hour 59 minutes to 2 hours and then added 15 minutes. Then we counted back one minute.

"What problem solving strategy did we use, and how did it help us?"

We *made the problem simpler* by rounding the length of the movie to an even amount. This made it easier to mentally calculate the total length of the previews and movie.

Alternate Strategy
Act It Out or Make a Model

Students can use their manipulative clocks to demonstrate the elapsed time. Choose a starting time, then have students move the hands forward 15 minutes for the previews and then 1 hour 59 minutes for the movie. Demonstrate how to simplify the problem by moving the hands forward 2 hours and then counting back 1 minute.

LESSON 69

• Triangles

Texas Essential Knowledge and Skills
(3.8) identify, classify, and describe two-dimensional geometric figures by their attributes and compare two-dimensional figures by their attributes using formal geometry vocabulary
(3.14)(A) identify the mathematics in everyday situations
(3.16)(B) explain the solution process

Power Up

facts   Power Up 69

jump start
 Count up by 12s from 0 to 120.
Count up by 10s from 6 to 96.

 Write "fourteen thousand, three hundred eighty" using digits. What digit is in the thousands place?   14,380; 4

Label the number line by 100s from 0 to 1,000.   0, 100, 200, 300, 400, 500, 600, 700, 800, 900, 1,000

mental math

a. **Money:** $1.30 + $0.40 $1.70

b. **Time:** A **decade** is 10 years. How many years are in 10 decades?   100 years

c. **Number Sense:** 55 + 7   62

d. **Measurement:** What is the perimeter of the rectangle?   14 in.

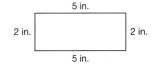

problem solving

Francesca and Sophie are going to the theater to see a movie. The movie is 1 hour 59 minutes long. The previews before the movie last 15 minutes. What is the total length of the previews and the movie? Explain how you found your answer.   2 hours 14 minutes; sample: We rounded 1 hour 59 minutes to 2 hours and then added 15 minutes. Then we counted back one minute.

New Concept

A **triangle** is a three-sided polygon.

Examples of triangles are shown in example 1.

Lesson 69   373

Facts   Multiply:

6 × 1 = 6	9 × 9 = 81	8 × 1 = 8	11 × 1 = 11	2 × 12 = 24	9 × 8 = 72	4 × 0 = 0	7 × 9 = 63
0 × 6 = 0	7 × 7 = 49	0 × 3 = 0	9 × 3 = 27	2 × 2 = 4	10 × 11 = 110	8 × 8 = 64	10 × 3 = 30
11 × 0 = 0	1 × 7 = 7	4 × 9 = 36	3 × 3 = 9	9 × 6 = 54	6 × 6 = 36	12 × 10 = 120	4 × 4 = 16

LESSON 69

Power Up

▶ **Facts**
Distribute **Power Up 69** to students. See answers below.

▶ **Jump Start**
Before students begin the Mental Math exercise, do these exercises as a class.

▶ **Mental Math**
Encourage students to share different ways to mentally compute these exercises. Strategies for exercises are listed below.

  a. **Think 13 dimes + 4 dimes**
    13 dimes + 4 dimes = 17 dimes, so
    $1.30 + $0.40 = $1.70.

  b. **Count by 10s**
    10, 20, 30, 40, 50, 60, 70, 80, 90, 100 years
    Multiply
    10 sets of 10 = 10 × 10 = 100 years

▶ **Problem Solving**
Refer to **Problem-Solving Strategy Discussion**, p. 373B.

New Concept

Connection
Remind students that any four-sided polygon can be classified as a quadrilateral and that there are different types of quadrilaterals.

"Different types of quadrilaterals have different names. What are some of these names?" parallelogram, rectangle, and square

List the names students call out on the board. Then draw an example of each. Explain to students that a triangle is a polygon that has only three sides.

"Triangles are the simplest polygon because we cannot make a closed figure with only 2 sides."

Tell students that triangles are like quadrilaterals in that there are different kinds with different names. We name triangles according to the kinds of angles and sides they have.

(continued)

Lesson 69   373

New Concept (Continued)

Example 1
Remind students that an obtuse angle is larger than a right angle. A right angle makes a square corner. "Equal sides" means that the sides are the same length.

Active Learning
Ask students to draw the four different types of triangles shown in their textbooks on their paper. Once students are finished, have them label each angle in their triangles as acute, right, or obtuse. Students should then mark the longest side and the shortest side of their triangles where appropriate (an equilateral triangle will not have a longer or shorter side). Ask students which angle is across from the longest side and which angle is across from the shortest side.

Students should see that larger angles are across from the longer sides and smaller angles are across from the shorter sides.

Example 2
Active Learning
"How do we know if two figures are congruent?" They are the same shape and the same size.

"Look at the lengths of the sides of the triangle. Is it equilateral, isosceles, or scalene?" scalene

"What types of triangles are shown in the answer choices?"

A scalene

B scalene

C isosceles

D scalene

"Which triangle is not congruent to the triangle shown?" C

(continued)

Example 1
Refer to the triangles to answer the questions below.

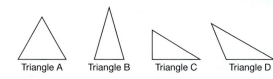

Triangle A   Triangle B   Triangle C   Triangle D

a. Which triangle has a right angle?
b. Which triangle has three equal sides?
c. Which triangle has an obtuse angle?
d. Which triangle has just two equal sides?

a. Triangle **C** has a right angle.
b. Triangle **A** has three equal sides.
c. Triangle **D** has an obtuse angle.
d. Triangle **B** has just two equal sides.

The table below shows some special kinds of triangles.

Types of Triangles

Name	Example	Characteristic
Equilateral		three equal sides
Isosceles		two equal sides
Right		one right angle
Scalene		all sides different lengths

Example 2
Which triangle below is *not* congruent to the triangle at right?

A   B   C   D

Math Background

Students are beginning to generalize the concept of perimeter to polygons other than quadrilaterals. They know that the perimeter of a triangle is the sum of three sides while the perimeter of a hexagon is the sum of six sides. In more advanced math, students will learn to find the area of a triangle by multiplying one half of the length of the base by the vertical height. Students can begin to explore area by figuring the area of a rectangle, and then dividing the rectangle in half to form two triangles. The area of each triangle will be half the area of the rectangle.

English Learners

To **refer** means to use or look at a thing or a person to get information. Ask:

"Refer to your multiplication chart and quickly tell me the products of 8 × 9, 8 × 7, and 9 × 4." 72; 56; 36

Ask:

"What book do you refer to when you need to know the spelling or definition of a word?" sample: dictionary

Have students refer to their dictionary or glossary to look up a math word.

The triangle in example 2 is a right triangle with sides that are three different lengths. The triangles in A, B, and D are congruent to this triangle because they are all the same size and the same shape. The triangle in **C** is not congruent because it is a different shape.

Activity
Make Equilateral and Right Triangles

Follow the directions on **Lesson Activity 24** to make triangles.

Lesson Practice

a. Kristin fit triangular pattern blocks together to make a hexagon. How many triangles did she use? 6

b. What type of triangles did Kristin use to make the hexagon? equilateral

c. Draw a right angle by tracing the side and bottom of a square tile. Then make a right triangle by drawing one more side. See student work.

▶ d. **Multiple Choice** Which shape below is a triangle? D

A   B   C   D

Written Practice
Distributed and Integrated

▶ 1. **Multiple Choice** Astra works 7 hours each day. How many hours does she work in 5 days? B
(60)
   A 28 hrs   B 35 hrs   C 42 hrs   D 56 hrs

2. Write the fractions or mixed numbers shown on each number line.
(48)
   a. 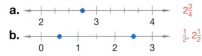 $2\frac{3}{4}$
   b. $\frac{1}{2}, 2\frac{1}{2}$

Lesson 69 375

Inclusion

Identify Triangles
Some students may have difficulty classifying the different kinds of triangles. Making and practicing with flash cards will give them extra practice with this skill.

Materials: index cards

- Place students in pairs and hand them index cards. Have students write the type or name of a triangle on one side and draw the shape on the other side.
- Have students take turns identifying the name or feature that matches each triangle on the card.

New Concept (Continued)

Activity
Distribute a copy of Lesson Activity 24 to students.

Lesson Practice
Guided Practice
Use these problems as guided practice to check the students' understanding of today's concept.

Problem d Multiple Choice
Test-Taking Strategy
Since all of these figures are different, students must apply the definition of a triangle to each shape to eliminate all invalid choices.
A: not a triangle because all sides are not straight
B: not a triangle because the figure is not closed
C: not a triangle because it has more than three sides
D: meets the definition

 Closure The questions below help assess the concepts taught in this lesson.

"What must we look at in order to name triangles?" the sides or the angles

"If a triangle has all sides of equal length, what do we call it?" an equilateral triangle

"If a triangle has no sides the same length, what do we call it?" a scalene triangle

"Can a right triangle also be an isosceles triangle? Why or why not?" Yes, if the two sides forming the right angle are the same length, it can be both.

Written Practice

Math Conversations
Independent Practice and Discussions to Increase Understanding

▶ **Problem 1 Multiple Choice**
Test-Taking Strategy
Students should recognize this as an "equal groups" story, which has a multiplication pattern. Since Astra worked five days, the number of hours will be a multiple of five, so it must end with a 0 or 5. Students can mark out any answer choice not ending in 0 or 5.

(continued)

Lesson 69 375

Written Practice (Continued)

Math Conversations
Independent Practice and Discussions to Increase Understanding

Problem 3 Multiple Choice
Test-Taking Strategy

Students should imagine tracing the tile and overlaying it on each answer choice. Students who have difficulty conceptualizing this method should actually trace the tile and test each answer. They should mark out any that do not match.

Problem 5 Explain

Tell students that one way to find how many tiles Andersen used is to count them. Students can also divide this room into two rectangles and then use multiplication and addition to find the area.

"Divide the room into rectangles that are 4 × 6 and 3 × 4. We can multiply and then add to get 24 + 12 = 36 tiles."

Extend the Problem

"If we wanted to make Andersen's room a rectangle, how many more tiles would we need to add?" 6 tiles

(continued)

---

3. **Multiple Choice** Donnell has a piece of tile in the shape of the figure at right. He wants to find a congruent shape among the scraps of tile. Which piece is congruent? **c**

A B C D

Andersen laid 1-ft-square tiles on the floor of a room with this shape. Look at the picture to help you answer problems **4–6**.

4. What is the perimeter of the room? **26 ft**

5. a. How many tiles did Andersen use? **36 tiles**

   b. **Explain** What is the area of the room? Explain how you found the area. **36 square feet; sample: I counted the number of 1-ft tiles Andersen used.**

6. a. The shape of the floor has how many sides? **6**

   b. What is the name of a polygon with this number of sides? **hexagon**

There are blue marbles, white marbles, and gray marbles in a bag. Look at the picture and table to help you answer problems **7–10**.

7. What fraction of the marbles are gray? $\frac{3}{10}$

8. Compare the fraction of the marbles that are white to the fraction that are blue. $\frac{3}{10} < \frac{4}{10}$

9. Which color is most likely to be picked from the bag? **blue**

10. Which two colors are equally likely to be picked from the bag? **white and gray**

11. The distance around the Earth is about 25,000 miles. Use words to write that number. **twenty-five thousand**

Marbles in Bag

Color	Number
Blue	4
White	3
Gray	3

12. What is the place value of the 2 in 25,000?   ten thousands
(32)

13. What fraction of the circle at right is shaded? $\frac{3}{8}$
(41)

▶ **14.** (Represent) Draw a circle and shade $\frac{7}{8}$ of it.
(42)   See student work.

15. Write a fraction equal to 1 that has a denominator of 9. $\frac{9}{9}$
(46)

16. Find each product.
(61)
   a. 6×6 36   **b.** 7×7 49   **c.** 8×8 64

17. Find each product.
(64)
   a. 9×5 45   **b.** 9×10 90   **c.** 9×8 72

Look at the parallelogram and triangle to help you answer problems **18–20**.

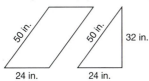

18. What is the perimeter of the parallelogram?   148 in.
(58, 66)

▶ **19.** What is the perimeter of the triangle?   106 in.
(58, 69)

20. The perimeter of the parallelogram is how much greater than the
(39)   perimeter of the triangle?   42 in.

Real-World
Connection

Jamal made a spinner divided into four equal sections with a different number written in each section. He wrote the numbers 25, 15, 30, and 10 on the spinner. Draw a picture of the spinner. Is the spinner more likely, less likely, or equally likely to stop on an even number?   See student work; equally likely

Lesson 69   377

Looking Forward

Understanding and naming different triangles problem prepares students for

- **Investigations 7 and 9,** identifying lines of symmetry.
- **Lesson 75,** identifying geometric solids.
- **Lesson 104,** sorting geometric shapes.
- **Lessons 106 and 108,** estimating area.
- **Lesson 109,** locating and naming points on a grid.

Written Practice (Continued)

Math Conversations
Independent Practice and Discussions to Increase Understanding

▶ **Problem 14** (Represent)
Invite a volunteer to draw the circle on the board or overhead. Students should follow along at their desks. The circle should be divided with 4 lines all passing through the center to make 8 equal segments. Students should shade all parts but one.

Extend the Problem
"Which is greater, $\frac{7}{8}$ or $\frac{3}{4}$?" $\frac{7}{8}$

▶ **Problem 19**
Extend the Problem
"If we were to double the length of all sides of the triangle, what would the new perimeter be?" 212 inches

Errors and Misconceptions

▶ **Problem 6**
A hexagon is a six-sided figure. A "regular hexagon" with six sides equal in length will be the shape most students bring to mind when they picture a hexagon. So students might classify the room as a rectangle with a corner missing. Remind students that polygons can be many different shapes and sizes because their sides do not have to be equal in length. Students can review the lesson on polygons if necessary.

▶ **Problem 15**
Watch for students who mistakenly write the fraction as $\frac{1}{8}$ instead of as $\frac{8}{8}$. Remind students that a fraction is equal to one if the numerator is equal to the denominator.

Have students show the picture of the spinner they drew. Then have them use the picture to explain the likelihood of the spinner landing on an even number.

Lesson 69   377

LESSON 70

> **Texas Essential Knowledge and Skills**
> (3.4)(A) learn multiplication facts through 12 by 12 using objects
> (3.6)(A) identify/extend geometric patterns to make predictions
> (3.15)(A) record observations using numbers

Planning & Preparation

• Multiplication Facts: Memory Group

Objectives
- Learn ten multiplication facts called the "memory group."
- Find the memory group multiplication facts on a multiplication table.
- Practice multiplication facts with flashcards.

Prerequisite Skills
- Use "product" and "factor" to describe numbers in multiplication number sentences and on the multiplication table.
- Use a multiplication table to find products of given multiplication problems.

Materials

Instructional Masters
- Power Up 70
- Lesson Activity 25

Manipulative Kit
- Rulers
- Fraction circles*

Teacher-provided materials
- Student fraction manipulatives

optional

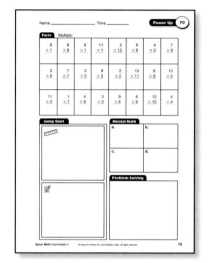
Power Up 70

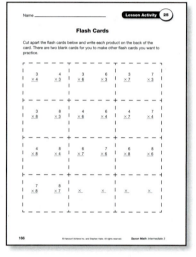
Lesson Activity 25

Differentiated Instruction

Reaching All Special Needs Students

Special Education Students	At-Risk Students	English Learners	Advanced Learners
• Adaptations for Saxon Math	• Reteaching Masters	• English Learners (TM) • English Learner Handbook	• Extend the Problem (TM) • Early Finishers (SE) • Online Activities

TM = Teacher's Manual
SE = Student Edition

Math Language

Maintained	English Learners
product	consider

378A *Saxon Math* Intermediate 3

Problem Solving Discussion

Problem

Draw the next two shapes in this pattern.

B, ⏶, ꓭ, ⏷, B, ⏶, ___, ___, …

Focus Strategy  **Find/Extend a Pattern**

Understand Understand the problem.

"What information are we given?"

We are shown a pattern with 6 terms.

"What are we asked to do?"

We are asked to draw the next two shapes in the pattern.

Plan Make a plan.

"What problem solving strategy will we use?"

We will *find a pattern* and *extend the pattern* to find the next two shapes.

Solve Carry out the plan.

"Let's number the terms of the sequence to help us identify the pattern."

Teacher Note: Draw the following on the board. Write the numbers 1–6 beneath the terms and label the blanks "7" and "8."

B, ⏶, ꓭ, ⏷, B, ⏶, ___, ___, …
1   2   3   4   5   6   7   8

"Does this pattern appear to be a repeating pattern? Why or why not?"

The pattern does appear to repeat. The fifth term is the same as the first term, and the sixth term is the same as the second term.

"If we assume that the first four shapes repeat, what will the seventh and eighth terms look like?"

The seventh and eighth terms will match the third and fourth terms:

B, ⏶, ꓭ, ⏷, B, ⏶, ꓭ, ⏷, …
1   2   3   4   5   6   7   8

"What pattern do you see in the shapes?"

The sequence is the letter B turned clockwise (to the right).

Check Look back.

"Did we complete the task?"

Yes, we drew the next two terms in the pattern.

"Are our answers reasonable?"

Yes, our answers fit the pattern.

"What problem solving strategy did we use?"

We *found a pattern* and then *extended the pattern* by drawing the next two shapes.

LESSON 70

Power Up

Facts
Distribute **Power Up 70** to students. See answers below.

Jump Start
Before students begin the Mental Math exercise, do these counting exercises as a class.

Mental Math
Encourage students to share different ways to mentally compute these exercises. Strategies for exercises are listed below.

a. Add and Then Attach Two Zeros
   $8 + 5 = 13$
   $800 + 500 = 1,300$

b. Think $45 - 10 + 1$
   $45 - 9 = 45 - 10 + 1 = 35 + 1 = 36$

c. Add and Then Attach One Zero
   $12 - 6 = 6$
   $120 - 60 = 60$

Problem Solving
Refer to **Problem-Solving Strategy Discussion**, p. 378B.

New Concept

Instruction
Draw students' attention to the multiplication table in the lesson. Remind them that they already know most of the products highlighted in gray. In this lesson they will learn the products highlighted in blue. Ask students to give examples of some of the facts they will learn in this lesson. *sample: $3 \times 4 = 12$; $6 \times 7 = 42$; $8 \times 6 = 48$*

(continued)

LESSON 70

• **Multiplication Facts: Memory Group**

Texas Essential Knowledge and Skills
(3.4)(A) learn multiplication facts through 12 by 12 using objects
(3.6)(A) identify/extend geometric patterns to make predictions
(3.15)(A) record observations using numbers

Power Up

facts   Power Up 70

jump start
- Count down by 3s from 45 to 0.
- Count down by 9s from 90 to 0.
- Draw a rectangle that is $1\frac{1}{2}$ inches long and 1 inch wide. *See student work.*
- Use these clues to find the secret number. Write the secret number on your worksheet.   16
  - two-digit number
  - perfect square
  - product of the two digits is 6

mental math
a **Number Sense:** $800 + 500$ 1,300
b **Number Sense:** $45 - 9$ 36
c **Time:** 120 minutes − 60 minutes   60 min
d **Estimation:** Round the value of these bills to the nearest ten dollars. $30.00

problem solving   Draw the next two shapes in this pattern.

, B, B, ...

New Concept

The products of 20 facts we will practice in this lesson are marked in blue on the multiplication table. If we learn 10 of these facts, we will know all 20 facts.

Facts   Multiply:

6 × 1 **6**	9 × 9 **81**	8 × 1 **8**	11 × 1 **11**	2 × 12 **24**	9 × 8 **72**	4 × 0 **0**	7 × 9 **63**
0 × 6 **0**	7 × 7 **49**	0 × 3 **0**	9 × 3 **27**	2 × 2 **4**	10 × 11 **110**	8 × 8 **64**	10 × 3 **30**
11 × 0 **0**	1 × 7 **7**	4 × 9 **36**	3 × 3 **9**	9 × 6 **54**	6 × 6 **36**	12 × 10 **120**	4 × 4 **16**

For example, consider 8 × 7 and 7 × 8. If we memorize the product of 8 × 7, then we also know the product of 7 × 8.

The 8s column and the 7s row meet at 56.
The 7s column and the 8s row meet at 56.

	0	1	2	3	4	5	6	7	8	9	10	11	12
0	0	0	0	0	0	0	0	0	0	0	0	0	0
1	0	1	2	3	4	5	6	7	8	9	10	11	12
2	0	2	4	6	8	10	12	14	16	18	20	22	24
3	0	3	6	9	12	15	18	21	24	27	30	33	36
4	0	4	8	12	16	20	24	28	32	36	40	44	48
5	0	5	10	15	20	25	30	35	40	45	50	55	60
6	0	6	12	18	24	30	36	42	48	54	60	66	72
7	0	7	14	21	28	35	42	49	56	63	70	77	84
8	0	8	16	24	32	40	48	56	64	72	80	88	96
9	0	9	18	27	36	45	54	63	72	81	90	99	108
10	0	10	20	30	40	50	60	70	80	90	100	110	120
11	0	11	22	33	44	55	66	77	88	99	110	121	132
12	0	12	24	36	48	60	72	84	96	108	120	132	144

(**Represent**) Draw an array showing 8 × 7 and an array showing 7 × 8. See student work.

Activity

Flash Cards

Cut apart **Lesson Activity 25.** On the back of each flash card, write the product shown in the table. Practice the flash cards with a partner. Then clip the cards together and save them for practice.

Lesson Practice   Find each product.

▸ a. 3 × 4 = 12   ▸ b. 4 × 6 = 24   ▸ c. 6 × 7 = 42   ▸ d. 3 × 7 = 21   ▸ e. 6 × 8 = 48

▸ f. 4 × 8 = 32   ▸ g. 3 × 6 = 18   ▸ h. 4 × 7 = 28   ▸ i. 7 × 8 = 56   ▸ j. 3 × 8 = 24

Lesson 70   379

Math Background

Students who can recite multiplication facts from memory will be able to extend their knowledge to more complicated mathematical results. Long division, fractions, and algebraic manipulations will all be easier with instant recollection of multiplication facts.

English Learners

To **consider** means to think about carefully. Ask:

"Consider the two facts 6 × 4 and 4 × 6. How are they related? What are the answers to both?" sample: They have the same product; 24

Ask:

"Consider why it is important to look both ways before you cross the street." sample: to avoid being hit by a car

Ask students to consider what they will do after school that day.

New Concept

Activity

Distribute one copy of Lesson Activity 25 to each student.

Active Learning

Another way to effectively drill with flashcards is to organize the class into two teams. Have each team line up in two rows. Show the first two students a flash card. The first student to call out the correct answer earns a point for his or her team.

For a less competitive game, divide students into teams of four. Give each team a page of multiplication facts. One team member writes the answer to one problem and passes the paper to the next team member. This member writes the answer to another problem and passes the paper on to the next team member. When all the questions are answered, the team that has the most correct answers wins.

Lesson Practice

Guided Practice

Use these problems as guided practice to check the students' understanding of today's concept.

Problems a–j

Encourage students to complete the problems on their own and then use a multiplication table to check their work.

Alternate Method

If students are having trouble memorizing the facts for this lesson, suggest that they draw an array representing each multiplication fact to solve each problem.

Closure

The questions below help assess the concepts taught in this lesson.

"Why do we memorize things?" We memorize things because they are important and so we don't have to look them up.

"Why is it important to memorize multiplication facts?" It will make learning new math concepts easier if we don't have to think about the multiplication facts.

Discuss real-world situations where the multiplication facts might be helpful. Examples are given below.

- We are buying 8 of something at the store. Instead of ringing it up 8 times, the sales clerk multiplies the price by 8.
- We want to find out if we have enough money to buy 7 stamps.

Lesson 70   379

Written Practice

Math Conversations
Independent Practice and Discussions to Increase Understanding

Problem 4 Multiple Choice
Test-Taking Strategy
Students may use the corner of a piece of paper to check for right angles in the answer choices.

Extend the Problem
Ask advanced learners,
"Can a triangle have two right angles? Explain." no; if you have two right angles, the sides will form parallel lines that never meet to form the third corner.

Problem 6 Multiple Choice
Test-Taking Strategy
Students should be looking for two figures that are the same size and shape. Students can imagine tracing one of the shapes and then placing this over the second shape. If they would not match, then the answer choice should be marked out. Students with difficulty conceptualizing this process should actually trace the figures.

Problem 8 Analyze
Point out to students that Points *A* and *B* can be eliminated because 662 is greater than 650; so it is after, or to the right of 650 on the number line. 662 is closer to 650 than to 700, so the answer is point *C*.

(continued)

380   Saxon Math Intermediate 3

Written Practice   Distributed and Integrated

1. What multiplication fact is represented by this rectangular pattern of tiles? $9 \times 4 = 36$ or $4 \times 9 = 36$
(53, 54)

2. One foot is 12 inches. Glenna jumped 8 feet. Use a multiplication table to find how many inches Glenna jumped. 96 inches
(55)

3. The tile factory makes tile in special shapes. Name each shape shown below.
(66, 67)

   a.   b.   c.
      parallelogram   hexagon   octagon

4. **Multiple Choice** Which triangle below has a right angle? C
(65, 69)
   A   B   C   D

5. a. A yard is how many feet? 3 ft
(34, 63)
   b. A square yard is how many square feet? 9 sq ft

6. **Multiple Choice** Which pair of figures are congruent? D
(68)
   A   B
   C   D

7. There were 89 students eating lunch in the cafeteria. Round 89 to the nearest ten. 90
(15)

8. **Analyze** Which point best represents 662? C
(33)

380   Saxon Math Intermediate 3

9. Round 662 to the nearest hundred. 700
(15)

10. Find the missing number: 831 − ☐ = 294. 537
(40)

▶ **11.** (Analyze) Will measured the distance he could ride his bike in 60 seconds. He recorded the results in a table. Write the distances in order from least to greatest. 1,303 ft; 1,312 ft; 1,320 ft; 1,332 ft
(27, 32)

Distance in 60 Seconds

Attempt	Feet
1st try	1,312
2nd try	1,320
3rd try	1,303
4th try	1,332

12. When dinner was over, Misha looked at the clock. Write the time in digital form. 6:42 p.m.
(38)

▶ **13.** (Conclude) Which two fractions below are equivalent? $\frac{1}{3}$ and $\frac{2}{6}$
(47)

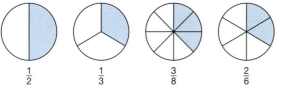

$\frac{1}{2}$ $\frac{1}{3}$ $\frac{3}{8}$ $\frac{2}{6}$

14. Compare: $\frac{1}{2}$ ⊙ $\frac{3}{8}$ >
(49)

15. Find each product.
(70)
   a. 3 × 4 12   **b.** 3 × 6 18   **c.** 3 × 7 21

16. Find each product.
(70)
   a. 6 × 4 24   **b.** 6 × 7 42   **c.** 6 × 8 48

17. Find each product.
(70)
   a. 7 × 4 28   **b.** 7 × 8 56   **c.** 3 × 8 24

Lesson 70 381

Written Practice (Continued)

Math Conversations
Independent Practice and Discussions to Increase Understanding

Problem 11 (Analyze)
Remind students to look at the thousands place first, then the hundreds, then the tens, and finally the ones to compare the digits and find which number is greater.

Extend the Problem
"Will went the fastest in which try?"
the 4th try

Problem 13 (Conclude)
Students may use fraction manipulatives to help solve the problem. Equivalent fractions will cover the same area of the circle. Students can trace only the shaded areas to compare and see which two are the same sizes.

(continued)

Lesson 70 381

Written Practice (Continued)

Math Conversations
Independent Practice and Discussions to Increase Understanding

Problem 20
Students should see that the tick marks represent the counting numbers. Choice **C** can be eliminated because it represents 4. Choice **A** is between 1 and 2, so it can be eliminated. Choice **B** is the correct answer since it is located halfway between 2 and 3.

Errors and Misconceptions

Problem 5
Students may mistakenly add 3 and 3 or multiply 3 × 2 to find the number of square feet in one square yard. Encourage students to draw an array representing a square yard to illustrate the correct multiplication.

Problem 14
When comparing fractions, students often compare numerators with numerators and denominators with denominators. This method only works if the denominators are equal. Encourage students to create a sketch to illustrate the size of each fraction before making the comparison.

Students may need a reminder to include a spare tire for each model in their pictures and calculations. Have students use their pictures to explain how they found the number of tires.

---

18. $1.98 + $3.65 $5.63
(22)

19. $603 − $476 $127
(23)

20. Which point on the number line best represents $2\frac{1}{2}$?   B
(48)

Early Finishers
Real-World Connection

Jackie bought 4 model tricycles and 7 model cars from Stan's Hobby Shop. Each model comes with a spare tire. How many tires came with the models altogether? You may draw pictures to help you find the answer.   51 tires

---

Memorizing multiplication facts prepares students for

- **Lesson 73,** finding volume.
- **Lesson 76,** multiplying 11s and 12s.
- **Lesson 77,** multiplying three numbers.
- **Lesson 78,** multiplying multiples of 10.
- **Lessons 81 and 84,** multiplying two-digit numbers.
- **Lesson 89,** using a multiplication table to divide by a one-digit number.
- **Lessons 91 and 97,** multiplying three-digit numbers.

Assessments
Distribute **Power-Up Test 13** and **Cumulative Test 13** to each student. Have students complete the **Power-Up Test** first. Allow 10 minutes. Then have students work on the **Cumulative Test**.

Performance Task
The remaining class time should be spent on **Performance Task 7.** Students can begin the task in class or complete it during another class period.

Flexible Grouping

Flexible grouping gives students an opportunity to work with other students in an interactive and encouraging way. The choice for how students are grouped depends on the goals for instruction, the needs of the students, and the specific learning activity.

Assigning Groups

Group members can be randomly assigned, or can be assigned based on some criteria such as grouping students who may need help with a certain skill or grouping students to play specific roles in a group (such as recorder or reporter).

Types of Groups

Students can be paired or placed in larger groups. For pairing, students can be assigned partners on a weekly or monthly basis. Pairing activities are the easiest to manage in a classroom and are more likely to be useful on a daily basis.

Flexible Grouping Ideas

Lesson 62, Example 1
Materials: grid paper, paper

Divide students into groups of 4. Choose a leader, recorder, checker, and presenter.
- Each group writes an area word problem using example 1 as a model. The leader helps every member stay on task.
- The recorder writes the word problem and records the solution as the group works together to solve the problem.
- The checker verifies their work. The presenter leads the group as they present the problem and solution for the class.

Lesson 63, Example 2
Materials: paper

After guiding the students through example 2, write 3 similar area problems on the board. Divide the students into groups of 4.
- Each group works together to solve the first problem.
- Divide groups into pairs to solve the second problem.
- Direct students to work on the last problem independently and then check their solutions with the group.

Lesson 69, Example 1
Materials: none

Divide students into groups of 4. The groups should be of varying abilities. Assign each student a number: 1, 2, 3, or 4.
- Students read example 1 and discuss the answers.
- Any member of the group should be able to present the answers to the problem and explain how they solved it.
- Call out a number from 1–4. The student assigned that number should present his or her group's solution and strategy for solving the problem.

Lesson 70, Activity
Materials: paper

Divide students into groups of 4.
- After guiding students through the activity, have students combine flashcards, mix them up, and place them in a stack face down.
- Each player takes turns flipping a card over. The player with the largest product keeps all 4 cards. If two players have the same high product, those players each flip another card. The highest product wins all cards.
- When all cards in the middle stack have been used, the player with the most cards wins.

INVESTIGATION 7

Texas Essential Knowledge and Skills

(3.9)(B) create two-dimensional figures with lines of symmetry using concrete models

(3.9)(C) identify lines of symmetry in two-dimensional geometric figures

(3.15)(A) record observations using pictures

Planning & Preparation

• Symmetry, Part 1

Objectives
- Find a symmetrical object's line of symmetry.
- Use concrete objects to create a pattern with a line of symmetry.

Prerequisite Skills
- Model shapes and angles using concrete objects.
- Identify angles as right, acute, or obtuse.
- Identify, classify, and describe polygons by their attributes.

Materials
Instructional Masters
- Lesson Activity 26

Manipulative Kit
- Color tiles or pattern blocks
- Mirrors*

    *optional

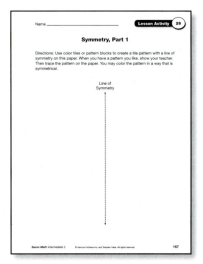

Lesson Activity 26

Reaching All Special Needs Students

Special Education Students	At-Risk Students	English Learners	Advanced Learners
• Adaptations for Saxon Math	• Error Alert (TM) • Reteaching Masters	• English Learners (TM) • English Learner Handbook	• Online Activities

TM=Teacher's Manual

Math Language

New	**Maintained**	**English Learners**
line of symmetry symmetry	halves (half)	nature

383B *Saxon Math Intermediate 3*

INVESTIGATION 7

Texas Essential Knowledge and Skills
- (3.9)(B) create two-dimensional figures with lines of symmetry using concrete models and technology
- (3.9)(C) identify lines of symmetry in two-dimensional geometric figures
- (3.15)(A) record observations using pictures

Focus on

• Symmetry, Part 1

In nature we often see a balance in the appearance of living things. For example, when a butterfly folds up its wings, the two sides match. We call this kind of balance **symmetry.**

The line in the middle of this image of a butterfly is called the **line of symmetry.** The line of symmetry divides the butterfly into two equal halves. One half is a mirror image of the other half. If we hold a mirror along the line and look at the reflection, we see the complete image of the butterfly.

Visit www.SaxonMath.com/Int3Activities for an online activity.

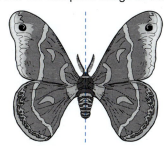

Miguel makes a pattern with tiles, as shown.

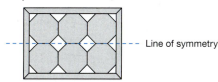
Line of symmetry

The tile pattern below the line of symmetry is a mirror image of the pattern above the line of symmetry.

sample: The other line of symmetry is a vertical line that divides the rectangle in half.

Discuss Find another line of symmetry in the pattern above. Explain where the line of symmetry is.

Activity
Symmetry, Part 1

Materials: **Lesson Activity 26,** color tiles or pattern blocks

Investigation 7   383

English Learners

Nature is anything that comes from the natural world, like plants, animals, land, air and water. Ask:

"What are some examples of things you find in nature?" samples: birds, roses, waterfalls, the ocean

Ask:

"What are some things we can do to take care of nature?" sample: pick up trash; only use one paper towel; use less water; turn the light off when we leave a room

In small groups, students make lists of things they might see in nature on land, in the water, and in the air.

Math Background

This investigation presents line symmetry or reflective symmetry. A figure has reflective symmetry if it can be divided with a line into two identical parts that are mirror images of each other. Another kind of symmetry is rotational symmetry. A figure has rotational symmetry if it can be rotated (or turned) less than a full turn and still look exactly the same. A pinwheel is a common example of a figure that has rotational symmetry.

INVESTIGATION 7

Symmetry, Part 1

In this investigation, students examine the concepts of symmetry and lines of symmetry. They are asked to find a line of symmetry and to use color tiles or pattern blocks to construct a pattern with visible symmetry.

Math Language
Have a volunteer read the first paragraph of the investigation aloud. Ask for a second volunteer to describe in his/her own words what symmetry means. Encourage the student to give an example for which he/she can describe a line of symmetry. Ask the class if anyone else can think of a good example of symmetry.

Observation
Students are required to visualize the mirror image of objects and patterns in this investigation. It might be beneficial to have students look at their image and the image of other objects in a mirror before performing the activity. Ask students to comment on the similarities and differences between objects and their mirror images. Help students see that when they raise their right hand, the image raises the left hand and vice versa.

For the *Discuss* question, point out to students that a vertical line that divides the rectangle in half is another line of symmetry because it marks the place where a mirror could be set to show an image of the other half of the pattern. There are no other lines of symmetry for this pattern because if we place a mirror in other places across the pattern, we will not get an image that matches the other half of the pattern.

Activity
Make one copy per student of **Lesson Activity 26.** Make sure that students have enough color tiles or pattern blocks to make a pattern on the activity sheet. Students may need to work in pairs to have enough pattern blocks.

(continued)

Investigation 7   383

Error Alert

Some students may mistakenly color their pattern asymmetrically. Tell students:

"Imagine what the other half of your pattern would look like in a mirror."

Real-World Connection

Point out the following examples of symmetry in the world around us:

- plants such as flowers, leaves, and grass
- man-made structures like railroad tracks, roads, and bridges
- ancient architecture like the Egyptian pyramids or the Greek Parthenon

Have students make their own suggestions about objects they have seen that have symmetry.

Closure — The questions below help assess the concepts taught in this lesson.

"What is symmetry?" When two sides of an object are mirror images of each other.

"What is a line of symmetry?" The line of symmetry is where an object could be folded to show that both sides match or where a mirror could be placed to show the matching half of the figure.

"If we say that half of an object is a 'mirror image' of the other half, is the object symmetrical?" Yes, if the halves are the same when a mirror is placed on a line of symmetry, then the object is symmetrical.

Discuss real-world situations where symmetry might be helpful. Examples are given below.

- We draw a picture of a person.
- We examine a butterfly's wings.
- We see a pattern of tiles on the floor which is the same in both directions.

In the activity, you will make a symmetrical pattern using color tiles or pattern blocks. Place the tiles or blocks on both sides of the line of symmetry on **Lesson Activity 26**. Make sure both sides match. Then trace the pattern on paper. You may color the pattern so that the coloring is symmetrical. Here is an example.

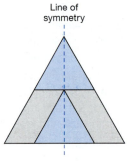

a. Cut pictures from newspapers and magazines of objects that have symmetry. Draw each picture's line of symmetry and paste the pictures on construction paper or cardboard to be displayed in the classroom.   See student work.

384   *Saxon Math* Intermediate 3

Recognizing and creating patterns that have symmetry and understanding lines of symmetry prepares students for

- **Lesson 75,** identifying geometric solids.
- **Investigation 8,** learning more about geometric solids.
- **Investigation 9,** identifying multiple lines of symmetry.
- **Lesson 104,** sorting geometric shapes.

384   *Saxon Math* Intermediate 3

SECTION 8 OVERVIEW

Lesson Planner

Lesson	New Concepts	Materials	Resources
71	• Rectangular Prisms	• Boxes (rectangular prism, cube)	• Power Up 71
72	• Counting Cubes	• Manipulative kit: 1-inch cubes	• Power Up 72 • Lesson Activity 27
73	• Volume	• Manipulative kit: 1-inch cubes, rulers • Empty boxes (shoe boxes or tissue boxes)	• Power Up 73 • Lesson Activity 28
74	• Weight: Ounces, Pounds, and Tons	• Manipulative kit: balance scale	• Power Up 74
75	• Geometric Solids	• Manipulative kit: Geosolids • Magazines • Scissors • Glue	• Power Up 75
Cumulative Assessment			• Cumulative Test 14 • Power-Up Test 14 • Test-Day Activity 7
76	• Multiplication Facts: 11s and 12s	• Manipulative kit: rulers, tape measures • $8\frac{1}{2}$ by 11 inch sheets of paper	• Power Up 76
77	• Multiplying Three Numbers	• Manipulative kit: 1-inch cubes, rulers	• Power Up 77
78	• Multiplying Multiples of Ten	• Manipulative kit: base ten rods	• Power Up 78
79	• Length: Centimeters, Meters, and Kilometers	• Manipulative kit: rulers, meterstick	• Power Up 79
80	• Mass: Grams and Kilograms		• Power Up 80
Cumulative Assessment			• Cumulative Test 15 • Power-Up Test 15 • Performance Task 8
Inv. 8	• More About Geometric Solids	• Manipulative kit: geosolids	• Lesson Activity 29

 All resources are also available on the Resources and Planner CD.

Additional Resources

- Instructional Masters
- Reteaching Masters
- Resources and Planner CD
- Calculator Activities
- Assessment Guide
- Performance Tasks
- Instructional Transparencies
- Answer Key CD
- Power Up Workbook
- Written Practice Workbook

SECTION 8

Math Highlights

Enduring Understandings — The "Big Picture"
After completing Section 8, students will understand that:
- figures that take up space are called solids.
- multiplication can be used to find area and volume.
- centimeters, meters, and kilometers are units for measuring length.
- ounces, pounds, tons, grams, and kilograms are units for measuring weight and mass.

Essential Questions
- What are the attributes of prisms and solids?
- How can we use multiplication to help us find area and volume?
- What units do we use to measure length?
- What units do we use to measure weight and mass?

Math Content Highlights	Math Processes Highlights

Number Sense
• Multiplication Facts: 11s and 12s Lesson 76
• Multiplication up to Two Digits Times One Digit Lesson 78
 	
Algebraic Thinking
• Patterns in Multiplication Lesson 76
 	
Geometry and Measurement
• Three-Dimensional Geometric Figures Lessons 71, 75, Inv. 8
• Two-Dimensional Geometric Figures Lesson 75
• Volume Lessons 72, 73, 77
• Ounces, Pounds, and Tons Lesson 74
• Centimeters, Meters, and Kilometers Lesson 79
• Perimeter Lesson 79
• Grams and Kilograms Lesson 80
	Problem Solving
	• Strategies
	  – Act It Out or Make a Model Lesson 72
	  – Draw a Picture or Diagram Lesson 75
	  – Find or Extend a Pattern Lesson 77
	  – Guess and Check Lessons 73, 78
	  – Make or Use a Table, Chart, or Graph Lesson 76
	  – Make an Organized List Lesson 80
	  – Use Logical Reasoning Lessons 73, 75, 77
	  – Work Backwards Lesson 79
	  – Write a Number Sentence Lessons 71, 74, 76, 78, 79
	• Real-World Applications Lessons 71–80, Inv. 8
	
	Communication
	• Analyze Lesson 76
	• Classify Lesson 75
	• Conclude Lesson 76
	• Discuss Lessons 73, 77
	• Verify Lesson 74
	
	Connections
	• Math to Math Lessons 73, 76
	• Math and Other Subjects
	  – Math and History Lessons 74, 76, 77
	  – Math and Geography Lessons 71, 72, 74–76, 78
	  – Math and Science Lesson 79
	  – Math and Sports Lesson 80
	
	Representation
	• Model Lessons 74–76, 79
	• Represent Lessons 71–73, 77–80
	• Manipulative Use Lessons 71–80, Inv. 8

LESSONS 71–80, INVESTIGATION 8

Differentiated Instruction

Support for differentiated instruction is included with each lesson. Specific resources and features are listed on each lesson planning page. Features in the Teacher's Manual to customize instruction include the following:

Teacher's Manual Support

Alternative Approach	Provides a different path to concept development. *Lessons 72, 76*
Manipulative Use	Provides alternate concept development through the use of manipulatives. *Lessons 71–73, 75, 78–80*
Flexible Grouping	Provides suggestions for various grouping strategies tied to specific lesson examples. *TM page 440A*
Inclusion	Provides ideas for including all students by accommodating special needs. *Lessons 71, 73, 75, 78–80*
Math Language	Provides a list of new and maintained vocabulary words along with words that might be difficult for English learners. *Lessons 71–80, Inv. 8*
English Learners	Provides strategies for teaching specific vocabulary that may be difficult for English learners. *Lessons 71–78, Inv. 8*
Errors and Misconceptions	Provides information about common misconceptions students encounter with concepts. *Lessons 73, 74–76, 79*
Extend the Example	Provides additional concept development for advanced learners. *Lessons 73–80*
Extend the Problem	Provides an opportunity for advanced learners to broaden concept development by expanding on a particular problem approach or context. *Lessons 71–75, 77, 79, 80, Inv. 8*
Early Finishers	Provides additional math concept extensions for advanced learners at the end of the Written Practice. *Lessons 71, 73, 75, 76, 79*
Investigate Further	Provides further depth to concept development by providing additional activities for an investigation. *Inv. 8*

Additional Resources

The following resources are also available to support differentiated instruction:

- Adaptations for Saxon Math
- English Learner Handbook
- Online Activities
- Reteaching Masters

Technology

Student Resources

- Student Edition eBook
- Calculator Activities
- Online Resources at
  www.SaxonMath.com/Int3Activities
  — Real World Investigations *Inv. 7*
  — Online Activities *Lessons 71–80, Inv. 8*
  — Online Calculator Activity *Lesson 73*

Teacher Resources

- Resources and Planner CD
- Test and Practice Generator CD
- Monitoring Student Progress: eGradebook CD
- Teacher Manual eBook CD
- Answer Key CD
- Adaptations for Saxon Math CD
- Online Resources at www.SaxonMath.com

Section Overview 8   385C

SECTION 8

Cumulative Assessment

The assessments in Saxon Math are frequent and consistently placed to offer a regular method of ongoing testing.

Power-Up Test: Allow no more than ten minutes for this test of basic facts and problem solving skills.

Cumulative Test: Next administer this test, which checks mastery of concepts in previous lessons.

Test-Day Activity and Performance Task: The remaining class time can be spent on these activities. Students can finish the Test-Day Activity for homework or complete the extended Performance Task in another class period.

After Lesson 75

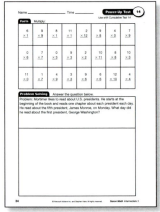
Power-Up Test 14

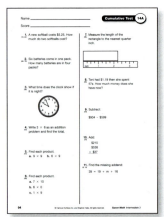
Cumulative Test 14

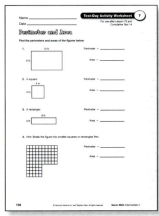
Test-Day Activity 7

After Lesson 80

Power-Up Test 15

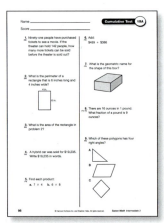
Cumulative Test 15

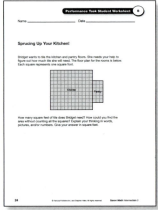
Performance Task 8

Evidence of Learning — What Students Should Know

By the conclusion of Section 8, students should be able to demonstrate the following competencies:

- Learn and apply multiplication facts. **TEKS (3.4)(A)**
- Identify patterns in multiplication facts. **TEKS (3.6)(B)**
- Identify, describe, classify, and compare geometric figures using formal geometric vocabulary. **TEKS (3.8)**
- Identify congruent figures and identify lines of symmetry in geometric figures. **TEKS (3.9)(A, C)**
- Locate and name points on a number line, including fractions. **TEKS (3.10)**
- Identify the mathematics in everyday situations. **TEKS (3.14)(A)**

Reteaching

Students who score below 80% on assessments may be in need of reteaching. Refer to the Reteaching Masters for reteaching opportunities for every lesson.

LESSONS 71–80, INVESTIGATION 8

Benchmarking and Tracking Standards

Benchmark Tests

Benchmark Tests correlated to lesson concepts allow you to assess student progress after every 20 lessons. An End-of-Course Test is a final benchmark test of the complete textbook. The Benchmark Tests are available in the Assessment Guide.

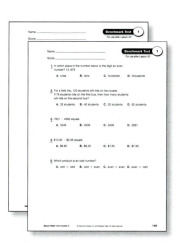

Monitoring Student Progress: eGradebook CD

To track TEKS mastery, enter students' scores on Cumulative Tests and Benchmark Tests into the Monitoring Student Progress: eGradebook CD. Use the report titled *Benchmark Standards Report* to determine which TEKS were assessed and the level of mastery for each student. Generate a variety of other reports for class tracking and more.

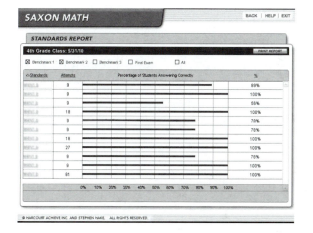

Test and Practice Generator CD

Test items also available in Spanish.

The Test and Practice Generator is an easy-to-manage benchmarking and assessment tool that creates unlimited practice and tests in multiple formats and allows you to customize questions or create new ones. A variety of reports are available to track student progress toward mastery of the TEKS throughout the year.

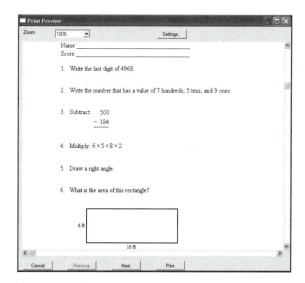

Northstar Math offers you real time benchmarking, tracking, and student progress monitoring.

Visit www.northstarmath.com for more information.

Section Overview 8   **385E**

SECTION 8

Content Trace

Lesson	New Concepts	Practiced	Assessed	Looking Forward
71	• Rectangular Prisms	Lessons 71, 72, 73, 77, 78, 79, 80, 81, 92	Test 15	Lessons 72, 73, 75, 87, Inv. 8
72	• Counting Cubes	Lessons 72, 73, 74, 76, 77, 79, 81, 82, 84, 85, 86, 92, 95, 101	Tests 15, 16	Lessons 73, 75, 87, Inv. 8
73	• Volume	Lessons 73, 74, 75, 76, 77, 79, 80, 81, 82, 84, 85, 86, 95, 97, 99, 108, 109	Tests 15, 16, 19	Lessons 75, 87, Inv. 8
74	• Weight: Ounces, Pounds, and Tons	Lessons 74, 75, 76, 77, 78, 79, 80, 84, 86	Test 15	Lessons 79, 87, 98
75	• Geometric Solids	Lessons 75, 76, 77, 78, 80, 82, 84, 86, 93, 94, 96, 100, 106, 108, 110	Tests 15, 16, 18, 21	Lessons 87, 104, Inv. 8
76	• Multiplication Facts: 11s and 12s	Lessons 76, 77, 78, 80, 106, 109	Test 16	Lessons 77, 78, 81, 84, 90, 91, 97
77	• Multiplying Three Numbers	Lessons 77, 78, 80, 81, 82, 83, 85, 86, 87, 88, 89, 90, 92, 94, 102, 109, 110	Tests 16, 17, 18	Lessons 78, 81, 84, 90, 91, 93, 97
78	• Multiplying Multiples of Ten	Lessons 78, 79, 80, 81, 82, 83, 84, 85, 86, 88, 89, 90, 92, 94, 95, 96, 97, 98, 100, 104, 105, 109	Tests 16, 17, 18, 19	Lessons 81, 84, 90, 91, 97, 100
79	• Length: Centimeters, Meters, and Kilometers	Lessons 79, 80, 81, 82, 83, 84, 85, 86, 87, 89, 92, 93, 97, 99, 100, 101, 103, 105, 109	Test 16	Lessons 87, 106, 108
80	• Mass: Grams and Kilograms	Lessons 80, 82, 86, 89, 104, 105	Test 17	Lessons 87, 98
Inv. 8	• More About Geometric Solids	Lessons 94, 103	Test and Practice Generator	Lessons 102, 104, 105

LESSON 71

Planning & Preparation

• Rectangular Prisms

Objectives
- Use proper vocabulary to describe attributes of rectangular solids.
- Identify, classify, and describe rectangular solids by their attributes.
- Sketch a rectangular solid.
- Compare and contrast rectangular solids.

Prerequisite Skills
- Identify, classify, and describe rectangles by their attributes.
- Identify parallel and perpendicular sides of rectangles.

Materials
Instructional Masters
- Power Up 71

Manipulative Kit
- Rulers
- Geosolids (rectangular prism and cubes)*

Teacher-provided materials
- Boxes (rectangular prism, cube)
- Pictures of rectangular prism and cube*
- Index cards*

   *optional

▶ Texas Essential Knowledge and Skills
(3.8) describe three-dimensional geometric figures by their attributes and compare three-dimensional figures by their attributes using formal vocabulary
(3.9)(A) identify congruent two-dimensional figures
(3.14)(A) identify the mathematics in everyday situations
(3.14)(D) use tools such as real objects to solve problems

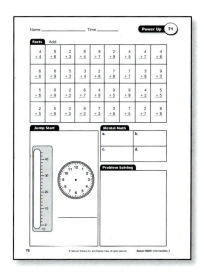

Power Up 71

Reaching All Special Needs Students

Special Education Students	At-Risk Students	English Learners	Advanced Learners
• Inclusion (TM) • Adaptations for Saxon Math	• Reteaching Masters	• English Learners (TM) • English Learner Handbook	• Extend the Problem (TM) • Early Finishers (SE) • Online Activities

TM=Teacher's Manual
SE=Student Edition

Math Language

New	Maintained	English Learners
cube	congruent	transparent
edge	parallel	
face	perpendicular	
rectangular prism	vertex	
rectangular solid		

Lesson 71   385G

LESSON 71

Problem Solving Discussion

Problem

Quinh plans to watch his favorite television show tonight. He told his mother that the show will begin in 14 minutes and will be over in 74 minutes. How long is Quinh's favorite television show?

Focus Strategy **Write a Number Sentence**

Understand Understand the problem.

"What information are we given?"

1. Quinh's favorite television show will begin in 14 minutes.
2. The show will end in 74 minutes.

"What are we asked to do?"

We are asked to find how long the television show is.

Plan Make a plan.

"What problem solving strategy can we use?"

We can *write a number sentence*.

"What kind of number sentence should we write to find the length of the show?"

We need to write a subtraction number sentence to find the difference of 74 minutes and 14 minutes.

Solve Carry out the plan.

"What number sentence can we write to solve the problem?"

We write this subtraction number sentence:

$$74 \text{ minutes} - 14 \text{ minutes} = 60 \text{ minutes}$$

Check Look back.

"Did we complete the task?"

Yes, we calculated the length of Quinh's favorite television show (60 minutes or 1 hour).

"Is our answer reasonable?"

Yes, our answer is reasonable because 74 minutes is 60 minutes greater than 14 minutes. Also, we might reason that 1 hour is a typical length of a television show.

"What problem solving strategy did we use, and how did it help us?"

We *wrote a number sentence* to find the length of the show.

Alternate Strategy

Make It Simpler

Students might notice that 74 minutes is the same as 1 hour 14 minutes. Since the television show begins in 14 minutes and ends in 1 hour 14 minutes, we immediately know that the difference between the starting and ending times is **1 hour.**

LESSON 71

• **Rectangular Prisms**

Texas Essential Knowledge and Skills
(3.8) describe and compare three-dimensional figures by their attributes using formal vocabulary
(3.9)(A) identify congruent two-dimensional figures
(3.14)(A) identify the mathematics in everyday situations
(3.14)(D) use tools such as real objects to solve problems

Power Up

facts Power Up 71

jump start
Count up by 25s from 0 to 250.
Count up by 7s from 0 to 77.

It is 5:05 in the morning. Draw hands on your clock to show the time in 15 minutes. Write the time on a digital clock.   5:20 a.m.

The temperature in a restaurant kitchen was 28°C. It was 9 degrees cooler in the dining room. Mark your thermometer to show the temperature in the dining room.   19°C

mental math
a. **Number Sense:** 35 + 9   44
b. **Number Sense:** 5 + 4 + 4 + 5   18
c. **Time:** 45 minutes + 15 minutes   60 min
d. **Fractions:** What fraction of the marbles are white? $\frac{3}{6}$ or $\frac{1}{2}$

problem solving
Quinh plans to watch his favorite television show tonight. He told his mother that the show will begin in 14 minutes and will be over in 74 minutes. How long is Quinh's favorite television show?   60 min or 1 hr

New Concept

Boxes come in different sizes and can be made of different materials. However, most boxes are alike in many ways. In this lesson we will study the shape of rectangular boxes. The shape of a rectangular box is called a **rectangular prism** or **rectangular solid**.

Lesson 71   385

Facts   Add:

4 + 4 = 8	8 + 6 = 14	2 + 3 = 5	8 + 4 = 12	9 + 7 = 16	2 + 9 = 11	4 + 5 = 9	4 + 7 = 11	4 + 6 = 10
6 + 6 = 12	8 + 9 = 17	5 + 3 = 8	3 + 4 = 7	2 + 8 = 10	7 + 8 = 15	7 + 7 = 14	3 + 6 = 9	9 + 3 = 12
5 + 6 = 11	6 + 9 = 15	2 + 2 = 4	6 + 7 = 13	4 + 9 = 13	9 + 5 = 14	9 + 9 = 18	4 + 2 = 6	5 + 5 = 10
2 + 5 = 7	5 + 8 = 13	3 + 3 = 6	6 + 2 = 8	7 + 3 = 10	3 + 8 = 11	7 + 5 = 12	2 + 7 = 9	8 + 8 = 16

LESSON 71

Power Up

Facts
Distribute **Power Up 71** to students. See answers below.

Jump Start
Before students begin the Mental Math exercise, do these exercises as a class.

Mental Math
Encourage students to share different ways to mentally compute these exercises. Strategies for exercises are listed below.

a. **Think 35 + 10 − 1**
    35 + 9 = 35 + 10 − 1 = 45 − 1 = 44
d. **Count and Write the Fraction**
    total marbles = 6; white marbles = 3
    fraction of white marbles = $\frac{3}{6}$ or $\frac{1}{2}$

Problem Solving
Refer to **Problem-Solving Strategy Discussion**, p. 385H.

New Concept

Instruction
Review some of the concepts of basic shapes that apply to rectangular prisms. Remind students that a square or rectangle has two dimensions: length and width. The shapes they draw on paper are two-dimensional, like triangles and circles. But real objects are three-dimensional.

"We can describe the sides of a real object as being two-dimensional shapes. What two-dimensional shapes would you use to describe the sides of a box?"   squares or rectangles

Math Language
Explain to students that "rectangular prism" and "rectangular solid" are two ways to describe the same shape. Have a volunteer read the second paragraph aloud. Hold up a box and point to its faces, edges, and vertices as the volunteer reads these words. Then discuss which edges of the box are parallel and which edges are perpendicular.

(continued)

Lesson 71   385

New Concept (Continued)

Active Learning

Draw a rectangular prism on the board. Write the following words on index cards: face, edge, vertex, parallel edges, and perpendicular edges. One term should be written on the front and back of each card. Make enough cards for each student to have at least one card. Explain to students that you will be pointing to different parts of the rectangular prism. Students with the word *face* on their card will hold up their card and say "face" when you point to a face of the prism. Students with *edge* on their card will do the same for edges and so on. Begin pointing to various parts of the prism and continue until all parts have been identified by the students.

Instruction

Demonstrate the method of drawing a "transparent" rectangular prism described in the text on the board or overhead. Encourage students to follow along and draw their own prisms at their desks. Students can draw their rectangular prisms using all solid lines or using some dotted lines.

Example 1
Instruction

Demonstrate the answer to example 1 using a tissue box or other rectangular container.

(continued)

Rectangular prisms have flat sides shaped like rectangles. These flat surfaces are called **faces**. Two faces meet at an **edge**. Three faces meet at a point. These corner points are called *vertices*. Each corner point is a **vertex**.

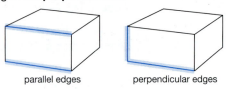

Rectangular Prism

Some of the edges of a rectangular prism are **parallel** and some edges are **perpendicular**.

parallel edges   perpendicular edges

If we draw a "transparent" rectangular prism, we can see all the faces, edges, and vertices. First, we draw two overlapping rectangles that are **congruent**.

Then we connect the four vertices of one rectangle to the matching vertices of the other rectangle.

(**Represent**) Practice drawing a rectangular prism.
See student work.

Example 1

How many faces does a box have?

Place a box in front of you. See that it has a front and a back, a top and a bottom, and a left side and a right side. **A box has six faces.**

386 *Saxon Math Intermediate 3*

Math Background

The descriptive vocabulary learned in this lesson will be extended and applied to other three-dimensional figures. A triangular prism has 6 vertices, 5 faces, and 9 edges, with two faces that are triangles. A pyramid is a solid figure that has four or more faces that are triangles. Students will learn that some figures have curved surfaces rather than flat surfaces. A cone is an example of a figure that has a curved surface.

English Learners

If something is **transparent** we can see through it.

"Clear drinking water is transparent. What objects can you think of that are transparent?" samples: clear glass jars, plastic water bottles, resealable plastic bags

Draw a transparent prism on the board. Ask:

"This prism is transparent so you can see all the faces. Which faces are of equal size?" Students should identify each pair of opposite sides as equal.

Have students draw transparent figures.

Example 2

Compare these two boxes. Describe how they are alike and how they are different.

Both boxes are rectangular prisms. They each have 6 faces, 12 edges, and 8 vertices. Both boxes have rectangular faces. The boxes are different because the faces of the box on the left are longer than they are wide. The faces of the box on the right are all squares.

If every face of a rectangular prism is a square, then the figure is a **cube**. The box on the right in example 2 is a cube. All the edges of a cube are the same length.

Cube

Lesson Practice

a. Draw a picture of a transparent box.   a. sample:
b. How many vertices does a box have?
   8 vertices
c. How many edges does a box have?
   12 edges
d. Describe a cube.   sample: A cube is a rectangular prism with square faces.

Written Practice   Distributed and Integrated

1. **Formulate** Molly counted the cars as the train rolled by the
(20, 28) intersection. There were 103 cars, counting four engines and the caboose. How many cars were there not counting the engines and caboose? Write a number sentence. Then write your answer in a complete sentence. $103 - 5 = \square$; sample: There were 98 cars.

2. Hawkins bought two round-trip train tickets to Grant's Pass for
(22) $9.75 each. What was the cost for both tickets? $19.50

3. Hawkins paid for the two tickets in problem **2** with a $20 bill. How
(26) much money should he get back?   50¢

Lesson 71   387

Inclusion

Match It and Count It

Some students may have difficulty identifying the attributes of a three-dimensional shape in a picture. These students will benefit from more experiences that connect tactile examination of the object with visual examination of the picture.

Materials: a rectangular prism and a cube; pictures of a rectangular prism and a cube

- Students match the object to the picture.
- Students identify and count the faces, edges, and vertices on the object.
- Then students identify and count the faces, edges, and vertices on the picture.

New Concept (Continued)

Example 2
Alternate Method
Have boxes that match the shapes in the picture available for students to examine. Students need experience with concrete objects to fully comprehend the concepts and vocabulary displayed in the pictures.

Lesson Practice

Guided Practice
Use these problems as guided practice to check the students' understanding of today's concept.

Problem a Extend the Problem
Have the students use a crayon or marker to outline a set of parallel lines and a set of perpendicular lines.

 Closure   The questions below help assess the concepts taught in this lesson.

Ask students to identify a face, edge, and vertex of a rectangular prism on a real object and in a picture. Then ask:

"What is an example of a rectangular prism?" sample: a square or rectangular box

"What is another word for the flat side of a box?" face

"What do you call the place where two faces meet?" edge

"What is another word for the corner of a box?" vertex

"What is a cube?" sample: a rectangular prism with six square faces

Written Practice

Math Conversations
Independent Practice and Discussions to Increase Understanding

Problem 1 **Formulate**
Students should always read word problems carefully and look for key words. Point out the words "counting four engines and the caboose" and "not counting the engine and caboose" to the students. They are clues that this is a "some went away" story.

(continued)

Lesson 71   387

Written Practice (Continued)

Math Conversations
Independent Practice and Discussions to Increase Understanding

Problem 11 (Represent)
Students should use straight lines and draw square corners as best they can. Remind students to draw parallel edges the same length.

Problem 12
Encourage students to draw a rectangular prism and count the faces. Remind students that *face* is another word for "side."

(continued)

---

4. Multiple Choice Which picture below shows the mixed number $1\frac{4}{5}$? **D**
(46)

A   B

C   D

5. It is morning. The clock shows the time the train arrived in Chicago. Write the time in digital form. **10:23 a.m.**
(38)

6. Are the rails of train tracks parallel or perpendicular? **parallel**
(Inv. 4)

7. The distance from the Upland Station to Burns Crossing is $17\frac{3}{10}$ miles. Use words to name $17\frac{3}{10}$. **seventeen and three tenths**
(46)

8. Find each product.
(70)
   a. 8×7 56   **b.** 4×7 28   **c.** 6×7 42

9. Find each product.
(70)
   a. 3×8 24   **b.** 4×8 32   **c.** 6×8 48

10. Find each product.
(64)
   a. 9×4 36   **b.** 9×6 54   **c.** 9×8 72

11. (Represent) Follow the directions in this lesson to draw a rectangular prism. sample:
(71)

12. A rectangular prism has how many faces? 6
(71)

13. Use your inch ruler to find the length of the sides of the right triangle.
(35, 69)
   a. side *AB* $\frac{3}{4}$ in.
   b. side *BC* 1 in.
   c. side *CA* $1\frac{1}{4}$ in.

▶ **14.** (Represent) On your paper draw a triangle congruent to the
(68, 69) triangle in problem **13.**   See student work.

▶ **15. Multiple Choice** Which polygon shows a line of symmetry?   **C**
(Inv. 7)

A   B   C   D

16. Martin has three quarters in his pocket. What fraction of a dollar is
(29) three quarters? $\frac{3}{4}$

17. If every face of a rectangular prism is a square, then
(71) what is the name of the solid?   **cube**

18. $32 + $68 + $124   **$224**
(24)

19. $206 − $78   **$128**
(26, 28)

20. Which number on the number line does point *M* represent?   **128**
(33)

Early Finishers
Real-World Connection

Mr. Tuff is making a rectangular table that is 4 feet long and 3 feet
wide. Draw the table using the scale $\frac{1}{2}$ inch = 1 foot.   See student work.

Lesson 71   389

Looking Forward

Recognizing, drawing, and building rectangular prisms and identifying parts of a rectangular prism prepares students for

• **Lesson 72,** finding volume by counting cubes.
• **Lesson 73,** finding volume.
• **Lesson 75,** identifying geometric solids.
• **Investigation 8,** building solids.
• **Lesson 87,** understanding capacity.

Written Practice (Continued)

Math Conversations
Independent Practice and Discussions to Increase Understanding

▶ **Problem 14** (Represent)
Remind students that *congruent* means the same size and the same shape, so the triangles should be identical.

▶ **Problem 15**
Extend the Problem
For advanced learners ask:

"If all sides of this triangle are the same length, how many total lines of symmetry does it have?" 3

Errors and Misconceptions

▶ **Problem 7**
Students may try to write "seventeen plus three tenths" instead of using the word "and." Have students review the rules for writing mixed numbers.

▶ **Problem 14**
Students often incorrectly draw congruent shapes as similar shapes that are the same shape but different sizes. Remind them that congruent shapes are the same size and the same shape.

▶ **Problem 20**
The labels on the number line may lead students to count by 4s to get the incorrect answer of 132. Instruct students to count the number of segments between labels. Ask:

"How many units does each tick mark represent?" 2

Early Finishers

Suggest to students that they figure out the lengths of the lines before they begin drawing the table. Have them show their drawings and explain how they determined the lengths of the sides.

Lesson 71   389

LESSON 72

> **Texas Essential Knowledge and Skills**
> (3.11)(F) use concrete models that approximate cubic units to determine the volume of a given container or other figure
> (3.15)(A) explain observations using objects

Planning & Preparation

• Counting Cubes

Objectives
- Use skip counting or multiplication to find the number of small cubes in a larger rectangular solid.
- Determine the number of inch-cube manipulatives needed to build a given rectangular solid.
- Build rectangular solids with inch cubes to model volume.

Prerequisite Skills
- Identify, classify, and describe rectangular solids by their attributes.
- Use square units to measure area.
- Multiply the length and width of a rectangle to find its area in square units.

Materials
Instructional Masters
- Power Up 72
- Lesson Activity 27

Manipulative Kit
- 1-inch cubes
- Rulers

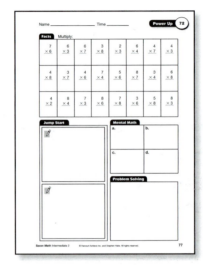
Power Up 72

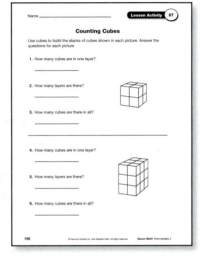
Lesson Activity 27

Differentiated Instruction

Reaching All Special Needs Students

Special Education Students	At-Risk Students	English Learners	Advanced Learners
• Adaptations for Saxon Math	• Alternative Approach (TM) • Reteaching Masters	• English Learners (TM) • English Learner Handbook	• Extend the Problem (TM) • Online Activities

TM = Teacher's Manual

Math Language

Maintained
multiplication
multiply

English Learners
layer

390A   Saxon Math Intermediate 3

Problem Solving Discussion

Problem

A sheet of paper is folded in half and then cut with scissors as shown. How many pieces of paper will there be after the cut?

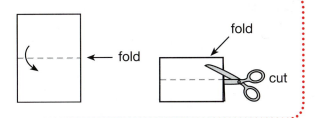

Focus Strategy Act It Out or Make a Model

Understand) Understand the problem.

Teacher Note: You will need a sheet of notebook paper and scissors to demonstrate the problem, or if desired, enough of each for students to act out the problem.

"What information are we given?"
We are shown a diagram of a sheet of paper folded in half and then cut.

"What are we asked to do?"
We are asked to find how many pieces of paper there will be after the cut is made.

Plan) Make a plan.

"What problem solving strategy can we use?"
We can *act out the problem* with paper and scissors.

Solve) Carry out the plan.

"Let's predict how many pieces will result from cutting the paper as shown."
Teacher Note: Discuss student responses.

"Let's act out the problem. How many pieces do we get after cutting?"
The two pieces at the top and bottom of the sheet are the same size, and the third piece from the middle has the fold in it.

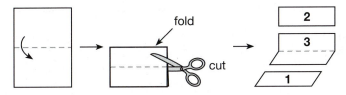

We get 3 pieces of paper after cutting the sheet.

"Did the result match your prediction?"
Teacher Note: Discuss student responses.

Check) Look back.

"Did we complete the task?"
Yes, we found the number of pieces that resulted from the fold and cut.

"What problem solving strategy did we use?"
We *acted out the problem* to find the answer.

Alternate Strategy
Use Logical Reasoning

Students can *use logical reasoning* and spatial sense to predict the result without actually cutting a sheet of paper. Have students study the picture given in the problem. Explain that the top edge of the sheet is folded over to line up with the bottom edge. After cutting, the top and bottom of the sheet would be separated from the middle portion of the sheet, which results in 3 pieces.

LESSON 72 • Counting Cubes

Texas Essential Knowledge and Skills
(3.11)(F) use concrete models that approximate cubic units to determine the volume of a given container or other figure
(3.15)(A) explain observations using objects

Power Up

Facts
Distribute **Power Up 72** to students. See answers below.

Jump Start
Before students begin the Mental Math exercise, do these exercises as a class.

Mental Math
Encourage students to share different ways to mentally compute these exercises. Strategies for exercises are listed below.

a. Compare the Digits from Left to Right
thousands: 2 = 2
hundreds: 5 < 6
2,560 < 2,690

c. Think 200 − 100 + 20
200 − 80 = 200 − 100 + 20 = 100 + 20
= 120

Problem Solving
Refer to **Problem-Solving Strategy Discussion,** p. 390B.

Power Up

facts Power Up 72

jump start
 Count up by 11s from 0 to 110.
Count up by 5s from 3 to 53.

 Write 10,550 as words. ten thousand, five hundred fifty

Draw an isosceles triangle. Trace the sides that have equal length with a crayon. See student work.

mental math

a. **Number Sense:** Compare these numbers using the symbol <, >, or =

2,560 < 2,690

b. **Money:** $10.00 − $5.25 $4.75

c. **Number Sense:** 200 − 80   120

d. **Time:** It is afternoon. Marta went to the library at the time shown on the clock. She left 1 hour later. What time did she leave the library? 1:15 p.m.

problem solving
A sheet of paper is folded in half and then cut with scissors as shown. How many pieces of paper will there be after the cut? 3 pieces

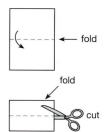

390 Saxon Math Intermediate 3

Facts   Multiply:

7 × 6 = 42	6 × 3 = 18	6 × 7 = 42	3 × 8 = 24	2 × 3 = 6	6 × 4 = 24	4 × 7 = 28	4 × 3 = 12
4 × 8 = 32	3 × 7 = 21	4 × 6 = 24	7 × 4 = 28	5 × 6 = 30	8 × 7 = 56	3 × 4 = 12	6 × 8 = 48
4 × 2 = 8	8 × 4 = 32	7 × 3 = 21	8 × 6 = 48	7 × 8 = 56	3 × 6 = 18	5 × 8 = 40	8 × 3 = 24

390   Saxon Math Intermediate 3

Andre uses a forklift to load boxes into a boxcar. Look at this stack of boxes. Can you count the number of boxes in the stack?

We cannot see all the boxes in the stack. One way to find the total is to first find the number of boxes in each layer.

Looking at the top of the stack, we see that there are nine boxes in the top layer.

Looking at the side, we see that there are three layers of boxes.

To find the total number of boxes, we can add: $9 + 9 + 9 = 27$. We can also multiply: $3 \times 9 = 27$.

(Formulate) If we add two more layers of boxes to the stack, how many boxes will we have altogether? Write a multiplication fact to show the answer. $5 \times 9 = 45$

Activity
Counting Cubes

Use cubes to build the stacks of cubes shown on **Lesson Activity 27**. Answer these questions for each stack of cubes.

- How many cubes are in one layer?
- How many layers are there?
- How many cubes are there in all?

Example 1

The picture shows a stack of cubes.

a. How many cubes are in each layer?
b. How many layers are there?
c. How many cubes are there in all?

a. There are **12 cubes** in each layer.
b. There are **three layers.**

Lesson 72 391

Math Background

In this lesson, cubes are presented as a concrete representation of the space inside a box. The next lesson will build on this concept with a formal definition of volume: the number of cubic units an object holds, or the amount of space an object occupies. When students find the number of cubes in one layer of a stack, they are actually finding the area of a rectangle. When they multiply the area times the number of layers, they are finding the volume of a rectangular prism. The formula for finding volume is *length × width × height*. The use of concrete materials to represent volume is critical for the development of this concept.

English Learners

When we put a group of objects on top of another group of objects, we call each group a **layer**.

Draw a picture of a brick wall with 5 layers of 10 bricks on the board.

Ask:

"Mr. Smith built a brick wall. He built a total of 5 layers, with 10 bricks in each layer. How many bricks did he use?" $10 \times 5 = 50$ bricks

Ask:

"What are other things that have layers or are used in layers?" samples: clothes, paint, the atmosphere

Have students draw a rainbow with 7 layers of color.

New Concept

Instruction

Show students 3 groups of 4 cubes (arranged 2×2). Skip count all the cubes by 4s, then stack the groups to make a box. Ask,

"Is the number of cubes different since you cannot see all of them?" no

Write the following incomplete multiplication facts on the board or overhead. Have students restate the multiplication as repeated addition and complete the facts verbally. Write each product in the correct space.

$1 \times 5 =$ ___ $3 \times 4 =$ ___
$4 \times 7 =$ ___ $8 \times 8 =$ ___

"Each of these multiplication facts could represent a stack of cubes."

Point to each fact as you say:

"1 layer of 5 cubes has 5 total cubes."

"3 layers of 4 cubes has $4 + 4 + 4$, or 12 total cubes."

"4 layers of 7 cubes has $7 + 7 + 7 + 7$, or 28 total cubes."

"8 layers of 8 cubes has $8 + 8 + 8 + 8 + 8 + 8 + 8 + 8$, or 64 total cubes."

For the *Formulate* question, build the stack with cubes and add two more layers.

Activity

Arrange students in pairs. Provide each student with **Lesson Activity 27** and each pair with about twenty 1-inch cubes.

Students should use the activity sheet as a guide for building their model. It is intended for students to find the volume in terms of the total number of cubes in the stack. Make sure students understand that they are to count all of the cubes, not just the ones they can see.

Example 1
Alternate Method

Tell students that if the number of cubes in one layer is an easy number to count by, then they can skip count by that number to find how many cubes there are in all. For this example, since there are 3 layers with 12 cubes in each layer, students could skip count to get 36 cubes in all: "12, 24, 36."

(continued)

Lesson 72 391

New Concept (Continued)

Lesson Practice

Guided Practice

Use these problems as guided practice to check the students' understanding of today's concept.

Problems a–c
Extend the Problem
Ask students what the total number of cubes in the stack would be if they were to double the number of layers from three to six. 60 cubes

"Describe how the number of cubes in the stack has changed." sample: The total number of cubes doubled too.

Closure The questions below help assess the concepts taught in this lesson.

"What three steps do you follow to find the total number of cubes in a stack?" sample: First, count the number of cubes in one layer. Next, count the number of layers. Then multiply the two numbers to find the total number of cubes.

"If we have a stack of cubes that has 4 layers and there are 8 cubes in each layer, how many cubes are there altogether?" 32 cubes

Discuss real-world situations where counting cubes might be helpful. Examples are given below.

- We have a stack of cracker packages at the store and need to know how many packages are in the display.
- We have a pallet of bricks and need to know how many bricks there are altogether.

Written Practice

Math Conversations
Independent Practice and Discussions to Increase Understanding

Problem 2 Formulate
Help students recognize this problem as a "some and some more" story. Tell students:

"You would travel 'some' and then turn around and travel 'some more.'"

(continued)

392 Saxon Math Intermediate 3

---

c. Three layers with 12 cubes in each layer means there are **36 cubes in all.**

12 + 12 + 12 = 36 *or* 3 × 12 = 36

Lesson Practice A box is filled with cubes, as shown at right.

▸ a. How many cubes are in each layer? 10 cubes
▸ b. How many layers are there? 3 layers
▸ c. How many cubes are there? 30 cubes

Written Practice — Distributed and Integrated

1. Sidney was on a 480-mile trip. When the train stopped in Omaha, Sidney had traveled 256 miles. How much farther did Sidney have to travel? 224 miles
(20)

▸ 2. **Formulate** It is 185 miles from Elam to Junction City. How far is it from Elam to Junction City and back? Write a number sentence.
(18) 185 + 185 = 370 miles

3. Livestock were hauled east from Denver, Colorado, to Chicago, Illinois. Use the scale and your ruler to find the approximate distance from Denver to Chicago. 1,000 mi
(Inv. 4)

Denver •———————————————————————————• Chicago
1 inch = 200 miles

4. It is morning in Chicago. Write the time shown at right in digital form. 8:44 a.m.
(38)

5. Find each product. You may use the multiplication table.
(59, 64)
   a. 7 × 2   14
   b. 7 × 5   35
   c. 7 × 9   63

6. Find each product.
(70)
   a. 8 × 4   32
   b. 8 × 6   48
   c. 8 × 7   56

7. Find each product.
(70)
   a. 6 × 3   18
   b. 6 × 4   24
   c. 6 × 7   42

392 Saxon Math Intermediate 3

Alternative Approach: Using Manipulatives

If students need a more concrete representation of the relationship between layers and total cubes, have them build the example and Lesson Practice stacks before answering the questions.

Advanced learners can see how many different stacks they can build with 36 cubes.

8. Find each product.
(64)
   a. 9 × 3   27
   b. 9 × 7   63
   c. 9 × 9   81

▶ **9.** (Represent) In Lesson 71 we learned how to draw a rectangular prism. Use the same process to draw a cube. (Hint: Begin by drawing two overlapping squares.)
(71)

9. sample:

10. What is the shape of every face of a cube?   square
(71)

11. A rectangular prism has how many edges?   12
(71)

12. **Multiple Choice** Which polygon does *not* show a line of symmetry?
(Inv. 7)
D
   A   B   C   D
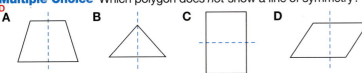

▶ **13.** Harold put some small cubes together to make this larger cube. How many small cubes make the larger cube?   8 cubes
(72)

Use polygon ABCD and a ruler to answer problems 14–16.

14. a. How long is each side of the polygon?   1 in.
(35, 58)
   b. What is the perimeter of the polygon?   4 in.

15. What is the shape of the polygon?   parallelogram
(66)

16. a. Which two angles are obtuse?   angles B and D
(65, 66)
   b. Which two angles are acute?   angles A and C

▶ **17.** (Conclude) The numbers below make a pattern on a multiplication table. What are the next three numbers in this pattern?   36, 49, 64
(55, 61)

0, 1, 4, 9, 16, 25, ___, ___, ___, ...

18. 36¢ + 74¢ + $2 $3.10
(22, 24)

19. $2.00 − $1.26 $0.74
(26, 28)

20. A driveway is 10 yd long and 7 yd wide. What is the area of the driveway?   70 sq. yd
(62, 63)

7 yd
10 yd

Lesson 72   393

Looking Forward

Counting cubes and representing totals with addition facts and multiplication facts prepares students for

- **Lesson 73,** finding volume.
- **Lesson 75,** identifying geometric solids.
- **Investigation 8,** building geometric solids.
- **Lesson 87,** understanding capacity.

Written Practice (Continued)

Math Conversations
Independent Practice and Discussions to Increase Understanding

▶ **Problem 9** (Represent)
Students need to realize that each view of the cube (front, side, and top) should give the impression that all faces are the same size.

▶ **Problem 13**
Extend the Problem
"If you added one more layer, the smaller cubes would not make a larger cube anymore. What shape would they make?"
rectangular prism

▶ **Problem 17** (Conclude)
Help students find the pattern on a multiplication table. Give them the following hint:
"Look for a diagonal pattern."
This pattern flows down diagonally across the table from the upper left to the bottom right. Students should investigate and note that these numbers are the result of multiplying two numbers that are the same:
0 × 0 = 0,
1 × 1 = 1,
2 × 2 = 4,
3 × 3 = 9, and so on.

Errors and Misconceptions

▶ **Problem 13**
Students may try to count only the visible cubes. Remind students to count all of the cubes, even the ones they cannot see.

▶ **Problem 20**
Students often forget the units in problems involving area.
"When we find the area of an object, we multiply one length by another. This means the units are squares which we read 'square units.'"

Lesson 72   393

LESSON 73

Texas Essential Knowledge and Skills

(3.11)(F) use concrete models that approximate cubic units to determine the volume of a given container or other figure

(3.15)(A) explain observations using objects

Planning & Preparation

- **Volume**

Objectives
- Use inch-cube manipulatives to measure the approximate volume of a box.
- Recognize that the number of small cubes used to fill a box is given by the number of cubes in one layer times the number of layers.
- Find the volume of a box from a pictorial model.

Prerequisite Skills
- Use skip counting or multiplication to find the number of small cubes in a larger rectangular solid.
- Build rectangular solids with inch cubes to model volume.

Materials
Instructional Masters
- Power Up 73
- Lesson Activity 28

Manipulative Kit
- 1-inch cubes
- Rulers

Teacher-provided materials
- Empty boxes (shoe boxes or tissue boxes)

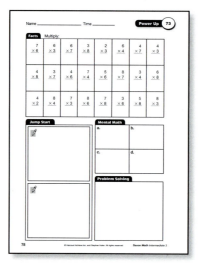

Power Up 73

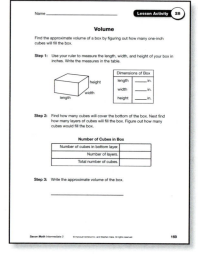

Lesson Activity 28

Differentiated Instruction

Reaching All Special Needs Students

Special Education Students	At-Risk Students	English Learners	Advanced Learners
• Inclusion (TM) • Adaptations for Saxon Math	• Error Alert (TM) • Reteaching Masters	• English Learners (TM) • English Learner Handbook	• Extend the Example (TM) • Extend the Problem (TM) • Early Finishers (SE) • Online Activities

TM=Teacher's Manual
SE=Student Edition

Math Language

New	Maintained	English Learners
cubic units volume	edge	occupy

Saxon Math Intermediate 3

Problem Solving Discussion

Problem

Denair wrote an addition problem and then erased some of the digits. Find the missing digits in the problem.

```
  _ 2
+ 1 _
-----
  2 7
```

Focus Strategies

- **Guess and Check**
- **Use Logical Reasoning**

Understand *Understand the problem.*

"What information are we given?"

We are shown an addition problem with some missing digits.

"What are we asked to do?"

We are asked to find the missing digits.

Plan *Make a plan.*

"What problem solving strategies can we use?"

We can *use logical reasoning* and *guess and check* to find the missing digits.

Solve *Carry out the plan.*

"Copy the problem onto your paper."

Teacher Note: Allow students to copy the problem onto their worksheet.

"Let's start by looking at the ones column, just as if we were adding numbers. How can we find the missing digit?"

We think, "2 plus what number equals 7?" We know that $2 + 5 = 7$, so we write a 5 in the blank.

"How can we find the missing digit in the tens column?"

We think, "What number plus 1 equals 2?" We know that $1 + 1 = 2$, so we write a 1 in the blank.

```
  1 2
+ 1 5
-----
  2 7
```

Check *Look back.*

"Is our answer reasonable?"

Yes, we check our guess by adding 12 and 15. We find that the sum is 27, so our guesses are correct.

"What problem solving strategies did we use, and how did they help us?"

We *used logical reasoning* to help us make educated guesses. Then we *checked our guesses* by adding the numbers.

Lesson 73 394B

LESSON 73

Power Up

Facts
Distribute **Power Up 73** to students. See answers below.

Jump Start
Before students begin the Mental Math exercise, do these exercises as a class.

Mental Math
Encourage students to share different ways to mentally compute these exercises. Strategies for exercises are listed below.

a. Think 38 + 10 − 2
38 + 8 = 38 + 10 − 2 = 48 − 2 = 46

c. Add the Lengths of the Sides
4 inches + 4 inches + 4 inches
= 12 inches

Problem Solving
Refer to **Problem-Solving Strategy Discussion**, p. 394B.

New Concept

Explanation
Explain to students that objects in the real world occupy space. Point to a box to show that three-dimensional objects take up space and have length, width, and height. Tell students that the length, width, and height of the box can be measured.

(continued)

LESSON 73 • Volume

Texas Essential Knowledge and Skills
(3.11)(F) use concrete models that approximate cubic units to determine the volume of a given container or other figure
(3.14)(D) use tools such as technology to solve problems
(3.15)(A) explain observations using objects

Power Up

facts   Power Up 73

jump start
- Count up by halves from 5 to 10.
- Count up by fourths from 2 to 4.
- Write two multiplication facts using the numbers 9, 7, and 63. $9 \times 7 = 63; 7 \times 9 = 63$
- Write these money amounts in order from least to greatest. $10.05, $10.50, $10.95, $11.50
$10.50 $10.95 $10.05 $11.50

mental math
a. **Number Sense:** 38 + 8   46
b. **Number Sense:** 3000 + 100 + 50 + 8   3,158
c. **Measurement:** What is the perimeter of the triangle?   12 in.
d. **Geometry:** What type of triangle is shown in problem **c**?   equilateral

problem solving
Denair wrote an addition problem and then erased some of the digits. Find the missing digits in the problem.

New Concept

Visit www.SaxonMath.com/Int3Activities for a calculator activity.

One way to describe the size of a box is to say how much space there is inside the box. If we fill up the box with cubes we can describe the space inside the box in **cubic units.** Instead of saying how many raisins or apples or oranges a box can hold, we might say how many cubic inches it can hold. We might describe the size of a boxcar by saying how many cubic feet or cubic yards it can hold.

394   *Saxon Math Intermediate 3*

Facts   Multiply:

7 × 6 = 42	6 × 3 = 18	6 × 7 = 42	3 × 8 = 24	2 × 3 = 6	6 × 4 = 24	4 × 7 = 28	4 × 3 = 12
4 × 8 = 32	3 × 7 = 21	4 × 6 = 24	7 × 4 = 28	5 × 6 = 30	8 × 7 = 56	3 × 4 = 12	6 × 8 = 48
4 × 2 = 8	8 × 4 = 32	7 × 3 = 21	8 × 6 = 48	7 × 8 = 56	3 × 6 = 18	5 × 8 = 40	8 × 3 = 24

The amount of space an object occupies is called its **volume**. A cube with edges one inch long has a volume of one cubic inch.

1 cubic inch

The activity below will help us understand volume. We will find the number of one-inch cubes needed to fill a box.

Volume

Materials: **Lesson Activity 28,** empty boxes such as shoe boxes or tissue boxes, rulers, one-inch cubes

For this activity, you will work together in small groups. Use your ruler to measure the length, width, and height of your box.

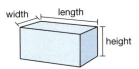

Record the length, width, and height in the table on **Lesson Activity 28.** Write the number of inches without a fraction. For example, if the length is $11\frac{3}{4}$ inches, just write 11 inches.

Dimensions of Box	
length	_____ in.
width	_____ in.
height	_____ in.

Next, figure out how many cubes are needed to make one layer on the bottom of the box. If you do not have enough cubes to cover the bottom of the box, you might need to multiply to find the number.

Lesson 73   395

To **occupy** means to take up space. Ask:

"How many seats are occupied right now?" Answers will vary.

Ask:

"What else occupies or takes up space in this room?" Answers will vary.

Have students name things that occupy space in their own rooms at home.

New Concept (Continued)

Math Language

Read the definition of volume aloud. Then ask volunteers to describe in their own words what volume means. Ask the students:

"What object can you think of that would have a large volume?" sample: a water tower

"What object can you think of that would have a small volume?" sample: a pencil

Math-to-Math Connection

Tell students that when we counted the total number of cubes in a stack, we also found the volume of the stack. The number of cubes told us how much space the stack occupied.

Explanation

Explain to students that a volume in cubic inches tells how many one-inch cubes would fill the object. A volume in cubic feet tells how many one-foot cubes would fill the object. A volume in cubic yards tells how many one-yard cubes would fill the object.

Activity

Arrange students in small groups. Provide each student with **Lesson Activity 28** and each group with about 20 one-inch cubes. Each group will also need one ruler and one box.

Remind students to drop fractions from measures when recording dimensions.

Students should have enough cubes to show the length and width of the bottom layer. Multiplying these two numbers gives the number of cubes that fill the bottom layer.

Instruction

Students can find the number of layers by stacking a column of cubes in the box.

Students can add the number of cubes in each layer to find the total number of cubes that would fill the box.

(continued)

New Concept (Continued)

Example

Extend the Example

"*What is the area of one layer?*"
20 square inches

"*How do we know this?*" sample: There are 4 rows of 5 cubes: 4 × 5 = 20.

Lesson Practice

Guided Practice

Use these problems as guided practice to check the students' understanding of today's concept.

Problem a

Point out to students that the problem says that the boxes are 1 cubic foot.

Problem b Error Alert

Students may try to count only the boxes they can see. Remind them to count the boxes in one layer. Then multiply by the number of layers.

Remind students to include the correct units as part of their answer.

Closure — The questions below help assess the concepts taught in this lesson.

"*How would you describe volume?*" The amount of space an object occupies.

"*How do we find the volume of a box?*" sample: We count the number of cubes it would take to fill the box.

"*When we write the volume, do we write the answer in square units?*" No, volume is given in cubic units. Area is given in square units.

Discuss real-world situations where volume might be helpful. Examples are given below.

- We have a package we need to mail and want to find out if it will fit inside a box.
- An astronaut going into space can take some things from home along, but he only has a small space to put them in. He needs to know the volume of the space to know how much he can bring.

396 *Saxon Math* Intermediate 3

Record the number of cubes that will fit on the bottom of the box. This is the bottom layer. Then figure out how many layers the box could hold without going over the top. Finally, figure out the total number of cubes the box will hold. This is the approximate volume of the box in cubic inches.

Number of Cubes in Box	
number of cubes in bottom layer	____
number of layers	____
total number of cubes in box	____

Write the approximate volume of the box as a number of cubic inches.

Example

Millie filled a small gift box with 1-inch cubes. The picture shows the top layer. There are two layers of cubes. How many cubes are in the box? What is the volume of the box in cubic inches?

We see the top layer. There are 4 rows of cubes and 5 cubes in each row.

4 × 5 = 20

There are 20 cubes in the top layer. Since there are 2 layers, there are **40 cubes in the box.**

20 + 20 = 40

The volume of the box is **40 cubic inches.**

Discuss Could you find the volume of Millie's box in cubic feet? Why or why not? sample: no; 1 cubic foot is 1 foot wide and that would not fit in Millie's box.

Lesson Practice Jorge stores work supplies in 1-foot cubic boxes in his garage.

▶ a. What is the volume of each box?
1 cubic foot
▶ b. What is the volume of this stack of boxes? 24 cubic feet

396 *Saxon Math* Intermediate 3

 Inclusion

Fill It Up

Some students will need more concrete experiences with finding volume.

Materials: a variety of small boxes that can be filled with cubes; 1-inch cubes

- Students cover the bottom of a box with cubes in rows and columns.
- They repeat that layer until they get to the top.
- Students remove the cubes from the box and reassemble the stack so that they can see all the blocks.
- They count the cubes in the top layer and skip count or add to find the total number of cubes in all the layers.

Written Practice *Distributed and Integrated*

1. A round-trip ticket to Topeka cost $149. Cory has $98. How much more money does he need to buy a ticket? $51
   (36)

2. **Analyze** In a common year, June 30 is the 181st day of the year. How many days are there in the last six months of the year?   184 days
   (40)

3. The railroad tie cutters worked 9 hours a day, 6 days a week. How many hours did the tie cutters work in a week?   54 hours
   (60, 64)

4. The ride to Pawtucket lasts an hour and a half. The train left the station at 8:45 a.m. The clock showed the time it arrived in Pawtucket. Write the time in digital form.   10:15 a.m.
   (39)

5. A pallet is loaded with boxes, as shown.
   (72)
   a. How many boxes are in each layer?   6 boxes
   b. How many layers are there?   4 layers
   c. How many boxes are there?   24 boxes

   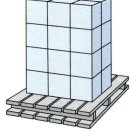

6. If each box in problem **5** is one cubic foot, then what is the volume of the stack of boxes?   24 cubic feet
   (73)

7. Find each product:
   (70)
   a. 3×6 18
   b. 3×8 24
   c. 3×7 21

8. Find each product:
   (64)
   a. 5×9 45
   b. 9×2 18
   c. 9×9 81

9. Change this addition into multiplication and find the total: $6 \times \$5 = \$30$
   (54)
   $$\$5 + \$5 + \$5 + \$5 + \$5 + \$5$$

10. **Represent** Draw a cube.   See student work.
    (71)

11. A cube has how many vertices?   8
    (71)

Lesson 73   397

Written Practice

Math Conversations
Independent Practice and Discussions to Increase Understanding

Problem 2 **Analyze**
Students should remember that June 30 is the last day of the first six months of the year and that a year has 365 days. Help students see that they should subtract the days that have passed from the total number of days in the year to find the days left. Some students may see this as a "some and some more" story and write a number sentence, $181 + d = 365$, to solve.

Problem 10 **Represent**
Students should first draw two overlapping squares and then connect the corresponding vertices with line segments. Remind students that each view of the cube (front, side, and top) should give the impression that all faces are the same size.

(continued)

Lesson 73   397

Written Practice (Continued)

Math Conversations
Independent Practice and Discussions to Increase Understanding

▶ **Problem 13** (Connect)
Students should recognize the "count by 7s" pattern or subtract consecutive terms to find the rule "add 7."

▶ **Problem 19**
Extend the Problem
"What do we call the shape that looks like a box?" rectangular prism or rectangular solid

Errors and Misconceptions

▶ **Problem 6**
Students may mistakenly write "24 boxes" instead of writing "24 cubic feet." Remind students that the total number of boxes indicates the volume, and that volume is written with both a number and a unit such as cubic inches, cubic feet, or cubic yards.

▶ **Problem 20**
Students often forget the units in problems about area. Remind them to use square units to name the area.

Students should be careful to multiply the correct numbers describing the length and width of the top of the box.

Early Finishers
Students may recognize this as a "some and some more" story with a missing addend. Have students explain how they found the weight of the passengers.

---

12. Which letter does not show a line of symmetry?   F
(Inv. 7)
C   D   E   F

▶ **13.** (Connect) Find the next three numbers in this sequence: 42, 49, 56
(2)
14, 21, 28, 35, ___, ___, ___, ...

14. Find each product:
(61, 70)
   a. 6×7 42   **b.** 7×7 49   **c.** 8×7 56

Add or subtract, as shown:

15. $800 − $724 $76   **16.** $6.49 + $5.52 $12.01
(28)   (22)

17. $9 + 9 + 9 + 9 + 9 + 9 + 9 + 9 + 9$ 81
(10, 54)

18. Use words to write each fraction or mixed number.
(41, 46)
   a. $\frac{3}{7}$ **b.** $3\frac{1}{2}$ **c.** $\frac{9}{10}$ **d.** $2\frac{3}{4}$
   a. three sevenths; b. three and one half; c. nine tenths; d. two and three fourths

▶ **19.** A drawing of a box is shown at right.
(71)
   a. What is the length of the box?   10 inches
   b. What is the width of the box?   6 inches
   c. What is the height of the box?   4 inches

20. What is the area of the top of the box in problem **19**?   60 sq. in.
(62)

Real-World Connection

Mr. Crosby's mini van weighs 2,746 pounds. When he drives his daughter and four of her friends to softball practice the car weighs 3,273 pounds with the weight of the passengers. How much do the passengers of the car weigh altogether? Write 2,746 and 3,273 using words.   527 pounds; two thousand seven hundred forty-six, three thousand two hundred seventy-three

---

Looking Forward

Finding the volume of boxes and stacks of cubes and using the correct units to describe volume prepares students for

- **Lesson 75,** identifying geometric solids.
- **Investigation 8,** building geometric solids.
- **Lesson 87,** understanding capacity.

LESSON 74

Planning & Preparation

• Weight: Ounces, Pounds, and Tons

Texas Essential Knowledge and Skills

(3.11)(D) identify concrete models that approximate standard units of weight/mass

(3.14)(A) identify the mathematics in everyday situations

(3.15)(A) record observations using numbers

Objectives
- Learn the relationships between ounces, pounds, and tons.
- Identify real-world benchmarks for each unit of weight.
- Use a scale to weigh objects in ounces and pounds.

Prerequisite Skills
- Learn the relationships between units of length in the U.S. Customary System.

Materials

Instructional Masters
- Power Up 74

Manipulative Kit
- Balance scale

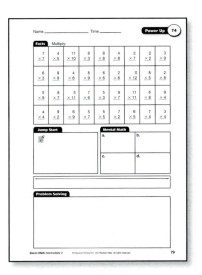

Power Up 74

Differentiated Instruction

Reaching All Special Needs Students

Special Education Students	At-Risk Students	English Learners	Advanced Learners
• Adaptations for Saxon Math	• Error Alert (TM) • Reteaching Masters	• English Learners (TM) • English Learner Handbook	• Extend the Example (TM) • Extend the Problem (TM) • Online Activities

TM = Teacher's Manual

Math Language

New	Maintained	English Learners
ounce pound ton weight	equals	buy

Lesson 74 399A

LESSON 74

Problem Solving Discussion

Problem

Jim, Ron, and George were standing in line. There were 38 people in front of them and 3 people behind them. Altogether, how many people were standing in line?

Focus Strategy 2+3=5 **Write a Number Sentence**

Understand Understand the problem.

"What information are we given?"

1. Jim, Ron, and George were standing in line.
2. There were 38 people in front of them.
3. There were 3 people behind them.

"What are we asked to do?"

We are asked to find how many people were standing in line altogether.

Plan Make a plan.

"What problem solving strategy can we use to solve the problem?"

We can *write a number sentence*.

Solve Carry out the plan.

"We are looking for a total number of people. What kind of number sentence can we write to find a total?"

To find a total, we can write an addition number sentence.

"What three numbers do we need to add to find the total?"

There were 38 people in front of Jim, Ron, and George. There were 3 people behind them. Jim, Ron, and George are 3 people. So we can write this number sentence:

$$38 \text{ people} + 3 \text{ people} + 3 \text{ people} = 44 \text{ people}$$

Check Look back.

"Did we complete the task?"

Yes, we found how many people were standing in line altogether (44 people).

"Is our answer reasonable?"

Yes, we know that our answer is reasonable because $38 + 3 + 3 = 44$.

"What problem solving strategy did we use, and how did it help us?"

We *wrote a number sentence* to find a total number of people.

"Why might it have been difficult to use the strategy of 'draw a picture' or 'act it out' to solve this problem?"

Since there are many people in line, drawing a picture or acting out the problem would be too time consuming. Writing a number sentence was a faster way to solve the problem.

LESSON 74

- **Weight: Ounces, Pounds, and Tons**

Texas Essential Knowledge and Skills
(3.11)(D) identify concrete models that approximate standard units of weight/mass
(3.14)(A) identify the mathematics in everyday situations
(3.15)(A) record observations using numbers

Power Up

facts   Power Up 74

jump start
- Count down by 4s from 40 to 0.
- Count down by 8s from 80 to 0.
- Draw an array to show the multiplication fact 4 × 2. *See student work.*
- Label the number line by 25s from 0 to 250. *0, 25, 50, 75, 100, 125, 150, 175, 200, 225, 250*

mental math
a. **Number Sense:** 900 + 400 + 300   *1600*
b. **Measurement:** How many inches are in 5 feet?   *60 in.*
c. **Money:** $5.75 + $1.00   *$6.75*
d. **Patterns:** What number is missing in the pattern below?   *16*

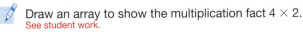

| 1 | 4 | 9 | ___ | 25 | 36 |

problem solving
Jim, Ron, and George were standing in line. There were 38 people in front of them and 3 people behind them. Altogether, how many people were standing in line? *44 people*

New Concept

The **weight** of an object is a measure of how heavy it is.

Weight can be measured in ounces. A metal spoon weighs about one **ounce.**

Weight can also be measured in pounds. A playground ball might weigh about a **pound.** A pound is equal to 16 ounces.

Very heavy objects can be measured in tons. A small car weighs a **ton.** A ton is equal to 2,000 pounds.

Lesson 74   399

Facts   Multiply:

7×7=49	4×5=20	11×10=110	8×3=24	8×8=64	4×8=32	3×7=21	2×2=4	3×9=27
6×3=18	9×9=81	4×6=24	8×9=72	6×6=36	2×6=12	0×12=0	8×5=40	2×8=16
5×9=45	8×7=56	5×11=55	7×6=42	5×3=15	9×7=63	11×11=121	6×8=48	9×4=36
4×4=16	9×2=18	6×9=54	5×7=35	5×5=25	7×2=14	6×5=30	7×4=28	3×4=12

LESSON 74

Power Up

Facts
Distribute **Power Up 74** to students. See answers below.

Jump Start
Before students begin the Mental Math exercise, do these exercises as a class.

Mental Math
Encourage students to share different ways to mentally compute these exercises. Strategies for exercises are listed below.

- **a. Think Hundreds**
  9 hundreds + 4 hundreds + 3 hundreds = 16 hundreds or 1600
- **b. Think 5 × 12**
  1 foot = 12 inches
  5 feet = 5 × 12 inches = 60 inches
- **d. Use a Multiplication Chart**
  1, 4, 9, <u>16</u>, 25, 36

Problem Solving
Refer to **Problem-Solving Strategy Discussion,** p. 399B.

New Concept

Explanation
Help students grasp the concept of weight by comparing the weight of a pencil and a book. Have students take a pencil and a book out of their desks. Ask which is heavier.

"Which might weigh about an ounce?" *pencil*

"Which might weigh about a pound?" *book*

Active Learning
Ask students to name items that they think might weigh:
- about 1 ounce
- about 1 pound
- about 1 ton

List the items on the board. Revisit the list after students have had more practice with weight in this lesson.

(continued)

Lesson 74   399

New Concept (Continued)

Example 1
Extend the Example
"How much would a pair of the man's shoes weigh in ounces?" about 32 ounces

Example 2
Alternate Method
Count by 2s for each ton: 2, 4. Then add three zeros to the end to get the number of pounds. So two tons would equal 4,000 pounds.

Extend the Example
"If four large cars weigh about eight tons, about how many pounds would they weigh?" about 16,000 pounds

(continued)

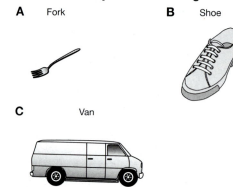

Metal spoon — 1 ounce
Playground ball — 1 pound
Small automobile — 1 ton

Units of Weight

| 1 pound = 16 ounces |
| 1 ton = 2,000 pounds |

Verify A 1-pound box of cereal costs the same as three 4-ounce boxes. Which is the better buy? Three 4-ounce boxes is less than one pound. So the one pound box of cereal is the better buy.

Example 1

Which of these objects would weigh about a pound?

A Fork
B Shoe
C Van

Choice **B, a shoe,** weighs about a pound. A fork weighs about an ounce. A small van might weigh two tons.

Example 2

If a large car weighs about two tons, then it weighs about how many pounds?

A ton is 2,000 pounds. We can add to find the number of pounds in two tons.

2,000 pounds + 2,000 pounds = 4,000 pounds

A car that weighs about two tons weighs **about 4,000 pounds.**

Math Background

Students may find it useful to know the abbreviations for words such as pounds and ounces since these abbreviations often appear on food packages purchased at a store. The abbreviation for pound is *lb*. This comes from the Latin word *libra* meaning "scales." The constellation *Libra* looks like the scales of a two-pan balance. The word *ounce* also originates from a Latin word, in this case *uncia*. However, the abbreviation for ounce, *oz*, appears to come from the Italian word *onza* which is now spelled *oncia*.

English Learners

A **better buy** means something that you paid less money for.

Ask:

"If a game costs $11.50 at one store and $12.00 at another store, which is the better buy?" the game that costs $11.50

Ask:

"If one CD costs $15.00 and two CDs together cost $25.00, which is the better buy? Why?" two CDs; sample: If you buy two CDs together, each one costs less than $15.00.

Have students discuss the best buy they've ever gotten at a store.

Activity
Weighing Objects

Use a scale to weigh various objects in the classroom. Make a table like the one below to record the name of each object and its weight. Can you find an object that weighs one ounce? Can you find an object that weighs one pound?

Weights of Objects

Name of Object	Weight

Lesson Practice

a. Would you describe the weight of a large dog in ounces, pounds, or tons?   pounds

b. **Multiple Choice** Which object weighs about an ounce?   A

  A Birthday card   **B** Box of cereal   **C** Brick wall

▶ c. The kitten weighed about two pounds. About how many ounces did the kitten weigh?   32 ounces

▶ d. **Multiple Choice** The horse weighed about one half of a ton. About how many pounds did the horse weigh?   B

  A 500 pounds   **B** 1,000 pounds
  C 1,500 pounds   **D** 2,000 pounds

Lesson 74   401

New Concept (Continued)

Activity

If more than one scale is available, arrange students in groups so that each group has a scale. If only one scale is available, have students rotate its use in small groups. Encourage students to weigh various objects, but not the same objects as other groups. Instruct each group on how to use and read the scale. Remind students to record both the weight and the unit of each object.

Lesson Practice

Guided Practice

Use these problems as guided practice to check the students' understanding of today's concept.

Problem c Error Alert

Watch for students who will try to find how many times 2 will go into 16. Ask students:

"One pound equals 16 ounces, so two pounds equal how many ounces?"
32 ounces

Problem d   Multiple Choice
Test-Taking Strategy

Since half of a ton is less that one ton, students can mark out any answer of 2000 or more. That eliminates answer choice **D**. Students may double each of the remaining answers and mark out the ones that do not total 2000 pounds.

 Closure The questions below help assess the concepts taught in this lesson.

"What is weight?" Weight is a measure of how heavy an object is.

"What are some things you might measure in ounces?" samples: a pencil, a drink, some foods

"What are some things you might measure in pounds?" samples: people, potatoes, animals

"How many pounds are there in a ton?" There are 2,000 pounds in one ton.

Discuss real-world situations where weight and weighing things might be helpful. Examples are given below.

- We need to buy three pounds of apples.
- A nurse weighs a child to make sure that she is healthy.
- We want to know if a 20-ounce bag of carrots for $2 is a better deal than a 12-ounce bag of carrots for $1.50.

Lesson 74   401

Written Practice

Math Conversations
Independent Practice and Discussions to Increase Understanding

Problem 2 (Formulate)
Students should always read word problems carefully and look for key words. Point out the words "loaded 16 tons" and "How many more tons" to the students. They are clues that this is a "some and some more" story. Help students recognize the clue words and write a number sentence for this story problem.

(continued)

Written Practice — Distributed and Integrated

1. Jefferson sat by the window and watched the train go by. He counted thirty-eight coal cars and twenty-seven boxcars. Altogether, how many coal cars and boxcars did he count? **65 cars**

2. (Formulate) The miners loaded 16 tons of ore in the morning. Their goal was 28 tons by nightfall. How many more tons of coal did they need to load to reach their goal? Write a number sentence **16 + ☐ = 28; 12 tons**

3. Automobiles were shipped west from Jonestown to Seagraves. Use the scale to find the approximate distance from Jonestown to Seagraves. **200 mi**

   Jonestown •————————————————————• Seagraves
   1 inch = 50 miles

4. It is noon in Detroit. Write the time in digital form. **12:00 p.m.**

5. Are the stripes on a United States flag parallel or perpendicular? **parallel**

6. The work crew was paid $16,000 for laying a mile of track on flat land. Use words to name $16,000. **sixteen thousand dollars**

7. How many ounces are equal to one pound? **16 ounces**

8. The tunnel was four tenths of a mile long. Write four tenths as a fraction. $\frac{4}{10}$

9. The first rail line connecting the east coast of the United States to the west coast was completed in 1869. How many years ago was that? **Answer will vary depending on current year.**

10. Find each product.
    a. 6×2 **12**   b. 8×5 **40**   c. 5×6 **30**

402   Saxon Math Intermediate 3

11. Change this addition to multiplication and find the total.
(54)

$$3 \text{ ft} + 3 \text{ ft} + 3 \text{ ft} + 3 \text{ ft} \quad 4 \times 3 \text{ ft} = 12 \text{ ft}$$

12. How many pounds are equal to
(74)
    a. one ton?   2,000 pounds   **b.** two tons?   4,000 pounds

13. Find each product.
(70)
    a. 6×7 42   **b.** 7×8 56   **c.** 6×8 48

Add or subtract, as shown:

14. $6.75 - $4.48 $2.27   **15.** $1 - 1¢   99¢
(26)   (26, 28)

16. Find the missing addend: $10 + 20 + m = 100$ 70
(9)

▶ **17.** Dora made this rectangular prism using 1-inch cubes.
(72, 73)
    a. How many cubes did she use?   30

    b. What is the volume of the rectangular prism?   30 cubic inches

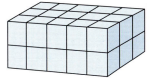

▶ **18.** (Model) Each quarter inch on this map represents 10 miles. How many miles is it from
(Inv. 4)
    a. Calmer to Seaton?   60 mi

    b. Calmer to Bayview?   90 mi

    c. Bayview to Seaton?   150 mi

▶ **19. Multiple Choice** Which of these polygons does *not* have at least one right angle? How can you tell?   B; sample: The shape does not have any square corners.
(65, 67)

20. **a.** The polygon in problem **19**, choice **D** has how many sides?   5
(67)
    b. What is the name for a polygon with this number of sides?
    pentagon

Lesson 74   403

Looking Forward

Using the concept of weight in units of ounces, pounds, and tons to describe and compare objects and converting between different measures of weight prepares students for

- **Lesson 79,** working with length in the metric system.
- **Lesson 87,** understanding capacity.
- **Lesson 98,** estimating by weight.

Written Practice (Continued)

Math Conversations
Independent Practice and Discussions to Increase Understanding

Problem 17
Extend the Problem

Ask students to add two layers to the rectangular prism and then answer **a** and **b** again.

a. 60

b. 60 cubic inches

Problem 18 (Model)

To help students convert quarter inches to miles, draw an inch ruler on the board showing quarter-inch tick marks to 2 inches. Use the drawing to show students how to count by 10s for every quarter inch of their measurement.

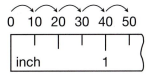

Problem 19   Multiple Choice
Test-Taking Strategy

Remind students to read the test question carefully and notice the word *not*. The question asks which polygon does *not* have a right angle, so they should eliminate every figure that *does* contain a right angle; the figure left over is the correct answer.

Errors and Misconceptions

Problem 17

Students may only count the cubes they can see in part **a**. Remind them to count all of the cubes including the ones in the middle of the stack that they cannot see in part **b**.

Students may forget to write the units.

"When describing volume, we use both a number and a cubic unit like cubic inches, cubic feet, or cubic yards."

Lesson 74   403

LESSON 75

Planning & Preparation

• Geometric Solids

Objectives
- Identify, classify, and describe geometric solids by their attributes.
- Use proper vocabulary to name geometric solids.
- Compare and contrast geometric solids with two-dimensional shapes and figures.

Prerequisite Skills
- Use proper vocabulary to describe attributes of rectangular solids.
- Identify, classify, and describe rectangular solids by their attributes.
- Compare and contrast rectangular solids.

Materials

Instructional Masters
- Power Up 75

Manipulative Kit
- Geosolids
- Rulers

Teacher-provided materials
- Examples of flat shapes (square, triangle, circle)
- Magazines
- Scissors
- Glue

🚩 **Texas Essential Knowledge and Skills**

(3.8) identify/classify three-dimensional geometric figures by their attributes and compare two- and three-dimensional figures by their attributes using formal vocabulary

(3.15)(A) explain observations using pictures

(3.16)(A) make generalizations from sets of examples and nonexamples

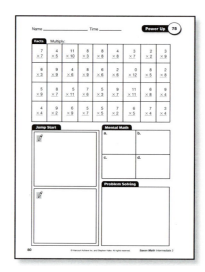

Power Up 75

Reaching All Special Needs Students

Special Education Students	At-Risk Students	English Learners	Advanced Learners
• Inclusion (TM) • Adaptations for Saxon Math	• Error Alert (TM) • Reteaching Masters	• English Learners (TM) • English Learner Handbook	• Extend the Example (TM) • Extend the Problem (TM) • Early Finishers (SE) • Online Activities

TM = Teacher's Manual
SE = Student Edition

Math Language

New		Maintained	English Learners
cone	solid	circle	rectangular prism	combination
cylinder	sphere	cube	triangle	
geometric solid	triangular prism	rectangle		
pyramid				

404A   Saxon Math Intermediate 3

Problem Solving Discussion

Problem

Four students can sit at a square table (one student on each side). If two tables are joined together, six students can sit. (Notice that nobody can sit at the edges where the tables touch.) Predict how many students can sit at four tables that are joined into one big square. To check your prediction, draw a diagram of the tables and place numbers where students can sit along the edges.

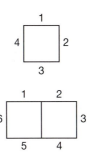

Focus Strategies

 Draw a Picture or Diagram

 Use Logical Reasoning

Understand *Understand the problem.*

"What information are we given?"

1. Four students can sit at a square table (one on each side).
2. Six students can sit at two square tables that are joined together.

"What are we asked to do?"

We are asked to predict how many people can sit at four square tables arranged into a large square. We are also asked to check our prediction by drawing a diagram.

Plan *Make a plan.*

"What problem solving strategy will we use?"

We will *use logical reasoning* to make a prediction, then *draw a diagram* to check our prediction.

Solve *Carry out the plan.*

"First, we will make a prediction. How many students can sit around two tables? Why?"

The diagram shows that six students can sit around two tables. Two of the sides touch, and there is no room for students to sit at those sides.

"If we add two tables to make a large square, there will be two tables along each side. Can you mentally picture how many students will be able to sit?"

Two tables along each side leaves room for 2 + 2 + 2 + 2 = 8 students to sit.

"We are told to draw a diagram to check our prediction. What might our diagram look like?"

Our diagram might look like this. We place numbers along the sides where students can sit.

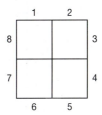

Check *Look back.*

"Did we complete the task?"

Yes, we predicted and found the number of students who could sit around a large square table made up of four smaller square tables (8 students).

"Is our answer reasonable?"

Yes, our answer is reasonable because there are 2 places to sit along each side of the large square. A square has four sides, so there are 2 + 2 + 2 + 2 = 8 places to sit.

Lesson 75   404B

LESSON 75

Power Up

Facts
Distribute **Power Up 75** to students. See answers below.

Jump Start
Before students begin the Mental Math exercise, do these exercises as a class.

Mental Math
Encourage students to share different ways to mentally compute these exercises. Strategies for exercises are listed below.

a. **Picture a Number Line**
Think of a number line from 400 to 500. Since 450 is in the middle, compare 466 to 450.
466 > 450
466 rounds to 500

d. **Count and Write the Fraction**
total parts = 8
parts not shaded = 3
fraction not shaded = $\frac{3}{8}$

Problem Solving
Refer to **Problem-Solving Strategy Discussion**, p. 404B.

LESSON 75 • Geometric Solids

Texas Essential Knowledge and Skills
(3.8) identify/classify three-dimensional geometric figures by their attributes and compare two- and three-dimensional figures by their attributes using formal vocabulary
(3.15)(A) explain observations using pictures
(3.16)(A) make generalizations from sets of examples and nonexamples

Power Up

facts   Power Up 75

jump start
- Count up by 6s from 0 to 60.
- Count up by 12s from 0 to 120.
- Write "five and two fifths" using digits. $5\frac{2}{5}$
- Use the clues below to find the secret number. Write the secret number on your worksheet.   25
  - two-digit number
  - perfect square
  - sum of the digits is 7
  - odd number

mental math
a. **Estimation:** Round 466 to the nearest hundred.   500
b. **Number Sense:** 44 + 11   55
c. **Money:** $1.60 − $0.80 $0.80
d. **Fractions:** What fraction of the rectangle is *not* shaded? $\frac{3}{8}$

problem solving
Four students can sit at a square table (one student on each side). If two tables are joined together, six students can sit. (Notice that nobody can sit at the edges where the tables touch.)

Predict how many students can sit at four tables that are joined into one big square. To check your prediction, draw a diagram of the tables and place numbers where students can sit along the edges.   8 students

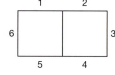

404   Saxon Math Intermediate 3

Facts   Multiply:

7 × 7 = 49	4 × 5 = 20	11 × 10 = 110	8 × 3 = 24	8 × 8 = 64	4 × 8 = 32	3 × 7 = 21	2 × 2 = 4	3 × 9 = 27
6 × 3 = 18	9 × 9 = 81	4 × 6 = 24	8 × 9 = 72	6 × 6 = 36	2 × 6 = 12	0 × 12 = 0	8 × 5 = 40	2 × 8 = 16
5 × 9 = 45	8 × 7 = 56	5 × 11 = 55	7 × 6 = 42	5 × 3 = 15	9 × 7 = 63	11 × 11 = 121	6 × 8 = 48	9 × 4 = 36
4 × 4 = 16	9 × 2 = 18	6 × 9 = 54	5 × 7 = 35	5 × 5 = 25	7 × 2 = 14	6 × 5 = 30	7 × 4 = 28	3 × 4 = 12

New Concept

Geometric shapes that take up space are sometimes called **solids.** Cubes and other rectangular prisms are examples of **geometric solids.** The chart below shows some more geometric solids.

Geometric Solids

Shape	Name
	Cube
	Rectangular prism
	Triangular prism
	Pyramid
	Cylinder
	Cone
	Sphere

Classify Are rectangles, triangles, and circles solids? Why or why not?   sample: No, they are not solids. They are flat shapes that do not take up space.

Example 1

Which of these figures does *not* represent a solid?

A   B   C   D

Figure **C**, the pentagon, is a flat shape. It is not a solid.

Lesson 75   405

New Concept

Instruction

Show examples of the following figures:

square rectangular prism
triangle pyramid
circle sphere

The figures in the chart are solids. They have length, width, and height and are called 3-dimensional figures.

Manipulative Use

Have geometric solids available for students to examine. Students should count the faces, edges, and vertices of each shape. Note that some shapes have flat surfaces while others have curved surfaces. Have students find an example of each.

Example 1

Since the problem asks which figure does not represent a solid, we can eliminate figures that are solids. Choices **A, B,** and **D** take up space, so they are solids. Choice **C** is flat and does not take up space. Choice **C** is a polygon and not a solid.

(continued)

Lesson 75   405

New Concept (Continued)

Example 2
Extend the Example
Have students label each of the remaining three shapes with the correct name.
A: rectangular prism
C: sphere
D: cone

Activity
You may want to ask students to bring some old magazines to school before performing this activity. If possible, students should have at least one magazine, scissors, and glue to perform the activity.

Lesson Practice

Guided Practice
Use these problems as guided practice to check the students' understanding of today's concept.

Problems a, d, and f Extend the Problem
Have students name the flat shapes that form the different sides of these solids.
a. triangles and rectangles
d. rectangles
f. rectangle or square and triangles

Closure The questions below help assess the concepts taught in this lesson.

"What is the difference between a polygon and a geometric solid?" A polygon is flat. A geometric solid takes up space.

"What are some things that are the shape of a sphere?" samples: a baseball, a basketball, a golf ball

"What are some things that are the shape of a rectangular prism?" samples: a box, a television, a book

Discuss real-world situations where understanding geometric solids might be helpful. Examples are given below.
- We build a pyramid out of blocks.
- We want to draw a house that looks like a real house.

The world around us is filled with objects that are shaped like solids and combinations of solids. In example 2 we show some common objects that are shaped like solids.

Example 2

Which object best represents a cylinder?

A   B

C   D

The object shaped most like a cylinder is choice **B**.

Activity
Solids
Find pictures in magazines or draw pictures of objects that are the shapes of the solids described in this lesson. Display the pictures on a classroom poster along with the names of the solid shapes.

Lesson Practice Write the geometric name for the shape of each figure below.

▶ **a.**   **b.**   **c.**

triangular prism   sphere   cylinder

▶ **d.** 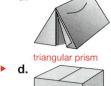 **e.**   ▶ **f.**

rectangular prism   cone   pyramid

Inclusion

Guess that Solid

Some students will have difficulty visualizing geometric solids by looking at pictures. These students need more tactile experience with the shapes.

Materials: geometric solids, paper and pencil

- Each student selects one geometric solid.
- Students trace the flat surfaces on the solid.
- Students exchange papers and try to guess which solid their partner traced.

English Learners

A **combination** is two or more things put together. Ask:

"Name a combination of numbers with a sum of 10." samples: 9 and 1; 8 and 2; 2, 3, and 5

Ask:

"If you had two pairs of shoes—one black, one white—and two pairs of colored socks—one green, one red—how many combinations of shoes and socks could you make?" black shoes, green socks; black shoes, red socks; white shoes, red socks; white shoes, green socks; four combinations

Have students discuss their favorite combination of colors.

Written Practice   Distributed and Integrated

▶ **1. (Analyze)** Bill wants to load a crate so it weighs 100 pounds. He placed the crate on a scale as shown at right. How many more pounds can he put into the crate?   **25 pounds**
(33, 36)

2. Hector bought two matinee tickets to a movie. Each ticket cost $7.75. What was the total cost of both tickets?   **$15.50**
(22)

▶ **3. (Formulate)** The train has seven boxcars. Each boxcar has eight wheels. How many wheels are there on all seven boxcars? Write a number sentence. Then write your answer in a complete sentence.   **7 × 8 = 56; sample: There are 56 wheels on all seven boxcars.**
(60, 70)

4. Vegetables were sent north from San Francisco, California, to Seattle, Washington. Find the approximate distance from San Francisco to Seattle.   **800 mi**
(Inv. 4)

San Francisco — 1 in. = 200 mi — Seattle

5. The clock shows the time the train arrived in Seattle Friday afternoon. Write the time in digital form.   **12:03 p.m.**
(38)

6. (Model) Draw pictures to show $1\frac{1}{4}$ and $1\frac{3}{8}$. Then compare the two mixed numbers using a comparison symbol.   **See student work; $1\frac{1}{4} < 1\frac{3}{8}$ or $1\frac{3}{8} > 1\frac{1}{4}$**
(46, 49)

7. Find each product.
(64)
  a. 9 × 5   **45**   **b.** 7 × 9   **63**   **c.** 2 × 9   **18**

8. Find each product.
(56)
  a. 5 × 0   **0**   **b.** 9 × 1   **9**   **c.** 10 × 8   **80**

Lesson 75   407

Written Practice

Math Conversations
Independent Practice and Discussions to Increase Understanding

▶ **Problem 1 (Analyze)**
Students may need help recognizing that the crate weighs 75 pounds. Draw a number line from 70 to 80 with three tick marks in between and an arrow pointing to the middle tick mark to represent the weight scale. Point out that the middle tick mark is halfway between 70 and 80, so the tick mark stands for 75 pounds. Students should recognize this as a "some and some more" story.

"Bill needs more to make 100 pounds."

Students may write a number sentence, 75 + m = 100, and then solve. Students should conclude that 75 pounds plus 25 pounds equals 100 pounds.

▶ **Problem 3 (Formulate)**
Sketch a picture of the problem on the board to help students visualize the multiplication.

(continued)

Written Practice (Continued)

Math Conversations
Independent Practice and Discussions to Increase Understanding

Problem 11
Have students count by 2,000s to 8,000:
2,000; 4,000; 6,000; 8,000

Students may also wish to make a table.

Tons	1	2	3	4
Pounds	2,000	4,000	6,000	8,000

Problem 18
Judging weights can be difficult for students if they do not have a firm grasp of the magnitude of various measures. Remind students that a metal fork weighs about one ounce, a soccer ball weighs about one pound, and a small car weighs about one ton.

(continued)

---

9. (Model) The drawing shows the top part of an old train rail. Use your ruler to find the distance across the top of the rail. $1\frac{3}{4}$ in.

10. Teresa bought a pencil for 22¢ and paid for it with a dollar bill. What coins should she get back in change?   sample: 3 quarters and 3 pennies

▶ **11.** How many pounds is
   a. two tons?   4,000 pounds
   b. four tons?   8,000 pounds

12. Find each product.
   a. 6×3 18
   b. 7×6 42
   c. 8×7 56

13. $472 - $396 $76

14. $354 + $263 + $50 $667

15. $5 + 5 + 5 + 5 + 5 + 5 + 5 + 5 + 5 + 5$ 50

16. Find the missing addend: $36 = 12 + a + 16$ 8

17. Wilson put 1-cubic-foot boxes into stacks like the one shown at right.
   a. How many boxes are in a stack?   27
   b. What is the volume of a stack?   27 cubic feet

▶ **18.** For **a–c**, describe the weight of each animal as about an ounce, a pound, or a ton.
   a. crow
   b. bison
   c. mouse

pound   ton   ounce

19. Name each solid in **a–c**.
(75)

a.
cylinder

b.
pyramid

c.
sphere

▶ **20. Multiple Choice** Which figure below does *not* show a line of symmetry?   C
(Inv. 7)

A   B   C   D

Real-World Connection

Jerry and Phil took a math test on Wednesday. They scored 178 points altogether. Jerry scored ten points higher than Phil. What is each student's score?   Jerry, 94; Phil, 84

Lesson 75   409

Written Practice (Continued)

Math Conversations
Independent Practice and Discussions to Increase Understanding

▶ **Problem 20   Multiple Choice**
Test Taking Strategy
Since the problem asks which figure does not show a line of symmetry, we can eliminate figures that *do* show a line of symmetry. Choices **A**, **B**, and **D** show a line that divides the figure so that one half is a mirror image of the other half. Choice **C** does not divide the figure in half.

Students might use a "guess and check" strategy to solve this problem. Have them show their work and explain how they found each student's score.

Looking Forward

Understanding solids, recognizing different solids, and drawing solids prepares students for

- **Investigation 8,** building geometric solids.
- **Lesson 87,** understanding capacity.
- **Lesson 104,** sorting geometric shapes.

Cumulative Assessments and Test-Day Activity

Assessments

Distribute **Power-Up Test 14** and **Cumulative Test 14** to each student. Have students complete the **Power-Up Test** first. Allow 10 minutes. Then have students work on the **Cumulative Test**.

Test-Day Activity

The remaining class time can be spent on **Test-Day Activity 7.** Students can begin the activity in class and complete it as homework.

Lesson 75   409

LESSON 76

Planning & Preparation

• Multiplication Facts: 11s and 12s

Objectives
- Recognize patterns in the 11 and 12 rows/columns of the multiplication table.
- Use patterns to learn the 11s and 12s multiplication facts.
- Use concrete objects to model and learn the 11s and 12s multiplication facts.
- Generate a table of related number pairs to show 11s or 12s multiplication facts.

Prerequisite Skills
- Understand the relationship between repeated addition and multiplication.
- Use "product" and "factor" to describe numbers in multiplication number sentences and on the multiplication table.
- Use a multiplication table to find products of given multiplication problems.

Materials
Instructional Masters
- Power Up 76

Manipulative Kit
- Rulers
- Tape measures
- Geosolids*

Teacher-provided materials
- $8\frac{1}{2}$-by-11-inch sheets of paper
- Grid paper*

    *optional

Texas Essential Knowledge and Skills

(3.4)(A) learn/apply multiplication facts through 12 by 12 using concrete models and objects

(3.6)(B) identify patterns in multiplication facts using concrete objects and pictorial models

(3.7)(A) generate a table of paired numbers based on a real-life situation

(3.7)(B) identify/describe patterns in a table of related number pairs based on a meaningful problem and extend the table

(3.15)(A) explain observations using objects

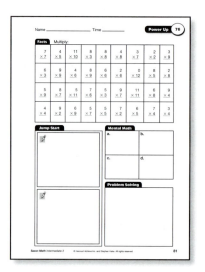

Power Up 76

Differentiated Instruction

Reaching All Special Needs Students

Special Education Students	At-Risk Students	English Learners	Advanced Learners
• Adaptations for Saxon Math	• Alternative Approach (TM) • Error Alert (TM) • Reteaching Masters	• English Learners (TM) • English Learner Handbook	• Extend the Example (TM) • Early Finishers (SE) • Online Activities

TM=Teacher's Manual
SE=Student Edition

Math Language

Maintained	English Learners
length	extend

410A *Saxon Math* Intermediate 3

Problem Solving Discussion

Problem

This graph shows the amount of time Layne spent on his homework last week.

Altogether, how many hours did Layne spend on his reading and math homework last week?

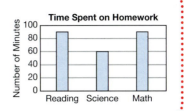

Focus Strategies

 Make or Use a Table, Chart, or Graph

 Write a Number Sentence

Understand *Understand the problem.*

"What information are we given?"

We are shown a bar graph that tells how much time Layne spent on reading, science, and math homework last week.

"What are we asked to do?"

We are asked to find how many hours Layne spent on reading and math homework.

Plan *Make a plan.*

"How can we use the information we know to solve the problem?"

We can *use the graph* to find how many minutes Layne spent on reading and math homework. We can *write a number sentence* to find the total number of minutes. We are asked for an answer in hours, so we will convert the minutes into hours.

Solve *Carry out the plan.*

"How much time did Layne spend on reading and math homework last week?"

The top of the "Reading" bar is halfway between 80 and 100, so Layne spent 90 minutes on reading homework. The top of the "Math" bar is at the same height as the "Reading" bar. So Layne spent 90 minutes on math homework.

"What number sentence can we write to find the total number of minutes?"

90 minutes + 90 minutes = 180 minutes

"How many hours is 180 minutes?"

Each hour is 60 minutes, and 60 + 60 + 60 = 180. So 180 minutes is 3 hours.

Check *Look back.*

"Did we do what we were asked to do?"

Yes, we found that Layne spent 3 hours on his reading and math homework last month.

"What problem solving strategies did we use, and how did they help us?"

We *used a graph* to find the information we needed. We *wrote number sentences* to find the number of minutes and to convert the minutes to hours.

Alternate Strategy
Use Logical Reasoning

Students might notice when reading the graph that 90 minutes equals $1\frac{1}{2}$ hours. Layne spent $1\frac{1}{2}$ hours on each of two subjects, so we can double $1\frac{1}{2}$ hours to find the total amount of time ($1\frac{1}{2} + 1\frac{1}{2} = 1 + 1 + \frac{1}{2} + \frac{1}{2} = 3$ hours).

LESSON 76

Power Up

Facts
Distribute **Power Up 76** to students. See answers below.

Jump Start
Before students begin the Mental Math exercise, do these counting exercises as a class.

Mental Math
Encourage students to share different ways to mentally compute these exercises. Strategies for exercises are listed below.

b. Think $10 + 19 + 1 + 5$
   First add $19 + 1 = 20$.
   $10 + 20 + 5 = 35$

c. Count Ahead
   $2:30 \rightarrow 3:30 \rightarrow 4:30$ p.m.
   Or Add Two Hours to 2:30 p.m.
   $2:30 + 2:00 = 4:30$ p.m.

d. Think 7×6
   1 week = 7 days
   6 weeks = $7 \times 6 = 42$ days

Problem Solving
Refer to **Problem-Solving Strategy Discussion**, p. 410B.

LESSON 76

- Multiplication Facts: 11s and 12s

Texas Essential Knowledge and Skills
(3.4)(A) learn/apply multiplication facts through 12 by 12 using concrete models and objects
(3.6)(B) identify patterns in multiplication facts using objects
(3.7)(A) generate a table of paired numbers
(3.7)(B) identify/describe patterns in a table of number pairs and extend the table
(3.15)(A) explain observations using objects

Power Up

facts Power Up 76

jump start   Count up by 11s from 0 to 110.
Count up by square numbers from 1 to 144.

 Write these numbers in order from least to greatest. 1,025; 1,250; 12,050; 12,500

1,025   12,050   12,500   1,250

Draw a square. Divide the square into 4 parts. Shade $\frac{3}{4}$ of the square. How much of the square is not shaded?
See student work; $\frac{1}{4}$

mental math
a. **Number Sense:** 18×10 180
b. **Number Sense:** $10 + 19 + 6$ 35
c. **Time:** It is afternoon. Stella's birthday party began at the time shown on the clock. It ended 2 hours later. What time did the party end? 4:30 p.m.
d. **Calendar:** How many days are in 6 weeks? 42 days

problem solving
This graph shows the amount of time Layne spent on his homework last week.

Altogether, how many hours did Layne spend on his reading and math homework last week? 3 hr

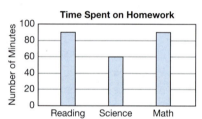

410   Saxon Math Intermediate 3

Facts Multiply:

7 × 7 = 49	4 × 5 = 20	11 × 10 = 110	8 × 3 = 24	8 × 8 = 64	4 × 8 = 32	3 × 7 = 21	2 × 2 = 4	3 × 9 = 27
6 × 3 = 18	9 × 9 = 81	4 × 6 = 24	8 × 9 = 72	6 × 6 = 36	2 × 6 = 12	0 × 12 = 0	8 × 5 = 40	2 × 8 = 16
5 × 9 = 45	8 × 7 = 56	5 × 11 = 55	7 × 6 = 42	5 × 3 = 15	9 × 7 = 63	11 × 11 = 121	6 × 8 = 48	9 × 4 = 36
4 × 4 = 16	9 × 2 = 18	6 × 9 = 54	5 × 7 = 35	5 × 5 = 25	7 × 2 = 14	6 × 5 = 30	7 × 4 = 28	3 × 4 = 12

New Concept

Since Lesson 56 we have been learning and practicing multiplication facts. In this lesson we will practice the remaining facts through 12 × 12.

	0	1	2	3	4	5	6	7	8	9	10	11	12
0	0	0	0	0	0	0	0	0	0	0	0	0	0
1	0	1	2	3	4	5	6	7	8	9	10	11	12
2	0	2	4	6	8	10	12	14	16	18	20	22	24
3	0	3	6	9	12	15	18	21	24	27	30	33	36
4	0	4	8	12	16	20	24	28	32	36	40	44	48
5	0	5	10	15	20	25	30	35	40	45	50	55	60
6	0	6	12	18	24	30	36	42	48	54	60	66	72
7	0	7	14	21	28	35	42	49	56	63	70	77	84
8	0	8	16	24	32	40	48	56	64	72	80	88	96
9	0	9	18	27	36	45	54	63	72	81	90	99	108
10	0	10	20	30	40	50	60	70	80	90	100	110	120
11	0	11	22	33	44	55	66	77	88	99	110	121	132
12	0	12	24	36	48	60	72	84	96	108	120	132	144

sample: From 1 × 11 through 9 × 11, the factor multiplying 11 appears in the tens place and ones place.

sample: 11 × 11 = 121 and 11 × 12 = 132; samples: The ones digit is a sequence of even numbers that repeats. For 1 × 12 through 4 × 12, the ones digit is double the tens digit.

On the multiplication table, look down the 11s column and notice a pattern.

Analyze Describe the pattern you see.

Conclude Which 11s facts do you need to practice so that you can remember them?

Look down the 12s column. What patterns can you find?

 Activity

Modeling 11s and 12s

We can model multiplying by 11 using $8\frac{1}{2}$-by-11-inch sheets of paper. On the floor or any other large surface, extend a tape measure to 66 inches.

Starting at the 0 mark, place a sheet of paper lengthwise along the tape measure. Make sure that the paper is lined up with the 0 tick mark and the 11 tick mark on the tape measure.

New Concept

Instruction

Review multiplication of numbers less than 11 with the students. Write the following problems on the board:

$1 \times 5 = 5$ $6 \times 5 = 30$
$2 \times 4 = 8$ $7 \times 8 = 56$
$3 \times 7 = 21$ $8 \times 5 = 40$
$4 \times 10 = 40$ $9 \times 9 = 81$
$5 \times 3 = 15$ $10 \times 6 = 60$

Have the class work through these problems. Write the answer given even if it is wrong and continue until all problems are solved. Have students use their multiplication tables to check the answers.

Math-to-Math Connection

Remind students that multiplication is often used to calculate area. If the length or width of a rectangular object is 11 or 12 units long, then the area can be represented by a multiplication fact from the 11s and 12s column in a multiplication table. For example, if a square has sides that are 12 inches long, then its area would be 144 square inches.

Write "12 in. × 12 in. = 144 square inches" on the board.

Instruction

For the *Analyze* question, tell students that the pattern does not have to extend through the whole column.

(continued)

Math Background

Rules for testing whether a number is divisible by 2 or 5 are well known. There is a lesser-known test for divisibility by 11 that might interest advanced students. Begin with a number, such as 4928. Is this number divisible by 11? The rule for answering this question quickly is to do the following: Starting with the right-most digit, alternately subtract and add the digits. In this case, we would compute 8 − 2 + 9 − 4 which equals 11. Since this answer (11) is divisible by 11, we know the original number (4928) is also divisible by 11. Similarly, since 7 − 2 + 9 − 1 + 9 = 22 and 22 is a multiple of 11, we know 91,927 is also a multiple of 11.

English Learners

To **extend** can mean to stretch or pull out. Say:

"Extend your arm. Extend your leg. Extend a pencil into the air." Students should follow the directions.

Ask:

"The teacher extended the number line. Did she make it longer or shorter?" She made it longer.

Have students practice extending tape measures to measure things around the room.

New Concept (Continued)

Activity
Instruction

Begin the activity by reviewing Lesson 60 on equal groups. Then demonstrate how to place sheets of paper end to end along a tape measure. As you add a sheet of paper to the row, name aloud the total length in inches of the row of paper: 11 inches, 22 inches, and so on.

Arrange students into groups of six. Each group will need a tape measure and a space at least 6 feet long. For the first part of the activity, each student should get one sheet of paper to place along the tape measure. For the second part of the activity, each student should get a ruler to place along the tape measure.

Example 1
Error Alert

Watch for students who try to continue the pattern of equal digits past 9 × 11 = 99. Suggest that students check their answers using a multiplication table after performing any multiplications.

Extend the Example

For advanced learners, demonstrate the method below for multiplying by 11.

To multiply 11 × 12:

- Locate the digit in the ones place of the factor being multiplied by 11. Write that digit in the ones place of the product.
- Add the digit in the ones place of the factor to the digit in the tens place. If the sum is a one-digit number, write it in the tens place of the product. If the sum is a two-digit number, write the digit in the ones place in the tens place of the product. Then add the digit in the tens place of the sum to the digit in the tens place of the factor.
- Write the digit in the tens place.

Ask students to extend the number of sheets to 14 and continue the table.
13 sheets = 143 inches
14 sheets = 154 inches

(continued)

Continue placing sheets of paper end to end along the tape measure until you reach 66 inches. Name the total length in inches as you put each sheet of paper in place.   11 in., 22 in., 33 in., 44 in., 55 in., 66 in.

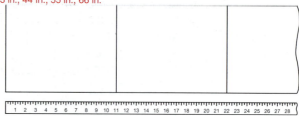

How many sheets of paper did you use?   6

Make a table showing the numbers of pages and inches for each page you placed.

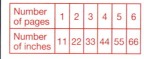

Recall from Lesson 60 that multiplying the number of groups times the number in each group gives us the total.

number of groups × number in each group = total

So 6 sheets × 11 inches for each sheet = 66 inches.

We can model multiplying by 12 using 1-foot rulers. Extend a tape measure to 72 inches. Arrange the rulers end to end along the tape measure. Name the total length in inches as you put each ruler in place.   12 in., 24 in., 36 in., 48 in., 60 in., 72 in.

How many rulers did you use?   6

6 rulers × 12 inches for each ruler = 72 inches

Formulate Write a multiplication fact to represent each ruler you placed.   1 × 12 = 12; 2 × 12 = 24; 3 × 12 = 36; 4 × 12 = 48; 5 × 12 = 60; 6 × 12 = 72

Example 1

Milton measured the total length of sheets of copy paper placed end to end. Each sheet of paper was 11 inches long. He recorded the results in a table. Make a table to show the total length of one through 12 sheets of paper.

Alternative Approach: Using Manipulatives

Have students outline the arrays that show the 12s facts on grid paper. They should write the multiplication fact in each array. Students can cut out the arrays if there is time.

We set up the table to show the number of sheets and the length in inches. We start with one sheet of paper with a length of 11 inches. We add 11 inches for each sheet of paper added to the row.

Number of Sheets	1	2	3	4	5	6	7	8	9	10	11	12
Length in Inches	11	22	33	44	55	66	77	88	99	110	121	132

Example 2

Use a multiplication table to find each product.

a. 3 × 12 b. 6 × 12 c. 12 × 12

a. 3 × 12 = **36**

b. 6 × 12 = **72**

c. 12 × 12 = **144**

Lesson Practice Find each product.

a. 11 × 11   121   b. 11 × 12   132   c. 12 × 5   60

d. 12 × 6   72   e. 7 × 12   84   f. 8 × 12   96

g. 9 × 12   108   h. 12 × 10   120   i. 12 × 12   144

▸ j. The word "dozen" means 12. John raises chickens and puts the eggs in cartons. Each carton contains a dozen eggs. Make a table to show the number of eggs in one through 12 cartons. How many eggs are in 9 cartons? How many eggs are in 12 cartons?   108; 144

Number of boxes	1	2	3	4	5	6	7	8	9	10	11	12
Number of eggs	12	24	36	48	60	72	84	96	108	120	132	144

Written Practice *Distributed and Integrated*

▸ 1. Jeff walked along the length of a rail. He took nine big steps. Each
(34, 60) big step was about 3 feet long. The rail was about how many feet long?   27 feet

2. The California Gold Rush was in 1849. The first railroad across the
(39) country was complete in 1869. How many years were there from 1849 to 1869?   20 years

Lesson 76   413

New Concept (Continued)

Lesson Practice

Guided Practice

Use these problems as guided practice to check the students' understanding of today's concept.

Problem j

Have students check their work by comparing their table to the 12s column in a multiplication table.

Closure The questions below help assess the concepts taught in this lesson.

"What is the pattern when you multiply 11 × 1 through 11 × 9?" The factor multiplying 11 appears in both the ones and tens column.

"What is 12 × 6?" 72

"11 × 12?" 132

"12 × 4?" 48

Discuss real-world situations where multiplying by 11s and 12s might be helpful. Examples are given below.

- We need to find out how many eggs there are in seven dozen.
- We have eleven markers for each student in the class.

Written Practice

Math Conversations
Independent Practice and Discussions to Increase Understanding

Problem 1

Students should recognize this as an "equal groups" story.

"There are nine groups with three feet in each group."

Encourage students to represent the story with a multiplication fact: 3 × 9 = 27.

(continued)

Lesson 76   413

Written Practice (Continued)

Math Conversations
Independent Practice and Discussions to Increase Understanding

▶ **Problem 9**
Have students count by 2,000s to 8,000:
2,000; 4,000; 6,000; 8,000

Students may also make a table.

▶ **Problem 14**
Students should recognize this as an "equal groups" story.

"There are 12 equal groups with 12 inches in each group."

Encourage students to represent the story with a multiplication fact and solve using a multiplication table.

12 feet × 12 inches per foot = 144 inches

(continued)

---

3. Fruit was shipped from Plains to Westcott. Find the approximate
(Inv. 4) distance from Plains to Wescott.   300 miles

   Plains   Westcott
   •————————————————————————————————————•
                        1 inch = 100 miles

4. Name each shape below.
(75)
   a. cone   b. cylinder   c. sphere

5. Find each product:
(64)
   a. 9 × 6   54   b. 4 × 9   36   c. 9 × 9   81

6. This picture is an old Santa Fe Railroad logo. Are the two
(Inv. 4) dark stripes inside the circle parallel or perpendicular?
   perpendicular

7. The work crew was paid $48,000 for laying a mile
(32) of track in the mountains. Use words to name
   $48,000.   forty-eight thousand dollars

8. Change this addition to multiplication and find the total.   6 × 12 = 72
(54, 76)
   12 + 12 + 12 + 12 + 12 + 12

▶ 9. How many pounds are equal to
(74)
   a. three tons?   6,000 pounds   b. four tons?   8,000 pounds

10. The bridge is three tenths of a mile wide. Write three tenths as a
(41) fraction. $\frac{3}{10}$

11. Find each product:
(70)
    a. 8 × 7   56   b. 4 × 6   24   c. 6 × 7   42

12. 85¢ + 76¢ + $10 $11.61   13. $5.00 − $3.29 $1.71
(22, 24)   (26, 28)

▶ 14. The hallway was 12 feet wide. How many inches are equal to
(60, 76) 12 feet?   144 in.

15. Find each product:
(61, 76)
    a. 11 × 11   121   b. 11 × 12   132   c. 9 × 12   108

16. Boxes are stacked on the shelf as shown at right.
(72, 73)
   a. How many boxes are in the stack?   16

   b. What is the volume of the stack?   16 cubic feet

▶ **17.** (Formulate) The rows of desks in the classroom
(57) formed an array. Write a multiplication fact for this
array, which is shown at right.   5 × 5 = 25

18. Write the two fractions represented by the shaded
(41, 47) squares. Then compare the two fractions. $\frac{3}{4}$; $\frac{6}{8}$; $\frac{3}{4}$ = $\frac{6}{8}$

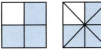

▶ **19.** (Model) On this map, how many inches is it from
(35)
   a. Granville to Lexington? $1\frac{3}{4}$ in.

   b. Lexington to Hampshire? $2\frac{1}{4}$ in.

   c. Granville to Hampshire through Lexington?   4 in.

20. If each $\frac{1}{4}$ inch on the map in problem **19** represents 10 miles, how
(Inv. 4) many miles is it from Lexington to Hampshire?   90 miles

Real-World
Connection

Mrs. Lee is sorting items by their shapes. She made a pile for items that are shaped like cylinders. She made a second pile for items that are shaped like rectangular solids. She made a third pile for items that are shaped like spheres. Make a list of items Mrs. Lee can put in each pile.   See student work.

Lesson 76   415

Written Practice (Continued)

Math Conversations
Independent Practice and Discussions to Increase Understanding

▶ **Problem 17** (Formulate)
Encourage students to think of an array as an "equal groups" story. There are 5 rows with 5 desks in each row.

▶ **Problem 19** (Model)
Students should read each question carefully to determine the correct segment to measure. Then they should measure the length of the route to the nearest quarter inch.

Errors and Misconceptions

▶ **Problem 7**
Students may forget the hyphen in "forty-eight thousand." Remind them that a hyphen is needed when two words are used to name a two-digit number, even when that number is used to label thousands.

▶ **Problem 16b**
When counting boxes or cubes to determine volume, units are easily forgotten. Remind students that volume is represented by both a number and a unit such as cubic inches or cubic feet.

Students might need to look at a set of Geosolids to make this list. Have them explain how they classified each item.

Looking Forward

Performing multiplication with a factor of 11 or 12 prepares students for

- **Lesson 77,** multiplying three numbers.
- **Lesson 78,** multiplying multiples of ten.
- **Lessons 81 and 84,** multiplying two-digit numbers.
- **Lesson 90,** more on equal groups problems.
- **Lessons 91 and 97,** multiplying three-digit numbers.

LESSON 77

> **Texas Essential Knowledge and Skills**
> (3.11)(F) use concrete models that approximate cubic units to determine the volume of a given container or other figure
> (3.15)(A) explain observations using words
> (3.16)(A) make generalizations from sets of examples and nonexamples

Planning & Preparation

• Multiplying Three Numbers

Objectives
- Find the product of three factors by multiplying two factors, then multiplying the product by the third.
- Multiply a box's length, width, and height to find its volume in cubic units.

Prerequisite Skills
- Learn the multiplication facts through 12s.
- Add three numbers by adding two numbers, then adding the third to the sum.
- Use skip counting or multiplication to find the number of small cubes in a larger rectangular solid.

Materials
Instructional Masters
- Power Up 77

Manipulative Kit
- 1-inch cubes
- Ruler

Teacher-provided materials
- Rectangular prism (such as a box or a book)*

  *optional

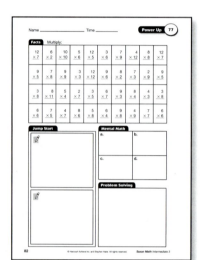

Power Up 77

Differentiated Instruction

Reaching All Special Needs Students

Special Education Students	At-Risk Students	English Learners	Advanced Learners
• Adaptations for Saxon Math	• Reteaching Masters	• English Learners (TM) • English Learner Handbook	• Extend the Example (TM) • Extend the Problem (TM) • Online Activities

TM = Teacher's Manual

Math Language

Maintained	English Learners
volume	relationship

Saxon Math Intermediate 3

Problem Solving Discussion

Problem

Here we show examples of figures with a special made-up name, Snips. We also show nonexamples (figures that are not examples) of Snips. Study the examples and nonexamples.

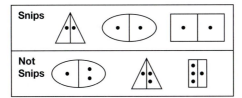

Which of these figures is a Snip? Explain your answer.

A   B   C

Focus Strategies

- Find/Extend a Pattern
- Use Logical Reasoning

Understand *Understand the problem.*

"What information are we given?"

We are shown 3 examples and 3 nonexamples of Snips.

"What are we asked to do?"

We are asked to find which of the choices is a Snip and to explain our answer.

Plan *Make a plan.*

"What problem solving strategy will we use?"

We will *look for a pattern* and *use logical reasoning*.

Solve *Carry out the plan.*

"What pattern do you find that separates the examples from the nonexamples?"

Each Snip is a figure that is divided into two halves with one dot in each half.

"Which figure—A, B, or C—is a Snip? Explain your answer."

Figure C is a Snip because it is divided into two halves and has one dot in each half.

Check *Look back.*

"Is our answer reasonable?"

Yes, we know that Figure A is not a Snip, because there are two dots in each half of the figure. Figure B is not a Snip, because one of the halves does not contain a dot. Figure C fits the pattern of the Snips that we are given.

"What problem solving strategies did we use?"

We *looked for a pattern* and *used logical reasoning* to find the figure that is a Snip.

LESSON 77

Power Up

Facts
Distribute **Power Up 77** to students. See answers below.

Jump Start
Before students begin the Mental Math exercise, do these exercises as a class.

Mental Math
Encourage students to share different ways to mentally compute these exercises. Strategies for exercises are listed below.

a. Think $10 − $7 Then Add One Quarter.
$10.00 − $6.75 = $10.00 − $7.00 + $0.25
= $3.00 + $0.25 = $3.25

d. Think "some and some more"
some + some more = total
35 minutes + x minutes = 60 minutes
x = 25 minutes

Problem Solving
Refer to **Problem-Solving Strategy Discussion**, p. 416B.

LESSON 77 • Multiplying Three Numbers

Texas Essential Knowledge and Skills
(3.11)(F) use concrete models that approximate cubic units to determine the volume of a given container or other figure
(3.15)(A) explain observations using words
(3.16)(A) make generalizations from sets of examples and nonexamples

Power Up

facts Power Up 77

jump start
Count up by 7s from 0 to 77.
Count up by 12s from 0 to 120.

There are 5,280 feet in one mile. Write this number using words.   *five thousand, two hundred eighty feet*

Write two multiplication facts using the numbers 6, 8, and 48.   *6 × 8 = 48; 8 × 6 = 48*

mental math
a. **Money:** $10.00 − $6.75   *$3.25*
b. **Number Sense:** 170 + 20   *190*
c. **Number Sense:** 20 × 10   *200*
d. **Time:** It is 7:35 a.m. How many minutes is it until 8:00 a.m.?   *25 min*

problem solving
Here we show examples of figures with a special made-up name, Snips. We also show nonexamples (figures that are not examples) of Snips. Study the examples and nonexamples.

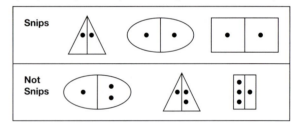

Which of these figures is a Snip? Explain your answer.

A   B   C

*Sample: Figure **C** is a Snip because it is divided into two halves and has one dot in each half.*

416   *Saxon Math* Intermediate 3

Facts   Multiply:

12 × 7 = 84	6 × 2 = 12	10 × 10 = 100	5 × 6 = 30	12 × 5 = 60	3 × 6 = 18	7 × 9 = 63	4 × 12 = 48	8 × 8 = 64	12 × 7 = 84
9 × 5 = 45	7 × 8 = 56	9 × 9 = 81	3 × 3 = 9	12 × 12 = 144	9 × 6 = 54	8 × 2 = 16	7 × 3 = 21	2 × 9 = 18	9 × 5 = 45
3 × 8 = 24	8 × 11 = 88	5 × 4 = 20	2 × 7 = 14	3 × 5 = 15	6 × 7 = 42	9 × 3 = 27	8 × 4 = 32	4 × 3 = 12	3 × 8 = 24
6 × 6 = 36	7 × 5 = 35	4 × 7 = 28	8 × 6 = 48	5 × 8 = 40	6 × 4 = 24	9 × 8 = 72	4 × 9 = 36	7 × 7 = 49	6 × 6 = 36

New Concept

In Lesson 10 we learned how to add three numbers. In this lesson we will learn how to multiply three numbers.

To find the product of $2 \times 3 \times 4$, we begin by multiplying two factors. We multiply 2×3. The product is 6.

$$2 \times 3 \times 4$$
$$\downarrow$$
$$6 \times 4$$

Next we multiply 6 by the remaining factor, 4.

$$6 \times 4 = 24$$

The product is **24**.

Example

Multiply: $4 \times 2 \times 7$

First we multiply 4×2 to get 8. Then we multiply 8×7 to find the product of all three factors: $8 \times 7 = $ **56.**

Activity

Multiplying to Find Volume

Materials: 1-inch cubes

In the activity in Lesson 73, we found the volume of a box by counting the total number of cubes the box would hold.

In this activity, we will use multiplication to find volume.

First, we will use cubes to build a rectangular prism. A rectangular prism has length, width, and height.

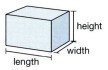

Math Background

In this lesson, students learn to multiply three factors. They are using the Associative Property of Multiplication even though they won't learn to define or name the property until later grades. According to the Associative Property of Multiplication, the grouping of factors does not affect their product. In other words, factors can be multiplied in any order. The Associative Property facilitates quicker computation because factors can be switched around. For example, if students are asked to compute $73 \times 25 \times 4$, they could first compute $73 \times 25 = 1825$ and then $1825 \times 4 = 7300$. But it would be much quicker to first compute $25 \times 4 = 100$ and then $73 \times 100 = 7300$. Students have already used the Associative Property of Addition. Subtraction and division are *non-associative* because changing the order in which the numbers occur will change the result.

New Concept

Instruction

Compare addition of three numbers with multiplication of three numbers. Write the following on the board:

$\underline{2 + 3} + 5 = 5 + 5 = 10$

$2 + 3 + 5 = \underline{3 + 5} + 2 = 8 + 2 = 10$

$2 + 3 + 5 = \underline{2 + 5} + 3 = 7 + 3 = 10$

Use these calculations to explain that the additions can be performed in any order. Students can look for combinations of addends that make the calculation easier, such as making doubles in the first problem.

Use the next set of calculations to show that the same is true for multiplication.

$\underline{2 \times 3} \times 5 = 6 \times 5 = 30$

$2 \times 3 \times 5 = \underline{3 \times 5} \times 2 = 15 \times 2 = 30$

$2 \times 3 \times 5 = \underline{2 \times 5} \times 3 = 10 \times 3 = 30$

Students should see that the multiplications can also be performed in any order. They can look for factors that will make the calculation easier for them.

Example
Extend the Example

Have students add 1 to each factor to form a new problem, then solve the problem.
$5 \times 3 \times 8 = 120$

Activity

Each student will need a total of twelve 1-inch cubes for this activity.

Demonstrate

Consider holding up a rectangular prism such as an art supply box, a tissue box, or a dictionary. Point out the object's length, width, and height. Then use a ruler to measure the object's dimensions to the nearest inch. Record the measurements on the board and write a number sentence demonstrating how to calculate the object's volume.

"Since the length, width, and height were measured in inches, what units will the volume have?" cubic inches

(continued)

New Concept (Continued)

Lesson Practice

Guided Practice

Use these problems as guided practice to check the students' understanding of today's concept.

Problem d Extend the Problem

Ask students to determine what reordering of the three factors would make the multiplication easier. $2 \times 5 \times 6$ is probably the easiest.

Problem e

Inform students that length is often (but not always) considered the longest side of an object, and width is considered the shortest.

Closure The questions below help assess the concepts taught in this lesson.

"How do we multiply three numbers together?" We multiply two of the numbers and then multiply their product by the third number.

"How can we use multiplication to find the volume of a box?" We can find the volume of a box by multiplying the length × width × height.

Discuss real-world situations where multiplying three numbers might be helpful. An example is given below.

- We need to find the volume of a rectangular suitcase.

Written Practice

Math Conversations

Independent Practice and Discussions to Increase Understanding

Problem 1 Formulate

Students should recognize this as a "some and some more" story.

"The boxcar holds some, but it can still hold some more."

Problem 3a Represent

Students should start by drawing two overlapping squares and then connect corresponding vertices with line segments. Each view (front, top, and side) should appear to be equal in size.

(continued)

418   Saxon Math Intermediate 3

Build a rectangular prism that is 3 units long, 2 units wide, and 2 units high, as shown below.

Count the number of cubes you used to build the rectangular prism. How many cubes are there in all?   12

What is the volume of the rectangular prism?   12 cubic units

What is the length, width, and height of the rectangular prism?
3; 2; 2
What is the product when you multiply $3 \times 2 \times 2$?   12

Discuss What is the relationship between the length, width, and height of a rectangular prism and its volume?
sample: Volume = length × width × height

Lesson Practice Find each product in **a–d**.

a. $2 \times 2 \times 2$ 8
b. $3 \times 3 \times 4$ 36
c. $1 \times 2 \times 11$ 22
▸ d. $6 \times 2 \times 5$ 60

▸ e. What is the length, width, and height of this figure?   3; 2; 3

f. Find the volume of the figure by multiplying its length, width, and height.   18 cubic units

Written Practice *Distributed and Integrated*

▸ 1. **Formulate** The boxcar could carry 36 tons of cargo. Fifteen
(36) tons of cargo were already in the car. How many tons of additional cargo could the boxcar carry? Write a number sentence. Then write your answer in a complete sentence. $15 + d = 36$; The boxcar could carry 21 additional tons.

2. Four round tables were in the room. There were eight chairs around
(60, 70) each table. Altogether, how many chairs were there?   32 chairs

▸ 3. a. **Represent** Draw a picture of a cube.   sample:
(71)
b. A cube has how many faces?   6 faces

c. A cube has how many vertices?   8 vertices

418   Saxon Math Intermediate 3

English Learners

A **relationship** is a connection between two things. Ask:

"What things can be connected by a relationship?" samples: number families, animals that belong to the same species or family, fruits or vegetables that come from the same group

"What is the relationship between 3, 5, and 8?" They form an addition/subtraction fact family.

Have students name other numbers with a similar relationship.

4. (Represent) Draw a rectangle that is 4 inches long and 1 inch wide.
   (34, 52) See student work.

5. a. What is the perimeter of the rectangle you drew in problem 4?
   (58, 62) 10 in.
   b. What is the area of the rectangle?   4 sq. in.

6. How many pounds are equal to
   (74)
   a. one ton?   b. two tons?   c. three tons?
   2,000 pounds   4,000 pounds   6,000 pounds

7. Draw a picture to show the fraction $\frac{3}{7}$.   See student work.
   (42)

8. A large horse weighs about half of a ton. A half ton is equal to
   (74) how many pounds?   1,000 pounds

9. The train was eight tenths of a mile long. Write eight tenths as a
   (41) fraction. $\frac{8}{10}$

10. Boxes were stacked on a pallet. Each box
    (72, 73) was one cubic foot.

    a. How many layers of boxes were there in
       the stack?   4

    b. How many boxes were in each layer?   9

    c. How many boxes were there in the
       stack?   36

    d. What is the volume of the stack of
       boxes?   36 cubic feet

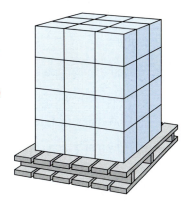

11. Draw an obtuse angle.   See student work.
    (65)

Lesson 77   419

Written Practice (Continued)

Math Conversations
Independent Practice and Discussions to Increase Understanding

Problem 4 (Represent)
Students should use a ruler. Their work should look like a rectangle and not like a parallelogram with angled sides. Students having difficulty making right angles can use the corner of a sheet of paper as an aid.

Problem 6c
Have students count by 2,000s to 6000: 2,000; 4,000; 6,000.

(continued)

Written Practice (Continued)

Math Conversations
Independent Practice and Discussions to Increase Understanding

▶ **Problem 19 Multiple Choice**
Test-Taking Strategy

Remind students that congruent shapes are the same size and same shape. Choice B can be eliminated because the triangles are not the same size. Choices C and D can be eliminated because the triangles are not the same shape. Only choice A will be left.

Errors and Misconceptions

▶ **Problems 12**

Students may try to include the word *and* or forget the units when writing the name for 107,400 pounds. Caution students against dropping the units and remind them that the word *and* is not used when naming counting numbers.

Judy saw these numbers on a boxcar. Refer to this illustration to answer problems **12** and **13**.

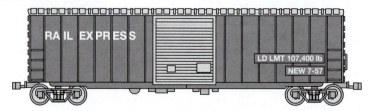

12. The "load limit" of this boxcar is 107,400 pounds. Use words to name this number.   one hundred seven thousand, four hundred pounds
  (32)

13. On the boxcar, Judy saw NEW 7-57. This shows the month and year the boxcar was built. Name the month and full year this boxcar was built.   July, 1957
  (1)

14. $648 + $286 $934
  (16)

15. $7.50 − $7.29 $0.21   **16.** 2 × 3 × 4   24
  (26)   (77)

17. a. Name the shape shown.   triangular prism
  (75)
   b. How many triangular faces does it have?   2
   c. How many rectangular faces does it have?   3
   d. How many faces does it have in all?   5

18. Find each product:
  (76)
   a. 8 × 12   96   **b.** 9 × 12   108   **c.** 11 × 12   132

▶ **19. Multiple Choice** Which pair of triangles are congruent?   A
  (68, 69)

20. a. What fraction of the face of the spinner is blue? $\frac{3}{4}$
  (41, 45)
   b. If the spinner is spun once, is the arrow more likely to stop on blue or white?   blue

420   Saxon Math Intermediate 3

Looking Forward

Performing multiplication with three factors and modeling and calculating volume as the product of three factors prepares students for

- **Lesson 78,** multiplying multiples of ten.
- **Lessons 81 and 84,** multiplying two-digit numbers.
- **Lesson 90,** solving equal groups problems.
- **Lessons 91 and 97,** multiplying three-digit numbers.
- **Lesson 93,** estimating products.

LESSON 78

🔻 **Texas Essential Knowledge and Skills**

(3.4)(B) solve/record multiplication problems (up to two digits times one digit)

(3.14)(A) identify the mathematics in everyday situations

Planning & Preparation

• Multiplying Multiples of Ten

Objectives
- Multiply multiples of ten by single-digit factors.
- Recognize shortcuts that can be taken when multiplying multiples of ten.

Prerequisite Skills
- Describe the value of a digit by its place value.
- Learn the multiplication facts through 12s.

Materials
Instructional Masters
- Power Up 78

Manipulative Kit
- Money manipulatives (bills)*
- Base ten rods

Teacher-provided materials
- Student money manipulatives (bills)*

  *optional

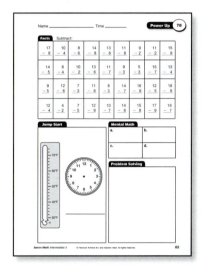

Power Up 78

Differentiated Instruction

Reaching All Special Needs Students

Special Education Students	At-Risk Students	English Learners	Advanced Learners
• Inclusion (TM) • Adaptations for Saxon Math	• Reteaching Masters	• English Learners (TM) • English Learner Handbook	• Extend the Example (TM) • Online Activities

TM=Teacher's Manual

Math Language

New	Maintained	English Learners
multiple	digit factor multiply product	shortcut

Lesson 78   421A

LESSON 78

Problem Solving Discussion

Problem

Megan inserted 4 coins into the vending machine to purchase a snack bar that cost 65¢. The machine returned 1 nickel in change. What coins did Megan use in the vending machine?

Focus Strategies

 Guess and Check

 Write a Number Sentence or Equation

Understand Understand the problem.

"What information are we given?"

1. Megan used 4 coins.
2. The snack bar cost 65¢.
3. Megan received 1 nickel in change.

"What are we asked to do?"

We are asked to find the coins that Megan used.

Plan Make a plan.

"How can we use the information we know to solve the problem?"

We can *write a number sentence* to find the total value of the 4 coins Megan used. Then we can *guess and check* to find the coins.

Solve Carry out the plan.

"Are we given the total value of the coins that Megan used?"

No, we are given the cost of the snack bar and the amount of change received.

"How can we find the total value of the 4 coins that Megan used?"

We can add the cost of the snack bar to the change received. The snack bar cost 65¢, and Megan received 1 nickel in change: 65¢ + 5¢ = 70¢.

"We now know that Megan used 4 coins worth 70¢. Did she use any pennies?"

No, Megan would have needed at least 5 pennies and other coins to make a money amount that ends in 0, so we know she did not use pennies.

"If we guess that Megan used quarters, what combinations can we find that total 70¢?"

If we guess that Megan used 2 quarters (50¢), we look for 2 more coins to raise the total to 70¢. Two dimes is 20¢, so Megan could have used 2 quarters and 2 dimes. We can use a table to show our answer.

Coin	Number
Q	2
D	2
N	0
P	0

Check Look back.

"Is our answer reasonable?"

Yes, we know that our answer is reasonable, because 2 quarters and 2 dimes have a total value of 70¢. If Megan inserted these coins and purchased a 65¢ snack bar, she would receive 1 nickel in change.

"What problem solving strategies did we use, and how did they help us?"

We *wrote a number sentence* to find the total value of the coins. We *guessed and checked* to find the coins.

Alternate Strategy
Act It Out

Students can work in pairs to *act out* this problem using their money manipulatives. Have them find combinations of four coins equal to 70¢.

421B *Saxon Math* Intermediate 3

LESSON 78

- Multiplying Multiples of Ten

Texas Essential Knowledge and Skills
(3.4)(B) solve/record multiplication problems (up to two digits times one digit)
(3.14)(A) identify the mathematics in everyday situations

Power Up

facts   Power Up 78

jump start
Count down by 3s from 45 to 0.
Count down by 6s from 60 to 0.

It is 2:20 in the afternoon. Draw hands on your clock to show the time in 2 hours. Write the time in digital form.   4:20 p.m.

The high temperature on the first of the month was 48°F. The high temperature on the last day of the month was 7 degrees warmer. Mark your thermometer to show the high temperature at the end of the month.   55°F

mental math

a. **Time:** How many years are in 8 decades?   80 years

b. **Number Sense:** $10 + 18 + 5$ 33

c. **Money:** Compare these money amounts using the symbol $<$, $>$, or $=$.

    5 quarters $>$ 12 dimes

d. **Measurement:** What is the perimeter of the parallelogram?   14 in.

3 in.
4 in.

problem solving
Megan inserted 4 coins into the vending machine to purchase a snack bar that cost 65¢. The machine returned 1 nickel in change. What coins did Megan use in the vending machine?   2 quarters, 2 dimes

LESSON 78

Power Up

Facts
Distribute **Power Up 78** to students. See answers below.

Jump Start
Before students begin the Mental Math exercise, do these exercises as a class.

Mental Math
Encourage students to share different ways to mentally compute these exercises. Strategies for exercises are listed below.

a. **Count by 10s**
10, 20, 30, 40, 50, 60, 70, 80
→ 80 years
Multiply 8×10
$8 \times 10 = 80$ years

c. **Count and compare**
Count by quarters.
25, 50, 75, 100, 125 → 125¢
Multiply 10×12.
$10 \times 12 = 120$¢
Compare 125¢ with 120¢.
125¢ > 120¢

Problem Solving
Refer to **Problem-Solving Strategy Discussion,** p. 421B.

Facts   Subtract:

17 − 8 = 9	10 − 4 = 6	8 − 6 = 2	14 − 8 = 6	13 − 8 = 5	11 − 8 = 3	9 − 2 = 7	11 − 2 = 9	15 − 9 = 6
14 − 5 = 9	6 − 4 = 2	10 − 2 = 8	13 − 6 = 7	11 − 7 = 4	9 − 3 = 6	5 − 3 = 2	15 − 7 = 8	13 − 4 = 9
9 − 5 = 4	12 − 6 = 6	7 − 3 = 4	11 − 6 = 5	8 − 3 = 5	14 − 7 = 7	16 − 9 = 7	12 − 5 = 7	18 − 9 = 9
12 − 4 = 8	4 − 2 = 2	7 − 5 = 2	12 − 9 = 3	10 − 7 = 3	14 − 6 = 8	15 − 8 = 7	17 − 9 = 8	16 − 7 = 9

New Concept

The **multiples of ten** are the numbers that we say when we count by tens.

10, 20, 30, 40, 50, …

Each multiple of ten can be written as a number times 10.

20 = 2 × 10
30 = 3 × 10
40 = 4 × 10

One way to multiply multiples of ten is to multiply three factors. Below we multiply 4 × 30 by writing 30 as 3 × 10.

4 × 30
∧
4 × 3 × 10

Next we multiply 4 × 3, which is 12. Then we multiply 12 × 10.

4 × 3 × 10
∨
12 × 10 = 120

A shortcut is to multiply the digit in the tens place and then attach a zero to the product. For 4 × 30, we multiply 4 × 3 = 12. Then we add a zero to the 12 to make 120.

④ × ③0 = 120

Example 1

Diana has seven $20 bills. How much money is that?

Instead of adding seven 20s, we can multiply $20 by 7. We know that 7 × 2 is 14, so 7 × $20 is **$140**.

Example 2

There are 40 cubes in each layer of this figure. How many cubes are there in all 4 layers?

Instead of adding four 40s, we multiply 40 by 4. Since 4 × 4 is 16, we know that 4 × 40 is 160. The figure contains **160 cubes**.

New Concept

Instruction

Review multiplication by 10s with students. Ask for a volunteer to count by 10s from zero to 120 as you write the numbers on the board. Follow this by writing the multiplication facts from a multiplication table in a vertical list on the board as well.

"What pattern do we notice about the digits in the ones place?" They are all zero.

"What pattern do we notice about the digits in the tens place?" They are the same as the factors multiplied by 10.

Example 1
Alternate Method: Manipulative Use

Students can model this problem using their money manipulatives. Students count out 7 sets of two $10 bills. Next, students should combine all of the $10 bills and then count the total. Remind students to trade ten $10 bills for one $100 bill.

Example 2
Extend the Example

Have students calculate the total number of cubes in 10 layers. **400 cubes**

(continued)

Math Background

Numbers that are multiples of 10 are found often in the real world because our number system is based on the number 10. Most of the U.S. bill denominations are in multiples of ten; examples include $10 bills, $20 bills, $50 bills, and $100 bills. The metric system of measurement is also based on the number 10. Fluency in multiplying numbers by powers of 10 will make conversions from one metric unit to another much easier for students.

English Learners

A **shortcut** is a shorter, or easier, way to get somewhere or do something. Ask:

"You need to find out how many eggs are in three dozen. What is a math shortcut to find the answer?" Multiply 12 × 3 to get 36 eggs.

Draw a map on the board with the main streets around school. Ask:

"Who knows a shortcut to school?" Have students show various shortcuts.

Have students discuss ways they use shortcuts to make their lives easier.

Lesson Practice

a. How much money is eight $20 bills? $160

b. If 5 classrooms each have 30 students, then how many students are in all 5 classrooms? 150

Find each product for problems **c–f**.

c. 4 × 60   240
d. 7 × 30   210
e. 8 × 40   320
f. 3 × 80   240

Written Practice *Distributed and Integrated*

1. **Formulate** Clovis bought eight new railroad cars for his model train. Each car cost seven dollars. How much did Clovis pay for all eight cars? Write a number sentence.   8 × 7 = $56
(60, 70)

2. One hundred ninety people crowded into the model train show. The room could hold 240 people. How many more people could be in the room?   50
(36)

3. Lilly bought a ticket for $14.75. She paid for the ticket with two $10 bills. How much money should Lilly get back? $5.25
(26, 28)

4. What solid is the shape of a can of soup?   cylinder
(75)

5. a. **Represent** Draw a picture of a rectangular prism.
(71)

5. a. sample:

b. A rectangular prism has how many vertices?   8 vertices

c. A rectangular prism has how many edges?   12 edges

6. Judith made the rectangle at right with square tiles. The sides of each tile are one inch long.
(52, 62)

a. How long is the rectangle?   6 inches

b. How wide is the rectangle?   4 inches

c. How many tiles did she use?   24 tiles

d. What is the area of the rectangle?   24 sq. in.

7. What is the perimeter of the rectangle in problem **6**?   20 in.
(58)

Lesson 78   423

Multiplying 10s

Some students may have difficulty multiplying by multiples of 10. Use this hands-on activity with base ten blocks as a concrete representation of this concept.

Materials: twenty 10-sticks per student or pair of students

- Write 3 × 40 on the board.
- Tell students to make 1 group of 40 using 10-sticks.

"How many tens are equal to 40?" 4

- Students make 3 groups of 40 using 10-sticks.

"How many tens are there altogether?" 12

"What is the value of 12 tens?"
Count by 10 to 120 or regroup to find 1 hundred and 2 tens.

- Write the answer to the number sentence on the board: 3 × 40 = 120.

New Concept (Continued)

Lesson Practice

Guided Practice

Use these problems as guided practice to check the students' understanding of today's concept.

Problem a
Some students may need to use money manipulatives to solve this problem. Remind them to regroup ten $10 bills as one $100 bill.

Problem b
Point out to students that this is an "equal groups" story. Have students write a number sentence, 5 × 30 = t, and solve.

Closure — The questions below help assess the concepts taught in this lesson.

"What are the first ten multiples of ten?"
10, 20, 30, 40, 50, 60, 70, 80, 90, 100

"What is an easier way to multiply 6 × 50?"
Multiply 6 × 5 = 30. Then add a zero to the 30 to make 300.

Discuss real-world situations where multiplying tens might be helpful. Examples are given below.

- We have to buy 5 pencils for 30 students and need to know how many to buy.
- A man earns $20 an hour at his job and works 8 hours a day.

Written Practice

Math Conversations
Independent Practice and Discussions to Increase Understanding

Problem 1 **Formulate**
Help students recognize this as an "equal groups" story.

Problem 5a **Represent**
Students can draw a rectangular prism several ways. They can start with two overlapping rectangles, two non-overlapping rectangles, or two non-overlapping squares. Students should connect the corresponding vertices of these shapes with segments of equal length.

(continued)

Lesson 78   423

Written Practice (Continued)

Math Conversations
Independent Practice and Discussions to Increase Understanding

Problem 12
Manipulative Use

Suggest that students solve these problems using their money manipulatives. For each multiplication, students should count out equal groups of $10 bills and combine them, regroup to a $100 bill when needed, and count out the total.

Problem 17   Multiple Choice
Test-Taking Strategy

Students should start by eliminating answers that are not reasonable. Choice **C** can be eliminated because 8 tons is not a reasonable weight for a cat. Choice **A** can be eliminated because a full-grown cat will weigh more than 8 metal spoons, or 8 ounces. That leaves choice **B**, or 8 pounds.

Errors and Misconceptions

Problems 5b and 5c
When naming parts of a cube or rectangular solid, students often confuse edges with faces and vertices with edges. Have students review the parts of a rectangular prism in Lesson 75.

Problem 6d
When calculating area, some students forget to record the units. Remind students that area is described with both a number and a unit, such as square inches or square feet.

---

8. Find each product:
   (59, 64)
   a. 7 × 0   0
   b. 7 × 5   35
   c. 7 × 9   63

9. Ten miles is 52,800 feet. Use words to write 52,800.
   (32) fifty-two thousand, eight hundred

10. Find each product:
    (76)
    a. 5 × 12   60
    b. 6 × 12   72
    c. 7 × 12   84

11. Find each product:
    (64, 70)
    a. 6 × 7   42
    b. 6 × 8   48
    c. 6 × 9   54

▶ 12. Find each product:
    (78)
    a. 3 × 20   60
    b. 6 × 30   180
    c. 4 × 40   160

13. $676 + $234 $910
    (16)

14. $1.00 − 73¢   27¢
    (26, 28)

15. 3 × 3 × 3   27
    (77)

16. 7 × 50   350
    (78)

▶ 17. **Multiple Choice** A full-grown cat could weigh   **B**
    (74)
    A 8 ounces.
    B 8 pounds.
    C 8 tons.

18. a. **Connect** How many ounces equal a pound?   16 ounces
    (41, 74)
    b. An ounce is what fraction of a pound? $\frac{1}{16}$

This map shows where Leslie and Monica live. Use this map to answer problems **19** and **20**.

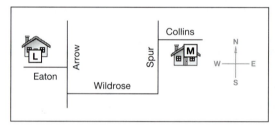

19. Name two roads perpendicular to Wildrose.   Arrow and Spur
    (Inv. 4)

20. Write directions that describe how to get to Monica's home from
    (31) Leslie's home.   sample: Go east on Eaton to Arrow, south on Arrow to Wildrose, east on Wildrose to Spur, north on Spur to Collins, and east on Collins to Monica's home.

424   Saxon Math Intermediate 3

Looking Forward

Performing multiplication with multiples of 10 and solving equal groups problems that involve multiples of 10 prepares students for

- **Lessons 81 and 84,** multiplying two-digit numbers.
- **Lesson 90,** solving equal groups problems.
- **Lessons 91 and 97,** multiplying three-digit numbers.
- **Lesson 100,** multiplying dollars and cents.

LESSON 79

Planning & Preparation

- **Length: Centimeters, Meters, and Kilometers**

Objectives
- Learn the relationships between centimeters, meters, and kilometers.
- Identify real-world benchmarks for each unit of length.
- Use a metric ruler or meterstick to measure objects in centimeters or meters.

Prerequisite Skills
- Understand the relationships between inches, feet, and yards in the U.S. Customary System.
- Select the appropriate unit to measure a given object.
- Use a ruler to measure length to the nearest half- and quarter-inch.

Materials

Instructional Masters
- Power Up 79

Manipulative Kit
- Rulers
- Meterstick

Teacher-provided materials
- Rectangles of varying sizes*

optional

Texas Essential Knowledge and Skills
- (3.11)(A) use linear measurement tools to estimate/measure lengths using standard units
- (3.11)(B) use standard units to find the perimeter of a shape
- (3.14)(C) select/develop an appropriate problem-solving plan/strategy, including working backwards to solve a problem
- (3.15)(A) record observations using numbers

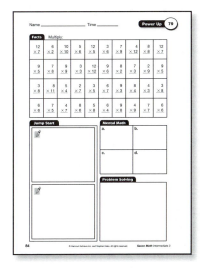

Power Up 79

Differentiated Instruction

Reaching All Special Needs Students

Special Education Students	At-Risk Students	English Learners	Advanced Learners
• Inclusion (TM) • Adaptations for Saxon Math	• Error Alert (TM) • Reteaching Masters	• English Learner Handbook	• Extend the Activity (TM) • Extend the Example (TM) • Extend the Problem (TM) • Early Finishers (SE) • Online Activities

TM = Teacher's Manual
SE = Student Edition

Math Language

New	Maintained
centimeter	area
kilometer	length
meter	perimeter
metric system	width
square centimeter	yard

Lesson 79   425A

LESSON 79

Problem Solving Discussion

Problem

Alex is half as old as Beyonce. Beyonce is 2 years older than Chandra. Chandra is 10 years old. How old is Alex?

Focus Strategies

 Work Backwards

 Write a Number Sentence

Understand Understand the problem.

"What information are we given?"

1. Alex is half as old as Beyonce.
2. Beyonce is 2 years older than Chandra.
3. Chandra is 10 years old.

"What are we asked to do?"

We are asked to find Alex's age.

Plan Make a plan.

"How can we use the information we know to solve the problem?"

We know how old Chandra is. We know that Beyonce is 2 years older, so we can *write a number sentence* and *work backwards* to find Beyonce's age, then Alex's age.

Solve Carry out the plan.

"How old is Beyonce?"

Beyonce is 2 years older than Chandra, so Beyonce is 12 years old.

"How can we use Beyonce's age to find Alex's age?"

We are told that Alex is half as old as Beyonce. Half of 12 is 6, so Alex is 6 years old.

Check Look back.

"Did we complete the task?"

Yes, we found Alex's age (6 years old) using the clues.

"Is our answer reasonable?"

Yes, Chandra is 10 years old, and Beyonce is 2 years older, which makes her age 12. Half of 12 is 6 years old, which is the age we found for Alex.

"What problem solving strategies did we use, and how did they help us?"

We *wrote a number sentence* to find Beyonce's age. We *worked backwards* to solve the problem: we started with Chandra's age, then found Beyonce's age, and then used that information to find Alex's age.

Alternate Strategy

Draw a Picture or Diagram

Students can also *draw a picture* to solve this problem. First have them draw 3 circles to represent Alex, Beyonce, and Chandra with 10 tally marks by the circle representing Chandra. Then use the information in the problem and the picture to find Alex's age.

LESSON 79

• **Length: Centimeters, Meters, and Kilometers**

Texas Essential Knowledge and Skills
- (3.11)(A) use linear measurement tools to estimate/measure lengths using standard units
- (3.11)(B) use standard units to find the perimeter of a shape
- (3.14)(C) select/develop an appropriate problem-solving plan/strategy, including working backwards to solve a problem
- (3.15)(A) record observations using numbers

Power Up

facts Power Up 79

jump start
Count down by 4s from 40 to 0.
Count down by 8s from 80 to 0.

Write the largest 4-digit number that uses each of the digits 3, 2, 6, and 4. What is the value of the digit in the hundreds place? 6,432; 400

Draw an isosceles triangle in the workspace on your worksheet. Then draw a line to show the triangle's line of symmetry. See student work.

mental math

a. **Measurement:** Which of these units would you use to measure a sheet of paper? inches
  feet   pounds   miles   inches

b. **Number Sense:** 26×10 260

c. **Number Sense:** 12×100 1,200

d. **Algebra:** The table below shows costs for a long-distance phone call. Find the missing money amount in the table. 32¢

Minutes	1	2	3	4	5
Cost	8¢	16¢	24¢	___	40¢

problem solving
Alex is half as old as Beyonce. Beyonce is 2 years older than Chandra. Chandra is 10 years old. How old is Alex?
6 years old

Lesson 79   425

LESSON 79

Power Up

Facts
Distribute **Power Up 79** to students. See answers below.

Jump Start
Before students begin the Mental Math exercise, do these exercises as a class.

Mental Math
Encourage students to share different ways to mentally compute these exercises. Strategies for exercises are listed below.

c. **Add Two Zeros**
 Add two zeros to the number multiplied by 100.
 $12 \times 100 = 1,200$

d. **Look for a Pattern**
 Each minute costs 8¢.
 $8 \times 4 = 32$
 The cost was 32¢.

Problem Solving
Refer to **Problem-Solving Strategy Discussion,** p. 425B.

Facts Multiply:

12×7 = 84	6×2 = 12	10×10 = 100	5×6 = 30	12×5 = 60	3×6 = 18	7×9 = 63	4×12 = 48	8×8 = 64	12×7 = 84
9×5 = 45	7×8 = 56	9×9 = 81	3×3 = 9	12×12 = 144	9×6 = 54	8×2 = 16	7×3 = 21	2×9 = 18	9×5 = 45
3×8 = 24	8×11 = 88	5×4 = 20	2×7 = 14	3×5 = 15	6×7 = 42	9×3 = 27	8×4 = 32	4×3 = 12	3×8 = 24
6×6 = 36	7×5 = 35	4×7 = 28	8×6 = 48	5×8 = 40	6×4 = 24	9×8 = 72	4×9 = 36	7×7 = 49	6×6 = 36

Lesson 79   425

New Concept

Instruction
To help students develop the relationship between customary units of length and metric units of length, direct them to look at their rulers and compare an inch and a centimeter.

"Which is longer?" an inch

Show them a meterstick. Point out the length of a yard and the length of a meter.

"Which is longer?" a meter

Explain that metric units of length are used the same way as inches, feet, yards, and miles. When we measure something in inches, we find how many inches long it is. To measure the same object using metric units, we would find how many centimeters long the object is.

Activity
Make sure each student has a ruler that measures centimeters. Students will start this activity by measuring items at their desks to answer the first four questions. Then students should be arranged in small groups and a meterstick should be given to each group.

Problems 1–4
Extend the Activity

Have students repeat questions **1–4** using inches as the unit of measure instead of centimeters.
1. $8\frac{1}{2}$ inches
2. 11 inches
3. answers vary
4. about 4 inches

Problems 5–6
Extend the Activity

Have students repeat questions **5–6** using a yardstick to measure the lengths instead of a meterstick.
5. about 1 yard
6. a little more than 2 yards

(continued)

426 **Saxon Math** Intermediate 3

New Concept

We have measured lengths in inches, feet, yards, and miles. These units are called customary units and are used mostly in the United States.

Nearly every other country uses the **metric system**. Metric units of length include **centimeters, meters,** and **kilometers.**

A ruler that is 12 inches long is about 30 centimeters long. A meter is 100 centimeters and is a little longer than a yard. A kilometer is 1000 meters and is a little more than half of a mile.

Metric Units of Length

Unit	Abbreviation	Reference
centimeter	cm	width of a finger
meter	m	one BIG step
kilometer	km	$\frac{6}{10}$ mile

1 meter = 100 centimeters
1 kilometer = 1000 meters

Activity
Metric Units of Length

Most rulers have an inch scale on one side and a centimeter scale on the other side. Find the centimeter scale on your ruler. Use it to measure some objects at your desk in centimeters.

1. How wide is your paper?   about 22 cm
2. How long is your paper?   about 28 cm
3. How long is your pencil?   See student work.
4. How long is this segment?   10 cm
   _____

Work in small groups to measure with a meterstick.

5. About how many meters wide is the classroom door?
   about 1 m
6. About how many meters high is the classroom door?
   about 2 m

426   **Saxon Math** Intermediate 3

Math Background

Many historical figures endorsed a change from the U.S. Customary System of measurement to a system based on powers of 10. In 1790, Thomas Jefferson proposed such a system to the House of Representatives in his role as the Secretary of State of the United States. At about the same time, Louis XVI authorized studies of a similar system of measurement in France that was actually adopted. The French system evolved into the metric system, as we know it today. While the Customary System is still widely used in the United States, most other countries use the metric system. Scientists use the metric system as their standard of measurement for research and reporting. The metric system is based on the base-ten number system. Metric measurements can be converted from one unit to another by multiplying or dividing by powers of 10. For example, 100 centimeters equals one meter, so two meters equals 200 centimeters.

7. About how many meters long is the chalkboard or bulletin board in your classroom? See student work.

8. About how many meters long (or wide) is your classroom? See student work.

Example 1

Multiple Choice Which length could be the length of a pencil?

A 15 centimeters   B 15 meters
C 15 kilometers   D 15 feet

A 15 centimeters

Example 2

The train engine pulled a line of 50 boxcars that was about a kilometer long. How many meters is a kilometer?

A kilometer is **1000 meters**.

Example 3

A 12-inch ruler is about 30 centimeters. If 3 rulers are laid end to end, about how many centimeters long would the 3 rulers be?

Since each ruler is about 30 cm long, 3 rulers would be 3 × 30 cm, which is about 90 cm long.

$$3 \times 30 \text{ cm} = 90 \text{ cm}$$

Analyze Is the length of 3 rulers more or less than a meter?
less than a meter

Example 4

Find the length and width of this rectangle in centimeters. Then find the perimeter of this rectangle in centimeters and find its area in square centimeters.

Lesson 79   427

New Concept (Continued)

▶ **Example 1 Multiple Choice**
Test-Taking Strategy

Students should mentally picture items they know for each answer choice and mark out ones that are not reasonable.

A: 15 centimeters is about the length of a spoon.
B: 15 meters is the height of a tree.
C: 15 kilometers is a long distance run.
D: 15 feet is about the length of a pickup truck.

▶ **Example 2**
Extend the Example

"About how many meters long would a line of 150 boxcars measure?"
about 3,000 meters

▶ **Example 3**
Extend the Example

"About how many centimeters long would ten rulers be?" 300 centimeters

Ask advanced learners,

"About how many meters long would ten rulers be?" 3 meters

For the *Analyze* question, explain that three rulers are equivalent to 12 in. + 12 in. + 12 in. = 36 in., which is the same as one yard. Since one yard is a little less than one meter, students can conclude that the length of three rulers is a little less than the length of a meter.

▶ **Example 4**
Instruction

Instruct students to read directions carefully in measurement activities. Look for phrases like "find the length in centimeters" or "find the width in inches" to determine which unit of measurement to use.

Students may need to review the concept of perimeter and area before reading this example.

(continued)

Lesson 79   427

New Concept (Continued)

Lesson Practice

Guided Practice

Use these problems as guided practice to check the students' understanding of today's concept.

Students need their rulers to answer the questions. Make sure students' rulers measure both inches and centimeters.

Problem c
Extend the Problem
"How many meters is 200 cm?" 2 meters

Problem d
Tell students that *kilo* means thousand.

Closure The questions below help assess the concepts taught in this lesson.

"What are some units of length in the metric system?" centimeter, meter, and kilometer

"Which unit is about half a mile?" a kilometer

"Which unit is about half an inch?" a centimeter

"If you were going to measure the width of our classroom, which unit of measurement would you use?" meters

Discuss real-world situations where using the metric system might be helpful. Examples are given below.

- In our science book, the measurements are all given in centimeters and meters.
- The doctor says a child is 94 centimeters tall.

Written Practice

Math Conversations
Independent Practice and Discussions to Increase Understanding

Problem 2 Analyze
Students should remember that a year has 365 days. They should subtract the days that have passed from the total number of days in the year to find the days left. Some students may see this as a "some and some more" story and write an addition number sentence, $90 + d = 365$, to solve.

(continued)

428   Saxon Math Intermediate 3

Using a centimeter ruler, we find the length and width.

Length **4 cm**
Width **3 cm**

We use these measures to find the perimeter and area.

Perimeter   4 cm + 3 cm + 4 cm + 3 cm = **14 cm**
Area   4 cm × 3 cm = **12 square cm**

Lesson Practice

a. Draw a segment 2 inches long. Then measure the segment in centimeters. Two inches equals about how many centimeters?   5 cm

b. How many centimeters long is the cover of your math book?   28 cm

c. A meter is how many centimeters?   100 cm

d. It takes about 10 minutes to walk a kilometer. How many meters is a kilometer?   1000 m

Refer to the rectangle to answer problems **e–h**.

e. How long is the rectangle in centimeters?   4 cm

f. How wide is the rectangle in centimeters?   2 cm

g. How many centimeters is the perimeter of the rectangle?   12 cm

h. How many square centimeters is the area of the rectangle?   8 square cm

Written Practice — Distributed and Integrated

1. The passenger car had nine rows of seats. Four passengers could sit in each row. How many passengers could sit in the passenger car?   36 passengers
   (60)

2. **Analyze** In a common year, March 31 is the ninetieth day of the year. How many days are in the last nine months of the year? (*Hint:* Think of how many days are in a whole year.)   275 days
   (1, 36)

428   Saxon Math Intermediate 3

3. The westbound crew laid four miles of track each day for six days. How many miles of track did the crew lay in six days?   24 miles of track
   (60)

4. a. (Represent) Draw a picture of a cube.   a. sample:
   (71)
   b. A cube has how many faces?   6 faces
   c. A cube has how many edges?   12 edges
   d. A cube has how many vertices?   8 vertices

5. Natalie arranged some wooden cubes to make the shape at right.
   (72, 73)
   a. How many cubes did she use?   12 cubes
   b. If each cube is one cubic inch, what is the volume of the shape?   12 cubic inches

6. (Represent) Use a centimeter ruler to draw a rectangle that is 5 cm long and 2 cm wide.   See student work.
   (52, 79)

7. a. What is the perimeter of the rectangle you drew in problem 6?   14 cm
   (58, 62)
   b. What is the area of the rectangle?   10 sq cm

8. a. (Model) How long, in centimeters, is each side of this triangle?   2 cm
   (69, 79)
   b. What is the name for a triangle with three equal sides?   equilateral

9. a. (Represent) Draw a triangle congruent to the triangle in problem 8.   See student work; All three sides of the triangle should measure 2 cm.
   (69, 79)
   b. What is the perimeter of the triangle you drew?   6 cm

10. Find each product.
    (64)
    a. 9 × 7   63   b. 6 × 9   54   c. 4 × 9   36

11. Find each product.
    (78)
    a. 2 × 40   80   b. 3 × 70   210   c. 4 × 50   200

12. Change this addition into multiplication and find the total.
    (54)   5 × 7 days = 35 days
    7 days + 7 days + 7 days + 7 days + 7 days

Lesson 79   429

Written Practice (Continued)

Math Conversations
Independent Practice and Discussions to Increase Understanding

▶ **Problem 4** (Represent)
Students should draw two overlapping squares and then connect the corresponding vertices with segments. The perspective of the cube should give the impression that all faces are the same size.

▶ **Problem 5**
Extend the Problem
"If Natalie uses twice as many cubes to make a second shape, what will be the volume of her new shape?"
24 cubic inches

"What is the name for Natalie's shape?"
rectangular prism or rectangular solid

▶ **Problem 6** (Represent)
Students should draw 2 sets of parallel line segments that meet at right angles. Students may use the corner of the ruler or a sheet of paper to draw straight right angles.

▶ **Problem 8** (Model)
Students may need to review types of triangles from Lesson 69.

▶ **Problem 9** (Represent)
Remind students that congruent figures are the same size and same shape.

Remind students that perimeter refers to the distance around the outside edge of a shape and that it is represented by a number and a unit of length.

(continued)

Inclusion

Measure Around

Some students may need additional hands-on experience with measurement. Provide opportunities to measure and reinforce the concept of perimeter with this activity.

Materials: ruler; rectangles of varying sizes

- Students measure each side of the rectangle in centimeters and record the measurement.
- Combine the lengths of the sides and record the perimeter.
- Continue as time allows.

Lesson 79   429

Written Practice (Continued)

Math Conversations
Independent Practice and Discussions to Increase Understanding

Problem 13
Have students count by 2,000s to 4,000: 2,000, 4,000. Two groups of 2,000 are equal to 4,000, so there are 2 tons in 4,000.

Problem 19
Extend the Problem

"How many one-inch cubes can you fit inside this prism?" 96 one-inch cubes

"What is the volume of this solid?" 96 cubic inches

Errors and Misconceptions

Problem 4
Students often confuse faces with edges and edges with vertices. Have students review the parts of a rectangular prism in Lesson 71.

Problems 5b, 7b, and 20
Units are often forgotten when calculating areas or volumes. Remind students that area and volume are represented by both a number and a unit.

Suggest that students draw a picture or table to solve this problem. Have them show what they drew and explain how they used it to find the answer.

---

13. A giraffe can weigh 4,000 pounds. How many tons is 4,000 pounds?   2 tons

14. Find each product.
    a. 8 × 4   32
    b. 8 × 6   48
    c. 8 × 7   56

15. $7.60 + $8.70 + $3.70 $20.00

16. $7.50 − $3.75 $3.75

17. Find the next four numbers in this sequence: $2\frac{1}{4}, 2\frac{1}{2}, 2\frac{3}{4}, 3$

    $1, 1\frac{1}{4}, 1\frac{1}{2}, 1\frac{3}{4}, 2, \_\_\_, \_\_\_, \_\_\_, \_\_\_, \ldots$

18. The thermometers show the boiling points of water on the Celsius and Fahrenheit scales. Write the temperatures.   100°C and 212°F.

19. A drawing of a rectangular prism is shown below.

    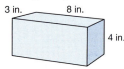

    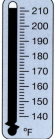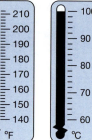

    a. What is its length?   8 in.
    b. What is its width?   3 in.
    c. What is its height?   4 in.

20. What is the area of the top of the rectangular prism in problem **19**?   24 sq in.

 Real-World Connection   Shantell is making bead necklaces for the craft fair. She can make 10 necklaces a day. She has to make 80 total for the craft fair. How many weeks will it take her to make all 80 necklaces if she only works 3 days a week?   3 weeks

---

Looking Forward

Measuring lengths in metric units, converting between metric units of length, and calculating the perimeter and area of shapes with metric units prepares students for

- **Lesson 87,** understanding capacity.
- **Lessons 106 and 108,** estimating area.

LESSON 80

> **Texas Essential Knowledge and Skills**
>
> **(3.11)(D)** use concrete models that approximate standard units to measure weight/mass
>
> **(3.14)(A)** recognize the mathematics in everyday situations
>
> **(3.15)(A)** explain observations using objects

Planning & Preparation

• Mass: Grams and Kilograms

Objectives
- Learn the relationship between grams and kilograms.
- Identify real-world benchmarks for each unit of mass.
- Use real-world benchmarks for mass to estimate the mass of other objects.

Prerequisite Skills
- Learn the relationships between ounces, pounds, and tons.
- Identify real-world benchmarks for each unit of weight.
- Use a scale to weigh objects in ounces and pounds.
- Learn the relationships between units of length in the metric system.

Materials
Instructional Masters
- Power Up 80

Manipulative Kit
- Scale*
- Rulers

Teacher-provided materials
- Large paper clips*

  optional

Power Up 80

Reaching All Special Needs Students

Special Education Students	At-Risk Students	English Learners	Advanced Learners
• Inclusion (TM) • Adaptations for Saxon Math	• Reteaching Masters	• English Learner Handbook	• Extend the Example (TM) • Extend the Problem (TM) • Online Activities

TM = Teacher's Manual

Math Language

New	Maintained
mass	metric system unit U.S. Customary System

Lesson 80   431A

LESSON 80

Problem Solving Discussion

Problem

Scott's basketball team will use two-digit numbers on their uniforms. Each player can choose a 1 or a 2 for the first digit. The second digit must be a 0, 1, or 2. What are the possible uniform numbers?

Focus Strategy **Make an Organized List**

Understand Understand the problem.

"What information are we given?"

1. Each player's uniform will have a two-digit number.
2. The first digit can be a 1 or a 2.
3. The second digit can be a 0, 1, or 2.

"What are we asked to do?"

We are asked to find the possible uniform numbers.

Plan Make a plan.

"What problem solving strategy can we use?"

We can *make an organized list* of the possible uniform numbers.

"How can we organize our list?"

To help us be sure that we list all the possibilities, we can first list all the two-digit combinations that begin with 1 and then list all the combinations that begin with 2.

Solve Carry out the plan.

"What are the possible combinations that begin with a 1?"

The second digit can be either 0, 1, or 2, so the possible combinations are: 10, 11, and 12.

"What are the possible combinations that begin with a 2?"

The second digit can be either 0, 1, or 2, so the possible combinations are 20, 21, and 22.

"List all the possible uniform numbers."

10	20
11	21
12	22

Check Look back.

"Did we complete the task?"

Yes, we found all the uniform numbers that the basketball team could use (10, 11, 12, 20, 21, and 22).

"Are our answers reasonable?"

Yes, our answers are reasonable because each combination has a first digit of 1 or 2 and a second digit of 0, 1, or 2.

"What problem solving strategy did we use, and how did it help us?"

We *made an organized list.* By concentrating first on all the combinations that begin with 1 and then concentrating on all the combinations that begin with 2, we made sure not to overlook any possible combinations.

LESSON 80

• **Mass: Grams and Kilograms**

Texas Essential Knowledge and Skills
(3.11)(D) use concrete models that approximate standard units to measure weight/mass
(3.14)(A) recognize the mathematics in everyday situations
(3.15)(A) explain observations using objects

Power Up

facts   Power Up 80

jump start
- Count up by 11s from 0 to 110.
- Count up by square numbers from 1 to 144.
- Use these clues to find the secret number. Write the secret number on your worksheet.   27
  - two-digit number
  - between 20 and 40
  - product of the digits is 14
- Draw a 10-centimeter segment on your worksheet. See student work.

mental math
a. **Calendar:** How many months are in 3 years?   36 months
b. **Number Sense:** 23 + 40   63
c. **Time:** 50 minutes − 15 minutes   35 min
d. **Number Line:** What year is shown by point G?   1935

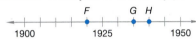

problem solving
Scott's basketball team will use two-digit numbers on their uniforms. Each player can choose a 1 or a 2 for the first digit. The second digit must be a 0, 1, or 2. What are the possible uniform numbers?   10, 11, 12, 20, 21, 22

New Concept

In the U.S. Customary System, ounces, pounds, and tons are units of weight. In the metric system, grams and kilograms are units of **mass**.

LESSON 80

Power Up

Facts
Distribute **Power Up 80** to students. See answers below.

Jump Start
Before students begin the Mental Math exercise, do these counting exercises as a class.

Mental Math
Encourage students to share different ways to mentally compute these exercises. Strategies for exercises are listed below.

a. Think 3 × 12
  3 × 12 = 36
  3 years equals 36 months.
c. Think 50 − 20 + 5
  50 − 15 = 50 − 20 + 5 = 30 + 5 = 35 minutes

Problem Solving
Refer to **Problem-Solving Strategy Discussion**, p. 431B.

Facts   Multiply:

12 × 7 = 84	6 × 2 = 12	10 × 10 = 100	5 × 6 = 30	12 × 5 = 60	3 × 6 = 18	7 × 9 = 63	4 × 12 = 4	8 × 8 = 64	12 × 7 = 84
9 × 5 = 45	7 × 8 = 56	9 × 9 = 81	3 × 3 = 9	12 × 12 = 144	9 × 6 = 54	8 × 2 = 16	7 × 3 = 21	2 × 9 = 18	9 × 5 = 45
3 × 8 = 24	8 × 11 = 88	5 × 4 = 20	2 × 7 = 14	3 × 5 = 15	6 × 7 = 42	9 × 3 = 27	8 × 4 = 32	4 × 3 = 12	3 × 8 = 24
6 × 6 = 36	7 × 5 = 35	4 × 7 = 28	8 × 6 = 48	5 × 8 = 40	6 × 4 = 24	9 × 8 = 72	4 × 9 = 36	7 × 7 = 49	6 × 6 = 36

New Concept

Real-World Connection

At the grocery store, many items are displayed in units of grams and kilograms.

- A bag of chips has a mass of about 500 grams.
- A large box of raisins has a mass of about 650 grams.
- A large bottle of ketchup has a mass of over 1 kilogram.

Activity
Instruction

Copy the table on the board as the students copy it on their papers. Then fill in some of the examples below to help get students started on their own tables.

Close to a gram: a small eraser, an envelope, a dime

More than a gram, less than a kilogram: a box of crayons, a shoe, a juice box

More than a kilogram: a gallon of milk, a stack of books, a bicycle

Encourage students to think of other examples that have not been mentioned before.

Example 1
Extend the Example

"Is the mass of a pencil closer to the mass of 12 paperclips or of 12 math books?"
12 paperclips

"Using that information, what would you estimate the mass of 8 pencils to be?"
about 96 grams

Example 2
Extend the Example

"If a pair of boots has a mass of about 2,000 grams, about how many kilograms is a single boot?" about 1 kilogram

For the *Analyze* question, students may solve the problem using multiplication by asking, "What number times 2 makes 1,000?" The answer, 500, will be about the mass of one shoe in grams.

(continued)

The mass of a dollar bill is about one gram. The mass of a large paper clip is also about one gram. A kilogram is 1,000 grams. The mass of your math textbook is about one kilogram. On Earth a kilogram weighs a little more than 2 pounds.

Metric Units of Mass

Unit	Abbreviation	Reference
gram	g	dollar bill or large paper clip
kilogram	kg	basketball
1 kilogram = 1,000 grams		

Activity
Metric Units of Mass

Copy the table below, and list two or three objects in each column of the table. Compare with a large paper clip to decide if an object is close to a gram or more than a gram. Compare with a basketball to decide if an object is more or less than a kilogram.

Mass of Objects

Close to a gram	More than a gram, less than a kilogram	More than a kilogram

Example 1

Which is the best estimate for the mass of a pencil?

12 grams   12 kilograms

The mass of a pencil is greater than a paper clip but much less than a basketball. So the mass is several grams but much less than a kilogram. The best estimate is **12 grams**.

Example 2

The mass of a pair of adult's shoes is about one kilogram. How many grams is a kilogram?

432   Saxon Math Intermediate 3

Math Background

Though the words *mass* and *weight* are sometimes used interchangeably to reflect everyday usage, there are important distinctions between the two in the physical sciences. Mass is very difficult to define in simple terms. A common simplified explanation is that mass is the amount of matter (stuff) in something. Weight is the measurement of the pull of gravity on something.

Grams and kilograms always measure mass. 100 grams has the same mass on the moon. However, the word "weight" is commonly applied to these units anyway. A person in a country where kilograms are often used will still say, "I weigh 70 kilograms."

Pounds may be used to measure mass or weight, and in some situations, the terms pound-mass and pound-force are used to distinguish between the two. A person weighing 150 pounds on Earth will have a mass of 150 pounds-mass on the moon, but their weight will decrease to 25 pounds-force.

A kilogram is **1,000 grams**.

Analyze About how many grams is one shoe?   Since 500 + 500 = 1,000, the mass of one shoe is about 500 grams.

Lesson Practice

▸ a. The mass of a dollar bill is about a gram. A kilogram of dollar bills would be about how many dollar bills?   1,000

▸ b. Which is the best estimate for the mass of a month-old baby?   5 kilograms

   5 grams   5 kilograms

▸ c. Arrange these objects in order from least mass to greatest mass: eyelash, paper clip, pencil, math book, desk

   your math book
   your desk
   a pencil
   an eyelash
   a paper clip

Written Practice   Distributed and Integrated

1. Rick and Antonia played a game with dot cubes. If they rolled a 2 or 4, Rick got a point. If they rolled a 1, 3, 5, or 6, Antonia got a point. Was their game fair? Why or why not?   no; sample: There are four ways for Antonia to get a point but only two ways for Rick to get a point.
(Inv. 5)

▸ 2. **Conclude** The train traveled across the prairie at a steady speed of 40 miles each hour. Copy and complete the table below to find how far the train traveled in 5 hours.   200 mi
(78)

Hours	1	2	3	4	5
Miles	40	80	120	160	200

3. The elevator had a weight limit of 4,000 pounds. How many tons is 4,000 pounds?   2 tons
(74)

4. What is the name for a parallelogram that has four right angles?
(65, 66)   rectangle or square

Lesson 80   433

Inclusion

How Many Grams

Some students will need more concrete experience with units of mass.

Materials: balance scale; several large paper clips; small classroom objects such as pencil, marker, scissors, glue stick

• Remind students that one large paper clip has a mass of about one gram.

• Students place one of the small objects on one side of the balance scale.

• Students place enough large paper clips on the other side of the scale to reach a balance.

• Students count the number of large paper clips to determine the approximate mass of the object in grams.

New Concept (Continued)

Lesson Practice

Guided Practice

Use these problems as guided practice to check the students' understanding of today's concept.

Problem a
Extend the Problem
"Half of a kilogram would be about how many dollar bills?"   500

Problem b
"Would a month old baby have about the same mass as five paper clips or as five textbooks?"

Problem c
Suggest that students compare the mass of the other three objects to the mass of a paper clip and the mass of a math book.

 Closure   The questions below help assess the concepts taught in this lesson.

"What are the basic units of mass in the metric system?" grams and kilograms

"If you want to find the mass of an adult, which unit would you use?" kilograms

"If you want to find the mass of a bag of potato chips, which unit would you use?" grams

Discuss real-world situations where metric measures of mass might be helpful. Examples are given below.

• In our science book, the mass of objects is given in kilograms.
• A child has a mass of 31 kilograms.
• We see that our bag of pretzels is labeled 100 grams.

Written Practice

Math Conversations
Independent Practice and Discussions to Increase Understanding

▸ **Problem 2** **Conclude**

Students should look for a pattern. The table can be completed if they skip count by 40s. Remind students to write the units.

(continued)

Lesson 80   433

Written Practice (Continued)

Math Conversations
Independent Practice and Discussions to Increase Understanding

Problem 6 Multiple Choice
Test-Taking Strategy

Students should start with the first answer and mark out any answers that *do* equal 12. Caution students to multiply the two numbers and not to add them.

Problem 10 Represent

Students should draw two overlapping squares and then connect the corresponding vertices with segments. The perspective of the cube should give the impression that all faces are the same size.

(continued)

---

5. Write the fraction of each rectangle that is shaded. Then compare the shaded rectangles. $\frac{2}{3}; \frac{5}{6}; \frac{2}{3} < \frac{5}{6}$
(61, 70)

6. Multiple Choice Which of these multiplications does *not* equal 12? **D**
(61, 70)

   A 1×12 **B** 2×6 **C** 3×4 **D** 6×6

7. What is the total value of four quarters, eight nickels, two dimes, and a penny? $1.61
(25)

8. An odometer shows the following display:
(32)

   0 5 7 6 3 0

  a. Use numbers to write the miles shown. 57,630

  b. Use words to state the number of miles the car has been driven. fifty-seven thousand, six hundred thirty miles

9. Name each figure below.
(67, 75)

  a. rectangle   **b.** rectangular prism

  c. triangle   **d.** triangular prism

10. Represent Draw a picture of a cube. A cube has how many edges? sample: ; 12 edges
(71)

11. Alberto made this rectangular shape with 1-centimeter square tiles.
(52, 62)

  a. How long is the rectangle? 6 cm

  b. How wide is the rectangle? 3 cm

  c. How many tiles did he use? 18 cm

  d. What is the area of the shape? 18 sq. cm

12. Change this addition to multiplication and find the total:
(54, 76) 6×12 in. = 72 in.
12 in. + 12 in. + 12 in. + 12 in. + 12 in. + 12 in.

13. Find each product:
(70)
a. 8×7 56   **b.** 7×6 42   **c.** 3×7 21

14. Find each product:
(78)
a. 4×30 120   **b.** 6×30 180   **c.** 8×30 240

▶ **15.** A meter is 100 cm. A door that is 2 meters tall is how many
(79)   centimeters tall?   200 cm

16. $587 − $295 $292   **17.** $5.45 + $3.57 $9.02
(23)   (22)

▶ **18.** What is the best estimate of the mass of a full-grown cat?
(80)   4 kilograms
       4 kilograms   4 grams

19. Which letter does *not* show a line of symmetry?   z
(Inv. 7)

▶ **20. a.** (Formulate) Show how multiplying three numbers helps you
(72, 77)   find the number of cubes in this stack. $4 \times 3 \times 2 = 24$

b. What is the volume of the stack of cubes?   24 cubic centimeters

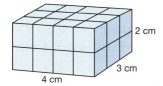

Lesson 80   435

Written Practice (Continued)

Math Conversations
Independent Practice and Discussions to Increase Understanding

▶ **Problem 15**
Extend the Problem
"If the door is one meter wide, what is its perimeter in centimeters?"   600 cm

▶ **Problem 18**
"Would a cat's mass be about the same as four paper clips or four textbooks?"

▶ **Problem 20a** (Formulate)
Multiply the length × width to find the number of cubes in one layer. Then multiply by the height to find the total number of cubes.

Errors and Misconceptions

▶ **Problem 4**
Some students may call this shape a square. A square is a rectangle and has four right angles, so it does correctly answer the question. But all parallelograms with four right angles will not be squares. All of them will be rectangles and some will be squares. So "rectangle" is the best answer.

▶ **Problem 8b**
Students may forget the hyphen in "fifty-seven" or try to include the word *and* in the name. Have students review the rules for naming counting numbers.

Assessments
Distribute **Power-Up Test 15** and **Cumulative Test 15** to each student. Have students complete the **Power-Up Test** first. Allow 10 minutes. Then have students work on the **Cumulative Test**.

Performance Task
The remaining class time should be spent on **Performance Task 8.** Students can begin the task in class or complete it during another class period.

Using the concept of mass in units of grams and kilograms to describe and compare objects and converting between different measures of mass prepares students for

- **Lesson 87,** understanding capacity.
- **Lesson 98,** estimating by weight.

Lesson 80   435

Flexible Grouping

Flexible grouping gives students an opportunity to work with other students in an interactive and encouraging way. The choice for how students are grouped depends on the goals for instruction, the needs of the students, and the specific learning activity.

Assigning Groups

Group members can be randomly assigned, or can be assigned based on some criteria such as grouping students who may need help with a certain skill or grouping students to play specific roles in a group (such as recorder or reporter).

Types of Groups

Students can be paired or placed in larger groups. For pairing, students can be assigned partners on a weekly or monthly basis. Pairing activities are the easiest to manage in a classroom and are more likely to be useful on a daily basis.

Flexible Grouping Ideas

Lesson 74, Example 2
Materials: paper, encyclopedias, internet

Divide students into groups of 4. Choose a leader, a recorder, a checker, and a presenter.
- After guiding students through example 2, direct groups to make a list of different objects that weigh about one ounce, one pound, and one ton. There should be at least one object for each unit.
- The leader makes sure all members are on task. The recorder writes the list. The checker verifies the weight of the objects either from a book or the internet.
- The presenter will share the group's list with the class.

Lesson 75, Example 2
Materials: paper, geosolids

Divide students into groups of 3. The groups should be of varying abilities and social skills. Choose a group leader, recorder, and presenter. Give each group 3–4 geosolids. Direct students to examine the geosolids and look for similarities and differences.
- The leader makes sure that all group members stay on task.
- The recorder lists the similarities and differences observed by the group.
- The presenter shares the group's observations with the class.

Lesson 76, Example 2
Materials: index cards

Students will work independently and then in pairs to reinforce multiplication facts.
- Direct students to choose 4 rows of the multiplication table and make flashcards showing the problem on one side and the answer on the other.
- Have students form pairs, combine and mix their cards, and use the table to solve the problems.

Lesson 78, Example 2
Materials: paper

Divide students into groups of 4. Write 3 multiplication problems with a multiple of ten as a factor on the board.
- Each group works together to solve the first problem.
- Divide the group into pairs to solve the second problem.
- Direct students to work on the last problem independently and then check their solutions with the group.

INVESTIGATION 8

Planning & Preparation

• More About Geometric Solids

Texas Essential Knowledge and Skills

(3.8) identify/classify/describe three-dimensional figures by their attributes and compare them by their attributes using formal vocabulary

(3.15)(A) explain/record observations using words

(3.15)(B) relate informal language to mathematical language

Objectives
- Identify, classify, and describe geometric solids by their attributes using proper vocabulary.
- Compare and contrast geometric solids.
- Group geometric solids based on similar attributes.
- Use informal language to describe geometric solids.

Prerequisite Skills
- Use proper vocabulary to name geometric solids.
- Compare and contrast geometric solids with two-dimensional shapes and figures.
- Use proper vocabulary to describe attributes of geometric solids.

Materials

Instructional Masters
- Lesson Activity 29

Manipulative Kit
- Geosolids

Teacher-provided materials
- Real-world objects that are geometric solids

Lesson Activity 29

Differentiated Instruction

Reaching All Special Needs Students

Special Education Students	At-Risk Students	English Learners	Advanced Learners
• Adaptations for Saxon Math	• Reteaching Masters	• English Learners (TM) • English Learner Handbook	• Extend the Problem (TM) • Investigate Further (SE) • Online Activities

TM=Teacher's Manual
SE=Student Edition

Math Language

Maintained
edge
face
geometric solid
rectangular prism
vertices

English Learners
classify

Investigation 8   **436B**

INVESTIGATION 8

More About Geometric Solids

In this investigation, students will learn to identify geometric solids, name the attributes of geometric solids, and identify geometric solids in everyday objects.

Observation

A face is the outside surface bounded by edges. Faces are the flat parts. The edge is where two faces meet and can be represented by a line segment. The vertex is where three faces meet. Vertices are sometimes called "corner points." Describe these facts to students using examples from the Relational GeoSolids for reference.

Math Conversations
Independent Practice and Discussions to Increase Understanding

Problems 1–4

If possible, have models of the Relational GeoSolids available for students to examine. Otherwise, a set of blocks should contain some of these solids. Divide students into groups to examine the example solids and to discuss the problems. Recommend that students answer the questions in the order that the models become available.

Problem 4
Extend the Problem

"What is the difference between this pyramid and the triangular prism above?"
The triangular prism has two triangular faces and three rectangular faces, while the pyramid has one square face and four triangular faces.

(continued)

INVESTIGATION 8

Texas Essential Knowledge and Skills
(3.8) identify/classify/describe three-dimensional figures by their attributes and compare them by their attributes using formal vocabulary
(3.15)(A) explain/record observations using words
(3.15)(B) relate informal language to mathematical language

Focus on
• More About Geometric Solids

In Lesson 75 we learned the geometric names of several different solids. In this investigation we will practice identifying, classifying, and describing geometric solids.

Recall from Lesson 71 that rectangular prisms have faces, edges, and vertices.

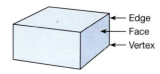

Other geometric solids made of flat surfaces also have faces, edges, and vertices.

Give the geometric name for each of the solids in problems **1–4**. Describe the solid by its number and shape of faces. Then count the numbers of edges and vertices. Use the Relational GeoSolids to help you answer the questions.

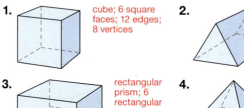

1. cube; 6 square faces; 12 edges; 8 vertices
2. triangular prism; 2 triangular faces and 3 rectangular faces; 9 edges; 6 vertices
3. rectangular prism; 6 rectangular faces; 12 edges; 8 vertices
4. pyramid; 1 square face and 4 triangular faces; 8 edges; 5 vertices

Some solids have surfaces that are not flat. Name each solid shown and described in problems **5–7**.

5. 1 curved surface, 2 flat surfaces shaped like circles — cylinder
6. 1 curved surface, 1 flat surface shaped like a circle — cone

Math Background

Students can find the surface area of rectangular solids by calculating the area of each face and combining all faces to get the total area. This can be modeled more concretely by cutting a cereal box along edges so that it can be flattened. Then students can readily see the different rectangles that make up the rectangular prism.

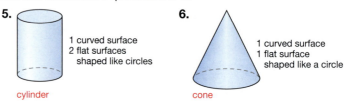

7. 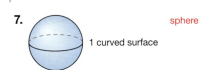 sphere

1 curved surface

Activity

Classifying Solids

Your teacher will show the class several objects labeled with letters from A–J. For each object, write its geometric name in the correct place on **Lesson Activity 29**. Then explain in your own words how you know that name is correct.

Use what you know about geometric solids and their attributes to answer problems **8–12**. Use your Relational GeoSolids to help answer the questions.

8. **Multiple Choice** Which geometric solid shown below does *not* belong? How do you know? **A;** sample: It is made of all flat surfaces. The other three solids have curved surfaces.

A   B

C   D

Investigation 8   437

 **English Learners**

Classify means to sort or assign things to a group. Ask:

"What information can we use to classify shapes?" samples: number of sides, size of angles, number of parallel sides

"What other objects might we classify?" samples: animals, food, stars, movies

Draw several four-sided shapes on the board. Have students classify the figures as rectangles, parallelograms, squares, or trapezoids.

Math Conversations
Independent Practice and Discussions to Increase Understanding

Problems 5–7
Extend the Problem

Have students list at least two real-world examples of each of these solids. Challenge them to be imaginative. samples:
5. a can of soup, a stick of lip balm
6. a funnel, the tip of a pencil
7. a baseball, a planet

Activity

Collect ten real-world objects representative of the geometric solids in this lesson. Label each object with letters from A–J.

Distribute one copy of Lesson Activity 29 to each student. Students may benefit from working in small groups.

Extend the Activity

Ask advanced learners,

"If we were to sort these solids into different bins, what might be some rules we could use for sorting?" sample: We could put all of the solids with curves in one bin and solids that have all flat faces into a different bin.

Problem 8
Extend the Problem

"Which geometric solid has no flat faces, and what is its name?" D; a sphere

(continued)

Investigation 8   437

Math Conversations
Independent Practice and Discussions to Increase Understanding

Problem 9
Extend the Problem

Have students identify each of the real-world objects in this problem and associate a geometric solid with it.
A: cracker box; rectangular prism
B: hat; cone
C: tent; triangular prism
D: dot cube; cube

Problem 10
Extend the Problem

"What do we call the flat surfaces of this geometric solid?" circles

Problem 11

Use this problem to help students make a connection between the number of vertices of a prism and the shape of its ends. A prism with quadrilateral ends will have four vertices per end for a total of 8 vertices. A prism with triangular ends will have three vertices per end for a total of 6 vertices. A prism with pentagonal ends will have five vertices per end for a total of 10 vertices. Students should start to see a pattern.

"What type of shape would form the ends of a prism with 16 vertices?" an octagon

(continued)

---

9. **Multiple Choice** Which object best represents a triangular prism? C

A    B

C   D

10. **Multiple Choice** Which geometric solid shown below has two flat surfaces and one curved surface? B

A   B

C   D

11. **Multiple Choice** Which geometric solid shown below has eight vertices? D

A   B

C    D

12. **Multiple Choice** What is the geometric name for this solid? A

   A pyramid   B rectangular prism
   C triangular prism   D cube

 Look around the classroom or around your house to find objects in the shape of each geometric solid we discussed in this investigation. Share the objects with the class, and choose an example of each to display.

Investigation 8   439

Identifying geometric solids prepares students for:

- **Lessons 102 and 104,** sorting objects.
- **Lesson 105,** using diagrams for sorting.

Math Conversations
Independent Practice and Discussions to Increase Understanding

Closure — The questions below help assess the concepts taught in this lesson.

"What are geometric solids?" geometric shapes that take up space

"What are faces, edges, and vertices?" Faces are the flat parts or outside surfaces of solids. The edge is where two faces meet. The vertex is where three faces meet (the "corner points").

Discuss real-world situations where understanding geometric solids might be helpful. Examples are given below.

- A manufacturer needs to decide if she wants to package her products in boxes or in cylinders.
- A boy is told to make a model of a pyramid for his history class.
- We want to make a set of dot cubes to play a board game.

Encourage students to bring items to the classroom or to find magazine pictures of objects representing different geometric solids.

Investigation 8   439

SECTION 9 OVERVIEW

Lesson Planner

Lesson	New Concepts	Materials	Resources
81	• Multiplying Two-Digit Numbers, Part 1	• Manipulative kit: yardstick • Student money manipulatives	• Power Up 81
82	• Fair Share	• Manipulative kit: color tiles or counters, ruler	• Power Up 82
83	• Finding Half of a Number		• Power Up 83
84	• Multiplying Two-Digit Numbers, Part 2		• Power Up 84
85	• Using Manipulatives to Divide by a One-Digit Number	• Manipulative kit: counters or color tiles	• Power Up 85
Cumulative Assessment			• Cumulative Test 16 • Power-Up Test 16 • Test-Day Activity 8
86	• Division Facts • Multiplication and Division Fact Families	• Manipulative kit: ruler	• Power Up 86
87	• Capacity	• Measuring cup • One-pint bottle • One-quart bottle • Half-gallon container • One-gallon container • Water or rice	• Power Up 87
88	• Even and Odd Numbers	• Manipulative kit: ruler, counters	• Power Up 88
89	• Using a Multiplication Table to Divide by a One-Digit Number	• Manipulative kit: ruler	• Power Up 89
90	• Equal Groups Stories, Part 2		• Power Up 90
Cumulative Assessment			• Cumulative Test 17 • Power-Up Test 17 • Performance Task 9
Inv. 9	• Symmetry, Part 2	• Manipulative kit: mirrors • Paper • Scissors	• Lesson Activity 30

 All resources are also available on the Resources and Planner CD.

Additional Resources

- Instructional Masters
- Reteaching Masters
- Resources and Planner CD
- Calculator Activities
- Assessment Guide
- Performance Tasks
- Instructional Transparencies
- Answer Key CD
- Power Up Workbook
- Written Practice Workbook

LESSONS 81–90, INVESTIGATION 9

Math Highlights

Enduring Understandings — The "Big Picture"

After completing Section 9, students will understand that:
- place value is fundamental to understanding the effects of multi-digit multiplication.
- division involves separating into equal groups.
- division is the inverse of multiplication.
- units of measuring capacity in the Customary System have doubles and halves relationships.

Essential Questions
- How does place value relate to multiplying a two-digit factor by a one-digit factor?
- How does division relate to subtraction? How is it different?
- How is division related to multiplication?
- What are the units of measuring capacity in the Customary System?

Math Content Highlights	Math Processes Highlights

Number Sense
• Multiplication *Lessons 81, 84, 86*
• Doubles and Halves *Lessons 81–83*
• Division *Lessons 82, 83, 85, 86, 88, 89*
 	
Algebraic Thinking
• Writing Number Sentences *Lesson 90*
• Solving Word Problems *Lesson 90*
• Related Multiplication and Division Facts (Fact Families) *Lessons 83, 86*
• Even and Odd Numbers *Lesson 88*
 	
Geometry and Measurement
• Measuring Capacity *Lesson 87*
• Symmetry *Inv. 9*
	Problem Solving
	• Strategies
	  – Act It Out or Make a Model *Lesson 81*
	  – Draw a Picture or Diagram *Lessons 82, 83, 86*
	  – Find or Extend a Pattern *Lessons 83, 86, 90*
	  – Guess and Check *Lesson 85*
	  – Make or Use a Table, Chart, or Graph *Lesson 90*
	  – Make It Simpler *Lessons 88, 89*
	  – Use Logical Reasoning *Lessons 84, 85*
	  – Work Backwards *Lesson 87*
	• Real-World Applications *Lessons 82, 84*
	
	Communication
	• Analyze *Lessons 86, 89*
	• Conclude *Lessons 87, 89, 90*
	• Connect *Lessons 85, 87*
	• Discuss *Lesson 87*
	• Explain *Lesson 88*
	
	Connections
	• Math to Math *Lessons 83, 85, 86*
	• Math and Other Subjects
	  – Math and Geography *Lesson 84*
	  – Math and Science *Lessons 81, 84, 86, 87, Inv. 9*
	  – Math and Sports *Lesson 89*
	
	Representation
	• Model *Lessons 83, 85, 86, 88*
	• Represent *Lessons 82, 83, 86, 89, 90*
	• Manipulative Use *Lessons 81, 82, 86, 89, 90, Inv. 9*

SECTION 9

Differentiated Instruction

Support for differentiated instruction is included with each lesson. Specific resources and features are listed on each lesson planning page. Features in the Teacher's Manual to customize instruction include the following:

Teacher's Manual Support

Alternative Approach	Provides a different path to concept development. *Lessons 81, 82, 86, 89, 90, Inv. 9*
Manipulative Use	Provides alternate concept development through the use of manipulatives. *Lessons 81, 82, 85, 90*
Flexible Grouping	Provides suggestions for various grouping strategies tied to specific lesson examples. *TM page 497A*
Inclusion	Provides ideas for including all students by accommodating special needs. *Lessons 81–86, 90*
Math Language	Provides a list of new and maintained vocabulary words along with words that might be difficult for English learners. *Lessons 81–90, Inv. 9*
English Learners	Provides strategies for teaching specific vocabulary that may be difficult for English learners. *Lessons 81, 83–90, Inv. 9*
Errors and Misconceptions	Provides information about common misconceptions students encounter with concepts. *Lessons 83, Inv. 9*
Extend the Example	Provides additional concept development for advanced learners. *Lessons 81, 82, 86–88, 90*
Extend the Problem	Provides an opportunity for advanced learners to broaden concept development by expanding on a particular problem approach or context. *Lessons 82, 84, 86, 87, Inv. 9*
Early Finishers	Provides additional math concept extensions for advanced learners at the end of the Written Practice. *Lessons 81, 83, 85, 89, 90*

Additional Resources

The following resources are also available to support differentiated instruction:
- Adaptations for Saxon Math
- English Learner Handbook
- Online Activities
- Reteaching Masters

Technology

Student Resources
- Student Edition eBook
- Calculator Activities
- Online Resources at www.SaxonMath.com/Int3Activities
  — Real World Investigations
  — Online Activities *Lessons 81–90, Inv. 9*
  — Online Calculator Activity

Teacher Resources
- Resources and Planner CD
- Test and Practice Generator CD
- Monitoring Student Progress: eGradebook CD
- Teacher Manual eBook CD
- Answer Key CD
- Adaptations for Saxon Math CD
- Online Resources at www.SaxonMath.com

LESSONS 81–90, INVESTIGATION 9

Cumulative Assessment

The assessments in Saxon Math are frequent and consistently placed to offer a regular method of ongoing testing.

Power-Up Test: Allow no more than ten minutes for this test of basic facts and problem solving skills.

Cumulative Test: Next administer this test, which checks mastery of concepts in previous lessons.

Test-Day Activity and Performance Task: The remaining class time can be spent on these activities. Students can finish the Test-Day Activity for homework or complete the extended Performance Task in another class period.

After Lesson 85

Power-Up Test 16

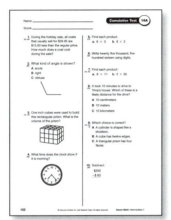
Cumulative Test 16

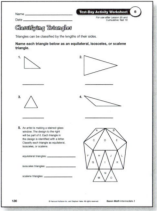
Test-Day Activity 8

After Lesson 90

Power-Up Test 17

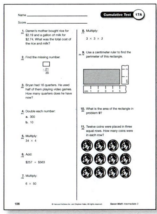
Cumulative Test 17

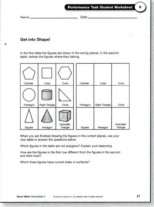
Performance Task 9

Evidence of Learning — What Students Should Know

By the conclusion of Section 9, students should be able to demonstrate the following competencies:

- Learn and apply multiplication facts. **TEKS (3.4)(A)**
- Locate and name points on a number line, including fractions. **TEKS (3.10)**
- Use linear measurement tools to estimate and measure lengths. **TEKS (3.11)(A, B, D)**
- Use standard units to find the perimeter, area, or volume of a shape. **TEKS (3.11)(A, B, F)**
- Identify the mathematics in everyday situations. **TEKS (3.14)(A)**
- Explain and record observations using words, pictures, and numbers. **TEKS (3.15)(A)**

Reteaching

Students who score below 80% on assessments may be in need of reteaching. Refer to the Reteaching Masters for reteaching opportunities for every lesson.

SECTION 9

Benchmarking and Tracking Standards

Benchmark Tests

Benchmark Tests correlated to lesson concepts allow you to assess student progress after every 20 lessons. An End-of-Course Test is a final benchmark test of the complete textbook. The Benchmark Tests are available in the Assessment Guide.

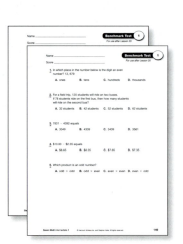

Monitoring Student Progress: eGradebook CD

To track TEKS mastery, enter students' scores on Cumulative Tests and Benchmark Tests into the Monitoring Student Progress: eGradebook CD. Use the report titled *Benchmark Standards Report* to determine which TEKS were assessed and the level of mastery for each student. Generate a variety of other reports for class tracking and more.

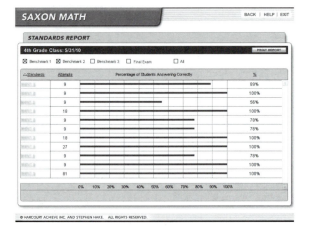

Test and Practice Generator CD

Test items also available in Spanish.

The Test and Practice Generator is an easy-to-manage benchmarking and assessment tool that creates unlimited practice and tests in multiple formats and allows you to customize questions or create new ones. A variety of reports are available to track student progress toward mastery of the TEKS throughout the year.

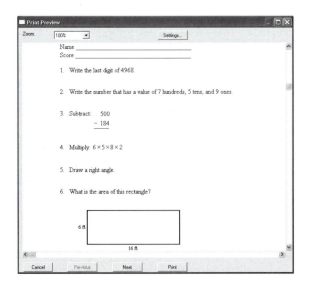

Northstar Math offers you real time benchmarking, tracking, and student progress monitoring.

Visit **www.northstarmath.com** for more information.

440E   *Saxon Math* Intermediate 3

LESSONS 81–90, INVESTIGATION 9

Content Trace

Lesson	New Concepts	Practiced	Assessed	Looking Forward
81	• Multiplying Two-Digit Numbers, Part 1	Lessons 81, 82, 83, 84, 85, 87, 88, 89, 91, 95, 97	Test 17	Lessons 84, 91, 97, 100, 101
82	• Fair Share	Lessons 82, 83, 85, 87, 91, 92, 105	Test and Practice Generator	Lessons 83, 85, 86, 89, 90, 101
83	• Finding Half of a Number	Lessons 83, 84, 85, 86, 87, 88, 89, 90, 91, 92	Tests 17, 18, 20	Lessons 85, 86, 89, 90, 101
84	• Multiplying Two-Digit Numbers, Part 2	Lessons 84, 85, 86, 87, 88, 89, 90, 91, 93, 94, 95, 96, 97, 98, 99, 101, 102, 108, 109, 110	Tests 17, 18	Lessons 90, 91, 97, 101
85	• Using Manipulatives to Divide by a One-Digit Number	Lessons 85, 89, 90, 92, 104	Test 17	Lessons 86, 89, 90, 101
86	• Division Facts	Lessons 87, 88, 89, 91, 93, 94, 95, 96, 97, 98, 99, 100, 101, 102, 103, 104, 105, 106, 107, 109	Tests 18, 19, 20, 21	Lessons 89, 90, 101
86	• Multiplication and Division Fact Families	Lessons 86, 87, 89, 98, 101, 102, 104, 105, 110		
87	• Capacity	Lessons 87, 88, 89, 91, 93, 94, 95, 96, 97, 98, 99, 102, 104, 108, 109	Tests 17, 18, 19	Lessons 90, 98
88	• Even and Odd Numbers	Lessons 88, 89, 90, 96, 102, 103, 105	Tests 18, 20	Lessons 89, 90, 101
89	• Using a Multiplication Table to Divide by a One-Digit Number	Lessons 92, 98, 105, 107	Test and Practice Generator	Lessons 90, 101
90	• Equal Groups Stories, Part 2	Lesson 90, 91, 93, 94, 100, 101, 102, 103, 104, 107	Tests 18, 20	Lesson 101
Inv. 9	• Symmetry, Part 2	Lessons 91, 97, 99, 100, 103, 105, 108, 110	Test 21	Lessons 104, 105, 109

Section Overview 9   440F

LESSON 81

Planning & Preparation

• Multiplying Two-Digit Numbers, Part 1

Texas Essential Knowledge and Skills

(3.1)(C) determine the value of a collection of coins and bills
(3.4)(B) solve/record multiplication problems (up to two digits times one digit)
(3.14)(D) use tools such as manipulatives to solve problems

Objectives
- Multiply two-digit numbers by 2.
- Use money manipulatives to demonstrate multiplying a two-digit number by 2.
- Learn the multiplication algorithm for multiplying two-digit numbers by one-digit numbers.

Prerequisite Skills
- Learn the multiplication facts through 12s.
- Understand the relationship between repeated addition and multiplication.

Materials

Instructional Masters
- Power Up 81

Manipulative Kit
- Rulers
- Money manipulatives (bills)*
- 1-inch unit cubes*
- Yardstick
- Meterstick*

Teacher-provided materials
- Student money manipulatives (bills)

optional

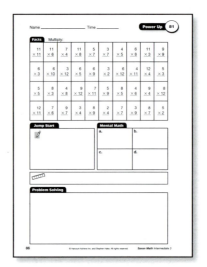

Power Up 81

Reaching All Special Needs Students

Special Education Students	At-Risk Students	English Learners	Advanced Learners
• Inclusion (TM) • Adaptations for Saxon Math	• Alternative Approach (TM) • Reteaching Masters	• English Learners (TM) • English Learner Handbook	• Extend the Activity (TM) • Extend the Example (TM) • Early Finishers (SE) • Online Activities

TM = Teacher's Manual
SE = Student Edition

Math Language

Maintained
digit
multiply
product

English Learners
either

440G Saxon Math Intermediate 3

Problem Solving Discussion

Problem

How many times does the minute hand go around a clock in one day?

Focus Strategy Act It Out or Make a Model

Understand Understand the problem.

"What are we asked to do?"

We are asked to find how many times the minute hand goes around a clock in one day.

Plan Make a plan.

"What problem solving strategy can we use?"

We can use our manipulative clocks to *model the problem*.

Solve Carry out the plan.

Teacher Note: Provide one manipulative clock per student.

"How many times does the minute hand go around a clock in one hour?"

Each hour, the minute hand starts at the 12 on the clock and goes all the way around (1, 2, 3, and so on) back to 12. This is one time around per hour.

Teacher Note: Have students demonstrate the movement of the minute hand in one hour.

"How many hours are in one day?"

There are 24 hours in one day.

"How many times does the minute hand move around a clock in one day?"

The minute hand moves around once each hour, so in one day it moves around the clock 24 times.

Check Look back.

"Did we complete the task?"

Yes, we found how many times the minute hand moves around a clock in one day (24 times).

"Is our answer reasonable?"

Yes, we know that there are 24 hours in one day, and the minute hand moves around once each hour. So it moves around the clock $24 \times 1 = 24$ times in one day.

"What problem solving strategy did we use, and how did it help us?"

We *modeled the problem* with a clock manipulative. This helped us to visualize the minute hand moving around once each hour.

Teacher Note: You may want to extend the problem by asking how many times the hour hand moves around the clock in one day. We can show that the hour hand moves 2 times around the clock each day using our manipulative clock. The hour hand moves around the clock once from midnight (12:00 a.m.) to noon (12:00 p.m.) and once more from noon to midnight.

Alternate Strategy

Use Logical Reasoning

If students already know that the minute hand goes around the clock once each hour, they can use logical reasoning to solve the problem. There are 24 hours in one day, so the minute hand moves around the clock 24 times in one day.

LESSON 81

Power Up

Facts
Distribute **Power Up 81** to students. See answers below.

Jump Start
Before students begin the Mental Math exercise, do these exercises as a class.

Mental Math
Encourage students to share different ways to mentally compute these exercises. Strategies for exercises are listed below.

b. Think 18 = 8 + 10
   82 + 8 = 90 + 10 = 100
d. Look at a Thermometer
   On the thermometer's scale, 5°C is higher than 32°F.
   Remember Benchmark Amounts
   32°F is the freezing point of water, as is 0°C. So 5°C is above freezing and is higher than 32°F.

Problem Solving
Refer to **Problem-Solving Strategy Discussion**, p. 440H.

New Concept

Instruction
As preparation for this lesson, review all of the "twos" multiplication facts. Write the "×2" line from a multiplication table on the board and ask students to recall the facts as you fill them in.

For the *Connect* question, discuss examples of things that come in pairs or doubles, then ask students to think of times in their lives that they have had to double numbers. List student responses on the board. **samples: buying two items of the same price, converting 2 feet to inches, playing games with two players, making a snack for two people**

(continued)

LESSON 81

• Multiplying Two-Digit Numbers, Part 1

Texas Essential Knowledge and Skills
(3.1)(C) determine the value of a collection of coins and bills
(3.4)(B) solve/record multiplication problems (up to two digits times one digit)
(3.14)(D) use tools such as manipulatives to solve problems

Power Up

facts Power Up 81

jump start Count up by 12s from 0 to 120.
Count up by 5s from 4 to 94.

Write two multiplication facts using the numbers 3, 7, and 21. $3 \times 7 = 21; 7 \times 3 = 21$

Draw a 7-centimeter segment on your worksheet.
See student work.

mental math
a. **Number Sense:** 56 + 27   83
b. **Number Sense:** 82 + 18   100
c. **Number Sense:** 450 − 400   50
d. **Measurement:** Which is the higher temperature, 32°F or 5°C?   5°C

problem solving How many times does the minute hand go around a clock in one day?   24 times

New Concept

When we double a number, we multiply the number by 2. For example, when we double 6, we have 2 groups of 6, or 12.

$$6 + 6 = 12$$
$$2 \times 6 = 12$$

We have learned multiplication facts for 2. In this lesson we will practice multiplying two-digit numbers by 2.

Connect List some things that you use or see in real life that come in pairs or doubles.   sample: gloves, shoes, socks, earrings

---

Facts Multiply:

11 × 11	11 × 6	7 × 4	11 × 8	5 × 7	3 × 7	4 × 5	6 × 8	11 × 3	9 × 9
121	66	28	88	35	21	20	48	33	81
6 × 3	6 × 10	3 × 12	6 × 5	6 × 9	3 × 2	6 × 12	4 × 11	12 × 4	5 × 3
18	60	36	30	54	6	72	44	48	15
5 × 5	8 × 3	4 × 8	9 × 12	7 × 11	5 × 9	8 × 5	4 × 6	9 × 4	8 × 12
25	24	32	108	77	45	40	24	36	96
12 × 11	7 × 6	9 × 7	3 × 4	8 × 9	2 × 4	7 × 7	3 × 9	8 × 7	5 × 2
132	42	63	12	72	8	49	27	56	10

Activity
Doubling Money

Use your money manipulatives to solve these problems.

1. Mariya has $24. If she doubles her money, how much money will she have?

   Step 1: Place 2 tens and 4 ones on your desk.

   Step 2: Double the money by placing 2 more tens and 4 more ones on your desk.

   Step 3: Combine the bills. What is the total? $48

2. Irena has $48. If she doubles her money, how much money will she have?

   Step 1: Place 4 tens and 8 ones on your desk.

   Step 2: Double the money by placing 4 more tens and 8 more ones on your desk.

   Step 3: Combine the bills. Trade with the bank if you can. Trade 10 ones for 1 ten.

   Step 4: What is the total? $96

Here is how we multiply $24 by 2 using pencil and paper:

Set up. Multiply 4 ones by 2. Multiply 2 tens by 2.

$$\begin{array}{r}\$24\\ \times\ \ 2\\ \hline\end{array} \qquad \begin{array}{r}\$24\\ \times\ \ 2\\ \hline 8\end{array} \qquad \begin{array}{r}\$24\\ \times\ \ 2\\ \hline \$48\end{array}$$

Here is how we multiply $48 by 2 using pencil and paper:

Set up. Multiply 8 ones by 2. Multiply 4 tens by 2.

$$\begin{array}{r}\$48\\ \times\ \ 2\\ \hline\end{array} \qquad \begin{array}{r}^{1}\\ \$48\\ \times\ \ 2\\ \hline 6\end{array} \qquad \begin{array}{r}^{1}\\ \$48\\ \times\ \ 2\\ \hline \$96\end{array}$$

When we multiply 8 ones by 2, the product is 16. Sixteen is 1 ten and 6 ones. We write the 6 in the ones place and the 1 ten above the 4 tens of 48.

When we multiply 4 tens by 2, the product is 8 tens. We add the 1 ten from 16 which makes 9 tens. The product is $96.

Lesson 81   441

Math Background

This is the students' first experience with multiplying two-digit numbers greater than 12. It is important for them to understand that the concept of multiplication as combining equal groups does not change because the algorithm looks different. For example, 2 × 27 is 2 groups of 27. The expanded form of 27 is 20 + 7. In the standard multiplication algorithm, the one-digit factor is first multiplied by the ones (2 × 7 = 14) and then the tens (2 × 20 = 40) of the two-digit factor. These two products are combined, which is why we add a 1 to the tens product when the ones product is regrouped. Showing students how the algorithm works will help them in later years when they are asked to represent problems such as 27 × 2 as 2 (20 + 7) = 2 × 20 + 2 × 7 using the Distributive Property.

New Concept (Continued)

Activity
Manipulative Use

Students will need their money manipulatives for this activity. They should take out the $10 bills and the $1 bills and clear enough room on their desks for two groups of money.

You may want to have students work with a partner.

1. While working in pairs, each student can count out one set of 2 tens and 4 ones from their money kits. Then the two students can combine the two groups of bills into one group.
2. In this problem, students will need to regroup their $1 bills. If students have difficulty with this, remind them to regroup ten $1 bills as one $10 bill.

Extend the Activity

Use the following problem to extend the activity:

After doubling her money, Elena had $78. How much money did Elena have before doubling it? Use your money manipulatives.

Step 1: Place 7 tens and 8 ones on your desk.

Step 2: Split the money into two groups.

   "The 8 ones are easily split into two groups of 4 ones. How do you split the 7 tens into two groups?" Exchange 1 ten for 10 ones. Then put 3 tens and 5 ones in each group.

Step 3: "How much money is in each group?" $39

Instruction

If students have difficulty remembering to add the extra ten from regrouping after multiplying, have them write "+1" to remind them to add.

Alternate Method

Point out to students that they double the digit in the ones place and get 16. Then they double the digit in the tens place and get 80: 16 + 80 = 96.

(continued)

Lesson 81   441

New Concept (Continued)

Example 1
Manipulative Use

Have students act out this story problem using their money manipulatives.

Example 2
Manipulative Use

Use a yardstick to remind students about the size of one yard. Use the yardstick to show that there are 36 inches in 1 yard. Draw a segment on the board that is 2 yards long, and label the number of total inches at the end of each yard.

Extend the Example

"If we double the number of yards, we also double the number of inches. What happens to the number of feet?" The number of feet has doubled from 3 to 6 feet.

Lesson Practice

Guided Practice

Use these problems as guided practice to check the students' understanding of today's concept.

Problems a and b
Extend the Problem

Challenge students to use the multiplication algorithm to triple or quadruple the larger number.

a. $42 or $56
b. 129 or 172

Problems a and c
Manipulative Use

Students may benefit from continuing to use their money manipulatives to model these problems, as they did in the activity.

(continued)

Example 1

A ticket to the amusement park costs $34. How much would two tickets cost?

To find the answer, we can add $34 and $34, or we can multiply $34 by 2. Either way, we find the cost of two tickets is **$68**.

Add	Multiply
$34	$34
+ $34	× 2
$68	$68

Example 2

One yard is 36 inches. How many inches is two yards?

We can find the answer by adding or multiplying. Either way, we find that two yards is **72 inches**.

$$\begin{array}{r} \overset{1}{36} \\ +36 \\ \hline 72 \end{array} \qquad \begin{array}{r} \overset{1}{36} \\ \times\ 2 \\ \hline 72 \end{array}$$

Lesson Practice Find each product.

a. $14 $28
   × 2

b. 43   86
   × 2

c. $27 $54
   ×   2

d. 39   78
   × 2

e. July and August each have 31 days. Altogether, how many days are in July and August? Find the answer by multiplying.   62 days

f. One pair of shoes costs $45. What would two pairs of the shoes cost? Find the answer by multiplying. $90

Written Practice — Distributed and Integrated

1. (60, 79) **Analyze** The ceiling is 3 meters high. How many centimeters is 3 meters?   300 cm

442 Saxon Math Intermediate 3

 Alternative Approach: Using Manipulatives

Have a student construct a small rectangular prism with 12 cubes that is 3 cubes wide, 2 cubes long, and 2 cube high.

"How many cubes are in this prism?" 12 cubes

Ask a second student to double the volume of the prism. This is most easily accomplished by doubling any one dimension such as height (double the number of layers).

"Use multiplication to find the number of cubes in the new prism" 2 × 12 = 24 cubes

English Learners

Either means one or the other. Say:

"You need to find out how much two CDs would cost at $15.99 each. You can either multiply or add. Who can write both equations on the board?" $15.99 + $15.99 = $31.98; $15.99 × 2 = $31.98

"Pretend we are having a talent show. You can either sing or dance. What would you choose and why?" See student work.

Ask students to draw either a circle or a square.

2. The class has collected 73 pounds of aluminum cans. The goal is to collect 100 pounds. How many more pounds of cans does the class need to collect to reach the goal?   27 pounds
(28, 36)

3. (Connect) Write the next three numbers in the sequence below.
(2, 32)
2,000, 4,000, 6,000, 8,000 , 10,000 , 12,000 , ...

4. It's time for lunch. Write the time shown on the clock in digital form.   11:45 a.m.
(3)

5. **Multiple Choice** Which of these multiplication facts equals 24? List all correct answers.   B, C, D
(55)
 A 3 × 6   B 2 × 12   C 1 × 24   D 4 × 6

6. What is the total value of five quarters, five dimes, five nickels, and five pennies? $2.05
(25)

7. **Multiple Choice** Which shows three tens and four thousands?   C
(32)
 A 34,000   B 4,003   C 4,030   D 30,004

▶ 8. (Analyze) Half of a dollar is equal to 50 cents. How many centimeters are equal to half of a meter?   50 cm
(79)

9. Multiply:
(81)
 a. 2 × 24   48   b. 2 × 48   96

10. A box is filled with cubes as shown at right.
(72, 73)
 a. How many cubes are in each layer?   10 cubes

 b. How many layers are there?   3 layers

 c. How many cubes are there?   30 cubes

 d. If each cube is one cubic inch, what is the volume of all of these cubes?   30 cubic in.

11. Write a fraction equal to one with a denominator of 5. Then write the mixed number one and one fifth using digits and symbols. Which number is greater? $\frac{5}{5}$; $1\frac{1}{5}$; $1\frac{1}{5}$
(46, 49)

Lesson 81   443

Inclusion

Look It Up

Students who are still struggling with multiplication facts can use a multiplication table for lessons involving multi-digit multiplication. This will give them an opportunity to learn the algorithm without getting hung up on basic facts.

Materials: multiplication table

• Write these multiplication problems on the board:

• Students multiply starting in the ones place.

• They use the multiplication table for any facts they do not know.

• If regrouping is necessary in the ones place, students write +1 above the digit in the tens place to remind them to add the ten.

• Students check their work with repeated addition.

New Concept (Continued)

Closure The questions below help assess the concepts taught in this lesson.

"What is another name for multiplying by two?"   doubling the number

"If we add a number to itself, is it the same as multiplying by two?"   yes

"What are the steps for multiplying a two-digit number by 2?"   1. Set up the problem. 2. Multiply the ones and regroup if needed. 3. Multiply the tens.

Discuss real-world situations where multiplying by two might be helpful. Examples are given below.

• We need to buy two items which cost the same amount.

• We have to find out how many people are in two classrooms that have an identical number of students.

Written Practice

Math Conversations
Independent Practice and Discussions to Increase Understanding

▶ **Problem 1** (Analyze)

Remind students how to convert from meters to centimeters. (Use the meterstick to demonstrate.)

▶ **Problem 8** (Analyze)

Remind students that 100 centimeters = 1 meter. (Use the meterstick to demonstrate.)

"How many cents are in a dollar?"   100 cents

"How many centimeters are in a meter?"   100 cm

"So if half of a dollar is 50 cents, half of a meter is how many centimeters?"   50 cm

(continued)

Lesson 81   443

Written Practice (Continued)

Math Conversations
Independent Practice and Discussions to Increase Understanding

▶ Problem 15   Multiple Choice
Test Taking Strategy

Point out the word *not* in the question. Three answer choices will be parallelograms. Students need to know that a parallelogram is a quadrilateral with two pairs of parallel sides. Answer **D** is the only choice that does not fit the definition.

Errors and Misconceptions

▶ Problem 9
Watch for students who write down these problems vertically with the 2 on top.

Remind students that the order of multiplication does not matter, so 2 × 24 = 24 × 2 and 2 × 48 = 48 × 2. So the two-digit number can be written on top.

Emphasize to students that the information they are given is in hours and minutes, whereas the question is asking for the answer in minutes only.

---

12. Find each product:
(70)
  a. 9 × 8   72
  b. 7 × 8   56
  c. 3 × 7   21

13. Here is a drawing of a brick:
(71)
  a. What is the length of the brick?   21 cm
  b. What is the width of the brick?   10 cm
  c. What is the height of the brick?   6 cm
  d. What is the name for the shape of the brick?   rectangular prism

14. What is the area of the top of the brick in problem **13**?   210 sq cm
(56, 62)

▶ **15. Multiple Choice** Which figure is *not* a parallelogram?   D
(66)
  A   B   C   D

16. Find each product:
(77, 78)
  a. 2 × 5 × 4   40
  b. 6 × 50   300

17. Find each product:
(78)
  a. 4 × 70   280
  b. 6 × 60   360
  c. 9 × 40   360

Add or subtract, as shown below:

18. $10.00 − $5.60 $4.40
(26, 28)

19. $95 + $85 + $75 $255
(24)

20. a. The spinner is least likely to stop on what number?   4
(44, 50)
  b. The spinner is most likely to stop on what number?   1
  c. What fraction of the face of the spinner has the number 2? $\frac{3}{10}$

Early Finishers
Real-World Connection

Nancy practiced basketball for 1 hour and 45 minutes on Friday and 1 hour and 15 minutes on Saturday. Jenny practiced for 1 and one half hours on Friday and 120 minutes on Saturday. How many minutes did each girl practice over two days? Who practiced longer?   Nancy 180 minutes, Jenny 210 minutes; Jenny

---

Looking Forward

Learning to multiply two-digit numbers prepares students for

- **Lesson 84,** multiplying two-digit numbers by factors greater than 2.
- **Lessons 91 and 97,** multiplying three-digit numbers.
- **Lesson 100,** multiplying dollars and cents.
- **Lesson 101,** dividing two-digit numbers.

LESSON 82

Texas Essential Knowledge and Skills
(3.4)(C) use models to solve division problems and number sentences to record the solutions

(3.14)(D) use tools such as manipulatives to solve problems

Planning & Preparation

- **Fair Share**

Objectives
- Model finding "fair share" (dividing by 2) with pictorial models and concrete objects such as counters or tiles.
- Use pencil and paper to write division number sentences to show dividing by 2.
- Draw arrays to model dividing by 2.

Prerequisite Skills
- Write a multiplication fact represented by a given array.
- Draw an array to represent a given multiplication fact.
- Use manipulatives such as counters or color tiles to model arrays.

Materials

Instructional Masters
- Power Up 82

Manipulative Kit
- Color tiles or counters
- Ruler

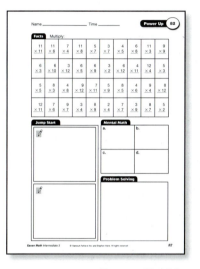

Power Up 82

Reaching All Special Needs Students

Special Education Students	At-Risk Students	English Learners	Advanced Learners
• Inclusion (TM) • Adaptations for Saxon Math	• Alternative Approach (TM) • Reteaching Masters	• English Learner Handbook	• Extend the Activity (TM) • Extend the Example (TM) • Extend the Problem (TM) • Online Activities

TM = Teacher's Manual

Math Language

Maintained
area
half

Lesson 82   445A

LESSON 82

Problem Solving Discussion

Problem

The area of Tandy's rectangular bedroom window is 12 square feet. The height of her window is 4 feet. What is the length of her window?

Focus Strategy

Understand Understand the problem.

"What information are we given?"

1. Tandy has a rectangular window.
2. The area of her window is 12 square feet.
3. The height of the window is 4 feet.

"What are we asked to do?"

We are asked to find the length of Tandy's window.

Plan Make a plan.

"How can we use the information we know to solve the problem?"

We can *draw a diagram* of the window.

Solve Carry out the plan.

"We can show area with an array of squares. The height of the window is 4 feet. If we draw a rectangle and make 4 rows to show the height in feet, how many columns do we need to show 12 square feet?"

We need to make 3 columns of squares. We can show this in a diagram like this:

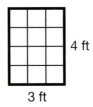

"What is the length of Tandy's window?"

We find that the length is 3 feet.

Check Look back.

"Is our answer reasonable?"

Yes, a window that is 3 feet long by 4 feet high has an area of 3 ft × 4 ft = 12 square feet.

"What problem solving strategies did we use, and how did they help us?"

We *drew a diagram* to show the dimensions of the window.

Alternate Strategy
Write a Number Sentence

Encourage students to write a number sentence to solve the problem. The area of the window equals the length times the height. So we know that 12 sq. ft = length × 4 ft. Since 3 ft × 4 ft = 12 sq. ft, the length of the window is 3 ft.

LESSON 82

• Fair Share

Texas Essential Knowledge and Skills
(3.4)(C) use models to solve division problems and number sentences to record the solutions
(3.14)(D) use tools such as manipulatives to solve problems

Power Up

facts Power Up 82

jump start
 Count up by halves from 0 to 5.
Count up by fourths from 0 to 2.

 Write these numbers in order from least to greatest: $\frac{1}{2}, \frac{3}{4}, 1\frac{1}{2}, 3$

$\frac{1}{2}$ $1\frac{1}{2}$ $\frac{3}{4}$ 3

Draw an equilateral triangle. Use a crayon to trace the sides that have equal length. *See student work.*

mental math
a. **Money:** $1.65 + $2.00 *$3.65*
b. **Number Sense:** 37 + 52 *89*
c. **Number Sense:** 620 − 100 *520*
d. **Probability:** Hector spins the spinner one time. Which number is the spinner most likely to land on? *2*

problem solving
The area of Tandy's rectangular bedroom window is 12 square feet. The height of her window is 4 feet. What is the length of her window? *3 ft*

New Concept

We saw in Lesson 81 that when we double a number, we multiply the number by 2. In this lesson, we will use manipulatives and pictures to find half of a number. When we find half of a number, we divide the number into two equal parts and find the number in each part.

Lesson 82   445

LESSON 82

Power Up

Facts
Distribute **Power Up 82** to students. See answers below.

Jump Start
Before students begin the Mental Math exercise, do these exercises as a class.

Mental Math
Encourage students to share different ways to mentally compute these exercises. Strategies for exercises are listed below.

b. Think 37 + 50 + 2
37 + 52 = 37 + 50 + 2 = 87 + 2 = 89
c. Think of Money
$6.20 − $1.00 = $5.20 ⟶ 520
Think 6 − 1 and Attach the 20
6 − 1 = 5 ⟶ 520
d. Count Spaces on the Spinner
There are three 2s, two 3s, and one 1. So 2 is the most likely.

Problem Solving
Refer to **Problem-Solving Strategy Discussion**, p. 445B.

New Concept

Discussion
Remind students that they learned to double a number in the last lesson. Ask,

"What is 4 doubled?" 8

"What does it mean to double a number?" to multiply it by 2

Write "2 × 4 = 8" on the board. Draw 2 groups of 4 tally marks and explain to students that this is a representation of the multiplication. Guide them to see that this is also a representation of half of 8.

"What examples can you think of where you would need to split a number in half?"

Write student responses on the board. samples: dividing a pack of juice boxes, a box of crayons, or a tray of watercolor paints

You might already have some of these items in the classroom for a demonstration.

(continued)

Facts Multiply:

11 × 11 = 121	11 × 6 = 66	7 × 4 = 28	11 × 8 = 88	5 × 7 = 35	3 × 7 = 21	4 × 5 = 20	6 × 8 = 48	11 × 3 = 33	9 × 9 = 81
6 × 3 = 18	6 × 10 = 60	3 × 12 = 36	6 × 5 = 30	6 × 9 = 54	3 × 2 = 6	6 × 12 = 72	4 × 11 = 44	12 × 4 = 48	5 × 3 = 15
5 × 5 = 25	8 × 3 = 24	4 × 8 = 32	9 × 12 = 108	7 × 11 = 77	5 × 9 = 45	8 × 5 = 40	4 × 6 = 24	9 × 4 = 36	8 × 12 = 96
12 × 11 = 132	7 × 6 = 42	9 × 7 = 63	3 × 4 = 12	8 × 9 = 72	2 × 4 = 8	7 × 7 = 49	3 × 9 = 27	8 × 7 = 56	5 × 2 = 10

Lesson 82   445

New Concept

Activity: Fair Share
Manipulative Use

For this activity, students will need counters or color tiles. Students can work in pairs, if desired. Each student or pair will need at least 24 counters.

Extend the Activity

Have each student place 10 counters in front of them. Then ask,

"If you had this amount after dividing a group into two equal groups, how would you find the amount in the original group?" samples: Put the two groups together and count up the total; Multiply the number of counters by 2.

"How many were in the original group before dividing it in half?" 20

Reading Math

Be sure that students know how to read long division notation correctly. Write a few extra examples of each on the board and ask for a volunteer to read them aloud. Point out that the division box is read from right to left with the answer on top.

For the *Connect* question, students may have trouble connecting division to repeated subtraction by thinking of doubles and halves. Show the following two examples on the board:

$3 + 3 + 3 + 3 = 4 \times 3 = 12$

"Combining four groups of 3 is the same as adding 3 four times."

$12 - 3 - 3 - 3 - 3 = 0$, so $12 \div 3 = 4$.

"12 can be divided into groups of 3 four times. This is like seeing how many 3s can be subtracted from 12 until nothing remains."

Example 1
Active Learning

"Since we don't know how many Xs to put in each row, how should we do this?" Put Xs in columns of two from left to right, counting as you go: 1, 2, then 3, 4, then 5, 6, ..., up to 14.

"How many Xs are in each row?" 7

Have students practice reading divisions properly by asking,

"How do you read each of these divisions?" "14 divided by 2 equals 7."

Point to each number as the students read each division.

(continued)

446 Saxon Math Intermediate 3

Below we show a **dozen** eggs in a carton. There are two rows of 6 eggs.

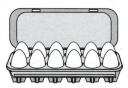

The picture shows that doubling 6 equals 12. The picture also shows that half of 12 is 6.

Fair Share

Materials: counters or tiles

1. Place 16 counters or tiles on your desk. Then separate the items into 2 equal groups. How many items are in each group? 8

2. Place 24 counters or tiles on your desk. Then separate the items into 2 equal groups. How many items are in each group? 12

There are two ways to show a number divided into 2 parts using pencil and paper.

$$24 \div 2 = 12 \qquad 2\overline{)24}^{\,12}$$

"24 divided by 2 equals 12."   "24 divided by 2 equals 12."

Connect If multiplication is the same as repeated addition, what do you think division is the same as? sample: repeated subtraction

Example 1

Draw a total of 14 Xs on your paper. Arrange the Xs in two rows like this:

X X X ...
X X X ...

How many Xs are in each row? Use digits and symbols to show two ways to write the division of 14 into 2 equal groups.

446 Saxon Math Intermediate 3

Math Background

The idea of separating a set of items into equal-sized groups is important as the students consider the concept of division. In this lesson, students are separating groups of manipulatives into two equal-sized groups. In the future, they can think of division by a larger number, like 7, as breaking a quantity of manipulatives into seven equal-sized groups.

We write 14 Xs in 2 rows. There are **7** Xs in each row.

X X X X X X X
X X X X X X X

The pattern of Xs shows that 14 divided by 2 is **7**.

$$14 \div 2 = 7 \qquad 2\overline{)14}^{\,7}$$

Example 2

Eighteen students line up in 2 equal rows. How many students are in each row? Use digits and symbols to show two ways to write the division of 18 into 2 equal groups.

We can use counters or draw pictures to help us divide 18 into 2 equal groups.

○ ○ ○ ○ ○ ○ ○ ○ ○
○ ○ ○ ○ ○ ○ ○ ○ ○

Since 18 divides into 2 equal groups of 9, there are **9 students** in each row.

$$18 \div 2 = 9 \qquad 2\overline{)18}^{\,9}$$

Lesson Practice

a. We find half of a number by dividing by 2. We can use two open hands to show 10 divided by 2. What number is half of 10? **5**

b. Use counters to find half of 12. **6**

c. Draw a total of 8 Xs on your paper arranged in 2 equal rows. How many Xs are in each row? Show two ways to write the division of 8 into 2 parts. ; **4; 8 ÷ 2 = 4, $2\overline{)8}^{\,4}$**

▶ d. Twenty students lined up in two equal rows. How many students were in each row? **10 students**

Lesson 82   447

Alternative Approach: Using Manipulatives

Students will need scratch paper and a ruler that measures in centimeters. Explain to students that their ruler can be used to divide numbers in half.

"We will be dividing 16, 24, and 28 into two equal groups."

Instruct students to measure and cut out three strips of paper: one of length 16 cm, one of length 24 cm, and one of length 28 cm. Students should fold each strip in half, crease the fold, and then unfold the strips. Have students measure to the crease mark to find half of each number.

"This method divides a length into two smaller, equal lengths." half lengths: 8 cm, 12 cm, and 14 cm

New Concept (Continued)

Example 2
Explanation
"What do you notice about all of the numbers we have divided in half in this lesson?" They are all even numbers.

Explain to students that only even numbers can be divided into two equal groups of whole numbers. An odd number will always have one extra.

Extend the Example
Ask students to explain how they would find the total number of students lined up in 2 rows of 12 students. samples: Count all the students; Count up by 2s; Multiply 12 by 2.

"How could you write that multiplication in two different ways?" 12 × 2 = 24 and 2 × 12 = 24

Lesson Practice

Guided Practice
Use these problems as guided practice to check the students' understanding of today's concept.

Problem d
Remind students that they can draw this problem (as in example 2) using small circles or dots to represent the students in 2 rows.

Extend the Problem
Have students write the division in two ways. 20 ÷ 2 and $2\overline{)20}$

 Closure   The questions below help assess the concepts taught in this lesson.

"True or false: when we divide a number by two, it is the same as dividing the number in half?" true

"Describe how we can use color tiles to divide 18 by 2 and find the answer." We take the 18 tiles and put them into two equal lines: 18 ÷ 2 = 9.

"Can every number be divided into 2 equal groups of color tiles?" No, only even numbers make equal groups when we use color tiles.

Discuss real-world situations where dividing by two might be helpful. Examples are given below.

- We need to find half the number of cups of flour in a recipe.
- We need to find a place to stop on a car trip which is halfway between where we started and our destination.

Lesson 82   447

Written Practice

Math Conversations
Independent Practice and Discussions to Increase Understanding

Problem 3 (Analyze)
"What does the problem ask?" for the number of pages Joni read on Tuesday

"What information does the problem tell us?" That Joni read 15 pages on Monday and twice as many on Tuesday.

"What is another way of saying 'twice as many'?" samples: "double", "times two"

"What is twice as many as 15?" 30

"How many pages did Joni read on Tuesday?" 30 pages

Problem 4   Multiple Choice
Test Taking Strategy
Since the question asks which is *not* equal, a good strategy for students to use is to find the opposite; that is, to find which choices *are* equal to 18 and cross them out.

Problem 8 (Represent)
Remind students that a square has four sides that are the same length. All four sides should be 5 cm long.

Problem 10
a. Remind students that they can multiply either set of numbers first:
$5 \times (4 \times 3) = 5 \times 12 = 60$ or
$(5 \times 4) \times 3 = 20 \times 3 = 60$

b. Many students will do this problem mentally by thinking of quarters. Other students may need to write the problem vertically and use the multiplication algorithm.

"What were the three steps we used for doing these multiplication problems?"
1. Set up the multiplication.
2. Multiply the ones and regroup if needed.
3. Multiply the tens.

Problem 11
Real-World Connection
Ask students if they know the significance of the number 5,280.

"Where have we seen the number 5,280 before?" It is the number of feet in one mile.

(continued)

448   Saxon Math Intermediate 3

Written Practice   Distributed and Integrated

1. Brandon ran 5 kilometers. How many meters is 5 kilometers?   5,000 m
(79)

2. Tamara bought a telescope for $189.00. Tax was $13.23. What was the total price with tax? $202.23
(22, 36)

▶ **3.** (Analyze) On Monday Joni read 15 pages. On Tuesday Joni read twice as many pages as she read Monday. How many pages did Joni read Tuesday?   30 pages
(81)

▶ **4.** **Multiple Choice** Which of these multiplication facts does *not* equal 18?   B
(55)

    A 3×6 B 9×9 C 18×1 D 2×9

5. **Multiple Choice** Bobby is five years old. Which of these could be his height?   B
(79)

    A 100 m   B 100 cm   C 100 km

6. What number is shown by this model?   130
(11)

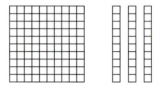

7. Marla arranged 16 counters to show half of 16. What number is half of 16?   8
(82)

▶ **8.** (Represent) Draw a square with sides 5 cm long.
(51, 79)   See student work.

9. a. What is the perimeter of the square in problem **8**?   20 cm
(58, 62)

    b. What is the area of the square?   25 sq cm

▶ **10.** Find each product.
(77, 81)
    a. $5 \times 4 \times 3$ 60   **b.** 2×25 50

▶ **11.** What is the place value of the 2 in 751,283?   hundreds
(32)

448   Saxon Math Intermediate 3

Inclusion

Deal It
Students who have difficulty dividing can use this strategy.

Materials: pencil and paper

- Students copy this division problem:
  $24 \div 2$

- They draw 2 circles on their paper.

- Then they "deal" 24 tally marks by drawing one in the first circle, then drawing one in the second circle, and so on back and forth, counting as they go.

- When the student has drawn 24 tally marks, they count the marks in one circle. That number is the quotient.

12. Cubes are stacked as shown at right.
(72, 73)
   a. How many cubes are in each layer? 12 cubes
   b. How many layers are there? 3 layers
   c. How many cubes are there? 36 cubes
   d. If each cube is one cubic centimeter, what is the volume of the stack of cubes? 36 cubic cm

▶ **13.** Multiply:
(70, 78)
   a. 6 × 7   42
   b. 7 × 80   560
   c. 8 × 90   720

Add or subtract:

▶ **14.** $4.58 + $8.97 $13.55
(22)

15. $800 − $735 $65
(28)

16. Find the missing addend: 24 + m = 100.   76
(9, 28)

17. Write 57,240 in expanded form.   50,000 + 7,000 + 200 + 40
(32)

18. What is the name of each polygon?
(67)
   a.
   b.
   c.

   pentagon   hexagon   octagon

19. What is the name of each solid?
(75)
   a.
   b.
   c.

   pyramid   triangular prism   cone

▶ **20.** Which of the measures below is reasonable for the mass of a grape?   6 grams
(80)
   6 grams   6 kilograms

Lesson 82   449

Looking Forward

Using manipulatives to divide by 2 prepares students for

- **Lesson 83**, finding half of a number.
- **Lesson 85**, using manipulatives to divide by a one-digit number.
- **Lesson 86**, learning division facts.
- **Lesson 89**, using a multiplication table to divide by a one-digit number.
- **Lesson 90**, solving equal groups problems.
- **Lesson 101**, dividing two-digit numbers.

Written Practice (Continued)

Math Conversations
Independent Practice and Discussions to Increase Understanding

Problem 13
For **b** and **c**, remind students to think of the single-digit multiplication facts, and then to add a 0.

   7 × 8 = 56, so 7 × 80 = 560
   8 × 9 = 72, so 8 × 90 = 720

Problem 14
A quick way to add these mentally is to add $9.00, and then to subtract $0.03.

   $4.58 + $9.00 = $13.58
   $13.58 − $0.03 = $13.55

Problem 20
Remind students that a paper clip has a mass of about 1 gram and that a textbook has a mass of about 1 kilogram.

"Would a grape weigh the same as 6 paper clips or as 6 textbooks?" 6 paper clips

Errors and Misconceptions

Problem 18
Math Language
Some students may still be confusing hexagons and octagons. Be sure to review the key prefixes with them:

tri- = 3
quad- = 4
pent- = 5
hex- = 6
oct- = 8

Students might remember *oct-* easily if they remember that an octopus has 8 tentacles.

Problem 19
Watch for students who get the pyramid and triangular prism confused. Drawings of these figures are often quite similar, so students may not visualize the differences in the three-dimensional figures. Using a concrete example or manipulative of each solid should help students understand the differences.

Lesson 82   449

LESSON 83

Planning & Preparation

• Finding Half of a Number

Objectives
- Use a multiplication table to find half a number.
- Find half of a number to solve a problem.

Prerequisite Skills
- Use pencil and paper to write division number sentences to show dividing by 2.
- Draw arrays to model dividing by 2.

Materials
Instructional Masters
- Power Up 83

Teacher-provided materials
- Highlighters*

optional

Texas Essential Knowledge and Skills
- (3.4)(C) use number sentences to record the solutions to division problems
- (3.6)(C) identify patterns in related multiplication and division sentences (fact families)
- (3.14)(C) select/develop an appropriate problem-solving plan/strategy, including looking for a pattern to solve a problem

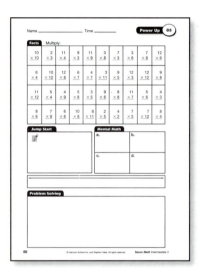

Power Up 83

Reaching All Special Needs Students

Special Education Students	At-Risk Students	English Learners	Advanced Learners
• Inclusion (TM)	• Error Alert (TM)	• English Learners (TM)	• Early Finishers (SE)
• Adaptations for Saxon Math	• Reteaching Masters	• English Learner Handbook	• Online Activities

TM=Teacher's Manual
SE=Student Edition

Math Language

Maintained	English Learners
column	price
half	
row	

450A *Saxon Math* Intermediate 3

Problem Solving Discussion

Problem

Shawntel used pennies to make the patterns below. How many pennies does she need to build the next triangular pattern?

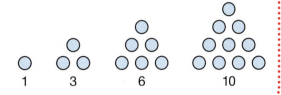

Focus Strategies

Understand Understand the problem.

"What information are we given?"

We are shown a picture of triangular patterns made with pennies.

"What are we asked to do?"

We are asked to find how many pennies are needed to make the next pattern.

Plan Make a plan.

"What problem solving strategies can we use?"

We can *draw a diagram* of the next pattern.

Solve Carry out the plan.

"What shape do you see in the patterns that Shawntel made?"

triangle

"What patterns do you see in the triangles?"

The first pattern has 1 row, the second pattern has 2 rows, the third pattern has 3 rows, and the fourth pattern has 4 rows.

The number of pennies in each row is one greater than the row above it. If we count the rows from the top, we also find that the number of pennies in a row equals the number of the row (for example, row 3 contains 3 pennies).

"Let's draw the next pattern. How many pennies are needed?"

The next pattern will have 5 rows of pennies. The first row has 1 penny, the second row has 2 pennies, the third row has 3 pennies, and so on. The total number of pennies in the pattern is 1 + 2 + 3 + 4 + 5 = 15 pennies.

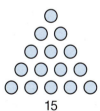

Check Look back.

"Did we complete the task?"

Yes, we found how many pennies Shawntel needs to build the next triangular pattern (15 pennies).

"Is our answer reasonable?"

Yes, the number of pennies in each row increases by one. The first row has 1 penny, so a triangular shape with 5 rows has 1 + 2 + 3 + 4 + 5 = 15 pennies.

"What problem solving strategies did we use, and how did they help us?"

We *drew a diagram* of the next triangular pattern to see the number of rows and the number of pennies in each row. We *extended a pattern* to find the total number of pennies.

Alternate Strategy

Act It Out or Make a Model

Students can act out this problem with pennies or counters. They should first make a triangular arrangement with 10 objects and then add a new row to the bottom of the triangle.

LESSON 83

Power Up

Facts
Distribute **Power Up 83** to students. See answers below.

Jump Start
Before students begin the Mental Math exercise, do these exercises as a class.

Mental Math
Encourage students to share different ways to mentally compute these exercises. Strategies for exercises are listed below.

c. Look for Amounts that Total 100
67 + 33 = 100, so 1 more than that is 101.

d. Count and Write the Fraction
The circle is divided into 3 equal parts. Only 1 part is not shaded, so the fraction not shaded is $\frac{1}{3}$.

Problem Solving
Refer to **Problem-Solving Strategy Discussion**, p. 450B.

LESSON 83 • Finding Half of a Number

Texas Essential Knowledge and Skills
(3.4)(C) use number sentences to record the solutions to division problems
(3.6)(C) identify patterns in related multiplication and division sentences (fact families)
(3.14)(C) select/develop an appropriate problem-solving plan/strategy, including looking for a pattern to solve a problem

Power Up

facts   Power Up 83

jump start
- Count up by 7s from 0 to 77.
- Count up by 100s from 0 to 2,000.
- Write "fifty thousand, four hundred one" using digits. What number is in the ten thousands place? *50,401; 5*
- Label the number line by halves from 5 to 10. (Show these numbers: 5, $5\frac{1}{2}$, 6, $6\frac{1}{2}$, 7, $7\frac{1}{2}$, 8, $8\frac{1}{2}$, 9, $9\frac{1}{2}$, 10.) *See student work.*

mental math
a. **Measurement:** How many inches are in 4 feet? *48 in.*
b. **Money:** $10.00 − $9.25 *75¢*
c. **Number Sense:** 67 + 34 *101*
d. **Fractions:** What fraction of the circle is *not* shaded? $\frac{1}{3}$

problem solving
Shawntel used pennies to make the patterns below. How many pennies does she need to build the next triangular pattern? *15 pennies*

1   3   6   10

---

450   *Saxon Math* Intermediate 3

Facts   Multiply:

10 × 10 = 100	2 × 3 = 6	11 × 4 = 44	9 × 3 = 27	11 × 9 = 99	3 × 8 = 24	7 × 3 = 21	3 × 6 = 18	7 × 8 = 56	12 × 6 = 72
6 × 4 = 24	10 × 12 = 120	12 × 8 = 96	6 × 7 = 42	4 × 7 = 28	3 × 11 = 33	9 × 5 = 45	12 × 3 = 36	12 × 12 = 144	9 × 8 = 72
11 × 12 = 132	5 × 4 = 20	4 × 9 = 36	5 × 8 = 40	3 × 5 = 15	9 × 6 = 54	8 × 8 = 64	11 × 7 = 77	5 × 6 = 30	4 × 3 = 12
8 × 6 = 48	7 × 9 = 63	6 × 6 = 36	10 × 8 = 80	6 × 11 = 66	2 × 5 = 10	4 × 2 = 8	7 × 5 = 35	7 × 12 = 84	8 × 4 = 32

New Concept

A multiplication table is a collection of multiplication facts. It is also a collection of division facts. In this lesson we will use a multiplication table to divide by 2.

	0	1	2	3	4	5	6	7	8	9	10	11	12
0	0	0	0	0	0	0	0	0	0	0	0	0	0
1	0	1	2	3	4	5	6	7	8	9	10	11	12
(2)	0	2	4	6	8	10	(12)	14	16	18	20	22	24
3	0	3	6	9	12	15	18	21	24	27	30	33	36
4	0	4	8	12	16	20	24	28	32	36	40	44	48
5	0	5	10	15	20	25	30	35	40	45	50	55	60
6	0	6	12	18	24	30	36	42	48	54	60	66	72
7	0	7	14	21	28	35	42	49	56	63	70	77	84
8	0	8	16	24	32	40	48	56	64	72	80	88	96
9	0	9	18	27	36	45	54	63	72	81	90	99	108
10	0	10	20	30	40	50	60	70	80	90	100	110	120
11	0	11	22	33	44	55	66	77	88	99	110	121	132
12	0	12	24	36	48	60	72	84	96	108	120	132	144

If we want to divide 12 by 2, we look at the row that begins with 2. Then we look across the row for 12. When we find 12, we look at the top of the column and find 6. We see that 12 divided by 2 is 6. We can write $12 \div 2 = 6$ or $2\overline{)12}^{\,6}$.

Connect What multiplication fact is related to $12 \div 2 = 6$? $2 \times 6 = 12$

Example 1

Use the multiplication table to find half of 22.

To find half of 22, we divide 22 by 2. We look across the 2s row for 22. We see 22 and look at the top of the column and find 11. Half of 22 is **11**.

Lesson 83   451

Math Background

Students have used the multiplication table for multiplication facts, but this is their first experience with using the table for division. Multiplication and division are inverse operations, and finding products and quotients on the multiplication table involves inverse processes. To multiply, you start with two factors and find the product. To divide, you start with one factor and the product (the divisor and dividend), then find the other factor (quotient). Students should already know about the skip-counting patterns on the table when multiplying. They may notice that when dividing, the same patterns are counting down. Seeing this pattern as skip counting down, or repeated subtraction, will help students as the division becomes more difficult.

New Concept

Connection

To start the lesson, first review all of the 2s multiplication facts. Write the 2s row from a multiplication table on the board, asking students the facts as you fill them in.

Have students practice finding products on the multiplication table. Ask them to find the row and column that begin with 2.

Math Language

Lessons 82 and 83 introduce students to two different ways of thinking about division. In Lesson 82, students divided by 2 by separating objects or representations of objects into two equal groups. In this lesson, students divide by 2 to find half of a number. As students solve story problems they will see phrases such as "shared equally," "split evenly," or "put in equal piles." Help students see that all these phrases tell them to separate a large group into smaller equal groups, or to divide. You might want to start a list of division phrases on a chart in your classroom that your class can add to when they encounter new ones.

For the *Connect* question, students might also give the fact $6 \times 2 = 12$.

Example 1
Math-to-Math Connection

Connect this example to a discussion of even and odd numbers.

"Can you find half of 21 in the multiplication table? Explain." no; samples: There is no 21 in the 2s row. Twenty-one is an odd number.

For advanced learners, ask,

"What can you say about half of 21 based on the multiplication table?" sample: Half of 21 is between 10 and 11.

(continued)

Lesson 83   451

New Concept (Continued)

Example 2
Instruction

Stress to students that $18 is being separated into 2 equal groups. You can use division to form equal groups.

Lesson Practice

Guided Practice

Use these problems as guided practice to check the students' understanding of today's concept.

Problems a and b

Help students spot the key words "half of," which indicate division in these problems.

Problem d Error Alert

Watch for students who mistakenly start looking along the 8s row in the multiplication table. Remind them to divide *by* 2 and look along the 2s row.

The questions below help assess the concepts taught in this lesson.

"How can we use a multiplication table to divide by two?" Find the number we are dividing in the 2s row. The number at the top of the column is the quotient.

"Use your multiplication tables to find the answer to 14 ÷ 2." 7

Discuss real-world situations where dividing by two might be helpful. Examples are given below.

- We need to divide the class into two equal groups.
- A boy needs to divide the money from watching the neighbor's dog with his sister.

Written Practice

Math Conversations
Independent Practice and Discussions to Increase Understanding

Problem 3 Multiple Choice
Test-Taking Strategy

Guide students to use the picture to solve this problem. There are 12 stars separated into 2 equal groups. There are 6 stars in one group, so half of 12 is 6.

(continued)

452 Saxon Math Intermediate 3

Example 2

Drew and his sister bought a game that cost $18. They both paid half of the price. How much money did Drew pay?

We find half of $18 by dividing $18 by 2. We find 18 in the row for 2. We look at the top of the column and see 9. Drew paid **$9**.

Lesson Practice

a. One day is 24 hours. How many hours is half of a day? **12 hours**

b. Sixteen ounces equals a pound. How many ounces is half of a pound? **8 oz**

Find each answer on the multiplication table.

c. $2\overline{)14}$ 7 d. $8 \div 2$ 4

Written Practice *Distributed and Integrated*

1. T-shirts were on sale for $2.00 off the regular price. If the regular price was $8.95, what was the sale price? **$6.95**
(20, 26)

2. **Analyze** Michelle bought ten pens for 89¢ each. What was the total price of the ten pens? **$8.90**
(21, 56)

3. **Multiple Choice** Divide 12 into two equal groups. What is half of 12? **B**
(82, 83)

   A $\frac{1}{2}$
   B 6
   C 2
   D 12

4. Computer chips were shipped from Fortner to Mesa. Use your ruler to find the distance from Fortner to Mesa. **300 miles**
(35)

   Fortner ●————————————● Mesa
   1 in. = 100 miles

452 Saxon Math Intermediate 3

English Learners

The **price** is how much something costs. Say:

"One pound of bananas is 89¢. What is the price for 2 pounds of bananas?" 89¢ × 2 = $1.78

Hold up a few items that you have recently purchased. Ask:

"Who can guess what the price was for each item?" Allow students to make guesses.

Have students make a list of items they would like to buy and list the price for each one.

Inclusion

Highlight the Table

Some students might have difficulty isolating numbers on the 2s row of the multiplication table. Give them a visual aid while reviewing patterns and skip counting.

Materials: multiplication table, highlighter

- Ask what pattern they see on the 2s row. counting up by 2s
- Students highlight the 2s row.
- Students count by 2s to 24 while touching the numbers on the table.

5. The clock shows the time that the computer chips arrived in Mesa on Friday morning. Write the time in digital form.   11:15 a.m.
   (3)

6. (Analyze) Two multiplication facts with a product of 8 are 1 × 8 and 2 × 4. Write two multiplication facts using different factors that have a product of 6.   1 × 6 and 2 × 3
   (55)

7. Write 560 in expanded form.   500 + 60
   (11)

8. Multiply:
   (56, 78)
   a. 10 × 25¢ $2.50
   b. 7 × 40   280

9. **Multiple Choice** Marion sprinted as fast as she could and won the race. Which of these is a likely distance for the length of the race?   A
   (79)

   A 100 m   **B** 100 cm   **C** 100 km

10. **Multiple Choice** Which addition is shown by the model below?   B
    (11)

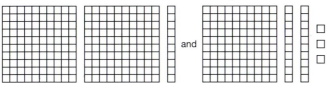

   A 201 + 123   **B** 210 + 123
   C 21 + 123   **D** 3 + 6

11. (Represent) Draw a picture of a rectangular prism. A rectangular prism has how many
    (51)
    a. faces?   6
    b. vertices?   8

12. Find the fraction of each circle that is shaded. Then write the fractions in order from least to greatest. $\frac{1}{2}, \frac{2}{3}, \frac{3}{4}, \frac{5}{6}$
    (49)

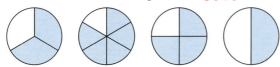

Lesson 83   453

Written Practice (Continued)

Math Conversations
Independent Practice and Discussions to Increase Understanding

Problem 6 (Analyze)
Remind students that *factors* are the numbers multiplied to get the product in a multiplication fact. Students can use a multiplication table to find two multiplication facts for 6. By looking down the rows of numbers smaller than 6, students should spot the number 6 in three different places. The corresponding row and column numbers are the factors that multiply to make 6.

Problem 9   Multiple Choice
Test-Taking Strategy
The key piece of information in this problem is that Marion "sprinted as fast as she could." If she ran for even one or two steps, she would go more than 100 cm, so choice **B** is not a good answer. Similarly, no one would be able to sprint as fast as they could for 100 km, so choice **C** is also a bad choice. This leaves only choice **A**, 100 m, which is a little more than the length of a football field.

Problem 10   Multiple Choice
Test-Taking Strategy
Students should notice that the first addend is different for each answer choice. Students only need to determine the first addend to eliminate all but one answer. The model shows two hundred grids and one ten strip, representing the number 210. Only answer **B** has this addend.

Problem 11 (Represent)
To remind students what a rectangular prism looks like, ask,

"What are some common examples of a rectangular prism?" samples: a shoebox, a cube, an art box, a book

(continued)

Lesson 83   453

Written Practice (Continued)

Math Conversations
Independent Practice and Discussions to Increase Understanding

Problem 18
Remind students of the three steps that were used for these multiplication problems in Lesson 81:
1. Set up the problem.
2. Multiply the ones and regroup if needed.
3. Multiply the tens.

Problem 20 (Model)
Since point *B* is on line segment *AC*, students can write an addition fact relating all three lengths shown: $AB + BC = AC$. Students can then solve for length *AC* by either measuring or adding.

Errors and Misconceptions

Problem 11
When identifying parts of a rectangular prism, students often confuse edges with faces and vertices with edges.

Problem 13
Students may forget to record the units when naming lengths and area. Remind students that length is reported using both a number and a unit of length such as inches, feet, or centimeters. Area is named using a number and a square unit such as square inches or square feet.

Watch for students who may forget to include Aiesha in their calculations and divide the number of pretzels by 5 instead of 6.

---

13. Carla made this rectangle out of floor tiles that were one-foot squares.
_(52, 62)
  a. How long is the rectangle? 4 feet
  b. How wide is the rectangle? 4 feet
  c. What is the area of the rectangle? 16 sq. ft
  d. What kind of rectangle is it? square

14. Change the addition below to multiplication and find the total.
₍₅₄₎ 5×10 cm = 50 cm
  10 cm + 10 cm + 10 cm + 10 cm + 10 cm

15. Find each product:
₍₇₈₎
  a. 4×80 320   b. 3×90 270   c. 6×70 420

16. $35 + $47 + $176 $258
₍₂₄₎

17. $12.48 − $6.97 $5.51
₍₂₆₎

▶ **18.** 2×57 114
₍₈₁₎

19. $3 \times 4 \times 5$ 60
₍₇₇₎

▶ **20.** (Model) Use a centimeter ruler to measure the distances between these points:
₍₇₉₎

  a. How many centimeters is it from point *A* to point *B*?   3 cm
  b. How many centimeters is it from point *B* to point *C*?   5 cm
  c. Use your answers to **a** and **b** to find the number of centimeters from point *A* to point *C*.   8 cm

Early Finishers
Real-World Connection

Aiesha has 2 bags of pretzels with 24 pretzels in each bag. She wants to share the pretzels with 5 friends. How many pretzels should Aiesha and her friends each have?   8 pretzels

---

Using a multiplication table to find half of a number prepares students for

- **Lesson 85,** using manipulatives to divide by a one-digit number.
- **Lesson 86,** learning about multiplication and division fact families.
- **Lesson 89,** using a multiplication table to divide by a one-digit number.
- **Lesson 90,** solving equal groups problems.
- **Lesson 101,** dividing two-digit numbers.

LESSON 84

Planning & Preparation

Texas Essential Knowledge and Skills
(3.4)(B) solve/record multiplication problems (up to two digits times one digit)
(3.15)(A) record observations using numbers

• Multiplying Two-Digit Numbers, Part 2

Objectives
- Multiply two-digit numbers by a one-digit number.
- Write and solve multiplication number sentences to solve problems.
- Continue practicing the multiplication algorithm for multiplying two-digit numbers by one-digit numbers.

Prerequisite Skills
- Learn the multiplication algorithm for multiplying two-digit numbers by one-digit numbers.
- Learn the multiplication facts through 12s.
- Use "product" and "factor" to describe numbers in multiplication number sentences and on the multiplication table.

Materials
Instructional Masters
- Power Up 84

Manipulative Kit
- Money manipulatives (bills)*

Teacher-provided materials
- Student money manipulatives (bills)

optional

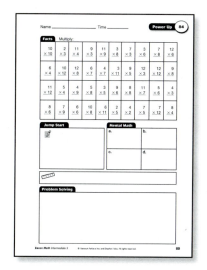

Power Up 84

Reaching All Special Needs Students

Special Education Students	At-Risk Students	English Learners	Advanced Learners
• Inclusion (TM) • Adaptations for Saxon Math	• Reteaching Masters	• English Learners (TM) • English Learner Handbook	• Extend the Problem (TM) • Online Activities

TM = Teacher's Manual

Math Language

Maintained
digit
multiply
square

English Learners
instead

Lesson 84 455A

LESSON 84

Problem Solving Discussion

Problem

Kelly has 26 square tiles. There is one tile for each letter of the alphabet. Kelly will place the tiles in a box, mix them up, and then draw one tile. Which one of these outcomes is most likely to happen? Explain your reasoning.

A Kelly will draw the letter R.
B Kelly will draw a vowel.
C Kelly will draw a consonant.

Focus Strategy  Use Logical Reasoning

Understand Understand the problem.

"What information are we given?"

1. There are 26 square tiles, one for each letter of the alphabet.
2. Kelly will mix up the tiles in a box and then draw one.

"What are we asked to do?"

We are asked to choose which of the three given outcomes is most likely.

Plan Make a plan.

"How can we use the information we know to solve the problem?"

We can *use logical reasoning* to determine which outcome is most likely.

Solve Carry out the plan.

"Let's look at Choice A. How many tiles have the letter R on them?"

There is one tile for each letter of the alphabet, so there is only one tile with an R.

"Let's look at Choice B. How many tiles have a vowel on them?"

Vowels are the letters A, E, I, O, and U. So there are five tiles with a vowel.

"Let's look at Choice C. How many tiles have a consonant on them?"

Any letter that is not a vowel is a consonant. So there are 26 − 5 = 21 tiles with a consonant on them.

"Which of the three outcomes is most likely? Why?"

Choice C is most likely because there are 21 tiles with a consonant. This is more tiles than there are for the letter R (1 tile) and for vowels (5 tiles).

Check Look back.

"Did we complete the task?"

Yes, we determined that Choice C is the most likely of the three given outcomes.

"Is our answer reasonable?"

Yes, Choice C is more likely than Choices A and B, because there are more ways to draw a consonant with one draw than there are ways to draw the letter R or a vowel.

Saxon Math Intermediate 3

LESSON 84

- Multiplying Two-Digit Numbers, Part 2

Texas Essential Knowledge and Skills
(3.4)(B) solve/record multiplication problems (up to two digits times one digit)
(3.15)(A) record observations using numbers

Power Up

facts   Power Up 84

jump start
- Count up by 25s from 0 to 250.
- Count up by 10s from 7 to 97.
- Draw an array to show the multiplication fact 3 × 4.   See student work.
- Draw a 12-centimeter segment on your worksheet. See student work.

mental math
a. **Number Sense:** 55 + 35   90
b. **Time:** How many years are in 9 centuries?   900 yr
c. **Measurement:** What is the perimeter of the triangle?   12 in.
d. **Geometry:** What type of triangle is shown in problem c?   right triangle

problem solving

Kelly has 26 square tiles. There is one tile for each letter of the alphabet. Kelly will place the tiles in a box, mix them up, and then draw one tile. Which one of these outcomes is most likely to happen? Explain your reasoning.

A Kelly will draw the letter R.
B Kelly will draw a vowel.
C Kelly will draw a consonant.

sample: Choice C is most likely because there are 21 consonants, so most of the tiles are labeled with a consonant. There is only 1 letter R, and there are only 5 vowels.

Lesson 84   455

LESSON 84

Power Up

Facts
Distribute **Power Up 84** to students. See answers below.

Jump Start
Before students begin the Mental Math exercise, do these exercises as a class.

Mental Math
Encourage students to share different ways to mentally compute these exercises. Strategies for exercises are listed below.

a. **Add 30, Then Add 5.**
55 + 35 = 55 + 30 + 5 = 85 + 5 = 90

b. **Skip Count by 100**
100, 200, 300, 400, 500, 600, 700, 800, 900
Nine centuries is 900 years.

Think 9 × 10
Think of 9 × 100 as 9 × 10, with an added zero on the end. So 9 centuries is 90 plus an extra zero, or 900 years.

Problem Solving
Refer to **Problem-Solving Strategy Discussion**, p. 455B.

Facts   Multiply:

10 × 10 = 100	2 × 3 = 6	11 × 4 = 44	9 × 3 = 27	11 × 9 = 99	3 × 8 = 24	7 × 3 = 21	3 × 6 = 18	7 × 8 = 56	12 × 6 = 72
6 × 4 = 24	10 × 12 = 120	12 × 8 = 96	6 × 7 = 42	4 × 7 = 28	3 × 11 = 33	9 × 5 = 45	12 × 3 = 36	12 × 12 = 144	9 × 8 = 72
11 × 12 = 132	5 × 4 = 20	4 × 9 = 36	5 × 8 = 40	3 × 5 = 15	9 × 6 = 54	8 × 8 = 64	11 × 7 = 77	5 × 6 = 30	4 × 3 = 12
8 × 6 = 48	7 × 9 = 63	6 × 6 = 36	10 × 8 = 80	6 × 11 = 66	2 × 5 = 10	4 × 2 = 8	7 × 5 = 35	7 × 12 = 84	8 × 4 = 32

Lesson 84   455

New Concept

Discussion

Students can build on their knowledge of the multiplication algorithm using their skills for multiplying two-digit numbers by 2. To begin, ask students to double the number 16 using the multiplication algorithm. 2 × 16 = 32

Have students write the multiplication as an addition. 16 + 16 = 32

Then ask students to add another 16 to the number sentence and solve. 16 + 16 + 16 = 48

Help students make the connection between 16 + 16 + 16 = 48 and 3 × 16 = 48.

For the *Analyze* question, think of the multiplication in terms of equal groups. Since there are 3 equal groups of 25, the total in all three groups is shown by adding three 25s to get a total of 75.

Ask advanced learners,

"What division fact can you write that is related to this multiplication of 3 quarters?" 75¢ ÷ 3 = 25¢

Example 1
Real-World Connection

Use this example to help students develop a sense of height measurements in inches.

"How many inches tall is someone who is 5 feet tall?" 60 inches

"What about someone who is 4 feet tall?" 48 inches

"The shortest grown adult on record was not quite 2 feet tall. How many inches is 2 feet?" 24 inches

"The tallest person on record was just under 9 feet tall. How many inches is 9 feet?" 108 inches

(continued)

New Concept

In Lesson 81 we multiplied two-digit numbers by 2. In this lesson we will multiply two-digit numbers by other numbers.

We know that a quarter is 25¢ and that 3 quarters total 75¢.

Below we show the multiplication:

Set up.   Multiply 5 ones by 3.   Multiply 2 tens by 3.

$$\begin{array}{r} 25¢ \\ \times\ 3 \\ \hline \end{array} \qquad \begin{array}{r} \overset{1}{25}¢ \\ \times\ 3 \\ \hline 5 \end{array} \qquad \begin{array}{r} \overset{1}{25}¢ \\ \times\ 3 \\ \hline 75¢ \end{array}$$

When we multiply 5 ones by 3 the product is 15, which is 1 ten and 5 ones. We write 5 ones in the ones place and write the 1 ten above the 2.

When we multiply 2 tens by 3 the product is 6 tens. After multiplying we add the 1 ten for a total of 7 tens.

Analyze Write the multiplication above as addition.
25¢ + 25¢ + 25¢ = 75¢

Example 1

One foot is 12 inches. Mr. Simms is 6 feet tall. How many inches tall is Mr. Simms?

We find the number of inches in 6 feet by multiplying 12 inches by 6.

Set up.   Multiply 2 ones by 6.   Multiply 1 ten by 6.

$$\begin{array}{r} 12 \\ \times\ 6 \\ \hline \end{array} \qquad \begin{array}{r} \overset{1}{12} \\ \times\ 6 \\ \hline 2 \end{array} \qquad \begin{array}{r} \overset{1}{12} \\ \times\ 6 \\ \hline 72 \end{array}$$

Mr. Simms is **72 inches** tall.

Math Background

The Commutative Property of Multiplication states that the order in which factors are multiplied does not impact the product. In other words, 3 × 2 = 2 × 3. Because of this property, the two numbers being multiplied do not need to be differentiated, so both are called factors. However, it is important for students to learn to perform the standard multiplication algorithm in the prescribed sequence. In the multiplication algorithm, shortcuts are used to record regrouping and place value. For example, writing down the regrouped digit above the tens column is just a shorthand way of recording the products of factors in the ones and tens places before adding them together. To get the correct answer using the algorithm, the digits in the ones place must be multiplied and regrouped first, then the regrouped product is added in the tens place. This sequence will become even more critical when both factors are multi-digit numbers. A third grader who does not perform the steps in sequence is likely to end up with this answer:

$$\begin{array}{r} 36 \\ \times\ 3 \\ \hline 918 \end{array}$$

Example 2

The walls of a square classroom are 32 feet long. What is the perimeter of the room?

Each side of the square is 32 feet. Instead of adding four 32s, we will multiply 32 ft by 4.

32 feet

Set up.	Multiply 2 ones by 4.	Multiply 3 tens by 4.
32 × 4	32 × 4 8	32 × 4 128

The perimeter of the room is **128 feet**.

Example 3

Find the product: 5 × 26

We write 26 above and 5 below with the 6 and 5 aligned in the ones place.

26
× 5

We multiply 6 ones by 5. The product is 30, which is 3 tens and 0 ones. We write 0 in the ones place and 3 above the 2.

3
26
× 5
0

Then we multiply 2 tens by 5. The product is 10 tens. Then we add the 3 tens for a total of 13 tens. We write 130, which is 1 hundred and 3 tens.

3
26
× 5
130

The product of 5 × 26 is **130**.

Lesson Practice

Find each product.

▶ a. 12
× 4
48

▶ b. 21
× 5
105

▶ c. 15
× 4
60

d. 35
× 3
105

e. A foot is 12 inches. The ceiling is 8 feet high. How many inches high is the ceiling? 96 in.

▶ f. A pound is 16 ounces. Leon weighed 7 pounds when he was born. How many ounces is 7 pounds?
112 ounces

Lesson 84   457

 **English Learners**

Instead of means in place of. Say:

"You want to find out the cost of 9 cards at 60¢ each. What can you do to find the answer instead of adding?"
sample: We can multiply 60¢ × 9 = $5.40.

Ask:

"Instead of watching television after dinner, what is a good activity?"
sample: reading a book, playing a game.

Have students talk about activities they like to do instead of watching television on the weekend.

New Concept (Continued)

Example 2
Alternate Method

Have students check their work by adding the sides to get the perimeter. Point out to students that adding 32 four times or counting by 32s is more difficult than using the multiplication algorithm.

Lesson Practice

Guided Practice

Use these problems as guided practice to check the students' understanding of today's concept.

Problems a–d
Remind students to start in the ones place when they multiply 2-digit numbers. Caution them to keep careful track of any tens from multiplication in the ones place.

Problem f
Extend the Problem

You may wish to extend the problem so that students convert from ounces back to pounds. Ask students to solve this problem:

"After one month, Leon weighed 144 ounces. How many ounces did Leon gain in the first month?"
144 − 112 = 32 ounces

"How many 16-ounce groups is that?" 2

"How many pounds did Leon gain the first month?" 2 pounds

 Closure The questions below help assess the concepts taught in this lesson.

"When we multiply a two-digit number by a one-digit number, should we write the problem horizontally or vertically?" vertically

"Explain how to multiply 24 × 8." Write the numbers in a vertical column with 8 underneath 4. Multiply 4 × 8. Write the 2 in the answer row and regroup the 3 to the top of the tens column. Multiply 2 × 8 to get 16 and add 3 to get 19 tens. The answer is 192.

Discuss real-world situations where multiplying a two-digit number by a one-digit number might be helpful. Examples are given below.

- We have three sweaters at $24 each and want to know the total cost.
- An artist wants to sell his 18 bowls for $7 each.

Lesson 84   457

Written Practice

Math Conversations
Independent Practice and Discussions to Increase Understanding

Problem 1 (Analyze)
Help students recognize the "equal groups" pattern.

"There are 7 classrooms, or equal groups, with 30 students in each group."

Problem 3 (Analyze)
Students should recognize this as an "equal groups" problem.

"There are 10 stamps, or groups, and each costs 42¢."

Some students may need to be reminded that 420¢ should be written as $4.20.

Problem 4 (Analyze)
You may need to remind students that a ton is equal to 2,000 pounds. Students can think of 7 times 2,000 as 7 × 2 with three zeros attached, or skip count by 2,000s seven times.

Problem 6 (Analyze)
"Half of a pound" indicates division by 2. Students may divide 16 by 2 using a multiplication table.

Problem 8 Multiple Choice
Test-Taking Strategy

"100 cm is the length of a meterstick. Do you think it would take an hour for a car to travel that distance?" no

"100 m is a little longer than the length of a football field. Is that a reasonable distance for a car to travel in 1 hour?" no

That leaves choice **C**, 100 km, as the only reasonable distance driven in an hour.

(continued)

Written Practice Distributed and Integrated

1. (Analyze) In each of the seven classrooms, there were 30 students. How many students were in all seven classrooms? 210 students
(60, 78)

2. Sixty-four students rode the bus for the field trip. The bus could hold 72 students. There was room on the bus for how many more students? 8 more students
(36)

3. (Analyze) Denise bought ten 42¢ stamps. How much did she pay for the stamps? $4.20
(56, 60)

4. (Analyze) An African elephant can weigh 7 tons. How many pounds is 7 tons? 14,000 pounds
(74)

5. Name the fraction or mixed number shown on each number line below.
(48)

a.  $\frac{2}{4}$ or $\frac{1}{2}$

b. $7\frac{1}{4}$

6. (Analyze) A pound is 16 ounces. How many ounces is half of a pound? 8 ounces
(74, 83)

7. Three multiplication facts that equal 12 are 1 × 12, 2 × 6, and 3 × 4. Write three multiplication facts that equal 18.
(55)
1 × 18; 2 × 9; 3 × 6

8. Multiple Choice The Olsens drove along the open highway. In one hour they could have traveled about how far? c
(79)
A 100 m **B** 100 cm **C** 100 km

9. Write an addition fact that is shown by this model: 143 + 260 = 403
(11)

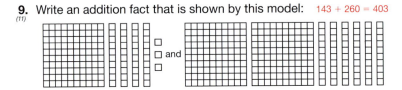

458 Saxon Math Intermediate 3

Inclusion

Multiplying Money

Some students will have difficulty multiplying two-digit numbers. Use money manipulatives to help them with regrouping in multiplication.

Materials: $1 bills and $10 bills

- Write 27 × 4 in vertical form on the board.

"Another way to say this is '4 groups of 27'."

- Students make 4 groups of $27.
- Students combine the $1 bills first and regroup ten $1 bills as a $10 bill.
- Show how the regrouping is recorded in the example on the board.
- Students combine the $10 bills. Record the answer on the board.

10. Find each product.
(78, 81)
   a. 2 × 30   60
   b. 2 × 31   62

11. Find each product.
(84)
   a. 3 × 31   93
   b. 4 × 31   124

12. One-inch cubes were used to build the rectangular prism at right.
(72, 73)
   a. How many inches long is it?   4 inches
   b. How many inches wide is it?   3 inches
   c. How many inches high is it?   2 inches
   d. What is its volume?   24 cubic inches

13. Multiply:
(78)
   a. 7 × 80   560
   b. 8 × 60   480
   c. 7 × 60   420

Add or subtract, as shown below:

14. $20.00 − $12.87 $7.13
(26, 28)

15. 96¢ + 87¢ + 79¢ $2.62
(22, 24)

16. Use money to multiply 3 × $24. $72
(84)

17. a. The shaded circle at right represents which fraction name for 1? $\frac{6}{6}$
(42, 46)
   b. Draw and shade a circle to represent $\frac{4}{4}$.

18. Marsha glanced at the clock while she was eating dinner. Write the time in digital form.   7:10 p.m.
(38)

▶ **19. Multiple Choice** Which figure shows a triangle inside of a square?   D
(67)

A   B   C   D

20. Multiple Choice Which word best names the shape of the Earth?   B
(75)
   A circle   **B** sphere   **C** rectangle   **D** cylinder

Lesson 84   459

 **Looking Forward**

Learning to multiply a two-digit number by a one-digit number prepares students for

- **Lesson 90,** solving equal groups problems.
- **Lessons 91 and 97,** multiplying three-digit numbers.
- **Lesson 100,** multiplying dollars and cents.

Written Practice (Continued)

Math Conversations
Independent Practice and Discussions to Increase Understanding

▶ **Problem 19   Multiple Choice**
Test-Taking Strategy

Students should first eliminate any answer choice that does not have a large square. Then students should make sure that any remaining answers also have a small triangle.

Errors and Misconceptions

▶ **Problem 1**
Reading Math

Students may struggle with the difference in meaning between the two similar phrases, "in each of the seven classrooms" and "in all seven classrooms."

> "Remember that when you see the words 'in each,' you should think of splitting items into equal groups. What operation involves splitting things into equal groups?" division

> "When you see the phrase 'in all' you should think of combining equal groups. What operation involves combining equal groups?" multiplication (or addition)

Lesson 84   459

LESSON 85

Planning & Preparation

Texas Essential Knowledge and Skills

(3.4)(C) use models to solve division problems and number sentences to record the solutions

(3.14)(D) use tools such as manipulatives to solve problems

- **Using Manipulatives to Divide by a One-Digit Number**

Objectives
- Model dividing by a one-digit number with pictorial models and concrete objects.
- Use pencil and paper to write division number sentences to show dividing by a one-digit number.
- Draw arrays to model dividing by a one-digit number.

Prerequisite Skills
- Learn the multiplication facts through 12s.
- Model finding "fair share" (dividing by 2) with pictorial models and concrete objects such as counters or tiles.
- Use pencil and paper to write division number sentences to show dividing by 2.
- Draw arrays to model dividing by 2.

Materials

Instructional Masters
- Power Up 85

Manipulative Kit
- Counters or color tiles
- Money manipulatives*

Teacher-provided materials
- Student money manipulatives*
- Index cards*
- Ribbon or yarn

    *optional

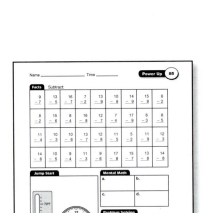

Power Up 85

Reaching All Special Needs Students

Special Education Students	At-Risk Students	English Learners	Advanced Learners
• Inclusion (TM) • Adaptations for Saxon Math	• Reteaching Masters	• English Learners (TM) • English Learner Handbook	• Early Finishers (SE) • Online Activities

TM = Teacher's Manual
SE = Student Edition

Math Language

New	Maintained	English Learners
division	equal	meaning

460A   *Saxon Math* Intermediate 3

Problem Solving Discussion

Problem

Tom is thinking of a number that is greater than 20 but less than 30. The sum of the digits is 6. What is Tom's number?

Focus Strategies

 Guess and Check

 Use Logical Reasoning

Understand Understand the problem.

"What information are we given?"

1. The number is greater than 20 but less than 30.
2. The sum of the digits is 6.

"What are we asked to do?"

We are asked to find the number.

Plan Make a plan.

"How can we use the information we know to solve the problem?"

We can find pairs of digits that equal 6. Then we can look for a pair that can make a two-digit number greater than 20 but less than 30.

Solve Carry out the plan.

"What are some pairs of digits that equal 6?"

0 and 6	3 and 3	6 and 0
1 and 5	4 and 2	
2 and 4	5 and 1	

"What is a number pair that we can guess as the answer to the problem?"

We are looking for a number between 20 and 30. If the first digit is 0 or 1, the number would be too small. If the first digit is a 3, 4, 5, or 6, the number would be too large. So we choose 24 as our guess.

Check Look back.

"Let's check our guess of 24. Is the number greater than 20 and less than 30? Do the digits have a sum of 6?"

Yes, the number 24 is greater than 20, less than 30, and $2 + 4 = 6$. Our guess checks out.

"What problem solving strategies did we use, and how did they help us?"

We *used logical reasoning* to help us narrow down our choices so that we could make an educated guess. Then we *guessed and checked* to find the answer.

LESSON 85

Power Up

Facts
Distribute **Power Up 85** to students. See answers below.

Jump Start
Before students begin the Mental Math exercise, do these exercises as a class.

Mental Math
Encourage students to share different ways to mentally compute these exercises. Strategies for exercises are listed below.

a. Think of 54 as 14 + 40
   54 + 60 = 14 + 40 + 60 = 14 + 100
   = 114

b. Multiply the First Two Numbers First
   7 × 5 × 10 = 35 × 10 = 350

d. Add, Then Round
   Adding the bills and coins gives $15.51. Rounding to the nearest dollar, $15.51 is more than $15.50. So it is closer to $16.00 than to $15.00.

Problem Solving
Refer to **Problem-Solving Strategy Discussion**, p. 460B.

LESSON 85

- Using Manipulatives to Divide by a One-Digit Number

Texas Essential Knowledge and Skills
(3.4)(C) use models to solve division problems and number sentences to record the solutions
(3.14)(D) use tools such as manipulatives to solve problems

Power Up

facts Power Up 85

jump start
Count up by 11s from 0 to 110.
Count up by square numbers from 1 to 144.

It is 11:50 in the morning. Draw hands on your clock to show the time. Write the time in digital form.   11:50 a.m.

In March the average daily high was 63°F. In January, the average high was 12 degrees cooler. Mark your thermometer to show the average high in January.   51°F

mental math
a. **Number Sense:** 54 + 60   114
b. **Number Sense:** 7 × 5 × 10   350
c. **Money:** $1.30 + 99¢ $2.29
d. **Estimation:** Round the value of these bills and coins to the nearest dollar. $16.00

problem solving
Tom is thinking of a number that is greater than 20 but less than 30. The sum of the digits is 6. What is Tom's number?   24

460   Saxon Math Intermediate 3

Facts Subtract:

9 − 7 = 2	13 − 5 = 8	16 − 7 = 9	7 − 2 = 5	13 − 9 = 4	10 − 8 = 2	14 − 9 = 5	15 − 8 = 7	6 − 2 = 4
8 − 2 = 6	15 − 6 = 9	8 − 4 = 4	16 − 8 = 8	12 − 7 = 5	7 − 4 = 3	17 − 9 = 8	6 − 3 = 3	8 − 5 = 3
11 − 4 = 7	10 − 3 = 7	10 − 6 = 4	13 − 7 = 6	12 − 8 = 4	11 − 5 = 6	5 − 2 = 3	11 − 9 = 2	12 − 3 = 9
14 − 6 = 8	10 − 5 = 5	9 − 4 = 5	11 − 3 = 8	9 − 6 = 3	17 − 8 = 9	15 − 7 = 8	13 − 8 = 5	14 − 8 = 6

New Concept

Using objects can help us understand the different meanings of **division**.

Activity
Equal Groups

Place 12 counters or tiles on your desk for problems **1** and **2**.

1. Tony has a collection of 12 rocks. He divided the rocks into 3 equal groups. How many rocks were in each group? (Act out the problem with your counters.) *4 rocks*

2. Then Tony arranged the 12 rocks into groups with 3 rocks in each group. How many groups did he make? (Act out the problem with your counters.) *4 groups*

We saw two different meanings of division in the activity. In the first problem we were looking for the **number in each group.** In the second problem we were looking for the **number of groups.** In both problems, we started with one large group and separated it into smaller equal groups.

Connect When we divide, we separate a group into smaller equal groups. How does this relate to multiplication? *sample: In multiplication, we combine equal groups. Multiplication is the opposite of division.*

Example 1

Fifteen students lined up in 3 rows. How many students were in each row? Use manipulatives or draw a picture to represent the problem. Then show how to write the division.

We arrange 15 counters in 3 equal rows or draw a picture.

○ ○ ○ ○ ○
○ ○ ○ ○ ○
○ ○ ○ ○ ○

We see that there were **5 students** in each row. We write the division this way:

$$15 \div 3 = 5 \text{ or } 3\overline{)15}^{\,5}$$

Lesson 85 461

New Concept

Instruction
Division can be viewed as a process of splitting one large group into smaller equal groups. Review the concept of dividing by 2 from Lesson 82. Have students go to the board to draw pictures that represent groupings of 2 and write the division fact shown above each sketch.

Activity
We recommend pairing students for this activity. Give each pair of students about 20 counters or tiles.

Example 1
Math-to-Math Connection

After drawing the array, ask students,

"What do we call a pattern like this?" an array

"What operation did we use arrays to represent before?" multiplication

"What multiplication fact would this array show?" $5 \times 3 = 15$

(continued)

Math Background

This lesson may be a good opportunity to mention prime numbers to advanced students. If you provide students with 13 tiles, you can then ask them whether they can divide the tiles into smaller groups of equal size. After attempting to do so, the students should come to the conclusion that they cannot split the tiles into smaller groups, and you can then point out that this means 13 is a prime number. Repeat the exercise with 12 tiles to demonstrate a composite number.

English Learner

A **meaning** is the intended purpose of something. Say:

"What is the meaning of a hug? A handshake? A frown?" See student work.

Ask:

"What is the meaning of a red light at an intersection?" stop

Have students think of other symbols and explain their meanings.

Lesson 85 461

New Concept (Continued)

Example 2
Reading Math

Ask for a volunteer to read the divisions aloud. Be sure the student understands to read the first one from left to right and the division box from right to left.

Lesson Practice

Guided Practice

Use these problems as guided practice to check the students' understanding of today's concept.

Problems a and b
Manipulative Use

Have students use actual books and do a classroom demonstration. Choose one or two students to arrange the books into equal piles. Have another student write the division fact on the board in two different ways.

Problem d
Active Learning

You can have students solve this problem using lengths of gift-wrapping ribbon or yarn.

"How can you cut the ribbon into four equal pieces?" sample: Fold the ribbon in half to find the middle, cut it there, and then repeat with the two smaller pieces.

"After you do that, how long is each piece?" 3 inches

Closure The question below helps assess the concepts taught in this lesson.

"Describe what happens when we divide." When we divide, we split a large group into smaller equal groups.

Discuss real-world situations where division might be helpful. Examples are given below.

- A gym teacher wants to make four teams of students to play basketball.
- We have $28 and want to buy packs of trading cards which are $4 each. We want to find how many packs we can buy.

Example 2

Fifteen students gathered in small groups of 3 students to work on the problem. How many groups were there? Use manipulatives or a picture to represent the problem. Then show how to write the division.

We separate 15 students into groups of 3.

There are **5 groups** of students. We show the division this way:

$$15 \div 3 = 5 \text{ or } 3\overline{)15}$$

Lesson Practice Use manipulatives or draw pictures to represent each problem. Then show how to write the division.

a. See student work;
6 books; $18 \div 3 = 6$ or $3\overline{)18}$

> **a.** Eighteen books were stacked in three equal piles. How many books were in each pile?

b. See student work;
6 stacks; $18 \div 3 = 6$ or $3\overline{)18}$

> **b.** Eighteen books were put in stacks with 3 books in each stack. How many stacks of books were there?

c. See student work;
5 stacks; $20 \div 4 = 5$ or $4\overline{)20}$

> **c.** Todd has 20 quarters. He put 4 quarters in each stack. How many stacks did he make?

d. See student work;
3 inches; $12 \div 4 = 3$ or $4\overline{)12}$

> **d.** Becki cut a 12-inch-long ribbon into 4 equal pieces. How long was each piece of ribbon?

Written Practice — Distributed and Integrated

1. The new pencil was 18 cm long. Mark used one half of the pencil. Then how long was the pencil? 9 cm
(79, 83)

2. Samantha bought some art supplies for $17.27 plus $1.22 sales tax. Write the total price. $18.49
(22)

3. The stamp cost 42¢. Jeremy gave the clerk a dollar bill. What coins should Jeremy get back for change? 2 quarters, 1 nickel, 3 pennies
(25, 26)

▶ **4.** (Analyze) Darren used 10 tiles to make the rectangle at right. If he doubles the length of the rectangle, then how many tiles will he use in all?   20 tiles
(56)

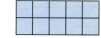

▶ **5.** Robin and Ashley shared $14 equally. How much money was there for each girl? $7
(82, 83)

▶ **6.** (Analyze) Multiply:
(84)
    a. 3 × $23 $69

    b. 4 × $23 $92

(Model) Use counters or draw a diagram to help you solve problems **7** and **8**.

7. Rob put 24 books in 3 equal stacks. How many books were in each stack?   8 books
(85)

8. Gwen put 24 books into stacks of 6 books. How many stacks were there?   4 stacks
(85)

9. Write an addition fact that is shown by the model below.   32 + 24 = 56
(11)

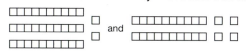

10. A box is filled with cubes as shown at right.
(72, 73)
    a. How many cubes are in each layer?   18 cubes

    b. How many layers are there?   2 layers

    c. How many cubes are there?   36 cubes

    d. If each cube is 1 cubic inch, what is the volume of all the cubes?   36 cubic inches

11. Find each missing addend:
(9)
    a. 15 + m = 25   10   **b.** n + 12 = 20   8

▶ **12.** Find each product:
(78)
    a. 9 × 90   810   **b.** 8 × 80   640   **c.** 7 × 70   490

Lesson 85   463

Inclusion

Division Stories

Some students may have difficulty visualizing division situations. This activity will give them additional hands-on experience.

Materials: 25 square color tiles per pair; 5 index cards per pair

- Tell students a simple division story such as: "I have 12 pencils. I want to give 3 students an equal number of pencils. How many pencils will each student get?"

"How many in all?" 12

- Students count out 12 color tiles.

"How many groups?" 3

- Students put one index card per group on their desk.

- Students separate 12 color tiles equally among the three index cards.

Written Practice

Math Conversations
Independent Practice and Discussions to Increase Understanding

▶ **Problem 4** (Analyze)
Have students use color tiles to show that doubling the length doubles the number of tiles needed. Doubling something means to multiply by 2, so students should multiply 10 × 2.

▶ **Problem 5**
Reading Math
Students need to interpret the words "shared equally" to mean that they will need to find half. Ask them,

"If Robin and Ashley share the money equally, how many equal groups are there?" 2

"How do you find the amount of money in each group?" samples: Divide $14 by 2, Find half of $14

▶ **Problem 6** (Analyze)
Encourage students to use mental math to solve these problems.

a. Think 3 × $20 plus 3 × $3.

b. Think 4 × $20 plus 4 × $3.

▶ **Problem 12**
Ask students,

"Before you added zeros at the end, what were the multiplication facts that you used to find these products?" 9 × 9 = 81, 8 × 8 = 64, 7 × 7 = 49

"Where are these multiplication facts found on the multiplication table?" along the diagonal

"Who remembers what these multiplication facts are called?" square numbers

(continued)

Lesson 85   463

Written Practice (Continued)

Math Conversations
Independent Practice and Discussions to Increase Understanding

Problem 17 Multiple Choice
Test-Taking Strategy

Since the problem asks for the figure that does *not* show a line of symmetry, a good strategy would be to identify the one picture that looks different from the others. Ask students which figure looks different from the others and why. choice **C**; The line does not divide the figure in half.

Errors and Misconceptions

Problem 8
Students may overlook the fact that this problem says "stacks of 6 books," not "6 equal stacks" as in the previous problem. Although the division that students do will be the same (24 ÷ 6 = 4), watch for students who write the answer as "4" or "4 books" instead of "4 stacks." Advise students to reread the problem and write the answer to the question that is being asked.

Problem 19
With the changing denominators in this sequence, the pattern might be difficult for students to see. Be sure that they look at the number line shown. Tell them to think of the number line as a ruler with half- and quarter-inch markings.

Students may use bills from their money kit or other manipulatives to solve this two-part "some went away" story problem.

Add or subtract, as shown below:

13. $786 − $694 $92
(23)

14. $3.50 + $0.97 + $0.85 $5.32
(22, 24)

15. 5 × 33 165
(84)

16. 4 × 4 × 4 64
(77, 84)

▶ **17. Multiple Choice** Which figure does *not* show a line of symmetry?
(Inv. 7) C

A   B   C   D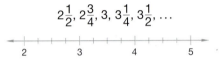

18. a. Draw a square with sides 6 cm long.   See student work.
(58, 62, 79)

b. What is the perimeter of the square?   24 cm

c. What is the area of the square?   36 square cm

19. Use the number line below to help you find the next four numbers
(2, 48) in this sequence: $3\frac{3}{4}, 4, 4\frac{1}{4}, 4\frac{1}{2}$

$2\frac{1}{2}, 2\frac{3}{4}, 3, 3\frac{1}{4}, 3\frac{1}{2}, \ldots$

20. Draw two parallel line segments. Then draw two more parallel line
(Inv. 4) segments that cross the first two segments and are perpendicular
to them. What game can you play using this design?   sample: ┼┼ ; tic-tac-toe

Early Finishers
Real-World Connection

Martina is a carpenter. She has a wooden board that is 182 inches long. She is working on 2 projects. She uses 41 inches for the first project and 64 inches for the second project. How many inches of the board are left for Martina to use?   77 inches

---

Using manipulatives to divide by a one-digit number prepares students for

- **Lesson 86**, learning multiplication and division fact families.
- **Lesson 89**, using a multiplication table to divide by a one-digit number.
- **Lesson 90**, solving equal groups problems.
- **Lesson 101**, dividing two-digit numbers.

Assessments

Distribute **Power-Up Test 16** and **Cumulative Test 16** to each student. Have students complete the **Power-Up Test** first. Allow 10 minutes. Then have students work on the **Cumulative Test**.

Test-Day Activity

The remaining class time can be spent on **Test-Day Activity 8**. Students can begin the activity in class and complete it as homework.

LESSON 86

Texas Essential Knowledge and Skills

(3.4)(C) use models to solve division problems and number sentences to record the solutions

(3.6)(C) identify patterns in related multiplication and division sentences (fact families)

Planning & Preparation

- **Division Facts**
- **Multiplication and Division Fact Families**

Objectives
- Use dividend, divisor, and quotient to describe parts of a division number sentence.
- Identify patterns in the relationships between related multiplication and division number sentences.
- Write a fact family when given three numbers.
- Use the inverse relationship of multiplication and division to find missing factors.

Prerequisite Skills
- Learn the multiplication facts through 12s.
- Write a multiplication fact represented by a given array.
- Model dividing by a one-digit number with pictorial models and concrete objects.
- Use pencil and paper to write division number sentences to show dividing by a one-digit number.

Materials

Instructional Masters
- Power Up 86

Manipulative Kit
- Ruler
- Counters or color tiles*
- 1-inch cubes*

Teacher-provided materials
- Index cards*

  *optional

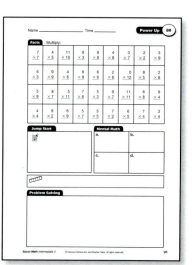

Power Up 86

Differentiated Instruction

Reaching All Special Needs Students

Special Education Students	At-Risk Students	English Learners	Advanced Learners
• Inclusion (TM) • Adaptations for Saxon Math	• Alternative Approach (TM) • Reteaching Masters	• English Learners (TM) • English Learner Handbook	• Extend the Example (TM) • Extend the Problem (TM) • Online Activities

TM = Teacher's Manual

Math Language

New	Maintained	English Learners
dividend	quotient	order
divisor	triangular numbers	fact family

Lesson 86 465A

LESSON 86

Problem Solving Discussion

Problem

In the problem solving exercise for Lesson 83, we found that we can use objects to make triangular patterns.

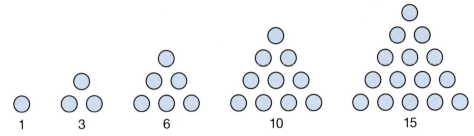

The numbers 1, 3, 6, 10, and 15 are examples of **triangular numbers**. Notice how the numbers increase:

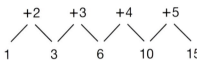

Continue the pattern to find the next two triangular numbers.

Focus Strategies

 Find/Extend a Pattern

 Draw a Picture or Diagram

Understand Understand the problem.

"What information are we given?"

1. We are shown diagrams of triangular patterns of objects.
2. We are told that the numbers 1, 3, 6, 10, and 15 are triangular numbers.
3. We are shown the increasing pattern formed by triangular numbers.

"What are we asked to do?"

We are asked to continue the pattern to find the next two triangular numbers.

Plan Make a plan.

"What problem solving strategies can we use?"

We can *draw a diagram* to help us *extend the pattern* of triangular numbers.

Solve Carry out the plan.

"Let's continue the diagram of the sequence of triangular numbers. What are the fifth and sixth terms of the pattern?"

We continue the diagram:
We find that the next two terms of the pattern are 21 and 28.

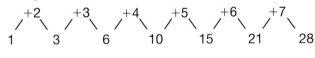

Check Look back.

"Are our answers reasonable?"

Yes, the numbers 21 and 28 fit the pattern of increase in triangular numbers.

"What problem solving strategies did we use, and how did they help us?"

We *drew a diagram* to keep track of the increase from one term to the next. We *extended the pattern* to write the next two numbers.

Alternate Strategy

Write a Number Sentence

Remind students that in triangular arrangements of objects, the number of objects in each row increases by 1. The number of objects in the arrangement with 5 rows is 1 + 2 + 3 + 4 + 5 = 15. So the next two triangular numbers are:

1 + 2 + 3 + 4 + 5 + 6 = 21

and

1 + 2 + 3 + 4 + 5 + 6 + 7 = 28.

LESSON 86

- Division Facts
- Multiplication and Division Fact Families

Texas Essential Knowledge and Skills
(3.4)(C) use models to solve division problems and number sentences to record the solutions
(3.6)(C) identify patterns in related multiplication and division sentences (fact families)

Power Up

facts Power Up 86

jump start
Count up by 2s from 0 to 30 and then back down to 0.
Count up by 5s from 0 to 60 and then back down to 0.

Write two multiplication facts using the numbers 5, 11, and 55.   5 × 11 = 55; 11 × 5 = 55

Draw a 5-centimeter segment on your worksheet. About how many inches long is the segment?   See student work; about 2 in.

mental math
a. **Calendar:** How many months are in 6 years?   72 months
b. **Number Sense:** 84 − 40   44
c. **Number Sense:** 77 + 25   102
d. **Money:** $3.49 + $7.00 $10.49

problem solving
In the problem solving exercise for Lesson 83, we found that we can use objects to make triangular patterns.

The numbers 1, 3, 6, 10, and 15 are examples of **triangular numbers.** Notice how the numbers increase:

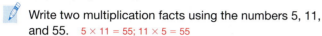

Continue the pattern to find the next two triangular numbers.   21, 28

Lesson 86   465

LESSON 86

Power Up

Facts
Distribute **Power Up 86** to students. See answers below.

Jump Start
Before students begin the Mental Math exercise, do these counting exercises as a class.

Mental Math
Encourage students to share different ways to mentally compute these exercises. Strategies for exercises are listed below.

a. Count by 12s
   12, 24, 36, 48, 60, 72 months
   Remember your Multiplication Facts
   6 × 12 months = 72 months

c. Think of 77 as 2 + 75
   77 + 25 = 2 + 75 + 25 = 2 + 100
   = 102
   Look for Pairs that Add up to 100
   75 + 25 = 100
   2 more than that is 102.

Problem Solving
Refer to **Problem-Solving Strategy Discussion,** p. 465B.

Facts Multiply:

7 × 7 = 49	4 × 5 = 20	11 × 10 = 110	8 × 3 = 24	8 × 8 = 64	4 × 8 = 32	3 × 7 = 21	2 × 2 = 4	3 × 9 = 27
6 × 3 = 18	9 × 9 = 81	4 × 6 = 24	8 × 9 = 72	6 × 6 = 36	2 × 6 = 12	0 × 12 = 0	8 × 5 = 40	2 × 8 = 16
5 × 9 = 45	8 × 7 = 56	5 × 11 = 55	7 × 6 = 42	5 × 3 = 15	9 × 7 = 63	11 × 11 = 121	6 × 8 = 48	9 × 4 = 36
4 × 4 = 16	9 × 2 = 18	6 × 9 = 54	5 × 7 = 35	5 × 5 = 25	7 × 2 = 14	6 × 5 = 30	7 × 4 = 28	3 × 4 = 12

Lesson 86   465

New Concepts

Connection
Remind students about addition and subtraction facts that form fact families.

Write the following facts on the board and point out the similarities:

$8 + 6 = 14$ $6 + 8 = 14$
$14 - 8 = 6$ $14 - 6 = 8$
$7 \times 2 = 14$ $2 \times 7 = 14$
$14 \div 7 = 2$ $14 \div 2 = 7$

Explain to students that just as addition and subtraction are opposites, so are multiplication and division. If one fact is known, then the other three can easily be written.

Math Language
Review multiplication vocabulary.

"What do we call the numbers that are multiplied?" factors

"What is the answer called?" product

Example 1
Active Learning
Send students to the board to practice writing fact families.

"What is an addition and subtraction fact family for the numbers 4, 5, and 9?"
$4 + 5 = 9, 5 + 4 = 9, 9 - 5 = 4, 9 - 4 = 5$

"What is a multiplication and division fact family that uses the numbers 4 and 5 as factors?" $4 \times 5 = 20, 5 \times 4 = 20,$
$20 \div 5 = 4, 20 \div 4 = 5$

Ask students to identify the name for the largest number in both a multiplication fact and a division fact. product, dividend

(continued)

New Concepts

Division Facts

We can learn division facts while we are learning multiplication facts. The same three numbers that make a multiplication fact also make a division fact.

$$20 = 4 \times 5$$
$$20 \div 4 = 5$$

When we multiply, we know the two factors, and we are looking for the product. When we divide, we know the product and one of the factors, and we are looking for the other factor. When dividing we call these numbers the **dividend, divisor,** and **quotient.**

$$\text{dividend} \div \text{divisor} = \text{quotient} \qquad \text{divisor} \overline{)\text{dividend}}^{\text{quotient}}$$

Example 1

Find each quotient:

a. $24 \div 6$ b. $4\overline{)24}$

a. We read $24 \div 6$ as "Twenty-four divided by six." We may think, "Six times what number equals 24?" Since $6 \times 4 = 24$, the quotient is **4**.

b. We read $4\overline{)24}$ as "Twenty-four divided by four." We think, "What number times 4 equals 24?" Since $6 \times 4 = 24$, the quotient is **6**.

Multiplication and Division Fact Families

The three numbers that make a multiplication fact can also be used to make a division fact. Together, the multiplication facts and their related division facts make up a **fact family.**

Fact Family

Multiplication Facts	Division Facts
$4 \times 6 = 24$	$24 \div 6 = 4$
$6 \times 4 = 24$	$24 \div 4 = 6$

Math Background

The *inverse relationship* between multiplication and division is similar to the inverse relationship between addition and subtraction. In multiplication, we multiply the factors to form the product. In division, we find a quotient by dividing the dividend by the divisor. The inverse relationship can be represented using the language of multiplication to describe division. The inverse of multiplying two factors to form a product is dividing the product by one factor to form the other factor. The Commutative Property of Multiplication tells us that we can change the order of factors without changing the product. Division is not commutative.

Example 2

Write two multiplication facts and two division facts using the numbers 6, 7, and 42.

The product is 42 and the factors are 6 and 7, which can be written in either order.

$$6 \times 7 = 42 \qquad 7 \times 6 = 42$$

By dividing 42 by 6 and by 7 we form two division facts.

$$42 \div 6 = 7 \qquad 42 \div 7 = 6$$

Example 3

Write two multiplication facts and two division facts shown by this array:

☆ ☆ ☆ ☆ ☆
☆ ☆ ☆ ☆ ☆
☆ ☆ ☆ ☆ ☆

There are 3 rows of 5 stars and 15 stars in all.

$$3 \times 5 = 15 \qquad 5 \times 3 = 15$$
$$15 \div 5 = 3 \qquad 15 \div 3 = 5$$

Analyze How many multiplication and division facts can be written to show an array of 3 rows of 3 stars? sample: one multiplication fact and one division fact: $3 \times 3 = 9$; $9 \div 3 = 3$

Example 4

Find each missing factor.

a. $3 \times \square = 18$ b. $m \times 4 = 36$

To find a missing factor we divide the product by the known factor.

a. Because $18 \div 3 = 6$, we know that $3 \times \mathbf{6} = 18$.

b. Because $36 \div 4 = 9$, we know that $\mathbf{9} \times 4 = 36$.

Lesson Practice

Find each quotient.

▸ a. $24 \div 3$ 8   ▸ b. 6   ▸ c. $18 \div 9$ 2

▸ d. 4   ▸ e. $30 \div 5$ 6   ▸ f. $4 \overline{)20}$ 5

g. Write two multiplication facts and two division facts using the numbers 56, 7, and 8. $7 \times 8 = 56$; $8 \times 7 = 56$; $56 \div 8 = 7$; $56 \div 7 = 8$

Lesson 86   467

Alternative Approach: Using Manipulatives

Students might benefit from modeling the multiplication and division facts in this lesson using counters or tiles. Have them arrange the counters in an array for each problem to model both multiplication and division facts all at once.

In example 2, for instance, an array of 6 rows and 7 columns will show students that there are two multiplication facts depending on whether they write the number of columns or rows first. There are also two division facts since the array represents both 42 items divided into 6 rows and 42 items divided into 7 columns.

English Learners

Order can mean the way we arrange or position items.

Ask:

"When multiplying, can we change the order of the factors? Show me on the board." yes; sample: $3 \times 8 = 24$, $8 \times 3 = 24$

Ask:

"What about when we subtract? Can we change the order without changing the answer?" no; sample: $8 - 3 = 5$, $8 - 5 = 3$

Have students discuss the order in which they do things to get ready for school in the morning.

New Concepts (Continued)

● **Example 2**
Math to Math Connection

You can use this pair of multiplication facts to point out the Commutative Property of Multiplication. Ask students to use the two multiplication facts to explain why the order does not matter in multiplication. Since 6×7 equals the same product as 7×6, the order does not matter when multiplying.

"Two numbers switch places in the division facts as well. How is this switch different from the switch in the multiplication facts?" sample: The numbers in multiplication switch places across the multiplication sign. The numbers in division switch places across the equal sign.

● **Example 3**
Extend the Example

Ask advanced learners:

"What three different sets of 3 numbers can you use to make a multiplication and division fact family for 16 stars?" 1, 16, 16; 2, 8, 16; 4, 4, 16

For the *Analyze* question, have students draw the array and write out all four facts for the numbers 3, 3, and 9. Students should surmise that equal factors can be represented by a single fact. This carries over to the division facts as well.

"What do we call numbers that are the product of factors that are equal?" square numbers

Remind students that an array for a square number is always a square.

● **Example 4**
Alternate Method

Students can also solve these missing-number problems by looking at a multiplication table. They can follow the row that starts with the known factor and look across to find the given product in that row. Then they can look up at what column the product is in. The number at the top of the column represents the unknown factor.

● **Lesson Practice**
Guided Practice

Use these problems as guided practice to check the students' understanding of today's concept.

Problems a–f

Have students practice reading the divisions aloud as you go through these practice problems. After solving the problems, ask students to name the dividend, divisor, and quotient.

(continued)

Lesson 86   467

New Concepts (Continued)

Lesson Practice

Problems i and j
Remind students to always divide the given product by the known factor in order to find the unknown factor.

Alternate Method: Manipulative Use
Have students use counters to determine the missing numbers by modeling the problem as an array.

Closure The questions below help assess the concepts taught in this lesson.

"How do we use fact families to help us divide?" If we know the multiplication fact for two numbers, we just need to find the third number—that will be the answer to the division problem.

"What is the name of the number we divide?" the dividend

"What is the name of the number that tells us how many groups we divide the first number into?" the divisor

"What do we call the answer to a division problem?" the quotient

Discuss real-world situations where division might be helpful. Examples are given below.
- We need to find out how many pages a day we must read to finish a 65 page book in 5 days.
- A doctor tells a mother how many pills she must give her child each day so that he finishes all 14 in one week.

Written Practice

Math Conversations
Independent Practice and Discussions to Increase Understanding

▶ **Problem 4** (Model)
Extend the Problem
This shape can be classified as two different types of triangles. Ask students to determine what type of triangle this is. right and scalene

(continued)

468 Saxon Math Intermediate 3

---

h. Write two multiplication facts and two division facts represented by the array below. $3 \times 7 = 21$; $7 \times 3 = 21$; $21 \div 3 = 7$; $21 \div 7 = 3$

Find each missing factor.

▶ i. $6 \times \square = 42$ 7

▶ j. $n \times 3 = 27$ 9

Written Practice — Distributed and Integrated

1. Oscar took his family to an amusement park. The fee to enter the park was $64. Oscar paid the fee with a $100 bill. How much money should he get back? $36
(20, 28)

2. Marcie purchased 10 greeting cards for $0.35 each. How much did she pay for all 10 cards? $3.50
(21, 60)

3. The odometer of the car showed this display:
(32)

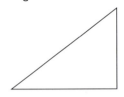

   a. Write the number of miles shown using digits. 76,304

   b. Write the number of miles shown with words. seventy-six thousand, three hundred four

▶ 4. (Model) Use a centimeter ruler to help you answer the following questions about this triangle:
(69, 79)

   a. How long are the three sides of the triangle? 3 cm, 4 cm, 5 cm

   b. What is the perimeter of the triangle? 12 cm

468 Saxon Math Intermediate 3

Inclusion

Fact Families
Some students may have difficulty remembering which symbols to use when recording fact families. Provide them with this visual aid.

Materials: one index card per student

- Write the following template on the board. Have students copy it on their index card.

Fact Family

___ × ___ = ___

___ × ___ = ___

___ ÷ ___ = ___

___ ÷ ___ = ___

- Students use the template to write a fact family for 3, 7, 21.

- Find the product of 4×8, then write related multiplication and division facts using the template.

5. a. (Represent) Draw a triangle that is congruent to the triangle in problem 4. See student work.

   b. What type of triangle did you draw? right triangle or scalene triangle

6. What is the total value of ten quarters, ten dimes, ten nickels, and ten pennies? $4.10

7. Recall that a dozen is 12. How many eggs are equal to half of a dozen? 6

8. The bridge had a weight limit of 8 tons. How many pounds is 8 tons? 16,000 lb

9. Write two multiplication facts and two division facts using the numbers 7, 8, and 56. $7 \times 8 = 56; 8 \times 7 = 56; 56 \div 8 = 7; 56 \div 7 = 8$

10. Choose the best measure. The mass of a raisin is about   1 gram
    1 gram.   1 kilogram.

11. **Multiple Choice** This picture shows the answer to which subtraction below? A

    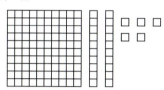

    A 375 − 250   **B** 125 − 50   **C** 750 − 200

12. Multiply:

    a. 8 × 42   336

    b. 4 × 34¢ $1.36

Written Practice (Continued)

Math Conversations
Independent Practice and Discussions to Increase Understanding

Problem 5 Represent
Remind students that the word *congruent* means the same shape and size. Students should trace the given triangle.

For part **b,** review the types of triangles that students have studied:

Equilateral – three equal sides
Isosceles – two equal sides
Right – one right angle
Scalene – all sides with different lengths

Problem 9
Help students write these multiplication and division facts by asking,

"Where does the largest number go in a multiplication fact?" the product

"Where does the largest number go in a division fact?" the dividend

Problem 10
Remind students of the benchmark measurements that were used to estimate mass:

"A paper clip is about 1 gram. A textbook is about 1 kilogram. Which one is closer to the mass of a raisin?" 1 gram

Problem 11 Multiple Choice
Test-Taking Strategy

Students should see that the answer is larger than 100, which eliminates answer choice **B.** By subtracting only in the ones place in the remaining answers, choice **C** is also eliminated since it results in no ones in the answer. Only answer **A** is left. Students can perform the subtraction to check.

(continued)

Written Practice (Continued)

Math Conversations
Independent Practice and Discussions to Increase Understanding

Problem 13 Analyze
To assist in answering all parts of the question, have students build a rectangular prism using 1-inch cubes to represent the box. Students can count cubes or multiply to determine the answers.

Problem 18
Remind students to divide the given product by the known factor in order to find the unknown factor.

Alternate Methods

Students could also find the missing factor by looking across the 6s row of a multiplication table to find 42, and then going up the column to see the 7 at the top or by writing the entire fact family for 6, n, and 42 to get $42 \div 6 = n$.

Problem 20 Multiple Choice
Test-Taking Strategy

A pyramid or a cone would have only one point or vertex on top instead of the two shown on the tent. This leaves the rectangular prism or triangular prism. The tent shown has two faces that are triangles and three faces that are rectangles. Since a rectangular prism has no triangular faces, the tent must be a triangular prism, so **D** is the correct choice.

▶ **13.** (Analyze) A box like the one shown below is completely filled with one-inch cubes.
(72, 73)

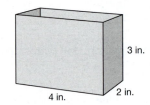

a. How many cubes are needed for the bottom layer?   8 cubes

b. How many layers of cubes are needed to fill the box?   3 layers

c. What is the volume of the box?   24 cubic inches

14. Find each product:
(78)
a. 6×90 540   b. 4×80 320   c. 3×60 180

15. $300 − $166 $134
(28)

16. $3.75 + $2.87 $6.62
(22)

17. $8 \times 9 \times 10$ 720
(77)

▶ **18.** Find the missing factor: $6 \times n = 42$ 7
(86)

19. Write "four and three fourths" using digits. $4\frac{3}{4}$
(46)

▶ **20. Multiple Choice** Which choice below best describes the shape of a tent like the one shown at right?   D
(75)

A pyramid   B rectangular prism
C cone   D triangular prism

470   Saxon Math Intermediate 3

Looking Forward

Learning division facts, writing multiplication and division fact families, and solving for missing factors using division prepares students for

- **Lesson 89,** using a multiplication table to divide by a one-digit number.
- **Lesson 90,** solving equal groups problems.
- **Lesson 101,** dividing two-digit numbers.

LESSON 87

Planning & Preparation

Texas Essential Knowledge and Skills

(3.4)(B) solve/record multiplication problems (up to two digits times one digit)

(3.11)(D) identify concrete models that approximate standard units of weight/mass and use them to measure weight/mass

(3.14)(A) identify the mathematics in everyday situations

• Capacity

Objectives
- Learn the relationships between ounces, cups, pints, quarts, half-gallons, and gallons.
- Identify real-world benchmarks for each unit of capacity.
- Use containers of each unit of capacity to model the doubles/halves relationship between units of capacity in the U.S. Customary System.
- Compare and contrast liters and quarts.

Prerequisite Skills
- Use pencil and paper to write division number sentences to show dividing by 2.

Materials

Instructional Masters
- Power Up 87

Manipulative Kit
- Rulers

Teacher-provided materials
- Measuring cup
- Pint, quart, half-gallon, and gallon containers
- Water or rice
- Funnel*

   *optional

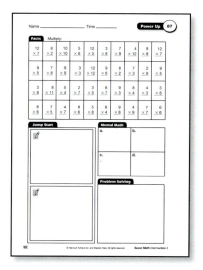

Power Up 87

Reaching All Special Needs Students

Special Education Students	At-Risk Students	English Learners	Advanced Learners
• Adaptations for Saxon Math	• Reteaching Masters	• English Learners (TM) • English Learner Handbook	• Extend the Example (TM) • Extend the Problem (TM) • Online Activities

TM = Teacher's Manual

Math Language

New	Maintained	English Learners
capacity fluid ounces liter	halves (half) ounce U.S. Customary System	contents

Lesson 87   471A

LESSON 87

Problem Solving Discussion

Problem

Perry's school starts classes at half past eight in the morning. If it takes Perry 1 hour to get to school, at what time does Perry need to leave home?

Focus Strategy  **Work Backwards**

Understand Understand the problem.

Teacher Note: You may want to use a geared clock or student clocks to help solve this problem.

"What information are we given?"

Perry's school starts classes at half past eight in the morning. It takes Perry 1 hour to get to school.

"What time is 'half past eight in the morning'?"

8:30 a.m.

"What are we asked to do?"

We are asked to find when Perry needs to leave home to get to school on time.

Plan Make a plan.

"What problem solving strategy can we use?"

We can *work backwards*.

Solve Carry out the plan.

"What time do the classes at Perry's school begin?"

8:30 a.m.

"If it takes Perry 1 hour to get to school, when does he need to leave home?"

We count back 1 hour from 8:30 a.m. and find that Perry should leave his home by 7:30 a.m. Perry can leave earlier than 7:30 and arrive at school early, but if he leaves after 7:30 he will arrive at school late.

7:30 a.m.
Leave home

8:30 a.m.
Arrive at school

Check Look back.

"Did we complete the task?"

Yes, we found the time by which Perry needs to leave for school (7:30 a.m.).

"Is our answer reasonable?"

Yes, it takes Perry 1 hour to get to school. One hour after 7:30 a.m. is 8:30 a.m., which is when Perry's school starts classes.

"What problem solving strategy did we use, and how did it help us?"

We *worked backwards* to find a starting clock time (leave from home) when we knew an ending clock time (start of school) and a duration (time to get to school).

Alternate Strategy
Act It Out or Make a Model

Use a geared clock (or have students use student clocks) to count back 1 hour from 8:30 a.m. Show students that we turn the minute hand counterclockwise one full turn to count back 1 hour.

LESSON 87

• Capacity

Texas Essential Knowledge and Skills
(3.4)(B) solve/record multiplication problems (up to two digits times one digit)
(3.11)(D) identify concrete models that approximate standard units of weight/mass and use them to measure weight/mass
(3.14)(A) identify the mathematics in everyday situations

Power Up

facts   Power Up 87

jump start
- Count down by 6s from 60 to 0.
- Count down by 12s from 120 to 0.
- Write two division facts using the numbers 3, 5, and 15. $15 \div 5 = 3$; $15 \div 3 = 5$
- Draw a rectangle and divide it into 8 parts. Then shade 3 parts. What fraction is not shaded? See student work; $\frac{5}{8}$

mental math

a. **Money:** $2.60 + 99¢ $3.59

b. **Number Sense:** $88 - 19$ 69

c. **Number Sense:** $7 \times 3 \times 10$ 210

d. **Algebra:** Jared made this table to show the number of pages he had read. Find the missing number in the table. 15

Pages read	10	20	30	40	50
Minutes	5	10	___	20	25

problem solving   Perry's school starts classes at half past eight in the morning. If it takes Perry 1 hour to get to school, at what time does Perry need to leave home?   7:30 a.m.

New Concept

The amount of liquid a container can hold is called its **capacity.** To measure capacity in the Customary System, we use the units **fluid ounces, cups, pints, quarts,** and **gallons.** Some of these units have a doubles and halves relationship. On the following page we show some common containers.

Lesson 87   471

Facts   Multiply:

12 × 7 = 84	6 × 2 = 12	10 × 10 = 100	5 × 6 = 30	12 × 5 = 60	3 × 6 = 18	7 × 9 = 63	4 × 12 = 48	8 × 8 = 64	12 × 7 = 84
9 × 5 = 45	7 × 8 = 56	9 × 9 = 81	3 × 3 = 9	12 × 12 = 144	9 × 6 = 54	8 × 2 = 16	7 × 3 = 21	2 × 9 = 18	9 × 5 = 45
3 × 8 = 24	8 × 11 = 88	5 × 4 = 20	2 × 7 = 14	3 × 5 = 15	6 × 7 = 42	9 × 3 = 27	8 × 4 = 32	4 × 3 = 12	3 × 8 = 24
6 × 6 = 36	7 × 5 = 35	4 × 7 = 28	8 × 6 = 48	5 × 8 = 40	6 × 4 = 24	9 × 8 = 72	4 × 8 = 36	7 × 9 = 63	6 × 6 = 36

LESSON 87

Power Up

Facts
Distribute **Power Up 87** to students. See answers below.

Jump Start
Before students begin the Mental Math exercise, do these counting exercises as a class.

Mental Math
Encourage students to share different ways to mentally compute these exercises. Strategies for exercises are listed below.

a. Think $2.60 + $1.00 − 1¢
   Think $2.60 + $1.00 = $3.60.
   Then $3.60 − $0.01 = $3.59.

b. Think $88 − 20 + 1$
   $88 − 20 = 68$
   $68 + 1 = 69$

Problem Solving
Refer to **Problem-Solving Strategy Discussion,** p. 471B.

New Concept

Instruction
Ask for a volunteer to give a definition for the term "capacity." Make sure students understand that capacity refers to the amount of something (usually liquids) that a container can hold.

(continued)

Lesson 87   471

New Concept (Continued)

Activity

Materials needed:

- Empty, clean plastic or paper containers of the following sizes (with labels that show the container's size):
  1 gallon, 1 half gallon, 1 quart, 1 pint, and 1 cup
- Supply of water or rice
- Funnel

If you are using water and do not have a sink nearby, you should also have a second one-gallon container to use for the water supply.

For the *Connect* question, discuss the connection between quarts and quarters, then ask students,

> *"Can you think of any other common uses of the word quarter?"* samples: a quarter mile; a quarter pound; telling time by saying "a quarter to" or "a quarter after" the hour

To solve the *Analyze* question, encourage students to use the large "G."

Active Learning

Draw the following chart on the board. Explain to students that the large G represents one gallon. The four Qs inside the G represent the four quarts in a gallon. The two Ps inside each Q represent the two pints in a quart. The two Cs inside each P represent the two cups in a pint. Have students copy the chart.

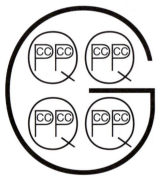

Almost every question about non-metric liquid measurement can be answered using this chart.

(continued)

Discuss How does the picture below show a doubles relationship? How does it show a halves relationship?
sample: × 2 shows a doubles relationship; ÷ 2 shows a halves relationship

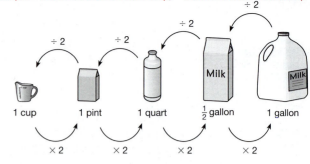

Activity

Measuring Capacity

Materials: measuring cup, one-pint bottle, one-quart bottle, half-gallon container, one-gallon container, water or rice

Do this activity in a small group or as a class.

1. Fill a measuring cup to the one-cup level and pour the contents into a one-pint bottle. Repeat until the bottle is full. How many cups were needed? **2**

2. Empty the full one-pint bottle into the one-quart bottle. Repeat until the one-quart bottle is full. What is another name for half a quart? **pint**

3. Fill the half-gallon container from the one-quart bottle. What is another name for two quarts? **half-gallon**

4. Then fill the one gallon container from the half-gallon container. How many quarts does it take to make a gallon? **4**

 Connect The word "quart" is in the word "quarter." In what way is a quart of water like a quarter of a dollar?

sample: Four quarts make a gallon; four quarters make a dollar. Both are a "quarter," or a "fourth," of the larger unit.

Analyze Doctors advise us to drink eight cups of water each day. What size liquid container equals eight cups? half-gallon

Math Background

Other less common units of measurement for capacity in the Customary System include the peck (2 gallons), the bushel (commonly 4 pecks), the barrel (officially 31.5 gallons), and the hogshead (2 barrels).

English Learners

The **contents** of a container are the things inside.

Ask:

"What are the contents of two full egg cartons?" 24 eggs

Ask:

"What could be the contents of a gallon jug?" samples: milk, juice, water, soda

Have students describe the contents of their desk, backpack, or lunch box.

Example 1

Multiple Choice Willow poured milk into her bowl of cereal. About how much milk did she pour?

　A 1 cup　　　**B** 1 quart　　　**C** 1 gallon

For a bowl of cereal, Willow would use about **one cup,** which is choice **A.**

Example 2

A cup is 8 ounces. How many ounces is a pint?

Two cups equal a pint; so a pint has twice as many ounces as a cup.

$$2 \times 8 \text{ ounces} = 16 \text{ ounces}$$

A pint is **16 ounces.**

A **liter** is used to measure capacity in the metric system. A liter is a little more than a quart.

　1 liter　　1 quart　　2 liters　　$\frac{1}{2}$ gallon

Example 3

Which is more, 2 liters of a beverage or $\frac{1}{2}$ gallon of a beverage?

Two quarts equal $\frac{1}{2}$ gallon. A liter is a little more than a quart; so 2 liters is close to, but **a little more than,** $\frac{1}{2}$ **gallon.**

Lesson Practice

▸ **a.** A gallon of milk is how many quarts?　4 quarts

▸ **b.** A pint is 16 ounces. How many ounces is a quart?
　32 ounces

▸ **c.** **Multiple Choice** Which unit would describe the amount of juice in a container?　A

　A quart　　　　　　**B** foot
　C pound　　　　　**D** meter

Lesson 87　473

New Concept (Continued)

Example 1
Remind students that when they buy milk at the store, it often comes in 1 quart or 1 gallon containers, so they should see that choices **B** and **C** are both too large. Only choice **A**, 1 cup, is a reasonable amount for a bowl of cereal.

Example 2
Have students draw two rectangles equal in size to show the relationship between ounces and cups. One rectangle should be whole (1 cup) while the other is divided into 8 equal parts (8 ounces).

Extend the Example
"How many ounces is a quart?"　32 ounces
"How many ounces is a half gallon?"
　64 ounces
"How many ounces is a gallon?"
　128 ounces

Have students look at the number of ounces in a cup, a pint, a quart, a half-gallon, and a gallon to see if they recognize the pattern. The numbers keep doubling, or multiply the previous number by 2.

Lesson Practice

Guided Practice
Use these problems as guided practice to check the students' understanding of today's concept.

Problems a and b
Students should refer to the picture of the containers at the beginning of the lesson or draw rectangles comparing the different measures to help with these problems.

Problem c **Multiple Choice**
Extend the Problem
Students should recognize that the only measure of capacity listed is choice **A**, quart. Extend the problem by asking students what each of the other units is used to measure and in which system.
B: foot – length in customary system
C: pound – weight in customary system
D: meter – length in metric system

(continued)

Lesson 87　473

New Concept (Continued)

Problem d Multiple Choice
Test-Taking Strategy

Since a glass holds about a cup, choice **B** can be eliminated because 10 cups is much more than a glass. The units in choices **C** and **D** are larger than a cup so those choices can be eliminated. Only choice **A** is reasonable.

Closure — The questions below help assess the concepts taught in this lesson.

"How many quarts are there in a gallon?" There are four quarts in a gallon.

"How many cups are in a quart?" There are 4 cups in a quart.

"How many cups are in a gallon?" There are 16 cups in a gallon.

"How many ounces are there in a cup?" There are eight ounces in a cup.

"How do the units that measure liquid in the Customary System show a doubles relationship?" There are two cups in a pint. There are two pints in a quart. There are two quarts in a half gallon. There are two half gallons in a gallon.

Discuss real-world situations where using liquid measurements might be helpful. Examples are given below.
- We need a gallon of milk, but the store only sells quarts.
- We want to double a soup recipe that calls for a pint of chicken broth.

▶ **d. Multiple Choice** Todd drank a glass of juice. Which measure below best describes the amount of juice in a glass? A

A 10 ounces **B** 10 cups **C** 10 pints **D** 10 quarts

Written Practice — Distributed and Integrated

1. **Analyze** Gabriel filled the ice tray with water from the tap and then put the ice tray in the freezer. If water from the tap is 62°F, how many degrees does it need to cool until it starts to freeze?
(4, 20) 30°F

2. Joey and Jermaine shared 18 pretzels equally. How many pretzels did each boy get? Draw a picture to represent the problem.
(82) 9 pretzels; See student work.

▶ 3. **Conclude** Jayne rode her bike one mile on Monday, two miles on Tuesday, and four miles on Wednesday. Each day she rode twice as far as she rode the day before. How many miles did she ride on Saturday? 32 mi
(81)

4. How many months is half of a year? 6 months
(83)

5. Steve paid two dollars for a toy that cost $1.39. What coins should he get back in change? 2 quarters, 1 dime, 1 penny
(25, 26)

6. Arrange these units in order of size from shortest to longest:
(79) centimeter, meter, kilometer
    meter   kilometer   centimeter

7. What fraction of a gallon is equal to a quart? $\frac{1}{4}$
(44, 87)

▶ 8. **Multiple Choice** This picture shows the answer to which multiplication below? C
(11, 84)

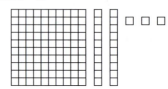

A 3 × 21   **B** 4 × 31   **C** 3 × 41   **D** 12 × 3

Written Practice

Math Conversations
Independent Practice and Discussions to Increase Understanding

Problem 3 Conclude
Help students find the answer by continuing the doubling pattern.

Problem 8 Multiple Choice
Test-Taking Strategy
The picture shows 3 ones. Only choices **A** and **C** multiply to give 3 ones. Of those two answer choices, only **C** will multiply to give you more than one hundred.

(continued)

▶ **9. Multiply:**
(84)
   a. 6 × 34   204
   b. 3 × 46¢ $1.38

▶ **10. Multiple Choice** What is a reasonable estimate of the
(87) amount of water in a full pitcher?   **B**

   A 2 ounces   **B** 2 quarts
   C 2 gallons   **D** 2 cups

11. Multiple Choice A liter is closest in measure to a
(87) **B**
   A pint.   **B** quart.
   C half-gallon.   **D** gallon.

12. Find the missing factor: 7 × m = 28.   4
(86)

13. Look at the sequence below. Each number is twice as big as the
(81) number before it. Find the next three numbers in the sequence.

   1, 2, 4, 8, 16, __32__, __64__, __128__, …

14. $8.96 + $4.78 $13.74
(22)

15. $11.00 − $5.75 $5.25
(26, 28)

16. 5 × 5 × 5   125
(77, 84)

17. 6)‾42   7
(86)

18. Write two multiplication facts and two division facts using the
(86) numbers 6, 7, and 42.   6 × 7 = 42; 7 × 6 = 42; 42 ÷ 7 = 6; 42 ÷ 6 = 7

19. A rectangle was formed with tiles that were 1-foot squares.
(58, 62)

   a. How long is the rectangle?   6 ft
   b. How wide is the rectangle?   4 ft
   c. What is the area of the rectangle?   24 square ft
   d. What is the perimeter of the rectangle?   20 ft

20. This paper clip is how many centimeters long?   3 cm
(79)

Lesson 87   475

Looking Forward

Learning the measures of capacity in the
Customary System and the metric system,
converting between measures, and
comparing different measures prepares
students for

• **Lesson 90,** solving equal groups problems.
• **Lesson 98,** estimating by weight.

Written Practice (Continued)

Math Conversations
Independent Practice and Discussions to Increase Understanding

▶ **Problem 9**
Some mental math strategies can be used for these two multiplications:
a. Think 6 × 30 plus 6 × 4. So 180 + 24 = 204
b. Think 3 × 40¢, then add 3 × 6¢. So $1.20 + $0.18 = $1.38

▶ **Problem 10   Multiple Choice**
Test-Taking Strategy
This question asks about the amount of water in a full pitcher. Since a cup is 8 ounces, 2 ounces would not be enough to fill a pitcher so you can eliminate choice **A**. Choice **C** can be eliminated because 2 one-gallon containers of milk would be too much to fill a pitcher. Two quarts is half a gallon, the size of a cardboard milk container, so choice **B** could be used to fill a pitcher.

Errors and Misconceptions

▶ **Problem 1**
Some students may mistakenly think that 0°F is the freezing point of water. Remind them that water freezes at 0° Celsius, or 32° Fahrenheit.

▶ **Problem 19**
When counting tiles to determine length, perimeter, and area, students often forget to record the proper units. Remind students that each of these measures has units associated with them. Students may also need to be reminded of the difference between area and perimeter.

Remind students that the perimeter is the distance around the outside of a shape, while the area shows how many square units fill a flat shape.

Lesson 87   475

LESSON 88

Planning & Preparation

• Even and Odd Numbers

Texas Essential Knowledge and Skills

(3.4)(C) use models to solve division problems

(3.14)(B) solve problems that incorporate understanding the problem, making a plan, carrying out the plan, and evaluating the solution for reasonableness

(3.14)(C) select/develop an appropriate problem-solving plan/strategy, including working a simpler problem to solve the problem

(3.16)(A) make generalizations from patterns

Objectives
- Classify numbers as even or odd.
- Understand that even numbers can be divided into two equal groups and odd numbers cannot.
- Use manipulatives such as tiles or counters to model even and odd numbers.
- Use pictorial models to model even and odd numbers.

Prerequisite Skills
- Model finding "fair share" (dividing by 2) with pictorial models and concrete objects such as counters or tiles.
- Draw arrays to model dividing by 2.

Materials
Instructional Masters
- Power Up 88

Manipulative Kit
- Ruler
- Counters

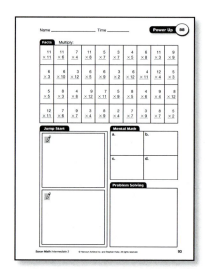

Power Up 88

Reaching All Special Needs Students

Special Education Students	At-Risk Students	English Learners	Advanced Learners
• Adaptations for Saxon Math	• Reteaching Masters	• English Learners (TM) • English Learner Handbook	• Extend the Example (TM) • Online Activities

TM = Teacher's Manual

Math Language

New	Maintained	English Learners
even numbers odd numbers	common year equal row	line up

476A   *Saxon Math* Intermediate 3

Problem Solving Discussion

Problem

What day of the week is 71 days after Monday?

Focus Strategy **Work a Simpler Problem**

Understand *Understand the problem.*

"What are we asked to do?"

We are asked to find which day of the week is 71 days after Monday.

Plan *Make a plan.*

"How can we use the information we know to solve this problem?"

Instead of counting each of the 71 days, we can *make the problem simpler*.

Solve *Carry out the plan.*

"What day is one week after Monday?"

One week after Monday is Monday.

"What day is two weeks after Monday?"

Two weeks after Monday is also Monday.

"We know that each week is 7 days. How can we use this fact to find a day that is close to 71 days after Monday?"

We can count up by 7s to reach 70, which is close to 71.

"What day is 70 days after Monday? What day is 71 days after Monday?"

We know that 70 days after Monday is Monday. This means that 71 days after Monday is the next day, which is Tuesday.

Check *Look back.*

"Did we complete the task?"

Yes, we found the day of the week that is 71 days after Monday (Tuesday).

"Is our answer reasonable?"

Yes, our answer is reasonable because 70 days is 10 weeks (10 × 7 days = 70 days). Ten weeks after Monday is Monday, so 10 weeks plus 1 day is Tuesday.

"What problem solving strategy did we use, and how did it help us?"

We *made the problem simpler*. Working a simpler problem helped us find the answer more quickly than if we had counted up the days one at a time.

LESSON 88

Power Up

Facts
Distribute **Power Up 88** to students. See answers below.

Jump Start
Before students begin the Mental Math exercise, do these exercises as a class.

Mental Math
Encourage students to share different ways to mentally compute these exercises. Strategies for exercises are listed below.

a. Multiply
$4 \times 4 \times 10 = 16 \times 10 = 160$

c. Look for a Pattern
The change in the numbers follows the pattern $+5, -4, +5, -4, \ldots$. The number after 9 should go down 4, so it is 5.

See the Pattern as 2 Counting Sequences.
Looking at every other number, you see the two sequences 2, 3, 4 and 7, 8, 9. The next number should be 5.

Problem Solving
Refer to **Problem-Solving Strategy Discussion**, p. 476B.

LESSON 88

• Even and Odd Numbers

Texas Essential Knowledge and Skills
(3.4)(C) use models to solve division problems
(3.14)(B) solve problems that incorporate understanding the problem, making a plan, carrying out the plan, and evaluating the solution for reasonableness
(3.14)(C) select/develop an appropriate problem-solving plan/strategy, including working a simpler problem
(3.16)(A) make generalizations from patterns

Power Up

facts Power Up 88

jump start
Count up by 8s from 0 to 88.
Count up by 4s from 0 to 44.

Draw a rectangle that is 3 centimeters long and 3 centimeters wide. *See student work.*

Write the largest 4-digit number that uses each of the digits 1, 7, 8, and 5. What is the value of the digit in the thousands place? *8,751; 8,000*

mental math
a. **Number Sense:** $4 \times 4 \times 10$ *160*
b. **Number Sense:** $96 - 30$ *66*
c. **Number Sense:** 2, 7, 3, 8, 4, 9, ___ *5*
d. **Measurement:** What is the perimeter of the pentagon? *20 in.*

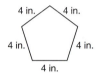

problem solving

Focus Strategy: Work a Simpler Problem

What day of the week is 71 days after Monday?

(**Understand**) We are asked to find which day of the week is 71 days after Monday.

(**Plan**) Instead of counting each of the 71 days, we can work a simpler problem.

(**Solve**) One week after Monday is Monday. Two weeks after Monday is also Monday. Each week is 7 days, so we can count up by 7s to reach 70, which is close to 71.

476 *Saxon Math Intermediate 3*

Facts Multiply:

11 × 11 **121**	11 × 6 **66**	7 × 4 **28**	11 × 8 **88**	5 × 7 **35**	3 × 7 **21**	4 × 5 **20**	6 × 8 **48**	11 × 3 **33**	9 × 9 **81**
6 × 3 **18**	6 × 10 **60**	3 × 12 **36**	6 × 5 **30**	6 × 9 **54**	3 × 2 **6**	6 × 12 **72**	4 × 11 **44**	12 × 4 **48**	5 × 3 **15**
5 × 5 **25**	8 × 3 **24**	4 × 8 **32**	9 × 12 **108**	7 × 11 **77**	5 × 9 **45**	8 × 5 **40**	4 × 6 **24**	9 × 4 **36**	8 × 12 **96**
12 × 11 **132**	7 × 6 **42**	9 × 7 **63**	3 × 4 **12**	8 × 9 **72**	2 × 4 **8**	7 × 7 **49**	3 × 9 **27**	8 × 7 **56**	5 × 2 **10**

We know that 70 days after Monday is Monday. This means that 71 days after Monday is the next day, which is **Tuesday.**

Check Our answer is reasonable because 70 days is 10 weeks (10 × 7 days = 70 days). Ten weeks after Monday is Monday, so 10 weeks plus 1 day is Tuesday.

New Concept

If we can divide a number of objects into two equal groups, then the number is **even.** We see that 12 is an even number because 12 objects can be divided into two equal groups.

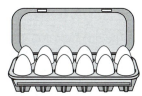

If a number of objects does not divide into two equal groups, the number is **odd.** So 11 is an odd number because it does not divide into two equal groups.

Activity

Even and Odd Numbers

Materials: counters

1. Place 10 counters on your desk. Can you divide 10 counters into two equal groups? Is 10 an even number or an odd number? *yes; even*

2. Place 9 counters on your desk. Can you divide 9 counters into two equal groups? Is 9 an even number or an odd number? *no; odd*

New Concept

Discussion

Ask students what numbers they say if they start at 1 and skip count by 2s: 1, 3, 5, 7, 9, …
Next ask students what numbers they say if they start at 2 and skip count by 2s: 2, 4, 6, 8, 10, …

Explain how these patterns are also the even and odd numbers. Point out that in each pattern two is added to each number to find the next number.

Explain that every even number can be formed by multiplying another number by 2. Every even number can also be divided by 2 to form two equal groups.

Math Language

Ask volunteers to give a definition for "even" and "odd" in their own words.

To help students remember the meanings, you could point out the fact that the word "even" has 4 letters, an even number, and the word "odd" has 3 letters, an odd number.

Activity

Manipulative Use

Students should work in pairs. Give each pair about 20 counters.

Instruction

Make sure students understand that any number ending in 0 is an even number.

(continued)

New Concept (Continued)

Example 1
Manipulative Use

While students still have their counters out from the activity, they can use them to model these even and odd numbers, making the patterns as shown in the solution.

Discussion

For the *Generalize* question, after students figure out the pattern for whole numbers, ask them to find the pattern for the sequence of numbers when they skip count by threes, fours, and fives:

For threes: odd, even, odd, even, …
For fours: even, even, even, even, …
For fives: odd, even, odd, even, …

"What pattern do these counting sequences follow?" sample: If counting by an odd number, the sequence has the pattern odd, even, odd, even, …; If counting by an even number, the sequence is all even numbers.

Example 2
Extend the Example

"Suppose you saw two rows of desks in the class. Without counting how can you tell if the total number of desks is odd or even?" sample: If the desks form two equal groups (rows), then the number of desks is even. If not, the number is odd.

(continued)

---

3. Place 8 counters on your desk. Divide the counters. Is 8 even or odd? even

4. Place 7 counters on your desk. Is 7 even or odd? How do you know? odd; sample: 7 counters cannot be divided into two equal groups.

Example 1

Are the numbers we say when we count by twos even numbers or odd numbers?

2, 4, 6, 8, 10, …

Each of these numbers can be divided into two equal groups. When we count by twos from 2, we say **even numbers.**

The numbers 1, 3, 5, 7, 9… are odd numbers. They cannot be divided into two equal groups.

Generalize You can name every whole number as either even or odd. What is the rule for the pattern of even/odd numbers in the sequence 1, 2, 3, 4, 5, 6, 7, 8, 9, …? odd, even, odd, even, …

Example 2

There are 21 students in the class. Can all the students line up into two equal rows?

The students can line up into two equal rows only if the number of students is even. Twenty-one is not an even number. It is an odd number.

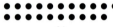

21

No, 21 students cannot line up into two equal rows.

A quick way to tell if a counting number is even or odd is to look at the last digit of the number. If the last digit is even (0, 2, 4, 6, 8), then the number is even. If the last digit is odd (1, 3, 5, 7, 9), then the number is odd.

English Learners

To **line up** means to place people or things one after the other.

Ask:

"Students lined up in 3 lines with 10 students in each line. How many students were there altogether?"
3 × 10 = 30 people

Ask:

"What else can you line up?" samples: cars, toys, bikes, markers, blocks

Have students line up counters in a row.

Example 3

There are 365 days in a common year. Is 365 even or odd?

The last digit of 365 is 5, which is odd. So 365 is **odd**.

Lesson Practice

a. **Multiple Choice** Which of these numbers is even?   D

   A 3   B 13   C 23   D 32

b. Can 28 students line up into two equal rows? Explain your answer.   yes; sample: Since 28 is an even number, 28 students can line up into two equal rows.

c. Simon has $7. Nathan has $7. If they put their money together, will they have an even number of dollars or an odd number of dollars?   even

d. **Multiple Choice** Which of these months has an even number of days?   C

   A July   B August
   C September   D October

Written Practice — *Distributed and Integrated*

1. Ramon bought a half gallon of milk for $2.24, a loaf of bread for $1.89, and a can of juice for $1.18. What was the total price of these groceries? $5.31
   (22, 60)

2. Ramon paid for the groceries in problem **1** with a $10 bill. How much money should he get back? $4.69
   (20, 28)

3. From the Earth to the moon is about two hundred fifty thousand miles. Use digits to write that number.   250,000
   (32)

4. How many inches are equal to half of a foot?   6 in.
   (83)

5. Draw a picture to represent $2\frac{1}{2}$.   See student work.
   (42, 46)

6. Double each number:
   (81)
   a. 100   200   b. 30   60

Lesson 88   479

New Concept (Continued)

Example 3
Extend the Example

After completing this example, write some longer numbers (with 4, 5, or 6 digits) on the board and ask students to tell you if they are even or odd.

Lesson Practice

Guided Practice

Use these problems as guided practice to check the students' understanding of today's concept.

Problem a   Multiple Choice
Test-Taking Strategy

Students should look at the ones digit and mark out all answer choices that have an odd number in the ones place. Only even numbers will be left.

Problem d
Math-to-Math Connection

Have students write down the number of days for each choice and choose the number that is even. **A:** 31, **B:** 31, **C:** 30, **D:** 31

Choices **A**, **B**, and **D** can be eliminated because they have an odd number of days. Choice **C** is the correct answer.

Closure — The questions below help assess the concepts taught in this lesson.

"What are three ways you can tell if a number is even or odd?" If a number divides evenly into two groups, it is even. When we skip count by twos starting with two, we say the even numbers. We can look at the last digit of a number. If this digit is even, then the whole number is even.

"Is the number 54,233 even or odd? How can you tell?" The last digit is 3. Three does not divide evenly into two groups. So 54,233 is an odd number.

Discuss real-world situations where understanding even and odd numbers might be helpful. Examples are given below.

- A teacher wanted to divide her class of 31 students into two teams.
- A boy wanted to read the same number of pages for two days in his book that was 48 pages long.
- We need to make two lines of students that are equal in length, but there are 77 students.

Lesson 88   479

Written Practice

Math Conversations
Independent Practice and Discussions to Increase Understanding

Problem 8 Multiple Choice
Test-Taking Strategy

Use the shortcut for identifying even and odd numbers. If the last digit of a number is even, then the number is even, and if the last digit is odd, then the number is odd. The only even number is **B, 536**.

Problem 9 Explain
Manipulative Use

Students can arrange 15 counters in the pattern shown. Then they can try separating the counters into 2 equal groups. They will have one counter too many, which means that the number is odd.

Problem 11
Students may need to refer back to the diagram of liquid measures in Lesson 87 to help them answer these questions.

Problem 15
A mental math shortcut for this problem is: Think of $496 as $500 − $4. Then mentally add: $500 + $467 = $967. Subtracting $4 makes it $963.

Problem 16
A mental math shortcut for this problem is: Think of the problem as $10 − $9.50 − 2¢ = $0.50 − 2¢ = $0.48.

Errors and Misconceptions

Problem 7b
Students may expect half of 30 to end in zero like half of 100. Suggest students make a sketch dividing thirty circles into two equal groups.

Problem 20
Students may need to be reminded of the difference between area and perimeter so that they do not confuse them. Remind students to record proper units.

---

7. Find half of each number:
   a. 10   5
   b. 30   15

8. **Multiple Choice** Which of the following numbers is an even number? **B**
   A 365   B 536   C 563   D 635

9. **Explain** Can John separate 15 counters into 2 equal groups? Explain your answer.   no; sample: 15 is an odd number, so it will not separate into two equal whole numbers. If John makes 2 groups of 7, there will be 1 extra counter.

10. Find each product.
    a. 5 × 30   150
    b. 4 × $24 $96

11. a. How many pints are equal to a quart?   2
    b. What fraction of a quart is a pint? $\frac{1}{2}$

12. Find each quotient.
    a. 8)48   6
    b. 36 ÷ 4   9

13. Write 521,769 in expanded form.   500,000 + 20,000 + 1,000 + 700 + 60 + 9

14. **Conclude** In the sequence below each number is half as big as the number before it. Find the next three numbers in the sequence.
    64, 32, 16, __8__, __4__, __2__, ...

15. $496 + $467 $963
16. $10.00 − $9.48 $0.52
17. 4 × 5 × 6   120
18. 3 × 36   108
19. Find the missing factor: 9 × n = 72   8

20. **Model** Use a centimeter ruler to help you answer the following questions about this rectangle.
    a. What is the length of the rectangle?   4 cm
    b. What is the width of the rectangle?   3 cm
    c. What is the perimeter of the rectangle?   14 cm
    d. What is the area of the rectangle?   12 sq. cm

Looking Forward

Learning about even and odd numbers prepares students for

- **Lesson 89,** using a multiplication table to divide by a one-digit number.
- **Lesson 90,** solving equal groups problems.
- **Lesson 101,** dividing two-digit numbers.

LESSON 89

Planning & Preparation

• Using a Multiplication Table to Divide by a One-Digit Number

Objectives
- Use a multiplication table to find a quotient.
- Solve problems by finding quotients on a multiplication table.

Prerequisite Skills
- Model dividing by a one-digit number with pictorial models and concrete objects.
- Use pencil and paper to write division number sentences to show dividing by a one-digit number.
- Draw arrays to model dividing by a one-digit number.

Materials
Instructional Masters
- Power Up 89

Manipulative Kit
- Ruler
- Meterstick*

Texas Essential Knowledge and Skills
(3.4)(C) use models to solve division problems and number sentences to record the solutions
(3.14)(A) identify the mathematics in everyday situations
(3.15)(A) explain observations using pictures

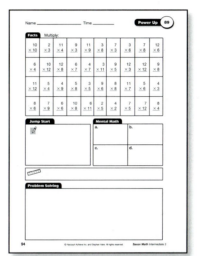

Power Up 89

Differentiated Instruction

Reaching All Special Needs Students

Special Education Students	At-Risk Students	English Learners	Advanced Learners
• Adaptations for Saxon Math	• Alternative Approach (TM) • Reteaching Masters	• English Learners (TM) • English Learner Handbook	• Early Finishers (SE) • Online Activities

TM=Teacher's Manual
SE=Student Edition

Math Language

Maintained
array
quotient

English Learners
orchard

Lesson 89   481A

LESSON 89

Problem Solving Discussion

Problem

Tristan's baby brother turned 13 months old in February. In what month was Tristan's brother born?

Focus Strategy **Work a Simpler Problem**

Understand Understand the problem.

"What information are we given?"

Tristan's brother turned 13 months old in February.

"What are we asked to do?"

We are asked to find in what month Tristan's brother was born.

Plan Make a plan.

"To find when Tristan's brother was born, will we count forward or backwards?"

Tristan's brother was born in the past, so we have to count backwards to find the month he was born.

"What problem solving strategy can we use?"

We can *make the problem simpler*.

Solve Carry out the plan.

"What prior knowledge do we have to help us make this problem simpler?"

We know that there are 12 months in one year.

"Instead of counting backwards 13 months, how can we quickly solve the problem?"

We can count back one year (12 months) and then count back one more month.

"In what month was Tristan's brother born?"

Twelve months before February is February. We count back one more month to find that Tristan's brother was born in January.

Check Look back.

"Did we complete the task?"

Yes, we found the month that Tristan's brother was born by finding that 13 months before February is January.

"Is our answer reasonable?"

Yes, we know that our answer is reasonable because February is 12 months before February, so January is 13 months before February.

"What problem solving strategy did we use, and how did it help us?"

We *made the problem simpler* so that we did not have to count the months one at a time.

LESSON 89

- Using a Multiplication Table to Divide By a One-Digit Number

Texas Essential Knowledge and Skills
(3.4)(C) use models to solve division problems and number sentences to record the solutions
(3.14)(A) identify the mathematics in everyday situations
(3.15)(A) explain observations using pictures

Power Up

facts	Power Up 89
jump start	Count up by odd numbers from 1 to 25.
	Count up by even numbers from 2 to 30.
	Write two division facts using the numbers 4, 6, and 24. $24 \div 6 = 4; 24 \div 4 = 6$
	Draw a 13-centimeter segment on your worksheet. About how many inches long is the segment? See student work; about 5 or $5\frac{1}{4}$ in.
mental math	**a. Time:** What is the time 3 hours after 3:47 a.m.? 6:47 a.m.
	b. Measurement: How many inches are in 7 feet? 84 in.
	c. Money: $5.15 + $0.99 $6.14
	d. Money: Find the value of these bills and coins: $4.15

problem solving	Tristan's baby brother turned 13 months old in February. In what month was Tristan's brother born? January

Lesson 89   481

LESSON 89

Power Up

Facts
Distribute **Power Up 89** to students. See answers below.

Jump Start
Before students begin the Mental Math exercise, do these exercises as a class.

Mental Math
Encourage students to share different ways to mentally compute these exercises. Strategies for exercises are listed below.

b. Use the Conversion and Multiply
1 foot = 12 inches
7 feet = 7 × 12 inches = 84 inches

Count by 12s
12, 24, 36, 48, 60, 72, 84
Seven feet is 84 inches.

c. Think $5.15 + $1.00 − $0.01
$5.15 + $1.00 = $6.15
Then subtract $0.01 to get $6.14.

Problem Solving
Refer to **Problem-Solving Strategy Discussion**, p. 481B.

Facts — Multiply:

10 × 10 = 100	2 × 3 = 6	11 × 4 = 44	9 × 3 = 27	11 × 9 = 99	3 × 8 = 24	7 × 3 = 21	3 × 6 = 18	7 × 8 = 56	12 × 6 = 72
6 × 4 = 24	10 × 12 = 120	12 × 8 = 96	6 × 7 = 42	4 × 7 = 28	3 × 11 = 33	9 × 5 = 45	12 × 3 = 36	12 × 12 = 144	9 × 8 = 72
11 × 12 = 132	5 × 4 = 20	4 × 9 = 36	5 × 8 = 40	3 × 5 = 15	9 × 6 = 54	8 × 8 = 64	11 × 7 = 77	5 × 6 = 30	4 × 3 = 12
8 × 6 = 48	7 × 9 = 63	6 × 6 = 36	10 × 8 = 80	6 × 11 = 66	2 × 5 = 10	4 × 2 = 8	7 × 5 = 35	7 × 12 = 84	8 × 4 = 32

Lesson 89   481

New Concept

Connection

Start this lesson with a review of division.

"What are the names of the parts of a division fact? (Write them out as a fact.)"

dividend ÷ divisor = quotient

"In what other way can this be written?"

$$\text{divisor}\overline{)\text{dividend}}^{\text{quotient}}$$

Remind students of the many methods they have used to divide numbers:

- manipulatives to divide numbers into equal groups
- sketches to show splitting numbers into equal groups
- arrays to represent a division problem
- related facts in fact families
- multiplication table to divide numbers by 2

Example 1
Alternate Method

A fact family can be used. The numbers 24 and 4 will both be part of a corresponding multiplication fact. Students should be able to write a multiplication number sentence describing this problem.

$$4 \times n = 24 \text{ or } n \times 4 = 24$$

Students can then solve this problem using the multiplication table in the same way as for the original division problem.

(continued)

New Concept

In Lesson 83 we used a multiplication table to divide by 2. In this lesson we will use a multiplication table to divide by other numbers. Read the following problem.

For an art project, 24 students will sit at 6 tables. If the students are divided equally, how many students will sit at each table?

To answer the question, we divide 24 into 6 equal groups. To divide 24 by 6, we will use a multiplication table. We look in the 6 row for 24. At the top of the column, we see 4. This means 24 ÷ 6 = 4. So, there are 4 students at each table.

Represent Draw a picture to show the solution to the problem above. See student work.

Multiplication Table

	0	1	2	3	4	5	6	7	8	9	10	11	12
0	0	0	0	0	0	0	0	0	0	0	0	0	0
1	0	1	2	3	4	5	6	7	8	9	10	11	12
2	0	2	4	6	8	10	12	14	16	18	20	22	24
3	0	3	6	9	12	15	18	21	24	27	30	33	36
4	0	4	8	12	16	20	24	28	32	36	40	44	48
5	0	5	10	15	20	25	30	35	40	45	50	55	60
6	0	6	12	18	24	30	36	42	48	54	60	66	72
7	0	7	14	21	28	35	42	49	56	63	70	77	84
8	0	8	16	24	32	40	48	56	64	72	80	88	96
9	0	9	18	27	36	45	54	63	72	81	90	99	108
10	0	10	20	30	40	50	60	70	80	90	100	110	120
11	0	11	22	33	44	55	66	77	88	99	110	121	132
12	0	12	24	36	48	60	72	84	96	108	120	132	144

Example 1

For Game Day the teacher divided the 32 students into 4 equal teams. How many students were on each team?

To find the answer to $4\overline{)32}$ on the table, we find 32 in the 4 row. Then we look at the top of the column and see 8. There were **8 students** on each team.

Math Background

Using a multiplication table to divide is actually the same as using related multiplication facts to divide. When we solve 24 ÷ 4 on the multiplication table, we start with 4 and find the other factor for the product of 24. This is the same as 4 × □ = 24. It is important at this level that students experience a variety of different models as they develop the concept of division.

Example 2

The farmer planted an array of 42 trees in the orchard with 6 trees in each row. How many rows of trees did the farmer plant?

To find the quotient of 42 ÷ 6, we look in the 6 row for 42. We see 7 at the top of that column. The farmer planted **7 rows** of trees.

Lesson Practice

a. There are 12 inches in a foot. How many feet is 60 inches? **5 feet**
b. Derek placed 32 books in 4 equal stacks. How many books were in each stack? **8 books**

Use a multiplication table to find each quotient.

c. 56 ÷ 8 **7**
d. 84 ÷ 7 **12**
e. 9)$\overline{72}$ **8**
f. 6)$\overline{54}$ **9**

Written Practice — Distributed and Integrated

1. An eraser costs 32¢. How much would five erasers cost? **$1.60**
(60)

2. The record was 900 points. Jan had 625 points. How many more points did Jan need to reach the record? **275 points**
(28, 36)

▶ 3. (**Analyze**) Half a dozen children were playing in the yard. Then half of them left. How many children were still in the yard? **3**
(83)

▶ 4. How many centimeters is half of a meter? **50 cm**
(79, 83)

▶ 5. (**Analyze**) One way to mentally multiply by 4 is by "double doubling" the other factor. That means to double the other factor, then double the result.
(78, 84)
   a. 4 × 20 **80**
   b. 4 × 21 **84**

6. Multiply:
(84)
   a. 6 × $14 **$84**
   b. 7 × 14¢ **98¢**

Lesson 89   483

English Learners

An **orchard** is a group of many fruit or nut trees. Ask:

"If there are 7 apple trees in the orchard, and each tree has 30 apples, how many apples are there in all?"
7 × 30 = 210 apples

Ask:

"What other types of trees can grow in an orchard?" samples: oranges, peaches, pecans, plums

Have students say what their favorite fruit or nut that grows in an orchard is.

Alternative Approach: Using Manipulatives

Students can use their rulers to divide numbers less than 30. Have students place their rulers on a sheet of paper so that they are measuring in centimeters. They should draw a line 30 cm long, marking the point at 0 cm and the point at 30 cm. To divide 30 into equal groups of 6, have students count 6 cm from the left and make a mark on their line. From the 6 cm mark, have students count another 6 cm, and so on. When they are finished, students can count the number of segments on their line. The answer can be checked using a multiplication table.

New Concept (Continued)

Lesson Practice

Guided Practice

Use these problems as guided practice to check the students' understanding of today's concept.

Problem a
Alternate Methods

Students can count by 12s to 60 to determine the answer.

Closure — The questions below help assess the concepts taught in this lesson.

"How can we use a multiplication table to divide 35 by 7?" Look at the row that begins with seven. Look across the row for the number 35. Then look at the top of the column and see which number is there. Five is the answer.

"What are two ways we can write thirty divided by six?" 30 ÷ 6 or 6)$\overline{30}$

Discuss real-world situations where division might be helpful. Examples are given below.

• 45 students sign up for the basketball team and the coach needs to know how many five-person teams he can make.

• A restaurant wants to put 42 people at 7 different tables.

Written Practice

Math Conversations
Independent Practice and Discussions to Increase Understanding

● **Problem 3** (**Analyze**)
This problem is asking students to divide 12 twice. Students may first need to be reminded that 1 dozen = 12.

● **Problem 4**
You may need to remind students of the following metric length conversion.

1 meter = 100 centimeters

Consider holding up a meter stick for the students to see before solving this problem.

● **Problem 5** (**Analyze**)
Write the following on the board to help students understand this method for problem **a**.

2 × 20 = 40
2 × 40 = 80
So we know that 4 × 20 = 80.

(continued)

Lesson 89   483

Written Practice (Continued)

Math Conversations
Independent Practice and Discussions to Increase Understanding

Problem 7 Multiple Choice
Test-Taking Strategy

Students can make this problem much easier by rewriting the four choices as the cent value of each coin. **A:** 1¢, **B:** 5¢, **C:** 10¢, **D:** 25¢

Students should then choose the answer that has an even number in the ones place.

Problem 8 Analyze

Students should first convert all measurements to quarts.

1 gallon = 4 quarts

$\frac{1}{2}$ gallon = 2 quarts

Students can then set up a subtraction problem to solve:

4 quarts − 2 quarts − 1 quart = 1 quart

Problem 11 Multiple Choice
Test-Taking Strategy

Choices **B** and **C** can be eliminated because they measure length, not mass. Students should recognize that ounces are too small a mass for barbells. The only reasonable measure of mass for a barbell is **A**, kilograms.

Problem 14 Conclude

A doubling sequence involves multiplication by 2. Help students recognize the following pattern:

Third term: 2 × 10 = 20

Fourth term: 2 × 2 × 10 = 4 × 10 = 40

Fifth term: 2 × 2 × 2 × 10 = 8 × 10 = 80

Sixth term: 2 × 2 × 2 × 2 × 10 = 16 × 10 = 160

(continued)

---

7. **Multiple Choice** Which of the following coins has a value that is an even number of cents?   **C**

   A penny   **B** nickel   **C** dime   **D** quarter

8. (**Analyze**) If a full gallon container of water is used to fill a half-gallon container and a quart container, then how much water is left in the gallon container?   1 quart

9. Write two multiplication facts and two division facts using the numbers 3, 9, and 27.   3 × 9 = 27; 9 × 3 = 27; 27 ÷ 9 = 3; 27 ÷ 3 = 9

10. What number goes in the square to complete the multiplication fact?   6

11. **Multiple Choice** Which unit is best for measuring the mass of a barbell?   **A**

   A kilograms   **B** feet   **C** meters   **D** ounces

12. **Multiple Choice** This picture shows the answer to which multiplication?   **B**

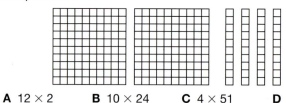

   A 12 × 2   **B** 10 × 24   **C** 4 × 51   **D** 20 × 4

13. The shirt was on sale for half price. If the regular price was $24, what was the sale price? $12

14. (**Conclude**) Find the next three numbers in this doubling sequence:

5, 10, 20, __40__, __80__, __160__, ...

15. Find each quotient:
(86)
  a. 24 ÷ 4   6
  b. 24 ÷ 6   4
  c. 24 ÷ 8   3

16. $1 − 42¢   58¢
(21, 28)

17. 38 + 47 + 163 + 9   257
(24)

18. $63 − $45 $18
(23)

19. 4 × 3 × 10   120
(77)

▶ **20. Multiple Choice** Which multiplication or division fact
(85, 86) below is *not* illustrated by this diagram?   D

  A 12 ÷ 4 = 3   **B** 4 × 3 = 12
  C 12 ÷ 3 = 4   **D** 2 × 12 = 24

Real-World Connection

Roderick's baby sister drinks 3 cups of milk a day. How many cups of milk does his baby sister drink in a week? How many cups of milk would she drink in the month of April?   21 cups; 90 cups

Lesson 89   485

Using a multiplication table to divide by a one-digit number prepares students for

- **Lesson 90,** solving equal groups problems.
- **Lesson 101,** dividing two-digit numbers.

Written Practice (Continued)

Math Conversations
Independent Practice and Discussions to Increase Understanding

▶ **Problem 20   Multiple Choice**
Test Taking Strategy

The question asks which fact is *not* illustrated, so one fact does not belong to the same family as the others. Choice **D** is the only choice to have the numbers 2 and 24 in it. Knowing that fact families share the same three numbers, choice **D** does not fit with the other choices, so it is the answer.

Errors and Misconceptions

▶ **Problem 5**
Explain that the phrase "double doubling" refers to multiplying a number by two twice, which is equivalent to multiplying by 4.

▶ **Problem 8**
Be sure that students are familiar with the relationships among gallons, half gallons, and quarts. Have them refer to the diagram of capacity measures from Lesson 87 for review.

You may wish to extend this question by having students calculate the amount of fruits and vegetables Roderick should eat in a week and in a month based on the U.S. Department of Agriculture's recommendation that a 9-year-old should eat about 2 cups of fruit and 2 cups of vegetables a day.

Lesson 89   485

LESSON 90

Planning & Preparation

Texas Essential Knowledge and Skills

(3.4)(C) use number sentences to record the solutions to division problems
(3.14)(C) select/develop an appropriate problem-solving plan/strategy, including looking for a pattern to solve a problem
(3.15)(A) explain observations using pictures
(3.15)(B) relate informal language to symbols

• Equal Groups Stories, Part 2

Objectives
- Translate a story problem about equal groups into a number sentence to solve the problem.
- Use division to solve story problems about equal groups.
- Use pictorial models to help visualize story problems about equal groups.

Prerequisite Skills
- Model dividing by a one-digit number with pictorial models and concrete objects.
- Use pencil and paper to write division number sentences to show dividing by a one-digit number.
- Use multiplication to solve story problems about equal groups.
- Draw arrays to model dividing by a one-digit number.

Materials
Instructional Masters
- Power Up 90

Manipulative Kit
- Color tiles or counters*
- Money manipulatives (coins)*
- Student clocks*

Teacher-provided materials
- Student money manipulatives (coins)*

optional

Power Up 90

Differentiated Instruction

Reaching All Special Needs Students

Special Education Students	At-Risk Students	English Learners	Advanced Learners
• Inclusion (TM) • Adaptations for Saxon Math	• Alternative Approach (TM) • Reteaching Masters	• English Learners (TM) • English Learner Handbook	• Extend the Example (TM) • Early Finishers (SE) • Online Activities

TM=Teacher's Manual
SE=Student Edition

Math Language

Maintained	English Learners
factor	available

486A   Saxon Math Intermediate 3

Problem Solving Discussion

Problem

The school principal's office has a water cooler. The big bottle of water that sits on top of the cooler is labeled "5 gallons." Cheyenne is making a table to help her find how many cups of water are in 5 gallons. Copy this table and fill in the missing numbers. How many cups are in 5 gallons?

Gallons	Cups
1	16
2	
3	
4	
5	

Focus Strategies

 Find/Extend a Pattern

 Make or Use a Table, Chart, or Graph

Understand Understand the problem.

"What information are we given?"

1. A water bottle has a capacity of 5 gallons.
2. We are shown a table that indicates there are 16 cups in 1 gallon.

"What are we asked to do?"

We are asked to copy the table and fill in the missing numbers. We are specifically asked to find how many cups are in 5 gallons.

Plan Make a plan.

"How can we use the information we know to solve the problem?"

There are 16 cups in 1 gallon. The "Gallons" column of the table counts up by 1 gallon for each row, so we can *complete the table* by *extending the pattern* in the "Cups" column.

Solve Carry out the plan.

"How many cups are in 2 gallons?"

Two gallons is 16 cups + 16 cups = 32 cups. We write 32 in the "Cups" column.

"How many cups are in 3 gallons? ... 4 gallons?"

32 cups + 16 cups = 48 cups

48 cups + 16 cups = 64 cups

"How many cups are in 5 gallons?"

64 cups + 16 cups = 80 cups

Gallons	Cups
1	16
2	32
3	48
4	64
5	80

Check Look back.

"Did we complete the task?"

Yes, we completed the table to show how many cups are in 1, 2, 3, 4, and 5 gallons. We found that 5 gallons is the same as 80 cups.

"Is our answer reasonable?"

Yes, there are 16 cups in 1 gallon, so there are 16 + 16 + 16 + 16 + 16 = 80 cups in 5 gallons.

Alternate Strategy

Write a Number Sentence

Students can write a multiplication number sentence to solve the problem. The number of cups in a given number of gallons is an equal-groups problem. Each gallon is a group of 16 cups. So we can multiply the number of gallons by 16. In this problem, we see that 5 × 16 cups = 80 cups.

Lesson 90   486B

LESSON 90

Facts
Distribute **Power Up 90** to students. See answers below.

Jump Start
Before students begin the Mental Math exercise, do these exercises as a class.

Mental Math
Encourage students to share different ways to mentally compute these exercises. Strategies for exercises are listed below.

a. **Think of 17 as 1 + 16**
  17 + 16 = 1 + 16 + 16 = 1 + 32 = 33
b. **Think 5 × 4, Then Add a Zero to the End**
  5 × 4 = 20 so 5 × 40 = 200
c. **Multiply**
  A hexagon has six sides. Three hexagons have 3 × 6 = 18 sides.

Problem Solving
Refer to **Problem-Solving Strategy Discussion**, p. 486B.

LESSON 90 • Equal Groups Stories, Part 2

Texas Essential Knowledge and Skills
(3.4)(C) use number sentences to record the solutions to division problems
(3.14)(C) select/develop an appropriate problem-solving plan/strategy, including looking for a pattern to solve a problem
(3.15)(A) explain observations using pictures
(3.15)(B) relate informal language to symbols

facts	Power Up 90
jump start	Count up by 3s from 0 to 45. Count up by 9s from 0 to 99. Draw a hexagon in the workspace on your worksheet. See student work. Use these clues to find the secret number. Write the secret number on your worksheet. 45 • two-digit number • sum of digits is 9 • product of the digits is 20 • odd number
mental math	a. **Number Sense:** 17 + 16 33 b. **Number Sense:** 5 × 40 200 c. **Geometry:** How many sides do 3 hexagons have? 18 sides d. **Time:** It is afternoon. Keyanna's little sister took a nap at the time shown on the clock. She woke up 1 hour later. What time did she wake up? 2:35 p.m.
problem solving	The school principal's office has a water cooler. The big bottle of water that sits on top of the cooler is labeled "5 gallons." Cheyenne is making a table to help her find how many cups of water are in 5 gallons. Copy this table and fill in the missing numbers. How many cups are in 5 gallons? See student work; 80 cups

Gallons	Cups
1	16
2	
3	
4	
5	

486 Saxon Math Intermediate 3

Facts Divide:

8 10)80	1 5)5	10 1)10	10 3)30	10 7)70	9 2)18	3 10)30	2 9)18	3 2)6
9 1)9	2 7)14	10 5)50	2 8)16	3 1)3	2 4)8	1 2)2	0 10)0	1 4)4
1 3)3	5 2)10	4 10)40	0 5)0	10 6)60	1 7)7	6 10)60	0 1)0	7 2)14
0 6)0	8 1)8	0 9)0	6 1)6	10 10)100	3 3)9	0 8)0	1 10)10	10 8)80

486 Saxon Math Intermediate 3

New Concept

Recall that an equal-groups story has three numbers.

If we know the number of groups and the number in each group, then we multiply to find the total.

Number of groups × Number in each group = Total

If we know the total and want to know the number of groups or the number in each group, we divide to find the answer.

Total ÷ Number of groups = Number in each group

Total ÷ Number in each group = Number of groups

Example 1

Twenty-eight children are going on a field trip. Seven cars are available to drive the children. If the children are divided into equal groups, how many children will ride in each car?

See how this story fits the equal groups pattern.

Number of groups × Number in each group = Total

7 cars × ? in each car = 28 children in all

This story has a missing factor.

7 × ? = 28

We can find a missing factor by dividing.

28 ÷ 4 = 7

We answer the question. **Four children** will ride in each car.

Example 2

Twenty-four people are coming to a party. They will sit at tables that will seat four people. How many tables will be needed to seat them all?

We see that the story fits the equal groups pattern.

Number of groups × Number in each group = Total

? tables × 4 people at each table = 24 people in all

Lesson 90   487

Math Background

The ability to solve a story problem might seem like a skill only applicable in math textbooks and on math tests. However, the components of efficient and accurate problem solving can be applied to any number of situations encountered in daily life. Let's say Fran needs to buy 128 bottles of juice for a meeting at work. The juice bottles come in packs of 6. Fran needs to understand the problem, or know that she will need to divide 128 by 6 to find how many packs to buy. She might want to estimate to determine a reasonable answer to decide which brand to buy.

English Learners

Available means ready for use. Ask:

"There were 20 students and 10 parents available for an after school clean-up day. How many people were available?" 10 + 20 = 30 people

Ask:

"What items are available for you to check out at the library?" samples: books, audio books, CDs, videos

Have students think about their schedule and tell what times they have available for play.

New Concept

Connection

In Lesson 60, students were introduced to equal groups problems with a multiplication pattern. In this lesson, students will solve equal groups problems using either multiplication with a missing factor or division. To solve this type of problem, students must be able to recognize related multiplication and division facts. Write the following number sentence on the board.

$b \times 12 = 36$

As a class, make up an equal groups story problem that follows this equation. sample: Ethan wants to put 12 books on each shelf. How many shelves will he need for 36 books?

Have students provide the remaining facts in the fact family, and write them on the board. Read these facts aloud and relate them to the story.

Example 1

Students can solve or check this problem using a multiplication table. By looking down the 7s row to find 28, students can check the answer by looking for the number at the top of the corresponding column.

Extend the Example

Have advanced learners determine the number of vans needed to carry 35 students on a field trip if each van can carry a maximum of 6 students. Since 35 is not a multiple of 6, students may need to divide by using a number close to 35, such as 36 or 30. The answer can be adjusted based on what number students choose to work with. Have students explain their answer. sample: 5 vans can carry a maximum of 30 students, which still leaves 5 students left to carry. 6 vans can carry a maximum of 36 students, leaving one open seat. So 6 vans are needed to carry all 35 students.

Example 2
Manipulative Use

Divide students into small groups. Each group should have 24 counters or tiles. Students divide the tiles into groups of 4 to find how many tables would be needed.

(continued)

Lesson 90   487

New Concept (Continued)

Lesson Practice

Guided Practice

Use these problems as guided practice to check the students' understanding of today's concept.

Problem a

Ask a volunteer to read the story aloud. Some students might want to act it out using their money manipulatives or counters. Ask students,

"What part of the equal groups pattern is the problem asking for?" the number of groups (stacks)

"What is the multiplication fact that represents this story?" $p \times 5 = 40$

Problem b

Students now have a number of different methods for solving an equal groups problem. Suggest that students use any of the following:

- Use a multiplication table to solve for the missing factor.
- Use counters to model the situation and divide 30 counters into six equal groups.
- Make a sketch of an array that illustrates 30 students in six rows.

Closure The questions below help assess the concepts taught in this lesson.

"What multiplication sentence will help us to solve an equal groups pattern?" Number of groups × Number in each group = Total

"How can we find the answer to an equal groups problem?" We first need to find out what the question asks. We find the two numbers we know, decide if we will multiply or divide, and solve.

Discuss real-world situations where using an equal groups pattern to solve a division problem might be helpful. Examples are given below.

- Jerry finished 15 math problems in 5 minutes and wants to know how many problems he did each minute.
- We have 18 socks and want to know how many pairs there are.

We know the total and the number in each group, but we do not know the number of groups.

$$? \times 4 = 24$$

We divide to find the missing factor.

$$4\overline{)24} \quad 6$$

We find that **6 tables** are needed.

Represent Draw a picture to show the equal groups story in example 2. See student work.

Lesson Practice

▶ **a.** Sylvester has 40 pennies. He puts them in stacks with 5 pennies in each stack. How many stacks does he make? 8 stacks

▶ **b.** There are 30 desks in the room. The teacher wants to arrange the desks in 6 equal rows. How many desks will be in each row? 5 desks

Written Practice Distributed and Integrated

1. Simon took twelve big steps to cross the street. Each step is about
(34) 1 yard long. The street is about how many feet wide? 36 feet

2. The television was on sale for $70 off the regular price. The
(20) regular price was $365. What was the sale price? $295

3. The population of the town is 16,000. Write the number using
(32) words. sixteen thousand

4. a. Round $389 to the nearest hundred dollars. $400
(15)
   b. Round $315 to the nearest hundred dollars. $300

5. Dixon bought a table for $389 and a chair for $315. Estimate the
(30) total cost of the desk and chair. $700

488   Saxon Math Intermediate 3

 Inclusion

Drawing Equal Groups

Some students may have difficulty visualizing a story problem. Drawing a picture of the problem may make it more concrete for them.

Materials: pencil and paper

- Write this story problem on the board. *Rachel had 24 erasers. She wanted to divide them equally among the 6 other students at her table. How many erasers would each student get?*

"What are we counting?" erasers

"How many groups of erasers?" 6

- Students draw a circle for each group.

"How many erasers are there altogether?" 24

"What will we do with the 24 erasers?" divide them equally among 6 students

- Students draw a tally mark in each circle, counting as they add one more to each circle until they have drawn 24 tally marks.

"How many erasers did each student get?" 4

6. On Monday, Max finished the fact practice quiz in 80 seconds. On Wednesday, he finished in half that time. In how many seconds did Max finish the quiz on Wednesday? 40 seconds
(83)

▶ 7. (Analyze) Mentally multiply by 4 by "double doubling" the other factor.
(78, 84)
   a. 4 × 30   120
   b. 4 × 15   60

▶ 8. Thirty desks were arranged in rows with 5 desks in each row. How many rows of desks were there? 6
(90)

9. (Multiple Choice) Which illustration below shows an even number of counters? B
(88)

   A ○ ○   B ○ ○   C ○ ○ ○
      ○ ○ ○ ○   ○ ○ ○ ○   ○ ○ ○
      ○ ○   ○ ○   ○ ○ ○
      ○   ○ ○

10. a. The shaded circle shows what fraction equivalent to $\frac{1}{2}$? $\frac{3}{6}$
(42, 47)

▶ b. (Represent) Draw and shade a circle to show a fraction equivalent to $\frac{1}{2}$ that has a denominator of 4. What is the fraction?

sample: $\frac{2}{4}$

▶ 11. Multiply:
(84)
   a. 6 × $25 $150
   b. 7 × 15¢ $1.05

12. Find the missing number: 48 − w = 29.   19
(40)

▶ 13. (Conclude) In this sequence each number is half the number before it. Find the next three numbers in this sequence.
(83)
   160, 80, 40, __20__, __10__, __5__, ...

14. Find each quotient:
(85)
   a. 25 ÷ 5   5
   b. 21 ÷ 3   7
   c. 20 ÷ 4   5

15. 5 × 6 × 7   210
(77)

16. $5.00 − $2.34 $2.66
(26, 28)

Lesson 90   489

Alternative Approach: Using Manipulatives

Provide each student with a small manipulative clock or use the large clock in the room to demonstrate how clocks can be used to solve equal groups problems. Division problems with a dividend less than 60 and a divisor equal to 5 can be solved using a clock. Have students use the clocks to solve the following problem:

"If we have 45 marbles that we want to arrange into groups of 5, how many groups will there be?"

Explain to students that the hours on the clock already show groupings of 5 minutes. So the hour corresponding to 45 minutes represents the number of groups. Help students recognize 9 as the answer, since 9 o'clock coincides with 45 minutes on a clock.

Written Practice

Math Conversations
Independent Practice and Discussions to Increase Understanding

● **Problem 7** (Analyze)
Write the following on the board to help students understand this method for problem a.
2 × 30 = 60
2 × 60 = 120
So we know that 4 × 30 = 120.

● **Problem 8**
Help students analyze this equal groups story problem by asking,
"What is the total number of desks?" 30
"What part of the equal groups pattern is the 5?" the number of desks in each row
"What does the problem ask for?" the number of rows
"What division fact could you use to solve this problem?" 30 ÷ 5 = r

● **Problem 10b** (Represent)
Since the denominator is four, students should draw a circle divided into four equal parts by marking two perpendicular diameters. Then students should shade two of the four parts.

● **Problem 11**
Remind students of the three steps they learned for multiplying two-digit numbers by one-digit numbers:
1. Set up the problem
2. Multiply the ones and regroup if needed
3. Multiply the tens

● **Problem 13** (Conclude)
Students may use counters to model this problem. Each term shows division of the previous term by 2. Students can keep splitting their counters into equal groups to get the next term of the sequence.

(continued)

Lesson 90   489

Written Practice (Continued)

Math Conversations
Independent Practice and Discussions to Increase Understanding

Problem 18
Extend the Problem

Ask students to name each figure.

A: scalene triangle

B: equilateral triangle

C: parallelogram

D: pentagon

Problem 19 Multiple Choice
Test-Taking Strategy

A line of symmetry divides a figure into two equal halves that are mirror images. Students should mark out any choices that do not show identical halves.

Problem 20 Represent

Students should decide on a realistic scale to use so that their sketches can fit on one piece of paper. Students should turn their paper sideways if most of the travel is in the east-west direction.

Errors and Misconceptions

Problem 7
"Double doubling" may confuse some students. Reinforce that the idea is to mentally multiply a number by 4 by doubling it twice.

Problem 9
Some students may be thrown off by the fact that choice **C** shows an array of counters with equal rows and columns. They may mistakenly believe the number is even. However, remind students that a number is even only if it can be put into *two* equal groups.

Have students act it out using differently colored counters or color tiles before drawing their pictures.

---

17. Find each product:
(56, 78)
   a. 4 × 90   360   **b.** 7 × 90   630   **c.** 10 × 23   230

18. Multiple Choice Which polygon below does *not* have at least
(65, 67) one obtuse angle? B

   A   **B**   **C**   **D**

19. Multiple Choice Which figure shows a line of symmetry? C
(Inv. 7)
   A   **B**   **C**   **D**

20. **Represent** Sketch a map that shows your school and your
(31) home. Make the top of the map north. Then write directions to your home from school. See student work.

Real-World Connection

Rosemary was making a costume. She sewed five buttons on her costume. The red button was below the blue one. The green button was above the blue one. The yellow button was between the blue and red ones. The purple button was above the green one. Which button is in the middle? Draw a picture to show your answer. blue; See student work.

Learning to solve equal groups story problems by dividing prepares students for

- **Lesson 101,** dividing two-digit numbers.

Assessments

Distribute **Power-Up Test 17** and **Cumulative Test 17** to each student. Have students complete the **Power-Up Test** first. Allow 10 minutes. Then have students work on the **Cumulative Test.**

Performance Task

The remaining class time should be spent on **Performance Task 9.** Students can begin the task in class or complete it during another class period.

Flexible Grouping

Flexible grouping gives students an opportunity to work with other students in an interactive and encouraging way. The choice for how students are grouped depends on the goals for instruction, the needs of the students, and the specific learning activity.

Assigning Groups

Group members can be randomly assigned, or can be assigned based on some criteria such as grouping students who may need help with a certain skill or grouping students to play specific roles in a group (such as recorder or reporter).

Types of Groups

Students can be paired or placed in larger groups. For pairing, students can be assigned partners on a weekly or monthly basis. Pairing activities are the easiest to manage in a classroom and are more likely to be useful on a daily basis.

Flexible Grouping Ideas

Lesson 82, Example 2
Materials: counters

Pair students before you teach Lesson 82. Then teach the lesson, stopping after you go over example 2.
- Direct pairs of students to use the counters to find other ways to divide 18 into equal groups.
- Volunteers share their comments with the class.

Lesson 83, Example 1
Materials: counters

Divide students into groups of 4. Have them choose a partner from the group. Write 2 even numbers less than 50 on the board.
- One partner divides the first number in half using counters, and the other partner does the same with the second number.
- Each student interviews their partner by asking questions about how to divide the number in half. (sample: How did you use the counters to find half of your number?)
- After partners have interviewed each other, they must share their answers with the team comparing solutions and strategies.

Lesson 84, Example 3
Materials: paper

After guiding students through example 3, write three multiplication problems with two-digit numbers on the board.
- Each group works together to solve the first problem.
- Divide the groups into pairs to solve the second problem.
- Direct students to work on the last problem independently and then check their solutions with the group.

Lesson 90, Example 1
Materials: counters

Have students form pairs to discuss equal groups.
- Guide students through example 1. Then write a similar multiplication problem on the board. Direct students to think about how to solve the problem using counters.
- Students work in pairs to solve the problem. Volunteers share their solutions with the class.

INVESTIGATION 9

Planning & Preparation

Texas Essential Knowledge and Skills
(3.9)(B) create two-dimensional figures with lines of symmetry using concrete models
(3.9)(C) identify lines of symmetry in two-dimensional geometric figures
(3.15)(A) record observations using pictures

• Symmetry, Part 2

Objectives
- Find one or more lines of symmetry on an object.
- Fold and cut paper to create objects with one or more lines of symmetry.
- Use a mirror to demonstrate symmetry.

Prerequisite Skills
- Find a symmetrical object's line of symmetry.
- Use concrete objects to create a pattern with a line of symmetry.

Materials
Instructional Masters
- Lesson Activity 30

Manipulative Kit
- Mirrors
- Geoboards*
- Rulers
- Rubber bands*

Teacher-provided materials
- Sheets of paper (2 per student)
- Scissors

optional

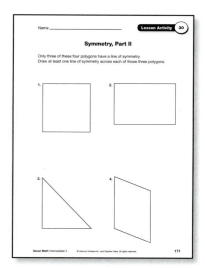

Lesson Activity 30

Differentiated Instruction

Reaching All Special Needs Students

Special Education Students	At-Risk Students	English Learners	Advanced Learners
• Adaptations for Saxon Math	• Alternative Approach (TM) • Error Alert (TM) • Reteaching Masters	• English Learners (TM) • English Learner Handbook	• Extend the Problem (TM) • Online Activities

TM=Teacher's Manual

Math Language

Maintained
half
line of symmetry

English Learners
upright

491B Saxon Math Intermediate 3

INVESTIGATION 9

Texas Essential Knowledge and Skills
(3.9)(B) create two-dimensional figures with lines of symmetry using concrete models and technology
(3.9)(C) identify lines of symmetry in two-dimensional geometric figures
(3.15)(A) record observations using pictures

Focus on

• Symmetry, Part 2

Recall from Investigation 7 that a line of symmetry divides a figure into mirror images.

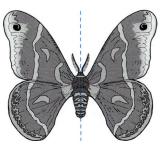

Visit www.SaxonMath.com/Int3Activities for an online activity.

A figure may have one line of symmetry, two lines of symmetry, or more. A figure may also have no lines of symmetry.

No lines of symmetry   One line of symmetry   Two lines of symmetry

A line of symmetry also shows where a figure could be folded in half so that one half exactly fits onto the other half. In the following activity, you will create shapes with one or two lines of symmetry by folding and cutting paper.

Activity 1

Creating Symmetrical Figures

Materials: two sheets of paper, scissors

Fold a sheet of paper in half. While the paper is folded, cut a shape out of the paper starting from one end of the folded edge to the other end.

Investigation 9   491

INVESTIGATION 9

Symmetry, Part 2

In this investigation, students will continue their study of symmetry. They will learn about figures with multiple lines of symmetry and create a symmetrical figure with paper and scissors.

Math Language

"When a figure has one or more lines of symmetry, we say that the figure is symmetrical."

Instruction

Not every figure has a line of symmetry. Ask students for examples of shapes and figures that have no line of symmetry.

Activity 1
Error Alert

Make sure that students start and end their cuts on the folded sides of the paper; otherwise they will have two separate figures instead of one symmetrical figure.

(continued)

Investigation 9   491

Math Conversations
Independent Practice and Discussions to Increase Understanding

Problem 1
Extend the Problem

"Which capital letters have lines of symmetry?" A, B, C, D, E, H, I, M, O, T, U, V, W, X, and Y

Problem 2
Extend the Problem

"A quadrilateral is a four-sided figure. Will a quadrilateral always have a line of symmetry?" no

"What is a parallelogram?" A parallelogram is a figure with two sets of parallel lines.

"Will a parallelogram always have a line of symmetry?" no

"How many lines of symmetry does a square have?" four lines of symmetry: one vertical, one horizontal, and two diagonal

(continued)

Here we show a heart shape being cut from the folded paper:

The opened figure you cut out has a line of symmetry along the fold.

Fold is line of symmetry

Repeat the activity with another sheet of paper folded twice.

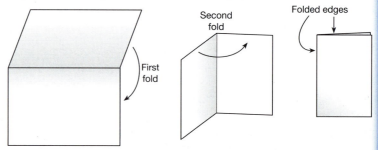

Cut a shape from the twice-folded paper, beginning the cut from one folded edge and ending in the other folded edge.

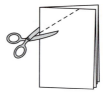

Have students make symmetrical figures using a geoboard. With one color of rubber band, have them make the figure, and with a second color, have them show the line of symmetry.

The opened figure you cut out has two lines of symmetry along the folds.

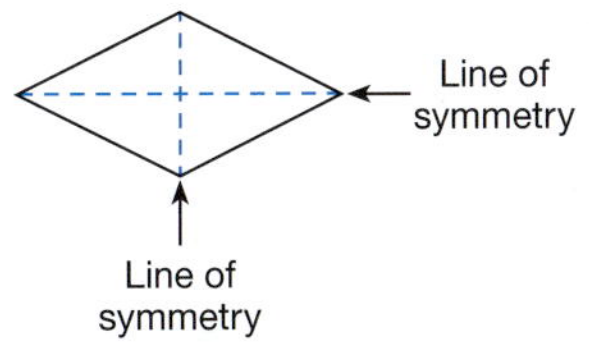

Recall from Investigation 7 that when we place an upright mirror on a line of symmetry, the reflection in the mirror completes the figure.

Place a mirror on the lines of symmetry in these figures to see the complete shape in the reflection.

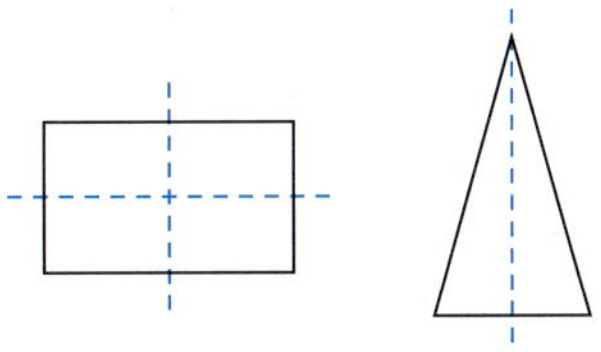

1. **Multiple Choice** Use a mirror to decide which of these letters has a line of symmetry. C

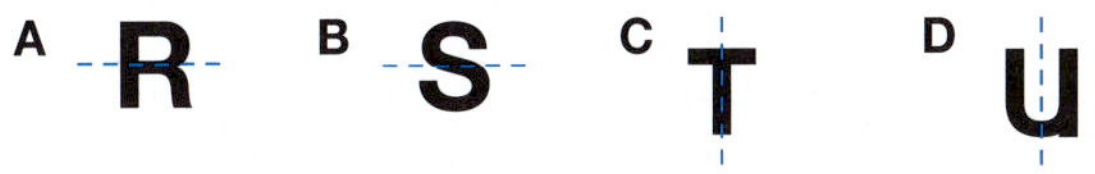

2. **Multiple Choice** Which of these quadrilaterals shows a line of symmetry? B

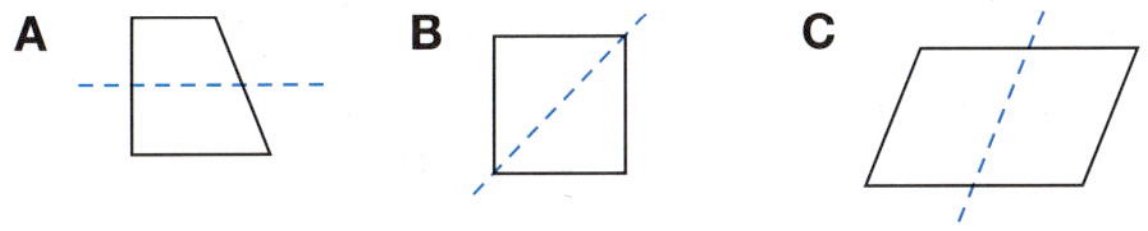

Activity 2

Lines of Symmetry

Materials: **Lesson Activity 30,** ruler, pencil

On **Lesson Activity 30,** there are four polygons. Three of the polygons have lines of symmetry. Draw at least one line of symmetry across each of those three polygons.

Discussion

Symmetry is all around us. Ask students if they can give examples of symmetry from the following categories: the ocean, cars, the dining room, sports, flowers, and food.

Activity 2

Distribute a copy of Lesson Activity 30 to each student.

Error Alert

Some students may draw a line of symmetry for all four polygons. For the polygon without a line of symmetry, show students that if they cut out the figure and fold it in half along the line they drew, the two halves will not match exactly.

Closure

The questions below help assess the concepts taught in this lesson.

"What does it mean when a figure is symmetrical?" sample: A figure can be folded along a line of symmetry and have both halves match exactly.

"Can a figure have more than one line of symmetry?" yes

"Give an example of a figure with more than one line of symmetry." a square, a rectangle, a circle.

Discuss real-world situations where symmetry might be helpful. Examples are given below.

- We want to make a mask that looks like a cat's face.
- A landscape architect is designing a garden and wants each side to be the same.

English Learners

Upright means that something is standing or sitting straight up and down or vertical. Say:

"Put your book upright on your desk. Sit upright at your desk." See student work.

Ask:

"Name some items in your refrigerator that will leak unless you set them upright." samples: drinks in bottles, salad dressing, a jar of pickles

Have students name objects in the classroom that are standing or sitting upright.

Looking Forward

Understanding symmetry and how to make a symmetrical figure prepares students for

- **Lesson 104,** sorting geometric shapes.
- **Lesson 105,** using diagrams for sorting.
- **Lesson 109,** placing points on a grid.

SECTION 10 OVERVIEW

Lesson Planner

Lesson	New Concepts	Materials	Resources
91	• Multiplying Three-Digit Numbers, Part 1	• Manipulative kit: ruler • 2 identical jars • Pennies	• Power Up 91 • Lesson Activity 31
92	• Parentheses • Using Compatible Numbers, Part 1		• Power Up 92
93	• Estimating Products	• Manipulative kit: geosolids	• Power Up 93
94	• Using Compatible Numbers, Part 2		• Power Up 94
95	• Using Estimation to Verify Answers	• Manipulative kit: ruler	• Power Up 95
Cumulative Assessment			• Cumulative Test 18 • Power-Up Test 18 • Test-Day Activity 9
96	• Rounding to the Nearest Dollar	• Manipulative kit: ruler • Student money manipulatives	• Power Up 96
97	• Multiplying Three-Digit Numbers, Part 2	• Manipulative kit: ruler	• Power Up 97
98	• Estimating by Weight or Mass	• Manipulative kit: ruler, balance scale • Penny jar from Lesson 91 • Extra penny rolls	• Power Up 98 • Lesson Activity 31
99	• Effects of Estimation	• Manipulative kit: ruler	• Power Up 99
100	• Multiplying Dollars and Cents	• Manipulative kit: ruler	• Power Up 100
Cumulative Assessment			• Cumulative Test 19 • Power-Up Test 19 • Performance Task 10
Inv. 10	• Evaluating Estimates	• Penny jar from Lesson 91 • "First Estimate" envelope • "Last Estimate" envelope	• Lesson Activity 31

 All resources are also available on the Resources and Planner CD.

Additional Resources

- Instructional Masters
- Reteaching Masters
- Resources and Planner CD
- Calculator Activities
- Assessment Guide
- Performance Tasks
- Instructional Transparencies
- Answer Key CD
- Power Up Workbook
- Written Practice Workbook

LESSONS 91–100, INVESTIGATION 10

Math Highlights

Enduring Understandings — The "Big Picture"
After completing Section 10, students will understand that:
- estimating can help us find "how many."
- rounding and compatible numbers may be used to estimate answers.
- estimating can be used to verify the reasonableness of computations.
- compatible numbers can help us add mentally.

Essential Questions
- What is the purpose of estimating?
- What are some strategies for estimating answers to arithmetic problems?
- How can we check our answers to arithmetic problems?
- What is a strategy for adding mentally?

Math Content Highlights	Math Processes Highlights

Number Sense
• **Compatible Numbers** Lessons 92, 94
• **Estimating** Lessons 93, 95, 96, 98, 99, Inv. 10
• **Multiplication** Lessons 91, 97, 100
• **Comparing Numbers** Lesson 99
 	
Geometry and Measurement
• **Weight and Mass** Lesson 98
	Problem Solving
	• Strategies
	  – Draw a Picture or Diagram Lessons 91, 94, 95
	  – Find or Extend a Pattern Lessons 91, 99, 100
	  – Guess and Check Lesson 97
	  – Make or Use a Table, Chart, or Graph Lessons 96, 98, 99
	  – Use Logical Reasoning Lessons 92, 93, 100
	  – Write a Number Sentence Lessons 92, 93, 95, 96
	• Real-World Applications Lessons 91–100, Inv. 10
	
	Communication
	• **Analyze** Lesson 94
	• **Discuss** Lesson 97
	• **Evaluate** Lessons 95, 99
	• **Explain** Lessons 94, 96
	• **Justify** Lessons 95–97
	
	Connections
	• **Math to Math** Lesson 91
	• **Math and Other Subjects**
	  – Math and Geography Lesson 93
	  – Math and Science Lesson 99
	
	Representation
	• **Model** Lessons 91–97, 100
	• **Represent** Lesson 100
	• **Manipulative Use** Lessons 92, 95, 97, 98, Inv. 10

SECTION 10

Differentiated Instruction

Support for differentiated instruction is included with each lesson. Specific resources and features are listed on each lesson planning page. Features in the Teacher's Manual to customize instruction include the following:

Teacher's Manual Support

Alternative Approach	Provides a different path to concept development. *Lessons 94, 95, 99*
Manipulative Use	Provides alternate concept development through the use of manipulatives. *Lessons 91, 99*
Flexible Grouping	Provides suggestions for various grouping strategies tied to specific lesson examples. *TM page 544A*
Inclusion	Provides ideas for including all students by accommodating special needs. *Lessons 91–95, 97, 98*
Math Language	Provides a list of new and maintained vocabulary words along with words that might be difficult for English learners. *Lessons 91–100, Inv. 10*
English Learners	Provides strategies for teaching specific vocabulary that may be difficult for English learners. *Lessons 91–100, Inv. 10*
Errors and Misconceptions	Provides information about common misconceptions students encounter with concepts. *Lessons 92–100*
Extend the Example	Provides additional concept development for advanced learners. *Lessons 92, 93, 95, 96, 98, 99*
Extend the Problem	Provides an opportunity for advanced learners to broaden concept development by expanding on a particular problem approach or context. *Lessons 91–98, 100, Inv. 10*
Early Finishers	Provides additional math concept extensions for advanced learners at the end of the Written Practice. *Lessons 97, 98*

Additional Resources

The following resources are also available to support differentiated instruction:
- Adaptations for Saxon Math
- English Learner Handbook
- Online Activities
- Reteaching Masters

Technology

Student Resources
- Student Edition eBook
- Calculator Activities
- Online Resources at www.SaxonMath.com/Int3Activities
  — Real World Investigations
  — Online Activities *Lessons 91–100, Inv. 10*
  — Online Calculator Activity

Teacher Resources
- Resources and Planner CD
- Test and Practice Generator CD
- Monitoring Student Progress: eGradebook CD
- Teacher Manual eBook CD
- Answer Key CD
- Adaptations for Saxon Math CD
- Online Resources at www.SaxonMath.com

LESSONS 91–100, INVESTIGATION 10

Cumulative Assessment

The assessments in Saxon Math are frequent and consistently placed to offer a regular method of ongoing testing.

Power-Up Test: Allow no more than ten minutes for this test of basic facts and problem solving skills.

Cumulative Test: Next administer this test, which checks mastery of concepts in previous lessons.

Test-Day Activity and Performance Task: The remaining class time can be spent on these activities. Students can finish the Test-Day Activity for homework or complete the extended Performance Task in another class period.

After Lesson 95

Power-Up Test 18

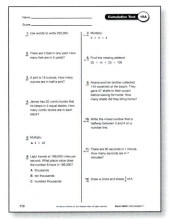
Cumulative Test 18

Test-Day Activity 9

After Lesson 100

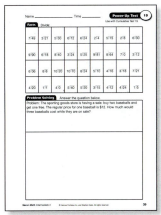
Power-Up Test 19

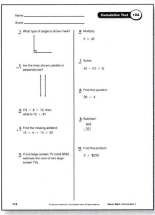
Cumulative Test 19

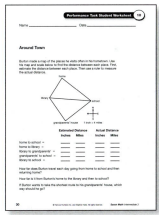
Performance Task 10

Evidence of Learning — What Students Should Know

By the conclusion of Section 10, students should be able to demonstrate the following competencies:

- Learn and apply multiplication facts through 12 by 12 and solve and record multiplication problems up to two digits times one digit. **TEKS (3.4)(A, B)**
- Use strategies including rounding and compatible numbers to estimate solutions to addition and subtraction problems. **TEKS (3.5)(B)**
- Identify, describe, classify, and compare geometric figures using formal geometric vocabulary. **TEKS (3.8)**
- Locate and name points on a number line, including fractions. **TEKS (3.10)**
- Identify benchmarks for units of weight/mass and capacity. **TEKS (3.11)(D, E)**

Reteaching

Students who score below 80% on assessments may be in need of reteaching. Refer to the Reteaching Masters for reteaching opportunities for every lesson.

SECTION 10

Benchmarking and Tracking Standards

Benchmark Tests

Benchmark Tests correlated to lesson concepts allow you to assess student progress after every 20 lessons. An End-of-Course Test is a final benchmark test of the complete textbook. The Benchmark Tests are available in the Assessment Guide.

Monitoring Student Progress: eGradebook CD

To track TEKS mastery, enter students' scores on Cumulative Tests and Benchmark Tests into the Monitoring Student Progress: eGradebook CD. Use the report titled *Benchmark Standards Report* to determine which TEKS were assessed and the level of mastery for each student. Generate a variety of other reports for class tracking and more.

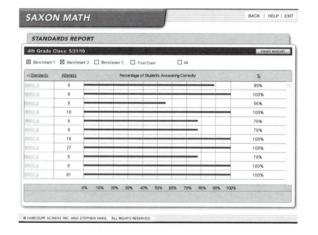

Test and Practice Generator CD

Test items also available in Spanish.

The Test and Practice Generator is an easy-to-manage benchmarking and assessment tool that creates unlimited practice and tests in multiple formats and allows you to customize questions or create new ones. A variety of reports are available to track student progress toward mastery of the TEKS throughout the year.

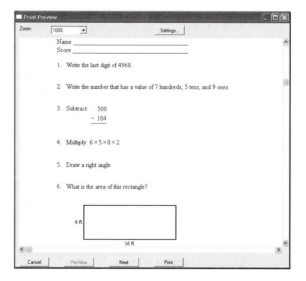

Northstar Math offers you real time benchmarking, tracking, and student progress monitoring.

Visit **www.northstarmath.com** for more information.

494E *Saxon Math* Intermediate 3

LESSONS 91–100, INVESTIGATION 10

Content Trace

Lesson	New Concepts	Practiced	Assessed	Looking Forward
91	• Multiplying Three-Digit Numbers, Part 1	Lessons 91, 92, 93, 95, 96, 98, 99, 102, 105, 106, 108	Test 19	Lessons 92, 93, 94, 95, 97, 98, 99, Inv. 10
92	• Parentheses • Using Compatible Numbers, Part 1	Lessons 92, 93, 94, 95, 96, 97, 98, 99, 100, 102, 103, 104, 107, 108, 109	Tests 19, 20, 21	Lessons 93, 94, 95, 97, 98, 99, Inv. 10
93	• Estimating Products	Lessons 93, 95, 96, 97, 100, 102, 103, 106, 108, 110	Tests 19, 20	Lessons 94, 95, 97, 98, 99, Inv. 10
94	• Using Compatible Numbers, Part 2	Lessons 94, 96, 99, 101, 104	Test 19	Lessons 95, 97, 98, 99, Inv. 10
95	• Using Estimation to Verify Answers	Lessons 95, 97	Test and Practice Generator	Lessons 97, 98, 99, Inv. 10
96	• Rounding to the Nearest Dollar	Lessons 96, 97, 98, 99, 100, 101, 102, 105, 107, 109, 110	Test 21	Lessons 97, 99, 100, Inv. 10
97	• Multiplying Three-Digit Numbers, Part 2	Lessons 97, 98, 99, 100, 101, 102, 104, 105, 106, 107, 108, 109	Test 21	Lessons 98, 99, 100, 101, 106, 108, Inv. 10
98	• Estimating by Weight or Mass	Lessons 98, 99, 100, 105, 109	Test and Practice Generator	Lessons 99, 106, 108
99	• Effects of Estimation	Lessons 99, 105, 108	Test 20	Lessons 106, 108
100	• Multiplying Dollars and Cents	Lessons 100, 101, 102, 103, 104, 105, 106, 107, 108, 109, 110	Test 21	
Inv. 10	• Evaluating Estimates	Investigation 10	Test and Practice Generator	Lessons 106, 108

Section Overview 10   494F

LESSON 91

Planning & Preparation

• Multiplying Three-Digit Numbers, Part 1

Objectives
- Multiply three-digit numbers ending in zero by one-digit numbers.
- Discuss different strategies to estimate the number of pennies in a jar.
- Multiply a three-digit number by a one-digit number to estimate the number of pennies in a jar.
- Write and solve multiplication number sentences to solve problems.

Prerequisite Skills
- Learn the multiplication algorithm for multiplying two-digit numbers by one-digit numbers.
- Learn the multiplication facts through 12s.

Materials
Instructional Masters
- Power Up 91
- Lesson Activity 31

Manipulative Kit
- Ruler
- 1-inch cubes*

Teacher-provided materials
- 2 identical jars
- Pennies
- Small tissue box or supply box*

optional

Texas Essential Knowledge and Skills

(3.2)(C) use symbols to describe fractional parts of whole objects
(3.6)(A) identify geometric patterns to make predictions and solve problems
(3.6)(C) identify patterns in related multiplication and division sentences (fact families)
(3.14)(A) identify the mathematics in everyday situations
(3.15)(A) explain/record observations using numbers

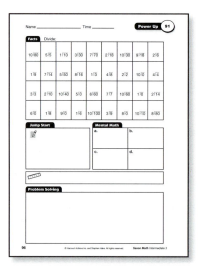

Power Up 91

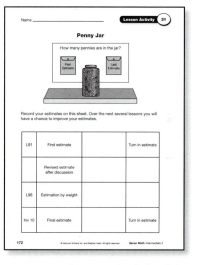

Lesson Activity 31

Differentiated Instruction

Reaching All Special Needs Students

Special Education Students	At-Risk Students	English Learners	Advanced Learners
• Inclusion (TM) • Adaptations for Saxon Math	• Reteaching Masters	• English Learners (TM) • English Learner Handbook	• Extend the Problem (TM) • Online Activities

TM = Teacher's Manual

Math Language

Maintained
estimate

English Learners
full

494G Saxon Math Intermediate 3

Problem Solving Discussion

Problem

Dina arranged dominoes into a repeating pattern. Below we show the first ten dominoes in the pattern.

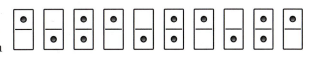

Draw the next two dominoes in the pattern.

Focus Strategies

Find/Extend a Pattern

Draw a Picture or Diagram

Understand   Understand the problem.

"What information are we given?"

We are shown the first ten dominoes in a repeating pattern.

"What are we asked to do?"

We are asked to draw the next two dominoes in the pattern.

Plan   Make a plan.

"What problem solving strategy will we use?"

We will *find the pattern* created by the dominoes and then *extend the pattern*.

Solve   Carry out the plan.

"Let's label the dominoes 1 through 10."

Teacher Note: Draw the dominoes on the board and label them 1–10.

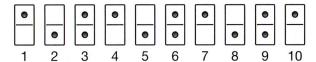

"What pattern do you see?"

The first domino has a dot in the upper half, the second domino has a dot in the lower half, and the third domino has a dot in each half. The pattern repeats starting at dominoes 4, 7, and 10.

"What are the next two dominoes in the pattern after the tenth domino?"

Dominoes 11 and 12 will match dominoes 2 and 3:

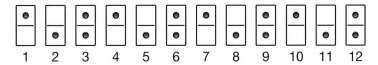

Check   Look back.

"Are our answers reasonable?"

Yes, the dominoes form a repeating pattern that starts over after every third domino. Dominoes 10–12 match dominoes 1–3.

"What problem solving strategy did we use, and how did it help us?"

We *found and extended a pattern*. We *drew a diagram* of the dominoes, which allowed us to label the dominoes and more easily see the repetitions.

Lesson 91   494H

LESSON 91

Facts
Distribute **Power Up 91** to students. See answers below.

Jump Start
Before students begin the Mental Math exercise, do these exercises as a class.

Mental Math
Encourage students to share different ways to mentally compute these exercises. Strategies for exercises are listed below.

a. Think 66 − 20 + 1
  66 − 19 = 66 − 20 + 1 = 46 + 1 = 47

b. Think 24 + 40 − 2
  24 + 38 = 24 + 40 − 2 = 64 − 2 = 62

Problem Solving
Refer to **Problem-Solving Strategy Discussion**, p. 494H.

LESSON 91

• Multiplying Three-Digit Numbers, Part 1

Texas Essential Knowledge and Skills
(3.2)(C) use symbols to describe fractional parts of whole objects
(3.6)(A) identify geometric patterns to make predictions and solve problems
(3.6)(C) identify patterns in related multiplication and division sentences (fact families)
(3.14)(A) identify the mathematics in everyday situations
(3.15)(A) explain/record observations using numbers

facts	Power Up 91
jump start	Count up by 11s from 0 to 121. Count up by 5s from 6 to 56. Write a multiplication and division fact family using the numbers 2, 4, and 8. $2 \times 4 = 8; 4 \times 2 = 8; 8 \div 4 = 2; 8 \div 2 = 4$ Draw a $2\frac{1}{2}$-inch segment on your worksheet. Then make it $2\frac{1}{2}$ inches longer. What is the total length of the segment? 5 in.
mental math	a. **Number Sense:** 66 − 19 47 b. **Number Sense:** 24 + 38 62 c. **Calendar:** How many days are in 7 weeks? 49 days d. **Estimation:** Round the value of these bills to the nearest ten dollars: $40.00

problem solving Dina arranged dominoes into a repeating pattern. Below we show the first ten dominoes in the pattern.

Draw the next two dominoes in the pattern.

Facts	Divide:							
$\frac{8}{10\overline{)80}}$	$\frac{1}{5\overline{)5}}$	$\frac{10}{1\overline{)10}}$	$\frac{10}{3\overline{)30}}$	$\frac{10}{7\overline{)70}}$	$\frac{9}{2\overline{)18}}$	$\frac{3}{10\overline{)30}}$	$\frac{2}{9\overline{)18}}$	$\frac{3}{2\overline{)6}}$
$\frac{9}{1\overline{)9}}$	$\frac{2}{7\overline{)14}}$	$\frac{10}{5\overline{)50}}$	$\frac{2}{8\overline{)16}}$	$\frac{3}{1\overline{)3}}$	$\frac{2}{4\overline{)8}}$	$\frac{1}{2\overline{)2}}$	$\frac{0}{10\overline{)0}}$	$\frac{1}{4\overline{)4}}$
$\frac{1}{3\overline{)3}}$	$\frac{5}{2\overline{)10}}$	$\frac{4}{10\overline{)40}}$	$\frac{0}{5\overline{)0}}$	$\frac{10}{6\overline{)60}}$	$\frac{1}{7\overline{)7}}$	$\frac{6}{10\overline{)60}}$	$\frac{0}{1\overline{)0}}$	$\frac{7}{2\overline{)14}}$
$\frac{0}{6\overline{)0}}$	$\frac{8}{1\overline{)8}}$	$\frac{0}{9\overline{)0}}$	$\frac{6}{1\overline{)6}}$	$\frac{10}{10\overline{)100}}$	$\frac{3}{3\overline{)9}}$	$\frac{0}{8\overline{)0}}$	$\frac{1}{10\overline{)10}}$	$\frac{10}{8\overline{)80}}$

New Concept

Gwen and Theo are guessing the number of pennies in a jar. They cannot empty the jar and count the pennies, so they think of other ways to estimate the number of pennies.

Sometimes we want to find the answer to a "how many" question when we cannot count. We can use math sense to estimate how many instead. In the next few lessons, we will practice different methods of estimating.

Gwen and Theo found an empty jar like the penny jar. They put 200 pennies in the jar. The jar was only partly filled.

Gwen and Theo estimated that they would need 8 times as many pennies to fill the jar completely. They multiplied 8 times 200 to estimate how many pennies would fill the jar.

$$\begin{array}{r} 200 \\ \times8 \\ \hline 1{,}600 \end{array}$$

Analyze What fraction shows about what part of the second penny jar was filled? $\frac{1}{8}$

Example 1

Find the product of 6 and 300.

Starting in the ones place, we multiply 0 ones by 6. The product is 0. Next, we multiply 0 tens by 6. The product is 0. Finally, we multiply 3 hundreds by 6. The product is 18 hundreds.

$$\begin{array}{r} 300 \\ \times6 \\ \hline 1{,}800 \end{array}$$

Lesson 91   495

Math Background

In this lesson, students apply the standard multiplication algorithm to three-digit by one-digit multiplication. It is important for students to practice the sequence of steps so they will be prepared to solve more difficult problems in the future. Some of the problems presented in this lesson end with two zeros and can be solved using mental math. The "appending of zeros" strategy will prove very helpful as a shortcut when figuring conversions among metric units of measurement. For example, to convert 13 kilometers to centimeters, multiply 100,000 by 13. We can do this quickly by appending five zeros after the 13 to obtain 1,300,000.

New Concept

Connection
Explain to students that multiplying a three-digit number works the same way as multiplying a two-digit number. Demonstrate by writing and solving the following problems on the board or overhead:

$$\begin{array}{r} 3 \\ 36 \\ \times5 \\ \hline 180 \end{array} \qquad \begin{array}{r} 1 \\ 620 \\ \times8 \\ \hline 4{,}960 \end{array}$$

"Where do we start when we multiply three-digit numbers?" ones place

Alternate Method
When students multiply a three-digit number that ends in one or two zeros by a one-digit number, they only need to multiply the first digit(s) and then attach the number of zeros at the end. For example, 400 × 5 can be thought of as 4 × 5 with two zeros attached to the product.

$$\begin{array}{r} 400 \\ \times5 \\ \hline 2{,}000 \end{array}$$

We can also think 4 × 5 = 20 plus two zeros attached to equal 2,000.

Math-to-Math Connection
For the *Analyze* question, help students see that this estimation problem can be modeled as an equal groups problem. Gwen and Theo estimate that they need 8 equal groups of 200 pennies each to fill the jar. The 8 equal groups also represent the total number of parts in the whole, of which Gwen and Theo have only 1 part. One part out of eight can be written as the fraction $\frac{1}{8}$.

Extend the Problem
"What is the fraction that would tell about what part of the second penny jar was *not* filled?" $\frac{7}{8}$

Example 1
Alternate Method
Multiply 6 and 3 to get 18, and attach the two zeros at the end to equal 1,800.

(continued)

Lesson 91   495

New Concept (Continued)

Example 2
Alternate Method

Students can solve this problem another way. From counting quarters students may know that 7 times 25 is 175. By attaching a zero to this product, students can find that 7 × $250 is $1,750.

Activity

Distribute a copy of Lesson Activity 31 to each student.

The number of pennies placed in the second jar should be a multiple of 100. Depending on the size of the jar, you might fill it to approximately $\frac{1}{4}$ or $\frac{1}{3}$ full.

Discussion

Some students may have a good sense of how to estimate the number of pennies in the jar. Ask for volunteers to describe how they arrived at their estimate. Encourage students to make further estimates if the comments of their peers spark ideas.

Real-World Connection

"Is it always important to have an exact count?" Student answers will vary.

Have students discuss situations where they would not be able to get an accurate count of the total. Some possible examples are the number of people at an outdoor concert or rally, the number of stars in the night sky, the number of whales in the oceans, and the number of pieces of gravel in a driveway.

Activity Problem 1

Add the pennies to the jar in groups of 10 and have students count by 10s as you fill the jar.

Activity Problem 2
Active Learning

Have a volunteer use his/her ruler to measure the height of the pennies in both jars. Write the two measurements on the board and have students count by the small measure until they get close to the big measure. The number of times they count represents the denominator of the fraction of the jar filled with pennies. Make sure students understand that this is still an estimate and not an exact answer.

(continued)

496 Saxon Math Intermediate 3

Example 2

Multiply: 7 × $250.

This multiplication is similar to multiplying a two-digit number. First, we multiply 0 ones by 7. The product is 0.

$250
× 7
0

Next, we multiply 5 tens by 7. The product is 35 tens, which is $350. We record the 5 tens in the tens place and write the 3 hundreds above the 2.

3
$250
× 7
50

Finally, we multiply 2 hundreds by 7. The product is 14 hundreds. We add the 3 hundreds, so the total is 17 hundreds.

3
$250
× 7
$1750

The final product is **$1,750**.

Estimation by Volume

Materials: **Lesson Activity 31**, jar filled with pennies, empty jar, extra pennies

Your teacher has filled a jar with pennies to help your class practice estimating. Guess the number of pennies in the jar and write your guess on **Lesson Activity 31**. You might want to talk about why you guessed your number.

Then watch and count as pennies are put into an empty jar like the penny jar.

1. How many pennies were put into the empty jar? See student work.
2. About what fraction of the jar is filled with pennies? See student work.
3. How many sets of pennies of this size would be needed to fill the jar? See student work.
4. What numbers would you multiply to estimate the number of pennies in the full jar? See student work.
5. If you would like to make a new estimate of the number of pennies in the full jar based on your work in this activity, record the new estimate on **Lesson Activity 31**. See student work.

496 Saxon Math Intermediate 3

English Learners

Full means having as much or as many inside as possible. Ask:

"Your parents' car has a 20-gallon gas tank. If it is only half full, about how many gallons would there be in the tank?" 10 gallons

Ask:

"An after-school art class can have 30 students. There are now 25 students in the class. How many more students can be added before the class is full?" 5 students

Have students name examples of things that might be full. samples: glass full of milk, box full of toys, jar full of marbles

Lesson Practice Find each product.

a. 7 × 400   2,800
b. 8 × $300 $2,400
c. 6 × 340   2,040
▸ d. 4 × $750 $3,000

Written Practice *Distributed and Integrated*

1. (90) Bertram divided 30 model cars into five equal groups. How many model cars were in each group?   6 model cars

2. (50, 83) Roderick has a bag of 18 marbles. Half of the marbles are red and half are blue. Is drawing a red marble more likely, equally likely, or less likely than drawing a blue marble?   equally likely

3. (Inv. 8) What geometric solid has one curved surface and one flat surface shaped like a circle?   cone

4. (82) Karen and Marie are sharing a bag of grapes. There are 18 grapes in the bag. If they share equally, how many grapes will there be for each of the girls?   9 grapes

5. (2, 59) Find the next three numbers in this doubling sequence: 4, 8, 16
$\frac{1}{2}$, 1, 2, ___, ___, ___, …

6. (81) Multiply 76 by 2 using pencil and paper.   152

▸ 7. (11, 84) **Multiple Choice** This picture shows the answer to which multiplication problem shown below?   B

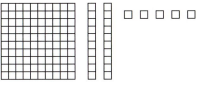

A 25 × 10   B 25 × 5   C 21 × 5   D 20 × 6

8. (87) A gallon of milk equals how many pints of milk?   8 pints

Lesson 91   497

Inclusion

Estimating Cubes

Some students will have difficulty visualizing the relationship between a partially filled jar and a full jar. This activity will give them an opportunity to solve an easier estimation problem.

Materials: twenty 1-inch counting cubes and a rectangular prism such as a small tissue box or supply box

- Give each pair of students one box and a set of counting cubes. Ask students to fill the bottom of the rectangular container with counting cubes.

- Students count the number of cubes they used to fill the bottom of the box.

- Students stack one column of cubes to determine how many layers will fill the box.

"How many layers will fill the box?" See student work.

"What fraction of the box is filled with the first layer?" See student work.

- Students add or multiply to estimate the number of blocks that will fill the box.

New Concept (Continued)

Lesson Practice
Guided Practice

Use these problems as guided practice to check the students' understanding of today's concept.

Problem d
Alternate Method

Students may think of sets of three quarters to solve this problem. Four sets of 3 quarters is 12 quarters. Twelve quarters have a value of 300 cents. Then we write the product with a dollar sign.

 Closure The questions below help assess the concepts taught in this lesson.

"What are some reasons we might estimate?" to solve problems more easily; to find an approximate answer if we do not need or cannot find an exact answer

"Explain how to find this product:
340
× 6"

Start in the ones place and multiply 0 ones by 6. The product is 0. Next, multiply 4 tens by 6 to get 24 tens. Write 4 in the tens place and write 2 above the 3. Multiply 3 hundreds by 6. The product is 18 hundreds. Add the 2 hundreds so the total is 20. The product is 2,040.

Discuss real-world situations where estimation and multiplication of a three-digit number might be helpful. Examples are given below.

- We want to guess how many people are in a crowded cafeteria.
- We want to know how much it would cost to buy four plane tickets that cost $320 each.

Written Practice

Math Conversations
Independent Practice and Discussions to Increase Understanding

Problem 7   Multiple Choice
Test-Taking Strategy

The picture shows 125 cubes.

Answer choices **A** and **D** do not result in a product that ends in 5, so they can be eliminated. The remaining answer choices need to be checked to see if either results in a product of 125.

(continued)

Lesson 91   497

Written Practice (Continued)

Math Conversations
Independent Practice and Discussions to Increase Understanding

▶ **Problem 9** (Formulate)
"If we have $\frac{1}{4}$, how many parts do we need to make the whole?" 4

Students should recognize this as an equal groups story and write the matching multiplication fact.

Extend the Problem
"We still need $\frac{3}{4}$ of the pennies to fill the jar. How many pennies would $\frac{3}{4}$ be?"
600 pennies

▶ **Problem 12** (Model)
Students should first draw two parallel lines $\frac{3}{4}$ inch long that are $1\frac{1}{4}$ inches apart. Suggest that students cut a strip of paper that is $1\frac{1}{4}$ inches long to act as a spacer. They can finish the rectangle by connecting the corresponding vertices.

▶ **Problem 16**
Tell students to think of doubling 132 as doubling $1.32: double $1, double 3 dimes, and double 2 pennies.

▶ **Problem 20a** (Model)
Students should first draw two parallel lines 3 inches long that are 4 inches apart. Suggest that students cut a strip of paper that is 4 inches long to act as a spacer. They can finish the rectangle by connecting the corresponding vertices.

Extend the Problem
"Draw two lines of symmetry for your rectangle."

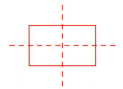

Errors and Misconceptions

▶ **Problem 3**
Students may think that the flat surface of a cone is curved because it is shaped like a circle. Show students a cone and point out the difference between the curved lateral surface and the flat base.

▶ **9.** (Formulate) A jar contains 200 pennies and is one fourth full. Write a multiplication number sentence to estimate about how many pennies would fill the jar. $200 \times 4 = 800$ pennies

10. Find m: $100 = 20 + 30 + 40 + m$ $m = 10$

11. Find each product:
a. 60×3 180
b. 40×9 360

▶ **12.** (Model) Draw a rectangle that is $1\frac{1}{4}$ inches long and $\frac{3}{4}$ inch wide. Then draw its two lines of symmetry.   See student work; sample:

13. Find each quotient:
a. $18 \div 3$ 6
b. $18 \div 2$ 9
c. $16 \div 8$ 2

14. $6.75 - 5.68$ $1.07
15. $1 - 47¢$ 53¢

▶ **16.** 132×2 264
17. 6×100 600

18. 5×32 160
19. 600×5 3,000

▶ **20. a.** (Model) Use a pencil and ruler to draw a rectangle 4 inches long and 3 inches wide.   See student work.
b. What is the perimeter of the rectangle?   14 inches
c. What is the area of the rectangle?   12 sq. in.

Looking Forward

Understanding estimation and multiplying three-digit numbers prepares students for

- **Lessons 92 and 94,** using compatible numbers to estimate.
- **Lesson 93,** estimating products.
- **Lesson 95,** using estimation to verify answers.
- **Lesson 97,** multiplying three-digit numbers.
- **Lesson 98,** estimating by weight or mass.
- **Lesson 99,** examining effects of estimation.
- **Investigation 10,** evaluating estimations.

LESSON 92

Planning & Preparation

- **Parentheses**
- **Using Compatible Numbers, Part 1**

Objectives
- Simplify expressions with more than one operation by calculating inside parentheses first.
- Use compatible numbers to estimate or quickly calculate the solutions to addition and subtraction problems.

Prerequisite Skills
- Add three or more addends.
- Multiply three or more factors.
- Round numbers to estimate solutions to addition or subtraction problems.

Materials

Instructional Masters
- Power Up 92

Manipulative Kit
- Money manipulatives (bills and coins)*

Teacher-provided materials
- Students' money manipulatives (bills and coins)*
- Number cards with numbers 0–20*

  *optional

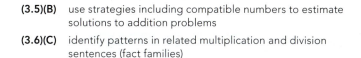

Texas Essential Knowledge and Skills

(3.5)(B) use strategies including compatible numbers to estimate solutions to addition problems

(3.6)(C) identify patterns in related multiplication and division sentences (fact families)

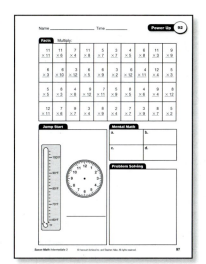

Power Up 92

Reaching All Special Needs Students

Special Education Students	At-Risk Students	English Learners	Advanced Learners
• Inclusion (TM) • Adaptations for Saxon Math	• Error Alert (TM) • Reteaching Masters	• English Learners (TM) • English Learner Handbook	• Extend the Example (TM) • Extend the Problem (TM) • Online Activities

TM=Teacher's Manual

Math Language

New
compatible numbers
parentheses

English Learners
recognize

Lesson 92   499A

LESSON 92

Problem Solving Discussion

Problem

The bookstore is advertising a special sale with this sign. The regular price for one book is $9. How much would it cost to buy 6 books while they are on sale?

Sale!
Buy 2 books, get 1 free!

Focus Strategies

💡 **Use Logical Reasoning**

2+3=5 **Write a Number Sentence**

Understand Understand the problem.

"What information are we given?"

1. Books are on sale. If you buy 2 books, you get one for free.
2. The regular price for one book is $9.

"What are we asked to do?"

We are asked to find how much it would cost to buy 6 books while they are on sale.

Plan Make a plan.

"How can we use the information we know to solve the problem?"

We *use logical reasoning* to help us *write a number sentence* to find the cost of 6 books.

Solve Carry out the plan.

"If a person gets 3 books on sale, the cost is equal to how many regular-price books?"

On sale, 3 books cost the same as 2 regular-price books.

"If a person gets 6 books on sale, the cost is equal to how many regular-price books?"

Six books is 3 books plus 3 more books. Since the cost of 3 books is equal to the cost of 2 regular-price books, 6 books have a cost of 2 + 2 = 4 regular-price books.

"What is the cost of 4 regular-price books?"

Each regular-price book is $9, so 4 regular price books have a cost of 4 × $9 = $36.

Check Look back.

"Did we complete the task?"

Yes, we found the cost of 6 books during the sale of "buy 2 books, get 1 free" ($36).

"Is our answer reasonable?"

Yes, we know that our answer is reasonable, because if we can "buy 2 books and get 1 free," we can "buy 4 books and get 2 free," which is a total of 6 books.

"What problem solving strategies did we use, and how did they help us?"

We *used logical reasoning* to apply the sale to 6 books instead of just 3 books. We *wrote a number sentence* to find the cost in dollars.

LESSON 92

- **Parentheses**
- **Using Compatible Numbers, Part 1**

Texas Essential Knowledge and Skills
(3.5)(B) use strategies including compatible numbers to estimate solutions to addition and subtraction problems
(3.6)(C) identify patterns in related multiplication and division sentences (fact families)

Power Up

facts — Power Up 92

jump start
- Count up by odd numbers from 1 to 25.
- Count up by even numbers from 2 to 30.
- It is 6:35 in the morning. Draw hands on your clock to show the time in 2 hours. Write the time in digital form. **8:35 a.m.**
- The temperature of the water at the beach was 76°F. The beach sand was 16 degrees warmer. Mark your thermometer to show the temperature of the beach sand. **92°F**

mental math

a. **Fact Family:** Find the missing number in this fact family: **4**

$3 \times \square = 12$ $12 \div \square = 3$
$\square \times 3 = 12$ $12 \div 3 = \square$

b. **Number Sense:** 46 + 22   **68**

c. **Number Sense:** 15 × 100   **1,500**

d. **Time:** It is 10:28 p.m. How many minutes is it until 11:00 p.m.?   **32 min**

problem solving

The bookstore is advertising a special sale with this sign. The regular price for one book is $9. How much would it cost to buy 6 books while they are on sale?   **$36**

> **Sale!**
> Buy 2 books, get 1 free!

Lesson 92   499

LESSON 92

Power Up

Facts
Distribute **Power Up 92** to students. See answers below.

Jump Start
Before students begin the Mental Math exercise, do these exercises as a class.

Mental Math
Encourage students to share different ways to mentally compute these exercises. Strategies for exercises are listed below.

c. **Multiply 15 × 1 and Attach Two Zeros**
Multiply 15 × 1 = 15.
Then add two zeros.
15 × 100 = 1500

d. **Picture the Face of a Clock**
10:28 is 2 minutes from 10:30. 10:30 is 30 minutes from 11:00.
30 minutes + 2 minutes = 32 minutes

Problem Solving
Refer to **Problem-Solving Strategy Discussion,** p. 499B.

Facts   Multiply:

11 × 11 = 121	11 × 6 = 66	7 × 4 = 28	11 × 8 = 88	5 × 7 = 35	3 × 7 = 21	4 × 5 = 20	6 × 8 = 48	11 × 3 = 33	9 × 9 = 81
6 × 3 = 18	6 × 10 = 60	3 × 12 = 36	6 × 5 = 30	6 × 9 = 54	3 × 2 = 6	6 × 12 = 72	4 × 11 = 44	12 × 4 = 48	5 × 3 = 15
5 × 5 = 25	8 × 3 = 24	4 × 8 = 32	9 × 12 = 108	7 × 11 = 77	5 × 9 = 45	8 × 5 = 40	4 × 6 = 24	9 × 4 = 36	8 × 12 = 96
12 × 11 = 132	7 × 6 = 42	9 × 7 = 63	3 × 4 = 12	8 × 9 = 72	2 × 4 = 8	7 × 7 = 49	3 × 9 = 27	8 × 7 = 56	5 × 2 = 10

New Concepts

Instruction

Students may not be familiar with parentheses or how to make them. Have students practice writing and using parentheses in a variety of expressions. Begin by writing the following problem on the board.

$$8 - 4 + 1$$

Instruct students to write this problem two different ways using parentheses. Students should use parentheses to mark which operation they do first.

$$(8 - 4) + 1 \quad 8 - (4 + 1)$$

Write "$(8 - 4) + 1$" on the board.

"Which operation should I do first?"
$8 - 4 = 4$

"Then what do I do?" $4 + 1 = 5$

Write "$8 - (4 + 1)$" on the board.

"Which operation should I do first?"
$4 + 1 = 5$

"Then what do I do?" $8 - 5 = 3$

Example 1
Error Alert

Problems with parentheses should be written horizontally. Some students may be accustomed to writing math problems vertically. If they are struggling to solve the problem horizontally, have them write and solve each individual operation vertically and then transcribe the answer horizontally.

Example 2
Discussion

"When we add or multiply, it does not matter in what order we perform the operations. But when we divide or subtract, the order does matter."

Write the following problems on the board and solve them as a class:

$10 + (5 + 3) = 18$ $8 \times (4 \times 2) = 64$
$(10 + 5) + 3 = 18$ $(8 \times 4) \times 2 = 64$

$(10 - 5) - 3 = 2$ $(8 \div 4) \div 2 = 1$
$10 - (5 - 3) = 8$ $8 \div (4 \div 2) = 4$

$10 + (5 - 3) = 12$ $8 \times (4 \div 2) = 16$
$(10 + 5) - 3 = 12$ $(8 \times 4) \div 2 = 16$

$10 - (5 + 3) = 2$ $8 \div (4 \times 2) = 1$
$(10 - 5) + 3 = 8$ $(8 \div 4) \times 2 = 4$

Use the problems to help students see when the order of operations changes the answer.

(continued)

New Concepts

Parentheses

Addition, subtraction, multiplication, and division are called **operations**. To solve some problems, we do more than one operation. In the expression below, we see there are two operations. The **parentheses** show us which operation to do first.

$$12 - (6 + 2)$$

Since $6 + 2$ is in parentheses, we first add $6 + 2$, which equals 8. Then we subtract 8 from 12.

$$12 - 8 = 4$$

Example 1

Simplify: $12 - (6 - 2)$

We do the operation inside the parentheses first: $6 - 2$ equals 4. Then we subtract 4 from 12.

$$12 - (6 - 2)$$
$$12 - 4 = \mathbf{8}$$

Example 2

Which is greater, $(12 \div 6) \div 2$ or $12 \div (6 \div 2)$?

We work inside parentheses first.

$(12 \div 6) \div 2$ $12 \div (6 \div 2)$
$\quad 2 \div 2$ $12 \div 3$
$\quad\quad 1$ 4

We see that $\mathbf{12 \div (6 \div 2)}$ **is greater.**

Using Compatible Numbers, Part 1

When adding three numbers, it does not matter which two numbers we add first; the sum is the same.

$12 + (6 + 2)$ $(12 + 6) + 2$
$\quad 12 + 8$ $18 + 2$
$\quad\quad 20$ 20

Math Background

In this lesson, students learn to perform calculations enclosed in parentheses first in multi-operation expressions. They have already had some experiences with the commutative and associative properties of addition and multiplication. They know that addition and multiplication can be done in any order but that subtraction and division cannot be done in any order. This is their first encounter with notation that dictates that operations must be performed in something other than left-to-right order. This lesson lays the foundation for the "order of operations" convention that students will learn in future math courses. According to that convention, you solve calculations within parenthesis first, and then exponents, then multiplication and division from left to right, and then addition and subtraction from left to right.

A strategy to help add three or more numbers quickly is to look for **compatible numbers.** Compatible numbers are numbers that, together, are easy to work with. For example, numbers whose sums are round numbers are compatible numbers.

$$50 + 40 + 160$$

If we add from left to right, we first add 40 and 50 to get 90. Then we must add 90 and 160.

However, we might notice that 40 + 160 = 200. If we add those numbers first, then our next addition is easy to perform mentally: 200 + 50 = 250. We can use parentheses to show which addition we will perform first:

$$50 + (40 + 160)$$

Numbers that end in 25, 50, or 75 are also easy to work with because we can imagine counting with quarters.

Example 3

> **The supply closet has 75 crayons, 80 pens, and 25 pencils. How many writing tools are there altogether?**
>
> We recognize this as a "some and some more" story with three addends. We know that 75 and 25 total 100, so we choose to mentally add those addends first. Then we mentally add 100 + 80 to get 180. There are **180 writing tools** altogether.

We can also use compatible numbers to estimate solutions to subtraction problems.

Example 4

> **Jasmine had $8.79. She spent $4.24 at lunch. About how much money does Jasmine have left?**
>
> To find the exact amount Jasmine has left, we would subtract $8.79 − $4.24. The amounts $8.79 and $4.24 are both very close to amounts we say when counting by quarters. We can rewrite the subtraction using compatible numbers this way: $8.75 − $4.25. We can perform this calculation quickly. **Jasmine has about $4.50 left.**

Lesson Practice

a. 12 − (6 ÷ 2)   9
b. (12 − 6) ÷ 2   3
c. 12 ÷ (6 − 2)   3
d. (12 ÷ 6) − 2   0

New Concepts (Continued)

Explanation

"When things are compatible, it means they fit well together. When numbers are compatible, they 'fit together' by adding up to a round number."

Remind students that a round number is one that ends in zero, such as 10, 60, 120, or 300.

Write the following numbers on the board or overhead: 2, 9, 6, 1, 4, 18.

"Which numbers are compatible and why?" 9 and 1, 6 and 4, and 18 and 2; They add up to round numbers.

Example 3
Extend the Example

"How could you write this problem with parentheses to make the compatible numbers easier to see?"

(75 + 25) + 80 or 80 + (75 + 25)

(continued)

 **English Learners**

To **recognize** is to see or understand. Ask:

"We recognize words in story problems that give us clues about how to solve the problem. Tell me a story problem using 'how many are left?'" Answers will vary.

Ask:

"If you had your eyes closed, what are some ways you could recognize another person?" samples: voice, footsteps, touching their hair or the features on their face

Have students cover their eyes and try to recognize an unknown classmate who is speaking.

New Concepts (Continued)

Lesson Practice

Guided Practice

Use these problems as guided practice to check the students' understanding of today's concept.

Problem e
Extend the Problem
"What does this comparison tell us about the order of the numbers in subtraction?" Changing the order of the numbers in subtraction changes the answer.

Problem g Error Alert
The second pair of compatible numbers may be missed by students. Advise them to look for sums of 10 when faced with a long addition problem such as this one. Using parentheses or lightly crossing off the pairs that equal 10 may help students keep track of the addition.

Closure The questions below help assess the concepts taught in this lesson.

"When we see parentheses in a number sentence, what should we do?" Do the part of the problem inside the parentheses first and then do the rest of the problem.

"What are compatible numbers?" Numbers that, together, are easy to work with.

Discuss real-world situations where using parentheses and finding compatible numbers might be helpful. Examples are given below.

- We have a list of 20 numbers that we need to add up quickly.
- We have to find the cost of four items at $2.25 each and add a final item which costs $3.15.

Written Practice

Math Conversations
Independent Practice and Discussions to Increase Understanding

Problem 2 (Model)
Extend the Problem
"How can we write $\frac{1}{2}$ using 4 as the bottom number of the fraction?" $\frac{2}{4}$

(continued)

---

e. Compare: $(12 - 6) - 2$ ⊙ $12 - (6 - 2)$

For **f** and **g**, first write the pairs of compatible numbers. Then find the total.

f. $30 + 90 + 110$
   90 and 110; 230

g. $2 + 7 + 3 + 9 + 1$
   7 and 3; 9 and 1; 22

h. Paolo spilled the puzzle pieces on the playground. The puzzle had 800 pieces but Paolo could only find 627. About how many puzzle pieces were lost? Write a subtraction number sentence using compatible numbers to find your answer. $800 - 625 = d$; sample: Paolo lost about 175 puzzle pieces.

Written Practice — Distributed and Integrated

1. (18, 22) The television cost $295. Sales tax was $20.65. What is the total price including tax? $315.65

2. (43) (**Model**) Use your fraction manipulatives to fit three $\frac{1}{4}$-pieces together to make $\frac{3}{4}$. Which is greater, $\frac{3}{4}$ or $\frac{1}{2}$? See student work; $\frac{3}{4}$

3. (82) The zookeeper wants to split a bag of peanuts between the zoo's two elephants. There are 24 pounds of peanuts in the bag. If the elephants share equally, how many pounds of peanuts will there be for each of them? 12 pounds

4. (71) Draw a regular prism. A rectangular prism has how many
   a. faces? 6
   b. edges? 12
   c. vertices? 8

5. (32) Write 895,283 in expanded form. $800,000 + 90,000 + 5,000 + 200 + 80 + 3$

6. (1, 91) Multiply to find the number of days in two common years. Use pencil and paper to show your work. 730 days; See student work.

7. (92) Rewrite this addition problem using compatible numbers, then add to estimate the sum: $824 + 747$. $825 + 750 = 1,575$

 **Inclusion**

Making 20

Some students will have difficulty recognizing compatible numbers. This activity will help them learn to pair numbers with sums that end in 0.

Materials: set of number cards with the numbers 0–20

- Give each student a set of number cards. Have students lay the cards out in random order. Instruct students to choose sets of two cards whose sum equals 20.
- Students should write each addition fact represented by their cards on a sheet of paper.
- If this activity proves too difficult, use number cards with digits 0–10 and find sums of 10.

8. Patricia built this shape with 1-inch cubes.
   (72)
   a. How many cubes are in each layer?   10 cubes

   b. How many layers are there?   4 layers

   c. How many cubes were used to make this shape?
      40 cubes
   d. What is the volume of the cube?   40 cubic inches

▶ 9. Estimate the sum of $395 and $598. $1,000
   (30)

10. 4 × 60   240
    (78)

11. 75 × 7   525
    (85)

▶ 12. **Analyze** Michael paid $5 for a model that cost $4.39 with tax.
    (20, 25) What coins should Michael get back in change?   2 quarters, 1 dime, 1 penny

▶ 13. **Formulate** Write a multiplication fact that shows how many
    (63) small squares cover this rectangle.   8 × 6 = 48 or 6 × 8 = 48

14. Find the next two numbers in this sequence: 6, 3
    (2, 83)

    48, 24, 12, ____, ____, …

15. Find each quotient:
    (89)
    a. 30 ÷ 6   5   b. 35 ÷ 5   7   c. 32 ÷ 4   8

16. $100 − ($62 + $9) $29
    (92)

17. $5.50 − $3.43 $2.07
    (26)

18. (7 × 80) + 40   600
    (77, 92)

19. 5 × 12   60
    (59)

20. The distance across a penny is about how many
    (79) centimeters?   2 cm

Lesson 92   503

Looking Forward

Using parentheses to specify order of operations and finding compatible numbers to assist in summing addends prepares students for

- **Lesson 93,** estimating products.
- **Lesson 94,** using compatible numbers to estimate.
- **Lesson 95,** using estimation to verify answers.
- **Lesson 97,** multiplying three-digit numbers.
- **Lesson 98,** estimating by weight or mass.
- **Lesson 99,** examining the effects of estimation.
- **Investigation 10,** evaluating estimations.

Written Practice (Continued)

Math Conversations
Independent Practice and Discussions to Increase Understanding

● **Problem 9**
Manipulative Use
Have students use money manipulatives to find the exact answer and see if their estimate is reasonable.

● **Problem 12** **Analyze**
Suggest students use money manipulatives to subtract first. Then decide which coins to use to make 61¢.

Alternate Method
Students can count up by different coins from $4.39 to $5.00. They would add one penny to get $4.40, one dime to get $4.50, and 2 quarters to get $5.

Extend the Problem
"How can we estimate the change?"
sample: $4.39 is close to $4.40. Sixty more cents would make $5.00, so the amount of change is close to 60¢.

● **Problem 13** **Formulate**
The number of small squares is equal to the area of the rectangle. Students should count the squares in one row and one column to write a multiplication fact.

Extend the Problem
"What is the perimeter of this rectangle?"
28 units

Errors and Misconceptions

● **Problem 16**
In addition to forgetting to complete the math inside the parentheses first, students may not line up the dollar amounts correctly. Remind students that work inside parentheses should be done first. Suggest that students write each part of the problem vertically.

Lesson 92   503

LESSON 93

Planning & Preparation

• Estimating Products

Objectives
- Round numbers to the nearest ten or hundred to estimate the solutions to multiplication problems.
- Record and solve multiplication number sentences to solve problems.
- Translate story problems about equal groups into multiplication number sentences.

Prerequisite Skills
- Multiply three-digit numbers ending in zero by one-digit numbers.
- Record and solve multiplication number sentences to solve problems.
- Learn the multiplication facts through 12s.
- Use "product" and "factor" to describe numbers in multiplication number sentences and on the multiplication table.

Materials

Instructional Masters
- Power Up 93

Manipulative Kit
- Geosolids

Teacher-provided materials
- Number cards 0–9 plus two extra zero cards*

  *optional

Texas Essential Knowledge and Skills

(3.4)(B) solve/record multiplication problems (up to two digits times one digit)

(3.5)(A) round whole numbers to the nearest ten or hundred in problem situations

(3.6)(C) identify patterns in related multiplication and division sentences (fact families)

(3.16)(B) explain the solution process

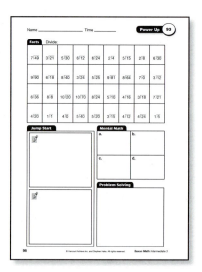

Power Up 93

Reaching All Special Needs Students

Special Education Students	At-Risk Students	English Learners	Advanced Learners
• Inclusion (TM) • Adaptations for Saxon Math	• Error Alert (TM) • Reteaching Masters	• English Learners (TM) • English Learner Handbook	• Extend the Example (TM) • Extend the Problem (TM) • Online Activities

TM = Teacher's Manual

Math Language

Maintained	English Learners
round	professional

504A *Saxon Math* Intermediate 3

Problem Solving Discussion

Problem

The Pitzer family ordered an extra large pizza for dinner. The pizza was cut into 16 slices.

Mr. and Mrs. Pitzer ate 4 slices altogether. The oldest child, Clint, ate 3 slices. The other two children, Elisha and Jason, each ate 2 slices.

How many slices were left over? Did the family eat more than half of the pizza? Explain your answer.

Focus Strategies

 Write a Number Sentence

 Use Logical Reasoning

Understand Understand the problem.

"What information are we given?"

1. The pizza was cut into 16 slices.
2. Mr. and Mrs. Pitzer ate 4 slices altogether.
3. Clint ate 3 slices.
4. Elisha and Jason each ate 2 slices.

"What are we asked to do?"

1. Find how many slices were left over.
2. Find whether the family ate more than half the pizza.
3. Explain our answer.

Plan Make a plan.

"What problem solving strategies can we use?"

We can *write number sentences* to find the total number of slices eaten and left over. We can *use logical reasoning* to find whether the number of slices eaten is more than half of the 16 slices.

Solve Carry out the plan.

"What number sentence can we write to find the total number of slices eaten?"

4 slices + 3 slices + 2 slices + 2 slices = 11 slices

"How many slices of pizza were left over?"

We write a subtraction number sentence, since this is a "some went away" story. We subtract the number of slices eaten from the number of slices in the pizza:

16 slices − 11 slices = 5 slices left over

"Did the family eat more than half of the pizza? Explain your answer."

Yes, half of 16 is 8. The family ate 11 slices, which is more than 8 slices.

Check Look back.

"Are our answers reasonable?"

Yes. The family ate 4 + 3 + 2 + 2 = 11 slices. Eight slices is half the pizza, so the family ate more than half of the pizza. There were 16 − 11 = 5 slices left over.

"What problem solving strategies did we use, and how did they help us?"

We *wrote a number sentence* to find how many slices were eaten and how many slices were left over. We *used logical reasoning* to find whether the number of slices eaten was more than half of the 16 slices.

Alternate Strategy
Draw a Picture or Diagram

Students can draw a diagram of a pizza with 16 slices and then mark off (or shade) the slices eaten by the parents and the children. The diagram will show 5 slices left over, and it will show that the family ate more than half the pizza.

LESSON 93

Power Up

Facts
Distribute **Power Up 93** to students. See answers below.

Jump Start
Before students begin the Mental Math exercise, do these exercises as a class.

Mental Math
Encourage students to share different ways to mentally compute these exercises. Strategies for exercises are listed below.

a. **Add Tens Then Ones**
   7 tens + 5 tens = 12 tens = 120, then add 8 ones; 120 + 8 = 128
   $78 + $50 = $128

b. **Think 6 × 3 and Attach a Zero**
   6 × 3 = 18
   60 × 3 = 180

Problem Solving
Refer to **Problem-Solving Strategy Discussion**, p. 504B.

LESSON 93 • Estimating Products

Texas Essential Knowledge and Skills
(3.4)(B) solve/record multiplication problems (up to two digits times one digit)
(3.5)(A) round whole numbers to the nearest ten or hundred in problem situations
(3.6)(C) identify patterns in related multiplication and division sentences (fact families)
(3.16)(B) explain the solution process

Power Up

facts   Power Up 93

jump start
 Count up by 7s from 0 to 84.
Count up by 10s from 8 to 98.

 Write a multiplication and division fact family using the numbers 2, 7, and 14.   2 × 7 = 14; 7 × 2 = 14; 14 ÷ 7 = 7; 14 ÷ 7 = 2

 Madison had a $10 bill. She bought a stamp set for $8.80. What is the fewest bills and coins she could receive for change? $1 bill and 2 dimes

mental math
a. **Money:** $78 + $50 $128
b. **Number Sense:** 6 × 30   180
c. **Number Sense:** 2 × 3 × 4   24
d. **Measurement:** Mohini's desk at home is 3 feet long and 2 feet wide. What is the area of her desk?   6 sq. ft

problem solving
The Pitzer family ordered an extra large pizza for dinner. The pizza was cut into 16 slices.

Mr. and Mrs. Pitzer ate 4 slices altogether. The oldest child, Clint, ate 3 slices. The other two children, Elisha and Jason, each ate 2 slices.

How many slices were left over? Did the family eat more than half of the pizza? Explain your answer.   5 slices; sample: Yes, the family ate more than half because they ate 4 + 3 + 2 + 2 = 11 slices. Half of 16 slices is 8 slices.

504   *Saxon Math* Intermediate 3

Facts   Divide:

7 7)49	7 3)21	6 5)30	2 6)12	4 6)24	2 2)4	5 5)15	4 2)8	5 6)30
10 9)90	3 6)18	5 8)40	8 3)24	5 5)25	9 9)81	8 8)64	0 7)0	4 3)12
6 6)36	1 8)8	2 10)20	7 10)70	3 8)24	2 5)10	4 4)16	6 3)18	3 7)21
5 4)20	1 1)1	0 4)0	8 5)40	4 5)20	5 3)15	3 4)12	6 4)24	5 1)5

New Concept

In Lesson 30 we estimated sums and differences. In this lesson we will estimate products.

Manny and two of his friends went to the amusement park. Each ticket cost $18. About how much did the three tickets cost altogether?

By rounding numbers before we multiply, we can estimate the answer to a multiplication problem. We round $18 to $20 and multiply to find the estimate: $20 × 3 = $60. The three tickets cost about $60 altogether.

Example 1

Tickets to the professional basketball game were $38 each. Mr. Jones wanted to buy 4 tickets. Estimate the total price of the 4 tickets.

To estimate the total price we will round $38 to $40 before we multiply.

$$4 \times \$40 = \$160$$

The total price of the tickets is about **$160**.

(Formulate) Write an estimating products story problem for the multiplication 4 × $40 = $160. *See student work.*

Example 2

Jamal counted 195 words on one page. About how many words would Jamal read on 5 pages?

We can round 195 to 200. If we assume that each page has about the same number of words, then each page has about 200 words. To estimate the number of words on 5 pages, we multiply 200 by 5.

$$5 \times 200 = \mathbf{1{,}000}$$

Jamal would read **about 1,000 words** on 5 pages.

Lesson Practice

a. Estimate the total price of 4 water-park tickets at $19 each. *$80*

b. If tickets to the football game are $32 each, about how much would 5 tickets cost? *about $150*

Lesson 93   505

Math Background

In Lesson 30, students learned to estimate sums and differences. In this lesson, students use their knowledge of place value and rounding to estimate products. The basic procedure is the same, only applied in a multiplication situation. Students will be able to solve multiplication problems mentally and evaluate the reasonableness of exact calculations.

English Learners

In athletics, a **professional** player earns money playing their sport. Ask:

"Which ticket would cost more: a high school football game or a professional football game?" professional

Ask:

"What kinds of professional sports are there?" samples: football, basketball, hockey, baseball, soccer, volleyball

Have students discuss their favorite professional sports team.

New Concept

Instruction

To emphasize the mechanics of estimating products, state the process as a series of two simple steps.

Step 1: Round the large number.
Step 2: Multiply.

Stress that students only need to round numbers which are two or more digits. One-digit numbers should be multiplied from memory.

Active Learning

Students going to an amusement park would need to take along enough money to pay for everything they would need, such as tickets, food, rides, and games. Have students brainstorm a list of things they would need to pay for at the amusement park and approximate costs.

Choose one item, round the number, and calculate the cost for Manny and his two friends.

Example 1
Extend the Example

Have students find both the exact price and the difference between the estimate and the exact price. *exact price: $152; difference: $8*

"Which was easier to calculate, the estimated price or the exact price?"
the estimated price

Lesson Practice
Guided Practice

Use these problems as guided practice to check the students' understanding of today's concept.

Problems a–b
Extend the Problem

Have students find the actual prices of the tickets in problems **a** and **b,** and then find the difference between the estimated prices and the exact prices.

Help students see that rounding a number up results in an estimate that is more than the exact value. Rounding down results in an estimate that is less than the exact value.

(continued)

Lesson 93   505

New Concept (Continued)

Closure The questions below help assess the concepts taught in this lesson.

"When we round a three-digit number, is it easier to multiply if we round it to the nearest ten or the nearest hundred?" It is easier to multiply if we round to the nearest hundred. We want every digit other than the first digit to be a zero.

"Will an estimated product be the same as the actual product?" No; an estimated product will be greater than the actual product if we round up and will be less if we round down.

"Why would we want to estimate?" sample: to get a general idea of the product, to get a quick answer which is close to the product, to check if the exact answer we got for the problem is reasonable.

Discuss real-world situations where using rounding and multiplication to estimate might be helpful. Examples are given below.

- A restaurant serves about 280 guests a night each week.
- We want to buy four pairs of sneakers that are $38 each.

Written Practice

Math Conversations
Independent Practice and Discussions to Increase Understanding

Problem 4 Multiple Choice
Test-taking Strategy
Students should eliminate answer choice **A** where a single unit would be too much for the height of a 10-year old. Then students can determine whether **B** or **C** is more reasonable.

Problem 7
Encourage students to use the large "G" discussed in Lesson 87 to understand how the units relate to one another.

Problem 8
Use parentheses to identify the compatible addends before solving.
$$(48 + 52) + 39$$

(continued)

506 Saxon Math Intermediate 3

---

c. Every day Alida walks around the track 4 times. She counted 489 steps for one lap. About how many steps does she take walking 4 laps? about 2,000 steps

Written Practice   Distributed and Integrated

1. (60) Leticia sleeps nine hours each night. How many hours does she sleep in one week?   63 hours

2. (26, 36) Bruce put stamps totaling 75¢ on the package. However, it cost $1.12 to mail the package. How much postage did Bruce need to add to the package?   37¢

3. (32) Luis flew a total of 2,200 miles from Los Angeles to Seattle and back to Los Angeles. Use words to write the number of miles that Luis flew.   two thousand, two hundred miles

▶ 4. (79) **Multiple Choice** Which of these measurements is a reasonable height for a ten-year-old person?   C
   A 140 km   B 140 m   C 140 cm

5. (32) Write 3,000 + 700 + 40 in standard form.   3,740

6. (35, 52) Measure the length and width of this rectangle to the nearest quarter of an inch.   length: $1\frac{1}{2}$ in.; width: $\frac{3}{4}$ in.

▶ 7. (87) List these units in order of size from smallest to largest: cup, pint, quart, gallon
   quart   gallon   pint   cup

▶ 8. (92) The total weight of two boxes is 147 pounds. The first box weighs 52 pounds. Use compatible numbers to estimate the weight of the second box.   about 100 pounds

9. (92) (21 − 10) + 33   44

10. (84) Multiply:
    a. 4 × 16   64
    b. 6 × 24   144

506 Saxon Math Intermediate 3

Inclusion

Estimation and Rounding
Some students will have difficulty rounding 3-digit numbers. This activity pairs tactile and visual learning to teach and reinforce rounding.

Materials: set of number cards with 0–9 plus two extra zero cards

- Give students a set of number cards. Write numbers on the board that do not have repetitive digits, such as 264, 709, and 58. Have students model the numbers using their number cards.

- Instruct students to point to the second digit of the number.

"Is this digit 5 or larger?"

If so, have the student replace the first digit with the next-higher number card. Have them replace all the other digits with the zero cards.

- Have students repeat the process using different sets of numbers: 123, 456, and 789; 147, 256, and 369; 159, 267, and 348.

11. Estimate the product of 4 and 683. 2,800
(93)

12. If 40 strawberries are placed equally in 5 bowls, how many strawberries will be in each bowl? 8 strawberries
(90)

▶ **13.** (**Model**) Fit two $\frac{1}{8}$-pieces together. What larger fraction piece do they match? $\frac{1}{4}$
(47)

14. Find each quotient:
(86)
    a. 40 ÷ 8   5   **b.** 42 ÷ 7   6   **c.** 45 ÷ 5   9

15. 412 × 2   824   **16.** $12.25 − $9.89 $2.36
(91)   (26)

17. 80 + (70 × 6)   500   **18.** (9 − 4) × 4   20
(92)   (92)

19. Use this map to answer the questions that follow:
(31, Inv. 4)

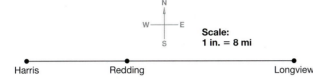

    a. Which town is east of Redding?   Longview

    b. How many miles is Longview from Harris?   32 mi

▶ **20.** (**Classify**) What is the geometric name for this figure? How many faces does it have?   triangular prism; 5 faces
(75)

Lesson 93   507

Looking Forward

Using rounded numbers to estimate the product in a multiplication problem prepares students for

- **Lesson 94**, using compatible numbers to estimate.
- **Lesson 95**, using estimation to verify answers.
- **Lesson 97**, multiplying three-digit numbers.
- **Lesson 98**, estimating by weight or mass.
- **Lesson 99**, examining the effects of estimation.
- **Investigation 10**, evaluating estimations.

Written Practice (Continued)

Math Conversations
Independent Practice and Discussions to Increase Understanding

▶ **Problem 13** (**Model**)
Extend the Problem

Ask advanced learners,

   "What fraction is made by fitting four $\frac{1}{8}$-pieces together?" $\frac{4}{8}$

   "What are two other names for this fraction?" $\frac{2}{4}$ and $\frac{1}{2}$

▶ **Problem 20** (**Classify**)

Show students the Geosolids from the manipulative kit and have them choose the one that matches the picture. Students may then examine the solid to help them answer the questions.

Extend the Problem

Have students name the other Geosolids in the manipulative kit.

Errors and Misconceptions

▶ **Problem 12**

It would be easy for students to misinterpret this problem and multiply the numbers to get 200. Remind students that the total is 40, so each bowl would have fewer than 40 strawberries in it.

Lesson 93   507

LESSON 94

Texas Essential Knowledge and Skills
(3.2)(C) use symbols to describe fractional parts of whole objects
(3.5)(A) round whole numbers to the nearest ten in problem situations
(3.5)(B) use strategies including compatible numbers to estimate solutions to addition problems

Planning & Preparation

• **Using Compatible Numbers, Part 2**

Objectives
- Practice using compatible numbers to estimate or quickly calculate the solutions to addition and subtraction problems.
- Use compatible numbers to estimate the solutions to multiplication problems.
- Estimate the solutions to addition, subtraction, and multiplication problems to solve real-world problems.

Prerequisite Skills
- Round numbers to estimate solutions to addition or subtraction problems.
- Use compatible numbers to estimate or quickly calculate the solutions to addition and subtraction problems.
- Round numbers to the nearest ten or hundred to estimate the solutions to multiplication problems.

Materials
Instructional Masters
- Power Up 94

Manipulative Kit
- Money manipulatives*

Teacher-provided materials
- Student money manipulatives*

*optional

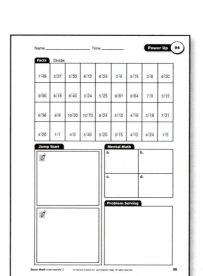

Power Up 94

Reaching All Special Needs Students

Special Education Students	At-Risk Students	English Learners	Advanced Learners
• Inclusion (TM) • Adaptations for Saxon Math	• Alternative Approach (TM) • Error Alert (TM) • Reteaching Masters	• English Learners (TM) • English Learner Handbook	• Extend the Problem (TM) • Online Activities

TM = Teacher's Manual

Math Language
Maintained
compatible numbers

English Learners
mentally

508A   Saxon Math Intermediate 3

Problem Solving Discussion

Problem

Ms. Braden's third grade class is planning a picnic. The class will bring blankets to sit on at the picnic. Each blanket has enough space for 3 people to sit. There are 19 students in the class. How many blankets are needed so that all 19 students and Ms. Braden can have a place to sit?

Focus Strategy  **Draw a Picture or Diagram**

Understand Understand the problem.

"What information are we given?"

1. Each blanket can seat 3 people.
2. There are 19 students and 1 teacher.

"What are we asked to do?"

We are asked to find how many blankets are needed so that everyone can sit.

Plan Make a plan.

"What problem solving strategy can we use?"

We can *draw a diagram* to help us find the number of blankets needed for the picnic.

Solve Carry out the plan.

"How can we draw a diagram to represent the problem?"

We want to keep our diagram as simple as possible. We can use ovals for blankets and draw dots inside the ovals to represent the students and teacher.

"Altogether, how many dots will we place in the diagram?"

There are 19 students and 1 teacher, so we will draw 19 + 1 = 20 dots.

"What will our diagram look like?"

We draw ovals and place dots within the ovals until we reach 20 dots:

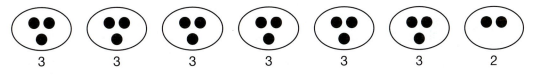

3 + 3 + 3 + 3 + 3 + 3 + 2 = 20 people

"How many blankets are needed for all 20 people?"

We count the ovals and find that 7 blankets are needed for the picnic.

Check Look back.

"Did we complete the task?"

Yes, we found that Ms. Braden's class needs 7 blankets if 3 people sit on each blanket and there are 20 people altogether.

"Is our answer reasonable?"

Yes, we see from our diagram that 6 blankets can seat 6 × 3 people = 18 people. There are 2 people left over, so another blanket (for a total of 7) is needed.

"What problem solving strategy did we use, and how did it help us?"

We *drew a diagram* to represent the blankets and people. We counted the ovals in the diagram to find how many blankets are needed.

Alternate Strategy

Guess and Check; Write a Number Sentence

Students might recognize that 3 students on each blanket is an "equal groups" problem. We can guess a number of blankets and then check whether there is enough space for all 20 people. Six blankets can seat a total of 6 × 3 people = 18 people. A seventh blanket is needed for the remaining 2 people.

Lesson 94   508B

LESSON 94

Power Up

Facts
Distribute **Power Up 94** to students. See answers below.

Jump Start
Before students begin the Mental Math exercise, do these exercises as a class.

Mental Math
Encourage students to share different ways to mentally compute these exercises. Strategies for exercises are listed below.

b. **Subtract Only the Hundreds Digits**
From the hundreds place, 5 − 3 = 2, so 591 − 300 = 291.

c. **Add Tens, Then Add Ones**
6 tens + 4 tens = 10 tens = 100
5 ones + 5 ones = 10 ones
100 + 10 = 110

Problem Solving
Refer to **Problem-Solving Strategy Discussion**, p. 508B.

New Concept

Instruction
Explain to students that we can estimate using compatible numbers which are close to the actual numbers but easier to work with when performing calculations.

Write the following examples of compatible numbers on the board or overhead:

27 → 25   48 → 50
71 → 75   103 → 100
245 → 250   522 → 525

Explain that the closer the compatible or rounded number is to the actual number, the closer the estimate will be to the true value.

Have students practice converting problems into compatible expressions. Write the problems below on the board or overhead, and then ask students to write a compatible expression and solve for the estimate.

79 + 55 → 75 + 50 = 125
146 − 73 → 150 − 75 = 75
4 × 53 → 4 × 50 = 200
412 ÷ 28 → 400 ÷ 25 = 16

(continued)

LESSON 94

• **Using Compatible Numbers, Part 2**

Texas Essential Knowledge and Skills
(3.2)(C) use symbols to describe fractional parts of whole objects
(3.5)(A) round whole numbers to the nearest ten in problem situations
(3.5)(B) use strategies including compatible numbers to estimate solutions to addition problems

Power Up

facts Power Up 94

jump start
Count up by 6s from 0 to 66.
Count up by 12s from 0 to 132.

Draw a rectangle and divide it into 8 parts. Then shade 6 parts. What fraction of the rectangle is shaded?
See student work; $\frac{6}{8}$ or $\frac{3}{4}$

Write "six hundred thirty four dollars and seventy two cents" using digits and a dollar sign. $634.72

mental math
a. **Estimation:** Round 525 to the nearest ten. 530
b. **Number Sense:** 591 − 300   291
c. **Number Sense:** 65 + 45   110
d. **Time:** It is afternoon. What will be the time 5 hours after the time shown on the clock? 8:48 p.m.

problem solving
Ms. Braden's third grade class is planning a picnic. The class will bring blankets to sit on at the picnic. Each blanket has enough space for 3 people to sit. There are 19 students in the class. How many blankets are needed so that all 19 students and Ms. Braden can have a place to sit? 7 blankets

New Concept

In Lesson 92 we learned to use compatible numbers in addition and subtraction problems. We also used compatible numbers to help estimate answers to arithmetic problems. Remember that instead of rounding addends or factors, we can choose nearby numbers that are easy to work with.

508   *Saxon Math* Intermediate 3

Facts Divide:

7)49	3)21	5)30	6)12	6)24	2)4	5)15	2)8	6)30
7	7	6	2	4	2	3	4	5
9)90	6)18	8)40	3)24	5)25	9)81	8)64	7)0	3)12
10	3	5	8	5	9	8	0	4
6)36	8)8	10)20	10)70	8)24	5)10	4)16	3)18	7)21
6	1	2	7	3	2	4	6	3
4)20	1)1	4)0	5)40	5)20	3)15	4)12	4)24	1)5
5	1	0	8	4	5	3	6	5

Problem		Easier Problem
76 + 73	→	75 + 75
26 × 4	→	25 × 4

We can mentally double 75 instead of adding 76 and 73. We can mentally multiply 25 × 4 by thinking of counting quarters instead of multiplying 26 × 4 with pencil and paper.

Example 1

Use compatible numbers to estimate each sum or difference.

a. $10.78 + $2.24

b. 294 + 74 + 322

c. $10.00 − $5.72

a. We can rewrite the addition as $10.75 + $2.25. The sum is **about $13.00.**

b. We can rewrite the addition as 300 + 75 + 325:

```
  300
   75
+ 325
  700
```

c. The second amount is close to $5.75:
$10.00 − $5.75 = **$4.25.**

Example 2

Use compatible numbers to estimate the cost of 4 board games at $24 each.

The cost ($24) is close to $25. Multiplying $25 by 4 is easy because it is similar to counting quarters. Since 25 × 4 is 100, we estimate that the cost of the four games is about **$100.**

Use Compatible Number $25	Actual Problem
$25 × 4 $100	$24 × 4 $96

 Analyze What is the difference between the estimate and the actual product? Explain the difference. $4; sample: $25 is 1 more than $24, and 4 × $1 = $4.

Lesson 94   509

Math Background

Accuracy and precision are important elements in mathematical computations. The use of compatible numbers increases the accuracy of an estimate because the compatible number is often closer than a rounded number to the original number. For example, 26 rounded to the nearest ten is 30. The nearest compatible number to 26 is 25. Twenty-five is easy for third graders to work with in computations because of their familiarity with money. It is also closer to 26 than 30, so any resulting estimates will be more accurate.

English Learners

To perform a task **mentally** means to do it in your mind without writing it down. Ask:

"How can we add 25 + 75 mentally?"
Think quarters: 1 quarter + 3 quarters = 4 quarters = 100.

Ask:

"How might you multiply 20 × 4 mentally?" Multiply 2 × 4 = 8 and add a zero: 20 × 4 = 80.

Have students practice mentally answering math facts.

New Concept (Continued)

Example 2
Instruction

Students can usually multiply by 25 mentally if they count by quarters. Counting by quarters is made easier if students group them into sets of four because four quarters equal $1.

(continued)

New Concept (Continued)

Lesson Practice

Guided Practice

Use these problems as guided practice to check the students' understanding of today's concept.

Problem a
Have students think, "25 × 4 = 100, so 250 × 4 = 1,000."

Problem b
Extend the Problem
"Alida was feeling adventurous one day and walked her dog for 5 miles. About how many minutes did this take her?"
5 × 25 = 125 minutes

Closure The questions below help assess the concepts taught in this lesson.

"Why don't we always round numbers to the nearest 10 or 100 when we estimate?" sample: Sometimes it is easier to round a number to the nearest multiple of 25, and doing this gives a better estimate. Since we know that a quarter is 25¢, it is like working with quarters.

"Would you round 77 to the nearest 10 or the nearest 25 and why?" sample: You could round it either way, but the estimate would be more accurate if you round to 75.

Discuss real-world situations where using rounding to compatible numbers might be helpful. Examples are given below.

- A school has about 26 students in each of the nine third grade classes.
- A family of four wants to travel on a bus trip and tickets cost $122 each.

Written Practice

Math Conversations
Independent Practice and Discussions to Increase Understanding

▶ **Problem 8** **Formulate**
Students should see that using the compatible number $25 will give a more accurate estimate than rounding to $20 because it is closer to $23. Students can think of 4 quarters plus one quarter to mentally solve for the product.

(continued)

510   *Saxon Math* Intermediate 3

Lesson Practice
Use compatible numbers to estimate in problems **a** and **b**.

▶ **a.** Estimate the product of 249 × 4.   250 × 4 = 1000

▶ **b.** When Alida walks her dog, she travels one mile in 24 minutes. About how long would it take Alida to walk 2 miles?   2 × 25 = 50; about 50 minutes

c. Use compatible numbers to estimate the difference between $678 and $354. $325

Written Practice — *Distributed and Integrated*

1. Phil bought an aquarium for $62.97. Sales tax was $4.41. What was the total price with tax? $67.38
(18, 22)

2. Brad is thinking of a number between 1 and 10. He gives this hint: "If I multiply the number by itself, the product is 49." What is Brad's number?   7
(61)

3. Estimate the product of 82 and 4.   320
(93)

4. There are 5,280 feet in a mile. Find the number of feet in two miles.   10,560 ft
(32)

5. What words go in the blanks?   quarters; quarts
(29, 87)
"Four ____ equal a dollar, and four ____ equal a gallon."

6. Janet placed 60 books on 5 shelves equally. How many books are on each shelf?   12 books
(90)

7. Is 254 closer to 200 or 300?   300
(15)

▶ **8.** **Formulate** Rosa bought tickets to a concert. She paid $23 for each ticket. Use compatible numbers to estimate how much Rosa spent if she bought 5 tickets. Write a number sentence for the problem. $25 × 5 = $125
(94)

9. Multiply:
(84)
   a. 4 × $25 $100   **b.** 8 × 34   272

510   *Saxon Math* Intermediate 3

Alternative Approach: Using Manipulatives

Write the following problem on the board or overhead:

27 × 9   25 × 9 = 225

Instruct students to use their money manipulatives to estimate the product. When students are finished, ask for volunteers to describe how they got the estimate. Several mental strategies can be used. Students can model it as $2 worth of quarters plus one quarter or as (10 × 25) − 25. If needed, use money manipulatives with the problems in the lesson. For additional practice, have students solve the following problems:

53 × 6   50 × 6 = 300
22 × 7   25 × 7 = 175
74 × 4   75 × 4 = 300

Inclusion

Rounding to the Nearest 25

Some students will have difficulty remembering the multiples of 25. Have them make a visual reminder and keep it handy to help with problems involving compatible numbers.

Materials: pencil and paper

- List the multiples of 25 on the board for students to copy and use as a reference.
- Have students find the multiples of 25 closest to 21, 69, 121, and 98.
- Let students use their list of multiples of 25 to help them with Lesson Practice and Written Practice.

▶ **10.** (Explain) How are a sphere and a cylinder different?
(75, Inv. 8) sample: A cylinder has two flat faces and a curved face. A sphere only has one curved face.

11. Name the place value of the 5 in each of these
(32) numbers:
   a. 45,321   thousands   **b.** 235   ones

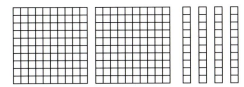

▶ **12.** Find each product:
(78)
   a. 30 × 4   120   **b.** 6 × 90   540

13. **Multiple Choice** This picture shows the answer to which
(78) multiplication?   A

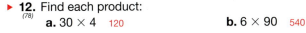

   A 6 × 40   **B** 20 × 7   **C** 2 × 12   **D** 2 × 40

14. Find each quotient:
(86)
   a. 48 ÷ 8   6   **b.** 49 ÷ 7   7   **c.** 42 ÷ 6   7

▶ **15.** 7 × 2 × 5   70   **16.** 50 × 9   450
(77)   (78)

17. 3 × 7 × 9   189   **18.** 100 − (3 × 30)   10
(77, 84)   (78, 92)

19. Find *a*: 36 + *a* + 17 + 42 = 99   4
(9, 24)

▶ **20.** (Model) Draw a rectangle 5 cm long and 4 cm wide. What is the
(52, 63) area of the rectangle?   See student work; 20 square cm

Lesson 94   511

Using compatible numbers to estimate answers in arithmetic problems prepares students for

- **Lesson 95,** using estimation to verify answers.
- **Lesson 97,** multiplying three-digit numbers.
- **Lesson 98,** estimating by weight or mass.
- **Lesson 99,** examining the effects of estimation.
- **Investigation 10,** evaluating estimations.

Written Practice (Continued)

Math Conversations
Independent Practice and Discussions to Increase Understanding

▶ **Problem 10** (Explain)
Tell students to think of the difference between the shape of a basketball and a can of soup.

Extend the Problem
"How is a cone different from a cylinder?"
A cone has a flat end like a cylinder, but the other end comes to a point like a pyramid.

"How is a sphere different from a circle?"
A circle is flat, but a sphere has three dimensions like a basketball.

▶ **Problem 13   Multiple Choice**
Test-Taking Strategy
The picture shows more than 200 cubes. Students can examine the answers and eliminate any that do not obviously result in a product that large. Only answer choice **A** is left. Students should find the product and match it to the picture to check their choice.

▶ **Problem 15**
Suggest that students look for compatible numbers to multiply first: 5 × 2 = 10 and 7 × 10 = 70.

▶ **Problem 20**
Extend the Problem
"What is the perimeter of this rectangle?" 18 cm

"What are two other names for this shape?" a quadrilateral, a polygon, or a parallelogram

Errors and Misconceptions

▶ **Problem 6**
Students may fail to notice that this problem needs to use division and will mistakenly give 300 as an answer. Remind students that if they see the word *equally*, it is a clue to use division.

Lesson 94   511

LESSON 95

Planning & Preparation

Texas Essential Knowledge and Skills

(3.5)(A) round whole numbers to the nearest ten or hundred in problem situations

(3.16)(B) justify why an answer is reasonable and explain the solution process

- **Using Estimation to Verify Answers**

Objectives
- Use estimation to verify that answers to addition and multiplication problems are reasonable.
- Analyze incorrect estimates to find the error made when estimating.

Prerequisite Skills
- Round numbers to estimate solutions to addition, subtraction, or multiplication problems.
- Use compatible numbers to estimate or quickly calculate the solutions to addition, subtraction, or multiplication problems.

Materials
Instructional Masters
- Power Up 95

Manipulative Kit
- Money manipulatives*
- Ruler

Teacher-provided materials
- Student money manipulatives*

    *optional

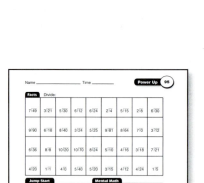

Power Up 95

Differentiated Instruction

Reaching All Special Needs Students

Special Education Students	At-Risk Students	English Learners	Advanced Learners
• Inclusion (TM) • Adaptations for Saxon Math	• Alternative Approach (TM) • Error Alert (TM) • Reteaching Masters	• English Learners (TM) • English Learner Handbook	• Extend the Example (TM) • Extend the Problem (TM) • Online Activities

TM = Teacher's Manual

Math Language

Maintained
estimate

English Learners
reasonable

512A   Saxon Math Intermediate 3

Problem Solving Discussion

Problem

Talia arranged one dollar in pennies in a square array on the table. Then Talia scooped some of the pennies into her hand. This diagram shows the pennies that remained. Without counting, find the number of pennies on the table. (*Hint:* Imagine the array of pennies that Talia scooped into her hand, and write a subtraction number sentence.)

Focus Strategies

 Draw a Picture or Diagram

 Write a Number Sentence

Understand   Understand the problem.

"What information are we given?"

1. Talia arranged one dollar in pennies in a square array.
2. Talia scooped some of the pennies into her hand.
3. We are shown a diagram of the pennies that remained on the table.

"What are we asked to do?"

We are asked to find how many pennies remain on the table without counting.

Plan   Make a plan.

"What problem solving strategies can we use?"

We will *use the diagram* to find the number of pennies that Talia scooped into her hand. Then we will *write a number sentence* to subtract this number from the total number of pennies she started with.

Solve   Carry out the plan.

"How many pennies did Talia use to make the larger square array?"

We are told that Talia used one dollar in pennies, which is 100 pennies.

"What is the size of the array of pennies that Talia scooped into her hand?"

The "missing array" in the corner of the given diagram has 4 rows and 5 columns.

"How many pennies did Talia scoop into her hand?"

Talia scooped 4 × 5 = 20 pennies altogether.

"How many pennies remained on the table?"

We subtract: 100 pennies − 20 pennies = 80 pennies.

Check   Look back.

"Did we complete the task?"

Yes, we found the number of pennies on the table (80 pennies) by writing a subtraction number sentence.

"Is our answer reasonable?"

Yes, Talia scooped a 4 × 5 array of pennies off the table, which is 20 pennies. There were 100 pennies in the original array, so 100 − 20 = 80 pennies remained.

LESSON 95

Power Up

Facts
Distribute **Power Up 95** to students. See answers below.

Jump Start
Before students begin the Mental Math exercise, do these exercises as a class.

Mental Math
Encourage students to share different ways to mentally compute these exercises. Strategies for exercises are listed below.

a. **Multiply in the Order Listed**
$3 \times 3 \times 5 = 9 \times 5 = 45$

c. **Add Compatible Numbers First**
$40 + 23 + 60 = (40 + 60) + 23$
$= 100 + 23 = 123$

Problem Solving
Refer to **Problem-Solving Strategy Discussion**, p. 512B.

New Concept

Instruction
Explain to students that a reasonable answer is one that makes sense. Tell them that one way we can check to see if our answer makes sense is to estimate and then compare the estimate to the answer to see if it is reasonable.

Have students practice spotting unreasonable answers using estimation. Write the following problems on the board and have students determine if the answer is reasonable or not.

$18 + 25 + 42 = 43$
$20 + 25 + 40 = 85$; sample: No, the answer is not reasonable because the estimate is twice as much. (43 is the sum of 18 and 25.)

$6 \times 45 = 270$
$6 \times 50 = 300$; sample: Yes, the answer is reasonable according to the estimate.

"Will estimation tell us if our answer is correct? Explain." no; sample: Estimation does not tell us the answer, but it will tell us if our answer is reasonable.

(continued)

LESSON 95

- **Using Estimation to Verify Answers**

Texas Essential Knowledge and Skills
(3.5)(A) round whole numbers to the nearest ten or hundred in problem situations
(3.16)(B) justify why an answer is reasonable and explain the solution process

Power Up

facts — Power Up 95

jump start
Count up by 5s from 7 to 57.
Count up by 4s from 0 to 44.
Draw a cube. How many vertices does a cube have? See student work; 8 vertices
Label the number line by fourths from 0 to $2\frac{2}{4}$. (Show these numbers: $0, \frac{1}{4}, \frac{2}{4}, \frac{3}{4}, 1, 1\frac{1}{4}$, and so on.) See student work.

mental math
a. **Number Sense:** $3 \times 3 \times 5$ 45
b. **Number Sense:** $72 + 28$ 100
c. **Number Sense:** $40 + 23 + 60$ 123
d. **Time:** Sharla finished the sack race in 55 seconds. Kevin finished in 70 seconds. How many more seconds did it take Kevin to finish the race than Sharla?   15 sec

problem solving
Talia arranged one dollar in pennies in a square array on the table. Then Talia scooped some of the pennies into her hand. This diagram shows the pennies that remained. Without counting, find the number of pennies on the table. (*Hint:* Imagine the array of pennies that Talia scooped into her hand, and write a subtraction number sentence.)   100 pennies − 20 pennies = 80 pennies

New Concept

We can use estimation to check whether a count, a measure, or a calculation is reasonable. Read the story on the following page and decide if Amber's total is reasonable.

512 *Saxon Math* Intermediate 3

Facts Divide:

7)49 = 7	3)21 = 7	5)30 = 6	6)12 = 2	6)24 = 4	2)4 = 2	5)15 = 3	2)8 = 4	6)30 = 5
9)90 = 10	6)18 = 3	8)40 = 5	3)24 = 8	5)25 = 5	9)81 = 9	8)64 = 8	7)0 = 0	3)12 = 4
6)36 = 6	8)8 = 1	10)20 = 2	10)70 = 7	8)24 = 3	5)10 = 2	4)16 = 4	3)18 = 6	7)21 = 3
4)20 = 5	1)1 = 1	4)0 = 0	5)40 = 8	5)20 = 4	3)15 = 5	4)12 = 3	4)24 = 6	1)5 = 5

512   *Saxon Math* Intermediate 3

Amber wants to buy 3 shirts for $28 each. She decides not to buy the shirts when she multiplies 3 × $28 and gets $624 for the total.

Amber could estimate to check if the total is reasonable. She could round $28 to $30. Then she could multiply 3 × $30 and find that the total price of the three shirts should be about $90. Since $624 is not close to $90, Amber's total is not reasonable.

Evaluate What mistake did Amber make when she multiplied 3 × $28 and got $624 for the total? sample: After she multiplied 3 × 8 = 24, she did not write the 2 at the top of the left column.

Example 1

Francine bought a bat for $32, a mitt for $49, and a pair of batting gloves for $13. She calculated that she would need $94 for all three items. Is her total reasonable?

Francine calculated a total price. We will use estimation to see if her answer is reasonable.

To estimate the total price, we round $32, $49, and $13 before we add.

$$\$30 + \$50 + \$10 = \$90$$

Our estimate is close to $94, so **Francine's total is reasonable.**

Example 2

Cody counted 213 words on one page. After reading 5 pages, Cody estimated that he had read 1050 words. Is Cody's estimate reasonable?

We can round 213 to 200. If we assume that each page has about the same number of words, then each page has about 200 words. To estimate the number of words on 5 pages, we multiply 200 by 5.

$$5 \times 200 = 1000$$

Since 1050 pages is close to 1000 pages, **Cody's estimate is reasonable.**

Lesson Practice

a. Roger bought a new bike seat for $31 and a helmet for $29. He calculated that he would need $90 to pay for both items. Is Roger's total reasonable? Explain your answer. no; sample: $29 and $31 both round to $30, and $30 + $30 = $60.

Lesson 95   513

Math Background

In real life, people examine known information and use logical reasoning to make decisions hundreds of times a day. They might check the weather forecast or look outside to determine if they need to wear a coat or take an umbrella when they leave home. Students can use known information to determine if their solution to a math problem is reasonable. Checking an answer for reasonableness is an essential component of the problem solving process. By rounding the numbers in a problem and using mental math to calculate an estimate, a student can readily see if their original answer is close to the estimated answer.

English Learners

To be **reasonable** means to be logical. Ask:

"Is it reasonable to ask for a 3-hour lunch?" No, there is too much to learn!

Ask:

"What are some reasonable school rules?" See student work.

Students make a list of some reasonable rules and consequences that can be used at home.

New Concept (Continued)

Connection

Write Amber's multiplication, showing her mistake, on the board or overhead.

Use this opportunity to stress the importance of aligning the digits correctly and keeping track of regrouping during multiplication.

Example 1

"Why did we round $13 and $32 to the nearest 10 instead of choosing compatible numbers like $25 or $50?" We want to choose numbers that will give the closest estimate. Since $13 is closer to $10 than $25, and $32 is closer to $30 than $25 or $50, rounding to the nearest 10 gives the closest estimate.

Active Learning: Manipulative Use

Have students find the exact total using money manipulatives.

Example 2
Extend the Example

Ask advanced learners,

"If Cody read 600 words, about what fractional amount of the five pages did he read?" Cody read about $\frac{3}{5}$ of the pages.

Active Learning

As a class choose two similar pages from the math textbook and count the words on half of one page. Use this number to estimate the total number of words on both pages. Assign a group of students to count the words on each page. Total the word counts of both pages on the board and check it against the estimate. Discuss why your estimate was or was not reasonable. Answers will vary.

Lesson Practice

Guided Practice

Use these problems as guided practice to check the students' understanding of today's concept.

Problem a
Extend the Problem

"If the tax on his helmet and bike seat was $3.90, how much was the actual total price?" $63.90

(continued)

Lesson 95   513

New Concept (Continued)

Lesson Practice

Problem b
Extend the Problem
"What is the exact cost of five tickets?" $160

Problem c
Extend the Problem
"If Alida can walk around the track in 4 minutes, how long will it take her to walk around the track five times?"
20 minutes

Closure The questions below help assess the concepts taught in this lesson.

"What are some reasons we might estimate?" to help us to solve problems more easily; to get an approximate answer if we cannot find an exact answer; to see if our answer is reasonable

"Will estimating tell us if our answer is right?" No, but if our answer is not close to the estimated answer, we probably made a mistake and should check our math.

Discuss real-world situations where using estimation to check the reasonableness of an answer might be helpful. Examples are given below.

- We want to order 6 dinners that cost $22 each at a nice restaurant.
- Marcie had $342 to spend on presents for 6 members of her family. She thinks she can spend $80 per person.

---

b. Jackson estimates that 5 tickets to the football game will cost more than $300. If tickets are $32 each, is Jackson's estimate reasonable? If not, about how much would 5 tickets cost? no; about $150

c. Every day Alida walks around the track 5 times. She counted 489 steps for one lap. She estimates that she will walk 2,500 steps in 5 laps. Is her estimate reasonable? Explain your answer. yes; sample: 489 rounds to 500, and 500 × 5 = 2,500.

Written Practice — Distributed and Integrated

1. (93) Estimate the cost of 7 uniforms at $62 each. $420

2. (40) After using 36 of the 100 stamps, how many stamps did Sidney have left? 64 stamps

3. (95) **Justify** Rachael bought 6 small bags of sunflower seeds. She found that there were 193 seeds in one bag. She estimated that there would be 1,800 seeds in all 6 bags. Is Rachael's estimate reasonable? Explain your answer. no; sample: 193 rounds to 200, and 200 × 6 = 1,200. 1,200 is not close to 1,800, so Rachael's estimate is not reasonable.

4. (91) Find each product.
   a. 3 × 400   1,200
   b. 6 × $500 $3,000
   c. 7 × 430   3,010
   d. 5 × $320 $1,600

5. (46, 48) What mixed number is halfway between 1 and 2? $1\frac{1}{2}$

6. (81) A yard is 36 inches. Multiply to find the number of inches in 2 yards. 72 inches

7. (93) A large bag of birdseed weighs about 38 pounds. Estimate the weight of 5 large bags of birdseed. 200 lb

8. (87) 1 quart = ___ cups   4

9. (42) **Model** Draw a circle. Then divide the circle into fourths and shade one fourth of the circle. sample:

514   Saxon Math Intermediate 3

Written Practice

Math Conversations
Independent Practice and Discussions to Increase Understanding

Problem 3 **Justify**
Dividing 1,800 by 6 results in 300, which is much higher than 200, so Rachael's estimate is not reasonable.

Extend the Problem
"If there were exactly 193 seeds in each bag, exactly how many seeds are in 6 bags?" 193 × 6 = 1,158 seeds

(continued)

Alternative Approach: Using Manipulatives

Tell students that people make estimates about things in daily life all the time.

"We estimate how long something will take, how much food we want to eat, and how much the total bill will be at a store."

Have students write down various activities they do during a day and estimate the time it takes to do them. Some ideas would be brushing teeth, getting dressed, eating breakfast, and making a bed. Ask students to estimate how much time it would take to do each of these activities for a week (multiply by 7). Have the students time themselves using a clock or watch as they complete these activities at home and record the times in a table. In class the next day, students should use the actual times to see if they were close in their estimates.

Inclusion

Is It Reasonable?

If some students have difficulty understanding the word "reasonable," connect it to concrete concepts.

Read the statements below. Have students indicate if the statement is reasonable (thumbs up) or not reasonable (thumbs down).

- A small car weighs about 1 ton.
- A new bicycle costs 35¢.
- A family can eat a dozen apples in a week.
- The temperature outside is 94° and it is snowing.
- There are 128 people in our classroom.

10. Estimate the difference when $298 is subtracted from $602. $300
(30)

11. Multiply:
(84)
a. 4 × $35 $140   b. 3 × 21   63   c. 2 × 43   86

12. 5 × 700   3,500   **13.** 3 × 460   1,380
(91)   (91)

14. 375 + 658 + 74   1107   **15.** 370 − (9 × 40)   10
(24)   (78, 92)

▶ **16.** ⟨Justify⟩ Each table in the restaurant can seat 6 people. Lori
(95) counted 31 tables in the restaurant. She estimates that the
restaurant can only seat a total of 100 people. Is her estimate
reasonable? Why or why not?   no; sample: The restaurant can seat about
30 × 6 = 180 people.

17. Find each quotient:
(86)
a. 28 ÷ 4   7   b. 36 ÷ 6   6   c. 48 ÷ 6   8

18. Use your ruler to find the length of this line segment to the nearest
(35) quarter of an inch. $2\frac{1}{4}$ in.   _____

▶ **19.** ⟨Conclude⟩ Counting by $\frac{1}{4}$s on a ruler, the order is
(2, 35)

$$\frac{1}{4}, \frac{1}{2}, \frac{3}{4}, 1, \ldots$$

Find the next four numbers in this sequence:

$\frac{1}{4}, \frac{1}{2}, \frac{3}{4}, 1, 1\frac{1}{4}, 1\frac{1}{2},$ ____, ____, ____, ____, ... $1\frac{3}{4}, 2, 2\frac{1}{4}, 2\frac{1}{2}$

20. This box is neatly filled with 1-centimeter cubes.
(72, 73)

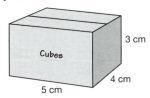

a. How many cubes fit in the bottom layer?   20

b. How many layers of cubes are there?   3

c. How many cubes are used to fill the box?   60

d. What is the volume of the box?   60 cubic cm

Lesson 95   515

Written Practice (Continued)

Math Conversations
Independent Practice and Discussions to Increase Understanding

▶ **Problem 16** ⟨Justify⟩
Encourage students to count by 6s to around 100 to estimate the number of tables that can seat 100 people. Since there are only about 16 groups of 6 in 100, many more people could be seated at 31 tables.

▶ **Problem 19** ⟨Conclude⟩
Tell students to think of the sequence as adding a quarter, or $\$\frac{1}{4}$, each time.

Extend the Problem
Ask advanced learners,

"In this counting pattern, we get a whole number how often?" Every fourth number is a whole number.

"What do you think the 16th term of this sequence would be?" 4

Errors and Misconceptions

▶ **Problem 5**
Some students may only write the fractional part, $\frac{1}{2}$, of the mixed number. Remind students that a mixed number is written with both a whole number like 1 or 2 and a fraction. Suggest that students sketch a number line to help visualize the answer.

▶ **Problem 15**
Remind students that they must do the multiplication inside the parentheses before they do any other math. If students fail to do so, they may get a wrong answer of 14,400.

Looking Forward

Verifying answers to arithmetic problems using estimation prepares students for

- **Lesson 97,** multiplying three-digit numbers.
- **Lesson 98,** estimating by weight.
- **Lesson 99,** examining the effects of estimation.
- **Lesson 100,** multiplying dollars and cents.
- **Investigation 10,** evaluating estimations.

Cumulative Assessments and Test-Day Activity

Assessments

Distribute **Power-Up Test 18** and **Cumulative Test 18** to each student. Have students complete the **Power-Up Test** first. Allow 10 minutes. Then have students work on the **Cumulative Test.**

Test-Day Activity

The remaining class time can be spent on **Test-Day Activity 9.** Students can begin the activity in class and complete it as homework.

LESSON 96

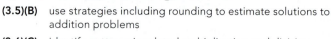

Texas Essential Knowledge and Skills

(3.5)(B) use strategies including rounding to estimate solutions to addition problems

(3.6)(C) identify patterns in related multiplication and division sentences (fact families)

(3.13)(B) interpret information from pictographs

Planning & Preparation

• Rounding to the Nearest Dollar

Objectives
- Round dollar-and-cent money amounts to the nearest whole dollar.
- Use a benchmark to quickly round amounts of money to the nearest whole dollar.
- Round dollar-and-cent money amounts to the nearest whole dollar to solve problems.

Prerequisite Skills
- Round numbers to the nearest ten and hundred.
- Round numbers to estimate solutions to addition, subtraction, and multiplication problems.

Materials

Instructional Masters
- Power Up 96

Manipulative Kit
- Ruler
- Money manipulatives*

Teacher-provided materials
- Students' money manipulatives

optional

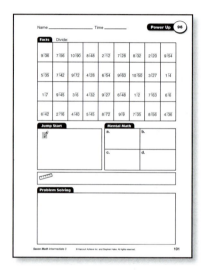

Power Up 96

Reaching All Special Needs Students

Special Education Students	At-Risk Students	English Learners	Advanced Learners
• Adaptations for Saxon Math	• Error Alert (TM) • Reteaching Masters	• English Learners (TM) • English Learner Handbook	• Extend the Example (TM) • Extend the Problem (TM) • Online Activities

TM = Teacher's Manual

Math Language

Maintained
estimate
round

English Learners
nearby

516A *Saxon Math* Intermediate 3

Problem Solving Discussion

Problem

The third grade students at Lincoln School made this pictograph to show the number of books read by each class.

Use the pictograph to find how many more books the students must read to reach a total of 180 books.

Focus Strategies

- Make or Use a Table, Chart, or Graph
- Write a Number Sentence

Understand Understand the problem.

"What information are we given?"

We are shown a pictograph that shows how many books were read by three classes.

"What are we asked to do?"

We are asked to find how many more books the students must read to reach a total of 180 books.

Plan Make a plan.

"How can we use the information we are given to solve the problem?"

We can *use the graph* to find how many books the students have read. Then we will *write a number sentence* to find the difference between that number of books and 180 books.

Solve Carry out the plan.

"How many books does each picture in the graph represent? Each half picture?"

Each small picture of a book stands for 10 books. Half of 10 is 5, so a half picture represents 5 books.

"How many books were read by the students in each room?"

Room 4: 10 + 10 + 10 + 10 + 5 = 45 books

Room 5: 10 + 10 + 10 + 10 + 10 + 10 = 60 books

Room 6: 10 + 10 + 10 + 10 + 10 + 5 = 55 books

"Altogether, how many books did the students read?"

45 books + 60 books + 55 books = 160 books

"How many more books must the students read to reach a total of 180?"

180 books − 160 books = 20 books

Check Look back.

"Did we complete the task?"

Yes, we found that the students must read 20 more books to reach a total of 180.

"Is our answer reasonable?"

Yes, we know that our answer is reasonable because the students have read 160 books. This amount is 20 less than 180 books.

LESSON 96

Power Up

Facts
Distribute **Power Up 96** to students. See answers below.

Jump Start
Before students begin the Mental Math exercise, do these exercises as a class.

Mental Math
Encourage students to share different ways to mentally compute these exercises. Strategies for exercises are listed below.

a. Think $7.80 + $2 − $0.01
   $7.80 + $1.99 = $7.80 + $2.00 − $0.01
   = $9.80 − $0.01 = $9.79

c. Think 8 × 6 and Attach a Zero
   8 × 6 = 48
   8 × 60 = 480

Problem Solving
Refer to **Problem-Solving Strategy Discussion**, p. 516B.

LESSON 96
• Rounding to the Nearest Dollar

Texas Essential Knowledge and Skills
(3.5)(B) use strategies including rounding to estimate solutions to addition problems
(3.6)(C) identify patterns in related multiplication and division sentences (fact families)
(3.13)(B) interpret information from pictographs

Power Up

facts — Power Up 96

jump start
- Count up by odd numbers from 1 to 25.
- Count up by even numbers from 2 to 30.
- Write a multiplication and division fact family using the numbers 3, 6, and 18.   3 × 6 = 18; 6 × 3 = 18; 18 ÷ 3 = 6; 18 ÷ 6 = 3
- Draw a $3\frac{1}{2}$-inch segment on your worksheet. Then make it $1\frac{1}{4}$ inches longer. What is the total length of the segment? $4\frac{3}{4}$ in.

mental math
a. **Money:** $7.80 + $1.99 $9.79
b. **Number Sense:** 39 + 22   61
c. **Number Sense:** 8 × 60   480
d. **Number Line:** Which point shows the number 370?   J

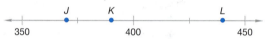
350   400   450
   J   K   L

problem solving
The third grade students at Lincoln School made this pictograph to show the number of books read by each class.

Use the pictograph to find how many more books the students must read to reach a total of 180 books.
20 more books

Number of Books Read	
Room 4	▢▢▢▢▢
Room 5	▢▢▢▢▢▢
Room 6	▢▢▢▢▢▢

Key ▢ = 10 books

516   *Saxon Math* Intermediate 3

Facts — Divide:

4 ÷ 9)36	8 ÷ 7)56	9 ÷ 10)90	6 ÷ 8)48	6 ÷ 2)12	4 ÷ 7)28	4 ÷ 8)32	10 ÷ 2)20	6 ÷ 9)54
7 ÷ 5)35	6 ÷ 7)42	8 ÷ 9)72	7 ÷ 4)28	9 ÷ 6)54	7 ÷ 9)63	5 ÷ 10)50	9 ÷ 3)27	4 ÷ 1)4
7 ÷ 1)7	5 ÷ 9)45	2 ÷ 3)6	8 ÷ 4)32	3 ÷ 9)27	8 ÷ 6)48	2 ÷ 1)2	9 ÷ 7)63	1 ÷ 6)6
7 ÷ 6)42	8 ÷ 2)16	10 ÷ 4)40	9 ÷ 5)45	9 ÷ 8)72	1 ÷ 9)9	5 ÷ 7)35	7 ÷ 8)56	9 ÷ 4)36

516   *Saxon Math* Intermediate 3

New Concept

We can estimate with money by rounding dollars and cents to the nearest dollar.

What is the price of these two items rounded to the nearest dollar?

The price of the ball is between $2 and $3. Halfway between $2 and $3 is $2.50. Since $2.95 is greater than $2.50, the price is closer to $3.

The price of the puzzle is between $4 and $5. Halfway between $4 and $5 is $4.50. Since $4.39 is less than $4.50, the price is closer to $4.

Example 1

Brad saw a game at the toy store that cost $5.85. The price is between what two nearby dollar amounts? Round the price to the nearest dollar.

The price $5.85 is **between $5 and $6.** Halfway from $5 to $6 is $5.50. Since $5.85 is more than $5.50, the price to the nearest dollar is **$6**.

Example 2

The price of a box of crayons is $3.15 and a set of colored markers is $1.89. Estimate the total price of the two items.

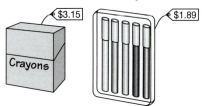

To estimate, we first round each price to the nearest dollar. Then we add to find the estimated total.

Lesson 96   517

New Concept

Explanation

Explain that when estimating money amounts to the nearest dollar, the amount representing the number of $1 bills is adjusted and the value of any change is dropped.

Alternate Method

To round $2.95 using money manipulatives, lay out two $1 bills and enough coins to make 95 cents. Explain that if the coins total 50 cents or more, we remove the coins and add one $1 bill to the amount.

To round $4.39, lay out four $1 bills and enough coins to make 39 cents. Explain that if the coins total less than 50 cents, we simply remove the coins and keep the dollar amount the same.

Example 1

Encourage students to use their money manipulatives to help show how the numbers were rounded in this example.

Extend the Example

"If Brad wanted to buy three of these games as presents for his friends, about how much money would he spend?" about $18.00

Example 2

Extend the Example

"What is the exact price for the items?" $5.04

"Would an estimate of $24 make sense for the cost of four boxes of crayons? Why or why not?" no; sample: Since 3 × 4 = 12, the actual price is close to $12, not $24.

(continued)

Math Background

In this lesson students are rounding to the nearest dollar. This may seem like an advanced skill for third graders since it involves rounding across decimal points. However, this is a skill that students can easily relate to their daily lives. Most students have been to a toy store or have seen an ad for a toy or game they would like to buy. They are very motivated to learn about and use money. They have worked with money amounts including dollars and cents throughout this book. Also, they have used fractions to describe parts of a dollar, so they should already know the concept of 50¢ as one half of a dollar.

English Learners

To be **nearby** means to be close by or close to. Say:

"A book costs $17.39. That price is nearby what two dollar amounts?" $17 and $18

Ask:

"Raise your hand if your house is nearby the school." Answers will vary.

Ask students to draw a map showing other locations nearby their house.

Lesson 96   517

New Concept (Continued)

Lesson Practice

Guided Practice

Use these problems as guided practice to check the students' understanding of today's concept.

Problem f
Extend the Problem

"*Derrick wants to buy eight bottles of milk. He has $20. Will this be enough money? Explain.*" Yes, because eight bottles of milk costs about $16 since $2.00 × 8 = $16.00.

Closure The questions below help assess the concepts taught in this lesson.

"*When we round money to the nearest dollar, how do we know whether to round up or down?*" We round up to the next dollar if the change is 50¢ or more. We leave the dollar amount the same and drop the change if it is less than 50¢.

"*How does estimating money help us to know if our answer is reasonable?*" When we estimate, it gives us a number to which we can compare our answer. If the estimate and the answer are very different, we know that we need to check our math.

Discuss real-world situations where rounding money might be helpful. Examples are given below.

- We want to know if we have enough money to buy a shirt for $9.95, a pair of socks for $2.18, and a hat for $3.81.
- We have $10 to buy as many pencils as possible at $0.48 each.

Written Practice

Math Conversations
Independent Practice and Discussions to Increase Understanding

Problem 4
Students may want to cross off numbers lightly as they pair them up into compatible numbers totaling ten. They can also rewrite the problem by changing the order of the addends and use parentheses to group pairs of compatible numbers.

(5 + 5) + (2 + 8) + 1 + 7

(continued)

518 *Saxon Math* Intermediate 3

---

sample: $3.15 is between $3.00 and $4.00. $3.50 is halfway between $3.00 and $4.00. $3.15 is less than $3.50, so we round down.

The $3.15 price rounds to $3.
The $1.89 price rounds to $2.
We add $3 and $2 and estimate that the total price is about **$5**.

Explain Explain why we rounded $3.15 down to $3.00.

Lesson Practice For problems **a–d**, round each dollar and cent amount to the nearest dollar.

a. $4.90 $5
b. $6.25 $6
c. $8.19 $8
d. $6.79 $7

e. Estimate the total price of a rubber ball that costs $2.95 and a plastic bat that costs $5.82. $9

▶ f. Estimate the total price of a bottle of milk at $1.89, a box of cereal at $3.92, and a bag of fruit at $4.17. $10

Written Practice — Distributed and Integrated

1. Bert is 150 cm tall. Lou is 118 cm tall. How many centimeters does Lou need to grow to be as tall as Bert?   32 cm
(39)

2. Jenny bought ten cartons of eggs. There were a dozen eggs in each carton. How many eggs were there in ten cartons?   120 eggs
(60)

3. The price of a box of greeting cards is $4.50. This price is between what two nearby dollar amounts? Round $4.50 to the nearest dollar.
(96) $4.00 and $5.00; $5.00

▶ 4. Add pairs of compatible numbers first to mentally find the total:
(92)
5 + 1 + 2 + 5 + 8 + 7   28

5. List the five odd numbers that are between 10 and 20.   11, 13, 15, 17, 19
(88)

6. Find each product:
(91)
a. 4 × 500   2,000
b. 3 × $800 $2,400
c. 5 × 720   3,600
d. 2 × $370 $740

7. (50 + 21) + 17   88
(92)

518   *Saxon Math* Intermediate 3

8. Kiondre and John put 300 pennies in the penny jar. They estimated that they would need 3 times that many pennies to fill the jar. About how many pennies would Kiondre and John need to fill the jar?
900

9. (Model) Draw a triangular prism. Begin by drawing two congruent triangular faces.   sample:

10. A half gallon is the same as how many quarts?   2 quarts

11. What number is halfway between 3,000 and 4,000?   3,500

```
0      1,000    2,000    3,000    4,000
```

12. Counting by quarters on a ruler, the order is:

$$\frac{1}{4}, \frac{1}{2}, \frac{3}{4}, 1$$

Find the next four numbers in this sequence: $2\frac{3}{4}, 3, 3\frac{1}{4}, 3\frac{1}{2}$

$$2, 2\frac{1}{4}, 2\frac{1}{2}, \underline{\quad}, \underline{\quad}, \underline{\quad}, \underline{\quad}, \ldots$$

13. Multiply:
   a. 4×15 60
   b. 9×21 189
   c. 8×45 360

14. One bouquet of flowers costs $12. Estimate the cost of 9 bouquets of flowers. $90

15. $20.00 − $1.99 $18.01

16. $(63 + 37) \times 2$ 200

17. (Justify) It took 11 minutes for Jonathan to ride his bike one mile. He estimates that it will take him about an hour to ride his bike for six miles. Is his estimate reasonable? Why or why not?
yes; sample: One hour is 60 minutes and $10 \times 6 = 60$.

18. Use compatible numbers to estimate the products in a and b.
   a. Estimate the product of 248×4. $250 \times 4 = 1,000$
   b. Estimate the product of 19×5. $20 \times 5 = 100$

19. Find each quotient:
   a. $27 \div 3$ 9
   b. $56 \div 7$ 8
   c. $63 \div 9$ 7

20. Which of these numbers are even?   152 and 438
   152   365   438

Lesson 96   519

Rounding money amounts to the nearest dollar to estimate arithmetic answers prepares students for

- **Lesson 97,** multiplying three-digit numbers.
- **Lesson 99,** examining the effects of estimation.
- **Lesson 100,** multiplying dollars and cents.
- **Investigation 10,** evaluating estimations.

Written Practice (Continued)

Math Conversations
Independent Practice and Discussions to Increase Understanding

Problem 9 (Model)
Invite a volunteer to draw the triangular prism on the board or overhead. If students have difficulty with their drawing, instruct them to draw two congruent triangles which are close, but not touching. Have students finish by drawing line segments connecting the corresponding vertices.

Problem 13
Encourage students to estimate their answers to check their calculations. Answers that do not seem reasonable should be recalculated.

Problem 17 (Justify)
The value of 6 times 11 equals 66 and is easy to compute mentally. This is the same as 1 hour and 6 minutes, so students can see right away that Jonathan's estimate is reasonable.

Errors and Misconceptions

Problem 12
Mixed-number patterns can be problematic for students because they are difficult to visualize. Have students use their rulers to continue this pattern. They can think of adding one quarter, $\frac{1}{4}$, or one quarter inch each time.

Problem 15
Watch out for students who hurriedly read this problem as $2.00 − $1.99 = $0.01. Suggest that students write this problem vertically or solve mentally by thinking $20 − $2 + 1 penny.

Lesson 96   519

LESSON 97

Texas Essential Knowledge and Skills
(3.13)(C) use data to describe events as more likely
(3.14)(A) identify the mathematics in everyday situations

Planning & Preparation

- **Multiplying Three-Digit Numbers, Part 2**

Objectives
- Multiply three-digit numbers by one-digit numbers.
- Multiply a three-digit number by a one-digit number to estimate the number of pennies in a jar.
- Write and solve multiplication number sentences to solve problems.

Prerequisite Skills
- Multiply three-digit numbers ending in zero by one-digit numbers.
- Discuss different strategies to estimate the number of pennies in a jar.
- Learn the multiplication algorithm for multiplying two-digit numbers by one-digit numbers.
- Learn the multiplication facts through 12s.

Materials
Instructional Masters
- Power Up 97

Manipulative Kit
- Ruler
- Money manipulatives (bills)*

Teacher-provided materials
- Index cards*
- Student money manipulatives (bills)*
  *optional

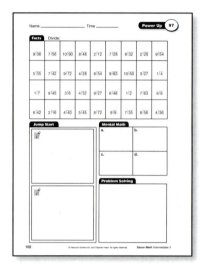

Power Up 97

Reaching All Special Needs Students

Special Education Students	At-Risk Students	English Learners	Advanced Learners
• Inclusion (TM) • Adaptations for Saxon Math	• Error Alert (TM) • Reteaching Masters	• English Learners (TM) • English Learner Handbook	• Early Finishers (SE) • Extend the Problem (TM) • Online Activities

TM=Teacher's Manual
SE=Student Edition

Math Language
English Learners
similar

520A   *Saxon Math* Intermediate 3

Problem Solving Discussion

Problem

Josh watched the night sky from 9:00 to 10:00 during the meteor shower. He saw twice as many meteors after 9:30 as he saw before 9:30. Josh counted 24 meteors altogether. How many meteors did Josh see before 9:30?

Focus Strategy

 **Guess and Check**

Understand — Understand the problem.

"What information are we given?"

1. Josh saw 24 meteors altogether from 9:00 to 10:00.
2. He saw twice as many meteors after 9:30 than he did before 9:30.

"What are we asked to do?"

We are asked to find how many meteors Josh saw before 9:30.

Plan — Make a plan.

"How can we use the information we know to solve the problem?"

We can *guess and check* to find the number of meteors Josh saw each half hour.

Solve — Carry out the plan.

"How many numbers are we looking for, and what is the sum of the two numbers?"

We are looking for two numbers whose sum is 24.

"We are told that Josh saw twice as many meteors after 9:30 as he saw before 9:30. How does this help us guess the two numbers?"

The greater number will be double the smaller number.

"Let's pretend that Josh saw the same number of meteors each half hour. How many meteors would that be for each half hour?"

Half of 24 is 12, so Josh would have seen 12 meteors during each half hour.

"Now let's count down from one of the 12s and count up from the other 12. By doing this, we make pairs of numbers that each have a sum of 24."

11 and 13   8 and 16
10 and 14   7 and 17
9 and 15   6 and 18

"Do any of these number pairs fit the situation described in the problem?"

Yes, we see that 16 is twice as many as 8, and that the sum of 16 and 8 is 24. Josh saw fewer meteors before 9:30 than after 9:30, so he saw 8 meteors before 9:30.

Check — Look back.

"Let's check our guess. Is our answer of 8 meteors correct?"

Yes, we know that our answer is correct because 8 is half as many as 16, and 8 + 16 = 24, which is the number of meteors Josh saw altogether.

"What problem solving strategies did we use, and how did they help us?"

We used the strategy of *guess and check* to find two numbers when we were given clues about how the numbers related to each other.

LESSON 97

Power Up

Facts
Distribute **Power Up 97** to students. See answers below.

Jump Start
Before students begin the Mental Math exercise, do these exercises as a class.

Mental Math
Encourage students to share different ways to mentally compute these exercises. Strategies for exercises are listed below.

b. Find Compatible Numbers and Add
Add 130 and 70 first because they are compatible numbers.
130 + 70 = 200
200 + 22 = 222

c. Multiply by 100
100 cm = 1 meter
3 meters = 3 × 100 cm = 300 cm
Count by 100s
100, 200, 300 cm

Problem Solving
Refer to **Problem-Solving Strategy Discussion**, p. 520B.

LESSON 97

- **Multiplying Three-Digit Numbers, Part 2**

Texas Essential Knowledge and Skills
(3.13)(C) use data to describe events as more likely
(3.14)(A) identify the mathematics in everyday situations

Power Up

facts   Power Up 97

jump start
- Count up by 25s from 0 to 250.
- Count up by 10s from 0 to 110.
- Aaron had a $10 bill. He bought a set of juggling balls for $4.65. Name the fewest bills and coins he could receive for change.   *1 $5 bill, 1 quarter, 1 dime*
- Use these clues to find the secret number. Write the secret number on your worksheet.   *80*
  - two-digit number
  - sum of digits is 8
  - product of the digits is 0

mental math
a. **Number Sense:** 2 × 4 × 6   *48*
b. **Number Sense:** 130 + 22 + 70   *222*
c. **Measurement:** How many centimeters are in 3 meters?   *300 cm*
d. **Probability:** Waverly spins the spinner one time. Which color is the spinner most likely to land on?   *yellow*

problem solving
Josh watched the night sky from 9:00 to 10:00 during the meteor shower. He saw twice as many meteors after 9:30 as he saw before 9:30. Josh counted 24 meteors altogether. How many meteors did Josh see before 9:30?   *8 meteors*

520   Saxon Math Intermediate 3

Facts   Divide:

4 9)36	8 7)56	9 10)90	6 8)48	6 2)12	4 7)28	4 8)32	10 2)20	6 9)54
7 5)35	6 7)42	8 9)72	7 4)28	9 6)54	7 9)63	5 10)50	9 3)27	4 1)4
7 1)7	5 9)45	2 3)6	8 4)32	3 9)27	8 6)48	2 1)2	9 7)63	1 6)6
7 6)42	8 2)16	10 4)40	9 5)45	9 8)72	1 9)9	5 7)35	7 8)56	9 4)36

520   Saxon Math Intermediate 3

New Concept

To help them estimate the number of pennies in a full jar, Chad and Jodi filled up one jar with pennies. Then they put 234 pennies in a second jar that is similar in size.

The second jar is only partly filled. Chad and Jodi estimate that they would need 4 times as many pennies to fill the second jar completely. So they estimate that the number of pennies in the full jar is about 4 × 234.

To multiply a 3-digit number with pencil and paper, we multiply the ones, then the tens, then the hundreds.

$$\begin{array}{r} \overset{1\,1}{234} \\ \times\ \ 4 \\ \hline 936 \end{array}$$

Discuss Look at the multiplication above. How many times do we need to regroup when we multiply 4 × 234? How can you tell?

2 times; sample: We can tell that there is regrouping in 4 × 234 because there is a number written above the 3 in the tens column and a number above the 2 in the hundreds column.

Example 1

Find the product: 8 × 125

First, we multiply the 5 by 8. The product is 40. We record 0 in the ones place. We write the 4 tens of 40 above the 2.

$$\begin{array}{r} \overset{4}{125} \\ \times\ \ 8 \\ \hline 0 \end{array}$$

Next, we multiply 2 tens by 8. The product is 16 tens. We add the 4 tens. The total is 20 tens. We record 0 in the tens place and write 2 above the 1.

$$\begin{array}{r} \overset{2\,4}{125} \\ \times\ \ 8 \\ \hline 00 \end{array}$$

Finally, we multiply 1 hundred by 8. The product is 8 hundreds. We add 2 hundreds. The total is 10 hundreds. The final product is **1,000**.

$$\begin{array}{r} \overset{2\,4}{125} \\ \times\ \ 8 \\ \hline 1,000 \end{array}$$

Lesson 97   521

New Concept

Instruction

Remind students that they multiplied three-digit numbers by a one-digit number in Lesson 91. In this lesson, students extend their experience by performing similar multiplications, but with regroupings in both the tens and hundreds places.

Manipulative Use

Three-digit numbers are easy to model using money manipulatives. To perform a multiplication, students can sort out a corresponding number of piles, each representing the three-digit number. Then they can combine the piles and use regrouping to count out the total.

Example 1
Mental Math

Students can solve this problem mentally if they think of 125 as $1.25 and separate the dollars from the quarters. Eight $1 bills will total $8.00, and eight quarters will total $2.00. Together that makes $10.00, which would correspond to an answer of 1,000.

(continued)

Math Background

As students progress to increasingly more complex algorithms, it is important to stress continued concept development and appropriate use of math vocabulary. Students should understand that to multiply 125 × 8, they actually multiply 100 × 8, 20 × 8, and 5 × 8, and then combine the three products. They need to understand that the algorithm is a "shortcut" method for performing these calculations. Numbers are aligned according to place value in algorithms to make regrouping easier. Third graders should be able to explain when and why regrouping is necessary. In later grades, students will build on these concepts to multiply decimals and fractions.

English Learners

Similar means to be almost the same. Ask:

"What objects have a similar size and shape to a tennis ball?" samples: an apple, an orange, a baseball

Say:

"I am wearing a [color] shirt. Raise your hand if you are wearing a similar color." Students should raise their hand if they are wearing a similar color.

Have students discuss with a partner their favorite hobbies and find ones that are similar.

Lesson 97   521

New Concept (Continued)

Example 2
Error Alert

If students attempted to add the number above the zero before multiplying, they may multiply 7 by 5. Point out that a number times zero results in zero.

Lesson Practice

Guided Practice

Use these problems as guided practice to check the students' understanding of today's concept.

Problems a–f

Encourage students to rewrite the problems vertically. Remind them to only write one digit under each column.

Closure The questions below help assess the concepts taught in this lesson.

"Explain how we would multiply 245 × 3."
First, write the problem vertically and line up the digits. Multiply 3 × 5 = 15. Write the 5 in the ones place and add the 1 ten above the 4 in the tens column. Multiply 3 × 4 tens = 12 tens. Add the 1 ten to get 13 tens. Write the 3 in the tens place and regroup the 1 to the hundreds column. 2 × 3 hundreds = 6 hundreds. Add the one to get 7 hundreds. The answer is 735.

Discuss real-world situations where multiplying a three-digit number might be helpful. Examples are given below.

- Mrs. Wilson ordered five packages of 125 daffodil bulbs.
- The Featherful Chicken Ranch sells 728 birds each month for four months and wants to know the total number of birds sold.

Written Practice

Math Conversations
Independent Practice and Discussions to Increase Understanding

Problem 1 (Model)
The capital letter "I" has both a vertical and a horizontal line of symmetry. Remind students that a line of symmetry marks the location of the start of an object's mirror image.

(continued)

Example 2

Chad compared the full penny jar with a jar that had 308 pennies. He thought the full jar had 7 times as many pennies, so he multiplied 308 by 7 to estimate the total. What was the product?

First, we multiply 8 by 7. The product is 56. We record the 6 in the ones place and write the 5 of 56 above the 0 in the tens place.

$$\begin{array}{r} \overset{5}{3}08 \\ \times\ \ 7 \\ \hline 6 \end{array}$$

Next, we multiply 0 tens by 7. The product is 0. We add 5 and record 5 in the tens place.

$$\begin{array}{r} \overset{5}{3}08 \\ \times\ \ 7 \\ \hline 56 \end{array}$$

Finally, we multiply 3 hundreds by 7. The final product is **2,156**.

$$\begin{array}{r} \overset{5}{3}08 \\ \times\ \ 7 \\ \hline 2,156 \end{array}$$

Lesson Practice
- a. 6 × 135   810
- b. 7 × 213   1491
- c. 4 × $275 $1,100
- d. 3 × $232 $696
- e. 8 × 706   5,648
- f. 9 × $204 $1,836

Written Practice — Distributed and Integrated

1. **(Model)** Write the uppercase form of the ninth letter of the alphabet. Then draw its lines of symmetry. *(Inv. 9)*   sample:

2. Tamara bought a dress for $39.95. Sales tax was $2.60. What was the total price with tax? $42.55 *(18, 22)*

3. Estimate the sum of $4.67 and $7.23 to the nearest dollar. $12.00 *(30, 96)*

4. **Multiple Choice** Which measurement is most likely the length of Vincent's pencil?   A *(79)*
   A 15 cm   **B** 15 m   **C** 15 km

5. Stuart stacked seventeen books in two piles as equally as possible. How many books were in each stack?   8 and 9 *(82)*

 Inclusion

Multiplication Template

Some students may be confused if regrouping is necessary in both the tens and hundreds places when multiplying a three-digit number by a one-digit number. Use this template as a visual reminder.

Materials: one index card for each student

- Write the following template on the board and have students copy it on their card.

$$\begin{array}{r} (\ )(\ ) \\ \_\ \_\ \_ \\ \times\ \ \ \ \_ \\ \hline \_,\_\_\_ \end{array}$$

- Demonstrate using the template below to solve 263 × 7.

$$\begin{array}{r} \overset{(4)\,(2)}{2\ 6\ 3} \\ \times\ \ \ \ 7 \\ \hline 1,8\ 4\ 1 \end{array}$$

- Remind students to use the template to solve similar problems until they can keep track of the numbers on their own.

6. The window was twice as wide as it was high. If the window was 35 inches high, then how wide was it?   70 in.
(81)

▶ 7. (Justify) Susan estimated that 3 tickets to the baseball game will cost about $60. If tickets are $22 each, is her estimate reasonable? Why or why not?   sample: Yes, because $22 is about $20, and $20 × 3 = $60.
(95)

8. (Analyze) What words should be used in place of w, y, and z in this description?   pint, quart, half gallon
(87)

> Doubling a cup makes a __w__. Doubling a __w__ makes a __y__. Doubling a __y__ makes a __z__. Doubling a __z__ makes a gallon.

▶ 9. (Formulate) Tyrone walks to school every day. He walks a total of 18 miles each month. Estimate the number of miles Tyrone walks in 5 months. Write a number sentence.   20 × 5 = 100 miles
(93)

10. Kumar used 1-inch cubes to build a rectangular solid like the one shown at right. How many 1-inch cubes did Kumar use to build the solid?   48 cubes
(73)

11. Multiply:
(84, 97)
   a. 4 × 210   840
   b. 7 × 34   238

12. Divide:
(86)
   a. 2)12   6
   b. 3)12   4

13. Round $5.38 to the nearest dollar. $5.00
(96)

14. 190 × 4   760
(97)

15. 230 × 5   1,150
(97)

16. $65 + $350 + $9 $424
(24)

17. 6 + (5 × 80)   406
(78, 92)

18. Find each quotient:
(86)
   a. 42 ÷ 7   6
   b. 36 ÷ 4   9
   c. 64 ÷ 8   8

Lesson 97   523

Written Practice (Continued)

Math Conversations
Independent Practice and Discussions to Increase Understanding

▶ **Problem 7** (Justify)
Students may also multiply 3 × 22 to get 66, the actual cost of three tickets. Since $66 is close to Susan's estimate of $60, students know the estimate is reasonable.

▶ **Problem 9** (Formulate)
The distance of 18 miles is closer to the rounded value of 20 than to the compatible number 25, so students should round and then multiply by 5 to get the estimate.

Extend the Problem
"Tyrone leaves his house and walks two blocks east on Maple Street. He then walks five blocks south on Acorn Lane and then one block east on School Street. Draw a map to show Tyrone's route to school." See student work.

(continued)

Lesson 97   523

Written Practice (Continued)

Math Conversations
Independent Practice and Discussions to Increase Understanding

▶ **Problem 20** Model

Students should first draw two parallel lines 3 cm long that are 5 cm apart. They can finish the rectangle by connecting the corresponding vertices.

Errors and Misconceptions

▶ **Problem 6**

Suggest that students draw a diagram of a window that is wider than it is tall and label its dimensions after rereading the problem.

▶ **Problem 20**

Students often forget to report the units for perimeter and area. Remind them that perimeter is a measure of length and should be reported with both a number and a unit such as centimeters, inches, or feet. Area is named with a number and a square unit such as square centimeters.

Students may also estimate the costs of the supplies by rounding to the nearest dollar—$10 for the can of paint, $5 for the paintbrush, and $4 for the stickers—for an estimated total of $19.

---

19. Name the mixed numbers represented by points A and B. $7\frac{1}{5}$; $8\frac{3}{5}$
(48)

▶ **20.** Model Draw a rectangle that is 5 cm long and 3 cm wide.
(58, 63)
  a. What is the perimeter of the rectangle? 16 cm
  b. What is the area of the rectangle? 15 sq. cm

Real-World Connection

Tony wants to paint his clubhouse. He has $15 to spend on supplies. At the paint store, he chose one can of blue paint for $9.99, a paint brush for $4.82, and a pack of reptile wall stickers for $3.62. Does Tony have enough money to buy all of the supplies he chose? Explain your answer. no; sample: He does not have enough because the total price for all items is greater than $18.

Multiplying three-digit numbers by one-digit numbers and making estimates prepares students for

- **Lesson 98,** estimating by weight and mass.
- **Lesson 99,** examining the effects of estimation.
- **Lesson 100,** multiplying dollars and cents.
- **Investigation 10,** evaluating estimations.
- **Lesson 101,** dividing two-digit numbers.
- **Lessons 106 and 108,** estimating area.

LESSON 98

Planning & Preparation

• Estimating by Weight or Mass

Objectives
- Use the weight or mass of a known quantity of objects to estimate an unknown number of objects whose weight or mass is known.
- Measure the weight or mass of the penny jar and of a known number of pennies and use that information to update the penny jar estimates from Lesson 91.

Prerequisite Skills
- Learn the relationships between ounces, pounds, and tons.
- Use a scale to weigh objects in ounces and pounds.
- Learn the relationship between grams and kilograms.
- Identify real-world benchmarks for each unit of weight or mass.

Materials
Instructional Masters
- Power Up 98
- Lesson Activity 31

Manipulative Kit
- Ruler
- Balance scale

Teacher-provided materials
- Penny jar from Lesson 91
- Extra penny rolls
- Blank two-row tables*

    *optional

Texas Essential Knowledge and Skills
(3.2)(C) use symbols to describe fractional parts of whole objects
(3.7)(A) generate a table of paired numbers based on a real-life situation
(3.11)(B) use standard units to find the perimeter of a shape
(3.11)(D) identify concrete models that approximate standard units of weight/mass and use them to measure weight/mass

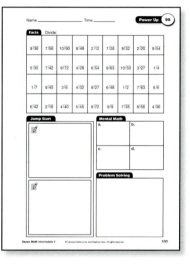

Power Up 98   Lesson Activity 31

Differentiated Instruction

Reaching All Special Needs Students

Special Education Students	At-Risk Students	English Learners	Advanced Learners
• Inclusion (TM) • Adaptations for Saxon Math	• Error Alert (TM) • Reteaching Masters	• English Learners (TM) • English Learner Handbook	• Extend the Example (TM) • Extend the Problem (TM) • Early Finishers (SE) • Online Activities

TM=Teacher's Manual
SE=Student Edition

Math Language

Maintained	English Learners
mass	pitcher

Lesson 98   525A

LESSON 98

Problem Solving Discussion

Problem

Ms. Hudson will pay to park her car in the parking garage. The cost is $3.50 for the first hour and $1.00 for each additional hour. Copy and complete this table to find the cost of parking a car in the garage for 6 hours.

Hours	Cost
1	$3.50

Focus Strategy Make or Use a Table, Chart, or Graph

Understand Understand the problem.

"What information are we given?"

The cost for the first hour of parking is $3.50. The cost is $1.00 for each additional hour.

"What are we asked to do?"

We are asked to complete the table and find the cost of parking a car for 6 hours.

Plan Make a plan.

"What problem solving strategy will we use?"

We will *make a table* to show the total cost for each hour.

Solve Carry out the plan.

"What numbers will we use to fill in the table?"

We count up by ones for the hours until we reach 6 hours. For each hour after the first hour, we count up by $1.00 (starting from $3.50) for the cost.

"What is the cost of parking a car in the garage for 6 hours?"

Our table shows that the parking cost for 6 hours is $8.50.

Hours	Cost
1	$3.50
2	$4.50
3	$5.50
4	$6.50
5	$7.50
6	$8.50

Check Look back.

"Is our answer reasonable?"

Yes, it is reasonable that the cost for 6 hours is $8.50, since the cost is $3.50 for the first hour and $5.00 for the next 5 hours.

"What problem solving strategy did we use, and how did it help us?"

We *made a table* to show the total cost of parking for each hour. Then we used the table to answer the question about the cost of parking for 6 hours.

Alternate Strategy

Write a Number Sentence

To find the total cost of parking, students can *write a number sentence*. We know that the cost for the first hour is $3.50. We also know that the cost for each additional hour is $1.00. Since 6 hours is 1 hour plus 5 additional hours, we can add to find the total cost: $3.50 + $5.00 = $8.50.

LESSON 98

• **Estimating by Weight or Mass**

🚩 **Texas Essential Knowledge and Skills**
(3.2)(C) use symbols to describe fractional parts of whole objects
(3.7)(A) generate a table of paired numbers based on a real-life situation
(3.11)(B) use standard units to find the perimeter of a shape
(3.11)(D) identify concrete models that approximate standard units of weight/mass and use them to measure weight/mass

Power Up

facts Power Up 98

jump start
 Count up by 9s from 0 to 108.
Count up by 5s from 8 to 58.

✏️ Write a multiplication and division fact family using the numbers 4, 4, and 16. $4 \times 4 = 16$; $16 \div 4 = 4$

✏️ Draw a rectangle and divide it into 6 parts. Then shade 1 part. What fraction is *not* shaded?   See student work; $\frac{5}{6}$

mental math

a. **Money:** $200 − $136 $64

b. **Number Sense:** 29 + 52   81

c. **Measurement:** What is the perimeter of this polygon? All sides are equal in length.   24 in.

d. **Geometry:** Name the polygon that is shown in problem c.   octagon

3 in.

problem solving

Ms. Hudson will pay to park her car in the parking garage. The cost is $3.50 for the first hour and $1.00 for each additional hour. Copy and complete this table to find the cost of parking a car in the garage for 6 hours. $8.50

Hours	Cost
1	$3.50
2	$4.50
3	$5.50
4	$6.50
5	$7.50
6	$8.50

Hours	Cost
1	$3.50

Lesson 98   525

LESSON 98

Power Up

● **Facts**
Distribute **Power Up 98** to students. See answers below.

● **Jump Start**
Before students begin the Mental Math exercise, do these exercises as a class.

● **Mental Math**
Encourage students to share different ways to mentally compute these exercises. Strategies for exercises are listed below.

a. **Think $200 − $140 + $4**
$200 − $136 = $200 − $140 + $4 = $60 + $4 = $64

c. **Multiply the Number of Sides by 3 in.**
The figure has 8 sides.
3 in. × 8 = 24 in.
Count by 3s
3, 6, 9, 12, 15, 18, 21, 24
The perimeter is 24 in.

● **Problem Solving**
Refer to **Problem-Solving Strategy Discussion,** p. 525B.

Facts   Divide:

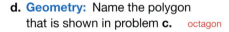

9)36	7)56	10)90	8)48	2)12	7)28	8)32	2)20	9)54
4	8	9	6	6	4	4	10	6

5)35	7)42	9)72	4)28	6)54	9)63	10)50	3)27	1)4
7	6	8	7	9	7	5	9	4

1)7	9)45	3)6	4)32	9)27	6)48	1)2	7)63	6)6
7	5	2	8	3	8	2	9	1

6)42	2)16	4)40	5)45	8)72	9)9	7)35	8)56	4)36
7	8	10	9	9	1	5	7	9

Lesson 98   525

New Concept

Instruction

In this lesson, students must be familiar with units of weight, mass, and capacity. Begin the lesson by reviewing these measures.

"What units do we use in the U.S. to describe the weight of different objects?" ounces, pounds, and tons

Have students match the appropriate unit to each item below:

an elephant   tons
a person   pounds
a bird   ounces

Ask students how many ounces are in a pound and how many pounds are in one ton.
1 pound = 16 ounces, 1 ton = 2,000 pounds

"What are the metric units used to measure mass?" grams and kilograms

Ask students to give some examples of objects that would have a mass of about one gram or one kilogram. samples: A dollar bill or a large paper clip would have a mass of about 1 gram; A textbook or a pair of shoes would have a mass of about one kilogram.

Remind students that there are 1,000 grams in a single kilogram. Next, write the following comparison of capacity measures on the board and have volunteers come to the board to fill it in, one conversion at a time.

1 gallon = 2 half gallons = 4 quarts
1 half gallon = 2 quarts = 4 pints
1 quart = 2 pints = 4 cups
1 pint = 2 cups

Example 1
Extend the Example

Challenge students to do this calculation mentally by thinking of 5 × 400 as 5 × 4 = 20 with two zeros attached at the end: 2,000.

For the *Analyze* question, encourage students to count by 50s.

Example 2
Extend the Example

This example estimates the number of pints in the pitcher. Have students convert this estimate to an equivalent value in ounces, cups, quarts, and half gallons. You may need to remind students that there are 8 ounces in one cup.

4 pints = 64 ounces, or 8 cups, or 2 quarts, or 1 half gallon

(continued)

526   Saxon Math Intermediate 3

New Concept

Gwen and Theo weighed the penny jar to help them estimate the number of pennies in the jar. They found that the mass of the jar was about 5 kilograms. Then they measured the mass of eight rolls of pennies. They found that the mass of eight rolls of pennies, or 400 pennies, was about 1 kilogram.

Use the information above to solve example 1.

Example 1

Create a table to help you estimate the number of pennies in 5 kilograms. Assume that 400 pennies has a mass of 1 kilogram.

Since the mass of 400 pennies is about 1 kilogram, we count up by 400 pennies for each kilogram.

Number of Pennies	400	800	1,200	1,600	2,000
Mass of Pennies	1 kg	2 kg	3 kg	4 kg	5 kg

We estimate that 5 kilograms of pennies is about **2,000 pennies**.

Analyze How many rolls of pennies can you make from 2,000 pennies?   40

Example 2

Alison knows that a pint of water weighs about a pound. She weighs a pitcher of water and finds that it weighs 7 pounds. The empty pitcher weighs 3 pounds. How many pints of water are in the pitcher?

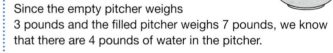

Since the empty pitcher weighs 3 pounds and the filled pitcher weighs 7 pounds, we know that there are 4 pounds of water in the pitcher.

```
  7 pounds   filled pitcher          4 pounds   water
− 3 pounds   empty pitcher         + 3 pounds   empty pitcher
  4 pounds   water                   7 pounds   filled pitcher
```

Since one pint of water weighs about one pound, we estimate that **4 pints** of water are in the pitcher.

526   Saxon Math Intermediate 3

English Learners

In this lesson, a **pitcher** is a container that holds liquids that we can drink. Ask:

"What might we serve in pitchers?" samples: lemonade, ice tea

Ask:

"If the pitcher holds a half of a gallon of water, how much water can two pitchers hold?" 1 gallon

Ask students to discuss places they have seen or used pitchers.

Activity

Estimating by Mass

Materials: full penny jar and **Lesson Activity 31** from Lesson 91, extra penny rolls, balance scale

Find the mass of the penny jar. Then find how many rolls of pennies have a mass of 1 kilogram. Use the information to help you estimate the number of pennies in the jar. You may use the results to improve your estimate on **Lesson Activity 31**.

Lesson Practice

a. An empty bucket weighs 1 pound. When filled with water, the bucket weighs 9 pounds. A pint of water weighs about 1 pound. About how many pints of water were in the bucket? 8 pints

b. If 1 kilogram of pennies is about 400 pennies, then 6 kilograms of pennies is about how many pennies? Make a table of number pairs to find the answer.

2,400 pennies; sample:

Kilograms	1 kg	2 kg	3 kg	4 kg	5 kg	6 kg
Pennies	400	800	1,200	1,600	2,000	2,400

Written Practice *Distributed and Integrated*

1. (39) Sal wants to buy a radio that costs $31.76 with tax. He has $23.50. How much more money does Sal need to buy the radio? $8.26

2. (87) A 5-gallon bucket is filled with water. How many quarts of water are in the bucket? 20 qt

3. (97) Find the products:
   a. 8 × 136   1,088
   b. 9 × $151 $1,359

4. (40) Find the missing number: 20 − n = 8   12

5. (96) The price of a pack of balloons is $5.49. The price of a pack of party hats is $3.29. Estimate the total price of the two items. $8

6. (86) Find the missing factor: 5 × m = 40   8

7. (87) A half gallon of milk is enough to fill how many cups? 8 cups

Lesson 98   527

Using a Table

Some students may have difficulty organizing information. Provide these students with a table template to write on. Keep a collection of templates on hand for students to use when needed.

Materials: blank two-row table

- See example 1.

- Students write "Number of Pennies" in the first row and "Mass of Pennies" in the second row.
- Write 400 in second column of first row.
- Skip count by 400 to complete first row.
- Complete second row with these masses: 1 kg, 2 kg, 3 kg, 4 kg, 5 kg.

Number of Pennies	400	800	1,200	1,600	2,000
Mass of Pennies	1 kg	2 kg	3 kg	4 kg	5 kg

New Concept (Continued)

Activity

Students will estimate the number of pennies in a jar by mass. They will measure the mass of the jar and the mass of one roll of pennies using a scale or balance. Inform students that one roll holds 50 pennies.

Lesson Practice

Guided Practice

Use these problems as guided practice to check the students' understanding of today's concept.

Problem a

Since one pint equals about one pound, students only need to find the number of pounds of water to determine the number of pints: 8 pounds will mean 8 pints.

 Closure The questions below help assess the concepts taught in this lesson.

"Explain how you could estimate how many jelly beans are in a jar by using weight or mass." Weigh the jar of jelly beans. Then weigh 50 jelly beans. See how many times you would have to add the weight of 50 jelly beans to get the weight of the whole jar. Multiply that number by 50 to find the estimated number of jelly beans.

Discuss real-world situations where using weight to estimate might be helpful. Examples are given below.

- Most packaged food is sold by weight. We want to know how many crackers are in a pound.
- We want to know how many scoops of flour it will take to fill a 5-pound bag.

Written Practice

Math Conversations
Independent Practice and Discussions to Increase Understanding

Problem 2

Suggest that students draw a row of 4 dots representing the number of quarts in one gallon, and then add four more rows for a total of 5 gallons.

(continued)

Lesson 98   527

> **Written Practice** (Continued)

Math Conversations
Independent Practice and Discussions to Increase Understanding

Problem 10
Extend the Problem

Challenge students to find the weight of 6 apples. Students may relate 4 apples in 1 pound to 4 quarters in one dollar and determine that each apple weighs a quarter pound. They can deduce that 6 quarters equal $1.50, which is the same as $1\frac{1}{2}$ dollars. So 6 apples equal $1\frac{1}{2}$ pounds.

Problem 13 **Multiple Choice**
Test-Taking Strategy

Each choice shows multiplication by 5, which produces a product that ends in only 0 or 5. The picture shows only hundreds and tens, so choice **A** can be eliminated because the product will end with a 5. Students can then complete the multiplication in the three remaining answer choices to determine which is represented in the picture.

(continued)

---

8. What number is halfway between 2,000 and 3,000? 2500

9. Katie is paid $7.75 per hour. Estimate how much Katie is paid for working 6 hours. 6 × $8 = $48

▶ **10.** (Formulate) If one pound of apples is about 4 small apples, then 6 pounds of apples is about how many apples? Make a table to help find the answer. 24; sample:

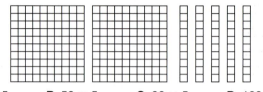

Pounds	1 lb	2 lb	3 lb	4 lb	5 lb	6 lb
Apples	4	8	12	16	20	24

11. Multiply:
a. 4 × 150   600
b. 3 × 630   1,890
c. 35 × 7   245

12. Divide:
a. 4)12   3
b. 6)12   2

▶ **13. Multiple Choice** This picture below shows the answer to which multiplication expression? B

A 25 × 5   **B** 50 × 5   **C** 20 × 5   **D** 100 × 3

14. Find each quotient:
a. 28 ÷ 4   7
b. 42 ÷ 6   7
c. 54 ÷ 9   6

15. $12.45 − $5.75 $6.70

16. 215 × 3   645

17. (70 × 5) − 50   300

18. 470 + 63 + 7 + 86   626

528   *Saxon Math Intermediate 3*

19. Refer to this rectangle to answer the questions that follow:
(58, 63)

   a. The rectangle is how many centimeters long?   5 cm

   b. The rectangle is how many centimeters wide?   2 cm

   c. What is the area of the rectangle?   10 sq. cm

   d. What is the perimeter of the rectangle?   14 cm

▶ **20.** Mark and two friends want to use the swing during a 15-minute recess. To find out how long each of them could use the swing, Mark divided 15 minutes by 3. What should Mark's answer be?
(89)
5 min

Early Finishers
Real-World Connection

Carlos wants to buy a bottle of apple juice from the vending machine. A bottle of apple juice costs $0.75. He has five coins that total exactly $0.75. What five coins does Carlos have? You may use money manipulatives to help you find the answer.
2 quarters, 2 dimes, 1 nickel

Lesson 98   529

Estimating quantity by weight or by mass prepares students for

- **Lesson 99,** examining the effects of estimation.
- **Lessons 106 and 108,** estimating area.

Written Practice (Continued)

Math Conversations
Independent Practice and Discussions to Increase Understanding

▶ **Problem 20**
Students can use a multiplication table to find the quotient. Remind them to find 15 in the 3s row, then look at the top of that column to see 5.

Errors and Misconceptions

▶ **Problem 3**
Both multiplication problems require students to regroup, which may still be a problem for some students. Consider writing these problems on the board in vertical format showing placeholders for numbers that need to be written above and below.

```
a.   ( ) ( )              b.    ( )
       1  3  6                 $ 1  5  1
   ×         8              ×          9
   ─────────              ─────────
     _, _ _ _                 $_, _ _ _
```

▶ **Problems 19 c and d**
Students may mix up the units for area and perimeter since many questions ask for the perimeter first. Remind students that the area is in square units, such as square centimeters, while perimeter has units of length, such as centimeters.

Students may recognize immediately that three quarters make $0.75. They may begin with the three quarters and then proceed systematically by exchanging one of the quarters for combinations of dimes, nickels, and pennies until they have the correct total of five coins.

LESSON 99

Texas Essential Knowledge and Skills

(3.1)(B) use place value to compare numbers through 9,999

(3.7)(A) generate a table of paired numbers based on a real-life situation

Planning & Preparation

• Effects of Estimation

Objectives
- Determine whether an estimate is greater than or less than the actual answer.
- Discuss the real-world effects of estimation.

Prerequisite Skills
- Round dollar-and-cent money amounts to the nearest whole dollar to solve problems.
- Round numbers to the nearest ten and hundred to solve problems.
- Round numbers to estimate solutions to addition, subtraction, and multiplication problems.

Materials
Instructional Masters
- Power Up 99

Manipulative Kit
- Ruler
- Fraction manipulatives*
- Money manipulatives*

Teacher-provided materials
- Student fraction manipulatives*
- Student money manipulatives*

   *optional

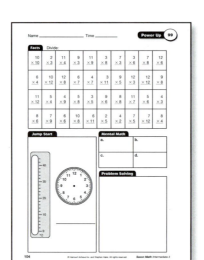

Power Up 99

Differentiated Instruction

Reaching All Special Needs Students

Special Education Students	At-Risk Students	English Learners	Advanced Learners
• Adaptations for Saxon Math	• Alternative Approach (TM) • Error Alert (TM) • Reteaching Masters	• English Learners (TM) • English Learner Handbook	• Extend the Example (TM) • Online Activities

TM = Teacher's Manual

Math Language

Maintained	English Learners
compatible numbers	actual

530A   *Saxon Math* Intermediate 3

Problem Solving Discussion

Problem

During a storm, we hear thunder after we see lightning. We can tell how far away lightning is by how long it takes us to hear the thunder after we see the lightning. The sound of thunder travels about 1 mile every 5 seconds. Make a table to show how many seconds it takes the sound of thunder to travel 1, 2, 3, and 4 miles. Use the table to find how far away lightning occurs if we hear thunder 20 seconds after we see lightning.

Miles	Seconds
1	5

Focus Strategies

 Make or Use a Table, Chart, or Graph

 Find/Extend a Pattern

Understand Understand the problem.

"What information are we given?"

1. We hear thunder after we see the lightning that caused it.
2. It takes 5 seconds for thunder to travel 1 mile.

"What are we asked to do?"

We are asked to complete the table. We are also asked to use the table to find how far away lightning occurs if we hear thunder 20 seconds after we see lightning.

Plan Make a plan.

"What problem solving strategy will we use?"

We can *make a table* and *extend the patterns* in the table.

Solve Carry out the plan.

"What numbers will we use to fill in the table?"

We count up by ones in the "Miles" column and count up by fives in the "Seconds" column.

"If we hear thunder 20 seconds after we see lightning, how far away is the lightning?"

In the table, we find that 20 seconds means that the lightning is 4 miles away.

Miles	Seconds
1	5
2	10
3	15
4	20

Check Look back.

"Is our answer reasonable?"

Yes, the delay is 5 seconds for each mile. For 4 miles, the delay would be 4 × 5 seconds = 20 seconds, which is the amount of time in the question.

"What problem solving strategies did we use, and how did they help us?"

We *made a table* to show the distance of lightning (in miles) and the delay of the thunder (in seconds). We *extended a pattern* of counting by fives in the "Seconds" column. We used the table to find the answer to the question.

LESSON 99

Power Up

Facts
Distribute **Power Up 99** to students. See answers below.

Jump Start
Before students begin the Mental Math exercise, do these exercises as a class.

Mental Math
Encourage students to share different ways to mentally compute these exercises. Strategies for exercises are listed below.

a. Think 50 − 20 + 2
   50 − 18 = 50 − 20 + 2 = 30 + 2 = 32

c. Think 9 × 5 and Attach a Zero
   9 × 5 = 45 so 9 × 50 = 450

d. Subtract Dollars, Then Subtract Cents
   $8 − $1 = $7
   50¢ − 30¢ = 20¢
   Combine the dollars and cents.
   $7 and 20¢ = $7.20

Problem Solving
Refer to **Problem-Solving Strategy Discussion**, p. 530B.

LESSON 99 • Effects of Estimation

Texas Essential Knowledge and Skills
(3.1)(B) use place value to compare numbers through 9,999
(3.7)(A) generate a table of paired numbers based on a real-life situation

Power Up

facts Power Up 99

jump start
- Count up by 4s from 0 to 48.
- Count up by 8s from 0 to 96.
- It is night. The plane will depart at 13 minutes before 9:00. Draw hands on your clock to show the departure time. Write the time in digital form.   8:47 p.m.
- The daily high on Wednesday was 32°C. That night, the low temperature was 17 degrees cooler. Mark your thermometer to show the low temperature.   15°C

mental math
a. **Number Sense:** 50 − 18   32
b. **Time:** The music lesson lasted 35 minutes. The science lesson lasted 35 minutes. Altogether, how many minutes were the two lessons?   70 min
c. **Number Sense:** 9 × 50   450
d. **Money:** Fiona had $8.50. Then she spent $1.30. How much money did Fiona have left? $7.20

problem solving During a storm, we hear thunder after we see lightning. We can tell how far away lightning is by how long it takes us to hear the thunder after we see the lightning. The sound of thunder travels about 1 mile every 5 seconds. Make a table to show how many seconds it takes the sound of thunder to travel 1, 2, 3, and 4 miles. Use the table to find how far away lightning occurs if we hear thunder 20 seconds after we see lightning.   4 miles

Miles	Seconds
1	5
2	10
3	15
4	20

Miles	Seconds
1	5

530   Saxon Math Intermediate 3

Facts   Multiply:

10 × 10 = 100	2 × 3 = 6	11 × 4 = 44	9 × 3 = 27	11 × 9 = 99	3 × 8 = 24	7 × 3 = 21	3 × 6 = 18	7 × 8 = 56	12 × 6 = 72
6 × 4 = 24	10 × 12 = 120	12 × 8 = 96	6 × 7 = 42	4 × 7 = 28	3 × 11 = 33	9 × 5 = 45	12 × 3 = 36	12 × 12 = 144	9 × 8 = 72
11 × 12 = 132	5 × 4 = 20	4 × 9 = 36	5 × 8 = 40	3 × 5 = 15	9 × 6 = 54	8 × 8 = 64	11 × 7 = 77	5 × 6 = 30	4 × 3 = 12
8 × 6 = 48	7 × 9 = 63	6 × 6 = 36	10 × 8 = 80	6 × 11 = 66	2 × 5 = 10	4 × 2 = 8	7 × 5 = 35	7 × 12 = 84	8 × 4 = 32

When we estimate an arithmetic answer, we often need to know whether our estimate is a little more than or a little less than the exact answer.

Example 1

Deb bought 4 gallons of milk for $2.89 per gallon. To estimate the total cost, Deb multiplied 4 × $3. Will Deb's estimate be greater than or less than the exact cost?

Deb rounded up the price of the milk. The rounded price is greater than the exact price.

$3.00 > $2.89

Therefore, **Deb's estimate will be greater than the exact price.**

```
Estimate   >   Exact
  $3.00        $2.89
×    4       ×    4
─────        ─────
 $12.00       $11.56
```

Example 2

There are 26 students in each of the three classrooms. Nelson estimates that the total number of students in the classrooms is about 75 since 3 × 25 = 75. How does Nelson's estimate compare with the exact number of students?

Nelson used compatible numbers to estimate the total number of students. To multiply he chose a number less than the actual number of students in each classroom.

25 < 26

Therefore, **Nelson's estimate is less than the actual number of students.**

```
Estimate   <   Exact
   25           26
 ×  3         ×  3
 ────         ────
   75           78
```

Lesson 99   531

Math Background

"Why do I need to know if my estimate is too high or too low?"

It is important that students understand the impact of estimates in real-world situations. If Deb's milk cost $2.39 per gallon in example 1, her estimate for 4 gallons might be $8.00 while the exact price will be $9.56. If she only takes $8.00 with her to the store, she will not have enough money. Hopefully Deb will compare the rounded price to the exact price, see that it is lower, and recognize that her estimate will be lower than the exact price. Then she will know to take extra money to the store.

 English Learners

Actual means to be true or real. Ask:

"A month is about 30 days. What is the actual number of days in this month?" If students are not sure, have them look at a calendar.

"Suppose you estimated that there were 58 pennies in a jar, and that your friend estimated that there were 89. The actual amount was 100. Whose estimate was closer?" sample: Your friend's estimate was closer.

Show students a cup of tiles and say:

"There are about 30 tiles in this cup. Count to find the actual number of tiles."

Have students count the tiles in the cup to find the actual number.

New Concept

Explanation

"Estimation is helpful in many situations. Can you think of a situation where estimation might be useful?" samples: We need to determine whether our answer is reasonable; We want to buy several items and need to be sure we have enough money to pay for them.

Example 1
Extend the Example

"Why might Deb need to know if her estimate will be greater than or less than the exact amount?" sample: Deb may need to know if she has enough money to buy 4 gallons of milk.

Explain

Students should understand that multiplying a number that has been rounded up results in an estimate that is greater than the exact value and that multiplying a number that has been rounded down results in an estimate that is less than the exact value.

"Round up and the estimate is greater; round down and the estimate is less."

Active Learning

Write the following amount on the board:

$6.23

Ask the students to round the number to either the nearest dollar or to a compatible amount and multiply it by 7.

"You have just estimated the cost of buying seven items that had a price of $6.23. Is your estimate greater or less than the exact cost of seven items? Explain."

Ask volunteers to show their work on the board and explain their answers.

Example 2
Extend the Example

"If Nelson rounded 26 to the nearest ten instead of rounding to a compatible number, how would it compare with the exact number of students?" It would be more than the actual number of students.

Use this as an opportunity to point out the usefulness of compatible numbers by having students compare the two estimates. They should note that being off by 3 when rounding down to 25 is a closer estimate than being off by 12 when rounding up to 30.

(continued)

Lesson 99   531

New Concept (Continued)

Lesson Practice

Guided Practice

Use these problems as guided practice to check the students' understanding of today's concept.

Problem a
Point out that each dollar amount was rounded up, so the estimate was more than the exact total.

Closure The questions below help assess the concepts taught in this lesson.

"When we round up, is our answer greater or less than the actual answer?" greater than the actual answer

"When we round down, is our answer greater or less than the actual answer?" less than the actual answer

Discuss real-world situations where knowing that rounding down gives a lesser total and rounding up gives a greater total might be helpful. Examples are given below.

- We estimate the cost of seven tickets priced at $23 each, and we only bring $150 to pay for them.
- We make treat bags for every member of the 18 soccer teams. There are 8 children on each team.

Written Practice

Math Conversations
Independent Practice and Discussions to Increase Understanding

Problem 3 Analyze
Since both rounded numbers are higher than the true prices, students should conclude that the estimate is higher than the exact price.

Problem 7 Multiple Choice
Test-Taking Strategy
Have students use their fraction manipulatives to model these fractions. Students can then eliminate choices **A, C,** and **D** where the fractions are equivalent.

(continued)

532 Saxon Math Intermediate 3

Evaluate Sam wants to buy four books for $3.29 each. He estimates that he will need $12 for the books. If Sam has $12, will he have enough money to buy all 4 books? Explain your answer. no; sample: Since $3.29 rounds down to $3.00, the estimate will be less than the actual total.

Activity

Estimating Capacity

Materials: gallon container, half-gallon container, quart container, water

Fill a gallon container with water. Pour water from the gallon container to fill a half-gallon container. Then fill a quart container from the gallon container.

1. **Estimate** About how much water is left in the gallon container?
2. Find out how much water is left in the gallon container. Write and solve a subtraction sentence to solve this problem.
3. **Analyze** Was your estimate greater than or less than the exact answer? Explain.

Lesson

a. Sal bought a gallon of milk for $2.89 and a box of cereal for $3.95. He added $3 and $4 to estimate the total price. Is Sal's estimate greater than or less than the exact price? greater than

b. Thom is paid $9.15 per hour. Estimate how much Thom is paid for working 8 hours. Is your estimate greater than or less than Thom's exact pay? sample: $8 \times \$9 = \$72$; less than

Written Practice *Distributed and Integrated*

1. From goal line to goal line on a football field is 100 yards. How many feet is 100 yards? 300 ft
   (34, 91)

2. **Formulate** Write a multiplication fact that shows how many small squares cover this rectangle.
   (53)
   $4 \times 7 = 28$ or $7 \times 4 = 28$

3. **Analyze** John bought a pair of sunglasses for $7.99 and a bottle of sunscreen for $8.90. He added $8 and $9 to estimate the total price. Is John's estimate greater than or less than the exact price? greater than
   (99)

532 Saxon Math Intermediate 3

Alternative Approach: Using Manipulatives

Have students use their money manipulatives to help visualize the effects of estimation. Instruct students to solve the problems below using their manipulatives. They should first round the values to the nearest dollar amount and determine an estimate. Then students should find the exact answer and compare it to the estimate.

$2.65 + $4.99 = $7.64
$3 + $5 = $8; estimate is greater by 36¢

$3.10 × 3 = $9.30
$3 × 3 = $9; estimate is less by 30¢

$6.58 × 4 = $26.32
$7 × 4 = $28; estimate is greater by $1.68

4. A plastic bag full of sweatshirts weighs 10 pounds. Two sweatshirts weigh about a pound. About how many shirts are in the bag?
   about 20 shirts

5. Multiply:
   a. 2 × 227   454
   b. 3 × $260 $780

6. $8.95 + $2.89 + 43¢ $12.27

7. **Multiple Choice** Which pair of fractions below is not equivalent?   B
   A $\frac{1}{2}, \frac{2}{4}$ B $\frac{2}{3}, \frac{3}{4}$ C $\frac{2}{6}, \frac{1}{3}$ D $\frac{3}{6}, \frac{1}{2}$

8. A gallon of punch is how many cups of punch?   16 cups

9. Estimate the difference when $2.95 is subtracted from $12.05. $9

10. How many small cubes were used to make this big cube?   125 cubes

11. Use compatible numbers to estimate the products in parts a and b.
    a. Estimate the product of 252 × 2.   250 × 2 = 500
    b. Estimate the product of 23 × 3.   25 × 3 = 75

12. Multiply:
    a. 4 × 40   160
    b. 6 × 62   372

13. Trace this figure. Then draw two lines of symmetry.

14. (25 + 75) × 4   400
15. 75 × 3   225
16. 1,306 − 567   739
17. 708 × 6   4,248

18. Find each quotient:
    a. 56 ÷ 8   7
    b. 45 ÷ 9   5
    c. 63 ÷ 7   9

19. Find the lengths of these segments to the nearest centimeter:
    a. ─────────── 5 cm
    b. ───────────── 6 cm

20. Write a fraction with a numerator of 2 and a denominator of 5. Then use words to name the fraction you wrote. $\frac{2}{5}$; two fifths

Lesson 99   533

Written Practice (Continued)

Math Conversations
Independent Practice and Discussions to Increase Understanding

▶ **Problem 13**
Students may want to cut out the traced figure and explore different ways of folding it to find the answer. Some students might benefit from holding the traced figure up to a mirror to examine possible lines of symmetry.

Errors and Misconceptions

▶ **Problem 11**
Students may round the larger numbers in the usual fashion rather than rounding them to a compatible number. Remind students that compatible numbers should be close to the true number.

▶ **Problem 16**
Subtracting large numbers that require regrouping can cause problems for some students. Caution them to align the digits correctly to minimize their chances of making an error when regrouping.

Looking Forward

Using estimation to solve addition and multiplication problems and understanding the effects of estimating compared to the exact result prepares students for

• **Lessons 106 and 108,** estimating area.

Lesson 99   533

LESSON 100

Texas Essential Knowledge and Skills
(3.16)(A) make generalizations from sets of examples and nonexamples

Planning & Preparation

• Multiplying Dollars and Cents

Objectives
- Multiply dollar-and-cent amounts by one-digit numbers.
- Write and solve multiplication number sentences to solve problems.

Prerequisite Skills
- Multiply three-digit numbers by one-digit numbers.
- Learn the multiplication algorithm.
- Learn the multiplication facts through 12s.

Materials
Instructional Masters
- Power Up 100

Manipulative Kit
- Ruler
- Money manipulatives*

Teacher-provided materials
- Student money manipulatives*

   *optional

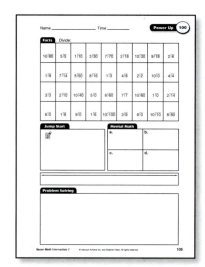

Power Up 100

Reaching All Special Needs Students

Special Education Students	At-Risk Students	English Learners	Advanced Learners
• Adaptations for Saxon Math	• Error Alert (TM) • Reteaching Masters	• English Learners (TM) • English Learner Handbook	• Extend the Problem (TM) • Online Activities

TM = Teacher's Manual

Math Language

Maintained
decimal point

English Learners
completely

534A *Saxon Math* Intermediate 3

Problem Solving Discussion

Problem

Look for a pattern in these figures. Which figure does *not* belong? Explain your answer.

Focus Strategies

💡 **Use Logical Reasoning**

🔺 **Find/Extend a Pattern**

Understand Understand the problem.

"What information are we given?"

We are shown four squares that contain both shaded and unshaded portions.

"What are we asked to do?"

We are asked to look for a pattern in the figures so that we can find which figure does not belong. We are also asked to explain our answer.

Plan Make a plan.

"How can we use the information we are given to solve the problem?"

We will *find a pattern* and *use logical reasoning* to find which figure does not fit the pattern.

Solve Carry out the plan.

"What do you notice about the shapes? Which figure does not belong?"

Teacher Note: Discuss student responses. If necessary, guide the discussion with the following questions.

"Look at the size of the shaded portion of each shape. What fractional part of each shape appears to be shaded?"

In figures A, C, and D, it appears that exactly one half of each square is shaded. In figure B, less than half of the square is shaded.

"Which figure does not belong? Explain your answer."

Figure B does not belong; figures A, C, and D each have one half of their area shaded. Less than half of figure B is shaded.

Check Look back.

"Is our answer reasonable?"

Yes, we found the figure that does not belong (Figure B). We also explained our answer.

"What problem solving strategies did we use, and how did they help us?"

We *used logical reasoning* to *find a pattern* among three of the four figures. By finding the pattern (shaded portion is one half of the square's area), we were able to name the figure that does not belong.

LESSON 100

Power Up

Facts
Distribute **Power Up 100** to students. See answers below.

Jump Start
Before students begin the Mental Math exercise, do these exercises as a class.

Mental Math
Encourage students to share different ways to mentally compute these exercises. Strategies for exercises are listed below.

a. Think 60 + 60 − 6
    54 + 60 = 60 + 60 − 6 = 120 − 6 = 114
b. Count by 6s
    6, 12, 18 faces
    Multiply
    3 × 6 = 18 faces

Problem Solving
Refer to **Problem-Solving Strategy Discussion**, p. 534B.

- **Multiplying Dollars and Cents**

Texas Essential Knowledge and Skills
(3.16)(A) make generalizations from sets of examples and nonexamples

Power Up

facts Power Up 100

jump start
- Count up by 6s from 0 to 72.
- Count up by 12s from 0 to 144.
- Write these amounts of liquid in order from least to greatest: 2 cups, 2 pints, 2 quarts, 2 gallons
    2 pints   2 gallons   2 cups   2 quarts
- Label the number line by tenths from 0 to 1. (Show these numbers: 0, $\frac{1}{10}$, $\frac{2}{10}$, $\frac{3}{10}$, $\frac{4}{10}$, and so on.) See student work.

mental math
a. **Number Sense:** 54 + 60   114
b. **Geometry:** One cube has 6 faces. How many faces do 3 cubes have? 18 faces
c. **Estimation:** Round 355 to the nearest ten. 360
d. **Patterns:** Find the missing number in this pattern: 108

| 144 | 132 | 120 | ___ | 96 | 84 |

problem solving
Look for a pattern in these figures. Which figure does *not* belong? Explain your answer.

B; sample: Figures A, C, and D each have one half of their area shaded. Less than half of Figure B is shaded.

Facts   Divide:

$10\overline{)80}$ = 8	$5\overline{)5}$ = 1	$1\overline{)10}$ = 10	$3\overline{)30}$ = 10	$7\overline{)70}$ = 10	$2\overline{)18}$ = 9	$10\overline{)30}$ = 3	$9\overline{)18}$ = 2	$2\overline{)6}$ = 3
$1\overline{)9}$ = 9	$7\overline{)14}$ = 2	$5\overline{)50}$ = 10	$8\overline{)16}$ = 2	$1\overline{)3}$ = 3	$4\overline{)8}$ = 2	$2\overline{)2}$ = 1	$10\overline{)0}$ = 0	$4\overline{)4}$ = 1
$3\overline{)3}$ = 1	$2\overline{)10}$ = 5	$10\overline{)40}$ = 4	$5\overline{)0}$ = 0	$6\overline{)60}$ = 10	$7\overline{)7}$ = 1	$10\overline{)60}$ = 6	$1\overline{)0}$ = 0	$2\overline{)14}$ = 7
$6\overline{)0}$ = 0	$1\overline{)8}$ = 8	$9\overline{)0}$ = 0	$1\overline{)6}$ = 6	$10\overline{)100}$ = 10	$3\overline{)9}$ = 3	$8\overline{)0}$ = 0	$10\overline{)10}$ = 1	$8\overline{)80}$ = 10

In Lesson 92 we learned how to multiply three-digit numbers. We multiply dollars and cents the same way. After multiplying, we must remember to write the dollar sign and decimal point in the product.

Example 1

Sergio bought 3 tickets to the movie for $7.75 each. What was the total price of the 3 tickets?

We can find the total by adding or by multiplying.

```
  2 1              2 1
  $7.75            $7.75
  $7.75          ×    3
+ $7.75          $23.25
 $23.25
```

Notice that we write the dollar sign and the decimal point as part of the answer. The total was **$23.25**.

Example 2

Gwen put 430 pennies in a jar. She estimated that she would need 6 times as many pennies to fill the jar completely. She multiplied $4.30 by 6 to estimate the value of the pennies in the jar. What is the product?

We multiply 0 pennies by 6. The product is 0, which we record. Next, we multiply 3 dimes by 6. The product is 18 dimes, which is 1 dollar and 8 dimes.

```
     1
  $4.30
×    6
    80
```

Finally, we multiply 4 dollars by 6. The product is 24 dollars. We add the dollar of dimes to make 25 dollars. The final product is **$25.80**.

```
     1
  $4.30
×    6
 $25.80
```

 Gwen estimated that the value of the pennies in the jar would be $25.80. How many pennies would be equal to $25.80? 2,580 pennies

Lesson 100   535

New Concept

Explanation
Students often make the mistake of leaving off the dollar sign or writing the decimal in the wrong place. Write the following on the board.

2 × $3.50 = 7.00
5 × $4.75 = $23.75
7 × $8.20 = $57.4

"Only one of these answers is correct. Which one is correct and what is wrong with the other two answers?" The second answer is correct. The first is wrong because it has no dollar sign. The last answer is also wrong because there is only one digit after the decimal point.

Explain to students that when writing money amounts, there will always be 2 digits after the decimal point, showing the cents. Remind students to estimate to determine if their final answer makes sense.

Example 2
Error Alert
When performing calculations with money amounts that end in zero, students may have a tendency to "lose" the zero. Call students' attention to the zero in the money amount $4.30.

Show students that a wrong answer of $2.58 could result from ignoring the zero. Encourage students to check the reasonableness of their answers to see if the number makes sense.

(continued)

Math Background

Students are introduced to multiplying dollars and cents in this lesson. This is their first experience with multiplying decimals. The second factor is a whole number in these problems. $3.27 × 3 is the same as 3 groups of $3.27. Decimal placement is simplified because there are always two places after the decimal to name the cents. However, in later grades, students will solve multiplication problems where both factors contain decimals. They will learn that the product should have the number of decimal places equal to the combined number of decimal places in both factors.

English Learners

Completely means all the way. Ask:

"Eight ounces of milk completely fills one cup. How many ounces of milk would you need to completely fill three cups?" 8 × 3 = 24 ounces of milk

Ask:

"What happens if you do not completely finish your homework one night?" samples: You might have to finish it the next morning; You might get a bad grade.

Have students draw a circle and completely shade it.

Lesson 100   535

New Concepts (Continued)

Lesson Practice

Guided Practice

Use these problems as guided practice to check the students' understanding of today's concept.

Problems a–d
Extend the Problems
Have students add one quarter to each money amount and solve the new problems.

a. 6 × $4.25 = $25.50
b. 7 × $3.30 = $23.10
c. 5 × $3.65 = $18.25
d. 4 × $2.60 = $10.40

Closure The questions below help assess the concepts taught in this lesson.

"What is different about multiplying dollars and cents and multiplying just dollars?" We need to add a decimal point to separate the dollars and cents when multiplying with dollars and cents.

"Where in the product do we put the decimal point?" We place it right before the last 2 digits, which name the cents.

Discuss real-world situations where multiplying dollars and cents might be helpful. Examples are given below.

• We buy three boxes of cereal which cost $2.89 each.
• Mr. Yan gives $6.75 to each of his four children for lunch on their field trip.

Written Practice

Math Conversations
Independent Practice and Discussions to Increase Understanding

Problem 8
Encourage students to check their math mentally by totaling the values of 4 dollars, 4 half dollars, and 4 pennies.

Problem 9 (Represent)
The word *mixed* implies that there is both a whole number and a fraction. Make sure students understand that the word *and* separates the whole number from the fraction.

(continued)

536   Saxon Math Intermediate 3

Lesson Practice   Find each product.
▸ a. 6 × $4.00 $24.00   ▸ b. 7 × $3.05 $21.35
▸ c. 5 × $3.40 $17.00   ▸ d. 4 × $2.35 $9.40

Written Practice   *Distributed and Integrated*

1. There were 32 books on the table arranged in four equal stacks. How many books were in each stack?   8
   (90)

2. Rob bought 5 bottles of juice for $2.29 per bottle. To estimate the total cost, Rob multiplied 5 × $2. Will Rob's estimate be greater than or less than the exact cost?   less than
   (99)

3. (Formulate) Change this addition to a multiplication and find the total: 5 × 4 qt = 20 qt
   (54)
   4 qt + 4 qt + 4 qt + 4 qt + 4 qt

4. (Model) The upper case letter A has one line of symmetry. Write the upper case letter B and show its line of symmetry.   sample: ---B---
   (Inv. 9)

5. Estimate the difference of $14.92 and $7.21. $8
   (96)

6. Use a pencil and a centimeter ruler to draw a segment 5 cm long. Then measure the segment with an inch ruler. The 5-cm segment is about how many inches long?   2 in.
   (79)

7. What is the geometric name for this solid? Describe the shape of its top and bottom faces.   cylinder; sample: Both faces are circles.
   (75, Inv. 8)

▸ 8. $1.51 × 4 $6.04
   (100)

▸ 9. (Represent) Use symbols to write the mixed number two and two thirds.   2⅔
   (46)

10. If 5 × 12 = 60, then what does 12 × 5 equal?   60
    (55)

536   Saxon Math Intermediate 3

11. Gia is looking at a map. Each inch on the map represents 5 miles. Two schools that are 4 inches apart on the map are how many miles apart?   20 mi
(Inv. 4)

12. What length is halfway between 1 inch and $1\frac{1}{2}$ inch? Use your ruler to find the answer. $1\frac{1}{4}$ in.
(35)

13. One plane ticket costs $415. Estimate the cost of two plane tickets. $800
(93)

14. Multiply:
(78, 97, 100)
   a. 5 × 40   200   b. 3 × 260   780   c. 4 × $1.25 $5.00

▶ 15. (Analyze) Use mental math to find the sum. Begin by adding pairs of compatible numbers.   250
(92)

$$50 + 90 + 110$$

16. Find each quotient:
(86)
   a. 32 ÷ 4   8   b. 48 ÷ 6   8   c. 63 ÷ 9   7

17. 4 × 60   240
(78)

18. 376 + 28 + 205 + 9   618
(24)

19. Find the missing number: $n - 3 = 15$ 18
(40)

20. If 1 box of pens has a mass of about 100 grams, then 6 boxes of pens have a mass of about how many grams? Make a table to help find the answer.   600 grams;
(98)

Grams	100 g	200 g	300 g	400 g	500 g	600 g
Boxes of Pens	1	2	3	4	5	6

Lesson 100   537

Written Practice (Continued)

Math Conversations
Independent Practice and Discussions to Increase Understanding

▶ **Problem 15** (Analyze)
The pair of compatible numbers, 90 + 110, should be added first.

$50 + 90 + 110 = 50 + 200 = 250$

Errors and Misconceptions

▶ **Problem 3**
In translating the addition into a multiplication, students may mistakenly include units with both factors. Explain to students that (quarts × quarts) equals square quarts, which does not make any sense.

▶ **Problem 12**
The wording of this question may lead some students to report half the *distance* from 1 inch to $1\frac{1}{2}$ inches, which is only $\frac{1}{4}$ inch. Remind students that length is measured from zero.

Looking Forward

Multiplying dollars and cents will be further developed in *Saxon Math Intermediate 4*.

Cumulative Assessments and Test-Day Activity

Assessments
Distribute **Power-Up Test 19** and **Cumulative Test 19** to each student. Have students complete the **Power-Up Test** first. Allow 10 minutes. Then have students work on the **Cumulative Test**.

Performance Task
The remaining class time should be spent on **Performance Task 10**. Students can begin the task in class or complete it during another class period.

Lesson 100   537

Flexible Grouping

Flexible grouping gives students an opportunity to work with other students in an interactive and encouraging way. The choice for how students are grouped depends on the goals for instruction, the needs of the students, and the specific learning activity.

Assigning Groups

Group members can be randomly assigned, or can be assigned based on some criteria such as grouping students who may need help with a certain skill or grouping students to play specific roles in a group (such as recorder or reporter).

Types of Groups

Students can be paired or placed in larger groups. For pairing, students can be assigned partners on a weekly or monthly basis. Pairing activities are the easiest to manage in a classroom and are more likely to be useful on a daily basis.

Flexible Grouping Ideas

Lesson 91, Example 1
Materials: paper

Have students form pairs to discuss multiplying three-digit numbers.
- Guide students through example 1. Then write a similar multiplication problem. Direct students to think about how to solve the problem.
- Students work in pairs to solve the problem. Volunteers share their solutions with the class.

Lesson 97, Example 1
Materials: paper

Divide students into groups of 4. The groups should be of varying abilities. Assign each student a number: 1, 2, 3, or 4.
- Guide students through example 1. Then write a similar multiplication problem on the board. Direct students to work together to solve the problem.
- Any member of the group should be able to present the answer to the problem and explain how they solved it.
- Call out a number from 1–4. Each member assigned that number must present his or her group's solution and strategy for solving the problem.

Lesson 98, Example 1
Materials: paper

Have students form pairs to extend the table in example 1.
- Direct students to think about how to extend the table to estimate the number of pennies in 10 kilograms.
- Students work in pairs to extend the table. Volunteers share their answers with the class.

Lesson 100, Example 2
Materials: paper

Students will work independently and then in pairs to reinforce multiplying with money.
- Guide students through example 2. Then instruct them to write their own word problem using money and multiplication.
- Have students form pairs and solve each other's multiplication problem.
- Students should explain their thinking to their partner.

INVESTIGATION 10

Texas Essential Knowledge and Skills
(3.1)(B) use place value to compare and order numbers through 9,999.
(3.14)(D) use tools such as real objects to solve problems.
(3.16)(B) explain the solution process.

Planning & Preparation

• Evaluating Estimates

Objectives
- Evaluate a group of estimates to find the best one by comparing them to the actual count.
- Discuss methods for evaluating estimates.

Prerequisite Skills
- Estimate the number of pennies in a penny jar by multiplying a three-digit number by a one-digit number.
- Estimate the number of pennies in a penny jar using weight or mass.

Materials

Instructional Masters
- Lesson Activity 31

Teacher-provided materials
- Penny jar from Lesson 91
- "First Estimate" envelope
- "Last Estimate" envelope
- Small cup or measuring scoop*
- Penny rolls or notebook paper*
  optional

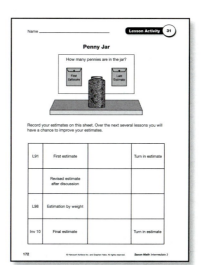
Lesson Activity 31

Differentiated Instruction

Reaching All Special Needs Students

Special Education Students	At-Risk Students	English Learners	Advanced Learners
• Adaptations for Saxon Math	• Reteaching Masters	• English Learner Handbook	• Extend the Problem (TM) • Online Activities

TM=Teacher's Manual

Math Language

Maintained	English Learners
estimate	evaluate

Investigation 10   538B

INVESTIGATION 10

Evaluating Estimates

In this investigation, students will learn to evaluate estimates of large totals first by determining if the estimate is reasonable, and then by counting the actual number.

Discussion
Remind students what they learned in Lesson 99 by asking,

"**What method did we learn in Lesson 99 for evaluating estimates?**" sample: We determined whether the estimate was greater than or less than the actual answer based on whether we rounded up or down.

Math Conversations
Independent Practice and Discussions to Increase Understanding

Problem 1
Explain to students that Ian assumed that each page in the lesson had about the same number of words as the page he used to count.

"**What things might make pages have different numbers of words?**" samples: If there are pictures or diagrams on some pages; If the page he counted was shorter or longer than the other pages.

"**If the page Ian counted was like the other five pages in the lesson, should Ian's estimate be greater than or less than the actual number of words in the lesson?**" sample: Since he rounded up, the estimate should be greater than the actual number of words.

Problem 3
Have students find the difference between each estimate and the actual count. Then have them compare the differences to determine which estimate was closest.

Activity
Students will need to use the class penny jar from Lesson 91 and the copies of **Lesson Activity 31** on which they have been recording their estimates. Paper rolls for wrapping pennies are also used while counting.

Problem 4
Before students make their final estimate, remind them of the strategies that were previously used to estimate the number of pennies:

- estimation by volume
- estimation by weight

INVESTIGATION 10

Texas Essential Knowledge and Skills
(3.1)(B) use place value to compare and order numbers through 9,999.
(3.14)(D) use tools such as real objects to solve problems.
(3.16)(B) explain the solution process.

Focus on
- **Evaluating Estimates**

In Lesson 99 we learned one way to evaluate estimates we make. In this investigation, we will talk about other ways to evaluate estimates, and we will evaluate the estimates we made on **Lesson Activity 31**.

Ian counted 198 words on one page of his science lesson.

1. How could he estimate the number of words in the whole lesson if it is six pages long? sample: He could round 198 to 200 and multiply 200 × 6 to estimate the number in the whole lesson.

Jerry, Talia, and Ian each estimated the number of words in the entire lesson. Their estimates are shown below:

Student	Estimate
Ian	1,200
Jerry	1,300
Talia	1,000

2. How can they find who made the closest estimate?

   The students counted the words on all six pages of the science lesson and found that there are 1,245 words altogether.

   2. sample: They could count the number of words in the lesson and compare their estimates to the actual total.

3. Whose estimate was closest?   Ian

Evaluating Estimates

In this activity, we will count the pennies in the penny jar we first saw in Lesson 91 and compare the estimates we made on **Lesson Activity 31** to the actual number of pennies.
See student work.

4. Before counting pennies, make your last estimate of the number of pennies in the jar. Record the estimate on your activity sheet. Also write your name and last estimate on a piece of scrap paper and give it to your teacher.

English Learners

In this investigation, to **evaluate** means to see how close an estimate is to being right or good.

Say:

"**Sam estimated that $38 + $22 is about $70. Evaluate his estimate.**"
sample: Sam's answer was $10 more than the correct answer because $38 + $22 = $60.

Ask:

"**You often evaluate things to decide if they are right for you or if you like them. What are some things you might evaluate?**"
samples: food, games, movies, clothes

Have students evaluate a movie they have seen recently.

7. With the class, sort the numbers in the "First Estimate" envelope until you find the closest estimate to the actual count.
8. Repeat the sorting for the "Last Estimate."
9. Which collection of estimates is closer to the actual count, the first estimate or the last estimate?
10. Look at **Lesson Activity 31.** Which one of your estimates was closest to the actual count?
11. **Justify** How do you decide which number is closest?
12. Which estimation strategy helped you improve your estimate the most?

Estimating Capacity

Materials: Two containers of different sizes, measuring cup, water or rice

Do this activity in a small group or as a class.

1. For each container, estimate the total number of cups of rice or water each will hold.
2. Fill a measuring cup to the one-cup level and pour the contents into one of the containers. Repeat until the container is full. How many cups were needed?
3. How does the number of cups compare to the estimate you made?
4. Estimate how much more or less the second container will hold compared to the first container.
5. Fill a measuring cup to the one-cup level and pour the contents into the second container. Repeat until the container is full. How many cups were needed?
6. How does the number of cups compare to the estimate you made?
7. How many more or less cups does the second container hold than the first container? How does this number of cups compare to the estimate you made for step 4?

Looking Forward

Evaluating estimates prepares students for:
- **Lessons 106 and 108,** estimating area.

Problem 5
You may want to have students work in groups of three or four to do the counting. Using a small cup or measuring scoop is a good way to quickly divide up the pennies between the groups.

If you do not have penny rolls, students can wrap rolls of 50 pennies in notebook paper. Suggest that students stack the extra pennies in groups of ten for easier counting.

Problem 9
To properly compare the estimates, ask two volunteers to go to the board and write all of the first estimates and all of the last estimates in ordered lists. This will highlight how the range of estimates changed. Ideally, the range in the list of last estimates will be "zeroing in" on the actual total.

Problem 12
Extend the Problem
Ask the following questions of individual students after having them respond to problem **12.**

"Why do you think that estimation strategy worked better?" Answers will vary.

"What assumptions did you make for each estimation strategy and were these assumptions reasonable?" Answers will vary.

Activity
One container used for this activity should be about a quart size and the other container should be about a half-gallon size.

 **Closure** The questions below help assess the concepts taught in this lesson.

"How can we evaluate our estimate?" We can count to find the actual number. Then we can compare the two amounts to find whether our estimate is too high or too low.

"How could we estimate how tall a building is?" sample: We could measure the height of one floor. Then we could multiply that number by the number of floors in the building to get an estimate.

Discuss real-world situations where estimating might be helpful. Examples are given below.

- Yuri is running a marathon and thinks he can run 2 miles in 15 minutes. He wants to estimate how long the 26-mile marathon will take him.
- We want to guess the number of marbles in a jar to win a prize at the school carnival.

SECTION 11 OVERVIEW

Lesson Planner

Lesson	New Concepts	Materials	Resources
101	• Dividing Two-Digit Numbers	• Manipulative kit: rulers	• Power Up 101
102	• Sorting		• Power Up 102
103	• Ordering Numbers Through 9,999	• Manipulative kit: rulers	• Power Up 103
104	• Sorting Geometric Shapes	• Manipulative kit: geosolids	• Power Up 104
105	• Diagrams for Sorting		• Power Up 105
Cumulative Assessment			• Cumulative Test 20 • Power-Up Test 20 • Test-Day Activity 10
106	• Estimating Area, Part 1	• Manipulative kit: rulers	• Power Up 106
107	• Drawing Enlargements	• Small-grid transparencies • Pictures	• Power Up 107 • Lesson Activities 23 and 32
108	• Estimating Area, Part 2	• Inch and centimeter transparency grids	• Power Up 108 • Lesson Activities 23 and 33
109	• Points on a Grid	• Manipulative kit: rulers	• Power Up 109
110	• Dot-to-Dot Design	• Manipulative kit: rulers	• Power Up 110 • Lesson Activity 34
Cumulative Assessment			• Cumulative Test 21 • Power-Up Test 21 • Performance Task 11
Inv. 11	• Planning a Design		• Lesson Activity 36

 All resources are also available on the Resources and Planner CD.

Additional Resources

- Instructional Masters
- Reteaching Masters
- Resources and Planner CD
- Calculator Activities
- Assessment Guide
- Performance Tasks
- Instructional Transparencies
- Answer Key CD
- Power Up Workbook
- Written Practice Workbook

LESSONS 101–110, INVESTIGATION 11

Math Highlights

Enduring Understandings — The "Big Picture"

After completing Section 11, students will understand that:

- the same set of objects, shapes, or numbers can be sorted in different ways, depending on the attributes chosen.
- an object, shape, or number can be placed into more than one group according to the rules.
- the area of an irregular shape can be estimated using standard square units.
- a location on a grid can be named using coordinates.

Essential Questions

- How can we sort objects, shapes, and numbers?
- How can an object, shape, or number be part of more than one group?
- How can we count partially filled squares on a grid to estimate area?
- How do coordinates tell us how many spaces to move to the right and up on a grid?

Math Content Highlights	Math Processes Highlights

Number Sense
• **Dividing Two-Digit Numbers** Lesson 101
• **Sorting** Lessons 102, 104, 105
• **Comparing and Ordering Numbers** Lesson 103
 	
Algebraic Thinking
 	
Geometry and Measurement
• **Estimating Area** Lessons 106, 108
• **Using a Grid to Draw Enlargements** Lesson 107
• **Finding Points on a Grid** Lesson 109
• **Using Coordinates to Draw Designs** Lessons 110, Inv. 11
	Problem Solving
	• **Strategies**
	  – Draw a Picture or Diagram Lessons 105, 106
	  – Find or Extend a Pattern Lessons 101, 102, 109
	  – Make an Organized List Lesson 102
	  – Use Logical Reasoning Lesson 104
	  – Work Backwards Lessons 107, 110
	  – Write a Number Sentence or an Equation Lessons 101, 103, 106, 107, 108
	• **Real-World Applications** Lessons 102, 108
	
	Communication
	• **Analyze** Lessons 105, 108
	• **Classify** Lesson 104
	• **Connect** Lesson 110
	• **Explain** Lessons 102, 108, 109
	• **Justify** Lesson 104
	
	Connections
	• **Math to Math** Lessons 105, 109
	• **Math and Other Subjects**
	  – Math and Geography Lessons 103, 108, 109, 110
	  – Math and Science Lesson 108
	  – Math and Sports Lessons 106
	
	Representation
	• **Model** Lessons 102, 104
	• **Represent** Lessons 107, 108, 110
	• **Manipulative Use** Lessons 103, 105, 108, 109

SECTION 11

Differentiated Instruction

Support for differentiated instruction is included with each lesson. Specific resources and features are listed on each lesson planning page. Features in the Teacher's Manual to customize instruction include the following:

Teacher's Manual Support

Alternative Approach	Provides a different path to concept development. *Lessons 103, 105, 108, 109*
Manipulative Use	Provides alternate concept development through the use of manipulatives. *Lessons 101–103, 105–108*
Flexible Grouping	Provides suggestions for various grouping strategies tied to specific lesson examples. *TM page 592 A*
Inclusion	Provides ideas for including all students by accommodating special needs. *Lessons 101, 102, 104–107, 109*
Math Language	Provides a list of new and maintained vocabulary words along with words that might be difficult for English learners. *Lessons 101–110, Inv. 11*
English Learners	Provides strategies for teaching specific vocabulary that may be difficult for English learners. *Lessons 101–110, Inv. 11*
Errors and Misconceptions	Provides information about common misconceptions students encounter with concepts. *Lessons 101–106, 108–110, Inv. 11*
Extend the Example	Provides additional concept development for advanced learners. *Lessons 101, 102, 105*
Extend the Problem	Provides an opportunity for advanced learners to broaden concept development by expanding on a particular problem approach or context. *Lessons 101–106, 109*
Early Finishers	Provides additional math concept extensions for advanced learners at the end of the Written Practice. *Lessons 104–110*

Additional Resources

The following resources are also available to support differentiated instruction:
- Adaptations for Saxon Math
- English Learner Handbook
- Online Activities
- Reteaching Masters

Technology

Student Resources
- Student Edition eBook
- Calculator Activities
- Online Resources at www.SaxonMath.com/Int3Activities
  — Real World Investigations *Lesson 105*
  — Online Activities *Lessons 101–110, Inv. 11*
  — Online Calculator Activity *Lesson 101*

Teacher Resources
- Resources and Planner CD
- Test and Practice Generator CD
- Monitoring Student Progress: eGradebook CD
- Teacher Manual eBook CD
- Answer Key CD
- Adaptations for Saxon Math CD
- Online Resources at www.SaxonMath.com

LESSONS 101–110, INVESTIGATION 11

Cumulative Assessment

The assessments in Saxon Math are frequent and consistently placed to offer a regular method of ongoing testing.

Power-Up Test: Allow no more than ten minutes for this test of basic facts and Problem Solving skills.

Cumulative Test: Next administer this test, which checks mastery of concepts in previous lessons.

Test-Day Activity and Performance Task: The remaining class time can be spent on these activities. Students can finish the Test-Day Activity for homework or complete the extended Performance Task in another class period.

After Lesson 105

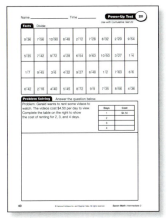
Power-Up Test 20

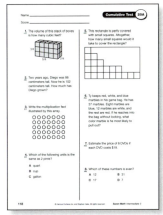
Cumulative Test 20

Test-Day Activity 10

After Lesson 110

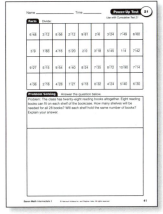
Power-Up Test 21

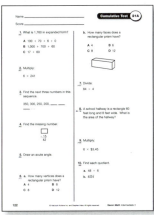
Cumulative Test 21

Performance Task 11

Evidence of Learning — What Students Should Know

By the conclusion of Section 11, students should be able to demonstrate the following competencies:

- Solve and record multiplication problems and use number sentences to solve/record division problems. **TEKS (3.4)(B, C)**
- Identify, describe, classify, and compare geometric figures using formal geometric vocabulary. **TEKS (3.8)**
- Identify lines of symmetry in figures. **TEKS (3.9)(C)**
- Use standard units to find the perimeter, area, or volume of a shape. **TEKS (3.11)(A, B, F)**
- Use data to describe the likelihood of events as compared to other events. **TEKS (3.13)(C)**
- Make generalizations from patterns or sets of examples and nonexamples. **TEKS (3.16)(B)**

Reteaching

Students who score below 80% on assessments may be in need of reteaching. Refer to the Reteaching Masters for reteaching opportunities for every lesson.

Section Overview 11   540D

SECTION 11

Benchmarking and Tracking Standards

Benchmark Tests

Benchmark Tests correlated to lesson concepts allow you to assess student progress after every 20 lessons. An End-of-Course Test is a final benchmark test of the complete textbook. The Benchmark Tests are available in the Assessment Guide.

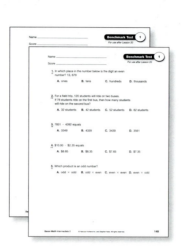

Monitoring Student Progress: eGradebook CD

To track TEKS mastery, enter students' scores on Cumulative Tests and Benchmark Tests into the Monitoring Student Progress: eGradebook CD. Use the report titled *Benchmark Standards Report* to determine which TEKS were assessed and the level of mastery for each student. Generate a variety of other reports for class tracking and more.

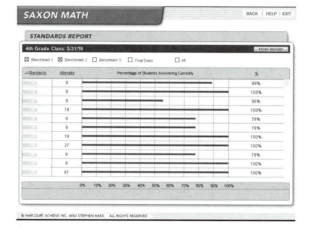

Test and Practice Generator CD

Test items also available in Spanish.

The Test and Practice Generator is an easy-to-manage benchmarking and assessment tool that creates unlimited practice and tests in multiple formats and allows you to customize questions or create new ones. A variety of reports are available to track student progress toward mastery of the TEKS throughout the year.

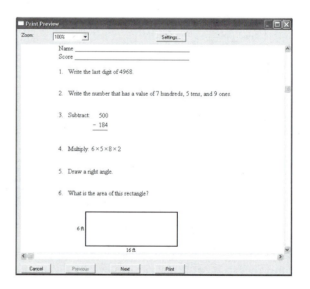

Northstar Math offers you real time benchmarking, tracking, and student progress monitoring.

Visit **www.northstarmath.com** for more information.

540E   *Saxon Math* Intermediate 3

LESSONS 101–110, INVESTIGATION 11

Content Trace

Lesson	New Concepts	Practiced	Assessed	Looking Forward
101	• Dividing Two-Digit Numbers	Lessons 101, 102, 103, 105, 106, 107, 108, 109, 110	Test 21	Saxon Math Intermediate 4
102	• Sorting	Lessons 102, 103, 108, 109	Test 21	Lessons 103, 104, 105
103	• Ordering Numbers Through 9,999	Lessons 103, 107, 108, 109, 110	Test 21	Saxon Math Intermediate 4
104	• Sorting Geometric Shapes	Lesson 110	Test and Practice Generator	Lesson 105
105	• Diagrams for Sorting	Lesson 107	Test and Practice Generator	Saxon Math Intermediate 4
106	• Estimating Area, Part 1	Lesson 106	Test and Practice Generator	Lessons 107, 108
107	• Drawing Enlargements	Lesson 107	Test and Practice Generator	Saxon Math Intermediate 4
108	• Estimating Area, Part 2	Lesson 108	Test and Practice Generator	Saxon Math Intermediate 4
109	• Points on a Grid	Lesson 109	Test and Practice Generator	Lessons 110, Inv. 11
110	• Dot-to-Dot Design	Lesson 110	Test and Practice Generator	Inv. 11
Inv. 11	• Planning a Design	Investigation 11	Test and Practice Generator	Saxon Math Intermediate 4

Section Overview 11 540F

LESSON 101

Planning & Preparation

• Dividing Two-Digit Numbers

Objectives
- Learn an algorithm for dividing two-digit numbers by a one-digit number using pencil and paper.
- Write and solve division number sentences to solve word problems.

Prerequisite Skills
- Model dividing by a one-digit number with pictorial models and concrete objects.
- Use pencil and paper to write division number sentences.
- Draw arrays to model dividing by a one-digit number.

Materials

Instructional Masters
- Power Up 101

Manipulative Kit
- Ruler
- Color tiles*

Teacher-provided materials
- Index cards*

    *optional

Texas Essential Knowledge and Skills

(3.4)(B) solve/record multiplication problems (up to two digits times one digit)

(3.4)(C) use number sentences to record the solutions to division problems

(3.6)(A) extend geometric patterns to make predictions and solve problems

(3.6)(C) identify patterns in related multiplication and division sentences (fact families)

(3.15)(D) explain/record observations using technology

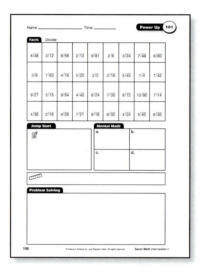

Power Up 101

Reaching All Special Needs Students

Special Education Students	At-Risk Students	English Learners	Advanced Learners
• Inclusion (TM) • Adaptations for Saxon Math	• Error Alert (TM) • Reteaching Masters	• English Learners (TM) • English Learner Handbook	• Extend the Example (TM) • Extend the Problem (TM) • Online Activities

TM = Teacher's Manual

Math Language

Maintained	English Learners
quotient	handful

540G Saxon Math Intermediate 3

Problem Solving Discussion

Problem

The number 10 is a triangular number because 10 objects can be arranged in the shape of a triangle. Notice how the number of objects in each row of the triangle increases:

```
•              1 dot
• •            2 dots     1 + 2 + 3 + 4 = 10
• • •          3 dots
• • • •        4 dots
```

Use this pattern to find the number of dots in a triangular shape with 8 rows of dots.

Focus Strategies

 Find/Extend a Pattern

 Write a Number Sentence

Understand — *Understand the problem.*

"What information are we given?"

We are shown a diagram of 10 dots arranged in a triangular pattern. The diagram divides the triangle into 4 rows of dots and shows how many dots are in each row.

"What are we asked to do?"

We are asked to use the pattern to find how many dots would be in a triangular shape with 8 rows of dots.

Plan — *Make a plan.*

"What problem solving strategy can we use?"

We can *write a number sentence* to *extend the pattern* shown in the diagram.

Solve — *Carry out the plan.*

"What pattern do you see in the triangular arrangement of dots?"

If we start at the top of the triangular arrangement, we find that each row has one dot more than the row above it. The first row has 1 dot, the second row has 2 dots, the third row has 3 dots, and so on.

"What number sentence can we write to find the number of dots in a triangular shape with 8 rows of dots?"

$1 + 2 + 3 + 4 + 5 + 6 + 7 + 8 = 36$ dots

Check — *Look back.*

"Did we complete the task?"

Yes, we used a pattern to find that there are 36 dots in a triangular shape with 8 rows of dots.

"Is our answer reasonable?"

Yes. We see in the diagram that there would be 10 dots in the top four rows of the triangular shape. The fifth through eighth rows would contain $5 + 6 + 7 + 8 = 26$ dots. Ten dots in the top four rows plus 26 dots in the next four rows is 36 dots altogether.

"What problem solving strategies did we use, and how did they help us?"

We *found a pattern* in the number of dots in the rows of the triangle. Then we *extended the pattern* to *write a number sentence* to find the total number.

Alternate Strategy

Draw a Picture or Diagram

Students may solve the problem by drawing a diagram and then counting the dots. Ensure that students who use this strategy are careful to use 1 dot in the first row, 2 dots in the second row, 3 dots in the third row, and so on.

LESSON 101

Power Up

Facts
Distribute **Power Up 101** to students. See answers below.

Jump Start
Before students begin the Mental Math exercise, do these exercises as a class.

Mental Math
Encourage students to share different ways to mentally compute these exercises. Strategies for exercises are listed below.

b. Add Tens, Then Add Ones
8 tens + 4 tens = 12 tens = 120
3 + 7 = 10
120 + 10 = 130

c. Multiply 7 times 12
7 × 12 = 84
Count by 12s
12, 24, 36, 48, 60, 72, 84

Problem Solving
Refer to **Problem-Solving Strategy Discussion**, p. 540H.

LESSON 101

• Dividing Two-Digit Numbers

Texas Essential Knowledge and Skills
(3.4)(B) solve/record multiplication problems (up to two digits times one digit)
(3.4)(C) use number sentences to record the solutions to division problems
(3.6)(A) extend geometric patterns to make predictions and solve problems
(3.6)(C) identify patterns in related multiplication and division sentences (fact families)
(3.14)(D) explain/record observations using technology

Power Up

facts Power Up 101

jump start Count up by halves from 5 to 10.
Count up by fourths from 4 to 6.

Write a multiplication and division fact family using the numbers 8, 4, and 32. $8 \times 4 = 32; 4 \times 8 = 32; 32 \div 4 = 8; 32 \div 8 = 4$

Draw a $3\frac{1}{4}$-inch segment on your worksheet. Then make it $2\frac{1}{4}$ inches longer. What is the total length of the segment? $5\frac{1}{2}$ in.

mental math
a. **Number Sense:** 98 − 39   59
b. **Number Sense:** 83 + 47   130
c. **Calendar:** How many months are in 7 years?   84
d. **Algebra:** This table shows costs for bookmarks at the school fair. How much do 5 bookmarks cost?   55¢

Bookmark	1	2	3	4	5
Cost	11¢	22¢	33¢	44¢	

problem solving
The number 10 is a triangular number because 10 objects can be arranged in the shape of a triangle. Notice how the number of objects in each row of the triangle increases:

• 1 dot
• • 2 dots
• • • 3 dots
• • • • 4 dots

1 + 2 + 3 + 4 = 10

Use this pattern to find the number of dots in a triangular shape with 8 rows of dots.   36

540   *Saxon Math* Intermediate 3

Facts   Divide:

$6\overline{)48}$ = 8	$3\overline{)12}$ = 4	$8\overline{)56}$ = 7	$2\overline{)12}$ = 6	$9\overline{)81}$ = 9	$2\overline{)6}$ = 3	$3\overline{)24}$ = 8	$7\overline{)49}$ = 7	$6\overline{)60}$ = 10
$3\overline{)9}$ = 3	$7\overline{)63}$ = 9	$4\overline{)16}$ = 4	$5\overline{)20}$ = 4	$2\overline{)0}$ = 0	$3\overline{)18}$ = 6	$5\overline{)45}$ = 9	$1\overline{)4}$ = 4	$7\overline{)42}$ = 6
$9\overline{)27}$ = 3	$5\overline{)15}$ = 3	$9\overline{)54}$ = 6	$4\overline{)40}$ = 10	$8\overline{)24}$ = 3	$7\overline{)35}$ = 5	$8\overline{)72}$ = 9	$10\overline{)90}$ = 9	$7\overline{)14}$ = 2
$4\overline{)36}$ = 9	$2\overline{)16}$ = 8	$4\overline{)28}$ = 7	$7\overline{)21}$ = 3	$9\overline{)18}$ = 2	$8\overline{)32}$ = 4	$4\overline{)24}$ = 6	$5\overline{)40}$ = 8	$6\overline{)30}$ = 5

540   Saxon Math Intermediate 3

New Concept

Visit www.
SaxonMath.com/
Int3Activities
for a calculator
activity.

To sort a number of objects into equal groups, we can divide. In previous lessons, we learned how to divide using pictures, manipulatives, and the multiplication table. In this lesson, we will learn how to divide two-digit numbers using pencil and paper.

Think about how to answer the question in the following story:

Dan has a stack of 90 baseball cards. He wants to put the cards into a photo album. Each page of the album can hold 6 cards. How many pages can he fill?

As Dan begins putting 6 cards on each page of the photo album, the number of cards in the stack becomes less and less.

$$\begin{array}{r} 90 \\ -6 \text{ cards on first page} \\ \hline 84 \\ -6 \text{ cards on second page} \\ \hline 78 \\ -6 \text{ cards on third page} \\ \hline 72 \end{array}$$

We could continue subtracting 6 cards until all the cards have been put into the album. A faster way to subtract the same number over and over is to divide. Here is how we can write the division:

$6\overline{)90}$

First, we look at the digit in the tens place. We think, "How many groups of 6 are there in 9?"

$6\overline{)90}^{\,1}$

○○○○○○ ○○○

We see that we can make 1 group of 6. So we write a 1 above the 9.

We also see that we have 3 circles left over. We show this by subtracting 6 from 9.

$$\begin{array}{r} 1 \\ 6\overline{)90} \\ -6 \\ \hline 3 \end{array}$$

Lesson 101 541

New Concept

Active Learning

To help prepare students for this lesson, have them review some of the concepts of division. First, ask students to write a division problem using the numbers 3, 10, and 30. 30 ÷ 10 = 3 or 30 ÷ 3 = 10

Next, have students complete the multiplication and division fact family for these numbers.
30 = 10 × 3   30 = 3 × 10
30 ÷ 10 = 3   30 ÷ 3 = 10

Ask students to write two division number sentences to describe the problem involving Dan's baseball cards. Give students a moment to write their number sentences down before showing the sentences on the board.
90 ÷ 6 = P and 90 ÷ P = 6

Ask two volunteers to go to the board and complete the fact family by writing the remaining two multiplication facts.
6 × P = 90 and P × 6 = 90

"If you look along the 6 row of a multiplication table, do you see the number 90?" no

"What is the multiplication fact for the largest number you see?" 6 × 12 = 72

Explain that the number of pages Dan can fill with his baseball cards must be more than 12 because only 72 cards fit on 12 pages with six cards per page. Ask students if anyone can think of a way, besides division, to solve the problem. samples: Count by 6s from 72 to 90 to find a total of 15 sixes; Subtract 72 from 90 to get 18 and then keep subtracting 6.

(continued)

Math Background

Students are beginning to learn the long-division algorithm in this lesson. The importance of memorizing multiplication facts becomes more apparent as the division becomes more complex. The long-division algorithm incorporates division, multiplication, and subtraction in a prescribed sequence of steps. Fluency in each of these operations is necessary for accurate and efficient long division. In later grades, division will become even more complex with the introduction of remainders and multi-digit divisors.

New Concept (Continued)

Example 1
Manipulative Use

Have students model this problem using 48 color tiles. Students divide the tiles into groups of 3 and count the number of groups.

Extend the Example

Students may wonder why they should solve division problems using the pencil-and-paper algorithm when they can use pictures, manipulatives, or a multiplication table instead. Inform them that this method is the easiest to use for dividends that are larger than 2 digits. To make this point, write the division problem below on the board and have students help you solve it using the division algorithm.

456,789 ÷ 3 = 152,263

Discuss with students why the algorithm is quicker than other methods.

(continued)

Next, we bring down the digit in the ones place.

$$\begin{array}{r} 1 \\ 6\overline{)90} \\ -6\downarrow \\ \hline 30 \end{array}$$

We think, "How many groups of 6 are there in 30?"

$$\begin{array}{r} 15 \\ 6\overline{)90} \\ -6 \\ \hline 30 \end{array}$$

We see that we can make 5 groups of 6. So we write a 5 in the quotient.

We also see that there are no circles left over. We show this by subtracting 30 from 30.

$$\begin{array}{r} 15 \\ 6\overline{)90} \\ -6 \\ \hline 30 \\ -30 \\ \hline 0 \end{array}$$

The quotient is 15. This means that Dan can fill 15 pages. We can be sure we are correct by multiplying 6 × 15.

$$\begin{array}{r} 3 \\ 15 \text{ pages} \\ \times 6 \text{ cards per page} \\ \hline 90 \text{ cards} \end{array}$$

Formulate Write another story problem for the division 6)90. See student work.

Example 1

Maria is putting a collection of 48 postcards into a photo album. Each page can hold 3 postcards. How many pages can she fill?

We can find the number of pages Maria can fill by dividing 48 by 3. We find that the number of pages is **16**. To make sure our answer is correct, we multiply:

$$\begin{array}{r} 16 \\ 3\overline{)48} \\ -3\downarrow \\ \hline 18 \\ -18 \\ \hline 0 \end{array}$$

$$\begin{array}{r} 1 \\ 16 \text{ pages} \\ \times 3 \text{ postcards per page} \\ \hline 48 \text{ postcards} \end{array}$$

Inclusion

Family Division

Some students will have difficulty remembering the sequence of steps for the division algorithm. Have them make a card with this mnemonic: Dad, Mother, Sister, Brother.

Materials: index cards

Dad	- Divide
Mom	- Multiply
Sister	- Subtract
Brother	- Bring down

• Write the mnemonic above on the board and have students copy it on their cards.

• Write this division problem on the board and practice using the steps: 5)70

Step 1: Divide 7 by 5 $\dfrac{1}{5\overline{)70}}$

Step 2: Multiply 1 × 5 $\begin{array}{r}1\\5\overline{)70}\\5\end{array}$

Step 3: Subtract 5 from 7 $\begin{array}{r}1\\5\overline{)70}\\-5\\\hline 2\end{array}$

Step 4: Bring down the 0 $\begin{array}{r}1\\5\overline{)70}\\-5\downarrow\\\hline 20\end{array}$

Example 2

Rob has a handful of nickels that total 80¢. How many nickels does Rob have?

To find the number of nickels, we divide 80 by 5. We find that Rob has **16 nickels**. We can multiply or quickly count by 5s to 80 to be sure that 16 nickels is 80¢.

$$\begin{array}{r} 16 \\ 5\overline{)80} \\ -5\downarrow \\ \hline 30 \\ -30 \\ \hline 0 \end{array}$$

Lesson Practice

a. To display his rock collection Juan glues 5 rocks on each card. How many cards does he need for 75 rocks? 15 cards

b. Shelley collected 54 shells that she will store in plastic bags. If she puts 3 shells in each bag, how many bags of shells will she have? 18 bags

c. If 76 horn players line up in 4 rows, how many players will be in each row? 19 horn players

Written Practice — Distributed and Integrated

1. Hanna arranged 36 books in stacks of nine books each. How many stacks of books did Hanna make? 4 stacks
   (90)

2. **Analyze** Lora wants to buy 3 folders for $2.39 each. She has $8. Estimate the total price of all three folders using compatible numbers. Does Lora have enough to pay for all three folders?
   (94, 99)
   $7.50; yes

3. $78 \div 6$ 13
   (101)

4. $54 \div 3$ 18
   (101)

5. Find the missing number: $24 - w = 3$ 21
   (40)

6. Use a pencil and a ruler to draw a segment 4 inches long. Measure the segment with a metric ruler. A 4-inch segment is about how many centimeters long? 10 cm
   (35, 79)

7. **Conclude** Simon began counting by hundreds:
   (2, 32)
   "100, 200, 300, 400, 500, …"

   What will be the fifteenth number Simon says? 1,500

Lesson 101   543

 **English Learners**

A **handful** is the amount of small objects that can fit in your hand. Ask:

"If you had two handfuls of color tiles, about how many would you have?" about 30–40

Ask:

"What else do we often grab in handfuls?" samples: rice, coins, erasers, grapes

Have students estimate how many 1-inch cubes would be in a handful. Have one student grab a handful of cubes out of a box and then count the cubes.

New Concept (Continued)

Example 2
Clarify for students that division by 5 is used because a nickel is equal to 5¢.

Lesson Practice

Guided Practice
Use these problems as guided practice to check the students' understanding of today's concept.

Problem a
Alternate Method
Students can solve this problem by thinking in terms of coins. Three quarters make 75¢. Students should see that five nickels make one quarter, so $5 \times 3 = 15$ nickels make three quarters, or 75¢. $75 \div 5 = 15$, so 15 cards are needed.

 Closure The questions below help assess the concepts taught in this lesson.

"When we divide, what are we really doing?" We are sorting or separating a number of things into equal groups.

"Explain the steps to divide 92 by 4 and show the math." Ask, "How many 4s are in 9?" Write a 2 above the 9, multiply $2 \times 4 = 8$, and write the answer underneath the 9. Subtract $9 - 8 = 1$ and bring down the 2. Ask, "How many 4s are in 12?" and write the 3 above the 2. Multiply $4 \times 3 = 12$ and write the answer below the 12. Subtract $12 - 12 = 0$ to show that there is nothing left over.

Written Practice

Math Conversations
Independent Practice and Discussions to Increase Understanding

Problem 2 **Analyze**
Students can round $2.39 to $2.50. Three folders at $2.50 each totals $7.50, which is less than the $8 Lora has. Since the price was rounded up, the estimated price was higher than the actual price, so Lora has plenty of money.

(continued)

Lesson 101   543

Written Practice (Continued)

Math Conversations
Independent Practice and Discussions to Increase Understanding

Problem 18
Extend the Problem

"What is the difference between the estimate and the actual sum? Is the estimate higher or lower?" The estimate is 4¢ lower.

Problem 19
Students can use their fraction manipulatives to help them see the comparisons.

Problem 20 Multiple Choice
Test-Taking Strategy

Students should look at the number after the equal sign and see that it is less than one of the numbers in the operation, so the operation will be either subtraction or division. Choices **A** and **C** can be eliminated. Students can easily see that $24 - 2 = 22$ and eliminate choice **B**. That leaves only choice **D**.

Errors and Misconceptions

Problem 16
Students may try to draw the other half of the circle to show symmetry.

Encourage students to trace the semicircle so that they can cut out the shape and fold it in half to show its line of symmetry.

---

8. **Formulate** Write two multiplication facts and two division facts
(86) using the numbers 8, 4, and 32. $8 \times 4 = 32$; $4 \times 8 = 32$; $32 \div 4 = 8$; $32 \div 8 = 4$

9. What length is halfway between $1\frac{1}{4}$ inches and $1\frac{3}{4}$ inches? $1\frac{1}{2}$ in.
(35)

10. A bike shop bought four *Midas Mountaineer* bicycles from the
(60, 97) factory for $248 each. What was the total cost of the four bikes? $992

11. Draw a square with sides $\frac{1}{2}$ inch long. Then trace around the
(35, 58) square with your pencil. How far is it around the square?
See student work; 2 in.

12. Marlinda is putting photos in a family album. She places
(90) 36 photos equally on 6 pages. How many photos does she place on each page?   6 photos

13. How many small cubes were used to build this
(72) rectangular solid?   54 cubes

14. From 1492 to 1992 was how many years?   500 years
(39)

15. Multiply:
(84, 100)
   a. 6×24 144   **b.** $5 \times \$2.30$ $11.50

16. Half of a circle is also called a semicircle. Copy this
(Inv. 7) semicircle and show its line of symmetry.

sample:

17. Find each quotient.
(86)
   a. $28 \div 7$ 4   **b.** $56 \div 8$ 7   **c.** $36 \div 9$ 4

▶ 18. Estimate the sum of $5.17, $6.98, and $8.89. $21
(96)

▶ 19. Write these fractions in order from least to greatest: $\frac{1}{2}, \frac{2}{3}, \frac{3}{4}$
(49)

   $\frac{3}{4}$ $\frac{1}{2}$ $\frac{2}{3}$

▶ 20. **Multiple Choice** Which symbol goes in the box: $24 \square 2 = 12$?   D
(86)
   A +   **B** −   **C** ×   **D** ÷

Looking Forward

Dividing two-digit numbers will be further developed in *Saxon Math Intermediate 4*.

LESSON 102

Texas Essential Knowledge and Skills
(3.15)(A) explain/record observations using words
(3.16)(A) make generalizations from sets of examples and nonexamples

Planning & Preparation

• Sorting

Objectives
- Look at groups of sorted objects and determine the rule used for sorting.
- Add objects to sorted groups based on the rules used for sorting.
- Sort a group of objects according to given rules.

Prerequisite Skills
- Use informal language to describe mathematical situations.
- Identify numbers as even or odd.

Materials
Instructional Masters
- Power Up 102

Manipulative Kit
- Pattern blocks*

  *optional

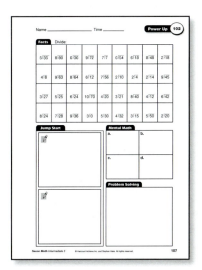

Power Up 102

Reaching All Special Needs Students

Special Education Students	At-Risk Students	English Learners	Advanced Learners
• Inclusion (TM) • Adaptations for Saxon Math	• Error Alert (TM) • Reteaching Masters	• English Learners (TM) • English Learner Handbook	• Extend the Example (TM) • Extend the Problem (TM) • Online Activities

TM = Teacher's Manual

Math Language

Maintained	English Learners
even numbers odd numbers	rule

Lesson 102   545A

LESSON 102

Problem Solving Discussion

Problem

A *palindrome* is a number or word that is the same whether it is written forward or backward. The word "noon" is a palindrome. The number 11 is also a palindrome. Predict the number of two-digit palindromes that are between the numbers 10 and 100. Then list the palindromes to check your prediction.

Focus Strategies

 Find/Extend a Pattern

 Make an Organized List

Understand *Understand the problem.*

"What information are we given?"

A palindrome is a number or word that is the same whether it is written forward or backwards.

"What are we asked to do?"

We are asked to predict the number of two-digit palindromes that are between the numbers 10 and 100. Then we are asked to list those numbers.

Plan *Make a plan.*

"What problem solving strategies will we use?"

We will *look for a pattern* to predict the number of palindromes between 10 and 100. Then we will check our prediction by *making an organized list*.

Solve *Carry out the plan.*

"Are there any palindromes between 10 and 20?"

Yes, the number 11.

"Are there any palindromes between 20 and 30?"

Yes, the number 22.

"Are there any palindromes between 30 and 40?"

Yes, the number 33.

"What pattern do we see?"

There is one palindrome for the 10s, one for the 20s, one for the 30s, and so on.

"How many palindromes do you predict to find between 10 and 100?"

Teacher Note: Discuss predictions with students.

"What are the two-digit palindromes between 10 and 100?"

We can find the two-digit palindromes by counting from 1 to 9 and repeating the digits. There are 9 palindromes; they are 11, 22, 33, 44, 55, 66, 77, 88, and 99.

Check *Look back.*

"Does our answer match your prediction?"

Teacher Note: Discuss student responses.

"Are our answers reasonable?"

Yes, it makes sense that there are 9 palindromes between 10 and 100, because a two-digit palindrome can be made with each of the digits from 1 to 9.

545B   *Saxon Math* Intermediate 3

LESSON 102

• Sorting

Texas Essential Knowledge and Skills
(3.15)(A) explain/record observations using words
(3.16)(A) make generalizations from sets of examples and nonexamples

Power Up

facts Power Up 102

jump start
- Count up by 11s from 0 to 132.
- Count up by 5s from 9 to 59.
- Write these fractions in order from least to greatest: $\frac{1}{4}, \frac{1}{3}, \frac{1}{2}, \frac{4}{5}$

  $\frac{1}{3} \quad \frac{1}{4} \quad \frac{4}{5} \quad \frac{1}{2}$

- A pair of shin guards costs $2.89. Marcy wants to buy 3 pairs. Write a number sentence to estimate the cost of the 3 pairs altogether. $3 \times \$3 = \$9$

mental math

a. **Measurement:** Which of these units would you most likely use to measure the amount of lemonade in a glass?
   ounces
   ounces   pounds   gallons   feet

b. **Number Sense:** 40 + 35 + 7   82

c. **Number Sense:** 480 − 110   370

d. **Time:** It is afternoon. The first clock shows the time the spelling bee began. The second clock shows the time the bee ended. How many minutes did the spelling bee last?
   45 min

problem solving
A *palindrome* is a number or word that is the same whether it is written forward or backward. The word "noon" is a palindrome. The number 11 is also a palindrome.

LESSON 102

Power Up

Facts
Distribute **Power Up 102** to students. See answers below.

Jump Start
Before students begin the Mental Math exercise, do these exercises as a class.

Mental Math
Encourage students to share different ways to mentally compute these exercises. Strategies for exercises are listed below.

a. **Units of Capacity**
   Both ounces and gallons measure amounts of liquid. One cup can hold 8 ounces while a gallon holds 16 cups. Ounces is the best unit since gallons is too large.

c. **Subtract Hundreds, Then Tens**
   4 hundreds − 1 hundred = 3 hundreds
   8 tens − 1 ten = 7 tens
   3 hundreds and 7 tens equals 370.

Problem Solving
Refer to **Problem-Solving Strategy Discussion**, p. 545B.

Facts   Divide:

7 5)35	10 8)80	6 6)36	8 9)72	1 7)7	9 6)54	3 6)18	6 8)48	9 2)18
2 4)8	7 9)63	8 8)64	2 6)12	8 7)56	5 2)10	2 2)4	7 2)14	5 9)45
9 3)27	5 5)25	4 6)24	7 10)70	5 4)20	7 3)21	5 8)40	3 4)12	7 6)42
3 8)24	4 7)28	4 9)36	0 3)0	6 5)30	8 4)32	5 3)15	10 5)50	10 2)20

New Concept

Real-World Connection

Provide students with some concrete examples of sorting in a real-world context.

"Grocery stores sort their products so that similar items can be found in the same place. Students often sort their supplies so that pencils are together, erasers are together, and paper is together."

Ask students to provide some examples of their own and list them on the board. As a class, discuss the possible sorting rules for each example. samples: sort books according to type, sort pencils from pens, sort girls from the boys

▶ Example 1

Ask students to identify some other ways that Sharon could sort her buttons into different groups.

samples: She could choose to arrange her buttons by size, shape, or color.

Have students choose one of their suggestions and develop the rule.

sample: Group 1 will be for round buttons, Group 2 will be for square buttons, and Group 3 will be for triangular buttons.

Error Alert

When sorting items, it is important to follow the specified rule because more than one rule can apply to the items being sorted.

(continued)

Predict the number of two-digit palindromes that are between the numbers 10 and 100. Then list the palindromes to check your prediction. 9 palindromes: 11, 22, 33, 44, 55, 66, 77, 88, 99

New Concept

People who have collections usually organize their collections in a logical way. They sort their collections by deciding what is similar and what is different.

Example 1

Sharon collects buttons. She has sorted the buttons into three groups. What rule does Sharon use to sort the buttons? In which group will she place the new button?

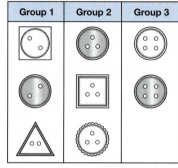

We look at the buttons in each group to see what is the same. We look at the buttons in different groups to see what is different. We see that the buttons in the same group have the same number of holes, and that the buttons in different groups have a different number of holes.

Sharon puts a button in Group 1 if it has 2 holes.

She puts a button in Group 2 if it has 3 holes.

She puts a button in Group 3 if it has 4 holes.

So, Sharon will place the **new button in Group 2**.

Math Background

Sorting may seem like a basic skill that students learned in kindergarten. However, sorting and classifying will remain integral parts of pattern recognition and geometry well beyond third grade math. To find the next term in a sequence, students find the rule that makes the pattern predictable. They sort numbers into two groups: those that follow the rule and those that don't follow the rule. They learn to make generalizations based on examples and nonexamples. Geometric figures can be sorted or classified according to rules based on attributes such as number of sides or types of angles. Classification will become more refined as students learn more attributes and properties of geometry.

Example 2

Sort the following numbers into two groups: even numbers and odd numbers.

26, 73, 54, 49, 31, 80

All even numbers end with a ones digit that is even. We make two lists.

Even numbers: 26, 54, 80

Odd numbers: 73, 49, 31

List List five more numbers that belong in the even numbers group. List five more numbers that belong in the odd numbers group. *See student work.*

Lesson Practice

sample: The numbers in Group A are multiples of 10. The numbers in Group B are not multiples of 10.

a. Describe the sorting rule for the numbers in these two groups.

Group A: 10, 60, 40, 20, 70

Group B: 12, 23, 74, 31, 58

b. Jill has a collection of action figures. Describe some ways she could sort the figures. *sample: Sort into "good guys" and "bad guys"; Sort by which movie or TV show they represent.*

Written Practice — Distributed and Integrated

1. (90) Twenty-four children separated into three teams with an equal number of children on each team. How many children were on each team? **8 children**

2. (88, 102) **Classify** Sort these numbers into two groups: even numbers and odd numbers. *Even: 98, 82, 90, 86; Odd: 75, 23, 43, 11*

   75, 23, 98, 43, 82, 11, 90, 86

3. (92) (275 + 375) − 200 **450**

4. (87) **Analyze** The recipe called for one cup of milk. If the recipe is doubled, how many pints of milk should be used? **1 pint**

5. (35, 47) Use your pencil and a ruler to draw a segment $\frac{2}{4}$ of an inch long. What is another fraction name for $\frac{2}{4}$ of an inch? $\frac{1}{2}$ in.

Lesson 102   547

Find the Rule

Some students may need more experience with sorting and classifying. Guide them through this hands-on activity.

Materials: 20 pattern blocks per student

- Instruct students to sort their tiles into two groups based on a rule.
- Have students trade places with a partner and identify each other's sorting rule.

 English Learners

A **rule** tells you what you should do or how you should do something. Divide the class into two groups, one group that wears shorts/skirts and the other that wears long pants. Ask:

"What rule did I use to sort these two groups?" See student work.

Ask:

"What are our classroom rules? Our school rules?" See student work.

Ask students to discuss and compare rules at home.

New Concept (Continued)

Example 2

Remind students that even numbers are the numbers we say when we count by 2s from zero: 0, 2, 4, 6, 8. Odd numbers are the numbers we say when we skip count by 2s starting with the number one: 1, 3, 5, 7, 9.

Extend the Example

Have advanced learners determine a new rule that divides the numbers into two equal but different groups. Students should list the numbers in each group. *sample: Group 1 has numbers less than 50: 26, 31, 49. Group 2 has numbers greater than 50: 54, 73, 80.*

Lesson Practice

Guided Practice

Use these problems as guided practice to check the students' understanding of today's concept.

Problem a
Extend the Problem

Ask students to determine other rules to sort the numbers into two groups that are not equal. *samples: Sort even and odd numbers; Sort numbers greater than 50 from numbers less than 50; Sort numbers that start with an even number from numbers that start with an odd number.*

 Closure The questions below help assess the concepts taught in this lesson.

"What is sorting?" Dividing things into groups based on a rule.

"What can we sort?" samples: numbers, people, books, crayons, collections

Write the numbers 2, 7, 8, 13, 15, and 16 on the board or overhead.

"What are some ways we could sort these numbers?" samples: We could sort them into even and odd numbers; We could sort them into one-digit and two-digit numbers.

Discuss real-world situations where sorting might be helpful. Examples are given below.

- A mother has clothes in different sizes for both boys and girls.
- We want to organize our books into categories.

Lesson 102   547

Written Practice

Math Conversations
Independent Practice and Discussions to Increase Understanding

Problem 6 (Model)
Students should draw an array with only three columns and begin placing Xs in these columns until they have a total of 27. By counting the number of rows the 27 Xs fill, students can find the answer.

Problem 10 (Explain)
Help students visualize the problem by drawing a jar on the board or overhead and dividing it into four equal parts. Write "300 pennies" in the bottom part of the jar.

Problem 13
Point out that more than one sorting rule will correctly describe the two groups of numbers. An alternate rule is that the numbers in Group A are less than 10 while the numbers in Group B are 10 or more.

Errors and Misconceptions

Problem 20
Students may not notice that they need to account for *two* boxes of cereal in their calculation and mistakenly solve $3 + $5 = $8.

---

6. (Model) Draw an array of 27 Xs with 3 Xs in each row. How many Xs are in each column of your array?   See student work; 9
(57, 86)

7. Polly calculated that $3 \times (4 \times 5) = 60$. What is $(3 \times 4) \times 5$?   60
(92)

8. Write 875,632 in expanded notation.
(11)   800,000 + 70,000 + 5,000 + 600 + 30 + 2

9. What number is halfway between 300 and 600?   450
(33)

10. (Explain) Kiondre and John have two large jars that are the same size. One jar is full of pennies. The other jar has 300 pennies and is about $\frac{1}{4}$ full. How can Kiondre and John estimate the number of pennies in the jar that is full? Estimate the number of pennies in the full jar.   sample: They can multiply 300 × 4 to find the number of pennies in the full jar; 1,200 pennies
(91)

11. Randall has 3 extra large boxes of crayons. Each box contains 108 crayons. How many crayons does Randall have in all?   324 crayons
(60, 97)

12. $3 \times 5 \times 8$ 120
(77)

13. Describe the sorting rule for the numbers in these two groups.
(102)   sample: The numbers in Group A have one digit. The numbers in Group B have two digits.

Group A: 0, 1, 4, 5, 8

Group B: 10, 32, 35, 57, 79

14. From 1776 to 1826 was how many years?   50 years
(39)

15. Multiply:
(84, 100)   **a.** 7×14 98   **b.** $3 \times \$2.50$ $7.50

16. Estimate the cost of 7 sleeping bags for $78 each. $560
(93)

17. Find each quotient.
(86)   **a.** $30 \div 6$ 5   **b.** $40 \div 5$ 8   **c.** $64 \div 8$ 8

18. $76 \div 2$ 38
(101)

19. $81 \div 3$ 27
(101)

20. Cheryl bought a gallon of milk for $3.19 and two boxes of cereal for $4.89 each. Estimate the total cost of the three items. $13
(96)

 **Looking Forward**

Sorting items or numbers into different groups and finding a rule to sort similar items prepares students for

- **Lesson 103,** ordering numbers through 9,999.
- **Lesson 104,** sorting geometric shapes.
- **Lesson 105,** using diagrams for sorting.

LESSON 103

Planning & Preparation

• Ordering Numbers Through 9,999

Texas Essential Knowledge and Skills

(3.1)(B) use place value to order numbers through 9,999
(3.14)(A) identify the mathematics in everyday situations
(3.14)(C) select/develop an appropriate problem-solving plan/strategy, including working backwards to solve a problem

Objectives
- Order numbers through 9,999 using place value.
- Order numbers according to rules other than greatest to least or least to greatest.

Prerequisite Skills
- Describe the value of a digit in a number by its place value.
- Compare and order numbers through 999.

Materials
Instructional Masters
- Power Up 103

Manipulative Kit
- Ruler
- Base ten blocks*

Teacher-provided materials
- Grid paper*

optional

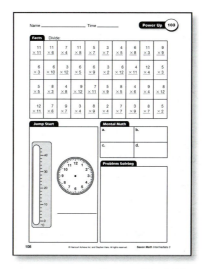

Power Up 103

Reaching All Special Needs Students

Special Education Students	At-Risk Students	English Learners	Advanced Learners
• Adaptations for Saxon Math	• Alternative Approach (TM) • Error Alert (TM) • Reteaching Masters	• English Learners (TM) • English Learner Handbook	• Extend the Problem (TM) • Online Activities

TM=Teacher's Manual

Math Language

Maintained
even numbers
odd numbers

English Learners
mail

Lesson 103   549A

LESSON 103

Problem Solving Discussion

Problem

Sera made up a riddle to tell people her age. She says that she is 14 years younger than the number of months in 2 years. How old is Sera?

Focus Strategy **Write a Number Sentence**

Understand Understand the problem.

"What information are we given?"

Sera is 14 years younger than the number of months in 2 years.

"What are we asked to do?"

We are asked to find Sera's age.

Plan Make a plan.

"What problem solving strategy can we use?"

We can *write a number sentence*.

Solve Carry out the plan.

"What prior knowledge do we have about the number of months in a year?"

There are 12 months in a year.

"How many months are in 2 years?"

There are 12 months + 12 months, or 24 months, in one year.

"Notice that Sera says she is '14 years younger' instead of '14 years older.' How can we use the word younger to know whether to add or to subtract?"

The word *younger* means we are looking for a number smaller than 24. So we will subtract 14 from 24. We write this number sentence:

$$24 - 14 = 10$$

We find that Sera is 10 years old.

Check Look back.

"Is our answer reasonable?"

Yes, there are 24 months in 2 years, so Sera is 14 years younger than 24 years old (10 years.)

"What problem solving strategy did we use, and how did it help us?"

We *wrote a number sentence* to solve the riddle.

Saxon Math Intermediate 3

LESSON 103

• Ordering Numbers Through 9,999

Texas Essential Knowledge and Skills
(3.1)(B) use place value to order numbers through 9,999
(3.14)(A) identify the mathematics in everyday situations
(3.14)(C) select/develop an appropriate problem-solving plan/strategy, including working backwards to solve a problem

Power Up

facts Power Up 103

jump start
Count up by odd numbers from 1 to 25.
Count up by even numbers from 2 to 30.

It is 19 minutes after 8 in the morning. Draw hands on your clock to show the time. Write the time in digital form. 8:19 a.m.

The temperature in the school library is 21°C. It is 14 degrees cooler on the playground. Mark your thermometer to show the temperature on the playground. 7°C

mental math
a. **Time:** The school lunch period lasts 35 minutes. Recess after lunch lasts 25 minutes. Altogether, how long are lunch and recess? 60 min or 1 hr

b. **Number Sense:** $3 \times 4 \times 4$ 48

c. **Money:** $3.30 − 99¢ $2.31

d. **Measurement:** Lindsey is making a lid for her jewelry box. The lid is 9 inches long and 5 inches wide. What is the area of the lid? 45 sq. in.

(5 in. by 9 in.)

problem solving
Sera made up a riddle to tell people her age. She says that she is 14 years younger than the number of months in 2 years. How old is Sera? 10 years old

---

LESSON 103

Power Up

Facts
Distribute **Power Up 103** to students. See answers below.

Jump Start
Before students begin the Mental Math exercise, do these exercises as a class.

Mental Math
Encourage students to share different ways to mentally compute these exercises. Strategies for exercises are listed below.
a. Think $10 + 25 + 25$
$35 + 25 = 10 + 25 + 25 = 50 + 10 = 60$
The time equals 60 minutes, or 1 hour.
b. Think $(3 \times 4) \times 4$
$(3 \times 4) \times 4 = 12 \times 4 = 48$

Problem Solving
Refer to **Problem-Solving Strategy Discussion**, p. 549B.

Lesson 103   549

Facts Multiply:

11 × 11 = 121	11 × 6 = 66	7 × 4 = 28	11 × 8 = 88	5 × 7 = 35	3 × 7 = 21	4 × 5 = 20	6 × 8 = 48	11 × 3 = 33	9 × 9 = 81
6 × 3 = 18	6 × 10 = 60	3 × 12 = 36	6 × 5 = 30	6 × 9 = 54	3 × 2 = 6	6 × 12 = 72	4 × 11 = 44	12 × 4 = 48	5 × 3 = 15
5 × 5 = 25	8 × 3 = 24	4 × 8 = 32	9 × 12 = 108	7 × 11 = 77	5 × 9 = 45	8 × 5 = 40	4 × 6 = 24	9 × 4 = 36	8 × 12 = 96
12 × 11 = 132	7 × 6 = 42	9 × 7 = 63	3 × 4 = 12	8 × 9 = 72	2 × 4 = 8	7 × 7 = 49	3 × 9 = 27	8 × 7 = 56	5 × 2 = 10

Lesson 103   549

New Concept

Instruction

Review the basics of ordering numbers. Point out to students that as we compare the digits with the greatest place value first, we compare from left to right. Draw a place-value chart on the board and write these numbers on it: 321; 3,210; 1,532. Beginning in the thousands place, have students identify the least number in each place as you write the numbers on the board in order from least to greatest. Make sure students understand that since 321 only has three digits, there is a zero in the thousands place.

Active Learning

Write each number from 0–9 on two small pieces of paper. Place all the papers in a bag or a box. Have a student draw three to four papers out of the bag. Let a different student arrange the digits to make a number. Continue with different students until you have four numbers. Write the numbers on a place-value chart on the board. As a class, list the numbers on the board from least to greatest and then from greatest to least.

Example 1
Alternate Method

Students can use grid paper or a table to list the three numbers with each digit in its proper position according to place value.

Example 2
Error Alert

When ordering 3- or 4-digit numbers that begin with the same digits, it is easy for students to confuse the digits being compared. Suggest that they write the numbers vertically in a column, aligning digits with the same place value, and then use two pieces of paper to cover up the digits not being compared. Students can also draw lines through digits in the same place value that are equal to avoid confusion.

(continued)

550 Saxon Math Intermediate 3

New Concept

We arrange numbers in order when we write or say the numbers from least to greatest (or from greatest to least). We use place value to help us order numbers.

Example 1

Write these numbers in order from least to greatest.

3,672   3,712   372

Writing the numbers in a column can help us order the numbers. We line up digits with the same place values.

Thousands	Hundreds	Tens	Ones
3	6	7	2
3	7	1	2
	3	7	2

We see that 372 is least. Both 3,672 and 3,712 have 3 in the thousands place; so we compare the digits in the hundreds place. Since 6 is less than 7, the order is:

372   3,672   3,712

Example 2

A mail carrier might arrange mail for a street using these two rules:

1. Order mail with even-numbered addresses from least to greatest.
2. Order mail with odd-numbered addresses from greatest to least.

Follow these two rules to arrange these "addresses" into an even numbered column and an odd-numbered column.

5327   5342   5353   5339   5352   5348

We start by sorting the addresses into an even-numbered group and an odd-numbered group.

Even: 5342, 5352, 5348
Odd: 5327, 5353, 5339

550 Saxon Math Intermediate 3

Math Background

In this lesson, students use their knowledge of place value to order numbers through the thousands place. The systematic approach taught in this lesson will apply to ordering larger numbers as students move into more advanced math classes. Students have been exposed to decimal numbers several times in this book through problems dealing with dollars and cents. Eventually, they will learn to order decimal numbers in the same way by comparing tenths, hundredths, thousandths, and so on.

English Learners

Mail is a letter, magazine, or package delivered to your home. Ask:

"If you received three letters one week and two the next, how much mail did you get altogether?" 5 pieces of mail

Ask:

"What are some things you have received in the mail?" Answers will vary.

Have students discuss a favorite piece of mail they received.

Then we order the even numbers in a column from least to greatest. Finally, we order the odd numbers in a column from greatest to least.

Even Addresses	Odd Addresses
5342	5353
5348	5339
5352	5327

Lesson Practice

a. The birth years in Roger's family are as follows:

1998   2002   1976   1974

Arrange these years from earliest to latest.   1974, 1976, 1998, 2002

b. In 2000, the population of Blanco County was 8,418. The population of Castro County was 8,285. The population of Archer County was 8,854. List the names of the 3 counties in order from least population to greatest.   Castro, Blanco, Archer

c. Robinson compared the price of a game at three different stores. Here are the prices:

$18.85 $19.25 $17.98

Arrange the prices in order from least to greatest.
$17.98, $18.85, $19.25

Written Practice   Distributed and Integrated

1. Burgess arranged twenty-four quarters into stacks with four quarters in each stack. How many stacks of quarters did Burgess form?   6 stacks
   (90)

2. Draw a polygon with six sides. What is the geometric name for the figure you drew?   See student work; hexagon
   (67)

3. 75 ÷ 5   15
   (101)

4. 88 ÷ 4   22
   (101)

5. Write an uppercase D and show its line of symmetry.   Sample:
   (Inv. 9)

6. Compare an inch ruler with a metric ruler. A 1-foot-long ruler is about how many centimeters long?   about 30 cm
   (35, 79)

Lesson 103   551

Alternative Approach: Using Manipulatives

Students may find it helpful to show the numbers being compared in expanded form using base ten blocks, as this provides more concrete visualization. Once students model the numbers, they should begin by comparing the largest values and working their way down. Have students practice by ordering the following numbers from least to greatest: 7,241; 7,219; 7,243.   least to greatest = 7,219; 7,241; 7,243

New Concept (Continued)

Lesson Practice

Guided Practice

Use these problems as guided practice to check the students' understanding of today's concept.

Problem a
Extend the Problem

"What does the listing of birth years of earliest to latest tell you?"   sample: the order of the members of Roger's family from oldest to youngest

"If Roger's family consists of his father, his mother, Roger, and his younger brother, in what year was Roger born?"   1998

Problem b

Encourage students to write the numbers in a column for comparison.

Closure   The questions below help assess the concepts taught in this lesson.

"What does it mean to order numbers?"
We arrange the numbers from least to greatest or from greatest to least.

"What helps you order?"   place value

"If I were ordering 2,752, 2,195, and 2,364 from greatest to least, which number would come first? Why?"   2,752 would come first because the numbers in the thousands place are the same, but 7 hundreds is more than 1 hundred or 3 hundreds.

Written Practice

Math Conversations
Independent Practice and Discussions to Increase Understanding

Problem 4
Tell students:

"The number 88 can be divided easily by 8, which is two times 4."

(continued)

Lesson 103   551

Written Practice (Continued)

Math Conversations
Independent Practice and Discussions to Increase Understanding

▶ Problem 10
Suggest that students write the numbers in a column with digits aligned according to place value. Once students know how a number compares to the others, they should write it in the proper place and then mark it out from its position in the column.

▶ Problem 16
Suggest that students draw rectangles for all faces of the rectangular prism. They should begin by drawing two congruent and overlapping squares for the cube and two congruent and overlapping rectangles for the prism. Encourage students to draw their shapes carefully to assist with the comparison.

▶ Problem 20
Point out that more than one sorting rule will correctly describe the two groups of numbers. An alternate rule is that the numbers in Group A are less than 100 while the numbers in Group B are 100 or more.

Extend the Problem
Have students sort the numbers into two new groups, one of even numbers and one of odd numbers.
Even numbers: 36, 48, 238, 374, 578
Odd numbers: 11, 25, 59, 125, 431

Errors and Misconceptions

▶ Problem 11
Watch for students who write the name for the sum as "one thousand, five hundred and ninety dollars." Remind students that the word *and* is not used in naming money amounts that do not involve coins.

---

7. There are 25 textbooks on the shelf. Can the books be separated into two equal stacks? no

8. 84 ÷ 7   12

9. 56 ÷ 8   7

▶ 10. Arrange these numbers from least to greatest: 2,398; 2,654; 2,913; 2,987
2,654   2,913   2,987   2,398

11. Use words to write the sum of $750 and $840.   one thousand, five hundred ninety dollars

12. Nadia collected 294 soda cans for a class recycling project. Raul collected about 3 times as many cans as Nadia collected. Estimate the number of cans Raul collected.   900 cans

13. Draw a rectangle that is one inch long and $\frac{1}{2}$ inch wide. Trace around the rectangle. How many inches is it around the rectangle?   See student work; 3 in.

14. Find the missing numbers:
  a. $6 + a = 24$ 18
  b. $6 \times c = 24$ 4

15. Multiply: $6 \times \$4.20$ $25.20

▶ 16. Draw a cube and a rectangular prism. How are the figures alike? How are they different?   See student work; sample: Both figures have six faces. Both figures have rectangular faces. sample: All six faces on the cube are the same size and shape, but the six faces of the rectangular prism are not.

17. Find each quotient.
  a. $27 \div 3$ 9
  b. $45¢ \div 5$ 9¢
  c. $\$36 \div 6$ $6

18. $10.00 − ($5.85 + 89¢) $3.26

19. Shaundra ran a 3-kilometer race. How many meters are in 3 kilometers?   3,000 m

▶ 20. Describe the sorting rule for the numbers in these two groups:
  Group A: 11, 25, 36, 48, 59
  Group B: 125, 238, 374, 431, 578
sample: The numbers in Group A are two-digit numbers. The numbers in Group B are three-digit numbers.

Looking Forward

Ordering numbers will be further developed in *Saxon Math Intermediate 4*.

LESSON 104

Planning & Preparation

• Sorting Geometric Shapes

Objectives
- Identify, classify, and sort two- and three-dimensional figures by their attributes.
- Use proper vocabulary and informal language to describe sorting rules.

Prerequisite Skills
- Look at groups of sorted objects and determine the rule used for sorting.
- Add objects to sorted groups based on the rules used for sorting.
- Sort a group of objects according to given rules.

Materials
Instructional Masters
- Power Up 104

Manipulative Kit
- Geosolids

Teacher-provided materials
- Flash cards of geometric figures*

optional

Texas Essential Knowledge and Skills

(3.8) identify/classify/describe two- and three-dimensional geometric figures by their attributes and compare them using formal vocabulary

(3.15)(A) explain/record observations using words

(3.16)(A) make generalizations from sets of examples and nonexamples

(3.16)(B) justify why an answer is reasonable and explain the solution process

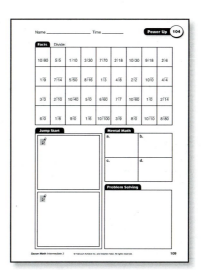

Power Up 104

Reaching All Special Needs Students

Special Education Students	At-Risk Students	English Learners	Advanced Learners
• Inclusion (TM) • Adaptations for Saxon Math	• Error Alert (TM) • Reteaching Masters	• English Learners (TM) • English Learner Handbook	• Extend the Problem (TM) • Early Finishers (SE) • Online Activities

TM=Teacher's Manual
SE=Student Edition

Math Language

Maintained	English Learners
polygon	curved

Lesson 104   553A

LESSON 104

Problem Solving Discussion

Problem

The kickoff to start the football game was at 1:00 p.m. During halftime, Tyrone looked at his watch and saw that it was 2:30 p.m.

Start of game   Halftime

What is a reasonable prediction for the time the football game will end? Explain how you made your prediction.

Focus Strategy **Use Logical Reasoning**

Understand Understand the problem.

"What information are we given?"

A football game started at 1:00 p.m. and it was 2:30 p.m. at halftime.

"What are we asked to do?"

We are asked to predict the ending time for the game and to explain our prediction.

Plan Make a plan.

"What problem solving strategy can we use to solve the problem?"

We can *use logical reasoning*.

Solve Carry out the plan.

"Who would like to share his or her prediction for when the game will end?"

Teacher Note: Discuss student predictions. If necessary, use the following questions to guide discussion.

"How much time passed from the start of the game to when Tyrone looked at his watch during halftime?"

From 1:00 to 2:30 is 1 hour 30 minutes, or $1\frac{1}{2}$ hours.

"Let's assume that the second half lasts the same amount of time as the first half. About what time would the game end?"

If the game ends $1\frac{1}{2}$ hours after 2:30 p.m., the game would end at 4:00 p.m. (One hour after 2:30 p.m. is 3:30 p.m., and 30 more minutes is 4:00 p.m.)

Check Look back.

"What is our reasoning for predicting 4:00 p.m. as the time the game will end?"

From the start of the game to halftime is $1\frac{1}{2}$ hours, so we can reasonably predict that it will take $1\frac{1}{2}$ hours from halftime to the end of the game.

"Are there other reasonable predictions for the time the game will end?"

Yes, we might say that any prediction from 3:30 p.m. to 4:30 p.m. is reasonable. We might predict a time slightly before or slightly after 4:00 p.m. because we do not know for certain that the second half will be as long as the first half.

553B   Saxon Math Intermediate 3

LESSON 104

• Sorting Geometric Shapes

Texas Essential Knowledge and Skills
(3.8) identify/classify/describe two- and three-dimensional geometric figures by their attributes and compare them using formal vocabulary
(3.15)(A) explain/record observations using words
(3.16)(A) make generalizations from sets of examples and nonexamples
(3.16)(B) justify why an answer is reasonable and explain the solution process

Power Up

facts — Power Up 104

jump start
- Count up by square numbers from 1 to 144.
- Count up by 10s from 9 to 99.
- Chris bought a book of maps for $12.90 plus $0.80 sales tax. He paid with a $20 bill. How much change should he receive? **$6.30**
- Write a multiplication and division fact family using the numbers 5, 9, and 45. **5 × 9 = 45; 9 × 5 = 45; 45 ÷ 9 = 5; 45 ÷ 5 = 9**

mental math
a. **Estimation:** Jerry will buy 4 bars of soap for 97¢ each. Estimate the total cost to the nearest dollar. **$4**
b. **Number Sense:** 900 − 450   **450**
c. **Number Sense:** 400 × 2   **800**
d. **Measurement:** How many quarts are in a gallon?   **4 qt**

problem solving
The kickoff to start the football game was at 1:00 p.m. During halftime, Tyrone looked at his watch and saw that it was 2:30 p.m.

Start of game

Halftime

What is a reasonable prediction for the time the football game will end? Explain how you made your prediction.
A reasonable prediction might be any time between 4:00 p.m. and 4:30 p.m. From the start of the game to halftime is 1½ hours, so we can predict that it will take about 1½ hours from halftime to the end of the game. Students might guess beyond 4:00 p.m. to account for extra time left in halftime.

Lesson 104   553

LESSON 104

Power Up

Facts
Distribute **Power Up 104** to students. See answers below.

Jump Start
Before students begin the Mental Math exercise, do these exercises as a class.

Mental Math
Encourage students to share different ways to mentally compute these exercises. Strategies for exercises are listed below.

a. **Round and Multiply**
   Round 97¢ to $1.
   4 × $1 = $4
d. **Think Double**
   2 quarts = $\frac{1}{2}$ gallon
   4 quarts = 1 gallon

Problem Solving
Refer to **Problem-Solving Strategy Discussion**, p. 553B.

Facts   Divide:

8 10)80	1 5)5	10 1)10	10 3)30	10 7)70	9 2)18	3 10)30	2 9)18	3 2)6	
9 1)9	2 7)14	10 5)50	2 8)16	3 1)3	2 4)8	1 2)2	0 10)0	1 4)4	
1 3)3	5 2)10	4 10)40	0 5)0	10 6)60	1 7)7	6 10)60	0 1)0	7 2)14	
0 6)0	8 1)8	0 9)0	6 1)6	10 10)100	3 3)9	0 8)0	1 10)10	10 8)80	

Lesson 104   553

New Concept

Instruction

Review by drawing the following shapes on the board: triangle, square, rectangle, parallelogram, pentagon, hexagon, octagon, and circle. Ask students to identify the shapes and describe their attributes.

"What are two characteristics that all of these shapes share?" They are all two-dimensional, flat shapes and are all closed figures.

Now draw a cube, a rectangular prism, a cone, and a cylinder on the board. Ask students to identify the shapes and describe their attributes.

"What characteristics do these shapes share?" sample: They are all three-dimensional shapes that take up space.

Ask students to determine a rule for dividing these new shapes into one group and the old shapes into another. Sort them into one group of flat figures and another that is three-dimensional.

"In what other way could we divide all of the shapes into two groups?" Sample: shapes with straight sides and shapes with one or more curved sides; shapes with a line of symmetry and shapes with no lines of symmetry

Example 1
Error Alert

Caution students against forming rules for sorting that are not exclusive for a given group of shapes. An example would be to sort shapes into two groups, one for shapes with straight edges and another for flat shapes. There are many shapes that qualify as both and could be placed in either group.

(continued)

New Concept

samples: All the shapes are closed shapes. Some shapes have curved sides and some only have straight sides. We could sort the shapes into polygons and non-polygons.

We sort or **classify** shapes by how they are alike or different. Look at the shapes below.

Discuss How are they alike? How are they different? How could we sort them into two different groups?

Example 1

Sort these figures into polygons and figures that are not polygons. Then describe your sorting rule.

We separate the figures into two groups.

Polygons   Not Polygons

Polygons are flat, closed shapes with straight sides. Shapes with curved sides are not polygons.

554   *Saxon Math* Intermediate 3

Math Background

One of the most common classifications for polygons is that of "regularity." A polygon is said to be regular if all of its sides are of equal length and all of its interior angles are equal. Thus, a square is a regular polygon while a rectangle with different length and width measurements is not. Similarly, an equilateral triangle is regular while a scalene triangle is not. Also, a hexagon is a figure with 6 sides and 6 angles. A regular hexagon has 6 sides of equal length, 6 interior angles of equal size, and 6 exterior angles of equal size.

English Learners

If something is **curved,** it is not straight. A circle, an oval, and a heart are made from curved lines. Ask:

"What other curved lines do you see in the classroom?" samples: edge of trash can, teacher's mug

Say:

"Draw a curved line on a blank piece of paper." See student work.

Have students write letters of the alphabet that have at least one curved line.

Example 2

These three-dimensional figures are sorted into two groups. Describe the sorting rule.

Solids

Group 1	Group 2

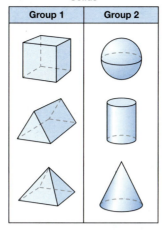

The solids in Group 1 have straight edges, and every face is a polygon. The solids in Group 2 have at least one curved surface.

Classify What is another rule we could use to sort these figures? *sample: solids that have one triangular face and solids that have no triangular faces*

Lesson Practice

a. Sort these polygons into two groups: triangles and quadrilaterals. *See student work.*

New Concept (Continued)

Example 2
Explain that another rule could be based on the number of vertices in each shape. The shapes in Group 1 have more than one vertex while the shapes in Group 2 have one or none.

Lesson Practice

Guided Practice
Use these problems as guided practice to check the students' understanding of today's concept.

Problem a
Extend the Problem
"What is another rule we could use that would sort these shapes into two different groups?" samples: We can sort based on whether or not the figure contains parallel sides; We can sort based on whether or not the figure contains lines of equal length.

(continued)

Lesson 104 555

Manipulative Use

Give each pair of students 6 geosolids and direct them to sort the figures into two groups based on a rule. Have each pair switch places with another pair and attempt to guess the other group's sorting rule. Remind students to use correct vocabulary to name the figures and describe their attributes.

Sorting Shapes

Some students will have difficulty naming geometric figures in pictures and identifying their attributes. This sorting activity will give them an opportunity to practice both skills.

Materials: premade flash cards with pictures of geometric figures on one side and names on the other

- Students work with a partner to name the figure on each flash card. They can look at the back of each card to self-check.
- After each group has named the shapes, they sort them and describe their sorting rule.

Lesson 104 555

New Concept (Continued)

Lesson Practice

Problem b Error Alert
Some students may have forgotten the definition of a prism. Review the definitions of the geometric solids students have learned about so far.

Closure The questions below help assess the concepts taught in this lesson.

"What are geometric shapes?" Polygons and rectangular solids are types of geometric shapes.

"What are some ways we can sort geometric shapes?" samples: closed or open shapes, polygons or solids, shapes with curved lines or without curved lines, shapes with a certain number of sides

Discuss real-world situations where sorting geometric shapes might be helpful. Examples are given below.

- A boy is building a block tower and wants to sort the different types of blocks.
- An art teacher has a box of construction paper cut-outs and wants to sort them according to their shape.

Written Practice

Math Conversations
Independent Practice and Discussions to Increase Understanding

Problem 4
Extend the Problem
"What is the difference between the estimate and the exact value? Is the estimate greater than or less than the exact value?"
a. $15; less than
b. $28; less than

(continued)

556   Saxon Math Intermediate 3

---

sample: The solids in Group 1 are prisms because they are the same at both ends and their other faces are rectangles. The solids in Group 2 are not prisms.

b. Describe how the solids in Group 1 are alike. Describe how the solids in Group 1 are different than the solids in Group 2.

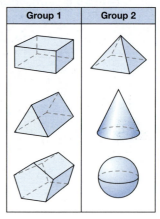

Written Practice — Distributed and Integrated

1. In Millie's backyard, 48 stalks of corn grow in 6 equal rows with an equal number of stalks in each row. How many stalks grow in each row?   8 stalks
(90)

2. Last year Kevin was 114 cm tall. This year he is 121 cm tall. How many centimeters did Kevin grow in a year?   7 cm
(39)

3. Draw an array of 20 dots with 4 dots in each column. How many dots are in each row?   5 dots
(57)

▶ 4. Estimate each answer by rounding each number to the nearest hundred dollars before you add or subtract.
(30)
   a. $396 + $419 $800
   b. $587 − $259 $300

5. Find the missing number: $18 - m = 3$ 15
(40)

6. How many grams equal one kilogram?   1,000 grams
(80)

556   Saxon Math Intermediate 3

▶ **7.** **Conclude** Simon began counting by thousands:
(2, 32)
1,000, 2,000, 3,000, 4,000, …

What will be the fifteenth number Simon says? Use words to write the answer.   15,000; fifteen thousand

▶ **8.** **Multiple Choice** Which of the following equals one quart?   C
(87)
A 3 cups   **B** 4 pints   **C** 2 pints   **D** 2 cups

9. If 56 ÷ 7 = 8, then what does 56 ÷ 8 equal?   7
(86)

10. This rectangle is partly covered with small squares. Altogether, how many small squares would cover the rectangle?   48
(63)

11. **Justify** Roderick has a bag of 10 marbles. There are 5 blue marbles. The rest of the marbles are red. Is drawing a red marble less likely, equally likely, or more likely than drawing a blue marble? How do you know?   equally likely; sample: There are 10 marbles. Five are blue. The rest are red, so five marbles are red (10 − 5 = 5). There are the same number of red and blue marbles, so drawing a marble of either color is equally likely.
(50)

12. A year is 365 days. Find the number of days in 4 years by multiplying 365 by 4. Then add one day for a leap year. Show your work.   See student work. 1461 days
(97)

13. (24 + 80) − 44   60
(92)

▶ **14.** **Model** Angela planted 24 flowers in 4 rows. How many flowers were in each row? Draw a picture to represent the problem.
(85)
6 flowers; See student work.

15. Multiply:
(100)
a. 5 × $0.24 $1.20   **b.** 4 × $0.24 $0.96

16. There are 70 crackers in each package. Each box contains 4 packages. How many crackers are in one box?   280 crackers
(78)

17. Find each quotient.
(86)
a. 36¢ ÷ 4   9¢   **b.** 36 ÷ 6   6   **c.** 35 ÷ 7   5

18. Write 6,877 in expanded form.   6,000 + 800 + 70 + 7
(32)

Lesson 104   557

Written Practice (Continued)

Math Conversations
Independent Practice and Discussions to Increase Understanding

Problem 7 Conclude
Students should see that counting by thousands is the same as counting by ones with three zeros added or with the word "thousands" added. So the fifteenth number would be 15 with three zeros attached or fifteen thousand.

Problem 8 Multiple Choice
Test-Taking Strategy
Since units of capacity are related by factors of two, students can mark out choice **A** because it is odd. Any remaining choices will have to be compared with one quart to determine which is the correct answer.

Problem 14 Model
Students should draw an array with four rows and begin placing circles (flowers) in these rows until they have a total of 24. By counting the number of columns the 24 circles fill, students can find the answer.

(continued)

Written Practice (Continued)

Errors and Misconceptions

Problem 19
Students may try to round to the nearest dollar instead of selecting a compatible number. Tell them that a compatible number should be close to the exact number, but easier to use when solving the problem.

Remind students that since there are 12 months in a year, Li read 12 books each year. Have students share the strategy they used to find how many books Li read in years.

---

19. Use compatible numbers to estimate the total price of 8 sandwiches for $2.56 each. $20.00
(94)

20. Multiply: 721 × 2   1,442
(97)

Real-World Connection

Li entered a reading contest every year for four years. He read one book each month for the first year. If he read the same number of books each year, how many books did he read in four years? 48 books

Sorting shapes according to a rule and recognizing a rule from a set of sorted shapes prepares students for

- **Lesson 105,** using diagrams for sorting.

LESSON 105

Planning & Preparation

• Diagrams for Sorting

Objectives
- Use circles to help sort groups of objects.
- Use Venn diagrams to sort groups of objects that have overlap.

Prerequisite Skills
- Identify, classify, and sort two- and three-dimensional figures by their attributes.
- Use proper vocabulary and informal language to describe sorting rules.
- Look at groups of sorted objects and determine the rule used for sorting.
- Sort a group of objects according to given rules.

Materials
Instructional Masters
- Power Up 105

Manipulative Kit
- Color tiles, counters, or money manipulatives*

Teacher-provided materials
- Handouts for the *Inclusion* activity*
- Yarn*

   *optional

Texas Essential Knowledge and Skills
(3.8) identify/classify/describe two-dimensional geometric figures by their attributes and compare them using formal vocabulary
(3.14)(A) identify the mathematics in everyday situations
(3.15)(A) record observations using pictures
(3.16)(A) make generalizations from sets of examples and nonexamples

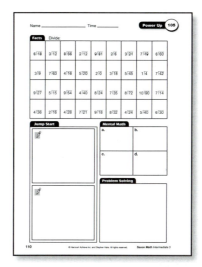

Power Up 105

Differentiated Instruction

Reaching All Special Needs Students

Special Education Students	At-Risk Students	English Learners	Advanced Learners
• Inclusion (TM) • Adaptations for Saxon Math	• Alternative Approach (TM) • Error Alert (TM) • Reteaching Masters	• English Learners (TM) • English Learner Handbook	• Extend the Example (TM) • Extend the Problem (TM) • Early Finishers (SE) • Online Activities

TM = Teacher's Manual
SE = Student Edition

Math Language
New
Venn diagram

English Learners
overlap

Lesson 105   559A

LESSON 105

Problem Solving Discussion

Problem

Twenty-three students are taking a field trip to the zoo. Each car can hold 4 students. How many cars will be needed for all 23 students? Will all the cars carry the same number of students? Explain your answer.

Focus Strategy  **Draw a Picture or Diagram**

Understand) Understand the problem.

"What information are we given?"

Twenty-three students will go on a field trip. Each car can hold 4 students.

"What are we asked to do?"

We are asked to find how many cars are needed and whether all the cars will carry the same number of students. We are also asked to explain our answer.

Plan) Make a plan.

"What problem solving strategy can we use?"

We can *draw a diagram*.

Solve) Carry out the plan.

"How can we draw a diagram to represent the situation in the problem?"

We can use dots for students and circles for cars. We place 4 dots inside each circle until we have placed 23 dots altogether.

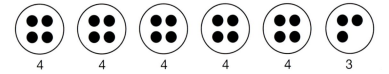

$4 + 4 + 4 + 4 + 4 + 3 = 23$ students

"Each circle stands for one car. How many cars are needed to take all the students on the field trip?"

We count the circles and find that 6 cars are needed.

"Will all the cars carry the same number of students?"

No, five cars will carry 4 students, and one car will carry only 3 students.

Check) Look back.

"Did we complete the task?"

Yes, we found how many cars will be needed for the field trip (6 cars), and we found that not all the cars will carry the same number of students. We explained that one car will carry only 3 students.

"Are our answers reasonable?"

Yes. This problem contains equal groups of 4 students. We know that 5 cars can hold 5×4 students $= 20$ students. A sixth car is needed to carry the other 3 students.

"What problem solving strategy did we use, and how did it help us?"

We *drew a diagram* to help us visualize the problem.

Alternate Strategy
Act It Out

Have students divide 23 color tiles into equal groups of 4 tiles and one group of 3 tiles to *act out* the problem.

LESSON 105

• Diagrams for Sorting

Texas Essential Knowledge and Skills
- (3.8) identify/classify/describe two-dimensional geometric figures by their attributes and compare them using formal vocabulary
- (3.14)(A) identify the mathematics in everyday situations
- (3.15)(A) explain and record observations using pictures and technology
- (3.16)(A) make generalizations from sets of examples and nonexamples

Power Up

facts Power Up 105

jump start
Count up by 3s from 0 to 45 and then back down to 0.
Count up by 9s from 0 to 108 and then back down to 0.

Write these years in order from earliest to latest: 1859, 1957, 1977, 1999
1977   1899   1957   1999

Draw a rectangular prism on your worksheet. How many vertices does a rectangular prism have? See student work; 8 vertices

mental math

a. **Fact Family:** Find the missing number in this fact family: 4

$5 \times \square = 20$ $20 \div \square = 5$

$\square \times 5 = 20$ $20 \div 5 = \square$

b. **Number Sense:** 687 − 200   487

c. **Measurement:** How many yards are equal to 9 feet?   3

d. **Number Sense:** Which point below represents the number $8\frac{1}{2}$?   H

problem solving
Twenty-three students are taking a field trip to the zoo. Each car can hold 4 students. How many cars will be needed for all 23 students? Will all the cars carry the same number of students? Explain your answer.   6 cars; no; sample: One car will carry only 3 students.

LESSON 105

Power Up

Facts
Distribute **Power Up 105** to students. See answers below.

Jump Start
Before students begin the Mental Math exercise, do these exercises as a class.

Mental Math
Encourage students to share different ways to mentally compute these exercises. Strategies for exercises are listed below.

b. Subtract the Hundreds
6 hundreds − 2 hundreds = 4 hundreds
687 − 200 = 487

c. Remember Conversions
3 feet = 1 yard, so 9 feet = 3 yards.
Think of Equal Groups
A yard is a group of 3 feet. Think, "9 feet can be divided into how many equal groups of 3 feet?" 9 ÷ 3 = 3

Problem Solving
Refer to **Problem-Solving Strategy Discussion,** p. 559B.

Facts   Divide:

8 ÷ 6)48	4 ÷ 3)12	7 ÷ 8)56	6 ÷ 2)12	9 ÷ 9)81	3 ÷ 2)6	8 ÷ 3)24	7 ÷ 7)49	10 ÷ 6)60
3 ÷ 3)9	9 ÷ 7)63	4 ÷ 4)16	4 ÷ 5)20	0 ÷ 2)0	6 ÷ 3)18	9 ÷ 5)45	4 ÷ 1)4	6 ÷ 7)42
3 ÷ 9)27	3 ÷ 5)15	6 ÷ 9)54	10 ÷ 4)40	3 ÷ 8)24	5 ÷ 7)35	9 ÷ 8)72	9 ÷ 10)90	2 ÷ 7)14
9 ÷ 4)36	8 ÷ 2)16	7 ÷ 4)28	3 ÷ 7)21	2 ÷ 9)18	4 ÷ 8)32	6 ÷ 4)24	8 ÷ 5)40	5 ÷ 6)30

New Concept

Instruction

This lesson introduces sorting circles and Venn diagrams. Since this is a new idea to students, try to connect it to examples of sorting in students' daily lives. Ask,

"What are some things that we have sorted in this class?" samples: money manipulatives, fraction circles, triangles

"What are some things that you sort at home?" samples: clothes, toys, game pieces, money, books

Example 1
Active Learning

Draw two large circles on the board and invite students to write the numbers in the correct circle. Students should follow along at their desks and draw the circles on their own paper. Continue by calling out additional numbers for students to place in the correct circle.

Discussion

"Suppose you were sorting clothes into dark colors and light colors, and you came to a shirt that was both black and white. Which pile would you put it in?" samples: both, neither, start a new pile

Tell students that there is a problem with sorting the black and white shirt because the black and white shirt actually belongs to both groups. Explain that since the black and white shirt has features common to both sorted piles, students might view it as overlapping a part of both piles.

"How could we place this shirt so that it looks like it is part of both piles?" sample: Move the piles close together and lay the shirt between the piles so that it is touching each pile.

Example 2
Instruction

Remind students what the multiples of 5 are by asking,

"What are 'multiples of 5'?" sample: The numbers you say when counting by 5s.

"Name the multiples of 5." 5, 10, 15, 20, 25, 30, …

(continued)

New Concept

We can use circles to help us sort collections of things.

Visit www.SaxonMath.com/Int3Activities for an online activity.

Example 1

Draw two circles. Label one circle "Even numbers" and the other circle "Odd numbers." Then write these numbers in the correct circles.

15, 26, 7, 14, 30, 21

We draw and label the circles and write the numbers.

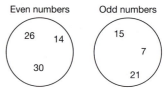

A **Venn diagram** is a special type of sorting circle. The circles in a Venn diagram overlap. The overlap part shows what the groups have in common.

Example 2

Copy the Venn diagram and write the following numbers in the correct parts of the circles.

15, 18, 20, 24, 25

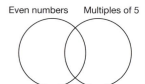

First, we sort the numbers into two groups.

Even Numbers	18, 20, 24
Multiples of 5	15, 20, 25

Notice that 20 belongs in both groups. On the Venn diagram, we write 20 in the space where the two circles overlap. Then we place the other numbers in the correct circle.

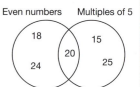

Math Background

Venn diagrams are named for John Venn (1834–1923), an English mathematician who used such diagrams to represent the relationships between sets. A Venn diagram is a valuable tool for comparing sets of objects. It provides a graphic representation of how members of a set are the same and how they are different. Two-circle Venn diagrams, as utilized in this lesson, can easily be extended to three-circles and more. In the case of three-circle Venn diagrams, we are attempting to sort items with three different characteristics rather than simply two.

English Learners

Objects **overlap** when part of one object covers part of the other object. Say:

"Take out two pieces of paper. Make them overlap. Make your math book overlap with your neighbor's book. Draw two overlapping circles on your paper." Students should follow directions.

Ask:

"What else might overlap?" samples: building materials like wood, tile, or metal; cloth used for sewing; shapes and colors in a painting

Have students draw shapes that overlap to make a design.

Example 3

Copy the Venn diagram and then draw the following polygons in the correct parts of the circle. One circle is labeled "P" for parallel sides and one circle is labeled "R" for right angle.

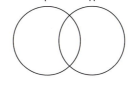

The triangle has a right angle but no parallel sides. The parallelogram has parallel sides but no right angles. Since the square has parallel sides and right angles, it is in both circles.

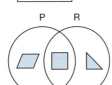

Analyze Where would you place an isosceles triangle in this diagram? *sample: outside both circles because it has no parallel sides or right angles*

Lesson Practice

a. Quadrilaterals   Triangles

a. Draw two circles that do not overlap. Label one circle "Quadrilaterals" and the other circle "Triangles." Then draw these shapes in the correct circles.

b. Q   R

b. Draw a Venn diagram. Label one circle "Q" for quadrilaterals and the other circle "R" for shapes that have a right angle. Then draw these shapes in the correct parts of the circles.

Written Practice — Distributed and Integrated

1. If each foot of molding costs 75¢, then what is the cost for each yard of molding? $2.25
   (100)

Lesson 105   561

New Concept (Continued)

Example 3
Extend the Example

Ask students where they would put a rectangle in this Venn diagram. *in the overlap region with the square*

Lesson Practice

Guided Practice

Use these problems as guided practice to check the students' understanding of today's concept.

Problem a

Before starting the solution, ask:

"What is the difference between a quadrilateral and a triangle?" A triangle is a polygon with three sides and a quadrilateral is a polygon with four sides.

Have students identify the four polygons shown. parallelogram, (equilateral) triangle, square, (right) triangle

Problem b
Instruction

Have students name the three polygons shown. quadrilateral, parallelogram, pentagon

Ask them to explain why they should use a Venn diagram for this problem instead of sorting circles. sample: Because some of the polygons are quadrilaterals and have right angles, so they belong in both groups. A Venn diagram can show this but sorting circles cannot.

 Closure The questions below help assess the concepts taught in this lesson.

"What is a Venn diagram?" two or more sorting circles

"What do the circles show us?" The circles show us which items are similar and which are different.

Draw a Venn diagram on the board or overhead. Label one side "Things that live in trees" and the other "Things with wings." List the following words near the Venn diagram: airplane, bird, squirrel, insects, butterfly

"Which circle would we put each item into, and which might go into both?" Things with wings: airplane, butterfly; Things that live in trees: squirrel; Overlap: bird, insect

Discuss real-world situations where using a Venn diagram might be helpful. Examples are given below.

- We want to show how many students are boys and have blue eyes in the school.
- A biologist makes a graph to show the animals which are both mammals and are nocturnal.

Inclusion

Sorting Circles (as individuals)

If students have difficulty understanding the concept of classification using a Venn diagram, provide them with these templates as a concrete visual model.

Materials: Worksheet with sorting circles and Venn diagrams for the examples and practice problems in this lesson. For the first few examples, fill in the labels and one or two numbers inside the circles. For the practice problems, provide blanks for students to fill in the labels. Be sure the overlapping parts of the circles have enough room for students to fill in the number or picture.

- Provide each student with one worksheet. Have them begin by working through each of the three examples in the lesson using the appropriate sorting diagram.
- Have the students attempt the two practice problems with the remaining diagrams.
- Instruct the students to exchange the last two diagrams with another student and check their work. For any mistakes that are made, have the two students pair up to solve the problem correctly.

Lesson 105   561

Written Practice

Math Conversations
Independent Practice and Discussions to Increase Understanding

● **Problem 4**
Analyze
Students should recognize that 2 dozen is equal to 2 × 12 = 24. Since one large paper clip has a mass of about 1 gram, 24 will have a mass of about 1 × 24 grams.

● **Problem 7**
Extend the Problem
After students make their estimates for this problem, have them add up the actual total to see if it is more or less than the estimate. Actual total: $10.00; It is the same as the estimate.

Ask advanced learners,

"Why did the actual answer come out the same as the estimate?" sample: We rounded the first amount up by $0.38. We rounded the next two amounts down by $0.18 and $0.20, which total $0.38. So the actual answer was the same as the estimate.

● **Problem 13**
Remind students that they should divide to find a missing factor. Ask them,

"What related division fact do you need to use to find n?" 48 ÷ 6 = n

● **Problem 17**
Encourage students to check their answers by multiplying:

2 × 46 = 92

(continued)

---

2. Forty-one students stood in two lines as equally as possible. How many students were in each line? 20 students and 21 students

3. Write an uppercase H. Show its two lines of symmetry. sample:

4. The mass of one large paper clip is about one gram. The mass of two dozen large paper clips is about how many grams? 24 grams

5. Round $395 to the nearest hundred dollars. $400

6. What is the geometric name for the shape of the object at right? sphere

7. Estimate the total price of a salad for $5.62, soup for $3.18, and juice for $1.20. $10.00

8. In what place is the 7 in each of these numbers?
a. 3,674   tens
b. 367   ones

9. What number is halfway between 500 and 1000? 750

10. Patrick wants to buy 4 yo-yos. Each yo-yo costs $3.23. He estimates that the total price will be $12.00. How does Patrick's estimate compare to the actual price? How do you know? Patrick's estimate is less than the actual price; sample: He rounded $3.23 down to $3.00 to find the total.

11. Draw a square with sides 2 cm long. Trace around the square. All the way around the square is how many centimeters? 8 cm

12. Change this addition to a multiplication and find the total: 5 × 60 sec = 300 sec
60 sec + 60 sec + 60 sec + 60 sec + 60 sec

▶ **13.** Find the missing factor: 6 × n = 48   8

14. 365 × 3   1,095

15. 400 × 8   3,200

16. 81 ÷ 9   9

▶ **17.** 92 ÷ 2   46

562   Saxon Math Intermediate 3

Alternative Approach: Using Manipulatives

Students who have difficulty conceptualizing the abstract representation of sets in this lesson may benefit from doing some actual sorting using manipulatives. Use the color tiles, counters, tangrams, money, or other manipulatives to make up a sorting activity that students can do in pairs or small groups. Loops of yarn could be used as the sorting circles. The loops can be overlapped to represent Venn diagrams.

18. Find each quotient.
₍₈₆₎
   a. 81 ÷ 9   9   **b.** 32 ÷ 4   8   **c.** 42 ÷ 7   6

19. Find the next three numbers of this sequence: 80, 160, 320
_(2, 91)
   5, 10, 20, 40, ____, ____, ____, …

▶ **20.** A rectangular floor like the rectangle shown at right will
₍₆₃₎   be covered with square tiles that are 1 foot on each
   side. How many tiles will cover the floor?   80 tiles

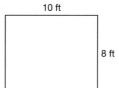
10 ft
8 ft

Real-World Connection

One python is 27 feet long and another is 22 feet long. Is the total length of the two pythons longer than an anaconda that is 44 feet long? What is the total length of all three snakes? Write number sentences and use a comparison symbol to show your answers.   yes; 27 + 22 = 49, 49 > 44; 49 + 44 = 93 feet

Lesson 105   563

Written Practice (Continued)

Math Conversations
Independent Practice and Discussions to Increase Understanding

● **Problem 20**
Math-to-Math Connection

Remind students how to find the area of a rectangle: length × width equals area in square units. Students need to determine how many squares will fit along each side and then multiply these numbers together.

Errors and Misconceptions

● **Problem 14**

Students may have trouble when regrouping more than once. In this problem regrouping is necessary in both the tens and hundreds places. Caution students to keep careful track of each number multiplied and each number added.

● **Problem 19**

Students may not recognize the "multiply by two" pattern as the numbers continue to double. Some students may be in the habit of adding or subtracting to find terms of a sequence. Encourage students to look for multiplication and division patterns in sequences as well as addition and subtraction patterns.

Point out to students that there is more than one question to answer for this problem. Have students share their number sentences as they explain their solutions.

Assessments

Distribute **Power-Up Test 20** and **Cumulative Test 20** to each student. Have students complete the **Power-Up Test** first. Allow 10 minutes. Then have students work on the **Cumulative Test**.

Test-Day Activity

The remaining class time should be spent on the **Test-Day Activity 10**. Students can begin the activity in class and complete it as homework.

Diagrams for sorting will be further developed in *Saxon Math Intermediate 4*.

Lesson 105   563

LESSON 106

> **Texas Essential Knowledge and Skills**
> (3.6)(A) identify/extend geometric patterns to solve problems
> (3.11)(C) use pictorial models of square units to determine the area of two-dimensional surfaces

Planning & Preparation

• Estimating Area, Part 1

Objectives
- Count whole and half squares to find or estimate the areas of irregularly shaped figures.

Prerequisite Skills
- Use square units to measure area.
- Draw rectangles on a 1-inch grid and determine their areas.
- Find the number of small squares inside a rectangle to determine its area.

Materials

Instructional Masters
- Power Up 106

Manipulative Kit
- Rulers

Teacher-provided materials
- Worksheets with copies of the lesson's art*
- Square and triangular paper tiles*

   *optional

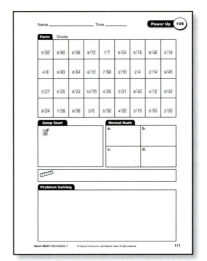

Power Up 106

Reaching All Special Needs Students

Special Education Students	At-Risk Students	English Learners	Advanced Learners
• Inclusion (TM) • Adaptations for Saxon Math	• Error Alert (TM) • Reteaching Masters	• English Learners (TM) • English Learner Handbook	• Extend the Problem (TM) • Early Finishers (SE) • Online Activities

TM=Teacher's Manual
SE=Student Edition

Math Language

Maintained	English Learners
area	surface

564A *Saxon Math* Intermediate 3

Problem Solving Discussion

Problem

This checkerboard pattern has 9 squares altogether. Five of the squares are dark and 4 of the squares are light.

Find the number of dark squares and light squares in a checkerboard pattern that has 16 squares altogether.

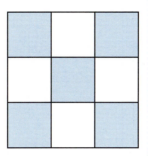

Focus Strategy Draw a Picture or Diagram

Understand *Understand the problem.*

"What information are we given?"

We are shown a checkerboard pattern with 9 squares. Five of the squares are dark and 4 are light.

"What are we asked to do?"

We are asked to find the number of dark squares and light squares in a checkerboard pattern that has 16 squares altogether.

Plan *Make a plan.*

"What problem solving strategy can we use?"

We can *draw a diagram*.

Solve *Carry out the plan.*

"In the diagram we are shown, there are 3 rows of 3 squares each. How can we make a checkerboard pattern with 16 squares?"

We can have 4 rows of 4 squares each; this is 4 × 4 squares = 16 squares altogether.

"If we use shading in our diagram to make a checkerboard pattern, how many squares will be dark and how many will be light?"

There will be 8 dark squares and 8 light squares.

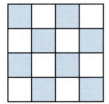

Check *Look back.*

"Did we complete the task?"

Yes, we found how many dark and light squares are in a checkerboard pattern of 16 small squares (8 dark and 8 light).

"Is our answer reasonable?"

Yes, eight is half of 16, and it makes sense that half of the squares would be shaded.

"What problem solving strategy did we use, and how did it help us?"

We *drew a diagram* of 16 squares and shaded the diagram like a checkerboard so that we could count the dark and light squares.

Alternate Strategy
Use Logical Reasoning

Students can use logical reasoning to solve the problem. In a checkerboard pattern with an even number of squares, half of the squares are dark and half are light. For a 16-square pattern, we logically reason that 8 of the squares are dark and the other 8 are light. Note that if there are an odd number of squares in the pattern, the number of dark and light squares differs by one (e.g., a 5-4 split in a 9-square pattern or a 13-12 split in a 25-square pattern).

Lesson 106   564B

LESSON 106

Power Up

Facts
Distribute **Power Up 106** to students. See answers below.

Jump Start
Before students begin the Mental Math exercise, do these exercises as a class.

Mental Math
Encourage students to share different ways to mentally compute these exercises. Strategies for exercises are listed below.

b. Think $13.40 − $2.00 + $0.01
$13.40 − $2.00 = $11.40
$11.40 + $0.01 = $11.41

d. Use the Compatible Number 50 for 47
50 × 4 = 200

Problem Solving
Refer to **Problem-Solving Strategy Discussion**, p. 564B.

LESSON 106

• Estimating Area, Part 1

Texas Essential Knowledge and Skills
(3.6)(A) identify/extend geometric patterns to solve problems
(3.11)(C) use pictorial models of square units to determine the area of two-dimensional surfaces

Power Up

facts Power Up 106

jump start   Count up by 4s from 0 to 48 and then back down to 0. Count up by 8s from 0 to 96 and then back down to 0.

 A board game costs $13.50. A small jigsaw puzzle costs $6.15. Write a number sentence to estimate how much they cost altogether. $14 + $6 = $20

Draw a $3\frac{3}{4}$-inch segment on your worksheet. Then make it $\frac{3}{4}$ inch longer. What is the total length of the segment? $4\frac{1}{2}$ in.

mental math
a. **Number Sense:** 25 × 3   75
b. **Money:** $13.40 − $1.99 $11.41
c. **Measurement:** Patrick jogged 700 meters and then walked 190 meters. How many meters did Patrick jog and walk altogether?   890 m
d. **Estimation:** Use compatible numbers to estimate 47 × 4.   200

problem solving
This checkerboard pattern has 9 squares altogether. Five of the squares are dark and 4 of the squares are light.

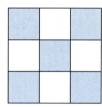

Find the number of dark squares and light squares in a checkerboard pattern that has 16 squares altogether.   8 dark squares and 8 light squares

564   *Saxon Math* Intermediate 3

Facts Divide:

5)35 = 7	8)80 = 10	6)36 = 6	9)72 = 8	7)7 = 1	6)54 = 9	6)18 = 3	8)48 = 6	2)18 = 9
4)8 = 2	9)63 = 7	8)64 = 8	6)12 = 2	7)56 = 8	2)10 = 5	2)4 = 2	2)14 = 7	9)45 = 5
3)27 = 9	5)25 = 5	6)24 = 4	10)70 = 7	4)20 = 5	3)21 = 7	8)40 = 5	4)12 = 3	6)42 = 7
8)24 = 3	7)28 = 4	9)36 = 4	3)0 = 0	5)30 = 6	4)32 = 8	3)15 = 5	5)50 = 10	2)20 = 10

New Concept

A grid of squares can help us estimate the area of a shape. Below we show a figure on a centimeter grid. Each square on the grid is one square centimeter. We can count squares to find the area of the figure.

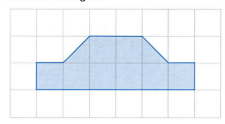

We count 8 whole squares and 2 half squares in the figure. The 2 half squares together equal 1 whole square. So the area of the figure is 9 square centimeters.

Example 1

In this diagram each square equals one square foot. What is the area of the figure on the grid?

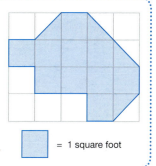

= 1 square foot

We count 10 whole squares and 4 half squares. The 4 half squares together equal 2 whole squares. So we add 10 whole squares and 2 whole squares and get 12 whole squares. The area is **12 square feet.**

Shapes do not always have straight edges or fit exactly onto grids. Monica drew this shape on a piece of centimeter grid paper:

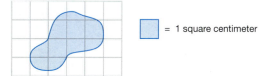

= 1 square centimeter

Lesson 106   565

New Concept

Connection

Students learned about area in Lessons 62 and 63. They learned to find the area of a rectangle by counting squares and also by multiplying the length by the width. Remind students of these concepts and point out that many figures do not have a shape that lends itself to simple area calculations.

"When shapes are more complicated than rectangles and squares, we often estimate the areas by counting squares on a grid. What polygons have areas that cannot be found by multiplying the length times the width?" samples: triangles, some quadrilaterals, pentagons, hexagons, and octagons

Have students examine the picture in the New Concept section of their textbook. Point out that the top edge of the figure is 2 units long, the bottom edge is 6 units long, and the height of the figure is 2 units. Explain that these measurements cannot be multiplied to give the area. Guide students through finding the area by counting the whole and the half squares. You could make a tally on the board to keep track of the whole and half squares.

Example 1
Active Learning

Make a table with two rows labeled "whole squares" and "half squares" on the board. Have a student record the tally while other students count the whole squares and the half squares. Then figure out the total area of the figure as a class.

(continued)

Math Background

In this lesson, students learn to estimate the area of an irregular polygon by counting squares and half squares in a grid. In later grades, students will learn to recognize this type of polygon as a composite figure. They will calculate area more precisely by breaking the composite figure apart into recognizable parts. They will use formulas to find the area of each part, then combine the areas of the parts to find the area of the whole figure.

English Learners

A **surface** is the outer area of something that can be seen and touched. Ask:

"If the surface of one desktop measures 480 square inches, and the surface of a second desktop measures 720 square inches, which table is larger?" sample: The second table is larger because 720 > 480.

Say:

"What are some words we use to describe different surfaces?" samples: smooth, rough, bumpy, wet, slippery

Have students work with a partner to list surfaces they cannot walk on. samples: water, a wall

Lesson 106   565

New Concept (Continued)

Example 2
Alternate Method

Another method for estimating the area of an irregular figure is to outline the largest complete rectangle or square that can be found inside the figure. In this example, point out that there is a complete 2-by-6-unit rectangle in the center of the figure. The area of this rectangle can be found by multiplying (6 × 2 = 12). Then students need to count the remaining whole and half squares surrounding this rectangle.

Error Alert

Students may find different answers for the area of irregular figures like this one and practice problem **b**. Slightly different answers are fine because we are only estimating. However, the figures in this book have been drawn to make estimation straightforward, so make sure that students are not counting any squares that have very little coverage.

Lesson Practice

Guided Practice

Use these problems as guided practice to check the students' understanding of today's concept.

Problems a and b

Make sure to check that students are including the square units as part of their answers to area problems.

(continued)

If a square is fully or mostly shaded, we count it as one whole square. If a square is about half shaded, we count it as a half square. If a square is only barely shaded, we do not count it. We see 5 squares that are whole or almost whole and 4 squares that are about half shaded. The area of Monica's shape is about 7 square centimeters.

Example 2

In this diagram, each square equals one square meter. Estimate the area of the surface of the pond.

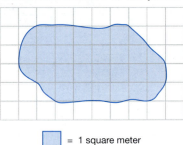

= 1 square meter

To estimate the area, we count each nearly whole square in the figure as a whole square. We count each nearly half square as a half square. We do not count a square if only a small part is in the figure. Altogether, we count 24 whole squares and 6 half squares. The 6 half squares together equal 3 whole squares. The area of the pond is about **27 square meters.**

Lesson Practice ▸ **a.** Find the area of this figure: 7 sq. in.

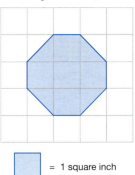

= 1 square inch

566 Saxon Math Intermediate 3

▶ **b.** Estimate the area of this figure: 14 sq. yd.

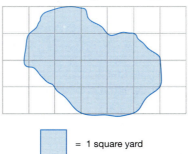

☐ = 1 square yard

Written Practice *Distributed and Integrated*

1. Robert carried the football and gained 11 yards, making a first down. How many feet is 11 yards?   33 ft
(34)

2. 72 ÷ 3   24
(101)

▶ 3. 575 × 3   1,725
(97)

4. Find the next three numbers in this sequence.   900, 1,000, 1,100
(2)
   … 600, 700, 800, ____, ____, ____, …

▶ 5. (Connect) Write a multiplication fact that shows the number of inches in 8 feet.   12 inches × 8 = 96 inches
(76)

6. What length is halfway between $1\frac{1}{2}$ inches and 2 inches? $1\frac{3}{4}$ in.
(35)

7. Estimate the product of 487 and 3.   1,500
(93)

8. a. Estimate the sum of $608 and $487. $1100
(16, 30)
   b. Calculate the sum of $608 and $487. $1095

9. If 11 × 12 = 132, then what does 12 × 11 equal?   132
(55)

10. Which digit is in the thousands place in each of these numbers?
(32)
    a. 23,478   3
    b. 375,129   5

Lesson 106   567

Inclusion

Estimating Area

Some students will have difficulty processing the abstract concept in this lesson. Use this hands-on activity with these students.

Materials: worksheets with reproductions of the figures on grids from this lesson, tiles made by cutting up a blank grid on colored paper (Make about 25 whole squares and 10 half squares (cut along a diagonal) for each group.)

- Using a figure from this lesson, have one student place square tiles on all of the whole squares inside the figure while another student keeps count. Then repeat this process with the half squares.
- Have the group add up their total, making sure to correctly add the half squares.
- For additional practice, draw other irregular figures on grids for students to use.

New Concept (Continued)

Lesson Practice

Problem b
Point out to students that there is a complete 2-by-3-unit rectangle inside the figure. Students can start by finding the area of this rectangle.

 Closure The questions below help assess the concepts taught in this lesson.

"Can we always multiply length times width to find the area of a shape?" No, we can only multiply length times width to find the area of rectangles.

"How can we estimate the area of a shape?" We can count the number of square units that would fit inside the figure.

Discuss real-world situations where estimating area might be helpful. Examples are given below.

- We have an irregularly shaped garden and want to know how much mulch we need to cover it.
- We bought a piece of land in the shape of a triangle and want to know the area.

Written Practice

Math Conversations
Independent Practice and Discussions to Increase Understanding

Problem 3
Alternate Method
Students could round, multiply, and then subtract to solve the problem mentally.
Think 600 × 3 = 1,800.
Then subtract 3 × 25 = 75:
1800 − 75 = 1,725.

Problem 5 (Connect)
Students can equate this to an equal groups story with 12 inches in one group (foot) and write the multiplication fact: 12 × 8 = ☐.

(continued)

Lesson 106   567

Written Practice (Continued)

Math Conversations
Independent Practice and Discussions to Increase Understanding

Problem 11 Represent
Students should begin by drawing two overlapping squares and then connect the corresponding vertices with line segments. Students might find it easier to count the vertices before drawing the line segments.

Extend the Problem
Continue the problem by asking,

"How many edges does a cube have?" 12

"How many faces does a cube have?" 6

Problem 14b
Alternate Method
Students can also do this problem mentally.

b. Round to $0.50, then subtract.

$4 \times \$0.50 = \$2.00$
$4 \times \$0.05 = \$0.20$
$\$2.00 - \$0.20 = \$1.80$

Problem 20 Analyze
Students can figure out the area of the shape by counting whole and half squares.

"How many whole squares are inside the figure?" 8

"How many half squares are inside the figure?" 4

"How many whole squares are equal to 4 half squares?" 2

Students should total the whole number of squares to get the area. $8 + 2 = 10$ square inches

Errors and Misconceptions

Problems 16 and 17
Students may have trouble when regrouping more than once. In these problems, regrouping is necessary in both the tens and hundreds places. Some students might benefit from first writing out a multiplication template with placeholders for the regrouped numbers that need to be added.

Have students use a multiplication table to find a number that meets the criteria. Refer students to Lesson 83 to review finding half of a number using a multiplication table.

568 *Saxon Math* Intermediate 3

▶ **11.** (Represent) Draw a picture of a cube. A cube has how many vertices? See student work; 8 vertices
(75)

12. A common year is 365 days. Write 365 in expanded form.
(11) $300 + 60 + 5$

13. Draw a rectangle that is 2 cm long and 1 cm wide.
(58, 63)
    a. What is the perimeter of the rectangle? 6 cm

    b. What is the area of the rectangle? 2 sq cm

14. Multiply:
(100)
    a. $7 \times \$1.45$ $10.15   ▶   b. $4 \times \$0.45$ $1.80

15. Find each quotient.
(86)
    a. $16 \div 2$ 8   b. $36 \div 6$ 6   c. $24 \div 3$ 8

16. 173×7 1,211   **17.** 322×8 2,576
(97)   (LRF)

18. 500×7 3,500
(91)

19. Find the next three numbers in this sequence: 275, 300, 325
(2)
    200, 225, 250, ____, ____, ____, ...

▶ **20.** (Analyze) Find the area of the figure at right.
(106) 10 square inches

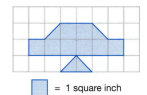

= 1 square inch

 Leon asked his brother to find out how many dollars he has in his pocket by solving a riddle. The first clue is that he has less than $30. The other clues are that the sum of the digits is four, and half of the total amount is an odd number of dollars. How much money does Leon have in his pocket? $22

Real-World Connection

568 *Saxon Math* Intermediate 3

Looking Forward

Learning to estimate the area of unusual shapes using grids prepares students for

- **Lesson 107,** drawing enlargements.
- **Lesson 108,** estimating area.

LESSON 107

Texas Essential Knowledge and Skills
(3.13)(C) use data to describe events as more likely than
(3.14)(A) identify the mathematics in everyday situations

Planning & Preparation

• Drawing Enlargements

Objectives
- Use a large and small grid to draw an enlargement of a figure or picture.

Prerequisite Skills
- Sketch a scale map of an object or location.

Materials

Instructional Masters
- Power Up 107
- Lesson Activity 23

Manipulative Kit
- Yardsticks*

Teacher-provided materials
- Small-grid transparencies
- Pictures
- Overhead projector, movie projector, or photo enlarger*
- Photo negatives, slides, filmstrips, movie film, or projection toys*
- Worksheets with simple figures on grids*

optional

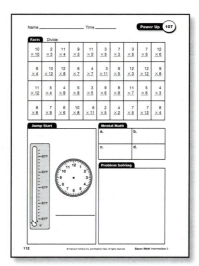

Power Up 107

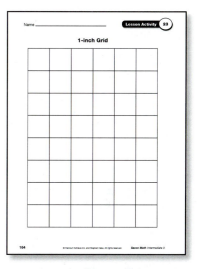

Lesson Activity 23

Differentiated Instruction

Reaching All Special Needs Students

Special Education Students	At-Risk Students	English Learners	Advanced Learners
• Inclusion (TM) • Adaptations for Saxon Math	• Reteaching Masters	• English Learners (TM) • English Learner Handbook	• Early Finishers (SE) • Online Activities

TM = Teacher's Manual
SE = Student Edition

Math Language

English Learners
produce

Lesson 107   569A

LESSON 107

Problem Solving Discussion

Problem

Jessica had a long piece of ribbon. She cut an 8-inch length from one end of the ribbon. Then she cut the rest of the ribbon into four equal lengths of 12 inches each. How long was the original piece of ribbon?

Focus Strategy **Write a Number Sentence**

Understand   Understand the problem.

"What information are we given?"

Jessica cut an 8-inch length from one end of a piece of ribbon. Then she cut the rest of the ribbon into 4 equal lengths of 12 inches each.

"What are we asked to do?"

We are asked to find the length of the original piece of ribbon.

Plan   Make a plan.

"How can we use the information we know to solve the problem?"

We can *write a number sentence* to find the total length of all the pieces of ribbon.

Solve   Carry out the plan.

"What is the total length of all the pieces of ribbon?"

After the cuts, there were four 12-inch pieces and one 8-inch piece. We show two different number sentences we could write below:

1. 12 in. + 12 in. + 12 in. + 12 in. + 8 in. = 56 in.
2. (12 × 4 in.) + 8 in. = 48 in. + 8 in. = 56 in.

Check   Look back.

"Did we complete the task?"

Yes, we found the length of the original piece of ribbon (56 inches).

"Is our answer reasonable?"

Yes, four pieces that are each 12 inches long plus one piece that is 8 inches long is a total length of 12 in. + 12 in. + 12 in. + 12 in. + 8 in. = 56 in.

"What problem solving strategy did we use, and how did it help us?"

We *wrote a number sentence* to add the lengths of the pieces.

Alternate Strategy

Draw a Diagram or Picture

Students might also solve this problem with the aid of a diagram. They can draw a long rectangle to stand for the original piece of ribbon, and then divide the rectangle into the pieces that were cut and label each piece with its length in inches.

LESSON 107

• Drawing Enlargements

Texas Essential Knowledge and Skills
(3.13)(C) use data to describe events as more likely than
(3.14)(A) identify the mathematics in everyday situations

Power Up

facts Power Up 107

jump start
- Count up by 6s from 0 to 72 and then back down to 0. Count up by 12s from 0 to 144 and then back down to 0.
- It is evening. The train will arrive at 18 minutes before 7. Draw hands on your clock to show the time the train will arrive. Write this time in digital form.   6:42 p.m.
- The ice at the hockey rink is 22°F. The temperature in the arena is 33 degrees warmer. Mark your thermometer to show the temperature in the arena.   55°F

mental math
a. **Number Sense:** 510 + 210   720
b. **Number Sense:** 80 × 9   720
c. **Probability:** Gracie spins the spinner one time. On which number is the spinner most likely to land?   3
d. **Fractions:** What fraction of the spinner is labeled with the number 2? $\frac{2}{8}$ or $\frac{1}{4}$

problem solving
Jessica had a long piece of ribbon. She cut an 8-inch length from one end of the ribbon. Then she cut the rest of the ribbon into four equal lengths of 12 inches each. How long was the original piece of ribbon?   56 in.

Lesson 107   569

LESSON 107

Power Up

Facts
Distribute **Power Up 107** to students. See answers below.

Jump Start
Before students begin the Mental Math exercise, do these exercises as a class.

Mental Math
Encourage students to share different ways to mentally compute these exercises. Strategies for exercises are listed below.

a. **Add Hundreds, Then Add Tens**
5 hundreds + 2 hundreds = 7 hundreds = 700
1 ten + 1 ten = 2 tens = 20
700 + 20 = 720

c. **Find the Label Used Most Often**
Three sections are labeled with 3s, two sections with 1s, two sections with 2s, and 1 section with a 4. The number that occurs most is 3.

Problem Solving
Refer to **Problem-Solving Strategy Discussion**, p. 569B.

Facts   Multiply:

10 × 10 = 100	2 × 3 = 6	11 × 4 = 44	9 × 3 = 27	11 × 9 = 99	3 × 8 = 24	7 × 3 = 21	3 × 6 = 18	7 × 8 = 56	12 × 6 = 72
6 × 4 = 24	10 × 12 = 120	12 × 8 = 96	6 × 7 = 42	4 × 7 = 28	3 × 11 = 33	9 × 5 = 45	12 × 3 = 36	12 × 12 = 144	9 × 8 = 72
11 × 12 = 132	5 × 4 = 20	4 × 9 = 36	5 × 8 = 40	3 × 5 = 15	9 × 6 = 54	8 × 8 = 64	11 × 7 = 77	5 × 6 = 30	4 × 3 = 12
8 × 6 = 48	7 × 9 = 63	6 × 6 = 36	10 × 8 = 80	6 × 11 = 66	2 × 5 = 10	4 × 2 = 8	7 × 5 = 35	7 × 12 = 84	8 × 4 = 32

Lesson 107   569

New Concept

Exploration

Transparencies on the overhead projector are a great way to demonstrate the concept of enlargement. Ask for a volunteer to trace his/her hand on a transparency. Place the transparency on the projector and have the student compare the actual size of his/her hand to the enlarged projection on the screen or wall.

Activity

You may wish to complete this as a whole group activity. Have students follow along at their desks while you demonstrate on the board or overhead how to copy the picture one square at a time onto large-grid paper. Be sure to provide each student with the same picture.

Students should position their small-grid transparency over the figure to be copied. Taping or clipping the transparency in place helps to avoid shifting. After the activity, save the transparency grid for Lesson 108.

The questions below help assess the concepts taught in this lesson.

"**How can we use a grid to enlarge an object?**" Tape a clear grid over the picture. Have a larger grid on a piece of paper and copy what is in each square one square at a time.

"**Why might someone want to enlarge a picture?**" samples: to show details, to have a bigger picture

Discuss real-world situations where enlarging might be helpful. An example is given below.

- A photo studio takes a picture and makes a poster to hang on the wall.

New Concept

Overhead projectors, movie projectors, and photograph laboratories produce a larger image. The larger image is called an *enlargement*. In this activity you will draw an enlargement using two different-sized grids.

Brenda placed a small-grid transparency over the picture of a horse. Then she copied on a large grid what she saw on the small grid. She copied one square at a time until she was done.

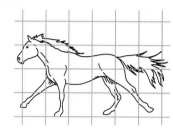

Activity

Drawing Enlargements

Materials: **Lesson Activity 23**, small-grid transparency, a picture you wish to copy

Tape or clip the small-grid transparency over a picture. Then copy the picture one square at a time onto **Lesson Activity 23**.

Estimate Each square on **Lesson Activity 23** has an area of one square inch. About how many square inches is the area of your enlargement? See student work.

Written Practice — Distributed and Integrated

1. Bea drew a marble from the bag without looking. Is she more likely to draw a blue marble or a black marble? blue marble
(45)

570 Saxon Math Intermediate 3

Math Background

Drawing enlargements is an example of what is known as a *projection* in higher mathematics. Various types of projections are used in mathematics with applications in *cartography*. Cartography is map drawing.

English Learners

To **produce** is to make or to create. Say:

"**A farm produces crops for food. What kinds of things can a carpenter produce?**" samples: bookshelves, cabinets, tables, bed frames

Ask students what an overhead projector produces. sample: an enlarged image

2. The table shows the years in which Matt and his siblings were
(103) born. Write the names in order from oldest to youngest.   Matt, Jessica, Paul, Samantha

Name	Birth Year
Jessica	1993
Matt	1980
Samantha	2000
Paul	1997

3. Draw a square with sides $1\frac{1}{2}$ inches long. What is the perimeter of
(58) the square?   6 in.

4. **Multiple Choice** Which of the following does *not* equal 15?   C
(6, 56)
   A 15 + 0   **B** 15 − 0   **C** 15 × 0   **D** 15 × 1

5. 90 ÷ 5   18
(101)

6. 111 × 3   333
(97)

▶ 7. Divide 39 by 3.   13
(101)

8. Gina puts 10 pennies in each pile. How many piles can Gina make
(90) with 100 pennies?   10 piles

9. In what place is the 5 in each of these numbers?
(32)
   a. 524   hundreds   **b.** 36,452   tens

10. Draw a rectangle 3 cm long and 2 cm wide. What is its area?
(63) See student work; 6 sq. cm

▶ 11. **Classify** Sort these figures into polygons and figures that are
(103) not polygons.

12. Round $5.58 to the nearest dollar. $6.00
(96)

13. $7.50 × 5 $37.50
(100)

14. $1.20 × 3 $3.60
(100)

Lesson 107   571

Written Practice

Math Conversations
Independent Practice and Discussions to Increase Understanding

▶ Problem 7
This problem is readily solved using long division, but encourage students to try to find the answer mentally first. Tell them that 13 is just off the edge of a multiplication chart, so knowing 12 × 3 will help.

▶ Problem 11 Classify
Remind students that polygons are flat, closed figures constructed of line segments. Based on the definition, two of the shapes are polygons but two are not: one is curved and the other is 3-dimensional.

(continued)

Teacher Tip

For this activity, you will need transparencies of **Lesson Activity 32** cut into fourths. Each student will need a small grid transparency to copy his/her picture. You may wish to present the New Concept, and then divide the class into groups. Some students can work on the activity while other students begin the Written Practice set.

Be sure to collect and save the transparencies at the end of class. They will be reused in Lesson 108.

Inclusion

Drawing Enlargements
Some students have difficulty drawing.

Materials: handouts with simple straight-line figures drawn on small grids (use figures like those in Lesson 106, example 1 or Lesson Practice a)

- Have students use the simpler straight-line figures for the enlargement activity rather than pictures with curves.

Lesson 107   571

Written Practice (Continued)

Math Conversations
Independent Practice and Discussions to Increase Understanding

Problem 16 (Classify)
Identify these as sorting circles to guide students in the right direction. Remind students that even numbers end in a 0, 2, 4, 6, or 8 and odd numbers end in a 1, 3, 5, 7, or 9.

Problem 19 (Represent)
Suggest that students start by using the corner of a piece of paper to draw a right angle. Then they should move the vertical segment back to form a larger angle. Connecting the open ends with a third line segment can complete the triangle. Using the corner of the same piece of paper for reference, students can label the angles in the triangle as acute or obtuse.

Errors and Misconceptions

Problem 2
Watch for students who mistakenly list the names in reverse order: Samantha, Paul, Jessica, and Matt. Remind them that earlier years correspond to older students. If necessary, have students write another column for the table, giving the age of each student. Then they just need to order the ages from oldest to youngest.

Early Finishers

Students may use manipulatives first to solve the problem. Also suggest that they guess and check to find the answer. Emphasize to students that it is not important what their sketches of the piles of snowballs look like, as long as each one has the correct number of snowballs.

---

15. Find each quotient.
(86)
   a. 56 ÷ 7   8
   b. 63 ÷ 7   9
   c. 24 ÷ 4   6

 16. (Classify) Draw two circles that do not overlap. Label one circle
(105) "Even Numbers" and the other circle "Odd Numbers." Then write each of these numbers in the correct circle.

   34   88   17   61   81   22   98   23

   See student work.

17. (50 + 50) − 25   75
(92)

18. (99 + 1) × 4   400
(92)

 19. (Represent) Draw an obtuse triangle. How many of its angles are
(65, 69) obtuse? How many are acute?   See student work; 1; 2

20. Betty ran 3 miles in 21 minutes. About how long did it take her to
(89) run one mile?   7 minutes

Real-World Connection

Curt, Bob, and Lee each made a pile of snowballs. Together they made 15 snowballs. Bob made two more than Lee. Lee made two more than Curt. How many snowballs did each boy make? Draw a picture showing what their piles of snowballs would look like.   Bob 7, Lee 5, Curt 3; See student work.

Looking Forward

Using grids will be further developed in *Saxon Math Intermediate 4*.

LESSON 108

Planning & Preparation

• Estimating Area, Part 2

Objectives
- Use transparency grids to estimate areas of figures.

Prerequisite Skills
- Count whole and half squares to estimate the areas of irregularly shaped figures.
- Use square units to measure area.
- Draw rectangles on a 1-inch grid and determine their areas.
- Find the number of small squares inside a rectangle to determine its area.

Materials
Instructional Masters
- Power Up 108
- Lesson Activities 23 and 33

Teacher-provided materials
- Inch and centimeter transparency grids
- Books and magazines*

optional

Texas Essential Knowledge and Skills

(3.6)(C)   identify patterns in related multiplication and division sentences (fact families)

(3.9)(C)   identify lines of symmetry in two-dimensional geometric figures

(3.11)(C)   use concrete and pictorial models of square units to determine the area of two-dimensional surfaces

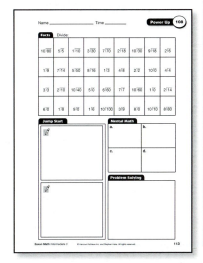
Power Up 108

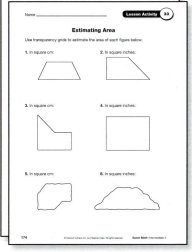
Lesson Activities 23 and 33

Differentiated Instruction

Reaching All Special Needs Students

Special Education Students	At-Risk Students	English Learners	Advanced Learners
• Adaptations for Saxon Math	• Alternative Approach (TM) • Error Alert (TM) • Reteaching Masters	• English Learners (TM) • English Learner Handbook	• Early Finishers (SE) • Online Activities

TM=Teacher's Manual
SE=Student Edition

Math Language

English Learners
figure

Lesson 108   573A

LESSON 108

Problem Solving Discussion

Problem

Julian opened a package of printer paper. He put 300 sheets into the black-and-white printer. He put half as many sheets into the color printer. Julian placed the remaining 50 sheets in his desk. How many sheets were in the package of printer paper that Julian opened?

Focus Strategy: 2+3=5 Write a Number Sentence

Understand Understand the problem.

"What information are we given?"

Julian used the sheets in a package of printer paper in this way:

1. 300 sheets in the black-and-white printer
2. half of 300 sheets in the color printer
3. 50 sheets in the desk

"What are we asked to do?"

We are asked to find the total number of sheets of paper in the original package.

Plan Make a plan.

"How can we use the information we know to solve the problem?"

We can *write a number sentence* to find the total number of sheets. We first need to find how many sheets Julian put in the color printer.

Solve Carry out the plan.

"How many sheets did Julian put in the color printer?"

Half of 300 sheets is 150 sheets. (We can think of 300 as 200 plus 100. Half of 300 is half of 200 plus half of 100, which is 100 plus 50.)

"What number sentence can we write to find the total number of sheets?"

We write this number sentence:

$$300 \text{ sheets} + 150 \text{ sheets} + 50 \text{ sheets} = 500 \text{ sheets}$$

Check Look back.

"Did we complete the task?"

Yes, we found the total number of sheets in the package of paper (500 sheets).

"Is our answer reasonable?"

Yes, half of 300 is 150, and 300 + 150 + 50 is 500.

"What problem solving strategies did we use, and how did they help us?"

We *wrote a number sentence* to find the total number of sheets.

LESSON 108

• Estimating Area, Part 2

Texas Essential Knowledge and Skills
(3.6)(C) identify patterns in related multiplication and division sentences (fact families)
(3.9)(C) identify lines of symmetry in two-dimensional geometric figures
(3.11)(C) use concrete and pictorial models of square units to determine the area of two-dimensional surfaces

Power Up

facts — Power Up 108

jump start — Count up by 5s from 0 to 60 and then back down to 0. Count up by 10s from 0 to 120 and then back down to 0.

Write a multiplication and division fact family using the numbers 9, 8, and 72. $9 \times 8 = 72$; $8 \times 9 = 72$; $72 \div 9 = 8$; $72 \div 8 = 9$

Draw an equilateral triangle. Then draw a line of symmetry. *See student work.*

mental math
a. **Number Sense:** $5{,}000 + 900 + 70 + 5$ 5,975
b. **Number Sense:** $300 - 199$ 101
c. **Number Sense:** Each tent uses 6 stakes to hold it to the ground. How many stakes are needed for 4 tents? 24 stakes
d. **Measurement:** Dana's backyard deck is 8 yards long and 4 yards wide. What is the area of the deck? 32 sq. yd

4 yd
8 yd

problem solving — Julian opened a package of printer paper. He put 300 sheets into the black-and-white printer. He put half as many sheets into the color printer. Julian placed the remaining 50 sheets in his desk. How many sheets were in the package of printer paper that Julian opened? 500 sheets

New Concept

We may use transparency grids to help estimate the area of figures.

Power Up (teacher)

Facts
Distribute **Power Up 108** to students. See answers below.

Jump Start
Before students begin the Mental Math exercise, do these exercises as a class.

Mental Math
Encourage students to share different ways to mentally compute these exercises. Strategies for exercises are listed below.

b. Think $300 - 200 + 1$
$300 - 199 = 300 - 200 + 1$
$= 100 + 1 = 101$

d. Multiply Length × Width
$8 \times 4 = 32$ sq. yd
Draw a Grid and Count Squares
Divide the rectangle into a grid 8 squares long and 4 squares wide. Count the squares by row or by column to get 32 sq. yd.

Problem Solving
Refer to **Problem-Solving Strategy Discussion**, p. 573B.

New Concept (teacher)

Instruction
In this lesson, students overlay transparency grids on figures to estimate area. There is some skill involved in placing a grid over a figure to make the most accurate estimate. Provide students with the following tips:

1. Demonstrate how best to align the grid with the figure. Students should try to align a corner or side of the figure on the edge or corner of a square on the grid.

2. Inform students that getting as many whole squares inside the figure as possible will usually make counting squares easier and will result in better area estimates.

Consider demonstrating on the overhead using a triangle, a pentagon, and a heart.

(continued)

Facts — Divide:

8 / 10)80	1 / 5)5	10 / 1)10	10 / 3)30	10 / 7)70	9 / 2)18	3 / 10)30	2 / 9)18	3 / 2)6
9 / 1)9	2 / 7)14	10 / 5)50	2 / 8)16	3 / 1)3	2 / 4)8	1 / 2)2	0 / 10)0	1 / 4)4
1 / 3)3	5 / 2)10	4 / 10)40	0 / 5)0	10 / 6)60	1 / 7)7	6 / 10)60	0 / 1)0	7 / 2)14
0 / 6)0	8 / 1)8	0 / 9)0	6 / 1)6	10 / 10)100	3 / 3)9	0 / 8)0	1 / 10)10	10 / 8)80

Lesson 108   573

New Concept (Continued)

Error Alert

In this lesson the figures do not always closely align to a grid. As a result, answers may vary somewhat from the given answers. Check for students whose answers are either consistently different or far removed from the given answers. Work through one area estimation problem with these students to help them understand the concept.

Active Learning: Real-World Connection

Using a map of your town, find some region like a park, lake, or neighborhood and have students estimate the area of the region with their transparency grids. Show advanced learners how to use the map's key to turn their estimate of the region's area into an estimate of the actual area.

Closure The questions below help assess the concepts taught in this lesson.

"How can we use a transparency grid to estimate area?" We lay the transparency on a figure and count the number of squares and partial squares that fill the figure. The total number of squares is the area.

"Why might we need to estimate area?" Sometimes we have a figure that has an irregular shape, and we can't multiply the length and width to find the area.

Discuss real-world situations where using a transparency grid to find area might be helpful. Examples are given below.

- We want to find the area of an irregularly shaped region on a map.
- Darlene uses a transparency grid to estimate the area of rooms on an architect's plans for her new home.

Justin placed a centimeter grid on a parallelogram and estimated its area. Kylie placed an inch grid on a triangle and estimated its area.

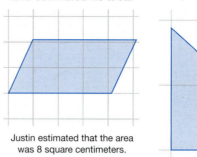

Justin estimated that the area was 8 square centimeters.

Kylie estimated that the area was 2 square inches.

Analyze Lucy estimated the area of a rectangle using a centimeter grid and again using an inch grid. Was the number of square units greater using the centimeter grid or the inch grid? centimeter grid

Activity

Estimating Area with a Grid

Materials: **Lesson Activity 33**, inch-grid transparency, centimeter-grid transparency

Use transparency grids to help you estimate the area of each figure on **Lesson Activity 33**.

Extension Use transparency grids to find the areas of other shapes in your books or in magazines.

Written Practice — Distributed and Integrated

1. On what number is the spinner least likely to stop? 2
(50)

574 **Saxon Math** Intermediate 3

English Learners

A **figure** is a shape or an outline. Ask:

"What are some figures that have more than four sides?" samples: pentagons, octagons, hexagons

Ask:

"Name a figure that is curved." samples: circles, ovals, some letters

Have students draw figures with a line of symmetry.

Teacher Tip

For the activity, you will need the small grid transparencies from Lesson 107 and transparencies of **Lesson Activity 23** cut into fourths.

This activity can be set up as a classroom center. Place copies of **Lesson Activity 33** and the transparency grids at a table. Groups of four students at a time can rotate to this center while the rest of the class works on the Written Practice problems. Each student should estimate the area individually, and then compare answers with their partner. If estimates differ, they should compare methods and decide which gives the better estimate.

2. The third grade at Larson elementary collected aluminum cans for a recycling drive. Room A collected 312 cans, Room B collected 624 cans, and Room C collected 511 cans. Estimate the total number of cans collected by the third grade.   1,400 cans
   (30)

▶ 3. (Analyze) Is the estimate you made for problem **2** greater than or less than the actual total number of cans?   less than
   (99)

4. Use a pencil and a ruler to draw a rectangle that is $1\frac{1}{2}$ inches long and $1\frac{1}{4}$ inches wide. Then show its two lines of symmetry.   See student work.   sample:
   (52, Inv. 9)

5. Joel compared the prices of teddy bears at three different stores.
   (103) $12.95, $17.95, $18.95
           $18.95 $12.95 $17.95

   Arrange the prices in order from least to greatest.

6. A roll of pennies is 50 pennies. A roll of dimes is 50 dimes. A roll of dimes is equal in value to how many rolls of pennies?   10
   (21)

▶ 7. A pint is 16 ounces. How many ounces is two quarts?   64 ounces
   (84, 87)

▶ 8. (Explain) Describe the sorting rule for the fractions in these two groups.   sample: The fractions in Group A are equal to 1. The fractions in Group B are not equal to one.
   (102)

       Group A: $\frac{2}{2}, \frac{3}{3}, \frac{4}{4}, \frac{5}{5}, \frac{6}{6}$

       Group B: $\frac{1}{2}, \frac{1}{3}, \frac{1}{4}, \frac{1}{5}, \frac{1}{6}$

9. (10 + 15) ÷ 5   5
   (92)

10. 68 ÷ 2   34
    (101)

11. Write these three numbers in order from least to greatest
    (103)   1,376, 1,859, 2,147
            1,376   2,147   1,859

12. How many small cubes were used to build this rectangular prism?   72 cubes
    (73)

Lesson 108   575

Alternative Approach: Using Manipulatives

Geoboards can be used to form shapes for this activity. Students should start with relatively easy shapes like triangles or polygons, and then create more challenging, irregular shapes.

Written Practice

Math Conversations
Independent Practice and Discussions to Increase Understanding

Problem 3 (Analyze)
Students should examine the rounded values used in making the estimation in the previous problem. Since each estimate was rounded down, students should conclude that the estimate is lower than the actual total number of cans.

Problem 5
Remind students to align the prices vertically to compare them:
    $18.95
    $12.95
    $17.95

Students should then look at the digits from left to right. The first digits are all ones, so we need to look at the next digit. The second digits are not in order, so rearrange them in the order 2, 7, 8:
    $12.95
    $17.95
    $18.95

The 3 numbers are now in order.

Problem 7
Students may need to be reminded that 1 quart = 2 pints.

Give the hint that students may need to double twice to find the answer.

Problem 8 (Explain)
Students should recognize that the numerators and denominators of the fractions in Group A are equal.

  "If you have all of the parts of something, then you have one whole thing."

This is not true in Group B.

There are other possible sorting rules that could have resulted in this grouping. Another possible sorting rule is that the fractions in Group B have numerators of 1 and the fractions in Group A do not.

(continued)

Written Practice (Continued)

Math Conversations
Independent Practice and Discussions to Increase Understanding

▶ **Problem 17**
Mental Math
Students can solve this problem mentally by thinking, $4 × 3 = $12 and $0.50 × 3 = $1.50, so the answer is $12 + $1.50 = $13.50.

▶ **Problem 20** Represent
Students should begin by drawing two congruent triangles that do not overlap. Then students can connect the corresponding vertices using line segments. It might prove easier to count the vertices before adding the line segments.

Errors and Misconceptions

▶ **Problem 6**
Students may find themselves confused because there are the same number of dimes as there are pennies. Suggest students make a sketch to help visualize the facts in the problem.

▶ **Problem 20**
A common mistake is to confuse triangular prisms with pyramids. Be sure that students know the meaning of *triangular prism* as well as *vertices* by asking,

"How would you describe a triangular prism?" sample: A triangular prism is a geometric solid with congruent triangles on two ends and rectangles on the sides.

"What are vertices?" sample: Vertices are the points at which the edges of a solid meet.

Have students act it out using different colors of counters or tiles to represent Pedro, Zack, and Alyssa. Students may then draw 13 rectangles or use 13 index cards to represent the blocks.

576   Saxon Math Intermediate 3

---

13. 700 × 3   2,100
(91)

14. 36 × 4   144
(84)

15. $0.75 × 6 $4.50
(100)

16. Cesar counted 153 raisins in a large box. Estimate the number of
(93) raisins that would be in 5 large boxes.   750 raisins

▶ **17.** $4.50 × 3 $13.50
(100)

18. 451 × 2   902
(97)

19. 61 − m = 24   37
(40)

▶ **20.** Represent Draw a triangular prism. How many vertices does
(75) it have?   See student work; 6 vertices

Real-World Connection

Pedro walks 13 blocks every morning to get to school. When he gets to the seventh block, he meets his friend Zack and they walk the rest of the way together. When Pedro and Zack get to the eleventh block, they meet Alyssa and all three walk to school together. How many blocks do Pedro and Zack walk together? Does Pedro walk more blocks alone or with his friends? You may use manipulatives or draw a picture to help you find the answer.   7 blocks; Pedro walks more blocks with his friends.

576   Saxon Math Intermediate 3

Looking Forward

Estimating area will be further developed in *Saxon Math Intermediate 4*.

LESSON 109

Texas Essential Knowledge and Skills
(3.6)(A) identify/extend geometric patterns to make predictions

Planning & Preparation

• Points on a Grid

Objectives
- Use coordinates to name points on a grid.
- Use coordinates to locate points on a grid.
- Name points on a grid with coordinates and with letters.

Prerequisite Skills
- Locate and name points on a number line.

Materials
Instructional Masters
- Power Up 109

Manipulative Kit
- Rulers
- Geoboards*

Teacher-provided materials
- Grid paper*
- Maps or bingo cards*

optional

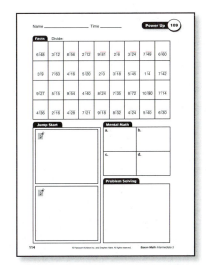

Power Up 109

Reaching All Special Needs Students

Special Education Students	At-Risk Students	English Learners	Advanced Learners
• Inclusion (TM) • Adaptations for Saxon Math	• Alternative Approach (TM) • Error Alert (TM) • Reteaching Masters	• English Learners (TM) • English Learner Handbook	• Extend the Problem (TM) • Early Finishers (SE) • Online Activities

TM=Teacher's Manual
SE=Student Edition

Math Language

New
coordinates

English Learners
sideways

Lesson 109   577A

LESSON 109

Problem Solving Discussion

Problem

Emma made a pattern with three different shapes. What two shapes are missing in the pattern?

Focus Strategy

Find/Extend a Pattern

Understand Understand the problem.

"What information are we given?"

1. Emma made a pattern with three different shapes.
2. We are shown the pattern that Emma made.

"What are we asked to do?"

We are asked to find and draw the two shapes that are missing.

Plan Make a plan.

"How can we use the information we know to solve the problem?"

We can *find a pattern* and then *extend the pattern* to find the missing shapes.

Solve Carry out the plan.

"What three shapes do you find in the pattern?"

We can see parallelograms, triangles, and squares.

"Do the shapes follow a repeating pattern?"

Yes, if we replace the first blank with a triangle and the second blank with a parallelogram, we find that that pattern is a repeating sequence of "parallelogram, triangle, square, parallelogram, triangle, square."

Check Look back.

"Did we complete the task?"

Yes, we found the two shapes missing from the pattern (triangle and parallelogram).

"Are our answers reasonable?"

Yes, we know that our answers are reasonable, because they fit the repeating pattern that we found.

"If we use letters to stand for the shapes in the pattern, how might we describe this pattern?"

To describe a repeating pattern, we can use letters of the alphabet. For this problem, we can use "A" to stand for parallelograms, "B" for triangles, and "C" for squares. We write at least two full repetitions of the pattern: ABCABC.

LESSON 109

• Points on a Grid

Texas Essential Knowledge and Skills
(3.6)(A) identify/extend geometric patterns to make predictions

Power Up

facts — Power Up 109

jump start
- Count up by 7s from 0 to 84 and then back down to 0.
- Count up by 11s from 0 to 132 and then back down to 0.
- A fishing rod costs $11.35. Write a number sentence to estimate the cost of 4 fishing rods to the nearest dollar. $11 × 4 = $44
- Use your ruler to draw a square with a perimeter of 8 inches. See student work.

mental math
- a. **Number Sense:** 25 × 5   125
- b. **Number Sense:** 87 + 37   124
- c. **Number Sense:** 50 ÷ 2   25
- d. **Patterns:** Find the missing number in this pattern: 260

| 248 | 252 | 256 | ___ | 264 | 268 |

problem solving
Emma made a pattern with three different shapes. What two shapes are missing in the pattern?

LESSON 109

Power Up

Facts
Distribute **Power Up 109** to students. See answers below.

Jump Start
Before students begin the Mental Math exercise, do these exercises as a class.

Mental Math
Encourage students to share different ways to mentally compute these exercises. Strategies for exercises are listed below.

- **a. Think of 5 Quarters**
  Five quarters are worth $1.25, so 25 × 5 = 125.
- **d. Find the Rule**
  The rule is "add 4."
  The missing number is 256 + 4 = 260.

Problem Solving
Refer to **Problem-Solving Strategy Discussion**, p. 577B.

Lesson 109   577

Facts Divide:

$6\overline{)48}$ = 8	$3\overline{)12}$ = 4	$8\overline{)56}$ = 7	$2\overline{)12}$ = 6	$9\overline{)81}$ = 9	$2\overline{)6}$ = 3	$3\overline{)24}$ = 8	$7\overline{)49}$ = 7	$6\overline{)60}$ = 10
$3\overline{)9}$ = 3	$7\overline{)63}$ = 9	$4\overline{)16}$ = 4	$5\overline{)20}$ = 4	$2\overline{)0}$ = 0	$3\overline{)18}$ = 6	$5\overline{)45}$ = 9	$1\overline{)4}$ = 4	$7\overline{)42}$ = 6
$9\overline{)27}$ = 3	$5\overline{)15}$ = 3	$9\overline{)54}$ = 6	$4\overline{)40}$ = 10	$8\overline{)24}$ = 3	$7\overline{)35}$ = 5	$8\overline{)72}$ = 9	$10\overline{)90}$ = 9	$7\overline{)14}$ = 2
$4\overline{)36}$ = 9	$2\overline{)16}$ = 8	$4\overline{)28}$ = 7	$7\overline{)21}$ = 3	$9\overline{)18}$ = 2	$8\overline{)32}$ = 4	$4\overline{)24}$ = 6	$5\overline{)40}$ = 8	$6\overline{)30}$ = 5

Lesson 109   577

New Concept

Observation

In this lesson, students learn to identify points on a grid by using coordinates. The points and coordinates that students will use are limited to positive whole numbers.

Math to Math Connection

Point out to students that the process for finding coordinate points is similar to finding products or quotients on a multiplication table.

Math Language

Help students remember the term *coordinate* by pointing out that *co-* means "together" and *ordinate* means "ordered."

"A set of coordinates is also called an 'ordered pair'."

Example 1

After finding the coordinates of point *A*, have students verify those coordinates by moving their finger sideways from 0 to 4, then up 2 spaces.

(continued)

New Concept

If we number the lines on a grid, we can name any point on the grid with two numbers.

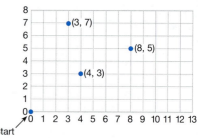

The two numbers in parentheses are called **coordinates.** Coordinates are like the address of a point. They tell us how to get to a point starting from (0, 0). The first number tells us how many spaces we move to the right. The second number tells us how many spaces we move up.

For example, to get to point (4, 3), we move sideways from (0, 0) to the 4. Then we move up 3 spaces. Starting from (0, 0), practice going to the right and then up to (3, 7) and to (8, 5).

Example 1

Write the coordinates of points *A*, *B*, and *C* on this grid.

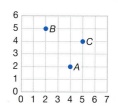

To find the first number of the coordinates, we place our finger on the point and move it straight down until we get to the number on the bottom of the grid. To find the second number of the coordinates, we place our finger on the point again and move it to the left until we get to the number on the side. We write the coordinates in parentheses.

A (4, 2)   B (2, 5)   C (5, 4)

To move **sideways** is to move to one side. Say:

"Turn your head sideways. Stand up and move sideways across the classroom." See student work.

Ask:

"Do elevators move sideways?" sample: No, they move up and down.

Have students face the front of the classroom and then walk sideways.

Example 2

Name the letter of the point that has these coordinates:

a. (6, 3)
b. (2, 4)

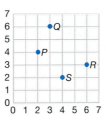

To find (6, 3) we start at (0, 0) and go sideways to 6. Then we go up 3 spaces. We see point **R**.

To find (2, 4) we go sideways to 2. Then we go up 4 spaces. The letter of the point is **P**.

Lesson Practice

Write the coordinates of the following points:

▶ a. Point *A*   (5, 3)
▶ b. Point *B*   (2, 1)
▶ c. Point *C*   (1, 4)
▶ d. Point *D*   (4, 6)

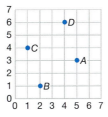

Name the letter of the point that has these coordinates.

e. (6, 3)   **X**
f. (1, 4)   **Z**

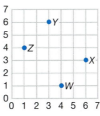

Written Practice   *Distributed and Integrated*

1. Vincent is reading a book that is 286 pages long. He has 72 pages left to read. How many pages has Vincent already read?   214 pages
(40)

2. Ginger ran to the fence and back twice. If it is 75 yards to the fence, how far did Ginger run?   300 yards
(84)

3. The distance from Olga's house to school on a map is 2 inches. If each inch on the map represents a distance of 4 miles, how many miles is Olga's house from school?   8 miles
(Inv. 4)

Lesson 109   579

Finding Coordinates on a Map

Using a real-world, concrete example of grids and coordinates should help some students who are having difficulty with the more abstract concept of points on a plane.

Materials: maps that have letters and numbers labeling the horizontal and vertical regions of a grid (like those from a phone book) or bingo cards.

- Find an easily identifiable city, street, or place on the map and have students identify the grid coordinates (for example, A-2, C-3, and so on) of the region it is in.

- Use the street locator on the map to have students find particular streets by locating the street's region from its coordinates.

- If maps still prove too difficult for some students, switch to Bingo cards. Call out a space on the card and have the students locate the space and write down its numerical coordinates. Do this for 7 or 8 different spaces.

New Concept (Continued)

Example 2
Error Alert

Watch for students who list point *Q* as the answer to **a** and point *S* as the answer to **b**.

Tell students that we must crawl before we can climb. We move along the horizontal axis for the first number and up the vertical axis for the second number.

Lesson Practice

Guided Practice

Use these problems as guided practice to check the students' understanding of today's concept.

Problems a–d

Reproduce the grid and points *A–D* on the board or overhead. Select different students to come up and explain how to find the coordinates of each point.

Extend the Problems

Have students write the coordinates for each point in reverse. Then ask them how to locate the new point.

a. (3, 5) Go sideways to 3 and then up 5 spaces.
b. (1, 2) Go sideways to 1 and then up 2 spaces.
c. (4, 1) Go sideways to 4 and then up 1 space.
d. (6, 4) Go sideways to 6 and then up 4 spaces.

  The questions below help assess the concepts taught in this lesson.

"What are coordinates?" Coordinates are like the address of a point.

"What does the first number of the coordinate tell us?" how many spaces to move to the right

"What does the second number of the coordinate tell us?" how many spaces to move up

Discuss real-world situations where using coordinates might be helpful. Examples are given below.

- A scientist graphs the values he found during an experiment.
- We are looking at a map of longitude and latitude and want to find a point which is 40° 48' N and 77° 52' W.
- Chrissy plotted a point on a street map and used coordinates to describe her point.

Lesson 109   579

Written Practice

Math Conversations
Independent Practice and Discussions to Increase Understanding

Problem 7 — Analyze
Math Language
Measures of capacity double each step from pints to quarts to half gallons to gallons. So students should multiply $2 \times 4 = 8$ to estimate the weight of one gallon. Multiplying this by 5 gives the weight of 5 gallons.

Problem 12 — Formulate
Students should recognize this addition problem as counting by 12s six times, which can be written with a multiplication symbol: 12×6.

Problem 13
Remind students to align the numbers vertically to compare them:
1,152
1,215
1,125

Problem 15
Mental Math
Students can multiply the 10s and 100s separately.
$400 \times 4 = 1{,}600$
$20 \times 4 = 80$
$1{,}600 + 80 = 1{,}680$

(continued)

---

4. $8 \times 5 \times 7$ 280
(77, 78)

5. Multiple Choice Which of the following is the best choice to estimate $579 - 329$?   A
(30)

A $600 - 300$ B $500 - 300$ C $600 - 400$ D $500 - 400$

6. Is $8.65 closer to $8 or $9? $9
(96)

▶ **7. Analyze** A pint of water weighs about one pound.
(87, 98)
  a. About how many pounds does a gallon of water weigh?   8 pounds
  b. About how many pounds does the water in a filled five-gallon aquarium weigh?   40 pounds

8. Use compatible numbers to mentally find the sum of 50, 90, 150, 20, and 10. List the pairs of compatible numbers you added first.
(92)
10 and 90; 50 and 150; 320

9. Use a comparison symbol in place of the circle to show each comparison.
(17)
  a. $123 \,\text{\textcircled{<}}\, 132$ **b.** $5 + 7 \,\text{\textcircled{=}}\, 7 + 5$

10. How many centimeters are in a meter?   100 centimeters
(79)

11. How many small cubes were used to build this rectangular solid?   40 cubes
(73)

▶ **12. Formulate** Change this addition to a multiplication and find the total. 6×12 in. = 72 in.
(54, 76)
12 in. + 12 in. + 12 in. + 12 in. + 12 in. + 12 in.

▶ **13.** Write these numbers in order from least to greatest:
(103)   1125, 1152, 1215
1,152   1,215   1,125

14. $78 \div 3$ 26
(101)

▶ **15.** 420×4 1,680
(97)

16. Find each quotient.
(86)
  a. $27 \div 3$ 9   **b.** $28 \div 7$ 4   **c.** $42 \div 6$ 7

Alternative Approach: Using Manipulatives

Students can use geoboards to gain practice with coordinates on a grid. Have students pair off into teams of two. Make sure each student has one geoboard. Tell one student to mark a peg on the geoboard and read its coordinates to his/her partner, who then marks that peg on his/her geoboard. Individual pegs, line segments, or other figures should be marked with string or rubber bands by one student and then described aloud using coordinates to his/her partner. Once finished, partners should compare geoboards to see if they made any mistakes.

17. 94 × 2   188
(84)

18. 52 ÷ 4   13
(101)

19. Multiply:
(100)
    a. 4 × $2.50 $10.00
    b. 8 × $2.50 $20.00

▶ **20.** ⬢Explain⬢ Describe the sorting rule for the numbers in these
(102)
two groups.   sample: The numbers in Group A are even numbers. The numbers in Group B are odd numbers.

        Group A: 0, 2, 4, 6, 8

        Group B: 1, 3, 5, 7, 9

Real-World Connection

Sonya played on a soccer team that practiced every day from the first of June through the end of October. How many days did Sonya's team practice in all?   30 + 31 + 31 + 30 + 31 = 153 days

Lesson 109   581

Looking Forward

Learning to identify points on a grid using coordinates and writing the coordinates of a given point prepares students for

- **Lesson 110,** drawing dot-to-dot designs.
- **Investigation 11,** planning a design.

Written Practice (Continued)

Math Conversations
Independent Practice and Discussions to Increase Understanding

▶ **Problem 20** ⬢Explain⬢
Since both groups do not contain any of the same numbers and all ten digits are accounted for, students should easily recognize that Group A has only even numbers and Group B has only odd numbers.

Errors and Misconceptions

▶ **Problem 2**
Students can become easily confused about the number of times Ginger ran a distance of 75 yards. Have students make a sketch to show the number of times Ginger ran to the fence and back. Tell them to label each trip to and from the fence with "75 yards" and then solve the problem.

Early Finishers

Refer students back to Lesson 1 if they do not remember the number of days in each month.

Lesson 109   581

LESSON 110

Texas Essential Knowledge and Skills

(3.6)(A) identify patterns in related multiplication and division sentences (fact families)

(3.14)(C) select/develop an appropriate problem-solving plan/strategy, including working backwards to solve a problem

Planning & Preparation

• Dot-to-Dot Design

Objectives
• Follow directions to sketch a dot-to-dot design on a grid.

Prerequisite Skills
• Use coordinates to name points on a grid.
• Use coordinates to locate points on a grid.
• Name points on a grid with coordinates and with letters.

Materials
Instructional Masters
• Power Up 110
• Lesson Activity 34

Manipulative Kit
• Rulers

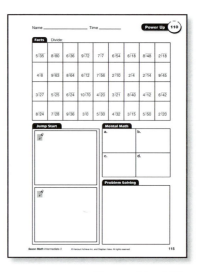

Power Up 110

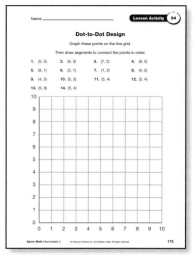

Lesson Activity 34

Reaching All Special Needs Students

Special Education Students	At-Risk Students	English Learners	Advanced Learners
• Adaptations for Saxon Math	• Reteaching Masters	• English Learners (TM) • English Learner Handbook	• Early Finishers (SE) • Online Activities

TM=Teacher's Manual
SE=Student Edition

Math Language
English Learners
design

582A   *Saxon Math* Intermediate 3

Problem Solving Discussion

Problem

It took Jack 25 minutes to walk from the U.S. Capitol to the White House. Then it took him 20 minutes to walk from the White House to the Lincoln Memorial. Jack arrived at the Lincoln Memorial at 2:50 p.m. At what time did Jack leave the U.S. Capitol?

Focus Strategy  Work Backwards

Understand *Understand the problem.*

"What information are we given?"

1. It took 25 minutes to walk from the U.S. Capitol to the White House.
2. It took 20 minutes to walk from the White House to the Lincoln Memorial.
3. Jack arrived at the Lincoln Memorial at 2:50 p.m.

"What are we asked to do?"

We are asked to find the time that Jack left the U.S. Capitol.

Plan *Make a plan.*

"What problem solving strategy can we use?"

We can *work backwards* from the ending time to find the starting time.

Solve *Carry out the plan.*

"Jack arrived at the Lincoln Memorial at 2:50 p.m. At what time did he leave the White House?"

The problem tells us that Jack walked 20 minutes to get from the White House to the Lincoln Memorial. So we count back 20 minutes from 2:50 p.m. to 2:30 p.m.

"Now we know that Jack left the White House at 2:30 p.m. At what time did he leave the U.S. Capitol?"

The problem tells us that Jack walked 25 minutes to get from the U.S. Capitol to the White House. So we count back 25 minutes from 2:30 p.m. to 2:05 p.m.

Check *Look back.*

"Did we complete the task?"

Yes, we found the time that Jack left the U.S. Capitol (2:05 p.m.).

"Is our answer reasonable?"

Yes, we know that our answer is reasonable, because Jack walked for a total of 45 minutes. He started walking at 2:05 p.m., and 45 minutes after that time is 2:50 p.m.

"What problem solving strategy did we use, and how did it help us?"

We *worked backwards* to find the starting time when we were given the ending time and the length of Jack's two walks.

Alternate Strategy
Act It Out or Make a Model

Use a geared clock (or use student clocks). Set the clock(s) to the time when Jack finished his walk (2:50). Move the hands to count back 20 minutes to 2:30 (when Jack left the White House). Then move the hands to count back 25 more minutes to 2:05 (when Jack left the U.S. Capitol).

LESSON 110

Power Up

Facts
Distribute **Power Up 110** to students. See answers below.

Jump Start
Before students begin the Mental Math exercise, do these exercises as a class.

Mental Math
Encourage students to share different ways to mentally compute these exercises. Strategies for exercises are listed below.

a. **Think of Money**
   4 quarters = $1.00
   $100 \div 4 = 25$

c. **Divide by 12**
   There are 12 inches in 1 foot. So divide by 12.
   48 inches ÷ 12 inches per foot = 4 feet

   Think of Equal Groups
   "48 inches can be divided into how many equal groups of 12 inches?"
   $48 = f \times 12$
   $f = 4$

Problem Solving
Refer to **Problem-Solving Strategy Discussion**, p. 582B.

LESSON 110
• Dot-to-Dot Design

Texas Essential Knowledge and Skills
(3.6)(A) identify patterns in related multiplication and division sentences (fact families)
(3.14)(C) select/develop an appropriate problem-solving plan/strategy, including working backwards to solve a problem

Power Up

facts Power Up 110

jump start
- Count up by 25s from 0 to 250.
- Count up by 100s from 0 to 2,000.
- Write a multiplication and division fact family using the numbers 11, 6, and 66. $11 \times 6 = 66$; $6 \times 11 = 66$; $66 \div 11 = 6$; $66 \div 6 = 11$
- Use these clues to find the secret number. Write the secret number on your worksheet.   121
  - three-digit number
  - less than 150
  - perfect square
  - palindrome

mental math
a. **Number Sense:** $100 \div 4$ 25
b. **Number Sense:** $201 - 199$ 2
c. **Measurement:** How many feet are equal to 48 inches?   4 ft
d. **Money:** Masa, Marta, and Naomi paid $24 altogether for tickets to the history museum. How much money did each ticket cost? $8

problem solving
It took Jack 25 minutes to walk from the U.S. Capitol to the White House. Then it took him 20 minutes to walk from the White House to the Lincoln Memorial. Jack arrived at the Lincoln Memorial at 2:50 p.m. At what time did Jack leave the U.S. Capitol?   2:05 p.m.

582   Saxon Math Intermediate 3

Facts Divide:

7 5)35	10 8)80	6 6)36	8 9)72	1 7)7	9 6)54	3 6)18	6 8)48	9 2)18
2 4)8	7 9)63	8 8)64	2 6)12	8 7)56	5 2)10	2 2)4	7 2)14	5 9)45
9 3)27	5 5)25	4 6)24	7 10)70	5 4)20	7 3)21	5 8)40	3 4)12	7 6)42
3 8)24	4 7)28	4 9)36	0 3)0	6 5)30	8 4)32	5 3)15	10 5)50	10 2)20

In this lesson you will draw a design on a grid by drawing line segments from point to point.

For example, we can draw an arrow on grid paper by first graphing these points:

1. (10,5)	2. (9,7)	3. (16,4)	4. (9,1)
5. (10,3)	6. (5,3)	7. (4,1)	8. (2,1)
9. (3,3)	10. (2,3)	11. (2,5)	12. (3,5)
13. (2,7)	14. (4,7)	15. (5,5)	16. (10,5)

To draw the lines, we start at point 1. From point 1, we draw a segment to point 2. From point 2, we draw a segment to point 3. We continue drawing segments from point to point in order. The drawing begins and ends at the same point.

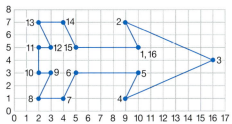

Classify The design above is a closed figure made up of line segments. What do we call a closed, flat shape with straight sides? polygon

Activity

Dot-to-Dot Design

Materials: **Lesson Activity 34**

On **Lesson Activity 34**, draw segments from point to point to complete the drawing.

Lesson 110   583

New Concept

Observation

Note that the beginning point and end point of the dot-to-dot design are the same and the line does not cross itself. This ensures that the design is one closed figure. Point this out to students and ask,

"Since the design is a closed figure and the dots are connected using straight line segments, what kind of figure will we make?" a polygon

Instruction

Before plotting the coordinates for the picture of the arrow, model the procedure on the board or overhead using a simpler dot-to-dot design, such as a parallelogram with coordinates (3,2), (5,4), (8,4), (7,2).

Activity: Dot-to-Dot Design

Distribute a copy of **Lesson Activity 34** to each student. You may wish to have students work in pairs or small groups so that they can check and assist each other.

For half of the points, one student could read coordinates while the other marks the points and draws the segments. Then they should switch roles for the other half of the points.

 The question below helps assess the concepts taught in this lesson.

"When we draw lines on a dot-to-dot design, why is it important to follow the order given?" If we don't follow the given order, we might not connect the correct dots to make the right picture.

Discuss real-world situations where using coordinates on a grid to make a picture might be helpful. An example is given below.

- A computer programmer uses the coordinates of pixels on a screen to make a picture.

A **design** is a drawing or a pattern that is used to make a picture. Direct the students' attention to the posters in the classroom and point out the different designs on each poster.

Ask:

"Which poster design do you like the best?" Answers will vary.

Show students a design made from multiple shapes, such as a design on a quilt.

Ask:

"What shapes do you see on this design?" Answers will vary.

Have students create a simple design using pattern blocks.

Written Practice

Math Conversations
Independent Practice and Discussions to Increase Understanding

Problem 4 — Classify
Help students see the difference between the two groups. Group A shows shapes constructed with only straight edges. Group B shows shapes that have at least one curved edge. Since a pyramid has only straight sides, students should sort it to Group A.

Problem 9 — Represent
Students should rewrite each comparison so that each side is in a similar numerical form.

a. Since the order of the factors in multiplication does not matter, students can rewrite the second expression as 2 × 3, or they can solve both multiplications.

b. Students should rewrite the first amount with a cent sign or the second amount with a dollar sign.

(continued)

Written Practice — Distributed and Integrated

1. (100) Sammy bought three pizzas for $7.50 each. What was the total cost of the pizzas? $22.50

2. (103) Write these numbers from least to greatest: 5,798; 7,862; 9,365
   7,862   5,798   9,365

3. (75) What is the geometric name for this shape? How many edges does it have? How many vertices? pyramid; 8 edges; 5 vertices

4. (104) **Classify** Mick sorted geometric shapes into Group A and Group B. Where should he put the shape shown in problem 3? Group A

5. (96) Round $7.75 to the nearest dollar. $8

6. (30) Estimate the difference when 395 is subtracted from 504. 100

7. (Inv. 9) Copy the figure at right and draw its line of symmetry.

8. (58) Use a ruler to draw a square with sides 2 inches long. What is the perimeter of the square? 8 in.

9. **(Represent)** Use a comparison symbol to show each comparison. Then write the comparison in words.
   a. $2 \times 3 \;\boxed{=}\; 3 \times 2$
   b. $\$0.05 \;\boxed{<}\; 50¢$

   a. sample: Two times three is equal to three times two.
   b. sample: Five cents is less than fifty cents.

10. If $60 \div 5 = 12$, then what does $60 \div 12$ equal? 5

11. A leap year contains 366 days. Write 366 in expanded form.
    $300 + 60 + 6$

12. Estimate the product of 92 and 9. 810

13. **Multiple Choice** If $1 \Diamond 1 = 1$ and $2 \Diamond 2 = 1$, then $\Diamond$ stands for which symbol? D

    A $+$
    B $-$
    C $\times$
    D $\div$

14. $38 \div 2$ 19

15. 51×3 153

16. Multiply: $4 \times \$1.25$ $5.00

17. Find each quotient.
    a. $64 \div 8$ 8
    b. $63 \div 9$ 7
    c. $60 \div 10$ 6

18. $5 \times 9 \times 2$ 90

19. **(Connect)** Use your ruler to help you find the next three numbers in this sequence: $2\frac{3}{4}, 3, 3\frac{1}{4}$

    $2, 2\frac{1}{4}, 2\frac{1}{2}, \underline{\quad}, \underline{\quad}, \underline{\quad}, \ldots$

20. **(Formulate)** Write a multiplication fact that shows how many small squares cover this rectangle. $7 \times 6 = 42$ or $6 \times 7 = 42$

Early Finishers — Real-World Connection

Jalicia went out for lunch. She spent half of the money she had on her meal. After she finished lunch and paid the bill, she had $2.25 left. How much money did she have before lunch? $4.50

Lesson 110   585

Looking Forward

Learning to draw dot-to-dot designs on grids using a set of directions prepares students for

- **Investigation 11,** planning a design.

Cumulative Assessments and Performance Task

Assessments

Distribute **Power-Up Test 21** and **Cumulative Test 21** to each student. Have students complete the **Power-Up Test** first. Allow 10 minutes. Then have students work on the **Cumulative Test.**

Performance Task

The remaining class time should be spent on **Performance Task 11.** Students can begin the task in class or complete it during another class period.

Written Practice (Continued)

Math Conversations
Independent Practice and Discussions to Increase Understanding

Problem 13   Multiple Choice
Test-Taking Strategy

Students should make a list showing each fact written with each one of the given answer choices. Students can then mark out the answer choices that have an untrue fact.
$1 + 1 = 1$ NO   eliminate choice **A**
$1 - 1 = 1$ NO   eliminate choice **B**
$1 \times 1 = 1$ YES $2 \times 2 = 1$ NO
eliminate choice **C**
$1 \div 1 = 1$ YES $2 \div 2 = 1$ YES

Only choice **D** will remain: division.

Problem 15
Mental Math

Students can work with the ones and tens separately and then combine at the end.
$50 \times 3 = 150$
$1 \times 3 = 3$
$150 + 3 = 153$

Problem 20 **(Formulate)**

The multiplication fact for this rectangle represents the calculation for its area. Students should recognize this and count only the squares in one row for one factor and one column for the other.

Errors and Misconceptions

Problem 12

Students may round 92 to 100 instead of to 90 before they multiply. Have these students write 90, 92, and 100 on a number line before they round.

Problem 13

Suggest that students rewrite the two listed facts with only a blank space between the two numbers instead of the unusual symbol shown.

Early Finishers

Suggest to students that they work backwards using money manipulatives.

Lesson 110   585

Flexible Grouping

Flexible grouping gives students an opportunity to work with other students in an interactive and encouraging way. The choice for how students are grouped depends on the goals for instruction, the needs of the students, and the specific learning activity.

Assigning Groups

Group members can be randomly assigned, or can be assigned based on some criteria such as grouping students who may need help with a certain skill or grouping students to play specific roles in a group (such as recorder or reporter).

Types of Groups

Students can be paired or placed in larger groups. For pairing, students can be assigned partners on a weekly or monthly basis. Pairing activities are the easiest to manage in a classroom and are more likely to be useful on a daily basis.

Flexible Grouping Ideas

Lesson 101, Example 1
Materials: paper

Divide students into groups of 4. Write 3 division problems with two-digit numbers on the board.
- Each group works together to solve the first problem.
- Divide the group into pairs to solve the second problem.
- Direct students to work on the last problem independently and then check their answer with the group.

Lesson 103, Example 2
Materials: paper

Have students individually answer example 2 without looking at the answers on the next page. Then divide the students into groups of 4.
- Students take turns sharing their strategies with the group. All strategies are acceptable.
- One person from the group should be chosen as the recorder. The group works together to write a summary of their strategies.

Lesson 105, Example 2
Materials: one Venn diagram per pair

Pair students before you teach Lesson 105. Then teach the lesson, stopping before you go over example 2. Give each pair a Venn diagram.
- Students read the example and discuss how to sort the numbers. Then they fill in the Venn Diagram.
- Have volunteers explain their thinking to the class.

Lesson 110, Activity
Materials: grid paper

Divide students into groups of 4. The groups should be of varying abilities and social skills. Choose a group leader, recorder, checker, and presenter. Give each group a blank sheet of grid paper. Direct groups to plot points on the grid to make their own dot-to-dot design.
- The leader makes sure that all group members are on task.
- The recorder works with the group to record the coordinates for the points on the grid.
- The checker verifies the coordinates to make sure the line segments form the intended picture.
- The presenter shares the group's new dot-to-dot activity and asks a volunteer from a different group to solve it.

INVESTIGATION 11

▶ **Texas Essential Knowledge and Skills**

(3.15)(A) explain/record observations using words, pictures, and numbers.

Planning & Preparation

• Planning a Design

Objectives
- Write directions for drawing a given dot-to-dot design on a grid.
- Make your own dot-to-dot design on a grid and write directions for drawing it.

Prerequisite Skills
- Follow directions to sketch a dot-to-dot design on a grid.
- Use coordinates to name points on a grid.
- Use coordinates to locate points on a grid.
- Name points on a grid with coordinates and with letters.

Materials

Instructional Masters
- Lesson Activity 36

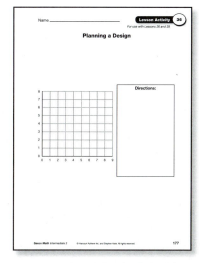

Lesson Activity 36

Reaching All Special Needs Students

Special Education Students	At-Risk Students	English Learners	Advanced Learners
• Adaptations for Saxon Math	• Error Alert (TM) • Reteaching Masters	• English Learner Handbook	• Online Activities

TM = Teacher's Manual

Math Language

Maintained	English Learners
estimate	continue

Investigation 11   586B

INVESTIGATION 11

Planning a Design
Math-to-Math Connection

The designs students will work with in this investigation are all polygons. Remind students that a shape is a polygon if it is both closed and constructed of only straight line segments. Mention the basic polygons that students have encountered so far: triangles, squares, rectangles, parallelograms, quadrilaterals, pentagons, hexagons, and octagons. Consider having volunteers come to the board to draw and label these shapes. Have them draw dots to mark the vertices of their shapes.

Math Conversations
Independent Practice and Discussions to Increase Understanding

Problem 1
Error Alert

When writing directions to describe a design, students need to read and write ordered pairs that coincide with the location of the vertices for the design. Students often confuse the two numbers and record the coordinates in reverse order. Remind students that the first number shows the distance along the bottom or horizontal direction and the second number shows the upward or vertical direction.

Problem 2

Make one copy per student of **Lesson Activity 35**.

Explanation

Students may not understand why a design begins and ends at the same point. Have students look at the triangle and imagine what it would look like if it were missing the segment connecting the points (2, 1) and (5, 2). Students can even physically cover up this segment with the corner of a piece of paper.

"The design no longer represents a triangle or even a polygon. Why?"
The shape is no longer closed.

Explain to students that closed shapes must always begin and end at the same point.

(continued)

INVESTIGATION 11

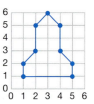

▶ Texas Essential Knowledge and Skills
(3.15)(A) explain/record observations using words, pictures, and numbers.

Focus on

• Planning a Design

In Lesson 110, we followed directions to draw a dot-to-dot design. In this investigation we will create a simple design and write directions for drawing the design.

1. Practice writing directions with your class. Look at the design at right. We can start the directions from any point. We will pick point (1,1) as the first point. We name (5,1) as the second point. Then we will continue around the figure, naming the point where each new segment ends. Below are the first three points.

   Continue naming the points in order all the way back to (1,1). You should have 10 points on your list when you are done.

   1. (1, 1)   4. (4, 3)   7. (2, 5)
   2. (5, 1)   5. (4, 5)   8. (2, 3)
   3. (5, 2)   6. (3, 6)   9. (1, 2)
                                10. (1, 1)

2. Practice drawing and writing directions by drawing a triangle on **Lesson Activity 35**. Begin by drawing three dots where grid lines intersect. Be sure the three dots are not lined up. Then draw segments between the dots to make a triangle.

   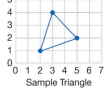
   Sample Triangle

   Now you are ready to write directions for someone else to make your triangle.

   For number 1, write the coordinates of one point (vertex) of your triangle.

   For number 2, write the coordinates of the second point of your triangle.

   For number 3, write the coordinates of the third point of your triangle.

   For number 4, write the coordinates of the first point of your triangle again so that the person following your directions will draw the third side of the triangle.

586   Saxon Math Intermediate 3

Math Background

In this investigation, students are naming and plotting points on a coordinate plane. The Cartesian coordinate system is used for graphing and has four quadrants.

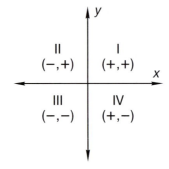

English Learners

To **continue** means to go on or to keep going. Begin reciting the alphabet, then ask:

"Who can continue reciting the alphabet?" See student work.

Ask:

"You are in third grade now. In how many years will you continue on to high school?" 6–7 years

Ask students to begin counting and to continue until you say "stop."

For our sample triangle, the directions look like this:

1. (5, 2) 3. (2, 1)
2. (3, 4) 4. (5, 2)

3. On **Lesson Activity 36,** you can draw your own dot-to-dot design. Then you can write directions for another student to follow so that they can make your design. Follow these rules:

- Use only segments—no curves.
- Make all segments end at points where lines on the grid intersect.
- Write the coordinates in order.
- Begin and end at the same point.
- Check your work by following your own directions.

Finding points on a grid will be further developed in *Saxon Math Intermediate 4*.

Math Conversations (Continued)
Independent Practice and Discussions to Increase Understanding

Problem 3
Explanation

Students can draw something more complicated than a single polygon in this part of the activity, so lines may cross each other. Make sure students understand that curved lines are still not allowed.

 Closure The questions below help assess the concepts taught in this lesson.

"How can we use coordinates to describe how to make a picture?" We can draw a picture on a graph by connecting grid points and write the ordered pairs of the points as we connect them.

"How can we check to make sure all the directions and ordered pairs that we wrote are correct?" Follow the directions we wrote and see if we draw the correct picture.

Discuss real-world situations where using ordered pairs to make a picture might be helpful. Examples are given below.

- We want to surprise a friend and have her draw a secret picture by connecting ordered pairs.
- A city has an electrical system on a power grid. An electrician plans a route to travel to check each relay station.

GLOSSARY

ENGLISH/SPANISH MATH GLOSSARY

A

acute angle (65) — An angle whose opening is smaller than a right angle.

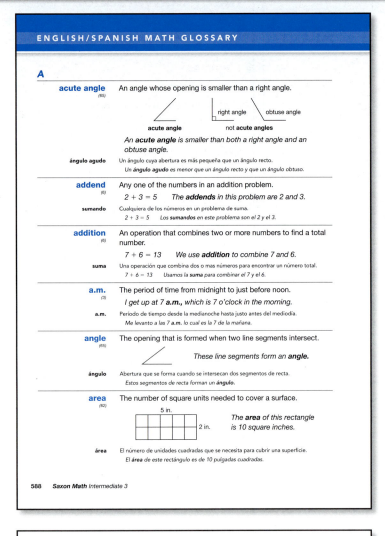

An acute angle is smaller than both a right angle and an obtuse angle.

ángulo agudo — Un ángulo cuya abertura es más pequeña que un ángulo recto.
Un *ángulo agudo* es menor que un ángulo recto y que un ángulo obtuso.

addend (6) — Any one of the numbers in an addition problem.
$2 + 3 = 5$ The *addends* in this problem are 2 and 3.

sumando — Cualquiera de los números en un problema de suma.
$2 + 3 = 5$ Los *sumandos* en este problema son 2 y el 3.

addition (6) — An operation that combines two or more numbers to find a total number.
$7 + 6 = 13$ We use *addition* to combine 7 and 6.

suma — Una operación que combina dos o más números para encontrar un número total.
$7 + 6 = 13$ Usamos la *suma* para combinar el 7 y el 6.

a.m. (3) — The period of time from midnight to just before noon.
I get up at 7 *a.m.*, which is 7 o'clock in the morning.

a.m. — Período de tiempo desde la medianoche hasta justo antes del mediodía.
Me levanto a las 7 *a.m.* lo cual es la 7 de la mañana.

angle (65) — The opening that is formed when two line segments intersect.
These line segments form an angle.

ángulo — Abertura que se forma cuando se intersecan dos segmentos de recta.
Estos segmentos de recta forman un *ángulo*.

area (62) — The number of square units needed to cover a surface.
The area of this rectangle is 10 square inches.

área — El número de unidades cuadradas que se necesita para cubrir una superficie.
El *área* de este rectángulo es 10 pulgadas cuadradas.

---

array (57) — A rectangular arrangement of numbers or symbols in columns and rows.
```
X X X
X X X    This is a 3-by-4 array of Xs.
X X X    It has 3 columns and 4 rows.
X X X
```

matriz — Un arreglo rectangular de números o símbolos en columnas y filas.
Esta es una *matriz* de Xs de 3 por 4. Tiene 3 columnas y 4 filas.

B

bar graph (Inv. 1) — A graph that uses rectangles (bars) to show numbers or measurements.

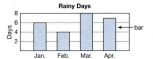

This bar graph shows how many rainy days there were in each of these four months.

gráfica de barras — Una gráfica que utiliza rectángulos (barras) para mostrar números o medidas.
Esta *gráfica de barras* muestra cuántos días lluviosos hubo en cada uno de estos cuatro meses.

C

calendar (1) — A chart that shows the days of the week and their dates.

SEPTEMBER 2009

calendario — Una tabla que muestra los días de la semana y sus fechas.

capacity (87) — The amount of liquid a container can hold.
Cups, gallons, and liters are units of *capacity*.

capacidad — La cantidad de líquido que puede contener un recipiente.
Tazas, galones y litros son medidas de *capacidad*.

Celsius (4) — A scale used on some thermometers to measure temperature.
On the *Celsius* scale, water freezes at 0°C and boils at 100°C.

Celsius — Escala que se usa en algunos termómetros para medir la temperatura.
En la escala *Celsius*, el agua se congela a 0°C y hierve a 100°C.

centimeter (79) — One hundredth of a meter.
The width of your little finger is about one *centimeter*.

centímetro — Una centésima de un metro.
El ancho de tu dedo meñique mide aproximadamente un *centímetro*.

century (57) — A period of one hundred years.
The years 2001–2100 make up one *century*.

siglo — Un período de cien años.
Los años 2001–2100 forman un *siglo*.

circle (67) — A closed, curved shape in which all points on the shape are the same distance from its center.

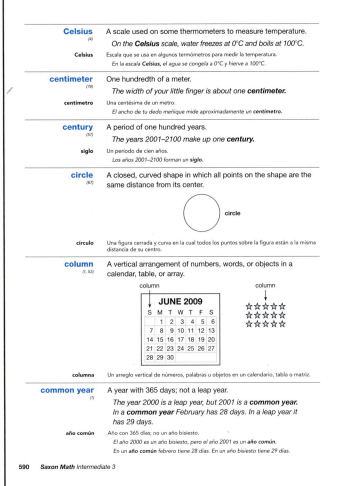

círculo — Una figura cerrada y curva en la cual todos los puntos sobre la figura están a la misma distancia de su centro.

column (1, 53) — A vertical arrangement of numbers, words, or objects in a calendar, table, or array.

JUNE 2009

columna — Un arreglo vertical de números, palabras u objetos en un calendario, tabla o matriz.

common year (1) — A year with 365 days; not a leap year.
The year 2000 is a leap year, but 2001 is a *common year*.
In a *common year* February has 28 days. In a leap year it has 29 days.

año común — Año con 365 días; no un año bisiesto.
El año 2000 es un año bisiesto, pero 2001 es un *año común*.
En un *año común* febrero tiene 28 días. En un año bisiesto tiene 29 días.

---

comparison symbol (17) — A mathematical symbol used to compare numbers.
Comparison symbols include the equal sign (=) and the "greater than/less than" symbols (> or <).

símbolo de comparación — Un símbolo matemático utilizado para comparar números.
Los *símbolos de comparación* incluyen al símbolo de igualdad (=) y los símbolos "mayor que/menor que" (> o <).

compatible numbers (92) — Numbers that are close in value to the actual numbers and are easy to add, subtract, multiply, or divide.

números compatibles — Números que están cerca en valor a los números reales y que son fáciles de sumar, restar, multiplicar o dividir mentalmente.

cone (75) — A three-dimensional solid with one curved surface, one flat, circular surface, and a pointed end.

cono — Un sólido tridimensional con una superficie curva, con una superficie circular plana y con un extremo puntiagudo.

congruent (68) — Having the same size and shape.
These polygons are congruent. They have the same size and shape.

congruente — De igual tamaño y forma.
Estos polígonos son *congruentes*. Tienen igual tamaño y forma.

coordinates (109) — A pair of numbers used to locate a point on a grid.
The coordinates of point B are (2, 3).

coordenadas — Un par de números que se utilizan para ubicar un punto sobre una cuadrícula.
Las *coordenadas* del punto B son (2, 3).

English	Definition
counting numbers (4)	The numbers used to count; the numbers in this sequence: 1, 2, 3, 4, 5, 6, 7, 8, 9, …. The numbers 12 and 37 are **counting numbers**, but 0.98 and $\frac{1}{2}$ are not.
números de conteo	Los números que se utilizan para contar; los números en esta secuencia: 1, 2, 3, 4, 5, 6, 7, 8, 9, … 12 y 37 son **números de conteo** pero 0.98 y $\frac{1}{2}$ no lo son.
counting patterns (2)	See **sequence**.
patrones de suma	Ver secuencia.
cube (71)	A three-dimensional solid with six square faces.
cubo	Un sólido tridimensional con seis caras cuadradas.
cubic unit (73)	A cube with edges of designated length. Cubic units are used to measure volume. The shaded part is 1 **cubic unit**. The volume of the large cube is 8 **cubic units**.
unidad cúbica	Un cubo con aristas de una longitud designada. Las unidades cúbicas se usan para medir volumen. La parte sombreada es de 1 **unidad cúbica**. El volumen del cubo mayor es de 8 **unidades cúbicas**.
cylinder (75)	A three-dimensional solid with two flat surfaces shaped like circles and one curved surface.
cilindro	Un sólido tridimensional con dos superficies planas como círculos y con una superficie curva.

D

English	Definition
data (Inv. 1)	Information gathered from observations or calculations. 82, 76, 95, 86, 98, 97, 93 These **data** are average daily temperatures for one week in Utah.
datos	Información reunida de observaciones o cálculos. Estos **datos** son el promedio diario de las temperaturas de una semana en Utah.
decade (69)	A period of ten years. The years 2001–2010 make up one **decade**.
década	Un período de diez años. Los años 2001–2010 forman una **década**.
decimal point (21)	A symbol used to separate dollars from cents in money. $34.15 ↑ decimal point
punto decimal	Un símbolo que se utiliza para separar los dólares de los centavos en dinero.
degree (°) (4)	A unit for measuring temperature. There are 100 **degrees** (100°) between the freezing and boiling points of water on the Celsius scale.
grado (°)	Una unidad para medir temperatura. Hay 100 **grados** (100°) de diferencia entre los puntos de ebullición y congelación del agua en la escala Celsius, o escala centígrada.
denominator (41)	The bottom number of a fraction; the number that tells how many parts are in a whole. The **denominator** of the fraction is 4. There are 4 parts in the whole circle.
denominador	El número inferior de una fracción; el número que indica cuántas partes hay en un entero. El **denominador** de la fracción es 4. Hay cuatro partes en el círculo entero.
difference (7)	The result of subtraction. 12 − 8 = 4 The **difference** in this problem is 4.
diferencia	El resultado de una resta. La **diferencia** en este problema es 4.

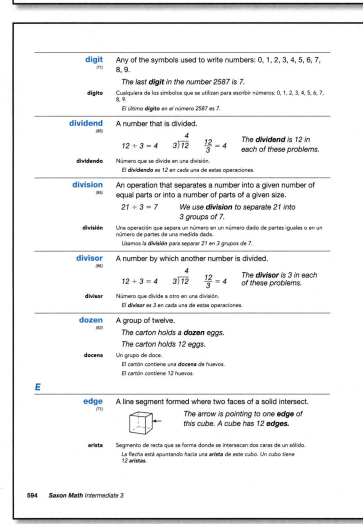

English	Definition
digit (11)	Any of the symbols used to write numbers: 0, 1, 2, 3, 4, 5, 6, 7, 8, 9. The last **digit** in the number 2587 is 7.
dígito	Cualquiera de los símbolos que se utilizan para escribir números: 0, 1, 2, 3, 4, 5, 6, 7, 8, 9. El último **dígito** en el número 2587 es 7.
dividend (86)	A number that is divided. $12 \div 3 = 4$ $3\overline{)12}$ $\frac{12}{3} = 4$ The **dividend** is 12 in each of these problems.
dividendo	Número que se divide en una división. El **dividendo** es 12 en cada una de estas operaciones.
division (85)	An operation that separates a number into a given number of equal parts or into a number of parts of a given size. $21 \div 3 = 7$ We use **division** to separate 21 into 3 groups of 7.
división	Una operación que separa un número en un número dado de partes iguales o en un número de partes de una medida dada. Usamos la **división** para separar 21 en 3 grupos de 7.
divisor (86)	A number by which another number is divided. $12 \div 3 = 4$ $3\overline{)12}$ $\frac{12}{3} = 4$ The **divisor** is 3 in each of these problems.
divisor	Número que divide a otro en una división. El **divisor** es 3 en cada una de estas operaciones.
dozen (62)	A group of twelve. The carton holds a **dozen** eggs. The carton holds 12 eggs.
docena	Un grupo de doce. El cartón contiene una **docena** de huevos. El cartón contiene 12 huevos.

E

English	Definition
edge (71)	A line segment formed where two faces of a solid intersect. The arrow is pointing to one **edge** of this cube. A cube has 12 **edges**.
arista	Segmento de recta que se forma donde se intersecan dos caras de un sólido. La flecha está apuntando hacia una **arista** de este cubo. Un cubo tiene 12 **aristas**.
equally likely (50)	Two events that have the same probability of happening. Drawing a blue marble and drawing a white marble are **equally likely**.
igualmente probables	Dos eventos que tienen la misma probabilidad de ocurrir. Sacar una canica azul y sacar una canica blanca son **igualmente probables**.
equals (6)	Has the same value as. 12 inches **equals** 1 foot.
es igual a	Con el mismo valor. 12 pulgadas **es igual a** 1 pie.
equilateral triangle (69)	A triangle in which all sides are the same length. This is an **equilateral triangle**. All of its sides are the same length.
triángulo equilátero	Un triángulo que tiene todos sus lados de la misma longitud. Éste es un **triángulo equilátero**. Sus tres lados tienen la misma longitud.
equivalent fractions (47)	Different fractions that name the same amount. $\frac{1}{2}$ and $\frac{2}{4}$ are **equivalent fractions**.
fracciones equivalentes	Fracciones diferentes que representan la misma cantidad. $\frac{1}{2}$ y $\frac{2}{4}$ son **fracciones equivalentes**.
estimate (30)	To find an approximate value. He **estimates** that the sum of 203 and 304 is about 500.
estimar	Encontrar un valor aproximado. Puedo **estimar** que la suma de 203 más 304 es aproximadamente 500.
even numbers (46)	Numbers that can be divided into 2 equal groups; the numbers in this sequence: 0, 2, 4, 6, 8, 10, …. **Even numbers** have 0, 2, 4, 6, or 8 in the ones place.
números pares	Números que se pueden dividir en grupos iguales; los números en esta secuencia: 0, 2, 4, 6, 8, 10, …. Los **números pares** tienen 0, 2, 4, 6 u 8 en el lugar de las unidades.

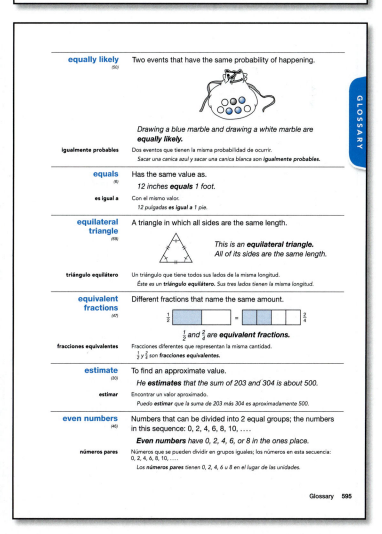

exchanging (Inv. 2)	See **regrouping**.	
intercambiar	Ver **reagrupar**.	
expanded form (11)	A way of writing a number that shows the value of each digit. The **expanded form** of 234 is 200 + 30 + 4.	
forma desarrollada	Una manera de escribir un número que muestra el valor de cada dígito. La **forma desarrollada** de 234 es 200 + 30 + 4.	

F

face (71)	A flat surface of a geometric solid. The arrow is pointing to one **face** of the cube. A cube has six **faces**.	
cara	Una superficie plana de un sólido geométrico. La flecha apunta hacia una **cara** del cubo. Un cubo tiene seis **caras**.	
fact family (8)	A group of three numbers related by addition and subtraction or by multiplication and division. The numbers 3, 4, and 7 are a **fact family**. They make these four facts: $3 + 4 = 7 \quad 4 + 3 = 7 \quad 7 - 3 = 4 \quad 7 - 4 = 3$	
familia de operaciones	Grupo de tres números relacionados por sumas y restas o por multiplicaciones y divisiones. Los números 3, 4 y 7 forman una **familia de operaciones**. Forman estas cuatro operaciones: $3 + 4 = 7 \quad 4 + 3 = 7 \quad 7 - 3 = 4 \quad 7 - 4 = 3$	
factor (55)	Any one of the numbers multiplied in a multiplication problem. $2 \times 3 = 6$ The **factors** in this problem are 2 and 3.	
factor	Cualquiera de los números que se multiplican en un problema de multiplicación. $2 \times 3 = 6$ Los **factores** en este problema son el 2 y el 3.	
Fahrenheit (4)	A scale used on some thermometers to measure temperature. On the **Fahrenheit** scale, water freezes at 32°F and boils at 212°F.	
Fahrenheit	Escala que se usa en algunos termómetros para medir la temperatura. En la escala **Fahrenheit**, el agua se congela a 32°F y hierve a 212°F.	
fluid ounce (87)	See **ounce**.	
onza líquida	Ver **onza**.	

596 Saxon Math Intermediate 3

fraction (5)	A number that names part of a whole. $\frac{1}{4}$ of the circle is shaded. $\frac{1}{4}$ is a **fraction**.	
fracción	Un número que representa una parte de un entero. $\frac{1}{4}$ del círculo está sombreado. $\frac{1}{4}$ es una **fracción**.	

G

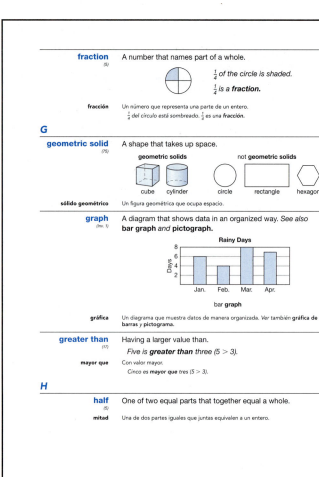

geometric solid (75)	A shape that takes up space. geometric solids: cube, cylinder. not geometric solids: circle, rectangle, hexagon	
sólido geométrico	Un figura geométrica que ocupa espacio.	
graph (Inv. 1)	A diagram that shows data in an organized way. See also **bar graph** and **pictograph**. Rainy Days bar **graph**	
gráfica	Un diagrama que muestra datos de manera organizada. Ver también **gráfica de barras** y **pictograma**.	
greater than (17)	Having a larger value than. Five is **greater than** three (5 > 3).	
mayor que	Con valor mayor. Cinco es **mayor que** tres (5 > 3).	

H

half (5)	One of two equal parts that together equal a whole.	
mitad	Una de dos partes iguales que juntas equivalen a un entero.	

Glossary 597

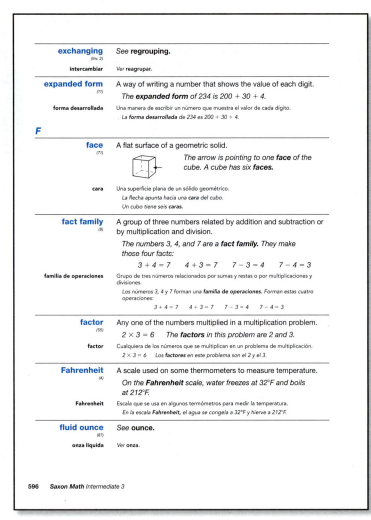

hexagon (67)	A polygon with six sides.	
hexágono	Un polígono con seis lados.	
horizontal (Inv. 6)	Side to side; perpendicular to vertical. **horizontal** line / not **horizontal** lines / vertical line	
horizontal	Lado a lado; perpendicular a la vertical.	

I

intersect (Inv. 4)	To share a common point or points. These two lines **intersect**. They share the common point M.	
intersecar	Compartir uno o más puntos en común. Estas dos rectas **se intersecan**. Tienen el punto M en común.	
isosceles triangle (69)	A triangle with at least two sides of equal length. Two of the sides of this **isosceles triangle** have equal lengths.	
triángulo isósceles	Un triángulo que tiene por lo menos dos lados de igual longitud. Dos de los lados de este **triángulo isósceles** tienen igual longitud.	

598 Saxon Math Intermediate 3

K

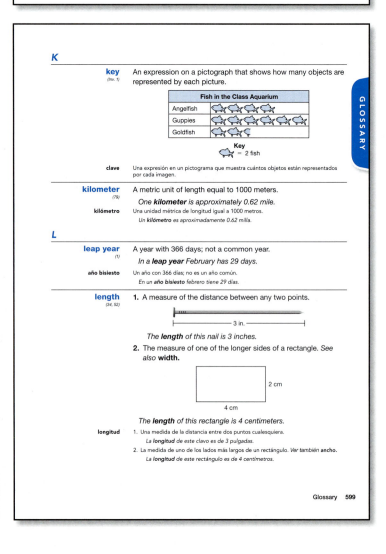

key (Inv. 1)	An expression on a pictograph that shows how many objects are represented by each picture. Fish in the Class Aquarium — Key = 2 fish	
clave	Una expresión en un pictograma que muestra cuántos objetos están representados por cada imagen.	
kilometer (79)	A metric unit of length equal to 1000 meters. One **kilometer** is approximately 0.62 mile.	
kilómetro	Una unidad métrica de longitud igual a 1000 metros. Un **kilómetro** es aproximadamente 0.62 milla.	

L

leap year (1)	A year with 366 days; not a common year. In a **leap year** February has 29 days.	
año bisiesto	Un año con 366 días; no es un año común. En un **año bisiesto** febrero tiene 29 días.	
length (34, 52)	1. A measure of the distance between any two points. The **length** of this nail is 3 inches. 2. The measure of one of the longer sides of a rectangle. See also **width**. The **length** of this rectangle is 4 centimeters.	
longitud	1. Una medida de la distancia entre dos puntos cualesquiera. La **longitud** de este clavo es de 3 pulgadas. 2. La medida de uno de los lados más largos de un rectángulo. Ver también **ancho**. La **longitud** de este rectángulo es de 4 centímetros.	

Glossary 599

less likely (45)	An event whose probability is less than another event.	
menos probable	Drawing a white marble is **less likely** than drawing a black marble. Un suceso cuya probabilidad es menor que la de otro suceso. Sacar una canica blanca es **menos probable** que sacar una canica negra.	
less than (17)	Having a smaller value than. Three is **less than** five (3 < 5).	
menor que	Con un valor menor. Tres es **menor que** cinco (3 < 5).	
line of symmetry (Inv. 7)	A line that divides a figure into two halves that are mirror images of each other. See also **symmetry**. lines of symmetry / not lines of symmetry	
eje de simetría	Recta que divide una figura en dos mitades, en la cual una mitad es la imagen especular de la otra. Ver también **simetría**.	
line segment (Inv. 4)	A part of a line with two distinct endpoints. $\overline{AB}$ is a **line segment**.	
segmento de recta	Parte de una recta con dos puntos extremos específicos. $\overline{AB}$ es un **segmento de recta**.	
liter (87)	A metric unit of capacity or volume. A **liter** is a little more than a quart.	
litro	Una unidad métrica de capacidad o volumen. Un **litro** es un poco más que un cuarto.	

M

mass (80)	The amount of matter an object contains. A kilogram is a metric unit of mass. The **mass** of the bowling ball is 7 kilograms.	
masa	La cantidad de materia que un objeto contiene. Un kilogramo es una unidad métrica de masa. La **masa** de la bola de boliche es de 7 kilogramos.	
meter (79)	The basic unit of length in the metric system. A **meter** is equal to 100 centimeters, and it is slightly longer than 1 yard. Many classrooms are about 10 **meters** long and 10 **meters** wide.	
metro	La unidad básica de longitud en el sistema métrico. Un **metro** es igual a 100 centímetros y es ligeramente más largo que una yarda. Muchos salones de clase miden como 10 **metros** de largo y 10 **metros** de ancho.	
metric system (79)	An international system of measurement in which units are related by tens. Also called the *International System*. Centimeters and kilograms are units in the **metric system**.	
sistema métrico	Un sistema internacional de medición en cual las unidades se relacionan por dieces. También es llamado el *Sistema internacional*. Centímetros y kilogramos son unidades del **sistema métrico**.	
midnight (3)	12:00 a.m. **Midnight** is one hour after 11 p.m.	
medianoche	12:00 a.m. La **medianoche** es una hora después de las 11 p.m.	
more likely (45)	An event whose probability is greater than another event.	
más probable	Drawing a blue marble is **more likely** than drawing a gray marble. Un suceso cuya probabilidad es mayor que la de otro suceso. Sacar una canica azul es **más probable** que sacar una canica gris.	
multiple (78)	A product of a counting number and another number. The **multiples** of 3 include 3, 6, 9, and 12.	
múltiplo	El producto de un número de conteo por otro número. Los **múltiplos** de 3 incluyen 3, 6, 9 y 12.	
multiplication (54)	An operation that uses a number as an addend a specified number of times. $7 \times 3 = 21$ — We can use **multiplication** to $7 + 7 + 7 = 21$ — use 7 as an addend 3 times.	
multiplicación	Una operación que usa un número como un sumando cierto número de veces. $7 \times 3 = 21$ — Podemos usar la **multiplicación** para usar $7 + 7 + 7 = 21$ — 7 como un sumando 3 veces.	
multiplication table (55)	A table used to find the product of two numbers. The product of two numbers is found at the intersection of the row and the column for the two numbers.	
tabla de multiplicación	Una tabla que se usa para encontrar el producto de dos números. El producto de dos números se encuentra en la intersección de la fila y la columna de los dos números.	
multiply (54)	See **multiplication**.	
multiplicar	Ver **multiplicación**.	

N

noon (3)	12:00 p.m. **Noon** is one hour after 11 a.m.	
mediodía	12:00 p.m. El **mediodía** es una hora después de las 11 a.m.	
number line (4)	A line for representing and graphing numbers. Each point on the line corresponds to a number. 0 1 2 3 4 5 number line	
recta numérica	Una recta para representar y graficar números. Cada punto de la recta corresponde a un número.	
number sentence (6)	A complete sentence that uses numbers and symbols instead of words. See also **equation**. The **number sentence** $4 + 5 = 9$ means "four plus five equals nine."	
enunciado numérico	Una oración completa que usa números y símbolos en lugar de palabras. Ver también **ecuación**. El **enunciado numérico** $4 + 5 = 9$ significa "cuatro más cinco es igual a nueve".	
numerator (41)	The top number of a fraction; the number that tells how many parts are counted. The **numerator** of the fraction is 1. One part of the whole circle is shaded.	
numerador	El número de arriba en una fracción; el número que indica cuántas partes se cuentan. El **numerador** de la fracción es 1. Una parte del círculo completo está sombreada.	

O

obtuse angle (65)	An angle whose opening is bigger than a right angle. obtuse angle / right angle / acute angle / not obtuse angles An **obtuse angle** is larger than both a right angle and an acute angle.	
ángulo obtuso	Un ángulo cuya abertura es mayor que un ángulo recto. Un **ángulo obtuso** es más grande que un ángulo recto y que un ángulo agudo.	
octagon (67)	A polygon with eight sides. octagon	
octágono	Un polígono de ocho lados.	
odd numbers (46)	Numbers that have 1 left over when divided into 2 groups; the numbers in this sequence: 1, 3, 5, 7, 9, 11, …. **Odd numbers** have 1, 3, 5, 7, or 9 in the ones place.	
números impares	Números que cuando se dividen en 2 grupos iguales tienen residuo 1; los números en esta secuencia: 1, 3, 5, 7, 9, 11, …. Los **números impares** tienen 1, 3, 5, 7 ó 9 en el lugar de las unidades.	
opposite sides (51)	Sides that are across from each other. opposite sides	
lados opuestos	Lados que están uno enfrente del otro.	
ordinal numbers (1)	Numbers that describe position or order. "First," "second," and "third" are **ordinal numbers**.	
números ordinales	Números que describen la posición u orden. "Primero", "segundo" y "tercero" son **números ordinales**.	
ounce (74, 87)	A unit of weight in the customary system. Also a measure of capacity. Sixteen **ounces** equals a pound. Sixteen **ounces** equals a pint.	
onza	Una unidad de peso en el sistema usual. También es una unidad de capacidad. Dieciséis **onzas** es igual a una libra. Dieciséis **onzas** es igual a una pinta.	

P

parallel lines (Inv. 4) — Lines that stay the same distance apart; lines that do not cross.

rectas paralelas — Rectas que siempre están a la misma distancia; rectas que no se cruzan.

parallelogram (66) — A quadrilateral that has two pairs of parallel sides.

paralelogramo — Un cuadrilátero que tiene dos pares de lados paralelos.

parentheses (92) — A pair of symbols used to show which operation to perform first: ( ).

$15 - (12 - 4)$

In the expression $15 - (12 - 4)$, the **parentheses** mean that $12 - 4$ should be calculated first. Then that difference should be subtracted from 15.

paréntesis — Un par de símbolos que se utilizan para mostrar que operación se debe de hacer primero: ( ).
En la expresión $15 - (12 - 4)$ los **paréntesis** significan que $12 - 4$ debe ser calculado primero. Después esa diferencia se debe de restar de 15.

pentagon (67) — A polygon with five sides.

pentágono — Un polígono con cinco lados.

perimeter (58) — The distance around a closed, flat shape.

The **perimeter** of this rectangle (from point A around to point A) is 32 inches.

perímetro — Distancia alrededor de una figura cerrada y plana.
El **perímetro** de este rectángulo (desde el punto A alrededor del rectángulo hasta el punto A) es 32 pulgadas.

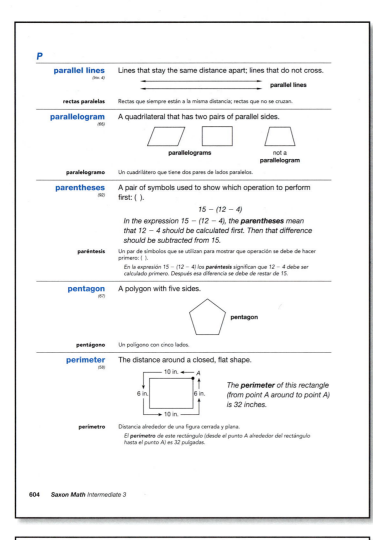

perpendicular lines (Inv. 4) — Two lines that intersect at right angles.

rectas perpendiculares — Dos rectas que se intersecan formando ángulos rectos.

pictograph (Inv. 1) — A graph that uses symbols to represent data.

This is a **pictograph**. It shows how many stars each person saw.

pictograma — Una gráfica que usa símbolos para representar datos.
Éste es un **pictograma**. Muestra el número de estrellas que vio cada persona.

place value (11) — The value of a digit based on its position within a number.

```
  341
   23
+   7
  371
```

Place value tells us that 4 in 341 is worth "4 tens." In addition problems we align digits with the same **place value**.

valor posicional — El valor de un dígito basado en su posición dentro de un número.
El **valor posicional** nos dice que 4 en 341 vale "4 dieces". En problemas de suma alineamos los dígitos con el mismo **valor posicional**.

p.m. (3) — The period of time from noon to just before midnight.
I go to bed at 9 **p.m.**, which is 9 o'clock at night.

p.m. — Período de tiempo desde el mediodía hasta justo antes de la medianoche.
Me voy a dormir a las 9 **p.m.**, lo cual es las 9 de la noche.

point (4, 109) — An exact location on a line or grid.
•A   This dot represents **point** A.

punto — Un lugar exacto en una línea o cuadrícula.
Esta marca representa el **punto** A.

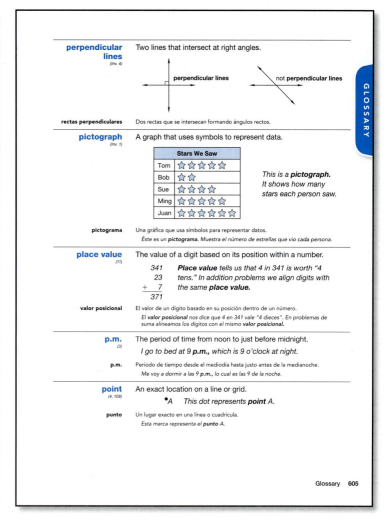

polygon (67) — A closed, flat shape with straight sides.

polígono — Una figura cerrada y plana que tiene lados rectos.

pound (74) — A customary measurement of weight.
One **pound** is 16 ounces.

libra — Una unidad usual de peso.
Una **libra** es igual a 16 onzas.

probability (45) — A way of describing the likelihood of an event.

The **probability** of the spinner landing on C is the greatest (it is the most likely).

probabilidad — Una manera de describir la posibilidad de ocurrencia de un suceso.
La **probabilidad** de que la flecha se detenga en C es la mayor (es la más probable).

product (55) — The result of multiplication.
$5 \times 3 = 15$ The **product** of 5 and 3 is 15.

producto — El resultado de una multiplicación.
$5 \times 3 = 15$ El **producto** de 5 por 3 es 15.

pyramid (75) — A three-dimensional solid with a polygon as its base and triangular faces that meet at a vertex.

pirámide — Un sólido tridimensional con un polígono en su base y caras triangulares que se encuentran en un vértice.

Q

quadrilateral (67) — Any four-sided polygon.

Each of these polygons has 4 sides. They are all **quadrilaterals**.

cuadrilátero — Cualquier polígono de cuatro lados.
Cada uno de estos polígonos tiene 4 lados. Todos son **cuadriláteros**.

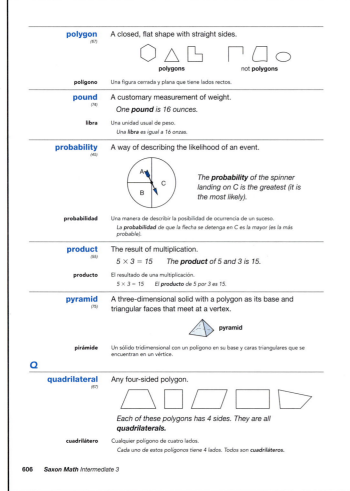

quarter (5) — A term that means one-fourth.

cuarto — Un término que significa un cuarto.

quotient (86) — The result of division.

$12 \div 3 = 4$ $3\overline{)12}$ $\frac{12}{3} = 4$ The **quotient** is 4 in each of these problems.

cociente — El resultado de una división.
El **cociente** es 4 en cada una de estas operaciones.

R

rectangle (51) — A quadrilateral that has four right angles.

rectángulo — Un cuadrilátero que tiene cuatro ángulos rectos.

rectangular prism (71) — A geometric solid with 6 rectangular faces.

prisma rectangular — Un sólido geométrico con 6 caras rectangulares.

rectangular solid (71) — See **rectangular prism**.

sólido rectangular — Ver **prisma rectangular**.

regrouping (14) — To rearrange quantities in place values of numbers during calculations.

```
  214  →   2̷1̷4
-  39     -  39
          ─────
            175
```

Subtraction of 39 from 214 requires **regrouping**.

reagrupar — Reordenar cantidades de acuerdo a los valores posicionales de los números cuando se hacen cálculos.
La resta de 39 de 214 requiere de **reagrupación**.

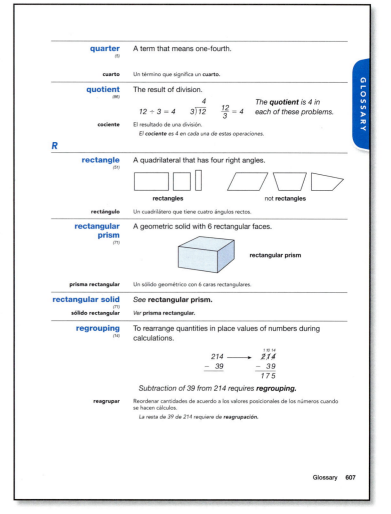

right angle (51)	An angle that forms a square corner. It is often marked with a small square.	

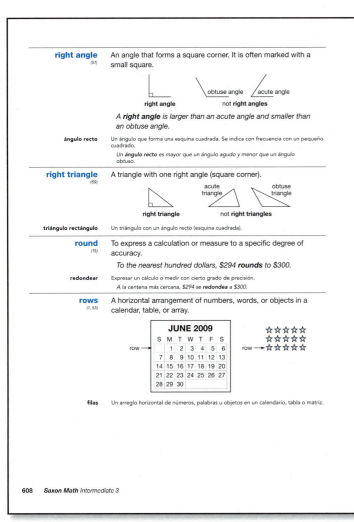

*A **right angle** is larger than an acute angle and smaller than an obtuse angle.*

ángulo recto — Un ángulo que forma una esquina cuadrada. Se indica con frecuencia con un pequeño cuadrado.
Un **ángulo recto** es mayor que un ángulo agudo y menor que un ángulo obtuso.

right triangle (69) — A triangle with one right angle (square corner).

triángulo rectángulo — Un triángulo con un ángulo recto (esquina cuadrada).

round (15) — To express a calculation or measure to a specific degree of accuracy.
*To the nearest hundred dollars, $294 **rounds** to $300.*

redondear — Expresar un cálculo o medir con cierto grado de precisión.
*A la centena más cercana, $294 se **redondea** a $300.*

rows (1, 53) — A horizontal arrangement of numbers, words, or objects in a calendar, table, or array.

filas — Un arreglo horizontal de números, palabras u objetos en un calendario, tabla o matriz.

S

scale (4) — A type of number line used for measuring.

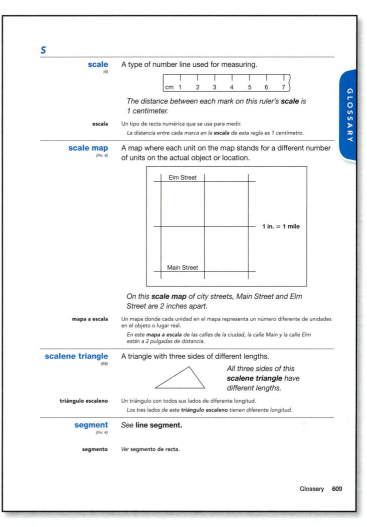

*The distance between each mark on this ruler's **scale** is 1 centimeter.*

escala — Un tipo de recta numérica que se usa para medir.
*La distancia entre cada marca en la **escala** de esta regla es 1 centímetro.*

scale map (Inv. 4) — A map where each unit on the map stands for a different number of units on the actual object or location.

*On this **scale map** of city streets, Main Street and Elm Street are 2 inches apart.*

mapa a escala — Un mapa donde cada unidad en el mapa representa un número diferente de unidades en el objeto o lugar real.
*En este **mapa a escala** de las calles de la ciudad, la calle Main y la calle Elm están a 2 pulgadas de distancia.*

scalene triangle (69) — A triangle with three sides of different lengths.

*All three sides of this **scalene triangle** have different lengths.*

triángulo escaleno — Un triángulo con todos sus lados de diferente longitud.
*Los tres lados de este **triángulo escaleno** tienen diferente longitud.*

segment (Inv. 4) — See **line segment**.

segmento — Ver segmento de recta.

sequence (2) — A list of numbers arranged according to a certain rule.
*The numbers 5, 10, 15, 20, … form a **sequence**. The rule is "count up by fives."*

secuencia — Una lista de números ordenados de acuerdo a una regla.
*Los números 5, 10, 15, 20, … forman una **secuencia**. La regla es "contar hacia adelante de cinco en cinco".*

side (65) — A line segment that is part of a polygon.

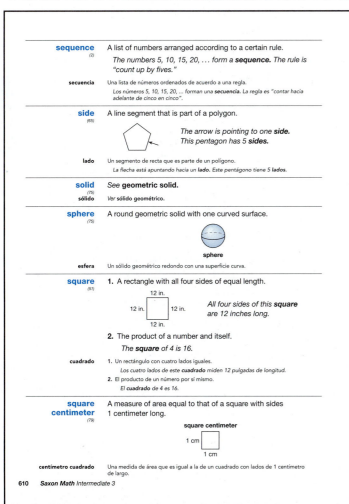

*The arrow is pointing to one **side**. This pentagon has 5 **sides**.*

lado — Un segmento de recta que es parte de un polígono.
*La flecha está apuntando hacia un **lado**. Este pentágono tiene 5 **lados**.*

solid (75) — See **geometric solid**.

sólido — Ver sólido geométrico.

sphere (75) — A round geometric solid with one curved surface.

esfera — Un sólido geométrico redondo con una superficie curva.

square (51)
1. A rectangle with all four sides of equal length.

*All four sides of this **square** are 12 inches long.*

2. The product of a number and itself.
*The **square** of 4 is 16.*

cuadrado
1. Un rectángulo con cuatro lados iguales.
*Los cuatro lados de este **cuadrado** miden 12 pulgadas de longitud.*
2. El producto de un número por sí mismo.
*El **cuadrado** de 4 es 16.*

square centimeter (79) — A measure of area equal to that of a square with sides 1 centimeter long.

centímetro cuadrado — Una medida de área que es igual a la de un cuadrado con lados de 1 centímetro de largo.

square inch (62) — A measure of area equal to that of a square with 1-inch sides.

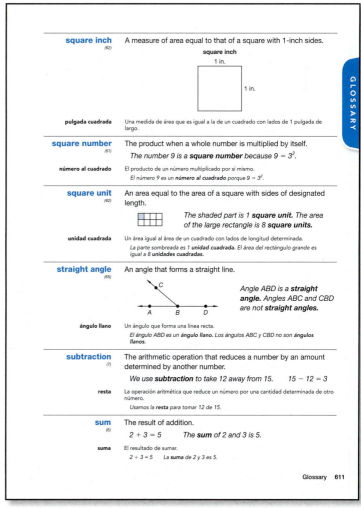

pulgada cuadrada — Una medida de área que es igual a la de un cuadrado con lados de 1 pulgada de largo.

square number (61) — The product when a whole number is multiplied by itself.
*The number 9 is a **square number** because $9 = 3^2$.*

número al cuadrado — El producto de un número multiplicado por sí mismo.
*El número 9 es un **número al cuadrado** porque $9 = 3^2$.*

square unit (62) — An area equal to the area of a square with sides of designated length.

*The shaded part is 1 **square unit**. The area of the large rectangle is 8 **square units**.*

unidad cuadrada — Un área igual al área de un cuadrado con lados de longitud determinada.
*La parte sombreada es 1 **unidad cuadrada**. El área del rectángulo grande es igual a 8 **unidades cuadradas**.*

straight angle (65) — An angle that forms a straight line.

*Angle ABD is a **straight angle**. Angles ABC and CBD are not **straight angles**.*

ángulo llano — Un ángulo que forma una línea recta.
*El ángulo ABD es un **ángulo llano**. Los ángulos ABC y CBD no son **ángulos llanos**.*

subtraction (7) — The arithmetic operation that reduces a number by an amount determined by another number.
*We use **subtraction** to take 12 away from 15. $15 - 12 = 3$*

resta — La operación aritmética que reduce un número por una cantidad determinada de otro número.
*Usamos la **resta** para tomar 12 de 15.*

sum (6) — The result of addition.
*$2 + 3 = 5$ The **sum** of 2 and 3 is 5.*

suma — El resultado de sumar.
*$2 + 3 = 5$ La **suma** de 2 y 3 es 5.*

survey (Inv. 6)	A method of collecting data about a particular population. *Mia conducted a **survey** by asking each of her classmates the name of his or her favorite television show.*	
encuesta	Un método para recolectar datos acerca de una población en particular. *Mia hizo una **encuesta** entre sus compañeros para averiguar cuál era su programa favorito de televisión.*	
symmetry (Inv. 7)	Correspondence in size and shape on either side of a dividing line. *See also* **line of symmetry**.	
simetría	Correspondencia en tamaño y forma entre cada lado de una línea divisoria. Ver también **eje de simetría**.	

T

table (Problem Solving Overview)	A way of organizing data in columns and rows.
	Our Group Scores
		Name	Grade	
		Group 1	98	
		Group 2	72	*This **table** shows the scores of four groups.*
		Group 3	85	
		Group 4	96	
tabla	Una manera de organizar datos en columnas y filas. *Esta **tabla** muestra las puntuaciones de cuatro grupos.*
tally mark (Problem Solving Overview)	A small mark used to help keep track of a count. ⅷ *I used **tally marks** to count cars. I counted five cars.*
marca de conteo	Una pequeña marca que se usa para llevar la cuenta. *Usé **marcas de conteo** para contar carros. Yo conté cinco carros.*
tick mark (4)	A mark dividing a number line into smaller portions.
marca de un punto	Una marca que divide a una recta numérica en partes más pequeñas.

612 Saxon Math Intermediate 3

---

timeline (33)	A type of number line for which each tick mark represents a date.
	Flight Timeline — 1903 Wright Brothers' powered flight; 1927 Lindberg's transatlantic flight; 1947 Yeager's supersonic flight; 1969 Armstrong/Aldrin moon landing (1900 – 2000)
línea cronológica	Un tipo de recta numérica donde cada marca de un punto representa una fecha.
ton (74)	A customary measurement of weight.
tonelada	Una medida usual de peso.
tree diagram (45)	A way to use branches to organize the choices of a combination problem.
	tree diagram
diagrama de árbol	Una manera de usar ramas para organizar las opciones de un problema de combinaciones.
triangle (69)	A polygon with three sides and three angles.
	triangles
triángulo	Un polígono con tres lados y tres ángulos.
triangular numbers (86)	Numbers that can be arranged in triangular patterns.
	1 3 6 10 15
	*The numbers 1, 3, 6, 10, and 15 are **triangular numbers**.*
números triangulares	Números que pueden ser ordenados en un patrones triangulares. *1, 3, 6, 10 y 15 son **números triangulares**.*

Glossary 613

---

triangular prism (75)	A geometric solid with 3 rectangular faces and 2 triangular faces.
prisma triangular	Un sólido geométrico con 3 caras rectangulares y 2 caras triangulares.

U

unit (53)	Any standard object or quantity used for measurement. *Grams, pounds, liters, gallons, inches, and meters are all **units**.*
unidad	Un objeto o cantidad estándar que se usa para medir. *Gramos, libras, litros, galones, pulgadas y metros son **unidades**.*
U.S. Customary System (34)	A system of measurement used almost exclusively in the United States. *Pounds, quarts, and feet are units in the **U.S. Customary System**.*
Sistema usual de EE.UU.	Un sistema de medición que se usa casi exclusivamente en EE.UU. *Libras, cuartos y pies son unidades del **Sistema usual de EE.UU.***

V

Venn diagram (105)	A type of diagram that shows how objects, numbers, or words are sorted.
	Venn diagram — Even numbers: 18, 24; 20 (center); Multiples of 5: 15, 25
diagrama de Venn	Un tipo de diagrama que muestra cómo y cuántos objetos, números o palabras se separan.
vertex (65, 71)	(Plural: *vertices*) A point of an angle, polygon, or solid where two or more line segments meet.
	*The arrow is pointing to one **vertex** of this cube. A cube has eight **vertices**.*
vértice	Punto de un ángulo, polígono o sólido donde se unen dos o más segmentos de recta. *La flecha está apuntando hacia un **vértice** de este cubo. Un cubo tiene ocho **vértices**.*

614 Saxon Math Intermediate 3

---

vertical (Inv. 6)	Upright; perpendicular to horizontal.
	vertical line not vertical lines
vertical	Hacia arriba; perpendicular a la horizontal.
volume (73)	The amount of space a solid shape occupies. Volume is measured in cubic units.
	*This rectangular prism is 3 units wide, 3 units high, and 4 units deep. Its **volume** is $3 \cdot 3 \cdot 4 = 36$ cubic units.*
volumen	La cantidad de espacio ocupado por una figura sólida. El volumen se mide en unidades cúbicas. *Este prisma rectangular tiene 3 unidades de ancho, 3 unidades de altura y 4 unidades de profundidad. Su **volumen** es $3 \cdot 3 \cdot 4 = 36$ unidades cúbicas.*

W

weight (74)	The measure of the force of gravity on an object. Units of weight in the customary system include ounces, pounds, and tons. *The **weight** of the bowling ball is 12 pounds.*
peso	La medida de la fuerza de gravedad sobre un objeto. Las unidades de peso en el sistema usual incluyen onzas, libras y toneladas. *El **peso** de la bola de boliche es 12 libras.*
width (52)	The measure of one of the shorter sides of a rectangle. *See also* **length**.
	(rectangle: 4 cm by 2 cm) *The **width** of this rectangle is 2 centimeters.*
ancho	La medida de uno de los lados más cortos de un rectángulo. Ver también **longitud**. *El **ancho** de este rectángulo es 2 centímetros.*

Y

yard (34)	A customary measurement of length.
yarda	Una medida usual de longitud.

Glossary 615

Symbols

Symbol	Meaning	Example
<	Less than	2 < 3
>	Greater than	3 > 2
=	Equal to	2 = 2
°F	Degrees Fahrenheit	100°F
°C	Degrees Celsius	32°C
∟	Right angle	⌐
…	And so on	1, 2, 3, …
×	Multiply	9 × 3
·	Multiply	3 · 3 = 9
÷	Divide	9 ÷ 3
+	Add	9 + 3
−	Subtract	9 − 3
⟌	Divided into	3⟌9

Símbolos/Signos

Símbolo/Signo	Significa	Ejemplo
<	Menor que	2 < 3
>	Mayor que	3 > 2
=	Igual a	2 = 2
°F	Grados Fahrenheit	100°F
°C	Grados Celsius	32°C
∟	Ángulo recto	⌐
…	Y más, etcétera	1, 2, 3, …
×	Multiplica	9 × 3
·	Multiplica	3 · 3 = 9
÷	Divide	9 ÷ 3
+	Suma	9 + 3
−	Resta	9 − 3
⟌	Dividido entre	3⟌9

Abbreviations

Abbreviation	Meaning
ft	Foot
in.	Inch
yd	Yard
mi	Mile
m	Meter
cm	Centimeter
km	Kilometer
L	Liter
ml or mL	Milliliter
lb	Pound
oz	Ounce
kg	Kilogram
g	Gram
qt	Quart
pt	Pint
c	Cup
gal	Gallon

Abreviaturas

Abreviatura	Significa
pie	pie
pulg	pulgada
yd	yarda
mi	milla
m	metro
cm	centímetro
km	kilómetro
L	litro
mL	mililitro
lb	libra
oz	onza
kg	kilogramo
g	gramo
ct	cuarto
pt	pinta
tz	taza
gal	galón

INDEX

¢ (cent sign), 115–117
: (colon), in telling time, 18
, (comma), in large numbers, 175–177
. (decimal point), 115–117
÷ (division sign), 446–447
$ (dollar sign), 60–62, 115–117
= (equal sign), 34–35, 93
> (greater than), 93–95
- (hyphen), 66
< (less than), 93–95
– (minus sign), 39–41
× (multiplication sign), 293–294
( ) (parentheses), 499–500
+ (plus sign), 34–35
$\frac{1}{4}$. See **Fourth**; **Quarter**
$\frac{1}{2}$. See **Half**

A

a.m. (before noon), 18–19, 207–208
Abbreviations
 cm, 426
 ft, 186
 g, 432
 in., 186
 kg, 432
 km, 426
 m, 426
 yd, 186
Act It Out or Make a Model. See **Alternate Strategy; Focus Strategy; Problem solving strategies**
Active Learning, 18, 34, 35, 45, 66, 76, 88, 94, 98, 99, 109, 120, 125, 126, 131, 136, 142, 144, 154, 158, 175, 186, 207, 222, 234, 240, 245, 255, 261, 266, 271, 278, 284, 289, 299, 335, 369, 374, 379, 386, 399, 446, 462, 466, 472, 496, 505, 513, 531, 541, 550, 560, 565, 574
Acute angles, 351–352, 357
Addend, 34–35. See also **Addition**
 missing, 49–50, 198–199
Addition, 34–35
 + (plus sign), 34–35
 addend, 34–35
 in columns, 131–132, 535
 estimating sums, 81–82, 162–163
 fact families, 45–46, 199
 missing addends, 49–50, 198–199
 modeling, 34–35, 70–73, 86–89, 120–121
 of money, 70–73, 85–89, 112–113, 120–121, 131–132, 509, 517–518, 535
 multiplication and, 293–294
 number sentences, 34–35, 198–199, 513
 place value and, 70–73, 131–132

 regrouping, 71–73, 87–90
 "some and some more" stories, 98–99, 197–199, 501, 513
 of three numbers, 53–54, 112, 131–132, 500–502, 509
 of three-digit numbers, 85–89, 112–113, 163
 of two-digit numbers, 70–73, 162–163
Alternate Strategy
 Act It Out or Make a Model, 38B, 108B, 140B, 169H, 206B, 211B, 270B, 287B, 292B, 306B, 316B, 334B, 361B, 373B, 421B, 450B, 471B, 559B, 582B
 Draw a Picture or Diagram, 197B, 425B, 504B, 540H, 569B
 Find/Extend a Pattern, 233B, 345B
 Guess and Check, 180B, 508B
 Make a Table, 260B
 Make It Simpler, 385H
 Use Logical Reasoning, 390B, 410B, 440H, 564B
 Write a Number Sentence, 350B, 368B, 445B, 465B, 486B, 508B, 525B
Alternative Approach: Using Manipulatives, 31, 35, 54, 94, 158, 167, 177, 193, 247, 262, 273, 278, 290, 295, 304, 308, 319, 330, 336, 342, 352, 357, 370, 392, 412, 442, 447, 467, 483, 489, 492, 510, 514, 532, 551, 562, 575, 580
Analog clocks, 17–19, 29–31, 207–208
Angles, 351–352
 acute, 351–352, 357
 obtuse, 351–352, 357–358, 374
 in polygons, 278–279, 356–358, 374–375, 561
 right, 278–279, 351–352, 356, 561
 straight, 351
Area, 335–337, 341–342, 427–428
 estimating, 341–342, 565–567, 573–574
 modeling, 288–289, 294, 329, 331, 335–337, 341–342, 347
Arrays, 307–308, 379

B

Bar graphs, 57–58, 326–327
Base-10 blocks, 61–62
Benchmarking and Tracking Standards. See **Section Overviews**
Boxes. See **Rectangular prisms**

C

°C (Celsius). See **Celsius**
Calendars, 9–10, 14–15
Capacity, 471–474
Celsius (°C), 23–25, 57

Cents (¢), 115–117. See also **Money**
Centimeter, 426–428
Circles, 362
Clocks
 analog, 17–19, 29–31, 207–208
 digital, 17–19, 207
Column addition, 131–132, 535. See also **Addition**
Columns
 in arrays, 307
 in calendars, 9–10, 14
Comma, in large numbers, 175–177
Common years, 8
Comparing numbers
 comparison symbols (<, >, =), 93–95, 142, 177, 234–235, 266–267, 502, 531
 fractions, 234–235, 266–267
 money, 93–95, 146–147, 551
 stories about, 212–213
 whole numbers, 93–95, 147, 177, 500, 502, 531–532, 538–539
Comparison symbols (<, >, =), 93–95, 142, 177, 234–235, 266–267, 502, 531
Compatible numbers, 500–502, 508–510, 531
Cones, 405–406, 436–439
Congruent shapes, 369–370, 374–375, 386
Content Trace. See **Section Overviews**
Coordinates, 578–579, 583, 586–587
Counting patterns. See **Patterns**
Cubes, 387, 405–406, 436–439. See also **Rectangular prisms**
Cubic units, 394–396. See also **Volume**
Cumulative Assessment. See **Section Overviews**
Cup, 471–474
Customary System. See **U.S. Customary System**
Cylinders, 405–406, 436–439

D

Data, 56–58
 collecting, 167–168, 326–327
 displaying, 57–58, 167–168, 327
Dates
 reading and writing, 8–11
 on timelines, 181–182, 212
Decimal point (.), 115–117
Degrees (°), 23–25
Denominator, 224–225, 240, 250, 261–262
Differences, 39–41, 212–213, 217. See also **Subtraction**
 estimating, 162–163, 501–502, 509–510

References in color indicate content exclusive to the Teacher's Manual.

Differentiated Instruction. *See* **Section Overviews**

Digital clocks, 17–19, 207

Digits, 60, 65–67, 76–77, 85–89, 103–105, 116–117, 131–132, 174–177, 478

Directions, writing, 169–171, 222

Distance, 186–188
    estimating, 201–203
    measuring, 186–188, 191–194, 202
    measuring on maps, 193–194, 221–222

Dividend, 466. *See also* **Division**

Division
    by 2, 445–447, 451–452
    dividend, 466
    divisor, 466
    equal groups stories, 487–488, 541–543
    fact families, 466–468
    facts, 451–452, 466–468
    halving, 445–447, 451–452
    modeling, 445–447, 461–462, 477–479, 541–542
    multiplication table and, 451–452, 482–483
    quotient, 466

Divisor, 466. *See also* **Division**

Dollars ($), 60–62, 115–117. *See also* **Money**

Dot-to-dot design, 582–583, 586–587. *See also* **Coordinates**

Doubling numbers, 440–441, 472, 509

Draw a Picture or Diagram. *See* **Alternate Strategy; Focus Strategy; Problem solving strategies**

E

Edges, 386–387, 436, 555

English Learners, 2, 10, 14, 20, 24, 30, 34, 39, 47, 49, 53, 57, 61, 66, 74, 76, 81, 86, 94, 99, 104, 109, 112, 115, 121, 127, 131, 137, 142, 148, 153, 159, 163, 166, 171, 176, 181, 187, 194, 198, 202, 207, 212, 217, 221, 227, 229, 234, 240, 245, 251, 256, 261, 266, 271, 279, 283, 288, 293, 298, 304, 308, 312, 317, 322, 327, 329, 335, 342, 347, 352, 357, 363, 369, 374, 379, 383, 386, 391, 395, 400, 406, 411, 418, 422, 437, 442, 452, 457, 461, 467, 472, 478, 483, 487, 493, 496, 501, 505, 509, 513, 517, 521, 526, 531, 535, 538, 543, 547, 550, 554, 560, 565, 570, 574, 578, 583, 586

Enlargements, 570

Equal groups stories, 322–323, 487–488, 510, 513–514, 522, 531–532, 535

Equal sign (=), 34–35, 93

Equilateral triangles, 374–375

Equivalent fractions, 254–257, 263

Errors and Misconceptions, 16, 20, 27, 32, 37, 42, 43, 47, 51, 55, 64, 68, 74, 83, 84, 91, 96, 101, 107, 111, 122, 129, 133, 139, 145, 155, 160, 165, 179, 184, 190, 200, 205, 210, 215, 220, 227, 232, 238, 243, 248, 253, 259, 264, 269, 274, 281, 286, 291, 296, 305, 310, 315, 325, 333, 339, 344, 349, 354, 360, 367, 372, 377, 382, 389, 393, 398, 403, 415, 420, 424, 430, 435, 444, 449, 454, 459, 464, 470, 475, 480, 485, 490, 498, 503, 507, 511, 515, 519, 524, 529, 533, 537, 544, 548, 552, 558, 563, 568, 572, 576, 581, 585

Estimating
    area, 341–342, 565–566, 573–574
    differences, 162–163, 501–502, 509–510
    effects of, 509, 531–532
    evaluating, 538–539
    length, 186, 187, 201–203
    mass, 432–433, 526–527
    products, 505–506, 509–510, 513–514, 531–532
    sums, 81–82, 162–163, 509, 513, 517–518, 532
    to verify answers, 512–514
    by volume, 495–496
    by weight or mass, 526–527

Even numbers, 477–479, 547, 550–551, 560

Exchanging money, 112–113, 115–116

Expanded form, 62–63, 175, 177

Extend the Example/Problem, 14, 35, 45, 46, 67, 68, 80, 82, 89, 95, 98, 100, 105, 109, 110, 136, 143, 157, 162, 171, 177, 183, 187, 202, 203, 204, 212, 214, 215, 221, 222, 225, 226, 227, 230, 235, 236, 240, 241, 246, 250, 252, 256, 257, 261, 262, 266, 267, 268, 271, 272, 308, 312, 329, 330, 331, 332, 336, 342, 344, 347, 349, 352, 354, 357, 358, 359, 363, 364, 365, 367, 369, 370, 372, 376, 377, 380, 381, 387, 389, 392, 393, 396, 398, 400, 403, 406, 412, 417, 418, 422, 426, 427, 428, 429, 430, 432, 433, 435, 436, 437, 438, 441, 442, 446, 447, 457, 467, 468, 473, 478, 479, 487, 490, 492, 495, 498, 501, 502, 503, 505, 507, 509, 510, 511, 513, 514, 515, 517, 518, 523, 526, 528, 531, 536, 539, 542, 544, 547, 551, 552, 555, 556, 561, 562, 568

F

°F (Fahrenheit). *See* **Fahrenheit**

Faces, 386–387, 436, 555

Fact families
    addition and subtraction, 45–46
    multiplication and division, 466–467

Factors, 298–299, 303–304, 317, 323, 329–331, 417, 422

Fahrenheit (°F), 23–25

Find/Extend a Pattern. *See* **Alternate Strategy; Focus Strategy; Problem solving strategies**

Fluid ounce, 471–474

Focus Strategy. *See also* **Problem solving strategies**
    Act It Out or Make a Model, 69B, 75B, 92B, 134B, 152B, 180B, 390B, 440H
    Draw a Picture or Diagram, 38B, 44B, 59H, 79B, 146B, 174B, 206B, 211B, 216B, 228B, 239B, 277H, 287B, 292B, 334B, 340B, 404B, 445B, 450B, 465B, 494H, 508B, 512B, 559B, 564B
    Find/Extend a Pattern, 7H, 13B, 17B, 33B, 48B, 59H, 85B, 130B, 156B, 201B, 223H, 265B, 297B, 311B, 350B, 378B, 416B, 450B, 465B, 486B, 494H, 530B, 534B, 540H, 545B, 577B
    Guess and Check, 97B, 124B, 169H, 191B, 260B, 270B, 302B, 394B, 421B, 460B, 520B
    Make an Organized List, 244B, 249B, 277H, 340B, 431B, 545B
    Make It Simpler, 361B, 368B, 373B, 481B, 476B
    Make or Use a Table, Chart, or Graph, 21B, 28B, 52B, 65B, 114H, 119B, 140B, 185B, 254B, 282B, 297B, 311B, 345B, 350B, 355B, 410B, 486B, 516B, 525B, 530B
    Use Logical Reasoning, 65B, 102B, 161B, 169H, 191B, 265B, 270B, 394B, 404B, 416B, 455B, 460B, 499B, 504B, 534B, 553B
    Work Backwards, 316B, 355B, 425B, 471B, 582B
    Write a Number Sentence, 108B, 114H, 119B, 185B, 197B, 233B, 239B, 282B, 306B, 321B, 328H, 334B, 345B, 385H, 399B, 410B, 421B, 425B, 499B, 504B, 512B, 516B, 540H, 549B, 569B, 573B

Foot, 186–188, 202–203

Fourth ($\frac{1}{4}$), 157–158, 225. *See also* **Quarter**

Fractions
    comparing, 234–235, 266–267
    denominators, 224–225, 240, 250, 261–262
    of a dollar, 157–158
    drawing, 229–230, 234–235, 250–251, 256–257
    equal to 1, 250–251
    equivalent, 250–251, 254–257, 263
    of groups, 239–241, 266–267
    of an hour, 29–31
    of an inch, 191–194
    manipulatives, 224–225, 234–235, 250, 255, 257, 266–267
    mixed numbers, 251, 262–263
    modeling, 157–158, 224–225, 234–235, 250–251, 255–257, 266–267
    on number lines, 261–262
    numerators, 224–225, 240, 250, 261–262

Fractions, continued
    pictures of, 157–158, 224–225, 229–230, 234–235, 239–241, 250–251, 255–257, 266–267
    reading and writing, 157–158, 224–225, 240–241, 250–251

ft (foot). *See* **Foot**

G

g (gram). *See* **Gram**

Gallon, 471–474

Geometric solids, 405–406, 436–439, 555–556

Gram (g), 431–433

Graphs, 56–58, 166–168, 326–327. *See also* **Bar graphs**; **Pictographs**

Greater – lesser = difference stories, 212–213

Greater than (>), 93–95. *See also* **Comparing**

Grids
    to estimate area, 565–567, 573–574
    points on, 578–579, 583, 586–587

Guess and Check. *See* **Alternate Strategy**; **Focus Strategy**; **Problem solving strategies**

H

Half ($\frac{1}{2}$), 29–31, 192–193, 257, 445, 472

Halving numbers, 445–447, 451–452

Hands (on clocks), 17–18, 207

Hexagons, 363–365, 375

Hyphen (-), 66

I

Inch, 186–188, 191–194, 202

Inch rulers. *See* **Rulers**

Inclusion, 3, 15, 19, 40, 45, 50, 62, 82, 89, 95, 99, 110, 121, 126, 132, 143, 154, 159, 182, 188, 199, 203, 218, 235, 241, 246, 263, 279, 294, 299, 309, 313, 318, 323, 337, 353, 358, 364, 370, 375, 387, 396, 406, 423, 429, 433, 443, 448, 452, 458, 463, 468, 488, 497, 502, 506, 510, 514, 522, 527, 542, 547, 555, 561, 567, 571, 579

Isosceles triangles, 374–375, 561

K

Keys, in pictographs, 56, 166–168

Kilogram, 431–433

Kilometer, 426–428

L

L (liter). *See* **Liter**

Later – earlier = difference stories, 210–211

lb (pound). *See* **Pound**

Leap years, 8

Length
    estimating, 186, 187, 201–203
    measuring, 186–188, 191–194, 202, 283–284, 426–428
    of rectangles, 263–264, 288–289
    units of, 186–187, 426–428

Less than (<), 93–95. *See also* **Comparing**

Lesson Planner. *See* **Section Overviews**

Lines of symmetry, 383–384, 491–493

Liter (L), 473

Looking Forward, 6, 12, 16, 20, 26, 32, 37, 43, 47, 51, 55, 58, 64, 68, 74, 78, 84, 91, 96, 101, 107, 111, 113, 118, 123, 129, 133, 139, 145, 151, 155, 160, 165, 168, 173, 179, 184, 190, 196, 200, 205, 210, 215, 220, 222, 227, 232, 238, 243, 248, 253, 259, 264, 269, 274, 276, 281, 286, 291, 296, 301, 305, 310, 315, 325, 333, 339, 344, 349, 354, 360, 367, 372, 377, 382, 384, 389, 393, 398, 403, 409, 415, 420, 424, 430, 435, 439, 444, 449, 454, 459, 464, 470, 475, 480, 485, 490, 493, 498, 503, 507, 511, 515, 519, 524, 529, 533, 537, 539, 544, 548, 552, 558, 563, 568, 572, 576, 581, 585, 587

M

m (meter). *See* **Meter**

Make an Organized List. *See* **Alternate Strategy**; **Focus Strategy**; **Problem solving strategies**

Make It Simpler. *See* **Alternate Strategy**; **Focus Strategy**; **Problem solving strategies**

Make or Use a Table, Chart, or Graph. *See* **Alternate Strategy**; **Focus Strategy**; **Problem solving strategies**

Manipulative Use, 39, 71, 72, 74, 76, 77, 78, 86, 87, 91, 93, 95, 98, 99, 103, 104, 105, 109, 111, 116, 120, 135, 137, 138, 141, 150, 153, 155, 207, 225, 227, 230, 234, 248, 256, 264, 267, 283, 290, 308, 405, 422, 424, 441, 442, 446, 462, 468, 477, 478, 480, 487, 503, 521, 542

Maps. *See* **Scale maps**

Mass, 431–433
    estimating, 432–433, 526–527

Math Background, 1, 9, 14, 18, 22, 29, 34, 39, 46, 53, 56, 60, 66, 70, 80, 93, 98, 103, 109, 120, 125, 131, 141, 147, 153, 157, 162, 170, 175, 181, 186, 192, 198, 202, 221, 229, 240, 245, 250, 255, 261, 271, 275, 278, 283, 288, 293, 298, 303, 307, 312, 317, 322, 326, 329, 335, 341, 351, 356, 362, 369, 374, 379, 383, 386, 391, 400, 411, 417, 422, 426, 432, 436, 441, 446, 451, 456, 461, 466, 472, 482, 487, 495, 500, 505, 509, 513, 517, 521, 531, 535, 541, 546, 550, 554, 560, 565, 570, 586

Math Highlights. *See* **Section Overviews**

Measuring
    area, 335–337
    capacity, 472
    length, 186–188, 191–194, 202, 283–284, 426–428
    mass, 431–433
    perimeter, 312–313, 427–428
    volume, 394–396
    weight, 401

Meter (m), 426–428

Metric system, 426–428, 431–433

Midnight, 18

Minus sign (–), 39–41

Mirror images (symmetry), 363–364, 491–493

Missing numbers, 49–50, 198–199, 217–218, 467–468

Mixed numbers, 251, 262–263
    on number lines, 262–263

Money
    adding, 70–73, 85–90, 112–113, 120–121, 131–132
    comparing, 93–95, 147
    counting, 135–138
    decimal point and, 115–117
    estimating with, 81–82, 517–518
    exchanging, 112–113, 115–116
    fractions and, 157–158
    modeling, 60–63, 70–73, 76–77, 86–90, 93–95, 103–106, 112–113, 115–117, 120–121, 125–127, 135–137, 141–143, 147–148, 153–154, 441
    multiplying, 441–442, 509, 522, 535–536
    naming, 115–117
    place value and, 60–62, 70–73
    rounding, 80–82, 517–518
    subtracting, 76–77, 103–105, 109–110, 112–113, 124–127, 153–154

Months, 8–11, 39–40, 41
    days in, 8–11

Multiples of ten, 422, 495–497, 505–506

Multiplication
    × (multiplication sign), 293–294
    by 0, 303–304
    by 1, 303–304
    by 2, 317–318
    by 5, 317–318
    by 9, 346–348
    by 10, 303–304
    by 11, 411–413
    by 12, 411–413
    arrays and, 307–308
    of dollars and cents, 535–536
    equal group stories, 322–323, 487–488, 510, 513–514, 522, 531–532, 535
    estimating products, 505–506, 509–510, 531–532
    fact families, 466–468
    facts, 299, 303–304, 317–318, 329–331, 346–348, 378–379, 411–413

memory group, 378–379
missing factors, 467–468
modeling, 288–289, 294, 307–308, 330–331, 411–412, 417–418, 441–442
of money, 441–442, 509, 522, 535–536
by multiples of ten, 422–423, 495–497, 505–506
as repeated addition, 293–294, 307
square numbers, 329–331
table, 298–300, 303, 317, 330, 346, 379, 411, 451, 482
of three numbers, 417–418
of three-digit numbers, 495–497, 521–522
of two-digit numbers, 440–442, 456–457, 509–510

Multiplication facts, 299, 466–468
0s, 303–304
1s, 303–304
2s, 317–318
5s, 317–318
9s, 346–348
10s, 303–304
11s, 411–413
12s, 411–413
memory group, 378–379
square numbers, 329–331

Multiplication table, 298–300, 303, 317, 330, 346, 379, 411, 451, 482

N

Noon, 18

Number lines, 22–23, 25, 39, 40, 181–183
comparing numbers using, 93–94
fractions and mixed numbers on, 261–263
rounding numbers using, 80–81

Number sentences, 34–35, 98–99, 109–110, 136–137, 217, 502, 513–514

Numerator, 224–225, 240, 250, 261–262

O

Obtuse angles, 351–352, 357–358, 374
Octagons, 363–364
Odd numbers, 477–479, 550–551, 560
Ordering numbers, 94–95, 146–150, 182, 551
Ordinal numbers, 9, 10–11
Ounce, 399–400
Ounce, fluid, 471–474

P

p.m. (after noon), 18–19
Parallel, 221–222, 278, 356–358, 386, 561
Parallelograms, 356–358, 561
perimeter of, 357–358
Parentheses, 500–502
Patterns
geometric, 7, 329
rules of, 14–15, 181

of whole numbers, 13–15, 181, 187–188, 331, 346–347, 411

Pentagons, 363
Perimeter, 312–313, 335–337, 357–358, 363–365, 427–428
Perpendicular, 221–222, 278, 386
Pictographs, 56–58, 166–168
Pint, 471–474
Place value, 60–63, 175–177, 550
money and, 60–62
ordering numbers, 94–95, 550
Plus sign (+), 34–35
Points
on grids, 578–579, 583, 586–587
on number lines, 22–23, 25, 181–182, 261–263
Polygons, 362–365, 373
Pound (lb), 399–401
Prisms. *See* **Rectangular prisms; Triangular prisms**
Probability, 245–246, 270–272, 275–276
games, 275–276
Problem solving, 1–6
process, 1–6, 7, 21, 36, 69, 97–98, 108, 161–162, 244–245, 316–317, 361–362, 476–477
strategy. *See* **Problem solving strategies**
Problem solving strategies, 5–6
act it out or make a model, 3–4, 5, 6, 69
draw a picture, 5, 6, 36
find/extend a pattern, 5, 6, 7
guess and check, 5, 6, 97–98
make a table, 2–3, 5, 6, 21
make an organized list, 6, 244–245
make it simpler, 5, 6, 361–362, 476–477
use logical reasoning, 5, 6, 161–162
work backwards, 5, 6, 316–317
write a number sentence, 5, 6, 108
Products, 298–300, 303–304, 317–318, 323, 329–331, 346–348, 378–379, 413, 417–418, 422–423, 441–442, 457, 521–522, 535–536
estimating, 505–506, 509–510, 513–514, 531–532
Pyramids, 405–406, 436–439

Q

Quadrilaterals, 363–365, 555
Quart, 471–474
Quarter ($\frac{1}{4}$), 29–31, 191–193. *See also* **Fourth**
Quotient, 466–467, 483. *See also* **Division**

R

Rectangles, 278–279, 356, 358
area, 335–336
length and width, 283–284

perimeter, 312–313, 335–337
Rectangular prisms, 385–387, 405–406, 436–439
volume, 394–396
Rectangular solids. *See* **Rectangular prisms**
Regrouping
in addition, 71–73, 87–90, 112–113, 162–163, 120–121
in multiplication, 521–522, 535–536
in subtraction, 76–77, 112–113, 141–144, 162–163
Right angles, 278–279, 351–352, 356, 374–375
Right triangles, 374–375
Rounding
money, 80–82, 162–163, 505, 513–514, 517–518
whole numbers, 80–82, 162–163, 505–506, 513–514
Rows
in arrays, 307
in calendars, 9–10
Rulers, 186–188, 191–194, 202, 221–222, 283–284

S

Scales, 23–24, 58, 207, 326–327
Scale maps, 221–222
Scalene triangles, 374
Section Overviews
Benchmarking and Tracking Standards, 7E, 59E, 114E, 169E, 223E, 277E, 328E, 385E, 440E, 494E, 540E
Content Trace, 7F, 59F, 114F, 169F, 223F, 277F, 328F, 385F, 440F, 494F, 540F
Cumulative Assessment, 7D, 59D, 114D, 169D, 223D, 277D, 328D, 385D, 440D, 494D, 540D
Differentiated Instruction, 7C, 59C, 114C, 169C, 223C, 277C, 328C, 385C, 440C, 494C, 540C
Lesson Planner, 7A, 59A, 114A, 169A, 223A, 277A, 328A, 385A, 440A, 494A, 540A
Math Highlights, 7B, 59B, 114B, 169B, 223B, 277B, 328B, 385B, 440B, 494B, 540B
Technology, 7C, 59C, 114C, 169C, 223C, 277C, 328C, 385C, 440C, 494C, 540C
Sequences, 13–15. *See also* **Patterns**
Shapes. *See* **Polygons; Circles**
Skip counting, 13–15, 18, 19, 207
Solids. *See* **Geometric solids**
"Some and some more" stories, 98–99, 197–199, 501, 513
"Some went away" stories, 109–110, 141–144, 217–218

Sorting, 546–547, 560–561
   diagrams for, 559–561
    geometric shapes, 554–556, 561
   Venn diagrams, 560–561

Spheres, 405–406, 436–439

Square corners. *See* **Right angles**

Square numbers, 329–331

Square units, 335–337, 341–342, 347, 565–567, 573–574. *See also* **Area**

Squares, 278–279, 329, 561
   perimeter, 312–313

Story problems
   about comparing, 212–213
   equal groups, 322–323, 487–488, 513–514, 522, 531–532, 535
   greater – lesser = difference, 212–213
   later – earlier = difference, 212–213
   some and some more, 98–99, 197–199, 501, 513
   some went away, 109–110, 141–144, 217–218

Straight angles, 351

Subtraction, 39–41
   – (minus sign), 39–41
   across zeros, 153–154
   estimating differences, 162–163
   fact families, 45–46
   greater – lesser = difference stories, 212–213
   later – earlier = difference stories, 212–213
   missing numbers, 216–217
   modeling, 39–41, 76–77, 103–105, 124–127, 141–144
   of money, 76–77, 103–105, 109–110, 112–113, 124–127, 141–144, 153–154, 509–510
   number sentences, 39–41, 213, 217–218, 502
   "some went away" stories, 109–110, 141–144, 217–218
   of three-digit numbers, 103–105, 112–113, 124–127, 162–163
   of two-digit numbers, 76–77, 109–110, 141–144, 217–218

Sums, 34–35, 49, 53, 86–89. *See also* **Addition**
   estimating, 81–82, 162–163, 509, 513, 517–518, 532

Surveys, 326–327

Symmetry, 363–364, 491–493

T

Tables
   creating/extending, 136, 138, 187–188, 271, 374, 526–527
   recording data in, 271

Tally, 56, 167, 275

Teacher Tip, 56, 61, 193, 224, 327, 574

Technology. *See* **Section Overviews**

Temperature, 23–25

Test-Taking Strategy, 36, 78, 83, 90, 101, 107, 122, 145, 155, 160, 189, 209, 215, 232, 242, 251, 258, 281, 285, 295, 301, 315, 332, 336, 337, 343, 354, 360, 364, 366, 370, 371, 372, 375, 376, 380, 401, 403, 409, 420, 424, 427, 434, 444, 448, 452, 453, 458, 459, 464, 469, 470, 474, 475, 479, 480, 484, 485, 490, 497, 506, 510, 528, 532, 544, 557, 585

Thermometers, 23–25

Tick marks, 17–18, 22–24, 58, 181, 183, 207, 261

Time, telling, 17–19, 29–31, 207–208. *See also* **Analog clock; Digital clock**

Timelines, 181–182, 212

Ton, 399–401

Tree diagrams, 245

Triangles, 363–364, 369–370, 373–375, 555
   angles in, 374–375
   equilateral, 374–375
   isosceles, 374–375, 561
   right, 374–375, 561
   scalene, 374

Triangular numbers, 465

Triangular prisms, 405–406, 436–439

U

U.S. Customary System, 186, 426, 431, 471

Use Logical Reasoning. *See* **Alternate Strategy; Focus Strategy; Problem solving strategies**

V

Venn diagrams, 560–561

Vertex, 351–352, 386–387, 436, 438

Volume, 394–396, 417–418
   estimating, 495–496
   modeling, 391–392, 395–396, 417–418, 422

W

Weight, 399–401

Width, 283–284

Work Backwards. *See* **Focus Strategy; Problem solving strategies**

Write a Number Sentence or Equation. *See* **Alternate Strategy; Focus Strategy; Problem solving strategies**

Y

Yard, 186, 188, 202–203

Yardstick, 186, 202

Years, 8–9, 10

NOTES

NOTES

NOTES

NOTES

NOTES

NOTES